Spiritual Kinship
as Social Practice

The University of Delaware Press Series

The Family in Interdisciplinary Perspective

General Editor:
Tamara Hareven, Unidel Professor of Family Studies and History

Charbonneau, Hubert, Bertrand Desjardins, André Guillemette, Yves Landry, Jacques Legare, and François Nault; Paola Colozzo (trans.). *The First French Canadians: Pioneers in the St. Lawrence Valley.*

De Singley, François. *Modern Marriage: A Sociological Look at Its Costs to Women.*

Guillemard, Anne-Marie. *Aging and the Welfare-State Crisis.*

Jussen, Bernhard; Pamela Selwyn (trans.). *Spiritual Kinship as Social Practice.*

Wall, Richard, Tamara K. Hareven, and Joseph Ehmer, with the assistance of Marcus Cerman. *Family History Revisited: Comparative Perspectives.*

Spiritual Kinship as Social Practice

Godparenthood and Adoption in the Early Middle Ages

Bernhard Jussen

Revised and expanded English edition
translated by Pamela Selwyn

Newark: University of Delaware Press
London: Associated University Presses

© 2000 by Associated University Presses, Inc.

All rights reserved. Authorization to photocopy items for internal or personal use, or the internal or personal use of specific clients, is granted by the copyright owner, provided that a base fee of $10.00, plus eight cents per page, per copy is paid directly to the Copyright Clearance Center, 222 Rosewood Dr., Danvers, Mass. 01923. [0-87413-632-6/00 $10.00 + 8¢ pp, pc.]
Other than as indicated in the foregoing, this book may not be reproduced, in whole or in part, in any form (except as permitted by Sections 107 and 108 of the U.S. Copyright Law, and except for brief quotes appearing in reviews in the public press.

Associated University Presses
440 Forsgate Drive
Cranbury, NJ 08512

Associated University Presses
16 Barter Street
London WC1A 2AH, England

Associated University Presses
P.O. Box 338, Port Credit
Mississauga, Ontario
Canada L5G 4L8

The paper used in this publication meets the requirements
of the American National Standard for Permanence of Paper
for Printed Library Materials Z39.48-1984.

Library of Congress Cataloging-in-Publication Data

Jussen, Bernhard.
 Spiritual kinship as social practice : godparenthood and adoption in the early Middle Ages / Bernhard Jussen : translated by Pamela Selwyn.
  p. cm. — (The University of Delaware Press series. The family in interdisciplinary perspective)
 Includes bibliographical references and index.
 ISBN 0-87413-632-6 (alk. paper)
 1. Sponsors—Europe—History. 2. Social history—Medieval, 500–1500. 3. Adoption—Europe—History—To 1500. 4. Kinship--Europe—History—To 1500. I. Title. II. Series.
BV1478.J89 2000
306.83—dc21   99-41732
                                                              CIP

PRINTED IN THE UNITED STATES OF AMERICA

Contents

Preface to the English Translation 7
Abbreviations 9

Part I: An Overview

1. Examining Sponsorship and Adoption in the Realm of Kinship Studies 15
2. Kinship Strategies: The Example of King Gunthchramn 46

Part II: Adoption

3. Adoption Contextualized: Legal Culture 53
4. King Gunthchramn: Interventions in Kinship 65
5. Counterstrategies: Gunthchramn's Nephews and Their Nobles 90
6. A Failed Attempt 109

Part III: Sponsorship

7. Practices in Antiquity 115
8. The Rule of the Merovingians and the Power of the Bishops 139
9. Sponsorship Bonds (1): Bishops and Kings 145
10. Sponsorship Bonds (2): Nobles and Bishops, Kings and Outsiders 171
11. An Exemplary Case: Gunthchramn as Chlothar's Godfather 181
12. Sponsorship as a Social Practice 210

Notes	239
Bibliography	328
Index	357

Preface

When this study was published in German, it bore the subtitle *Artificial Kinship as Social Practice (Künstliche Verwandtschaft als soziale Praxis)*. At the time, my chief concern was that my empirical work with the early medieval sources would live up to an epistemological standard that had been developed particularly in the "theory of practice". This central idea runs through the book's twelve chapters.

I paid less attention to the framework within which research on sponsorship has tended to be discussed. In keeping with the usual scholarly terminology, I referred to both sponsorship and adoption as "artificial kinship." I have adopted a different concept for the English-language edition. The translation of the book has offered me the opportunity to undertake a new discussion of an aspect that seems important to me: the scholarly notions of kinship familiar to us continue to suffer from internal inconsistencies and to conceptualize the research field of "kinship" in a manner that is not particularly plausible. I discuss these problems in the expanded first chapter of this edition. The brief chapter on the conception of kinship ("Patenschaft und Adoption als Instrumentarien der Verwandtschaftsbildung") included in the German edition has been omitted here.

Since my book appeared in German Martin Heinzelmann and Adriaan Breukelaar have published major works on the text at the center of the present study, Gregory of Tours' *History of the Franks*. Both have heightened our sense of the extent to which Gregory's history is a composition whose historical figures are characters typifying good or evil, and the extent to which the selection of stories told follows the interests of argumentation or composition. For social historians interested in the social constellations "behind" the text, the text's presence is always unsettling. We know that works such as Gregory's *History* are compositions and yet cannot avoid mining them for information. In exposing the structure of the *History*, works such as those by Heinzelmann and Breukelaar make it easier for social historians to handle the (for us) frequently perturbing presence of the text as *text*. With this in mind, I have changed a few passages in the German edition when I believed that I was not attentive enough to textual issues, and have tried to do greater justice to Gregory's work in its place between the analytical gaze and the social practices of the Merovingians. The following studies of cases and events in Merovingian history are, however, largely identical to those in the German edition.

So much for the revisions to my arguments of 1991. I have Tamara Hareven, David Sabean, and Patrick Geary to thank for the opportunity to rethink my approach and conclusions. I thank them warmly for their interest in this book, for many conversations and for their commitment to getting a translation published. Many thanks also to Pamela Selwyn for her careful, scholarly, and fluid translation.

Abbreviations

AASS	Acta sanctorum
BKV	Bibliothek der Kirchenväter
CCSL	Corpus Christianorum. Series Latina
CSEL	Corpus scriptorum ecclesiasticorum latinorum
DA	Deutsches Archiv für Erforschung des Mittelalters
DACL	Dictionnaire d'archéologie chrétienne et de liturgie
FMSt	Frühmittelalterliche Studien
HRG	Handwörterbuch der deutschen Rechtsgeschichte
L.H.	Gregorii episcopi Turonensis libri historiarum X
HF	Gregory of Tours. History of the Franks. Translated by O. M. Dalton, 2 vols. Oxford, 1927
Mansi	Sacrorum conciliorum nova et amplissima collectio
MGH	Monumenta Germaniae Historica
- AA	Auctores antiquissimi
- Cap.	Capitularia
- Conc.	Concilia
- DD	Diplomata
- Epp.	Epistolae
- LL nat. Germ.	Leges nationum Germanicarum
- SS	Scriptores
- SS rer. Germ.	Scriptores rerum Germanicarum in usum scholarum
- SS rer. Lang.	Scriptores rerum Langobardicarum
- SS rer. Merov.	Scriptores rerum Merovingicarum
PG	Migne Patrologiae cursus completus. Series graeca
PL	Migne Patrologiae cursus completus. Series latina
RAC	Reallexikon für Antike und Christentum
SC	Sources Chrétiennes
TRE	Theologische Realenzyklopädie

ZRG	Zeitschrift der Savigny-Stiftung für Rechtsgeschichte
- Germ.	Germanistische Abteilung
- Kan.	Kanonistische Abteilung

Spiritual Kinship
as Social Practice

Part I:
An Overview

1
Examining Sponsorship and Adoption in the Realm of Kinship Studies

When the Anglo-Saxon Wynfrid-Boniface (d. 754), a veritable expert on matters of sin and atonement, looked about him on the Continent, he realized to his own astonishment that, despite his intensive study of the Church fathers, he was not yet acquainted with all the sins. Around 735, he wrote to the Scottish Bishop Pehthelm: "As to the nature of this sin, if it is a sin, I was entirely ignorant, nor have I seen it mentioned by the fathers in the ancient canons, nor in the decrees of the popes, or by the Apostles in their catalogue of sins."[1] He also requested of Nothelm, Archbishop of Canterbury, "If you find that this is accounted so great a sin in the decrees of the catholic fathers or in the canons or even in Holy Writ, pray let me know it...."[2]

What worried the missionary was that the "priests throughout Gaul and Frankland maintain that for them a man who takes to wife a widow, whose son he had adopted, lifting him from the baptismal font *(cuius filium in baptismo adoptivum suscipiebat)*, is guilty of a very serious crime."[3] The conscientious specialist wished to know "what is the authority for such an opinion" about which he harbored severe misgivings. "I cannot possibly understand," he remarked, "how on the one hand, spiritual kinship *(spiritalis propinquitas)* in the case of marital intercourse can be so great a sin, while on the other hand, it is well established that by holy baptism we all become sons and daughters, brothers and sisters of Christ and the Church."[4] According to the interpretation of the Gallic priests, he argued, every Christian marriage would be criminal incest since the community of all Christians—like baptismal sponsorship—was, after all, described using the vocabulary of kinship.

Boniface's observation is substantiated by much other evidence. Those "priests throughout Gaul and Frankland" transposed the marriage restrictions incurred through relations of blood and alliance onto the bond established through an *adoptio* in baptism: godparenthood. And they did so with the utmost thoroughness: from the Carolingian era to Gratian's *Decretum* and beyond, in council acts, penitentials, or capitularies, canon and secular lawmakers applied the ever more broadly interpreted rules regarding incest among consanguineous and affinal kin to godparents and godchildren.[5] To be sure, even when Boniface voiced his objections to these rules, he nevertheless regarded sponsorship as another means to create kinship, beyond birth or marriage. He called it "spiritual kinship" and several other medieval authors followed suit.

Both notions—the one held by Boniface and that favored by the Gallic priests—point, in an initial crude classification, to sponsorship's role as a form of kinship. For a society in which belonging was primarily expressed in terms of kinship, in which kinship was the dominant medium of group formation, this is hardly surprising and, at this level of generalization, scarcely helpful. When it came to self-representation and establishing norms, most social groups in the early Middle Ages drew on the repertoire of kinship. We are thus compelled to hone our analytical instruments more sharply. How might we, as social historians, conceive of baptismal kinship in relation to kinship based on descent and alliance? What is "spiritual kinship," and how did it work?

Questions of this kind are far from new for historians, let alone for anthropologists, who have been studying godparenthood since the 1950s. With the publication of works by Arnold Angenendt and Joseph Lynch in the 1980s, sponsorship (in German, *Patenschaft*) was staked out as an area of research within the social history of the Middle Ages.[6] Both scholars have described sponsorship as a medieval form of kinship with considerable social and political relevance; indeed, as the most popular method of acquiring new relations in the Middle Ages.[7] Angenendt emphasizes that, from the eighth century on, sponsorship frequently was called *adoptio*, a word referring to another means of creating kinship, one with a rich tradition in the Roman world.[8] In Boniface's words, becoming a godparent meant adopting a child in baptism *(filium in baptismo adoptivum suscipere)*.

This link between adoption and godparenthood is a good starting point from which to unfold the problematic discussed in this book. It is not easy to tell what the description of godparenthood as *adoptio* was intended to convey. The fact that Boniface protested against the simple equation of descent and alliance with godparent kinship merely confirms the all too obvious insight that what we know about the antique Roman legal practice of *adoptio* is of little help in interpreting the social relevance of baptismal *adoptio* in the Middle Ages. Yet our search for other modes of interpretation quickly runs up against substantial difficulties. Any attempt to locate *adoptio* and godparenthood in the scholarly discourse reveals some basic inconsistencies in the common conceptions of "kinship." The terminology for kinship current in the literature appears to present a significant obstacle to the interpretation of medieval sponsorship—and perhaps medieval kinship in general. The ways in which "medieval godparenthood" has been constructed as a field of research have depended largely on scholarly notions of "kinship."

Kin Relations and Kinlike Relations?
Inconsistencies in Scholarly Concepts of "Kinship"

During the past twenty years or so, historians' understanding of kinship practices in the Middle Ages has undergone considerable refinement, thanks not least to a greater openness toward the questions and insights of other disciplines, especially sociology and social anthropology, but also to scholarship on the phenomenology of religion and liturgy.[9] Like the majority of anthropologists, historians too have uncoupled the scholarly notion of kinship from biology and now restrict themselves to assuming that there is some kind of relationship between biological reproduction and kinship. This kind of relationship is, however, hard to define. The difficulty lies in the tightrope walk involved in retaining some connection between biology and kinship while conceiving of kinship as a *mental* system used to structure social relations of *all kinds*. How authors define the ties between kinship and biological reproduction depends on their membership in a particular intellectual camp. When it comes to the relationship between kinship and biology, authors tend to remain vague and are often inconsistent. I will limit myself here to three examples from encyclopedias, which will elucidate this pattern:

In the *Encyclopedia of Social Anthropology*, published in 1996, David Kronenfeld begins by noting that "in all known cultures" there is "some cultural recognition (whether direct or indirect) of a genealogical basis for kinterms."[10] There can be little objection to such a cautious formulation, which we might rephrase as "the terminology of kinship is derived from the semantic field of biological reproduction." This does not get us very far, however, since the origin of the terminology says nothing about the relationship between biology and kinship. Some scholars express this radically: "There is no procedure for inferring the existence of the one from the existence of the other."[11] In social usage, according to Kronenfeld, kinship terms tell us little about biological circumstances: "The normal communicative information carried by kinterms in normal conversational usage in most cultures has much more to do with affect and behavioral expectations than it does with genealogical relatedness per se." All this caution does not, however, prevent Kronenfeld from subjecting his entire article to a biologistic classification: he treats everything outside of descent and marriage as a metaphor.[12]

Charlotte Seymour-Smith makes a similarly inconsistent argument in the 1986 *Macmillan Dictionary of Anthropology*. She too insists on the distinction between biology and kinship. The association between the two derives from our own culture's "intuitive definition," but cultural determinist analysts, she states, have rightly shown us that "kin classifications are social and cultural constructions which do not necessarily refer to the biological facts." Seymour-Smith, too, attempts to define the relationship between biology and kinship: "Most anthropologists today would agree that kinship relations involve some kind of modelling on 'natural' or 'biological' ties." Despite her obvious efforts to avoid a simple equation between blood and kinship, in a number of sentences Seymour-Smith, too, gives free reign to her "intuitive definition." "Kinship," she explains in the very first sentence, "in its broadest sense [!] includes marriage alliance and relations of affinity [= related by a marriage link]."[13]

To take a third example, in 1968, Julian Pitt-Rivers wrote the third section of the article "Kinship," entitled "Pseudo-kinship," for the *International Encyclopedia of the Social Sciences*. Here, he briefly discusses the suggestion that every relation which employs a kin term should be labeled as a kin relationship. This, he argues, would not evade the necessity of establishing distinctions. Pitt-Rivers suggests that "genuine" kinship be distinguished from "pseudo" kinship, intending this—at least in one of his recommendations—in a genuinely culturalist sense: "It seems advisable to consider as genuine kin those to whom the custom of the society ascribes such status, whatever the criteria for ascription may be, and to regard as pseudo-kin those who achieve the role otherwise." The tie between kin and biology would consequently be the object of and not the prerequisite for studies of kinship. Pitt-Rivers refers to the Eskimos to show that, for some societies, it is difficult to discover what is considered "genuine." Among the Eskimos, "genuine" kin are defined by residence, not biology. Pitt-Rivers doubtless would have found it similarly difficult had he been interested in medieval clerics. But these culturalist approaches in Pitt-Rivers' contribution were doomed to failure, since the larger article on "kinship" followed a clear concept: it does not divide kinship into "pseudo-" and "genuine" kinship (which would provide a place for the Eskimo variant), but rather into "pseudo-kinship" and "descent groups." Pitt-Rivers cannot escape this framework, and thus offers a biologistic solution alongside the culturalist one: "Pseudo-kinship includes those relationships in which persons are described or addressed by kin terms, . . . but do not stand in such a relationship by virtue of the principles . . . of descent or marriage."[14]

All three articles exhibit the same pattern, and it would not be difficult to provide further examples. The same contradiction is present in each. In a sort of theoretical tightrope walk, the author reflects on the distance and connections between kinship and biology, arguing in culturalist terms. At the same time, the direct identification or "intuitive definition" (Seymour) derived from the author's own culture soon breaks through.

This fact has had a simple consequence for historical studies. Practically all work on kinship continues to focus on descent and marriage bonds without ever specifically reflecting on this restriction of the field of kinship. We can find this limitation even in the work of scholars who claim to be interested in social practices or to study the subject from the perspective of the sociology of knowledge (although the sociology of knowledge is quite capable of distinguishing the terminology of kinship from biological reproduction). In short, whatever theoretical conclusions may have been drawn about kinship, in empirical work the concept of what kinship is suddenly becomes very narrow: blood and marriage. A study such as David Sabean's *Kinship in Neckarhausen* represents an exception. In order to understand strategies for securing subsistence and of social reproduction, Sabean paid equal attention to the manner in which descent, alliance, and godparent relations functioned—as three kinds of social networks that overlap and intermingle, reinforcing and supplementing each other.[15]

At first glance, it appears that the theoretical principles were being applied with greater consistency in medieval studies. During the past twenty years or so, many scholars have expanded the spectrum of what they refer to as kinship. They repeatedly, if obliquely, hint that in the Middle Ages, kinship was the most common way of putting social relations into words and linking individuals into diverse forms of groups. Oath brotherhoods, confraternities, sponsorship bonds, *amicitiae*—indeed, entire *gentes*—were referred to as forms of kinship.

This perspective would seem to signal a radical change, one requiring a total reorientation of the field of "kinship" studies. Kinship should thus refer to much more than a mere mode of constituting familial groups (descent, marriage, adoption). How, then, do medievalists define the various aspects of "kinship" as an object of study? Do they also use this term as a tool for analyzing a mode of constituting religious groups (monastic communities, confraternities, godparenthood) or *amicitiae*? Is kinship also treated as a notion involved in defining hierarchies (the bishop as *pater* of the diocesans and *frater* of the other bishops, the emperor as *pater patriae*), for the community of Christians as a whole (God's children) or for an individual parish? In short, do medievalists take Saint Boniface seriously when, writing in the eighth century, he claimed that "by holy baptism we all become sons and daughters, brothers and sisters of Christ and the Church?"[16]

They do not take him seriously. Almost no one associates the argument made by the baffled missionary with what scholars mean when they speak of kinship. We reach all too readily for the label "metaphor," a sort of panacea that promises a speedy return to order. It may be a result of the adoption of culturalist perspectives that medievalists in recent years have become more sensitive to the types of early medieval group formation that existed outside of descent and marriage—forms such as oath brotherhoods *(coniurationes)*[17] and ritual friendships *(amicitiae)*.[18] Their significant role had previously been largely ignored. However keen some medievalists may be to label this or that social form outside of descent and marriage as "kinship," such exercises involving "culturalist" concepts of kinship are relegated to subordinate clauses. Even patently untenable positions go unchallenged. According to a widely used handbook, it is a "peculiarity of primitive thinking that tribal identity can be understood only in terms of consanguinity," and that consequently tribes like the Franks were "imagined as an enormous clan . . . , as a group of blood-relations embracing many clans."[19] The fact that what is "true" or "false" about such positions goes undiscussed is merely an expression of how little these exercises in subordinate clauses expect to be taken seriously. The reader is quickly left to his or her own devices.

Serious studies of kinship in the Middle Ages, like those on the modern period, limit themselves to those forms of kinship associated with the transmission of property and status identity. They do not, however, relate these forms—descent and alliance—to those social relations that use kin terms merely to establish normative conditions of authority and behavioral expectations. If they appear in kinship studies at all, relationships such as godparenthood have an unsatisfactory status, "somehow" integrated theoretically, but not taken very seriously empirically.

In order to understand this curious disjunction, it is useful to take a closer look at the implications of the scholarly terminology of kinship. This terminology does not appear to have incorporated the theoretical reflections on the relationship between biology and kinship. Biologistic notions continue—via terminology—to exercise a great influence over scholarly systems.

Since the earliest documents that have come down to us from the period around the year 500, sponsorship ties have been referred to using the vocabulary of descent relations: *pater (mater, filius, filia)* "from the font," *adoptio*, and later derivative terms such as *matrina* and *patrinus*.[20] We are accustomed in the literature to distinguish this form of kinship from descent and alliance by means of a scholarly systematology that reveals something of its presuppositions: godparenthood is a form of "artificial kinship" or "pseudo-kinship,"[21] of "putative"[22] or "ritual kinship."[23] It is regarded as a "kin like" relation,[24] as "fictive" or even "metaphoric" kinship.

It is not difficult to show that these scholarly conceptions of kinship are inconsistent. They are incompatible with the broadly accepted proposition that kinship is an instrument for conceiving of social relations, and that it has no clear-cut relationship to biological reproduction. It is, however, far more difficult to tell what conclusions we should draw to avoid these inconsistencies. Only a few approaches within medieval studies appear to resist biologism and seek out new scholarly differentiations.[25]

The empirical studies in the chapters that follow are not intended as interventions in the discussion about new scholarly classifications of the field of "kinship." They aim to understand the practical value of "sponsorship" and "adoption" as instruments. When and to what ends were sponsorship ties and adoptions initiated, used, (re)interpreted, circumvented, or ignored? What I have provided here are empirical close-ups, which may at least offer a material basis for discussing the profile of the research field known as "kinship." The remarks in this first chapter stake out the field in order, on the one hand, to introduce the framework for the close-ups that follow, and, on the other, to point out the methodological inconsistencies inherent in this framework. The three categories most frequently used to distinguish godparenthood from descent and alliance—fiction, ritual, and legal consequences—will be discussed briefly.

Fiction: The problems with the concept of godparenthood as "fictive kinship" are particularly obvious, and have occasionally been noted. Following a tradition in legal history that goes back to Henry Maine, one may regard as fictive descendants those persons to whom particular rights belonging to official descendants (such as inheritance rights) have been transferred through a *conscious* act of *legal fiction*. Maine regarded the legal fiction as one of the "first steps towards civilization." The example he used was adoption as it appears in ancient Roman law. Adoption is understood here as a strategically deployed legal fiction of descent, a legally binding "as if." This concept of fictive descent draws on the assumption that the "as if" is the most universal characteristic of fiction (in the nonliterary sense).[26] One accords someone the *status* of a blood relative through a formal act of naming. The range of this form of fictive descent was as variable as its consequences and motives, and in many cases the fiction remained incomplete and the adoptee acquired only certain of the filial rights and duties.[27] This scholarly concept of adoption is obviously not a very useful way of understanding godparenthood. Baptismal kinship was used to meet very different needs. It was never associated with inheritance rights and was never intended to establish descent through a conscious act of legal fiction. It was not a corrective to biological chance, nor a fiction.

Other concepts, however, raise similar problems. What they all have in common is the wish to define godparenthood as something that is not quite "real" kinship ("ritual," "putative"); indeed, they explicitly refer to it sometimes as false kinship ("pseudo," "fictive") or as something else altogether ("kin like," "metaphoric"). The notion that some forms of kinship are somehow (scarcely anybody comes right out and says it) "proper" and that some are "not proper" runs through the scholarly terminology.

Ritual: English-speaking scholars often describe godparenthood as "ritual kinship." That this concept is ill suited to capture the specific quality of godparenthood is all too apparent. Any form of kinship that has a social reality is constituted, defined, and represented ritually. This applies as much to baptismal kinship as it does to kinship by marriage or birth. Even in the case of kinship by birth, it is always an initiation rite that establishes the kinship bond. The notion of "illegitimate children" is clear enough. The rite of godparenthood was no more artificial, contractual, or voluntarist than a marriage ritual. Even descent, it should be recalled, was an act of will: a newborn child had to be acknowledged before becoming a descendant. In classical Roman law, for example, this occurred through the rite of the *tollere liberum* (lifting up of the child), and the Germanic tribes had a similar practice. If the abandonment of children truly was an ever-present option in the Middle Ages, as John Boswell has indicated, then in the medieval period the voluntarist element was also not inconsiderable even in relationships of descent.[28]

For this reason, it is surprising that the ritual element should be declared the decisive characteristic of kinship, particularly in the case of godparenthood. What is the baptismal bond being distinguished *from* in this way? We might expect to find the opposition "ritual versus biological kinship" lurking behind the notion of godparenthood as "ritual kinship." This suspicion makes even more sense when it comes to concepts such as "artificial kinship" or "pseudo-kinship." It seems as if scholars try to find subtle definitions for the relationship between biology and kinship only on the level of epistemological professions. The step from epistemological profession to empirical method and the categories used to structure the field of research seems a problematic one. But why do scholars almost always define godparents, adoptees, or oath brothers as "pseudo"-kin, as false, artificial kin? What is wrong—"pseudo-," "fictive," "artificial," "putative"—with them? And how does this classification influence researchers' conclusions?

Legal consequences: Doubtless, the legal consequences varied. Here, too, though, the implicit division of the field of research along the lines of biological and "non-genuine" kinship is scarcely tenable. Even within relationships of descent and alliance, the social and legal positions held by individuals—for example, between firstborn children and later ones, between sons and daughters, men and women, kin by blood and marriage—varied widely. The treatment of illegitimate children in particular shows that it was not nature but the law that mattered. Legal texts occasionally distinguished between legitimate children *(liberi)* and "natural children" *(liberi naturales)*—that is, the children of concubines. In this case "natural" plainly denoted a lower status, an arbitrarily chosen but significant example.[29]

There is no characteristic of (and no deficiency in) a "ritual" relationship that does not have its counterpart in a characteristic of (or deficiency in) some biological relationship or other. The criteria of the usual scholarly terminology quickly reach their limits, limits whose origins should be sought in the history of scholarship rather than in epistemology. Especially at a time when the cultural sciences have become thoroughly permeated by semiotics, it would seem appropriate to follow other criteria than, ultimately, "blood." In order even to recognize other possibilities, we need to take into account those social relations in which kin terms may not have been used to define descent and alliance, yet still played a key role in describing behavioral norms and relations of authority. If we wish to understand what is specific about medieval kinship, shouldn't we be taking the social fields of the monastery, godparenthood, and the confraternity as seriously as we do those of marriage alliance and lineage?

If kinship is considered a culturally specific mental construct, then we can restrict our research on it to descent and alliance only if the society (or segment of society) under analysis also limited kinship in this way. Such a narrow view is unlikely to prove fruitful for work in medieval studies. Those contemporaries who possessed broad powers of definition did not, at any rate, accept this restriction. In their everyday interactions, the laity may have had different ideas about kinship than those preached by the clergy. Perhaps their thoughts on the subject were closer to those of present-day scholars. The notions held by priests, however, belonged to their store of knowledge, and we can occasionally catch glimpses of how they applied them.[30] In any case, this presumed discrepancy of perspective is already part of our object of study.

We should not forget the simple proposition that kinship was one of a whole series of categories of perception with which people at one and the same time ordered their social environment and legitimated that order. Each mode of perception claimed to do no more than render conceivable a specific aspect of social reality. As such a category, kinship, like many others in the Middle Ages (that is, social metaphors such as the house or the body, patterns of interpretation such as the famous *tria genera hominum*), was normative and at the same time made reality imaginable.[31] Viewed from this perspective, we may regard as kin relations all those social ties that were described in the Middle Ages using the vocabulary of kinship—and they were many. The logic according to which the research field of "kinship" is delimited from others, and internally differentiated, is the object of—not (as in biologistic concepts) the prerequisite for—research.

A Framework for the Analysis of Parenthood: A Functionalist Alternative

The usual divisions of kinship were already obsolete for the purposes of a structural functionalist approach such as that suggested by Esther Goody in her *Framework for the Analysis of Parent Roles*. Goody played through an alternative perspective, taking the term "parents" as an example. She proposed a functional scientific term, "a universally applicable definition of parenthood" in place of the everyday term "parents." To investigate the techniques of social reproduction in cultural comparison, she considered as an individual's "parents" all those who fulfilled "the critical tasks which have to be dealt with in producing a society's new member, so that they can effectively assume adult roles in society": bearing and begetting, endowment with civil and status identity, nurturance, training, sponsorship into adulthood. "Parenthood is about social replacement," she notes. In order to understand the logic of these reproductive processes, Goody proposes that "the full range of problems involved in reproducing a new generation be treated together." She distinguishes between different kinds of parenthood (physiological, jural, educational) that are expressed in different parent roles. Only in exceptional cases are all these roles fulfilled by an individual's genitors. To learn something about a society's specific contours we need to understand "how these tasks are linked or distributed in different societies," as well as how they are "differently weighted." According to Goody's framework, we must analyze the "culturally prescribed distribution of parent roles" (allocation) and the possibilities of a "transfer of one or more roles to pro-parents" (delegation) in a given society.[32]

Goody's framework positions society's new members within the network of their culturally prescribed set of "significant others." Where the literature often views individuals as surrounded by "real," "artificial," and "metaphoric" kin, Goody examines them within a network of ties to persons with parent roles, founded on childbearing and rearing, nurturing, teaching, sponsoring, and the endowment with status identity. Society's profile is revealed in the way in which the tasks of social reproduction (the parent roles) are allocated.

Esther Goody's framework thus provides an instructive comparison because she seeks to reinterpret a concept few of her readers regard as problematic, yet which has massively influenced the delineation of research fields. Here, too, what is at stake is a querying of the connections among biological vocabulary, social vocabulary, and scholarly concepts. Adoption and sponsorship, both important in Goody's framework, are understood not as "fictive" or "pseudo" but rather within the context of the physiological, jural, and educational aspects of parenthood that are allocated to a culturally specific set of persons.

To be sure, the scholarly climate is no longer conducive to structural functionalist approaches. Goody's proposals are based on a list of tasks within social reproduction that she regards as objectively necessary. The semiotically oriented approaches widespread today tend not to proceed from such scholarly definitions of the objectively necessary, instead taking as their starting point the collective conceptions of the society under investigation. Goody's proposals already make clear that this is, in part, merely a question of argumentative strategies. She marshals culturally specific notions of parenthood in order to counter biologistic approaches. Not every society shares the notion of today's European cultures that the physiological parents are the "real" parents. In many societies, those who transmit civil and kinship status are considered the "real" parents. In a few societies (for example, some poor black urban communities in the United States), it is the child-rearing relationship that is the key criterion for parenthood.[33] Historians could supply further examples. For example, in the society of Roman antiquity, which gave us the terminology of sponsorship, *pater* was a juridical term referring not to the biological father but to the head of household *(dominus)*, and the *familia* was a purely legal term for all those persons subject to the authority of this *pater*.[34] Put another way, the *familia* of the Roman jurists was constituted through the idea of authority, and it was the *pater* who wielded that authority.[35] It thus remains to be investigated whether the baptismal *pater* was modeled on biology or perhaps more on such legal constructions. Medieval historians may be more inclined to think of all the "spiritual fathers" and "spiritual mothers" *(pater/mater spiritalis)* who populate our sources. There was no shortage of contemporaries who referred to these spiritual parents as the "real" parents.

Ex Anima et Corpore: Approaches to Medieval Kinship

How, then, might research on medieval kinship proceed without projecting current ideas of kinship onto its object of study? We may begin with the hardly controversial proposition that kinship is a *terminological* structuring system which can be used to define social relationships of *all kinds*. If we wish to measure the accomplishments of this terminological system within a particular culture, we must examine everything the society in question regarded as being connected with kinship. The relationship between kinship and biological reproduction must be examined anew in each case: what was the position of illegitimate children, who was considered the "real" father, and so forth.

The western Middle Ages would appear to be an especially appropriate object on which to test such an approach. After all, in medieval culture a particularly large proportion of the relationships referred to as "kin" were based on neither birth nor marriage. In contrast to medievalist research on kinship in the tradition of economic and social history, we need to show how a highly productive mental structuring system was used to define a large number of social relationship types and what these relationship types had to do with each other. In a dialogue with kinship research by cultural anthropologists, another aspect probably would be more central: in medieval society—especially that of the early and high Middle Ages—"kinship" was, to be sure, a dominant system for structuring social relations, but also one that had to assert itself alongside other structuring systems that functioned in completely different ways. Vassalage—for many scholars the epitome of what we call the "Middle Ages"—was a system of social relationships that dispensed with the terminology of kinship altogether. It would be interesting, especially with regard to macrohistorical cultural developments, to ask what kind of relationship existed between those social fields defined primarily in terms of kinship (from the diocese to descent) and those not defined in such terms (such as vassalage, university, guild, municipality) and how this relationship changed over time.

We do have some studies that, while concentrating solely on the modes of argument used by the clergy, at least play through the possibilities of non-biologistic kinship research taking this social group as an example. They proceed from the observation that in their sermons and tracts, the clerics developed two systems of thinking about kinship, in analogy to the human duality of spirit and body *(ex anima et corpore)*: a carnal one *(cognatio carnalis*, constituted through birth and marriage), and a spiritual one *(cognatio spiritalis*, constituted through baptism). Although often constructed as pairs of opposites *(carnis-spiritus*, sin-redemption, etc.), the two systems were thoroughly intertwined (the incarnation of Christ, the union of spirit and flesh in the redemption).[36]

The difference between *cognatio spiritualis* and *cognatio carnalis* is especially apparent in the way in which the boundaries of the kin group were conceived in each case.[37] Carnal kinship had an inside and an outside; there were kin and non-kin. Marriage was a constitutive element of the change in status. The act referred to in ancient Rome (as in our present-day societies) as "adoption" could also have been a constitutive element of a change in status. At present, however, the assumption dominates that in the western Middle Ages this form of status change was not practiced.[38] In contrast, according to the concept of spiritual kinship, all Christians were, in principle, kin. Legitimate ways of life beyond this kinship bond were barely conceived of, and a place outside existed at most for heretics, Jews, and heathens. Baptism, the initiation into life, was constitutive of entry into spiritual kinship. Specific forms (kinship through godparenthood, monastic vows, ordination, membership in a parish, etc.) signified only modifications in status, which varied from close kinship, such as godparenthood, to kinship relations that were little more than conventions of speech.

There is no doubt that this concept of kinship was the product of theologians. It has its roots in an image of humanity developed by and constantly repeated by theologians. It would be interesting to know how the techniques for securing social status among the laity were influenced by this concept, and what competing ways of thinking about kinship (which may have been more significant for social practice) existed. This interpretation is, however, a plausible one (at least in regard to clerical culture), which does not make presumptions about the place of biological reproduction in the kinship system but, rather, seeks to derive it from the culture itself.

To reiterate: in Roman antiquity, an adoptee was considered a blood relation and (although everyone knew that this was not true) was claimed as a descendant. In one of the cases I will discuss later, the chronicler has the Merovingian king Gunthchramn claiming that his adopted son was "from my offspring" *(de stirpe mea)*.[39] Nobody would have made such an assertion about a godchild. Kinship, like baptismal sponsorship or the brotherhood and sisterhood of all Christians, was meant to establish a *quality of behavior*, it was a mode of conceiving of and ritually stabilizing a set of behavioral norms among kinsmen. The two conceptions of kinship, carnal and spiritual, were used simultaneously; they had different functions and were intertwined but seldom confused. A kinsman *ex anima* was not, for example, drawn by these ties into family feuds, nor did he inherit. Similarly, one does not speak of a spiritual kinsman "twice removed": carnal kinship bound groups, spiritual kinship bound individuals. Not infrequently, strict lines were drawn by the clerics between carnal and spiritual kinship and the spiritual variety was considered the more binding—based, of course, on the biblical texts that disparaged blood ties (Matthew 10:35–38; Luke 12:52–53; Genesis 12:1). Medieval baptismal sponsorship is a particularly good example.

Kinship Happens: Sponsorship and Adoption between Official Portrayals and Actual Practice

Angenendt stressed that godparenthood was labeled as adoption from the eighth century onward. Others have argued that Roman adoption practices did not survive in the Frankish kingdoms. Married couples could no longer choose a descendant through an act of legal fiction.[40] Only in the context of this altered legal situation does the religious linguistic convention take on contours: in the eighth century, when theologians began referring to godparenthood as *adoptio*, the term was no longer a legal one. The social place of this word was in the liturgy and in theology. The Merovingian sources that are the focus of the following chapters provide insights into this transition. They offer a unique opportunity to follow in narrative sources the process by which the legal fiction of *adoptio* came into direct competition with godparenthood. The chronicler Gregory of Tours recounts the history of two generations of Merovingians, which is, among other things, the tale of how the Merovingian rulers sought to pit the institutions of adoption and godparenthood against each other. His account throws light on the moment of transition between what the works of scholars of Roman law describe and the claim made at every baptism in the Frankish kingdom: that adoption was a spiritual matter. When the present study analyzes both adoptions and godparenthood under the heading of "Spiritual Kinship," it is already anticipating the state of affairs that would come to prevail from the eighth century on. The chapters that follow, which only seldom touch on the eighth century, focus on showing how the Roman legal institution of *adoptio* ceased to function during the period of transition.

As long as one does not confront it with concrete practices, the equation of sponsorship with *adoptio*—already expressed by one sixth-century Merovingian—says little about how and to what ends sponsorship was used and what this had to do with *adoptio*. Questions, particularly in regard to the specific social value of this form of kinship, remain which can scarcely be answered using Angenendt's and Lynch's main sources, but which are significant for social historians. The title of this book stresses my perspective on godparenthood and adoption: the analysis of practice. The proposition E. P. Thompson once summarized as "class happens" has since become a scholarly commonplace. Research on kinship has also been transformed by the basic assumption that kinship does not simply *exist*, but *happens*.[41] This insight directs our attention more closely to the material and symbolic transactions that take place both within kin groups and between kin groups and the world around them. Scholars have abandoned their privileging of the legal texts, their fixation on descent and alliance and structuralist methodologies, in favor of an analysis of kinship as practice. Constantly altered, whether perceptibly or imperceptibly, by the most diverse interpretations, kinship now appears as variable in its boundaries and definitions as the situations in which it exists and as the perspectives of its various representatives. This applies equally to descent and alliance groups and to baptismal kin relations. Recent scholarship on the Staufers and the Welfs, which has described these dynasties systematically from the perspective of their constantly changing self-interpretations and representations, demonstrates how powerfully explanatory the interpretation of historical descent and alliance groups can be when such an approach is used.[42]

Chapters 7 to 12 of this book aim to show how one can grasp the widely varying social value of godparenthood relations even in times and areas for which the source material is relatively sparse. The material allows us at least glimpses of answers to numerous questions, such as whether the relationship was permanent or dependent on occasion and context and thus temporary, whether it was largely predetermined by custom, whether it allowed the actors much scope for decision making (for example in the number and sex of a baptizee's godparents), whether it affected only the parties involved or their kin as well,[43] and finally, whether their roles were defined within the kinship system (as in the case of adoption) or in competition to it (as, for example, in the case of the *fraternitas* of guild members).

Sponsorship could either provide an official framework for useful relationships that already existed in practice[44] or create such practically useful relationships in the first place. The strategy of Theodoric the Great, who employed both marriage and adoption to secure his political position, may serve as an example of the latter function: in the year 500, Theodoric gave his sister Amalafrida in marriage to Trasamund, king of the Vandals, after already having given his daughter Thiudigotho to the Visigoth Alaric II a few years earlier. Another daughter, Ostrogotho, was married off to the Burgundian Sigismund, while Theodoric himself wedded the sister of the Frank Clovis, who in turn took the Burgundian Clotild as his wife. Rodulf, king of the Heruli, on the other hand, did not provide Theodoric with a wife, but rather "adopted" him as a *Waffensohn*,[45] a procedure his father, Thiudimir, had already used with Hunimund, leader of the Suevi.[46]

It is easier to identify such acts of kinship creation than to demonstrate their value in terms of social relations in a given case. To cite one of the central episodes in this area: when the Burgundian king Gunthchramn (reigned 561–93) assumed the sponsorship of his Neustrian nephew Chlothar, his Austrasian nephew Childebert protested,[47] arguing that this alliance brought with it consequences for the succession and endangered his own rights. Gunthchramn's reply was that he had had to agree to stand as godfather since "the call to perform this office is one that no Christian [is permitted to] refuse."[48] We need not question Gunthchramn's piety and subjective honesty here in order to look for the interests he was doubtless pursuing at the same time, which are also necessary to explain the importance of his argument in this concrete situation. In this case Gunthchramn suppressed half of the rule—the half that stated that one may only make a request after the other party has already agreed to it.[49]

The norm Gunthchramn cites, like his obedience to it, must always be taken into account as part of his calculations and of the "objective" conditions which led him to resort to particular strategies in the first place. Ultimately, it belonged to the conditions which, at once objective and internalized, he always *also* acknowledged and reproduced in his actions.[50]

This episode is not representative, however, if only because it is the sole case in the period under consideration of someone actually being called upon to justify an act of sponsorship. Usually we learn of sponsorship relationships only in passing without any reference to norms. It is even less common for a chronicler or hagiographer to refer to the concrete interests of a child's parents when choosing a particular person as godparent.[51] Such information on concrete interests is necessary, though, if we are to show that—and especially *how*—baptismal sponsorship functioned and was deployed. The Merovingian sources generally refer to kings who frequently, but not always, chose bishops as godparents. If we do not wish to attribute such choices to coincidence or chance—for example, by assuming that the godfather's bishopric just happened to be the birthplace of the king's son[52]—the only possibility left is to search for unmentioned motives. In what follows, we will analyze the possible motives behind each of the sixth-century cases that have come down to us.

If we regard the various forms of kinship from the standpoint of their social value or their respective purposes, we can distinguish among the various forms of kinship which, though always similar, had their own specificity and were formed and cultivated with different ends in mind. At the same time, this approach allows us to recognize where and how in practical terms they resembled each other and overlapped, where they had comparable effects and where they did not. No less important is the ever-present distinction between two aspects of kinship practice: on the one hand, we must investigate how kinship or a concrete kin relationship was portrayed and defined publicly by those who were legitimated to do so (that is, by the representatives of a kin group themselves or by experts in canon and secular law). On the other hand, we must undertake the far more difficult task of studying how people dealt with the rules that kin obeyed in their everyday interactions with each other and with outsiders. The following section outlines a few basic reflections on this question.

The fact that the protagonists had a number of options for creating kinship links with particular persons who interested them and for establishing more or (usually) less[53] fixed rules governing relations with these persons tells us nothing about the practical value of the resulting kinship group. The "rules" of kinship allow us to draw conclusions about kinship practice only to a limited extent. To be sure, these rules, which were demanded and at the same time internalized, helped determine behavior, but at the same time they competed with momentary interests or also with other potentially opposing "rules" from other social contexts.

Whenever a group of persons was expected, as a kin group, to fulfill this function of ordering and legitimation—for instance, in family trees, at weddings, or inheritance proceedings—it represented the universally "known" specific morality of the kin group to the outside world and at the same time enforced that morality among its members. In displaying its (occasionally fictive) genealogical and affinal alliances, a kin group ostensibly defined its inner and outer boundaries. A single captured image, such as the drawing up of a genealogical table, might suggest that kinship was "natural" and static, whereas in reality it was mutable. Consider, to name but a few well-known examples, the genealogies, continually modified over the course of time and in some cases fictive, with which medieval ruling dynasties sought to legitimate themselves.[54] Or let us recall Theodoric the Great: when after the death of Alaric II there was no eligible successor to the throne of the Visigothic kingdom, Theodoric quickly "discovered" *(comperit)* a suitable kinsman, and, in order to ensure that his legitimacy was beyond question, gave him his daughter Amalasuintha in marriage.[55] Think of the case of James II, king of Aragon (1267–1327), who at the opportune moment declared two of his marriages to have been incestuous and in both cases received a papal dispensation and thus the opportunity to marry again.[56] Other instances of the fluctuation of kin groups wholly lack the political imagination we happily attribute to Theodoric and James II. Thus, in early medieval *libri memoriales* we not infrequently encounter the same circle of relatives in several places—sometimes in the same book—with changing members. In the many eleventh- and twelfth-century deeds of donation in which kin proclaimed their consent *(laudatio, consensus)* to pious donations, the composition of the kinship group was equally mutable and assembled according to no recognizable method.[57] A final example: through the custom of dividing property in the case of inheritance into scattered parcels, families continually produced new neighbor property relations among their members, so that the intensity of relationships among the individual members must have shifted constantly.[58]

In its own way, each of these examples portrays kinship and its norms as a medium for social and political action—constantly changed by the actors, who staked out the scope for modifications and sometimes also manipulations, presenting different interpretations to suit the situation, adroitly "forgetting" inconvenient facts, casting doubt on kin relationships here and suddenly "discovering" kinsmen there, craftily fulfilling an unwelcome duty here and cultivating one relationship and neglecting another there,[59] dodging and delaying here, reactivating an old alliance there, and so forth.

All this can be shown more clearly for kinship groups beyond descend and alliance, whose activities are the focus of attention here, than for biological ones, since the aspect of their deliberate establishment is more apparent. Medieval narrators describe them similarly, to be sure, using the same pattern of "kinship," but as specifically differentiated among themselves, and thus render visible the techniques with which, in a given case, those involved reconciled publicly assumed duties with current interests.

So much for the preliminary discussion of the approach to godparenthood in the early Middle Ages, which I am testing here. For the sake of greater precision, I shall begin by sketching how the material used by Angenendt and Lynch appears in a new light when viewed from this perspective.

The Churchmen's Version: Baptismal Sponsorship as an All-Embracing Family Network

Angenendt and Lynch attribute the unusual success and expansion of baptismal sponsorship over the course of the early Middle Ages in particular to certain advantages sponsorship offered over traditional methods of creating artificial kinship. The first advantage of sponsorship was that a desired alliance could also be established through female offspring.[60] In addition, sponsorship—unlike, for example, oath brotherhood or *Waffensohnschaft*—could create ties among an entire group of people: the godchild and godparent, the godparent's spouse, the godchild's biological parents, and occasionally also the cleric performing the baptism.[61] From the late ninth century on, parents also began to invite several sponsors to their child's baptism, although the Church initially had forbidden this, so that two or three and, in the late Middle Ages, six or even twelve sponsors might be named and thus the number of those with whom parents could ally themselves apparently increased several fold.[62] In addition, in the eighth century churchmen then extended the office of sponsor to the newly introduced rite of confirmation,[63] so that parents could now choose not only a baptismal sponsor for each child but also a confirmation sponsor *(patrinus/ matrina de confirmatione episcopi)*. As in the modern period, confirmation sponsorship appears to have enjoyed a lesser status and thus also less social relevance[64] (at least it is much more rarely documented in the Middle Ages than baptismal sponsorship), but rulers nevertheless occasionally made use of it for political purposes. When he came to the Frankish kingdom in 754, Pope Stephen II may have stood as confirmation sponsor to Pippin's sons, Charles and Carlomann, while Otto III and Henry II were confirmation sponsors to the sons of the doges of Venice, and Alfred the Great acted as confirmation sponsor for the Welsh king Anarawd ap Rhodri.[65] Rulers appear to have resorted to confirmation sponsorship when they were in need of an alliance but had no unbaptized child.[66]

Scholars looking for confirmation sponsorship in canon and secular legal texts of the early Middle Ages—in penitentials, canonical collections and council acts, capitularies and *"leges barbarorum"*—are in for a surprise.[67] Here, where churchmen and kings articulated their claim officially to formulate the rules, there is no evidence of lesser social relevance. The "familial" consequences of confirmation sponsorship are (except in the case of Ine)[68] treated no differently from those of baptismal sponsorship.[69] According to these documents, the institutions of baptismal and confirmation sponsorship were equally well placed to provide every parent-child relationship with a substantial kin network. For every two or three surviving children we may assume per family, we should count the same number who died in childhood[70] but were still baptized. Thus, each set of parents might have been allied to half a dozen baptismal sponsors, together with their spouses, a few confirmation sponsors, and finally to the kin groups of their own godchildren. In this way, a couple could easily acquire twenty to thirty spiritual cofathers and comothers.

According to the churchmen, this was still not enough. The *Canons of Theodore* (between 690 and 755) refer to a further expansion. Apart from sponsorship at confirmation, the *Canons* mention another offshoot of baptismal sponsorship, which the author describes as a "custom" to be followed: a third sponsor should be engaged just for the preparatory rite preceding actual baptism. In this preparatory rite, the child was made a *catechumenus*, someone ready to be initiated into the secrets of the creed. According to the *Canons*, the same person could fulfill all three roles only in exceptional cases.[71] This "custom" is documented for at least one case, though, and an illustrious one at that. When the future William of Dijon was baptized, Adelheid, the wife of Emperor Otto I, served as godmother, and Otto himself received William on the occasion of his becoming a *catechumenus*.[72] Other normative sources enumerate even more separate occasions for sponsorship than Theodore. In a letter allegedly written by Pope Deusdedit (615–18) to the Spanish bishop Gordianus, for example, the author divides the act of baptism into seven stages, each of which was said to entail a prohibition on marriage.[73] These stipulations found their way into no lesser legal compilations than those of Burchard of Worms and Gratian,[74] and they appear in similar terms in two Norwegian laws for the *Thing* at Gule and that at Frosta. The law book for the *Thing* at Gule mentions six occasions for sponsorship, which, if the parents took advantage of all the possibilities and chose only one sponsor per rite, would have produced sixteen new kin relationships out of a single baptism.[75]

> The occasions of coparenthood are six, in which we should exercise abstinence as we do with our female blood kin. The first is that of holding the child during the first benediction, and the second, receiving it from the font, the third, taking it from its christening gown, the fourth, holding it under the bishop's hand, the fifth, loosening the confirmation band, the sixth, leading a woman to church [after the birth of a child?]. We should heed the last coparenthood only towards the woman, but all of the other five coparenthoods we should keep towards the father and mother as well as the child.[76]

All these regulations might lead us to conclude that from the early Middle Ages on, baptism produced a powerful set of social interconnections which, because of the ever-growing number of bonds, must have severely restricted the possibilities for marriage. This picture does not seem very realistic, though, if we consider the size of settlements in the early Middle Ages[77] and the necessarily limited spatial radius of social contacts (and hence opportunities for marriage). Furthermore, if the spiritual interconnections with which churchmen concerned themselves had possessed anything approaching a practical reality beyond learned discussions, then one could have demanded familial *pax* and *amor* from practically everyone in the social field of a village or regional noble society. At this level of universality, though, sponsorship would have been so unspecific and lacking in exclusivity that its social value would have been practically nonexistent.

Limited Efficacy

We need to begin by looking at individual cases and asking whether and to what extent sponsorship ties are recognizable as practically relevant ties. Even here, early medieval accounts are not exactly forthcoming. To cite just one example: when a ninth-century chronicler writes that two Ravenna merchants had made an alliance *(foedus)* with the help of sponsorship, and goes on to note that "from that day, on which the child was christened, forward, they were fathers together and loved each other in the holy spirit and the kiss of peace," his narrative apparently describes only the concrete conduct of these two merchants. What he is actually describing is the norm of kinship, as the chronicler himself indicates when he adds the words "as it is proper for persons as have such dealings with each other."[78] To be sure, this does not automatically render the account unrealistic, since even stereotypes such as those visible here tell us something about behavior.[79] However, we do not learn how the merchants actually behaved toward each other after they entered the baptismal alliance. Such examples tell us little about the practical reality of sponsorship relationships. They tell us little about whether people actually made use of their familial possibilities, and, if they did, what the implications were—for conduct toward each other, for group solidarity, the representation of kinship boundaries or marital behavior.

Studies of sponsorship in the early modern period can remind us of all the possibilities about which early and high medieval sources offer no information. Thus, David Sabean's research on sponsorship relationships in early modern Neckarhausen has yielded the surprising information that parents often chose the same person as godparent for all their children and that that person's son or daughter frequently "inherited" this function upon his or her death. In the face of all the lost potential for alliances that seems rather a waste, no less than the equally frequent practice of naming one's close relatives (father, mother, brother, sister) as sponsors. Here, apparently, less stress was placed on expanding social relationships than on intensifying them.[80] Such a setting of parental priorities[81] tends to remain hidden in the medieval sources, particularly the normative ones. But knowledge of such early modern practices at least serves as a warning against drawing inferences about an actual broad system of sponsorship bonds from the possibilities mentioned in the normative documents.

Sabean's work also suggests caution if we are to interpret the practice, already present in the early Middle Ages, of choosing two or more baptismal sponsors for a child. Here, too, evidence from early modern Neckarhausen shows that the issue may have been less an expansion of relationships than the differing interests of the two parents and their families, which could most easily be reconciled by choosing two godparents. Sabean has demonstrated for Neckarhausen that most often one sponsor was chosen according to the needs of the father and one according to the needs of the mother.[82] This, too, is something the medieval sources do not reveal, just as they do not show how strongly the potential network was reduced by overlapping, for example when a parent chose a sponsor for one child whose spouse then served as godparent to a further child. Thus, the interpretation of such practices becomes to a considerable extent a question of perspective. The opportunities for a given individual to use sponsorship to place himself or herself at the center of an extensive network of personal relationships may be much less spectacular if we look at families rather than individuals, that is, less at sponsorship's function in constituting groups than in creating, and, even more, cementing, alliances between kin groups. Viewed from this perspective, it is conceivable that all of an individual's spiritual kin could come from only a few families to whom sponsorship relations were continually being renewed.

If these qualifying remarks about the medieval sources are of a rather hypothetical nature, with no possibility of being tested against the material, on closer inspection the medieval sources also lend themselves to a few conspicuous reservations. These apply to the efficacy of incest rules and the efficacy of the opportunities for creating ever more spiritual kin through sponsorship relationships. One gains the impression that by no means everything the normative sources deemed possible, or even common (*consuetudo*)[83] actually occurred in this form and that, conversely, forbidden practices occurred not infrequently.

Incest Inflation

Using many examples from sixth-century and later narrative sources, Angenendt and Lynch have shown that sponsorship was an institution generally used in social practice. They have also shown that sponsorship was by no means inevitably linked to the notion of incest. If Boniface found the incest prohibitions disconcerting,[84] there is a good historical explanation for this: unlike the "normal" prohibitions against incest with blood kin[85] these prohibitions had no tradition in the West. Joseph Lynch has shown that Boniface indeed could not have been familiar with the rules governing incest because they had entered the West from Byzantium only around 692—and then at the highest official level. The Byzantine emperor Justinian II had sent them, as an outcome of the Trullan council of 692, to Rome for papal approval. The popes then agreed to the regulations in 711 and promulgated them ten years later at a Roman council,[86] that is, some fifteen years prior to the letters that have come down to us from Boniface. The incest prohibitions regarding baptismal kin went on, however, to conquer the whole spectrum of Western sources of law by the second half of the eighth century, within the space of only a few decades.[87]

This means that the demand of the "priests throughout the whole of Frankland and Gaul"[88] to treat baptismal kin like blood kin in marriage prohibitions was in no way obvious or immediately understandable to contemporaries; it was by no means the product of "primitive" ways of thinking or of an "archaic" culture.[89] What the "priests throughout the whole of Frankland and Gaul" maintained and canon and secular legal texts demanded was not necessarily what the "normal" laity thought, let alone practiced. If such an incest prohibition was "in force,"[90] this was initially the case only in learned writings. And was a prohibition "in force" if "people" knew about it or only if they also obeyed it? The actual relevance of these incest prohibitions on baptismal kin for determining who married whom is a question in its own right. Even if practice is harder to pin down than canon and royal law, one can point to details that help illuminate the relationship between the rules and actual practice.

The *Canons of Theodore*[91] provide some initial hints. They assert that inviting a separate godparent for the preliminary ritual—an action scarcely found in practice—was a custom, or *consuetudo*. The relationship between regulation and "compliance" is no more favorable if we view that alleged letter from Pope Deusdedit, which—in common with a few Nordic *leges*—divides the rite of baptism into seven stages, each with its separate sponsor and incest prohibition.[92] Although the letter appears in Burchard and Gratian, this division of baptism is nowhere reflected in the narrative sources describing the actions of those who applied it. Evidently the zeal for norms among liturgical and ecclesiastical specialists occasionally exceeded the requirements of liturgical and social practice. The churchmen—and, in their wake, the secular legislators—apparently were simply thinking ahead.[93]

Such examples do not indicate that incest prohibitions had any high practical relevance for the regulation of marriage behavior. To be sure, the popes pushed the dissemination of these prohibitions immediately after adopting the decrees of Trullo in 721. Two years later, King Liutprand, helped along, no doubt, by Pope Gregory II, incorporated the regulations into Langobard law.[94] Pope Zachary transmitted them to Pippin, who soon adopted them in his first capitulary.[95] The stipulations even found their way into a few Nordic legal texts.[96] The prohibitions were widely diffused in canonical collections, penitentials and council acts,[97] and we know that Ghaerbald of Liège (785/7–809), for example, instructed his priests to note precisely who had sexual contacts with which spiritual kin, and to bring these persons before the bishop.[98]

Nevertheless, we find scarcely a trace of these regulations, or of any intervention by the bishops against a concrete marriage which baptismal sponsorship had rendered incestuous, be it annulment or any form of punishment. When a chronicler does recount a "practical" case, such as in the *Liber historiae Francorum* (written in 727), it is an old, well-known story. According to this account, Fredegund, the second wife of King Chilperic, slyly convinced his first wife, Audovera, to receive her own son from the font. In so doing, Audovera became a spiritual kinswoman to her royal husband, who could now cast her off and become free to marry Fredegund. As Audovera's spiritual kinsman he was "compelled" by canon law to leave her.⁹⁹ In this account, the ecclesiastical prohibition was indisputably in effect. Even if the theme here was the "practical" and crafty manner of dealing with the regulation, the point could be made only because the rule was deemed binding.

Naturally, the fact that we cannot demonstrate that people obeyed the incest prohibitions should not lead us to assume that all these prohibitions existed only in learned discourse. There are indeed examples taken from the lives of "the people." But these do not show that the rules were being *obeyed*, rather that people were *aware* of them and knew how to use them in arguments when necessary. Where the rules on incest did have a practical value, they appear unexpectedly. Thus, the anecdote in the *Liber historiae Francorum* already suggested a practice which, a century later, the bishops meeting in council at Chalon-sur-Saône in 813 sought to halt: apparently, some people were using baptismal sponsorship as a trick to gain a divorce.¹⁰⁰ Centuries later, Gratian was still construing a highly complicated case in which, among other things, a woman "slyly" *(callide)* sought to receive her own son from the font.¹⁰¹

Another virtually classic example of the clever use of such regulations was recounted in the twelfth century by Petrus Cantor. A godfather whose godchild had died feared that he might now lose the favor *(gratia)* of his cofather (that is, the child's biological father) and asked the latter for a new godchild. The father, however, refused and handled the delicate situation of denying his spiritual cofather's *(compater)* request by means of two arguments. First, he noted that if he chose the same person twice as godfather to his child he would lose the opportunity to broaden his social alliances, or, as he put it, "Cofatherhood *(compaternitas)* was established to extend love *(caritas)*. You are, however, already bound to me through a co–fatherhood *(una compaternitas)* and I to you. Is it not better for me to make another man cofather, in order to extend love *(caritas)* further?"¹⁰² One *(una) compaternitas*, he argues, must suffice.

While the father fell back on an official definition of the *caritas* of spiritual kin, his cofather's anxiety probably arose more from the experience that such favor tended to fade *(timet ne langueat gratia)*¹⁰³ when because of the death of the godchild one could no longer renew the relationship. As if recognizing the weakness of his own argument, the father then immediately talked himself out of the precarious situation with a second, very different and much cleverer version: It was not permitted. "If," he argued, "I had a wife from a given family *(cognatio)*, I could not marry any other woman of the same family *(cognatio)* after her death. . . . Similarly, if your godson has died, I may not take you into cofatherhood *(compaternitas)* again."¹⁰⁴ The father behaved as (not because) the "rule" dictated, he cited a "rule" to justify his action.

In these episodes from the life of "the people" the incest prohibitions are part of the knowledge that they could deploy in everyday life to portray what they desired in a given situation as "objectively" necessary and prescribed. In contrast, these prohibitions, as widespread as they were, had at least no perceptible effect on actual marriage choices. Even if the odd document may be interpreted in this light, a glaring discrepancy remains between the efforts at regulation and their (perceptible) effects.[105] Who could have controlled incestuous unions so long as they were not recorded? Certainly not the priests, and the efficacy of neighborly control, for example, even if neighbors had been interested in it, should not be overestimated. The more godparents a baptizee had, the more difficult it was to keep track of them. A much later (but structurally comparable) case, chosen at random, illustrates this point nicely—the example of Joan of Arc. During the rehabilitation proceedings of 1456 all witnesses, among them four sponsors, including Joan's godfather, were questioned. Each of them, including the sponsors themselves, gave a different answer. One of them could name not one, another only two or three, and one woman six sponsors. The witnesses introduced a total of eight names of which only two were mentioned frequently (thirteen and ten times), and four names appear only once each. In 1431, Joan herself had named two godfathers and three godmothers in court. One witness each mentioned the two godfathers in 1456, while nobody remembered the three godmothers. A close investigation of this example and similar cases would show how complicated such collective memories were, how many factors they depended on and how unreliable they are as a means of verifying the application of such regulations.[106]

At least one theoretical qualification is possible, however. If sexual unions between baptismal kin were indeed taboo, as Lynch suspects[107] and we could thus assume that a kind of internalization of ecclesiastical regulations did take place, that might at least explain the absence of evidence of actual penalties for such offences or of clerical intervention. "People" simply did not enter such relationships. Anthropological studies indicating that sexual contacts between baptismal sponsors and their artificial kin are taboo in certain societies[108] make such a solution appear at least possible for the Middle Ages as well. Such a taboo becomes plausible if we take into account that, at least according to the norm, godparents were also supposed to help educate their godchildren. It does seem a bit foolhardy, though, to use these borrowings from anthropology to draw conclusions about medieval practice merely because the sources remain silent, especially since incest taboos are by no means as universal as we once believed.[109] It is also conceivable that incest taboos were operating in some of the incest prohibitions applying to baptismal sponsors, but hardly in all of the relationships which the specialists wished to treat as incestuous. Given the limited opportunities for marriage and the generally minimal efficacy of other legal norms, it makes more sense to assume that the incest prohibitions incurred by sponsorship, for whose practical application we have no evidence, likewise exercised little influence over marriage behavior.

Finally, the limited efficacy of other legal norms goes a long way towards rendering this conclusion less spectacular, since it does not differ from the results of *leges* studies, for example, or from the findings of research on other aspects of Frankish marriage practices. Thus, despite extensive efforts, it took the Church centuries to establish the biological incest prohibitions as well as its own notions of divorce and remarriage, concubinage or *Friedelehe*, a less formal kind of marriage.[110] Here, unlike the incest prohibitions connected with baptismal sponsorship, we have ample evidence of the discrepancy between church regulations and Frankish marriage practice[111] and of interventions by bishops in cases of concrete violations.[112] The same holds true for the prohibitions of spiritual incest in the *leges barbarorum* and capitularies. Initiators in the Frankish sphere do not even always appear to have intended the *leges* to have relevance for everyday legal practice, and the politics of the capitularies, by means of which the kings probably actually sought to standardize practice in the Frankish lands, apparently also enjoyed no great success.[113] And yet the various regulations of the *leges* or capitularies were, on the whole, at least practicable. The same can hardly be said for the rules governing incest among baptismal kin. They were not merely so extensive that, if applied consistently, they would have curtailed opportunities for marriage sharply. They were also—and this is the next point—highly obscure and (at least from the scholarly standpoint) resistant to systematization.

Diffuse Rules

Why were the prohibitions so inefficient? Structural difficulties more generally, and the limited opportunities for communication and inadequate apparatus of sanctions at the same time offer a partial explanation. The sources on sponsorship suggest an additional element as well: even professionals—the clergy—could not recognize in every case which bonds were to be considered "incestuous" since the bishops had not even composed rules to cover all the possible constellations. In his *capitula*, which was intended for the practical work of the clergy, Haito of Basel admitted that there were so many potential forms of incest that he could not possibly list the "almost countless" cases .[114] In the eighth century, Theodore of Pavia asked Pope Zachary whether it was permissible for a man to marry his father's goddaughter (which the pope forbade)[115] and whether the children of such illegitimate unions were allowed to marry (which the pope permitted).[116] In 895, the council of Tribur preferred not to, or could not, decide whether a godparent was permitted to marry the siblings of his or her godchild.[117] In a letter to Pippin, Pope Zachary claimed that the Church fathers had not prohibited spiritual kinship because they had been too afraid to mention such heinous crimes.[118] Such a line of argument was surely not simply the makeshift assertion of a pope with no authoritative texts to bring forward. He himself mentioned such an example of spiritual incest by name in a letter to Theodore of Pavia, but expressly added that it "is terrible to speak out loud."[119] The records of the council of Epaon (517) show that this kind of argument was not unusual: they expressly mention a series of prohibited incestuous unions (none of them spiritual) by name, omitting, however "those whose mention sullies."[120]

Apparently, the decision makers in a given locality themselves had to be familiar with these "sullying" prohibitions, which seems all the more difficult given the frequent lack of any recognizable system. Thus, for example, none of the Frankish sources prohibit marriage between the biological and spiritual children of the same father, that is, between the closest kin.[121] When a child had several godparents the latter were also apparently not prohibited from marrying one another.[122] The Scholastic Petrus Cantor noted much later that he did not know why "in many places" the Church did not forbid people from choosing two godparents from the same family *(cognatio)* given that a man was not permitted after his wife's death to choose a spouse from the same *cognatio*.[123]

Not even specialists in canon law, let alone "the people," then, extended the incest prohibitions on biological kin in strict analogy to spiritual kin. Departures, where they did occur, scarcely originated in any systematic logic. The early testimony of a Boniface, like that of the Scholastic authors, still shows that people were quite capable of conceiving of spiritual kinship without positing any impediment to marriage.[124] The bishops in Gaul also did not always demand that spouses leave each other when one became the sponsor of his or her own child. In order to ensure that nobody could use sponsorship as an occasion for divorce, the bishops sometimes only required penance in such cases.[125] At the same time, however—and it may have been not least this contradiction which provided the room for maneuver—the social effect of sponsorship rested precisely on the analogy between kinship by sponsorship and kinship by descent and marriage.

Such uncertainties, indeterminacies, and obscurities, which continued to produce a multiplicity of disagreements among commentators even in the twelfth century, doubtless did nothing to improve the efficacy of prohibitions.[126] If only for that reason, we cannot assume that the incest rules applying to sponsorship played a significant role in marital choices. We may be inclined to generalize Bishop Theodore of Pavia's lament in a letter to Pope Zachary that, in his experience, such (technically "incestuous") marriages occurred "extremely frequently *(enormiter contigisse)*."[127]

Kin Inflation

It is striking that, as in the case of the incest rules, the initiators and authors of the legal sources (canonical collections, council acts, penitentials, capitularies, *leges barbarorum*) adopted expanded definitions while the authors of the narrative sources did not. To be sure, the latter often report on baptismal sponsors, but much less frequently on confirmation sponsors. We are unlikely to find a catechumenate sponsor other than Otto I, or any of the other kinds of sponsors—for example, churching sponsors, or those who loosened the confirmation bands—who are listed in the Nordic *leges* or the letter attributed to Pope Deusdedit.[128]

Attempts at interpreting this reticence on the part of "users" can only suggest probabilities. The multiplication of sponsors in the normative texts that was brought about by the increasing splitting of rituals, which appears to have been followed in practice only to a limited extent, would have led to an inflation in godparent-godchild bonds and thus to a decline in their social utility. Anthropologists have encountered such a loss of value and function among sponsors who had a particularly large number of godchildren and were no longer in a position even to remember all of them. They cannot, therefore, have cultivated all of these relationships.[129] Just as it cannot have been socially very advantageous to limit opportunities for marriage severely by means of incest prohibitions, it was also not very useful to extend kin groups excessively through ever more kinds of sponsorship. Sponsorship bonds would have ceased to be practicable and maintainable, useless for that *caritas* and *gratia* for which people entered into such relationships in the first place.[130]

We thus cannot simply assume that an increase in the forms of sponsorship mentioned in legal texts reflected an increased need for kin in practice, let alone that an expansion of godparent-godchild bonds actually permitted a more efficient social utilization of relationships. On the contrary: if medieval narrative writers often mention baptismal sponsorship, but almost never other forms of sponsorship, the "users" appear to have had little interest in these other forms for their social relationships.

In this case, however, a practice that appears nonsensical at first sight remains to be explained. While in some regions people were satisfied with only one godparent even in the early modern period, in others parents in particular appear, over the course of time, to have invited several sponsors for each child, without it being clear whether these godparents served some ritual function.¹³¹ With such a group of baptismal sponsors, each of whom was less likely to serve any function the more of them there were, parents' primary interest cannot have been to create a social or political bond with all of the godparents. If during the rehabilitation proceedings for Joan of Arc many witnesses could recall one particular godparent, but scarcely anyone another godparent, this should lead us to reflect on the differing relevance of Joan's various godparents for social relationships.¹³²

The usefulness of such multiplications should be sought instead in another aspect of group relations: in the self-representation of parents—that is, in the prestige value of a particularly elaborate christening. This, too, was a means of using baptismal sponsorship to further the current interests of the parents, who could thereby demonstrate and solidify their place in the social structure. Some of the sixth-century examples treated here will show how people used this prestige value which could also—if not exclusively—be expressed in the form of multiple godparents. A few examples from the eighth to tenth centuries—albeit only indirectly applicable to the social practice of "the people"—show this particularly clearly: the imperial baptismal actions of the Anglo-Saxon, Carolingian, or Ottonian rulers which have been studied by Arnold Angenendt.

An Application: Imperial Sponsorship as Adoption

Arnold Angenendt has described the use of sponsorship in the interest of imperial politics, which he calls "imperial baptismal patronage," as an example of the particular political efficacy of sponsorship.¹³³ In all of western mission politics, he concludes, rulers deployed sponsorship in a virtually stereotypical manner. Angenendt's analysis demonstrates a technique of rule as apparently simple as it was successful: the ruler leading the mission received the king of the converted people from the font and by this act simultaneously declared the latter to be his adoptive son *(filius adoptivus)*. According to Rimbert, Louis the Pious, for example, received the Danish king Heriold "himself from the holy font and adopted him as a son *(in filium adoptavit)*." And Bede maintains that King Ethelwalh of Sussex "was received as a son" *(loco filii)* by the Mercian king Wulfhere "when he had emerged from the font" and was given "two lands, namely the Isle of Wight and the land of the Meonwares as a sign of his *adoptio*."¹³⁴ The godfather's duty to educate his spiritual son, Angenendt argues, then provided the imperial "father" with an argument for supplying the converted godchild with missionaries from his own imperial church. And because the land being proselytized belonged to the archbishopric that carried out the mission,¹³⁵ the newly founded bishoprics could thus be incorporated into the imperial church—and into the empire itself.[136] At the same time sponsorship had a high prestige value for the imperial rulers: sponsorship gave ritual expression to a self-representation in which they were not merely kings but also priests *(rex et sacerdos)*. In the reality of missions, the Frankish kings' claim to priestly status found visible expression in one place only: sponsorship. Only here did the ruler perform a liturgical service.[137] In so doing, the Frankish kings would not least have been following a practice already common among the Byzantine emperors, their models and competitors.[138]

With his "discovery" and interpretation of imperial sponsorship, Angenendt uncovered a political instrument previously ignored by medieval studies, and introduced sponsorship as an object of social historical research and discussion for medievalists.

My study, which was inspired by, and proceeded from, Angenendt's research, focuses on aspects of the topic whose treatment by Angenendt I find rather problematic. Thus one could object, first of all, that the Frankish kings by no means always used sponsorship for the purposes of ecclesiastical and political expansion. An oath of vassalage or the simple liquidation of leaders were no less effective methods.[139] There is also ample evidence of imperial conversion campaigns in which sponsorship is never mentioned.[140] At any rate, the missionaries were sent by the imperial church, whether or not the emperor could claim responsibility for the spiritual education of a godson. In either case, the emperors were powerful enough to enforce acts of sovereignty in the converted regions.[141] Sponsorship also did not replace the usual ritual of vassalage; instead, the two rituals were combined.[142] What, then, did those involved hope to attain with the sponsorship bond? According to Angenendt, the answer was "legal and political duties," "religious love" *(religiosus amor)*, mutual help, the "instruction" *(admonitio)* of the godchild by the godfather, and, finally, the duties that an *adoptio* brought with it.[143] Sponsorship, Angenendt has remarked of a Merovingian example, "in reality also included a politically significant adoption."[144]

All that this means in concrete terms, though, is that during the ritual act, to the extent that it was interpreted as a familial bond, the participants evoked the "legal and political duties" of kinship, or at most specifically named them using the usual vocabulary *(pax, amor)*. Put another way, baptism was one of the occasions at which a family could represent and define itself, demanding kin morality within and representing it to the outside world.[145] This statement still tells us nothing about the actual effects of such a formal act on the relationships among participants. Did the sponsorship bond make it more difficult for Charlemagne to overrun his "son" Widukind militarily and punish him? Conversely, was the rebellious Widukind forced to behave better because the tie of vassalage was now joined by a familial bond, and because he could now also portray his vassalage as filial duty? If the answer is yes, how are we to explain it?

The social value of sponsorship is more difficult to describe, and we need first to ask more precise questions: What were the relationships between baptismal kin really like? From which spiritual kin did one demand an act of peace and *caritas*, and what kind of acts were these? How did one collect on them? What moved someone to be peaceable (and what did others allow to pass for peaceable)? Naturally, we could also name numerous examples in which nobody seems to have paid any attention to peaceableness or *caritas*. What characterized these situations?

Furthermore, what did one achieve by referring to sponsorship as *adoptio*? The question here is not merely one about the value of equating the two acts, but rather one about what *adoptio* actually meant at the time, how and when an *adoptio* took place and what it was intended to accomplish. This is more complicated than it may appear at first sight, for we know little about the practice of *adoptio* in the early Middle Ages—whether something of the kind actually existed, how widespread it was, to what ends and under what circumstances people undertook something they called by that name. Suffice it to say that some scholars believe that the practice of adoption completely disappeared in the early Middle Ages,[146] while others apparently assume, on the basis of surviving adoption forms, the existence of practices along the lines of ancient Roman adoption.[147]

Scarcely any of this can be found in the sources on imperial baptismal patronage, which was the main focus of Angenendt's interest, because they never report concretely on how relationships developed after the sponsorship act itself. In many cases the only evidence we have that peace and *caritas* prevailed between the baptismal kin is that we hear nothing further about their relationship after the baptism. The only author of the early or high Middle Ages who reports in detail on the practical consequences of such sponsorship is Gregory of Tours (sixth century). He is also the only author who reports on a sponsorship bond that came into conflict with an *adoptio* and, finally, he is also the medieval chronicler with by far the most stories to tell about sponsorship. For this reason I have used Gregory's history as the main source for my investigation, supplementing his relatively extensive accounts from time to time with the much less plentiful references in the early medieval *Lives* and some normative texts.

2
Kinship Strategies: The Example of King Gunthchramn

The story to which Gregory of Tours repeatedly returns in his chronicle, and into which he weaves the most numerous and interesting details on the subjects of sponsorship and adoption, is that of King Gunthchramn of Burgundy, who had no sons, but two nephews—Childebert from the Austrasian and Chlothar from the Neustrian kingdom. In the course of his long, drawn-out efforts to organize his relationship to both and to secure the succession, he resorted both to sponsorship and, on several occasions, to *adoptiones*. Disputes repeatedly broke out over a period of some twenty years during which conditions were continually altered by deaths, uprisings or (to us) often inexplicable changes of heart on the part of the man whose inheritance stood to be divided up. The participants were also constantly devising all manner of cunning and seemingly contradictory plans for securing their interests. Let us give a summary of all of these comings and goings, as well as of what the literature has had to say about them up until now, as they will provide a central theme for the present study.

The chronicler Fredegar, who described the events from the distance of half a century, devoted but one succinct sentence to Gunthchramn's death in 592: "Childebert took over his kingdom."[1] This was by no means as obvious an outcome as Fredegar's remark would have us believe, for this succession contradicted the genealogical facts. King Gunthchramn had outlived both his own sons and his three brothers Charibert (d. 567), Sigibert (d. 575), and Chilperic (d. 584).[2] A *corpus fratrum* which could have inherited in common[3] was thus not available in this case. There were, however, two nephews. The Austrasian kingdom was ruled by the very Childebert II who, according to Fredegar's note of 592, was entitled to the entire inheritance. Neustria was ruled by his cousin Chlothar II, then still a child. By the logic of genealogy, Chlothar would have had just as much right to claim the inheritance as Childebert, but he apparently came away empty-handed in 592 all the same—contrary to Merovingian practice up to that time.⁴ This inheritance procedure may have been, not least, a matter of power and force, but Gunthchramn and Childebert had nevertheless laid the groundwork with legitimizing measures they used in order to circumvent custom, oriented as it was towards genealogical circumstances, in order to favor Childebert's claim.

Scholars largely agree in their accounts of how they achieved this: Childebert was adopted by Gunthchramn and also succeeded in cementing his claim to the inheritance in the famous Pact of Andelot (587), while Chlothar only—and much later—became Gunthchramn's godson, which brought him two or three *civitates* at most.⁵

Difficulties arise, however, when we try to describe the individual activities and their respective political benefits more precisely. To be sure, Gregory of Tours recounts in detail the tug-of-war between the two nephews and their mothers and nobles *(proceres)* over the inheritance, and he also describes Gunthchramn's constant maneuvering, but his accounts of the conduct of the Burgundian king, in particular, appear so mutually contradictory that it has proved extremely difficult up until now to interpret them.

The game began with the murder of Gunthchramn's brother Sigibert (575), the king of Austrasia, who left behind a single son, Childebert, still in his minority. The chronicler then recounts how, in 577, King Gunthchramn publicly took this Childebert as his son *(hic nepus meus mihi sit filius)*, thereby making him the heir to the Burgundian throne.⁶ A short time later the chronicler introduces Childebert's second uncle, Chilperic of Neustria, who, like Gunthchramn, had no sons of his own. Chilperic, too, is said to have taken his nephew Childebert as his heir and son.⁷ Unlike Gunthchramn, however, this uncle had another son shortly before he was murdered in 584, who, as an orphaned infant, was dragged into the conflicts of his royal kinsmen: the chronicler has the Burgundian King Gunthchramn assert, immediately following Chilperic's death, that he had adopted not only the Austrasian Childebert, but also his little nephew Chlothar *(qui mihi adoptivi facti sunt filii)*.⁸ In this case, however, the chronicler does not speak of a formal ritual comparable to the public *adoptio* of Childebert in 577. Shortly thereafter he then asserts that Gunthchramn had once again excluded Chlothar from the inheritance: during a meeting in 585 with Childebert, Gunthchramn is said to have expressly named him alone as a member of his lineage *(stirps)*, thus promising him his entire inheritance.⁹ This was then formally recorded in the Pact of Andelot in 587.¹⁰ At Andelot, too, Gunthchramn is said to have alluded to *adoptio*, not in the pact itself, but at the feast that followed.¹¹ According to the chronicler this was not, however, Gunthchramn's final word on the matter. Two years later in 589 Gunthchramn supposedly explained to Childebert's protesting ambassador that

Childebert would not receive the entire inheritance after all. Now, it seems, Gunthchramn wanted to provide Chlothar with two or three *civitates* "in some part of my dominions that he may not feel himself disinherited."[12] In 585 he had still expressly "shut out all others [apart from Childebert] from my succession."[13] Finally, in 591, Gunthchramn became Chlothar's godfather after the Neustrians had put off setting a date for the christening for years.[14] Fredegund and her nobles had allowed many dates for the baptism to pass since 584 before the queen finally invited Gunthchramn to be Chlothar's sponsor in 591, with the words that he might accept young Chlothar—whom he supposedly had already referred to in 584 as his adoptive son—as a foster child *(alumnus)*.[15] When Gunthchramn then received Chlothar from the font Childebert was moved to vehement protest, informing his legate that this was tantamount to appointing Chlothar his heir and thus a breach of the Pact of Andelot.[16]

Scholars' attempts at interpreting these actions have generally been inspired by a tacit effort to submit them to a certain juridical logic, without ever expressly discussing this standard and its suitability. Thus one author sees an "actual adoption" and another only an "adoption-like institution," one a political pact, a defensive alliance or a pact of friendship and succession, another a testamentary adoption.[17] Whether this procedure makes sense may depend on what exactly one wants to find out, and why. Juridical logic is not very helpful for understanding familial practices in the Frankish kingdom, as will be explained in more detail in the next chapter. This method leads, not least, to a tendency to gloss over rather than explain the contradictions in the chroniclers' accounts. Thus, for example, we may resort to positing that Chilperic must have had two sons, one after the other, both of whom were named Chlothar, and that Gunthchramn adopted one of them and became godfather to the other in 591.[18] Alternatively, we can take an easygoing approach to the problems surrounding how *adoptio* worked and not address this specifically.[19] A third option would be to sweep aside the *adoptio* of Chlothar mentioned by the chronicler with the remark that Gregory was using imprecise terminology here.[20]

But the problem does not "solve itself" when "one discovers that Gunthchramn only [1] took Chilperic's son [i.e., Chlothar] under his protection, [and] wanted to regard him [2] as an *alumnum proprium*, i.e., as a foster son, and [3] as a *filium spiritualem*, i.e., as a godchild."[21] The problem remains because, firstly, the chronicler does not say that Gunthchramn offered protection to Chlothar, but rather to Fredegund.[22] It was, secondly, not Gunthchramn who *"wanted* to regard [Chlothar] as a foster son," but rather Fredegund who suggested that Gunthchramn *should* take him as such.[23] Thirdly, and finally, a reading of the chronicler's assertion that Gunthchramn declared Chlothar his *adoptivus*, in 584, to mean that he "wanted to regard him as a godchild" (when he only actually became his godfather seven years later) would require some justification, especially since the political function of sponsorship remains to be explained.[24] Why should we assume that Gunthchramn only took the young Chlothar "under his protection"? Why not investigate whether he was pursuing his own interests in the kingdom of this underage nephew, aims for which he could make good use of aspects of an *adoptio*—paternal authority, for example?

On the whole, the proposed solutions cited here tend to create an illusory harmony among the sources. In so doing they obscure our view of the ways in which people handled problems, and of the diversity of situations to which they responded by deploying equally diverse social tactics (adoption, foster sonship, "protection"). From the standpoint of social history, many of the "contradictions" are less problems of the evidence than essential aids to understanding, and thus less in need of "resolution" than of acceptance and explanation.

Part II:
Adoption

3
Adoption Contextualized: Legal Culture

Replacing "Reception" with "Appropriation"

Ultimately, all that the division of Gunthchramn's and other contemporaries' actions into "genuine adoptions"[1] and less genuine ones means is that "genuine" adoptees were simply defined as those whose *adoptio* most closely corresponded to the notions of Roman juridical culture (or to our own concepts and practice).

Let us take one example: After the Burgundian Gunthchramn made his Austrasian nephew Childebert his *filius* in 577, Gunthchramn's brother, the Neustrian Chilperic, followed suit in 581 and named Childebert as *his* heir, and is said to have called him his "son."[2] German scholars have debated whether or not this constituted an adoption. Eduard Hlawitschka is skeptical about whether Childebert "even *could* be adopted by someone else [Chilperic] during the lifetime of his adoptive father [Gunthchramn] without officially abandoning his family ties."[3] Hlawitschka argues in terms of a norm without specifying the norms against which such an act should be measured. We must ask whose regulations would have been violated had Childebert been made a *filius* twice. To be sure, nobody will disagree that he contravened the regulations of the "classic" Roman jurists[4] or perhaps those of this or that Roman in the Merovingian kingdom. But how are we to prove that such Roman regulations were of any interest within the leading court circles, and that someone used such regulations to pass judgment on whether or not Childebert "could" be made a *filius* twice? We do not even know whether the *adoptiones* carried out by the Romans in the Merovingian kingdom approximated the prescriptions set down centuries before by the Roman jurists.[5] Is it not conceivable that Childebert was taking advantage of the very fact that the cultural differences within his kingdom also made for a certain pluralism in and greater ambiguity of the regulations?

A more serious objection is that such a norm, if it was indeed in place here, may *also* have determined Childebert's conduct (as an internalized element of social structures, or perhaps only as calculation, or both at once), but only as one factor in addition, for example, to his momentary interests or the political balance of power. Why should Childebert, Gunthchramn's *filius*, not also have become Chilperic's *filius* if he found it convenient and if nobody stood in his way? And who in Merovingian Gaul was in a position to confront him—successfully—with Roman legal norms?[6] Comparison with a single example, the practice of multiple vassalage, shows just how much one "could" do given the right balance of power. Furthermore, who would have cared whether Childebert changed his family ties "officially"[7] or not? And if nobody was interested, why regulate it? Naturally this is not to say that Chilperic *did* adopt Childebert, but we should be skeptical of assertions that this was not even *possible*.

Hlawitschka raises a further argument in this case: The agreement between Childebert and Chilperic cannot have been an adoption because it was negotiated only by emissaries.[8] Viewed with the eyes of a "classical" Roman jurist this might also be plausible, but it cannot simply be transferred to the act of a Merovingian king without relevant evidence.[9] Here, too, a comparison may prove useful: When Pope Paul I became the godfather of Pippin's daughter, Gisela, in 757, he was not himself present. Apparently it was considered sufficient to send him the christening cloth.[10] The Byzantine emperor Michael apparently also accepted the Bulgarian khan Boris as his godson via a deputy.[11] To be sure, these episodes do not tell us how the Merovingians made someone a *filius*, but they do demonstrate that the scope was greater and the regulations less clear-cut than a viewpoint proceeding from Roman jurisprudence (which, after all, was not even used universally in the old Roman empire)[12] would have us believe.

Hlawitschka's assumption that "particularly in the Merovingian royal family [we see] how quickly this legal concept must have been assimilated" reveals the nature of the difficulties surrounding the Merovingian *adoptiones*.[13] The problem lies in the assumption that Roman law entered Merovingian society through a process of *reception*. Such an approach runs the risk of portraying Merovingian society as an accumulation of more or less disparate elements to which adoption, for instance, was added—a view that ultimately assigns a passive role to society. Quite a few scholars appear to ascribe to the "received" legal institution a "nature" against which they can measure the conduct of actors independent of the society under investigation, and to distinguish "properly" received Roman law and "genuine" adoptions from what was "misconstrued," or even "alarmingly misunderstood" and "degenerate."[14]

Naturally misunderstandings did occur,[15] particularly in those intercultural relations that characterized Gaul in the sixth century. They are even of particular interest to social historians to the extent that the misunderstandings have a logic of their own and an internal coherence that we might expect to possess explanatory value. If there were "misunderstandings," however, which could indeed be demonstrated for individual cases, what the actors involved misunderstood was not the "nature" of adoption, to name just one example, but rather alien patterns of interpretation and practices which they perceived in terms of their own patterns. When we study such misunderstandings we are studying not the "nature" or "meaning" or "genuine essence" of *adoptio*, but rather social functions and relationships. Consequently, a Frankish legal practice that departs from Roman law is not improper, let alone "alarming" or "degenerate."

If we apply this approach consistently, then we can scarcely grasp an *adoptio* in the Merovingian kingdom using the model of "reception," valuable as reception studies may be in other fields. Individuals did not merely passively receive alien influences. Instead, as subjects of the events, they actively incorporated these influences into their own social networks turning them, in a process of active appropriation, into instruments of their own system. The deviation of a Merovingian *adoptio* from the "classical" Roman norm neither necessarily points to the terminological weakness of the chronicler who used a Roman term carelessly[16] (although he may well have done so), nor does it reveal the Merovingian act to have been an "improper" or "misunderstood" adoption. We might make more progress if we grasped the differences to Roman adoption as the result not of faulty reception but of a functional appropriation, of an ongoing multiperspectived shaping of the social system by all participants, each of whom appropriates his or her own world from his or her own standpoint and, in continual action, modifies the environment and thus the entire system by means of this *Eigensinn*.[17] The Merovingians needed and perceived something different from what the Romans needed and perceived. For a social historical study, at least, it makes no sense tacitly to declare Roman adoption law to be the proper and genuine article, particularly since in the everyday—and even political—life of the Merovingian world a "proper" understanding of Roman legal norms in this sense had no value.

If "proper" is an appropriate category at all, then it can only describe perception: how in their various contexts people perceived the procedure as "proper" or only made it out to be "proper" and to what extent that which was declared to be proper determined usage at a given time. It is precisely the departures from ancient Roman regulations (and, where possible, practices) that show how people in the sixth century took up influences and modified them to suit their own ends. In short, social historians could learn more by asking not about the (more or less passive) reception of *the* institution of adoption, but rather about the (functional) appropriation, within the respective concrete practical contexts, of a legal institution handed down from the Roman empire.

We must, of course, take account of the possibility that the context in which the *leges* compilers lived and thought was not the world of those actors who appear in the sources as political and social agents. These actors may thus have appropriated the *adoptio* of Roman legal cultural differently than the compilers incorporated this construction into their collections of laws. One need only recall baptismal sponsorship, which the churchmen—to the extent that they are accessible to us—also wanted to see regulated differently from the ways in which "the people" were using it. What we do know about the efficacy and relevance of Frankish legal texts should make us very cautious here.[18] Some of the more or less randomly chosen examples of early medieval *adoptiones* would seem to indicate the existence of such differences in appropriation between the scholarly practice of the compilers and everyday usage in the social arena.[19]

Let us imagine, then, Gunthchramn going before the Austrasian nobles desirous of "taking this, my nephew, as my son."[20] What did he mean by this?[21] What were the nobles supposed to make of it? What was Gunthchramn's aim? On what concepts and objectives did the adoption activities which the bishop of Tours, a Gallo-Roman, recounts in the case of Gunthchramn, rest? Why did Gunthchramn apply these practices (at least, in the chronicler's narrative) which he had somehow learned from the Romans? What benefits could he or the adoptee expect?

This was, not least, a question of the conditions that made possible such an appropriation of *adoptio*, which we can use to study both the tactics and power relations involved and the establishment and treatment of regulations and concepts. It will thus be useful to recall, at least in outline form, some Frankish legal customs and how they differed from their Roman counterparts.

The Roman Context

What scholars refer to as adoption ("in the true sense of the word") reveals itself, on closer inspection, as the product of a highly learned Roman juridical discourse of the imperial period. This discourse did not even affect practice in all provinces of the Roman Empire[22] and had, in this form, already given way by the end of the third century to a legal culture which we are accustomed to call "vulgar." One may define the *adoptio* of the "classical" jurists as an "imitation of a parent-child relationship with all the legal consequences of genuine legitimate filiation."[23] For these jurists, the notion of fictitious blood kinship was initially less important than the attempt to render reproducible the authority *(patria potestas)* of a head of household *(pater familias)* who was without male offspring. Since the head of household was responsible for household religious worship and family sacrifice for the spiritual welfare of his father and other ancestors every head of household had an interest in reproducing his authority and duties, if only for his own salvation.[24]

The "classical" Roman jurists were interested not in the biological paternity of the *pater (familias)* but rather in his authority within the household (as a *dominus*).[25] He was a *pater* whether he had children or not.[26] In the view of these specialists *(iure proprio)*[27] *familia* was, accordingly, not a group defined by blood ties but rather a simple legal unit comprising all those persons who were under the authority of the same *pater*.[28]

Even these jurists, however, did not exclude the more concrete notion of *familia* as kinship. Ulpian, who gave us the definition of the *familia* as a legal unit, believed at the same time that "adoption . . . creates blood kin *(consanguineos)*."[29] This was a far more effective notion than the abstract idea of a mere legal unit, particularly beyond the realm of "classical" legal scholarship. It increasingly found its way into law at a time, around the middle of the third century, when these jurists were just beginning to take account of altered social conditions. This is particularly apparent in the role of the paterfamilias. The all-encompassing authority *(patria potestas)* which the classical jurists had used to define the father was no longer the only point of interest for the legal construction of *familia*, which was also supposed to be a kinship unit. Once-effective extralegal counterbalances, which had substantially restricted the all-encompassing paternal authority of juridical logic and emphasized the loving and caring father, now gained greater visibility in legal practice as well.[30] Thus for example there was a move away from agnatic inheritance law, the obvious expression of strong *pater*-centeredness,[31] just as the interests of women and children gained increasing consideration in legislation.

With this different description of the *familia* by the "vulgar" jurists there also came a shift in the frame of reference for "classic" adoption, which had heretofore—at least according to the logic of the jurists—served to guarantee the reproduction of the head of household. It was not least the spread of Christianity, which favored other forms of remembering the dead, that rendered this necessity obsolete.[32] If the jurists now also permitted the adoption *of* women as well as adoption *by* women,[33] they appear to have oriented themselves toward other needs. This is apparent in the form of *adoptio* later sanctioned by Justinian. According to his provisions, "classic" adoption was to have only a marginal existence. In practical terms, only the maternal grandfather could, in the classic sense of the word, "properly" adopt a child. Instead, Justinian sanctioned forms of adoption concerned more with the welfare of the child (for example, an orphan) whose effect, according to the will of the Justinian legislator, should be restricted to "giving him [the adoptee], in addition to rights within his own [birth] family, an intestate inheritance right as *suus heres* after the death of the adoptive parent—but not toward the adoptive parent's family [as a whole]."[34] In other words, it was not supposed to do precisely what one tends to regard as the heart of a "proper" adoption. It was no longer intended to bring about a change of family, a transition to a new relationship of authority, or fiction of kinship, but only to transfer an inheritance claim.

This Justinian version of adoption is interesting for a study of the Merovingian period, in that it gives us an impression of the direction in which the practices of preceding centuries could take the legal structure. This is important because this development—particularly in the West—cannot be followed on a more detailed level. From the eastern provinces, where official imperial law never managed fully to assert itself over customary law,[35] contracts have survived which contain such less all-encompassing forms of adoption which were directed at concrete problems such as providing for orphans.[36] We cannot, however, learn much more about these "post-classical" adoptions, particularly in the West.[37] However well documented "classical" specialist law may be, we know comparatively little about the imperial law of the subsequent period, especially in the West and—much more important here—we apparently know next to nothing about the legal practices of the lower courts in the provinces.[38] Scholars assume that the practice of Roman vulgar law was not so far removed from what the barbarian rulers recorded,[39] and that even practices such as the oath and trial by ordeal may have been adopted from Roman vulgar law.[40]

In short, when it comes to adoption practices, it is unclear what example the Gallo-Romans provided the Franks in the fifth and sixth centuries. We must settle for knowing that on the one hand, the *adoptio* of specialist culture probably still existed in imperial law (whatever the consequences may have been for legal practice in the Roman provinces), but had little relevance anymore because of changes in commemorative practices, and had long since been modified, for example by the addition of greater rights for women. On the other hand, in everyday practice there were doubtless possibilities such as the pragmatic adoption contracts that have survived from the eastern provinces, which were quickly recognized by Justinian (for example, *adoptio per testamentum*).[41] It is thus well-nigh impossible to say how and why a Gallo-Roman of the fourth, fifth, or sixth century resorted to *adoptio*, nor which practices exactly the Franks encountered. The conditions under which classic *adoptio* had once established itself had long since ceased to exist. *Adoptio* was by no means strictly tied any longer to a concrete social practice—namely, the reproduction of paternal authority. In many, if not most cases, it was no longer a "proper" adoption according to "classical" Roman categories. Ambiguous as it was, without a fixed place and incorporated into a new context, this *adoptio* was in a good position to be taken up and modified by the Franks.

The Frankish Context

Legal historians agree that the Germanic peoples[42] did not know "true" adoption,[43] that is, adoption as it had been regulated by the learned jurists of antiquity. Legal scholars refer to the practices—such as regulations on legacies (*Affatomie*)[44] or in some regions on the raising of other people's children (foster-fatherhood)—that were established among the Germanic peoples as "adoption-like institutions."[45] Thus, when we do find *adoptiones* in sixth-century accounts of Frankish practices, these practices proceed—at least, terminologically—from the Franks' contacts with those diverse Gallo-Roman adoption customs and regulations which we can no longer reconstruct with any precision.

This vagueness seems tangible in the Frankish legal texts of the sixth to eighth centuries, and both the strict version of the learned Roman jurists and the more pragmatic "vulgar" forms appear to have been integrated. The latter are apparent in the Lex Ribuaria, for example. Here, *adoptio* has been taken up as adoption *per testamentum,* in that it is equated with the regulations for passing on inheritances (*Affatomie*) which the Franks already recognized: *adoptare in hereditate vel acfatimi(re).*[46] The compilers were doing nothing more than giving a Frankish inheritance practice a Roman name. The compilers of the Lex Salica took another tack: they took a more pedantic approach to the same institution, calling it not *adoptio,* but retaining, into the Carolingian period, the vernacular term *Affatomie.*[47] Whether this indicates that in their eyes "there were no absolutely equivalent terms in the Latin of their day" for *Affatomie*[48] remains an open question.[49] In any case these compilers used the Roman term *adoptio* neither in this nor in any other context of this codification.

By now most scholars agree that these documents convey information about legal practices at best very indirectly and only in conjunction with additional evidence from other sources. The image of a "Frankish judge of the sixth or eighth century running a trial with a copy of the Lex Salica or the Lex Ribuaria under his arm" has long been considered a naive one.[50] Indeed, he may not even have reached decisions with the *written* law in his head. In the Merovingian period, in particular, these written royal laws were, in short, irrelevant to everyday legal practice.[51] Whatever ideological or symbolic uses they may have been put to (perhaps as objects of royal prestige, for purposes of integration and solidarization),[52] in the Merovingian kingdom they served no function in the legal process. To be sure, this does not exclude the possibility that the notations were taken from practice and thus might serve as evidence of legal practice in some place at some period. It does mean, however, that sometimes they were outdated by the time they were written down, and that sometimes meaningless and contradictory regulations continued to be recorded.[53] It also means that the selection appears arbitrary and in some cases absurd, and that large and important areas of everyday life, which surely had as great a need of regulation as the areas of the law that were included, went unrecorded.[54] It also means that in the Merovingian period, references to the Lex Salica in other sources do not once refer to the written law, the Lex Salica *scripta*.[55] For the present context, it means that the silence of the Lex Salica (*scripta*), for example, regarding *adoptio* tells us nothing about practice. Conversely, borrowings from Roman *adoptio*—for example, in the terminology of the Lex Ribuaria—also have correspondingly little to say about actual practice.

The collections of formulae, which contain set texts abstracted from the documents for all manner of legal transactions, present a different picture. They must have had a closer connection to legal practice, and appear actually to have been used and thus to have greater value for those trying to learn about early medieval legal practice.[56] Markulf's collection (compiled in 650 or 721-35) already contained an adoption formula, which is similar to that found in Roman imperial law.[57] In Markulf's formula a man with no sons bequeathed his property to someone outside his family (*extranius*) under the condition that the heir not merely inherit from him, but also act as a son, caring for him when he was ill or frail. The heir, in turn, could also dispose of the inheritance even before his "father's" death. In a later collection of formulae the compiler added that the adoptee was transferred from the authority of his father to that of his new father before the *curia publica*.[58] This might call to mind the *curia* of the late Roman provincial towns before which the *adoptio* was consummated in late antiquity[59] were it not for the fact that this municipal administrative body had disappeared long before the formula was recorded.[60] Thus we may choose here between believing in a change in the meaning of the word *curia*, or simply in the "phantom existence"[61] of this practice in the Frankish documents, a legal practice retained although it was mere "dead wood"[62] and no longer used.[63] Both versions may be equally well suited to remind us that even texts designed for practical use and apparently "compiled with care and reference to concrete realities"[64] represented a conservative element within the context of a largely oral legal culture and could become quickly outdated both in terms of terminology and of the practices they promoted.[65]

When it comes to the practice of Frankish adoptions, the normative evidence should thus be used only with great caution. The transportation of obsolete laws—a conservative terminology with changing contents and, not least, the fact that legal texts transmit their social context only in encoded form—limits the usefulness of legal texts for a study of practical interests and actual behavior. In addition, there is no corresponding normative evidence from the Frankish kingdom for the period in which the Merovingians were practicing for the first time something the chronicler (a Gallo-Roman aristocrat) called "adoption." This alone would make us dependent on the narrative sources.

A first glance at a few rather randomly chosen adoptions from the period after the sixth century quickly reveals that in concrete cases, *adoptio* was adapted in ways we would never suspect from the normative sources.

In an account by Bede, the Anglo-Saxon Wilfrid, who was on his way to Rome, stopped in Lyon and made such an impression on Dalfinus, the local bishop, that the latter offered "to confer on him the government of a great part of Gaul, to give him his brother's maiden daughter as a wife, and to accept him henceforth as his adopted son."[66] According to an Icelandic saga, someone else had a similar idea much farther to the north and in what was surely a different cultural context: Torstein, son of a ruler from northern Norway, had killed the son of Ingimund, Jarl of Gautland. He then set off to see the very same Ingimund in order to marry his daughter Tordis and ensure peace through this familial affiliation. Ingimund, who now no longer had a son, is said to have replied in the following manner: "I shall not refuse it [the relationship by marriage] . . . but I want you to stay here with us." Here, too, the situation was resolved by means of a fictive filiation: "It would also be the best filial penitence if you were to take the place of my son and wished to stay here with me."[67] The son-in-law simultaneously became a fictive son so that he would not take the daughter away. Gratian still believed that it made sense specifically to ask whether one could adopt a son in order to give him one's daughter in marriage.[68] He forbade it, citing a tradition of legal experts ranging from Pope Nicholas to Justinian.[69]

The evidence may be sparse and widely scattered across space and time, but it does indicate that there was a practicable and apparently utilized area of application for *adoptio*, which many a legal expert was keen to make impossible. One could make a man one's fictive son and at the same time give him one's blood daughter in marriage. It is striking that in the cases mentioned here the issue was keeping one's son-in-law (and thus one's daughter) in one's own house. A borrowing from anthropological scholarship may help explain this phenomenon.[70] It is conceivable that such an adoption was intended to enable a man who had just married into a family, and whose status therein was only that of his wife's spouse, to define himself properly—that is, agnatically.

It would be interesting here to inquire after the notions associated with an *adoptio*. If there is anywhere we can expect to find knowledge of Roman traditions, such as we find perhaps in Markulf, it is doubtless in the southern Gaul of a Dalfinus. But how does the example of Dalfinus fit in with the possibility of such knowledge? Would the bishop of Lyon really conceive of *adoptio* as an "imitation of a parent-child relationship with all of the legal consequences of genuine legitimate filiation" as Markulf's roughly contemporaneous formula appears to presuppose?[71] Was he concerned with the fiction that he was marrying his own son to his cousin? Or did "the people" perhaps act differently here and have other notions, and did they have something else in mind when it came to *adoptio* than the professional norms of a Markulf would seem to indicate?

Let us leave these questions, which are not to be treated here, but which do admonish us to apply the yardstick of the legal sources only with the greatest caution to Gunthchramn and his activities in the realm of adoption. These norms, which are perhaps more our own than those of the actors, tend to obscure our view of actual practice.

The Logic of the Legal Sources versus Social Practice

A further factor militates against privileging the legal sources in an analysis of Merovingian *adoptiones*. It might lead to questionable results if we sought to fit statements made by Gunthchramn over a period of many years into a strict normative system, and to draw conclusions about normative distinctions from contradictions in practice. The contradictions in the utterances and conduct of actors are perhaps less indicative of normative differentiations than of strategies, of the capacity for remembering and forgetting, and also of people's tricks and knowledge of the ways and means of regulating social placement.[72] It is precisely the contradictions that show us when people were following the rules, when they were testing their room for maneuver and their tactics, applying the official rules at the right moment, wriggling their way out of the requirements, (re)interpreting and exploiting them, playing them off one another or simply ignoring them.

Any historian who compiles everything Gunthchramn and his contemporaries said and did on the topic of adoption over a period of many years and—of necessity, harmonizing them—seeks to derive from this Gunthchramn's (or even "the era's") understanding of adoption, ignores the possibility that such a harmonious regulation of adoption may never have existed.[73] He or she also ignores the influence of time on social processes: Gunthchramn never uttered these different and contradictory statements all at one time, and in practice it was insignificant that, and doubtless no one thought the worse of him because, the statements he made to different people at different places and times over a period of more than a decade were logically inconsistent—a fact that only scholars, from their detemporalized synoptic viewpoint, would be in a position to notice anyway.[74] If those involved could recall Gunthchramn's words precisely they doubtless did not do so during "that same year," that is, when it was still fresh in their minds or—as in Andelot—fixed by contract.[75] Where no documents existed and the time factor encouraged forgetfulness contradictions in legal logic were scarcely significant for social reality. And in his dealings with contemporaries (as opposed to latter-day scholars) Gunthchramn could channel and nuance the information and arguments he provided. He could say one thing about *adoptio* in Neustria and another in Austrasia; he could call his *adoptivus* Childebert his "son" on one occasion, emphasizing closeness and filial and paternal duties,[76] only to place him at a distance at the next opportunity by addressing him as his "nephew."[77]

All of this represents practice. As we shall see, practically speaking, Gunthchramn was consistent in his *adoptiones*. He always pursued his own interests. The example of an action by Childebert, who had to decide the same conflict over property twice during a five-year period, clearly demonstrates this practically oriented logic, which one could easily miss if one measured it against legal logic. A bishop presented his inherited property (*res patris*) to his sister as a gift. When he died, however, his mother claimed the property, which had formerly belonged to her husband (*res viri*), as her own and contested the gift.[78] The first time the case arose Childebert awarded a portion of the inheritance to both parties, along with a few of the bishop's orphaned nephews and nieces. The sister, however, did not obey the judgment and kept the entire inheritance. When, after years of disputes, the bishop's mother died, Childebert reassessed the case—as Gregory had already noticed—without any reference to his previous judgment.[79] This time the sister received everything, and the *nepotes* apparently nothing at all.

Had Childebert forgotten his earlier decision, and not noticed the contradictions? Did he possess new information? What was the relationship between the gift and the claim to the inheritance? Did Childebert perhaps not have a clear conception of the regulations that should have governed his decision, or were the rules themselves unclear?[80] Or was it not a matter of rules at all, but merely of ending the dispute? In that case, Childebert may have acted opportunely, the first time simply dividing the property rather than pitting the claim to the inheritance against the gift, and the second time "recognizing" that matters had to be as they were anyway.

We are confronted with numerous possibilities, as perhaps were the actors at the time, although Gregory's few words do not permit an adequate explanation. At any rate, this case suggests a method for dealing with the contradictions surrounding Gunthchramn's *adoptiones*: studying the statements and actions of Gunthchramn and the other actors in their respective practical contexts and trying to find out why they took a particular course in the given situation.

As we shall see, *adoptio* was a particularly troublesome area in the relationship between the Merovingian royalty and the nobility. Had Gunthchramn been able to establish them, the possibilities provided by Roman *adoptio*—particularly paternal authority and inheritance—might have helped radically to alter the power structure. For just this reason attempts to deploy *adoptio* within a sociopolitical arena in which it had no fixed and customary place immediately became part of a tug-of-war among the dominant groups. The position of *adoptio* within a Frankish society which had previously managed without such an instrument was bound to depend on political constellations and the attitudes and actions of the participating interest groups. The main protagonists in the surviving documents are King Gunthchramn, on the one hand, and the nobles surrounding his two nephews, on the other. All of them sought to bring their political possibilities to bear and ascertain the place and function of *adoptio* in the political game, but the driving force behind this struggle remained King Gunthchramn.

4
King Gunthchramn: Interventions in Kinship

Our knowledge of practically all contemporary statements and actions has been filtered through the perceptions and narrative constructions of Gregory of Tours, a Gallo-Roman senator with a late-classical education. Gregory frequently has his protagonists speak in the first person. Although it is quite likely that these speeches were less a faithful record of what actually was said than stylistic devices in the service of Gregory's narrative, they are all we have. At any rate, Gregory was an eyewitness to many of the events he describes.[1] A significant number of the stories he tells are devoted to the attitudes of King Gunthchramn and his, at first glance, contradictory policies. The narrator appears to have been far less interested in the Frankish nobility, who, it is generally assumed, were antagonistic toward the royal dynasty during the era of Gunthchramn and Brunechildis.[2]

Thus, I will focus on King Gunthchramn's actions, which also makes sense because—at least in the chronicler's account—only he explicitly had recourse to *adoptio* with which to assert his interests. Of these interests, there were two in particular for which adoption could be useful in various situations and in various ways. These were, first, Gunthchramn's interest in extending his rule to the kingdoms of his nephews, and second, his interest in a concrete outcome for the succession, one that deviated from established practice. The latter, however, interested him only under certain circumstances.

The Question of Power: Fictitious Sons and Real Force

Only twice does the chronicler have one of the protagonists of his *History* explicitly mention *adoptio*. The first time he himself is the actor, the second time it is King Gunthchramn. In both cases, political interests are at stake.

The first account refers to the year 584, or, to be more precise, to the period following the murder of Chilperic. After his death a conflict arose between the Burgundian Gunthchramn (d. 592) and his Austrasian nephew Childebert II (d. 596) over some Aquitanian towns, among them Tours and Poitiers.[3] When the *civitas* of Poitiers itself became involved in the conflict and wanted to open itself to Childebert, the neighboring bishop of Tours—our chronicler, Gregory—admonished the bishop and citizens to submit to Gunthchramn.

> For Guntram now stood in the place of a father *(esse pater)* to the two sons of Sigibert and Chilperic [that is, to Chlothar II and Childebert II], whom he had adopted *(qui ei fuerant adoptati);* therefore he held the whole kingdom *(regni principatus)* under his rule, as his father Lothar [I] had done before him.[4]

This is how Gregory quotes his own speech in the *History*. Let us recall that "his father, King Lothar [I]" had been supreme ruler over the entire Merovingian kingdom. Gregory's logic thus leaves no room for doubt about what was at stake here: *adoptio* meant *pater esse, regni principatus*, autocratic rule. In Gregory's version, *adoptio* is reduced to paternal authority. Taken alone, this statement by the Gallo-Roman chronicler for whom *adoptiones* might still have been a familiar affair, would not represent reliable testimony, had he not at the same time described rather precisely the actions he called *adoptiones*.

What actions were these? In the case of the *adoptio* of Childebert, it is easy to understand what Gregory meant. Gunthchramn had celebrated Childebert's *adoptio* in 577 near the Burgundian-Austrasian border town of Pompierre before a great entourage, an occasion Gregory describes in detail.[5] We do not know, in contrast, exactly how Chlothar, whom the chronicler also refers to as an *adoptivus* of Gunthchramn's, became his uncle's "son," but we can guess at the outlines from the surrounding narrative. The starting point is the second episode in the *History* in which someone mentions an *adoptio*, and this time it is King Gunthchramn himself. After Chilperic's death, Gunthchramn is said to have adjured the citizens of Paris not to slay him, the last surviving adult Merovingian, as well.[6] Gunthchramn presented his audience with a particularly noble reason for sparing him, expressing the hope that "it be granted to me, at least for three years, to bring up the nephews whom I have made my adopted sons *(qui mihi adoptivi facti sunt)*."[7]

Thus, Gunthchramn is said to have claimed that he intended to "bring up" his two orphaned nephews not as an uncle, closest agnate *(Schwertmage)*, senior member of the dynasty, "presumptive godfather," or what-have-you,[8] but as an adoptive father *(qui mihi adoptivi facti sunt)*. Naturally, it is unlikely that an uncle living at a distant court, even if he were a fictive father, actually intended to "bring up" his nephews. After all, the king's mother and the professional household staff *(nutritores)* were there for that purpose.[9] What Gunthchramn refers to here as the boys' "upbringing" is specified in the next sentence: the "protection" *(defensio)* of the population[10]—to this day, the classic euphemism for intervention. It was the claim to sovereignty over the kingdom of his dead brother. When he spoke to the *cives* of Paris of adoption, Gunthchramn appears to have been claiming that authority over the entire kingdom *(regni principatus)* which the chronicler Gregory portrayed as the quintessence of *adoptio*.[11] The only difference is that Gunthchramn, who was trying to win over the people of Paris, diplomatically portrayed this power to the *cives* as "upbringing" and "protection," whereas Gregory sought to warn his neighbors in Poitiers and thus baldly called the power of the adoptive father by its proper name.

The background to Gunthchramn's wooing of the Parisian *cives* provides further hints about the act of adoption. The story begins with an offer made by Chlothar's mother, Fredegund. Immediately after the death of her husband, Chilperic, she had fled to the capital, Paris, and sent an entreaty to Gunthchramn from there. He should come to Paris "and take the kingdom of his brother"; she longed to place her son "in his arms" and "submit [herself] to his governance *(dicio).*"[12] Even this offer emphasized authority in an attempt to appeal to Gunthchramn. He arrived, and shortly thereafter the chronicler has him speaking to the Parisian *cives* the above-cited words, in which he refers to Chlothar as his *adoptivus*.[13] To be sure, the chronicler does not explicitly say that a corresponding action took place, so that we also do not learn *how* Gunthchramn made his Neustrian nephew his son after his arrival in Paris or what Fredegund's offer to place her son "in his arms" actually meant.[14] We can at least assume from the course of events as described by Gregory *that* an action took place that the chronicler, and apparently also Fredegund and Gunthchramn, associated with the transfer of paternal authority *(esse pater, regni principatus, dicio, defensio, enutrire)*.[15]

Let us recapitulate. In 577 and 584 Gunthchramn participated in actions that permitted him to claim both of his nephews—if he so desired[16]— as "sons," and which, in his own opinion as well as that of Fredegund and Gregory, potentially gave him authority over the boys. If these two actions of 577 and 584 are the first evidence in the Frankish kingdom of Frankish actions referred to as *adoptio*, this appearance should explain, and show, the value such recourse to classical Roman law (or, at least, its vocabulary) had at this particular time and place. Do these two statements show that people—or, at least, Gunthchramn—were after something different than the usual? Or was the term *adoptio* being used merely to refer to a common Frankish practice, which a Gallo-Roman chronicler or a Frankish king spoke of only in Roman terms because they were addressing a Gallo-Roman audience? One might speculate, for example, that after the death of his two brothers, Gunthchramn, as the eldest member of his dynasty or the closest agnate, assumed the *munduburdium*.[17] And, since the *mund*, or guardian, of the Frankish father corresponded more or less to the authority of the Roman father *(patria potestas)*,[18] what Gunthchramn expressed to the Parisian *cives* may have been quite a common Frankish custom. One might be tempted to interpret the term *adoptio* as a kind of translation of what Gregory perceived into his own linguistic and mental world.[19] One might also conclude that Gunthchramn was adapting a Roman legal concept to a long-established Frankish practice. This would make sense when one considers that the words of both Gregory and Gunthchramn were addressed to town dwellers who, for the most part, probably were Gallo-Romans. However, such reflections, which make the use of the term more a phenomenon of perception and communication than of legal practice, presuppose that the practices so described were not unusual among the Frankish kings.

To anticipate the heart of my argument: this was *not* the case. It may have been the usual solution among subjects to place heirs still in their minority under the authority of the nearest agnate,[20] but the Frankish succession apparently took a different path. There was no certain claim, or even one suggested by precedent, which Gunthchramn could have cited in order to assume sovereignty over the lands of his minor nephews.[21] Indeed, tradition here tended to favor his opponents. For that reason, Gunthchramn had to adopt a legal course from outside this tradition. It was for this purpose that *adoptio* appears to have been useful. Fictitious paternal authority promised to benefit Gunthchramn in two ways. When it came to sovereignty over the two neighboring kingdoms, it created a claim he could stake, and at the same time it made this sovereignty, when Gunthchramn exercised it, appear to be legitimate. Frankish tradition could do neither.

It should be noted that *adoptio* was not the only strategy Gunthchramn employed to extend his rule, just as the extension of his rule was not the only benefit *adoptio* offered. Events, of course, did not depend on Gunthchramn alone. His nephews and their nobles, against whom he had to assert his interests, were a factor, just as were those allies he needed for his efforts at legitimation if naked force proved insufficient. Gunthchramn made repeated attempts to extend his power, and the chronicler apparently had excellent opportunities to observe how he proceeded in detail.

Admonitions and Prohibitions: Childebert

The chronicler reports for the year 577 that Gunthchramn "sent envoys to his nephew Childebert, seeking peace, and praying that they might meet."[22]

This does not, in itself, sound spectacular, just as the subsequent encounter at Pompierre would not have been dramatic[23] had Gunthchramn not staged the hitherto unusual ritual in the course of which he declared Childebert to be his "son."[24]

If, however, we examine the subsequent contacts between the two rulers, we are struck by another fact: Never again would Gunthchramn treat Childebert as courteously as he did in 577. The chronicler, at least, attributes quite another style to Gunthchramn thereafter: In 585, "the king summoned his nephew"[25] to a meeting, this time not at a location on their common frontier, but rather to an (unnamed) location where Gunthchramn happened to be staying at the time.[26] The invitation to Andelot two years later was also no longer formulated as a request, as it had been in 577 *(deprecans eum videre)*; rather, the king now ordered his nephew to "Put aside all delay, and come, that I may see thee."[27]

That this new tone may be attributed less to a whim of the narrator than to a new strategy on Gunthchramn's part is visible in the way Gunthchramn tried three times (albeit unsuccessfully)[28] to organize joint synods with Childebert: Gunthchramn's emissary Felix referred to the first synod, planned for 585, as that, "which thou [Childebert] and he together did appoint."[29] According to the surviving evidence, this must have occurred at the meeting between the two kings in 585,[30] about which the chronicler reports so extensively that any notion of a mutual decision appears in quite a different light: Gunthchramn had summoned *(arcessire iubet)*[31] the thirteen- or fourteen-year-old Childebert to Burgundy, where he isolated his young nephew from his entourage and instructed him "privily" on the details of his regency, naming "the men whom he should admit as his advisers and those whom he should keep from his counsels; those whom he might trust, and those whom he should avoid; those whom he should distinguish by rewards, and those whom he should degrade from their offices."[32] Indeed, he even "forbade" Childebert to have any contact with a certain bishop.[33] Thus, it doubtless was rather farcical when a messenger from Gunthchramn to Childebert later claimed that the two of them had together appointed a synod of both parts of the kingdom at this meeting. Here, Gregory is to be taken all the more seriously, since he himself was present at the appearance of the messenger who was supposed to admonish the Austrasian bishops to attend. Gregory himself even came to the aid of his king, "as the king [Childebert] remained silent," and repelled the messenger's attacks.[34] The choice of a site for the synod also would seem to indicate that Gunthchramn was acting alone here, and not "together" with his nephew. The synod was supposed to take place at Troyes—once again, not on the common border but inside Gunthchramn's kingdom.[35]

Later, Gunthchramn is no longer said to have invoked the fiction of a supposedly mutual decision. For a second synod in 588, Gunthchramn simply "made known" (*indecavit*) to his nephew that all of Gunthchramn's and Childebert's bishops were to meet at an appointed place. When Childebert protested through his legate—once again, Gregory of Tours—Gunthchramn did not cancel the synod but instead "commanded" that it be postponed.[36] Gunthchramn "commanded" the holding of a third synod in 589[37] in order to have judgment passed on Childebert's mother Brunechildis, whom he held responsible for his defeat by the Goths. The king's mother prevented the meeting by clearing herself of the charge by oath.[38] Gregory does not say which bishops were supposed to appear, but, under the circumstances, it is likely that Gunthchramn had summoned the Austrasians who, in this case, apparently were prepared to follow without resistance.

In short, after the meeting at Pompierre Gunthchramn repeatedly claimed supremacy over the Austrasians. His actions repeatedly invoked adoption, whether explicitly[39] or implicitly.[40] As we will see, Gregory described these efforts as having been thwarted by Austrasian resistance.[41]

An Unprecedented Intervention: Chlothar

Let us examine Gunthchramn's activities in the kingdom of Chilperic, who died at the end of 584. For the year 585, the chronicler expressly notes that "King Guntram, desiring to govern on his own account the kingdom of his nephew Lothar, son of Chilperic,"[42] intended to proceed in this region just as he had in Austrasia.

Gregory goes on to recount Gunthchramn's swift action to fill ecclesiastical and secular offices. Gunthchramn appointed Theodulf count of Angers and tried to push through Beppolen as duke in the region surrounding Rennes and Angers.[43] Gunthchramn also removed Bishop Melantius of Rouen, a favorite of Fredegund's, and returned Praetextatus, whom Chilperic had banished, to this see.[44] One of the ways in which he took Fredegund "under his protection"[45] was to banish her to a court near Rouen.[46] Not the least of Gunthchramn's actions was to intervene in Neustrian property relations immediately following Chilperic's death. He wrested the estate from Chilperic's vassals, who had appropriated it illegitimately, and returned it to the injured parties, "making large gifts to the churches"[47] and restoring his testamentary bequests to the church, which Chilperic "had suppressed."[48] It was Gunthchramn who now secured justice (*iustitia intercedente*)[49] for Chilperic's subjects, *the* demonstration of legitimate power par excellence. Finally, it was Gunthchramn who, in 590, waged war against the Bretons from Rennes and Angers.[50]

What was the underlying "rule" here? Was Gunthchramn acting as the "senior member of the royal dynasty"?[51] If so, this would be the only instance of a Merovingian doing so. In the only parallel case we know of, the filial succession of Theudebald (d. 555) to the throne of Theudebert (d. 548) in the eastern lands, the position of the senior—Childebert I of Paris—remained without consequences: Gregory and another author state, respectively, that Theudebald was still a *parvulus* and that he was "still very young, not yet having completed his education."[52] Nevertheless, he was able, apparently without difficulty, to enter into his inheritance from his father without the eldest member of the dynasty making any claims for himself. Thus, it does not seem logical to accord any great significance to the right of seniority.

Perhaps, as Eugen Ewig once suggested, Gunthchramn did all this as a "presumptive godfather,"[53] that is, with reference to a planned sponsorship that would actually come about years later? We have no evidence for this; whether the attempt to present such interventions as legitimate with the help of baptismal sponsorship made any great impression remains to be studied. To anticipate the subsequent chapters: there is little evidence that it did—none at all that the mere plan of baptismal sponsorship provided Gunthchramn with a necessary and politically efficacious legitimation for his actions.

The fact that Gunthchramn was Chlothar's nearest agnate, as Childebert I had been Theudebald's, might have been important in "normal" cases of inheritance, but not among kings. As we learn from Gregory's *History*, among the Franks, rule by noble guardians apparently was common in such cases. Guardians ruled on behalf of the minor Theudebald as well as Childebert II, and, as we shall see, they considered the same procedure to be natural in the case of Chlothar too, or at least claimed it as their self-evident right.[54]

It thus appears that in his quest "to govern on his own account the kingdom of his nephew Lothar," Gunthchramn did not succeed in producing any legitimation that was at once self-evident to all concerned and supported by traditional practice or precedent.[55] The fact that he nevertheless tried, appointing bishops and counts, enforcing testaments, restoring property to its rightful owners, and banishing the queen, would seem to be evidence of his actual power.

Seizing the Moment

The moment was not inauspicious: the tyrant Chilperic, whom Gregory describes as the "Nero and Herod of our time,"[56] was dead, his henchmen in a precarious situation. It was this circumstance that set the stage for Gunthchramn's intervention.

Let us take a closer look at the situation of the Neustrian potentates. Originally, in the partition of the kingdom in 561, Chilperic had received only a disproportionately small territory in the extreme northwest. The largest and best piece was ruled by his brother Charibert, whose capital was in Paris. After the latter's death in 567, the three surviving brothers—Sigibert, Gunthchramn, and Chilperic—made a complicated pact for the partition of his kingdom. It stipulated, among other things, that any partner violating the pact would forfeit his portion of Charibert's legacy to those who had honored the agreement. The heart of the kingdom—the *civitates* of Paris, Chartres, and Senlis (including the small quarter of Ressons-sur-Matz)—was divided in three, and the city of Paris itself rendered neutral.[57]

Subsequently, however, the kings came to bolster their arguments less with the pact than with the sword, so that finally, around the years 575–80, Chilperic, previously slighted, occupied the entire portion of his brothers Gunthchramn and Sigibert in Charibert's kingdom. This benefited not least his *duces* whose administrative districts Chilperic had expanded by the conquered territories, or who owed their appointments altogether to these new acquisitions.[58] Two *duces* in particular managed to amass large terrains. The *dux* Berulf ruled the *civitates* of Tours and Poitiers, which had been taken from Austrasia in 578, as well as the originally Burgundian Nantes and a section of Chilperic's portion of Charibert's kingdom. Another part of this legacy was under the rule of *dux* Desiderius, who had also captured the previously Austrasian Albi as well as the entire territory Gunthchramn had inherited by right from Charibert. Furthermore, in the Novempopulana a certain *dux* Bladast also ruled over parts of Charibert's Neustrian legacy. Finally, we also know of a *dux* Bobo, who probably presided over the Neustrian motherlands around Soissons and ruled the *civitas* of Paris. He alone ruled, at least in part, over indisputably Neustrian territory (that is, the motherlands). The others, in contrast, administered territories in which the legitimacy of their rule could easily be challenged. They ruled over what they had captured of Charibert's legacy, in the neighboring portions of the kingdom, or over sections of the Neustrian legacy to which, because of their violation of the pact, they no longer had any claim.

With the death of Chilperic in 584, the situation for these potentates apparently became precarious, less because the pact itself was against them, which had also been the case beforehand, than because only the death of the powerful Chilperic made this pact a weapon in Gunthchramn's hands. The bellicose Childebert immediately entered the scene with his mother Brunechildis, an archenemy of Fredegund's, penetrating the Neustrian ancestral territory and even capturing Soissons, the ancestral seat of the Neustrian Merovingians before setting forth for Paris with his army; but that was not all.⁵⁹ At the hour of Chilperic's death, Gunthchramn's chief capital was the regiment that Chilperic and his men had led and which now was sworn to revenge. Immediately, a "great outcry was raised against those who had been powerful by favour of King Chilperic."⁶⁰ It must have been Gunthchramn to whom the "great outcry" of the injured parties was addressed, for he would hardly have been able to restore their property to them otherwise.⁶¹ The victims of Chilperic and his men did not appeal to the nobles under whom they had suffered, but rather to their strong neighbor, who was preparing to intervene anyway.

The chronicler recounts the behavior of one petitioner in particular, who, however, met with no success. The man in question was a certain Promotus, whom Sigibert had installed as bishop in the Austrasian *castrum* of Châteaudun, but who was deposed by his fellow bishops after Sigibert's death because the *castrum* belonged to the diocese of Chartres.⁶² Promotus owed his promotion to the power politics of Sigibert, who probably had been seeking to remove the Austrasian *castrum* from the sphere of influence of the non-Austrasian episcopal see of Chartres.⁶³ With the death of his protector Sigibert in 574, Promotus could no longer maintain his position as bishop, particularly since Chilperic had occupied the diocese of Chartres since around 575–80. When Chilperic died, Promotus turned to Gunthchramn in the hope of regaining the *castrum* as his episcopal see. His lack of success is less interesting here than the fact that he clearly regarded Gunthchramn as the responsible authority, or at least as one capable of acting as such.

The citizens of Rouen took similar action. It was they who recalled Bishop Praetextatus from banishment after Chilperic's death and "restored [him] to the city in triumph." The chronicler notes especially that the king's widow was reluctant to take him back and thus apparently had to look on, powerless to intervene. Praetextatus then addressed himself to Gunthchramn, who had therefore been declared the responsible authority.⁶⁴

The political situation therefore became extremely favorable to Gunthchramn, although no traditional practice provided him with legitimation (as senior, agnate, or even presumptive godfather) for his intervention.

Pressured by their own subjects, their powerful neighbor Gunthchramn, and the aggressive Childebert, for the time being the *duces* and the king's mother had no choice but to arrive at a modus vivendi with Gunthchramn and, in some cases, also with Childebert—at least, initially. This is not yet the place to describe the individual strategies they developed.⁶⁵ At any rate, in this situation it was a bold move on Fredegund's part to turn to one of the men who was potentially most dangerous for her, Gunthchramn, and invite the intervention which she feared might be impending anyway.

Legitimation

We may assume that Gunthchramn, however favorably things stood, was compelled to portray his intervention as justified and to demonstrate his claim both to the *cives* of the cities and to the *duces* in order to impress or at least appease them. Here, he seems to have made good use of the partition pact of 567. In 584, when Chilperic was barely cold in the ground, Gunthchramn declared to an Austrasian legation that he regarded the entire legacy of Charibert, including Sigibert's and Chilperic's portions, as his own:

> Both of them [the brothers] by these transgressions forfeited their shares. Since, therefore, they have suffered God's doom, and the curse threatened in the pact, I intend, as the law alloweth, to take under my jurisdiction the whole kingdom of Charibert and all his treasures; nor will I make any grant of them, save as a free act of grace.[66]

As Gunthchramn portrayed it, the situation was clear and simple: none of the Neustrian *duces* ruled over a territory they could have reclaimed from Gunthchramn as Chilperic's property. Because Chilperic had violated the pact, the Neustrians had now lost their portion of Charibert's kingdom to Gunthchramn. Gunthchramn could have depicted his interventions in Rennes, Rouen, Angers, or the diocese of Chartres[67] as measures taken within his own kingdom. We do not know whether he took this position with the Neustrians, but his reply to the Austrasians shows that he knew how to use the pact to his own advantage. Further, according to this view of things, Gunthchramn would have appeared to be banishing the royal widow, Fredegund, from her kingdom to his own when he sent her to Rouen[68] while the young heir to the throne remained in Neustria with his governors. Such a measure would not have been unprecedented; a few years earlier Chilperic had banished the Austrasian king's mother, Brunechildis, to Rouen.[69]

This partition pact, however, could not justify every action; it applied only to those territories which had once belonged to Charibert's kingdom and thus could not be used to legitimize Gunthchramn's interventions in the Neustrian ancestral lands, nor his access to his small nephew. In order to present these, too, as justifiable, Gunthchramn needed something more, and this was precisely the point at which he brought up *adoptio*. Adoption legitimated his role in "bringing up" the boy[70] and his rule over the "whole kingdom" *(regni principatus)*.[71] In some respects, it was also more moderate and more acceptable to the Neustrians than the partition pact. After all, the territories in which the adoptive father Gunthchramn intervened could, if one so desired, continue to be regarded as "Neustrian," even if they continued to be ruled by the fictive father in Burgundy until Chlothar reached his majority. The partition pact was more radical. Had Gunthchramn actually enforced it—which he did not[72]—a large portion of the kingdom ruled by Chilperic would have become "Burgundian."

The protagonists not only needed access to such legitimations at the right moment, but they also needed to know how to use them. They had to refer to the right one at the right moment, and not to another—equally correct but less useful. When Gunthchramn considered it expedient to proclaim in Paris, of all places, a city already his alone, according to the partition pact, that he had adopted Chlothar and intended to "bring him up," we can see his deployment of such a technique of rule at work. He was interested in the accumulation of claims, in access to a reservoir out of which, depending on the situation, he could draw a gentler or harsher, structural or informal version of authority. Whether Gunthchramn's aim was to "take [everything] under my jurisdiction,"[73] to make a grant to no one,[74] to claim the "whole kingdom,"[75] or only to "bring up" and "protect,"[76] whether he was trying to woo the citizens as in Paris or to sack and pillage his opponents to their knees, as in the Austrasian towns of Tours and Poitiers,[77] depended on his feeling for the situation, on tactics, and in each case he had to search for the appropriate means. It was extremely helpful here that Fredegund not merely provided him with an opportunity to refer to *adoptio*, but also offered him the role of sponsor. Gunthchramn had a profound interest in this sponsorship relationship, of which the Neustrians, for their part, made extensive use.[78]

In short, Gunthchramn sought to buttress an intervention in the neighboring kingdom that was possible in terms of power politics but not legitimated by tradition by appropriating the alien, but not unfamiliar, institution of *adoptio*. It would have been a convenient legitimation for him to the extent that a segment of Fredegund's nobles, and particularly the *cives* to whom he turned, were Gallo-Romans anyway for whom *adoptio*, however defined,[79] was at least a familiar, accepted practice and associated with *potestas*. At this moment those who wielded power in Neustria apparently had no choice but to allow this to happen or, as Fredegund's behavior indicates, to seek their salvation in it. They were, however, soon to consolidate and change their stance, but that brings us to the question of their reaction to the legal import, which will be dealt with presently. [80]

We are concerned here, first, with Gunthchramn's adoption strategy, which proved as logical within its momentary context as it appears (at first sight) astonishing in regard to the inheritance process: when it came to the paternal authority of the adoptive father, Gunthchramn (in the chronicler's view, at least) made no distinction between Chlothar and Childebert. In both cases, he sought to establish his *regni principatus* and expressly referred to *adoptio*.

Why, then, did he not divide the inheritance and, more particularly, how did he find a legitimate means of naming only one of his two *adoptivi* as his heir? Gregory's *History* also contains a number of references to the ways in which Gunthchramn did indeed make distinctions in his relationships with his nephews.

The Inheritance Question: The Exclusion of Chlothar

Sudden "Doubts"

In July 585, less than a year after Chilperic's death and after Gunthchramn told the Parisian *cives* that he had adopted Chlothar, he returned to Paris, where, according to the chronicler, he said: "My brother Chilperic is said (*dicitur*) to have left a son behind him when he died."[81] He thus suddenly expressed doubts about the boy's legitimacy, and Gregory has him give a reason for these doubts:

> [Chlothar's] governors, at the mother's request, besought me to receive him from the holy font at the feast of the Lord's Nativity; but they never came. They next asked that the infant should be baptized at the holy Paschal feast; but on that occasion also he was not brought. A third time they prayed that he might be presented on St. John's Day; once again he came not. And now they have forced me from home in this hot season; here I am, and behold! the boy is kept hidden, and is not shown to me.[82]

According to this account, Gunthchramn must have been invited by Fredegund to become the infant's godfather immediately after Chilperic's death—that is, around the same time he says he adopted Chlothar—and he apparently accepted. The Neustrians thereupon offered him three dates, one after the other, but allowed all to pass by without the baptism taking place. Only now, when the fourth date had come and gone, did Gunthchramn react with a massive threat: "This leadeth me to think that they made an empty promise, and it is my present belief that one of our *leudes* is the real father of the boy. . . . Know, therefore, that I shall not receive him from the font unless I recognize certain proofs of his descent."[83] In the face of the weak position the Neustrian rulers found themselves in, these publicly expressed doubts about the boy's legitimacy (and thus about the royal *sanctitas*) represented a dangerous threat, one which the Neustrians had, however, themselves assiduously provoked. Only Gunthchramn's indication that they had made him undertake a special journey each time without bringing the boy reveals the full extent of the diplomatic game they were playing with him. At any rate, in the summer of 585, "in this hot season," Gunthchramn traveled to Paris especially for the baptism and later, in 591, when the christening finally did occur, it was again Gunthchramn who was expected to make the journey.[84] It is not specifically stated where Gunthchramn waited for the boy on the first three attempts, but there is no reason to assume that the protocol governing these three occasions was any different from that of the two subsequent occasions. From the end of 584 to the summer of 585, Gunthchramn made the journey in vain four times.

Clearly, the Neustrians were using the baptism for tactical purposes, stretching Gunthchramn's patience to the limit.[85] This was the situation in which Gunthchramn suddenly expressed public doubts about his nephew's legitimacy and threatened to refuse to act as his sponsor. It would be wrong to use his suspicions of 585 to interpret the actions taken shortly after Chilperic's death a year earlier, on the grounds, for example, that no *adoptio* could have taken place in 584, or that Gunthchramn had never seen the boy up to that point.[86] To do so would be to smooth over the tensions inherent in this situation and mask the explosive nature of the political actions. Gunthchramn's publicly expressed doubts seem, instead, to point to his resolve to take a harder line. Without having to decide whether he actually harbored doubts, or was merely airing them for tactical purposes (or perhaps both together), we may note that he did not choose just any moment to voice his suspicions, but rather just the right moment: when, namely, he required an enormously menacing response to an enormous provocation. To this extent, the case bears distinct similarities to that of Theoderich who, at the right moment, suddenly "found" a useful kinsman,[87] or that of the king of Aragon, who suddenly "recognized" that his marriage was incestuous and had it annulled.[88] However subjectively convinced these actors may have been of their misgivings and "discoveries," they arrived at them in concrete situations and with conspicuous convenience.

Neither should we ignore the fact that these perhaps subjectively genuine, but in any case politically targeted doubts were to have no consequences. Once again, the boy was not baptized but continued to be recognized as of legitimate birth, and Gunthchramn only became a godfather many years later. Apparently, Gunthchramn had an interest in his ties to Chlothar on which the Neustrian rulers could rely, and they apparently were more secure in the summer of 585 than they had been shortly after Chilperic's death. Fredegund's reaction is instructive. Doubts concerning the child's legitimacy represented a genuine threat to her position, which was defined solely in terms of the boy, so that she needed to react unequivocally, which she was quick to do: "When Queen Fredegund heard this, she assembled the principle men of the kingdom, three bishops and three hundred laymen of the highest birth, and all took solemn oath with her that the boy was the lawfully begotten child of Chilperic."[89] It need not concern us here whether or not "suspicion was [hereby] removed from the mind of the king."[90] Whatever the chronicler may assert, this can no longer be proven. If, however, Fredegund managed to assemble three hundred high-born men and the most important bishops, this demonstrated a collective solidarity that left Gunthchramn no choice but to withdraw his suspicions from the public arena. In Merovingian legal practice, oriented as it was more toward mediating disputes than reaching the truth,[91] this demonstration of solidarity must have been a central, if not *the* central, aspect of oath-helping.

The entire episode reads like a tense exercise in diplomatic muscle-flexing. First the Neustrians tried provocation and thus tested Gunthchramn's patience. Gunthchramn, in turn, used his sudden doubts to show that Chlothar's sovereignty could be saved only by securing the boy's kingdom, and neither served himself from it too generously nor allowed the Austrasian Childebert to do so. He also made the most of the fact that his sponsorship represented a recognition of Chlothar's legitimacy and that the people surrounding the royal child could scarcely afford a public refusal of this act by Gunthchramn.[92] The Neustrians responded to Gunthchramn's tactic with a display of unity, and henceforth there was no more talk of doubts about the boy's legitimacy—at least not to the Neustrians. Only to Childebert's emissaries did Gunthchramn apparently use this argument once again, at a much later date. When they complained because Gunthchramn had apparently once intended part of his inheritance to go to Chlothar, he used three arguments to mollify them. First, Chlothar would receive only two or three cities "somewhere." Second, he was merely trying to prevent a dispute. And third, he would have to see whether Chlothar was legitimate or not. However, the chronicler does not report that Gunthchramn ever initiated investigations into this matter in Neustria. The remark probably was simply one of his appeasement maneuvers, especially since Gunthchramn appears to have abandoned once again the plan to make Chlothar his heir.[93]

In Neustria, at any rate, the subject seemed to be closed, and for the time being—at least, according to the picture Gregory paints—there was no longer any talk of baptism. The test of strength had been shifted to another arena, as we shall see.

Imitatio naturae: stirps and *genus*

Gunthchramn's sudden "doubts" in the summer of 585 indicate a tension between him and the Neustrian rulers which found expression elsewhere as well. The terminology of kinship the chronicler puts in Gunthchramn's mouth suggests that he soon came to treat his nephews unequally in those cases where it was a matter not of his authority but of inheritance.

Scarcely had Gunthchramn announced (in 584) the adoption of his nephews *(mihi adoptivi facti sunt)* and his intention to raise them both, because, apart from himself, "there shall remain no strong man of our line *(de genere nostro robustus non fuerit),*"[94] than the chronicler has the Burgundian king telling Childebert at a meeting in 585 that "no male of my line *(de stirpe mea)* remaineth, save only thou, who art my brother's son. I shut out all others from my succession; do thou succeed as heir in all my realm."[95] We should read this to mean that Chlothar, the *adoptivus*, was apparently reckoned part of the *genus nostrum*, but not of the *stirps mea*. That, at least, was Gregory's interpretation. And his use of the words *stirps* and *genus* gives the impression that this reflected a commonly made distinction. Whenever the chronicler uses *genus* he does so to indicate, very generally, membership in a group defined in ethnic,[96] social[97] or genealogical[98] terms (tribe, royal or senatorial lineage, family). The same picture emerges when we compare this usage with the way in which Old High German translations of Latin texts render *genus*. There exists a multiplicity of variants that, in turn, are themselves unspecific: *kunni, chunne* (lineage), *slahta* (tribe, lineage, species, kind), *geslahta* (lineage), *edil(i)* (high birth, excellence, lineage, nobility), *zila* (line, series, kind), and *framchumft* (descent, lineage).[99] In specific cases, the term often remains ambiguous. For example, when Chlodwig I accusingly asked his near relative[100] Ragnachar, "why hast thou disgraced our *genus (cur humiliasti genus nostrum),*"[101] it remains an open question whether he was referring to the latter's kingly rank (both were kings)[102] or to their close familial ties.

In contrast, the chronicler uses *stirps* far less frequently and only in the sense of descent with clear reference to a common progenitor.[103] One could easily cite a similar usage in other authors such as Fredegar[104] or the Old High German Isidor *(framchumft)*, who provides the only evidence of an Old High German equivalent for *stirps*.[105]

Genus thus has a much broader and more diffuse spectrum of meaning and very generally indicates some sort of membership in a "lineage" or "race" *(Geschlecht)*, the more precise definition of which depends on context. Clearly, *stirps* always indicates a direct relationship of descent. For Gunthchramn, Chlothar II was, to be sure, *de stirpe nostra*,[106] since both of them were descended from Chlothar I; but, as a collateral relation, Gunthchramn may not have counted his nephew Chlothar II as part of his own *stirps*. If, however, he is said to have referred to Childebert II as *de stirpe mea*,[107] he was clearly anxious to claim him as a true descendant—quite in keeping with the fiction the Romans called *naturam imitari*: adoption creates blood kin.[108]

What the chronicler has to say about the act of adoption in 577, at Pompierre, may also be read in this manner. Gunthchramn placed Childebert in a relationship of fictive filiation by wishing "that this my nephew may now be a son to me *(mihi sit filius)*."[109] This is a conspicuous use of language, particularly because, in other, comparable, situations, the chronicler has the protagonists operate with "as" constructions. In the year 533, Childebert I intended to take his nephew, Theudebert I, "as my son."[110] In Andelot, it was stipulated that in the case of Childebert's death, Gunthchramn should treat his sons "as *(ut)* a true father" and Childebert's wife and daughter like *(tamquam)* "his own dear sister, with her daughters."[111] And in 591, when Gunthchramn's influence in Neustria was no longer a threat, Fredegund now offered him her son only "as a foster son."[112] This terminological difference may indicate that the idea of a legal fiction was being expressed in 577. For it was precisely the element of fiction *(mihi sit filius)*, the *naturam imitari*, that made this action suitable as a strategy for manipulating the inheritance process. Gunthchramn also had to choose a strong safeguard in Pompierre in 577, since his brother Chilperic was still alive, and it was not a matter, as it would to be later, of preferring one of two equal nephews but, rather, of displacing his brother Chilperic, the legitimate legatee, in favor of his nephew Childebert.[113] It would have made perfectly good sense for Gunthchramn to appropriate this idea of fictive kinship, which may have been widespread in the Gallo-Roman milieu. Years later, in a discussion with Gunthchramn's legates, the chronicler, who was involved in political dealings, once again claimed that the relationship between the two kings should be interpreted as a fiction: "Gunthchramn," says the chronicler, quoting himself, "had decided [!] to have no other son than him [Childebert]."[114] Childebert was thus supposed to count *as* a son, to be a son, not to be *like* a son.

According to Gunthchramn's interpretation, which, apparently, was unique in the Frankish milieu, Childebert was to be Gunthchramn's only "blood" offspring and thus his sole heir. The terms *stirps* and *genus* defined kinship in different ways. The terminology of kinship was deployed publicly to draw up boundaries against the Neustrians who surrounded both Chilperic and Chlothar, and the normative implications of the phrase *stirps mea* had a dual value for the relationship between Gunthchramn and the Austrasian royal dynasty, at once creating and stabilizing the group.

Enlisting Spiritual Support

Gunthchramn took a further measure, which doubtless served to establish both separation from the Neustrian and unity with the Austrasian side.

When he met with several bishops at Orléans on his way to Paris, where he intended to become Chlothar's godfather, he asked during a meal "that ye pray for the Lord's mercy on Childebert my son. . . . If, therefore, your prayers attend him, by God's grace he shall rule the land."[115] The chronicler describes Gunthchramn's entire sojourn in Orléans as an elaborate ceremony lasting several days, which we might well consider scrupulously stage-managed. Thus, the request for prayers was also a calculated political action.[116] Gunthchramn's request was a public demonstration of his politics toward his nephew. If the bishops granted the request, it would represent the public recognition and propagation of his politics on the part of a group that exercised great influence, especially in the Merovingian period,[117] and on whose loyalty Gunthchramn could by no means always rely.[118] On this occasion, the bishops played along, and "all uttered their prayer to the Lord that of His mercy He would preserve both *(utrumque)* kings."[119]

Like the *adoptio* that preceded it, the bishops' prayer advanced the close alliance *(utrumque)* the Burgundian king had sought to form with Childebert and to control. When, in Orléans, he used the royal prayer, a fundamental instrument of representation and rule in the Middle Ages as in antiquity,[120] for the benefit of only one of his nephews—namely, Childebert—he sent a political signal the participants understood well and would long remember. The chronicler Gregory, at least, recalled it clearly. During a sojourn at Childebert's court a few months later, he fell into a dispute with a delegation sent by Gunthchramn. It was in this dispute that the chronicler, a partisan of Childebert's, voiced the above-cited argument that Gunthchramn wanted "to have no other son *(habere disponit)* than him [Childebert]." He then deliberately added, "[H]ave we not heard him say it this very year?"[121] Gunthchramn's message at Orléans had achieved the desired effect.[122]

And Gregory described a king, Gunthchramn, who did not stop at the request for a royal prayer. We are informed that he added a story intended to cast the proper light on Childebert's fortunes: as Gunthchramn informed the bishops, Childebert had been born on Easter day while his father, Sigibert, was in church. Just as the Gospel was being read out, a messenger arrived. In Gregory's account, Gunthchramn told his listeners that "he who read the lection from the Gospel and the messenger spoke as it were with a single voice the words: 'Unto thee a son is born.'" The whole people thereupon responded "to a twofold message" by praising God. To make matters more auspicious still, Childebert had been baptized at Whitsun and crowned on Christmas Day.[123] Gunthchramn presented this one of his two nephews as the chosen one, and the bishops rewarded his interpretation with their public prayer for these two *(utrumque)* kings, "father" and "son."

The Question of Blood: A Fiction with Limits

Fiction and metaphor: *sit filius—tamquam filius—ut pius pater*

Gunthchramn appears to have tried in Pompierre to establish a fictive filiation and thus to change Childebert's kinship *status*. This is one way of reading his desire for Childebert to be his "son."[124] As scholarship in social anthropology has taught us, however, such fictions can be highly incomplete and restricted to certain specific cases.[125] Reinhard Schneider places the relationship of the Neustrian Chilperic to his nephew Childebert in just such a context: In 581, Chilperic promised his inheritance to his nephew Childebert, later referring to him as his "son."[126] After the birth of Chlothar, however, and after Chilperic's death, there is no further mention of this. In Schneider's interpretation, Chilperic offered only his inheritance to his new "son" for the eventuality that he himself produced no more biological sons. In the case of a later-born son of his own, he would leave his entire legacy to this child, and no longer to Childebert, and this was probably the "normal case."[127] To put it another way, the fiction was limited from the outset.

The trouble with the story about Chilperic is that no such restrictive clause is expressly mentioned, and because he was murdered in 584 he no longer had a chance to exclude his "son" Childebert after the birth of his biological son, Chlothar II. We, in turn, have no opportunity to see how he would have done this—whether it would have been necessary at all and, if not, whether it really would have been the pact that kept Childebert from asserting further claims. Gregory apparently was not sufficiently interested in the evidence Childebert produced in the Neustrian royal city of Soissons when he arrived there after Chilperic's death, or in whether the agreement of 581 possessed any diplomatic or legitimatory value, to record it for posterity. However vague this example may be, it nevertheless is at least plausible to posit that the birth of a biological son "normally" superseded such promises of legacies.[128]

Less plausible is the assumption that Gunthchramn made an exception to this "normal case" at Pompierre[129] when he immediately followed his wish that Childebert "be my son" with the promise that "'If I should yet have sons, I will nonetheless regard thee as one of them *(tamquam unum ex his)* that between them and thee there may abide the loving-kindness which to-day I promise thee, calling God to witness.'"[130] Can those present actually have understood this as an exception to the "normal case"? Is it not far more likely that, in adding this provision, Gunthchramn already had in mind the limitation of the fiction *(mihi sit filius)* and that he, too, intended only to imitate nature as long as he had no sons of his own?

Naturally, whereas the language chosen by the chronicler is insufficient proof, it certainly is conspicuous: Gunthchramn's later-born sons would have accorded the nephew and "son" Childebert—literally—a son*like* position *(tamquam unum ex his)*, promising him nothing more than *caritas*. To be sure, in the early Middle Ages *caritas* could mean many things, apparently sometimes also an "objective legally binding tie between two biological [!] brothers."[131] In such cases, *caritas* may suggest a right of inheritance, thus evoking the status, as well as a pattern, of behavior. The examples of such use of terminology are rare,[132] and the term is, on the whole (in the legal context as well) so unspecific that Gunthchramn could scarcely have formulated an exception in Pompierre that was comprehensible to the nobles present.

A more sensible conclusion is that Gunthchramn had no such exception in mind. After all, ten years later, the same partners, Gunthchramn and Childebert, made a pact at Andelot in which they once again addressed the same topic—the inheritance issue—this time in writing. The problem of later-born sons was expressly taken up, but more unambiguously this time. The pact states that "whichever of the two kings God shall cause to survive the other, if that other pass childless from . . . this present world, shall inherit his kingdom."[133]

If, therefore, Gunthchramn had had another son (whether he expected it or not, he provided for the eventuality), then Childebert would have inherited nothing. We could object that ten years had passed since the *adoptio* of Pompierre, and that the regulations of Pompierre and Andelot need not have been identical. This is correct, but there is no evidence that (and also no visible reason why) the inheritance should have been regulated differently at Andelot in 587 than at Pompierre in 577. If, then, an unambiguous regulation was adopted in 587 in the pact of Andelot, there is no reason why we should not use this regulation to interpret the *adoptio* of 577 as well: Childebert would, "if I [Gunthchramn] should yet have sons," no longer be an imitation, fictive son *(mihi sit filius)*, but at least be treated similarly to a son *(tamquam filius)*, that is, with *caritas*. Thus, at Pompierre— and this is the lesson the pact of Andelot teaches—Gunthchramn was simply contemplating the loss of the right of inheritance. "The same *caritas*" which Gunthchramn continued to promise his Austrasian nephew Childebert was, at least in its material effects, not the *caritas* of biological brothers but, rather, that of friendship, or of "Frankish oath brotherhood *(Schwurfreundschaft)*."[134] What Childebert could still expect was not a specific (materially beneficial) kinship status, but a specific way of behaving that was expected of kin. The fiction was to leave off where the biological sons began.

Incidentally, similar provisions were made at Andelot for the eventuality that Childebert might predecease Gunthchramn. Gunthchramn was then to take Childebert's two sons, Theudebert and Theuderic, "as a true father *(ut pius pater)* under his guardianship and protection . . . and . . . see that in all security they possess their father's kingdom."[135] Two aspects are striking here: first, that Gunthchramn intended to bring up the "sons of this my son Childebert," as he called them,[136] "*as* a true father"; and second, that Childebert's sons were to inherit "*their father's* kingdom." The pact gives no indication that this kingdom comprised more than Austrasia. The pact of Andelot shows an encounter between two autonomous rulers of autonomous kingdoms. It had been decided to preserve Austrasia for Childebert's sons, but they were not explicitly made their late father's heirs and were not assured of an explicit claim to Burgundy. Apparently, Gunthchramn was less interested in preserving for the "sons of this my son," Childebert, the materially effective status of "grandsons" than he was in protection and care: he promised to act as a father, to treat them as sons. Accordingly, he also promised to take Childebert's mother, sister, wife, and daughters "as it were his dear sister and daughters *(tamquam sororem bonam et filias)* . . . under his guardianship and defence in all spiritual affection."[137] In this phrasing, too, the terminology of kinship was used to lay claim to a behavior rather than a status.

The provisions for the case of Childebert's predeceasing Gunthchramn are instructive from the perspective of Gunthchramn's political tactics. Gunthchramn was confronted with the same problem he had faced in his attempts to rule in his nephews' kingdoms and to favor Childebert as his heir; that is, he had to circumvent tradition. This case shows clearly just how Gunthchramn proceeded, how purposefully he introduced legal material from a related context into a specific situation in order to counter a (for him) inconvenient traditional arrangement by means of a related but decidedly different legitimation.

To prevent the intervention of the nobles in the event of Childebert's premature death, the Burgundian king apparently was to be appointed the guardian ("as a true father") of Childebert's orphan sons.[138] That is, he was supposed to secure the boys' property as well as preserve the legacy for them. This, it is generally assumed, was the "normal" arrangement of guardianship among the Franks.[139] Especially in the royal family, however, this arrangement was, it seems, frequently not used, for example in the cases of Childebert II, Chlothar II, and Theudebald. In these instances, it seems that it was not the nearest agnate who took the role of guardian, but the mothers and nobles.[140] At Andelot, however, it was the closest agnate who was entrusted with the care of the child, apparently in an attempt to intervene in previous royal practice by means of a custom from a different social sphere.

It is this procedure which also appears to have caused Gunthchramn to make use of *adoptio*. In the neighboring kingdoms, he sought to usurp the nobles' right of guardianship and legitimated his action by invoking the hitherto unused but not wholly unfamiliar idea of fictive paternity. Similarly, he also tried to manipulate the customary inheritance process and to give preference to his nephew Childebert, first before his brother, Chilperic, and then before his nephew Chlothar, once again employing a previously neglected construction, that of "imitated nature."

A Parallel: Grimoald

Here, too, the course of historical events fails to tell us what we want to know. Gunthchramn had no sons of his own against whose lives we could test whether his affectionate promise to his *adoptivus* Childebert was more than a promise about behavior. Another adoption story from the Merovingian period, obscure though it may be on the whole, at least does not exhibit this defect. It is the story of the powerful Austrasian *maior domus*, Grimoald (d. 662), and his striving for royal power. This Grimoald, an early Carolingian, succeeded in promoting his son to *adoptivus* of the Merovingian king Sigibert III (d. 656) at a time when the king had no sons of his own. In addition, Grimoald called this son—whether only since the adoption or beforehand, we do not know—by the name of "Childebert," that is, after the only Merovingian up to that point who had managed to use an *adoptio* to extend his own rule. This was the first attempt of a Carolingian *maior domus* to attain the kingship,[141] and it was endangered when Sigibert III had a son after all, the future Dagobert II (d. 679).

For the purposes of historical understanding it would have been simpler if, upon Sigibert's death, sovereignty had either been divided between his biological son and his *adoptivus*, or Dagobert had simply become the sole ruler. The first case would at least have provided us with an example of a consistent and complete fiction. In the second case, it would have been obvious that the fiction was tied to a specific situation that no longer obtained after Dagobert's birth. Neither of the two occurred, though, making it unclear what utility this *adoptio* retained after Dagobert's birth. Instead, Grimoald had Dagobert, the biological Merovingian, tonsured and sent to an Irish monastery. His own biological son, the fictive Merovingian Childebert, then ascended the throne. This was a forceful solution, one that initially appeared to succeed. For several years, perhaps six, this *adoptivus* managed to reign alone, backed by the mighty Grimoald, before a group of nobles organized resistance, ambushed and captured Grimoald, and brought him before a Neustrian royal tribunal. Grimoald paid for his conduct with death in prison, while his son simply disappeared from the written record. Dagobert, the "real" Merovingian, was restored and reigned alone from then on.[142]

We do not know what crime Grimoald was charged with before the royal tribunal. Was he reproached for having violated the principle of partition when he removed Dagobert and set the *adoptivus* Childebert alone on the throne? Or was the argument that an *adoptivus* no longer had a function once a biological son had been born? We do not know and are thus still faced with the same question: what value could *adoptio* retain for the *adoptivus* when the "father" subsequently had a son of his own blood? Could he, indeed, still claim the rights of a son?

Naturally, he could—or, at least, try to. Whether the nobles played along, and whether he could enforce such an interpretation, is another question. The conviction of Grimoald does not help us here because the chroniclers and hagiographers do not name the charges against him. The fact that the adoptee Childebert managed to reign for a few years also does nothing to illuminate the problem, unless we equate power with its legitimation. Just because they tolerated Grimoald's actual rule for a time does not mean that the nobles adopted his arguments. Also, there is no evidence that they would have done so. On the contrary, those documents that contain an interpretation favorable to Grimoald appear to be "Carolingian." They are the *Life* of Bonitus of Clermont and two Carolingian regnal lists.

These regnal lists do mention a Childebert as an *adoptivus*, in chronological order after Sigibert III. They are silent, however, on the reign of Dagobert II, who returned from exile, and in them Childebert *adoptivus* is followed immediately by Childeric II. Dagobert II, then, who reigned for several years after the death of Grimoald and the disappearance of the adopted Childebert, is missing from these lists. This, at any rate, was the safest way of dealing with the issue of whether the *adoptivus* Childebert still had rights alongside a biological son. The question was simply avoided.[143]

The second piece of evidence for Grimoald's version at least hints at why this account came to be recorded. It is the work of a monk from the monastery of Manglieu (or Manlieu) near Clermont, who wrote the *Life* of Bonitus of Clermont shortly after the latter's death.[144] The monk also mentions in passing how the succession continued after the death of Sigibert III and his *sons* [sic].[145] With this modest plural (provided Sigibert III had no blood offspring unknown to us), the hagiographer treats the *adoptivus* just like Sigibert's biological son, plainly accepting, in this sentence, that the *adoptivus* also had a claim to the kingship. The *Life* leaves scarcely any doubt as to the source of the hagiographer's interpretation. He tells us enough about his hero to demonstrate that Bonitus can hardly be considered an enemy of the Carolingians. While still a boy, he arrived at the court of Sigibert III where the powerful *maior domus* Grimoald held sway. Bonitus embarked on his career there and ended up a referendarius—the second man at court after Grimoald. Later, when he was set to become bishop of

Clermont (apparently at the initiative not of the court but of his predecessor and kinsman), the hagiographer expressly mentions who actually provided the necessary assent: in his time "under King Theuderic," he asserts, the actual *maior domus* had been Pippin, who "occupied the first position in the kingdom and ran the affairs of the court and according to whose judgment all matters were arranged."[146] Finally, the hagiographer informs us that Bonitus withdrew for a time to the very same monastery in which the author himself sat and which belonged to the diocese of Bonitus.[147] The hagiographer thus appears to have heard at first hand the version of the *maiores* and his bishop and hero, who together ran the affairs of the Austrasian court for many years.

To be sure, contemporary statements from the opposing side exist, which inform us of the forced exile of Dagobert,[148] but not about the usefulness of the *adoptio* for Childebert after Dagobert's birth. Only one author reports on the events from another perspective than that of the pro-Carolingian witnesses, and he was writing centuries later. That author was Sigebert of Gembloux, the value of whose evidence is nevertheless by no means wholly diminished by the passage of time. Whatever texts he based his version on, the account must at least have appeared plausible to him. Precisely because of his temporal distance from the events he may have de-individualized the situation, so that his narrative contains elements from the storehouse of what he considered "normal." And this proves to be quite different from the version in the regnal lists and the pro-Carolingian *Life*, but similar to what Gunthchramn and Childebert decided at Andelot— and probably at Pompierre as well. Sigebert of Gembloux claimed to know for a fact that King Sigibert III withdrew his inheritance from the *adoptivus* Childebert after Dagobert's birth and instead made his *maior domus*, Grimoald, swear that he would raise Dagobert and preserve the kingdom for him.[149] In keeping with the provisions of the sixth-century pact of Andelot, which had been self-evident at the time, this eleventh-century author apparently also could not imagine an *adoptivus* retaining the right to inherit after a biological son had entered the picture. Indeed, there is no evidence of this having happened. Even the seeming exception of Pompierre can be read much more easily as the norm: as at Andelot, here, too, the fiction was to end if Gunthchramn produced a son of his own.

Fiction and "Blood"

Had Gunthchramn managed, after 577, to have a biological son, Childebert's adoption would have been reduced to the effect of an oath brother's *caritas*, and the status fiction *(sit filius)* to a mere rule of conduct *(tamquam filius)* entailing no inheritance claims.[150] After the birth of Chlothar, Chilperic's legacy to Childebert no longer was mentioned. Biological offspring rendered the fictive kinsman insignificant. Gregory's *History* relates other cases as well, in which a fictive son was of interest only so long as he had no biological counterpart. Whenever he describes any action directed in some way at the creation of sons, the chronicler repeats in stereotypical language the underlying purpose. Thus, in the year 533, Childebert I is supposed to have said to Theudebert I, "I have no sons and I would fain regard thee as my son."[151] And at Pompierre in 577, Gunthchramn supposedly told Childebert II, "'It is befallen me through my sins that I am left childless; and therefore I ask that this my nephew may now be a son to me.'"[152] Similarly, in 581, Gregory has Chilperic I telling Childebert II, "'So great were grown my sins that I have no sons more, nor remaineth there an heir to me, save only King Childebert, my brother Sigibert's son.'"[153] And the chronicler reports of King Childebert I and Gundovald that "The king [Childebert] received him, and kept him with him because he had no sons."[154]

After the death of Chlothar I, Gundovald was taken in by Charibert, who also had no sons of his own, and, as is mentioned above, Sigibert III also had no offspring of his own when he accepted Grimoald's son.[155] This motive is also specifically mentioned in the legal sources. Markulf's collection of formulas says: "*Dum, peccatis meis fatientibus, diu orbatus a filiis . . . , et te . . . in loco filiorum meorum visus sum adobtasse . . . et omnes res meas . . . in tua potestate recipere debias*";[156] and the Lex Ribuaria notes: "*Si quis procreatione filiorum vel filiarum non habuerit . . . adoptare in hereditate vel adfatimi*[*re*] *. . . licentiam habeat.*"[157]

A given man's interest in *adoptio* depended on whether he had biological sons or hopes of acquiring any. As the legal sources show, this applied not only in matters of royal succession. Even for those above-mentioned fathers who adopted grown men and simultaneously married them to their daughters, an *adoptio* made sense only because these fathers had no sons of their own.[158] If they did subsequently acquire a son they no longer needed these outsiders *(extranius)*.[159] In the history of kingship, at least—and it is only here that we have sources—the outsider was then allowed to disappear. If we examine the practices of social and political authority we find that the logic of the filial fiction remained subordinate to the logic of "blood."

Here, we can see a fundamental, functional distinction to that form of *adoptio* which people later claimed to accomplish by means of baptismal sponsorship. Someone who accepted a son in *adoptio* through baptismal sponsorship did not care whether he already had a biological son; nor did it matter whether or not he already had another such spiritual son. It may be that Gunthchramn's sponsorship of his nephew Chlothar "in reality [included] a politically significant adoption."[160] But what kind of adoption was this, in concrete terms? Did anyone actually confuse the *adoptio* of sponsorship with that which one usually sought to accomplish by means of an *adoptio*? It seems unlikely. The stereotypical repetition of childlessness in the case of secular *adoptiones* places such arrangements within a much different context from that of baptismal sponsorship.

It is striking as well that Gunthchramn did not emphasize his lack of a son in all situations. He did so only in circumstances in some way associated with inheritance. When he was interested in *adoptio* because it could ensure him a legitimate authority in Neustria not provided for by tradition, he did not mention that he already had an—albeit fictive—child from his own line *(stirps mea)*—namely, Childebert. In light of his objective, to ignore this aspect as far as possible represented the only sensible course.

Such nuances, however, belong not to the realm of the normative but rather to that of political technique, and their success did not depend on Gunthchramn alone. There were other actors as well—his nephews, their mothers and, not least, the nobles. It was on them that he had to test his strategies and to enforce his right " to govern on his own account" in his nephews' kingdoms.[161]

5
Counterstrategies: Gunthchramn's Nephews and Their Nobles

As we have seen thus far, Gunthchramn sought to stabilize the temporary advantage he was able to draw from the weak position of the regencies by means of *adoptiones* intended to lend an appearance of legitimacy to his rule over the neighboring kingdoms. Whether he was successful in exploiting this borrowed construction—which his own Frankish tradition did not provide in this form, and which was by no means advantageous for all parties interested in this political constellation—depended not least on the balance of power and the extent to which the different interest groups managed to assert themselves.

What, then, did Gunthchramn accomplish? Was his strategy successful? Was he able to establish his legitimacy, and if so, when was it accepted and when not? We now turn our attention to the interests of Gunthchramn's fellow actors, who tried, as he did, to make the best of every situation, appearing, in one case, as Gunthchramn's opponents, and, in the next, as his accomplices. These actors were his nephews, represented by their mothers and the heterogeneous group of the nobles.

The Austrasians

The Technique of Diplomacy

How, then, did Gunthchramn's allies and opponents react? How did they treat his claims? As for Austrasia, two incidents might initially give the impression that Childebert and his mother Brunechildis consented to Gunthchramn's claims of supremacy. The first occurred in 587, shortly after the two kings had settled their affairs in writing at Andelot. The Visigothic king Recared had sent a delegation at that time to Childebert, asking for the hand of Childebert's sister. "King Childebert and his mother" had replied to the envoys: "'As far as we are concerned the promise should be readily given, but we dare not give it without consulting our kinsman King Guntram; for we have pledged ourselves to do nothing in matters of moment without his counsel.'"[1] We might be tempted at first to consider whether Childebert and his mother were not simply looking for an elegant way out of answering Recared's request, but the course of events makes this improbable. They were conspicuously obliging to the legation, and "pledged themselves to maintain unbroken peace with Recared."[2] After Gunthchramn had been consulted, Childebert gave his sister to the Gothic king, despite Gunthchramn's overtly reluctant approval.[3]

If Gunthchramn was consulted not because Childebert and his mother wanted to evade the Goth, was it perhaps because his "son," Childebert, accorded (or was compelled to accord) him supremacy, even "paternal" authority? Gunthchramn's reply to Childebert's query seems, instead, to support the interpretation that his promise had less to do with the *adoptio* of Pompierre than with the recently sealed pact of Andelot. When, through envoys, Childebert consulted Gunthchramn a short while later, the latter at first expressed his reluctance, then replied: "'If my nephew shall fulfill all the conditions written at his own wish in this treaty, then I on my side will gratify his wishes on this matter.'"[4] In the pact of Andelot, the two kings had sworn to maintain faith (*fides*), harmony (*concordia*), and *caritas*.[5]

In their answer to the Gothic envoys, Childebert and Brunechildis seem to have taken the recent pact into consideration. The pact, however, did *not* define the asymmetrical relationship of an *adoptio*, nor did it cement the kind of paternal authority which Gunthchramn not infrequently claimed. Two equal yet sovereign kings had met at Andelot, and the most they could do was coordinate their actions. There is no evidence that Gunthchramn was granted any prerogatives as a "father" or that he was thus consulted *for that reason*. This example tells us nothing about the attitudes toward *adoptio* that prevailed in Austrasia ten years after Pompierre. Most likely, the consultation of Gunthchramn before such a marriage was a measure taken out of consideration for the pact.

To be sure, the Merovingians were, as we have seen,[6] by no means particularly devoted to duty, making it unlikely that Childebert consulted Gunthchramn simply to fulfill a contractual obligation. In fact, Gunthchramn expressly complained to the envoys that Childebert was violating central passages of the pact.[7] Pacts may also be honored at least in part because of a cost-benefit analysis, and one could easily find several good reasons why, in the matter of this marriage, the Austrasians should have consulted the neighboring king.

These reasons bring us to the second passage in the text, in which the

Austrasians appear to acknowledge Gunthchramn's rule as deriving from the *adoptio*. It is remarkable because the chronicler himself was involved, perhaps even personally speaking the words in question. When Childebert's envoys arrived at Gunthchramn's court to hear his advice on the matrimonial plans of the Gothic king, they, including Gregory, began with a striking salutation:[8] "'Childebert . . . [renders] thee thanks beyond measure for thy perpetual admonishment to do that which is pleasing in God's sight, acceptable to thee, and fitting his people's need.'"[9] Their greeting signalized acknowledgment of Gunthchramn's claim; they did not leave it at the terminology Gunthchramn had used years before in Paris to mask his designs on power.[10] Instead, they declared not merely that Gunthchramn had acted like a foster father, offering counsel and training (that is, that he had acted on behalf of the child's welfare or done "that which is pleasing in God's sight . . . and fitting his people's need"). They also specifically emphasized that he had asserted his own interests ("acceptable to thee"). If there was a difference between paternal authority and foster fatherhood, this must have been it.[11]

In their salutation the delegation appears to have defined a relationship that probably only *adoptio* could have legitimated. Gregory and his companions greeted Gunthchramn with the version Gregory had presented some years before to the citizens Poitiers.[12] We can only judge this properly, however, if we consider that, in other contexts, the same Gregory, acting in the service of the same King Childebert, had emphasized not this asymmetry but his parity. Thus, he had demanded "that each should equally *(pariter)* defend and love the other," and had conceded to the neighbor king no rights in Austrasia—for example, to convene synods.[13] How one described the relationship was a question not of legal logic but, rather, of diplomatic calculation. And this delegation, whose very greeting signaled an acknowledgment of the "father," had some matters to discuss that made it advisable to treat Gunthchramn with consideration: first, Gunthchramn was supposed to support his nephew in his exploits against the Langobards, and, second, Gunthchramn had made overtures to the Neustrians in a manner Childebert apparently regarded as dangerous. The envoys were supposed to protest against this.[14] Therefore, they had to offer something in return, and made (verbal) concessions to Gunthchramn, granting him not only supremacy but also acceding to some political claims he had made on the basis of the pact of Andelot.[15]

The Practice of Rule

These were, however, still few concessions compared with the assessment Gregory had made to the *cives* of Poitiers—namely, that Gunthchramn ruled "as his father, Lothar had done before him," that is, alone.[16] Despite all the acknowledgment and consultation, which Childebert "dared not" neglect,[17] there is no indication that Gunthchramn ever ruled in Austrasia.

Thus, a confrontation between Gunthchramn and a Saxon named Chulderic indicates just how strictly Gunthchramn's scope of action was circumscribed by the borders of his own kingdom. In 585, after committing numerous misdeeds and to avoid punishment by Gunthchramn, Chulderic had taken refuge in the church of St. Martin at Tours. He managed to escape Gunthchramn, as the chronicler relates somewhat ponderously: "Childeric the Saxon . . . sought the church of the holy Martin, leaving his wife in Guntram's dominions. The king had adjured her not to presume to see her husband until such time as he should be restored to the royal favour."[18] Gunthchramn and Childebert had fought over Tours during the years 584 and 585, but now the city belonged once again to Austrasia.[19] Chulderic was thus in a different part of the kingdom from his wife. If Gunthchramn now turned, instead, to the Saxon's wife, he must have been denied access to Chulderic himself. Gregory justifies Gunthchramn's turning to the wife by saying that she had been left behind "in Guntram's dominions," so that one may assume it was not Chulderic's asylum in the church of St. Martin but, rather, the frontier of the kingdom that prevented the king from arresting him.

As a further example, one might point to the case of Theodore of Marseilles. Gunthchramn was able to have the bishop arrested three times as long as the city was divided between Austrasia and Burgundy and the bishop stood between two kings.[20] In 584, however, Gunthchramn had returned his part of Marseilles to Childebert, thus losing his access to the city.

Nevertheless, "the king [Gunthchramn] sought with renewed efforts to pursue Bishop Theodore," because he suspected him of having supported the conspirator Gundovald. The chronicler describes these efforts on Gunthchramn's part as follows: "As the city of Marseilles had been already restored to his dominion, King Childebert sent thither Ratherius, in the quality of duke, to investigate the matter." Gunthchramn could no longer do this himself, but he was apparently the instigator behind Childebert's initiation of the investigation.[21] Childebert himself, as the chronicler notes, had no interest in pursuing Bishop Theodore.[22] The same cannot be said of the *quasi dux* Ratherius, who, "disregarding the method of action enjoined upon him by the king, besieged the bishop, demanded sureties, and sent him to king Guntram."[23] This time it was only through the disloyalty of one of Childebert's officials that Gunthchramn managed to seize the bishop. Like the Saxon Chulderic, Bishop Theodore was separated from Gunthchramn by the frontier of the kingdom. Despite *adoptio*, he had no jurisdiction in Austrasia. Conversely, once Theodore was in Gunthchramn's realm, Childebert's only options were entreaties and threats.[24]

When unrest also arose during the occupation of the Austrasian see of Uzès, apparently only the youthful Childebert was regarded as a legitimate decision maker. Dynamius—governor of Provence and, albeit Childebert's subject, always an ally of Gunthchramn's—played a key role in these conflicts.[25] After the death of Bishop Ferreolus, "Albinus the ex-prefect, through the influence of Dynamius, actual governor of Provence, assumed the episcopate without the royal sanction."[26] He was set to be deposed but died before this could be carried out. When "Jovinus, another ex-governor of Provence, received the royal nomination to the bishopric"[27] the governor Dynamius managed to thwart the king's plans, pushing through a candidate who asserted himself by force of arms and gifts against Childebert's appointee. A short time later, Gunthchramn had Childebert's pretendant, Jovinus, imprisoned.[28] Thus, Childebert's exclusive legitimation to fill such posts was not assailed even when Gunthchramn apparently had opposing interests. If Gunthchramn became involved, it was not because of his own legitimation but, rather, because he was drawn in by the intrigues of Dynamius.

Finally, one might also cite the meeting of 585. There, Gunthchramn instructed his small nephew on how to rule, and indeed even "forbade"[29] him to do certain things; but it was Childebert, not Gunthchramn, who governed thereafter.

Surveying these events, we are not left with the impression that any "unification" of the two parts of the kingdom under Gunthchramn's aegis ever took place, as is occasionally posited[30] and as the paternal authority attached to *adoptio* might lead us to expect. In other words, Gunthchramn evidently failed in his attempt to manipulate the tradition of the regency with the aid of *adoptio*, and extend his rule to Austrasia.

And yet he had not merely staked claims, but also tried to tempt the Austrasians. This, at least, is how one might interpret an attempt he undertook at the meeting of 585, the same meeting at which he presented his nephew with admonitions and prohibitions, purporting all the while to have made decisions "together" with him.[31] At this meeting he gave Childebert a spear, saying, "'This is the sign that I have bestowed all my kingdom on thee. By virtue of this, take under thy dominion all my cities as if they were thine own.'"[32] He had already done something similar at Pompierre: "And setting him upon his own seat, he gave over to him his whole kingdom. . . ."[33] Scholars have used these passages to continue the debate about Merovingian adoption. They have discussed whether this was the classic passage on Merovingian enthronements[34] or whether it was not an "actual" enthronement,[35] but merely a "provision in case of death in legal symbolic form through enthronement"[36]—that is a prefigurative ritual on the occasion of an enthronement or royal progress.[37] As in the discussion surrounding adoption, this perspective scarcely seems to take into account that the custom was still in an embryonic stage[38] and that the scope for shaping and interpreting actions was thus much broader than such a discussion would have us believe.

Gunthchramn had publicly set his nephew on the throne in 577, and we are familiar with at least one interpretation of this action. Gregory states that "he gave over to him his whole kingdom." He does not say, as one scholar has suggested, that all he meant here "was the takeover of the kingdom after Gunthchramn's death."[39] And when later, at the meeting of 585, Gunthchramn is said to have called upon his *adoptivus* to undertake a royal progress, he was not revealing any testamentary intentions. His nephew was to go forth and "take under thy dominion all my cities as if they were thine own."[40]

Nor was Gunthchramn giving up his kingdom voluntarily. But was that what this was all about? Certainly, he had repeatedly (in 577, 585, and 587) sought to settle the question of the succession. This was not the only recognizable measure of his actions, however. After the deaths of his brothers in 575 and 584, Gunthchramn engaged in activities in Austrasia and Neustria that clearly were directed at expanding his rule. His handling of *adoptio* repeatedly reveals how much the logic of his actions was determined by this interest and how little by the rigorousness of any legal construction.[41]

Matters were not much different when, in 577, Gunthchramn turned over his kingdom to his seven-year-old nephew, or when, in 585, he sent the youth off to receive homage. Both acts were ambiguous, leaving open to interpretation whether they were undertaken only in preparation for the time after Gunthchramn's death or whether, even during Gunthchramn's lifetime, the frontiers and jurisdiction were to be blurred between "father" and "son." Of course, it is possible the context is now lost to us and that contemporaries immediately understood the significance of these acts. It is equally possible that these actions were not unambiguous, and that it would be misguided to look for juridical logic when all that mattered at the time was the practical extension of power. In this case, the potential effects of an enthronement and a royal progress could remain open. What danger—and for whom—existed anyway, even if Gunthchramn's aim had been to promote a unification of the kingdoms by means of a royal progress (perhaps similar to *adoptio*)? The only possible danger was that Gunthchramn might gain a tighter grip on the boy than he already had. And that was, at most, a danger for the Austrasian nobles.

Even if we cannot detect even a "temporary"[42] unification of the two kingdoms, Gunthchramn's strenuous attempts to intervene in Austrasia show that such a unification would have been useful and attractive to him. If one interprets his activities in such a way that they were organized to this end, then both the enthronement and the request for a royal progress were deliberate attempts to bring both kingdoms under his rule and to lend institutional form to the officially "mutual" decisions of the year 585, which were, in fact, unilateral ones: the "father" as coregent in Austrasia and the "son" as coregent in Burgundy. This would at least explain why there is no mention of the progress taking place. Although it would officially have enlarged the area over which Childebert ruled and demonstrated his inheritance claims, the progress would, in fact, have facilitated Gunthchramn's access to his nephew, making it appear legitimate for Gunthchramn to take "the boy aside," speak to him "privily," and give him instructions on how to behave.[43] Childebert's progress through Burgundy would have endangered the Austrasian nobles' scope of action, which, quite possibly, is the reason Gunthchramn's gambit was unsuccessful, just as the *adoptio* had been. The potentates were quite capable of foiling such attempted interventions. Precisely how they did this can be shown for Neustria, but even better for the Austrasian bishops.

GUNTHCHRAMN AND THE AUSTRASIAN BISHOPS

Commands and Resistance

The success or failure of this attempt, born of power-political calculation, to enforce a new practice which flew in the face of Frankish tradition, and to legitimize it by means of a legal practice not previously used in this context, necessarily depended on the prevailing balance of power and political constellations, on the interests and weight of the monarchy on the one hand and of the kingdom's powerful men on the other. Gunthchramn's synodal policies are a good place to observe this, for it was here that he repeatedly asserted his claims vis-à-vis the Austrasians. Time and again, he "summoned" (*iussit, praecepit*)[44] Austro-Burgundian synods solely on his own authority. A glance at the assemblies that actually took place shows, however, that his success remained limited. Ultimately, none of the synods were conducted as joint Austro-Burgundian assemblies. The Austrasian episcopate apparently knew how to assert themselves.

In 585, when Gunthchramn was planning a meeting at Troyes to settle a score with the bishops who had opened their cities to the usurper Gundovald, Gregory found a simple reason for his failure: that "this had not suited the bishops of Childebert's kingdom."[45] When Gunthchramn protested through his legates, it was the chronicler himself who replied as Childebert's adviser. The episode shows how skillfully the bishops at one and the same time bound and resisted Gunthchramn. In this situation, which involved both resistance to intervention and the preservation of peace, Gregory sought to mollify Gunthchramn. He began with the remark that Childebert accepted his uncle as a father: "All men know that King Childebert hath no father save his uncle." But then he suppressed the very supremacy Gunthchramn had promoted by means of this fiction, choosing an interpretation that stressed equality and remarking of the two kings "that each should equally defend and love the other." He also slipped in the warning that people well remembered that Gunthchramn had decided to cultivate such a relationship only with Childebert.[46] The affront was thus mitigated verbally, but in the matter itself, Gunthchramn was left no choice but to hold the council without the Austrasians.[47]

The second synod, whose summoning Gunthchramn simply "made known" *(indecavit)* to his nephew in 588, suffered a similar fate.[48] Once again the bishops stayed away, and once again Gregory of Tours justified this to Gunthchramn in his capacity as Childebert's envoy. This time he stated that "our canonical use" did not provide for holding such a meeting when "the faith of the church is unshaken by any peril," and "no new heresy showeth its head." In this case it would be better for each metropolitan to maintain order and discipline in his own province.[49] Gunthchramn did not accept this either, and merely postponed the assembly.[50] It never took place, but the chronicler gives no further reason for the bishops' resistance.

Yet the Austrasians by no means entertained such fundamental misgivings about joint synods as their reference to principles suggests. When unrest broke out among the nuns of the convent of Radegundis at Poitiers, necessitating episcopal intervention, the matter was dealt with—if not by all bishops—at a joint Austro-Burgundian synod especially called for this purpose by the kings.[51] Typically enough, there were significant differences between this synod and the ones that had been rejected by the Austrasian episcopate. This time, the initiator was not Gunthchramn, but Childebert, the subject being discussed was a relatively internal Church matter, and, last but not least, the Austrasian bishops whose dioceses were affected by the tumult had an interest in a quick solution to the problem. Suddenly the Austrasians were no longer concerned "that each metropolitan should meet together with the bishops of his province, and amend by decree of such councils the disorders occurring in his own region."[52] Poitiers, the site of the events, was the only see in the province of Bordeaux under Childebert's rule. All the others were Burgundian, and the Austrasian affair would thus, "following our canonical use," have been decided by an almost purely Burgundian synod. In this case, Childebert sent two of his most influential bishops—the chronicler Gregory of Tours and Eberegisel from distant Cologne—as reinforcement.[53]

In general, there was apparently no objection to assemblies that crossed the boundaries of metropolitan districts. On the contrary, such assemblies tended to be the norm, and were by no means constantly deployed to combat heresies, as the bishops tried to present ecclesiastical custom to Gunthchramn.[54] Many synods of the two kingdoms and the Merovingian kingdom as a whole were held without any objections being raised, yet "the faith of the Church" was probably never more strongly "shaken by . . . peril" than in the year in which Gunthchramn wished to convene a synod and met with such resistance.

The advantage of the bishops' argument must have lain more in its vagueness and flexibility than in its soundness. It was a somewhat defter circumlocution for the motive which the chronicler had already named for resistance to the first synod: it had "not suited the bishops."[55] In this case, canon law suited the bishops better, and their allegiance to the rules was largely a political strategy.

Bad Experiences

Naturally, what did not suit some bishops may well have been the long journey and undoubted inconvenience involved in assembling "such a multitude in a single place."[56] There were, however, numerous occasions on which bishops did undertake such journeys. In 590, for example, when King Childebert wanted to pass judgment on Bishop Egidius of Reims, the bishops were expected to meet in council "in the middle of November." The weather could scarcely have been more miserable. "It was a season of heavy and unceasing rains, the cold was unbearable, the roads were deep in mire, and the rivers overflowed their banks. . . ." Nevertheless the chronicler was convinced that in this case "there might be no disobeying the King's [Childebert's] demands,"[57] although Egidius had by no means been spreading a "new heresy."[58] The bishops knew, then, when they could offer resistance and when they could not, and this did not necessarily have anything to do with false doctrines and "our canonical use."[59]

Gregory's account provides another hint to the "real" reasons for this resistance. He tells us, at least in outline, that the Austrasian bishops were hardly well-disposed toward Gunthchramn, for he does not seem to have maintained good relations with any of them.

To be sure, we know practically nothing about several of these bishops. Neither the names nor any actions of the Austrasian bishops of

Avranches, Châlons-sur-Marne, Chalon-sur-Saône, Javols, Cologne, Laon, Léscar Bearn, Maastricht, Meaux, S. Lizier, Speyer, Strasbourg, Tongeren, Toul, Velay, Viviers, or Worms have come down to us.[60] It is questionable whether the tiny episcopal see of Alais-Arisitum even still existed in 585, the year of the first synod called by Gunthchramn.[61] In any case, at the time when Gregory wrote his *History*, it apparently was administered by the bishop of the Austrasian see of Rodez.[62] All that we know of the bishop of Albi is his name,[63] which is also true of the bishops of Mainz during the period in question.[64] Accounts referring to Avitus of Clermont and Innocentius of Rodez offer no hints to their relations with Gunthchramn.[65] We may disregard Bigorre, whose status in the kingdom was disputed, since, during the years that interest us, it was ruled by Gunthchramn.[66] If Bishop Amelius of Bigorre was present at the synod called by Gunthchramn in 585 in Mâcon[67] it was simply because he was Gunthchramn's subject. Comminges, too, was most probably Burgundian and need not concern us here.[68]

What do we know about the others? Let us begin with Aix.[69]

Aix: About Pientius of Aix (born after 566, died before 596),[70] Gregory reports that he helped Theodore when he came to King Gunthchramn as a captive.[71] Michel Rouche has convincingly explained the presence at the rump synod of Mâcon (which was boycotted by the Austrasians) of an envoy from Pientius. According to Rouche, the southern bishops sought to oppose Gunthchramn's wrath with a united front. For this reason, no Austrasian bishop attended in person, but all of them, with the exception of the two bishops from Novempopulana and four from Provence, sent deputies. Gunthchramn's capitulary, which followed the council and contains no political decision,[72] demonstrates the success of this tactic.[73]

Avignon: Rouche's interpretation might also explain why John of Avignon sent an envoy. We know nothing further about him.[74] Perhaps part of his see lay in Gunthchramn's kingdom, which would provide an additional reason for sending a representative to Mâcon.[75]

Marseilles: Theodore of Marseilles,[76] who attended the council of Mâcon, had once again become a subject of Childebert II only after the 575 partition of Marseilles was rescinded in 584.[77] Because the *civitas* was no longer mentioned at Andelot, it must not have been disputed after 584. Gregory provides a detailed account of both Gunthchramn's relationship to Theodore and the reason for the latter's presence at Mâcon. According to a poem written by Fortunatus around 566, which already mentions the bishop,[78] he must have been appointed by the Austrasian King Sigibert. He was captured by Gunthchramn four times and imprisoned by him once.[79] When Childebert II sent out a *dux* Gundulf against the governor Dynamius, a partisan of Gunthchramn's, Theodore joined forces with Gundulf,[80] and similarly received the usurper Gundovald.[81] It was for this reason that Gunthchramn tried to pursue him after Gundovald's death in 585. Theodore was forced to participate in the synod after Childebert's *quasi dux* Ratherius, disobeying Childebert's command, captured the bishop and turned him over to King Gunthchramn.[82]

Poitiers: Bishop Maroveus of Poitiers also had his conflicts with Gunthchramn. Maroveus probably was appointed by Sigibert, since Poitiers had been annexed to Austrasia in 567.[83] After Sigibert's death, the Neustrian Chilperic had occupied the *civitas* around 575/577[84] and after his murder (late 584) it became a bone of contention between Austrasia and Burgundy. In 584, Childebert demanded that the citizens swear an oath of loyalty to him, which they willingly did. Gregory of Tours then admonished the bishop and inhabitants of the neighboring city to submit to the rule of Gunthchramn as the holder of the *regni principatus* lest they suffer the sad fate of Tours. The *civitas* at first resisted, then gave in to the pressure of Gunthchramn's troops.[85] In the following year, however, they withdrew their loyalty. Bishop Maroveus received Gunthchramn's envoy "harshly" *(dure suscepit)*, whereupon the king had the town sacked several times. Gunthchramn held Maroveus responsible for the townspeople's resistance, so that the latter could only ransom "the people and himself" by breaking a liturgical gold chalice and having it made into coins.[86] That same year, Gunthchramn returned the freshly conquered *civitas* to Childebert,[87] and Maroveus did not have to appear at Mâcon. Childebert's claim was finally recognized at Andelot.[88]

Reims: Bishop Egidius of Reims "had ever been his [Gunthchramn's] enemy,"[89] as Gregory emphasizes several times, illustrating the point with a story. The bishop had sojourned for some time at Gunthchramn's court as one of Childebert's envoys, and King Gunthchramn had "commanded putrid horse-dung to be flung upon their heads as they departed, with rotten woodchips and mouldy hay, and even the foul mud from the road."[90]

Tours: Gregory of Tours took an ambivalent attitude toward Gunthchramn. His overall assessment of the king was positive, going so far as to describe him as something akin to a man of God.[91] But the chronicler nevertheless suffered at the king's hands. Gregory had attained his bishopric in 573, with the help of the Austrasian Sigibert.[92] Since the partition of 567, Tours had belonged to the Austrasian kings; but, like Poitiers, the city had been occupied since around 577 by Chilperic, and after his death it became an object of dispute between Austrasia and Burgundy. Recalling the devastation Gunthchramn's troops had wreaked on Tours, Gregory opened the *civitas* to him in 584. This did not prevent the city from being ravaged again a year later[93] shortly before Gunthchramn ceded the city to Childebert, as he had done with Poitiers in 585.[94] The bishop and chronicler belonged henceforth to the inner circle around Childebert, and served as his legate to Gunthchramn.[95] It was Gregory who, as Childebert's envoy, spoke out against the second planned synod, and it was also Gregory who delivered to Gunthchramn the complaint that he was treating Fredegund, the archenemy of the Austrasian dynasty, with far too much courtesy.[96] He may have described Gunthchramn as a good and pious king; but, particularly on the "diplomatic" level, he managed to defend Austrasian autonomy unequivocally and, as we have seen, not without skill.[97]

Triers: Two events are mentioned which tell us something of Magneric of Trier's relations with King Gunthchramn. First, when Bishop Theodore of Marseilles was brought to Trier as a captive, Magneric took up his cause, gaining access to his heavily guarded colleague, bringing him fresh clothing, and praying for him. Presumably, the arrest had been ordered by Gunthchramn.[98] Second, when the kings resolved in 587 at Andelot that the insurgent Gunthchramn Boso must die, the latter fled to the house of Magneric of Trier, since he trusted in the bishop's *compaternitas* with Childebert II, and forced the bishop to support him. King Gunthchramn, believing that the bishop was shielding Boso, also decided that Magneric should be put to death and had his house set on fire.[99]

Verdun: Ageric of Verdun, whom the kings had entrusted with the rebel Gunthchramn Boso together with his children, is said to have told the children after Boso's death: "'On account of the hatred felt for me ye are now left orphans'."[100] The chronicler does not point directly to Gunthchramn as the person who hated Ageric, but he was careful to let the reader know that Childebert was trying to gain Ageric's favor. When the rebel Berthefred was murdered in Ageric's church—without Childebert's knowledge, as Gregory expressly adds—the king sent the bishop gifts "to distract him from his grief."[101] Here, it may be significant that Childebert was Ageric's godchild, for, as we shall see in another context, Childebert adhered, if cleverly, to the relevant duties.[102] On the other hand, it was Gunthchramn who had set in motion the events at Andelot. He had summoned Childebert to Andelot, and had had the rebel slain after "it had been decided," as Gregory puts it, to separate him from Ageric prior to his appearance before the royal tribunal.[103] All of this occurred in 587, so that it should not surprise us that a year later Ageric, too, preferred to refer to "our canonical use" rather than appear at a joint synod called by Gunthchramn.[104]

Uzès: The only exception among the Austrasian bishops known to us was Marcellus of Uzès, who had held this office since 581. We know nothing of his relations with Gunthchramn, but, at the instigation of Gunthchramn's partisan Dynamius, governor of Provence, and against Childebert II's candidate, he was consecrated through election by the *conprovinciales*.[105] We do not know who these electors were, since, apart from the vacant Austrasian Arisitum and Neustrian Toulouse, all the episcopal sees of the province were in Gothic hands.[106]

Thus, not a few Austrasian bishops, especially those involved in political events, had had unpleasant encounters with Gunthchramn. If Gunthchramn wanted to "summon" these bishops to synods, apparently as Childebert's *pater*, he had only two options at his disposal: actual dominance or the good will of the bishops. He apparently did not possess enough real power. Thus, Gunthchramn's only hope of enforcing his synodal policy was an Austrasian episcopate well disposed toward his claim to supremacy, for which Merovingian history provided no models, or at least one that did not regard his claim as inimical to their interests. These very Austrasians had, scarcely a generation earlier, found themselves under the rule of a minor without needing (and, thus, recognizing) the supremacy of a third man, a senior member of the dynasty.[107] Now, too, the bishops made no move to submit voluntarily to the rule of a king whom many of them had good reason to view with suspicion. Only an all-powerful Gunthchramn could have compelled the bishops to participate in his manipulation of tradition, accept his "rule over the whole kingdom" (*regni principatus*) on the basis of the *adoptio* and heed his summons to attend the synods. This, however, was not in their interest. A glance at the reaction of the Neustrians will show this even more clearly, although they were in a much more perilous situation politically. Here, Gunthchramn's opponents cited old law in order to parry the claims of the Burgundian uncle, senior, and *pater*.

The Neustrians

The Strategy of the Weaker Party

Let us recall that Fredegund had summoned Gunthchramn to Paris so that he might "take the kingdom of his brother."[108] We already know that Chlothar's status as a minor apparently did not demand this, and that, in fact, the nobles could just as easily have ruled as his guardians. We also know that the Neustrian nobles everywhere found themselves in a worrisome situation—in the motherlands, in which the people were "grumbling" and the nephew Childebert was intervening, even more so in the territories which Chilperic had inherited from Charibert, and most precariously in the lands Chilperic had annexed from his brothers. And we know that Gunthchramn had actually been exerting his authority by forceful means.[109] On closer examination, it becomes apparent just how dangerous Fredegund's situation was immediately following Chilperic's death, and her appeal to Gunthchramn makes more sense.

All the Neustrian *duces* we know of [110] tried the same tack in order to escape their difficult situation after the death of their overlord, by breaking with the Neustrian dynasty. Bladast turned to the usurper Gundovald and, after the latter's defeat, emerged unscathed. The victorious Gunthchramn pardoned him, taking his duchy but leaving him his property.[111] *Dux* Desiderius was cleverer. First, he plundered the bridal escort accompanying Chilperic's daughter, Rigunth, to Spain after his death. Then he, too, temporarily turned to Gundovald, but joined the party of Gunthchramn at an opportune moment. The success of this tactic is demonstrated by the fact that he later appeared with the same duchy in Gunthchramn's service.[112] *Dux* Berulf, who had ruled over the Austrasian cities of Tours and Poitiers, was less fortunate. He, too, broke with Neustria, and tried to regain the cities from Childebert, their new and legitimate sovereign, but was arrested and barely managed to escape with his life.[113]

The Neustrian kingdom—now represented by the king's widow, Fredegund, and her four-month-old son, Chlothar—suddenly was abandoned by all the *duces* (with the possible exception of Bobo) and rendered defenseless. The militarily significant *duces* were not the only ones to abandon the kingdom.[114] A part of the royal treasure was "now removed by officials of the treasury, who at once went off to King Childebert."[115] "After her lord's decease" Fredegund had invited the treasurer Eberulf "to abide with her, but he would not be persuaded."[116] Chilperic's former favorites evidently found it inopportune to ally themselves prematurely with Fredegund, not least because of the "great outcry [which] was raised against those who had been powerful by favour of King Chilperic."[117] The cities previously occupied by Neustria were at war with each other, and Childebert II captured Cambrai, Meaux, and even Soissons, the ancestral seat of the Neustrian Merovingians, then marched with his army toward Paris.[118] The situation was exacerbated by *dux* Beppolen whom Chilperic, in 583, had deprived of power over the large territory he administered and who now, after Chilperic's death, bestirred himself anew.[119]

The nobles at court and the *duces* seemed busy saving themselves. Under the circumstances, the king's widow, Fredegund, had little room to maneuver, and probably had no choice but to take the initiative and place herself under Gunthchramn's "protection" and "governance" (*patrocinium, dicio*), especially since the latter had already begun to enforce his claim to large portions of the territory ruled by Chilperic.[120] This is precisely what she seems to have been doing with her invitation, following which Gunthchramn claimed to the Parisian *cives* that he had adopted Chlothar: "'Let my lord [Gunthchramn] come [to Paris] and take the kingdom of his brother [Chilperic]. I have . . . a tender infant [Chlothar], whom I long to place in his arms; myself, too, I would submit to his governance (*dicio*).'"[121] And

Gunthchramn appealed to the *cives*: "'may it be granted me, at least for three years, to bring up the nephews whom I have made my adopted sons *(qui mihi adoptivi facti sunt).*'"[122] However vague the legitimation Fredegund transferred when she sought "to place her son in his [Gunthchramn's] arms,"[123] the offer at any rate explicitly included—and this was what counted—governance. For this reason, Gunthchramn preferred to present it, in whatever way it might be interpreted, as *adoptio*. If, as the chronicler tells us a short time later, "King Guntram [desired] to govern on his own account the kingdom of his nephew Lothar, son of Chilperic" and appointed counts, dukes and bishops, this offer of Fredegund's would have come as welcome legitimation.[124]

This offer of legitimation for Gunthchramn was, however, not the only action taken within Fredegund's camp to make the best of a bad situation. First of all, the powerful men of the kingdom soon began publicly to call the royal newborn "Chlothar" after his grandfather, who, for a few years, had ruled over all of Gaul.[125] This appellation was used to create social and political reality, assigning a place to the receiver and no less to the givers of the name: "The chief men of the kingdom . . . rallied," as the chronicler recounts,[126] around a figure whom they demonstratively declared through his very name to be a king, proclaiming at once their own social proximity to the king and the infant's position as successor to Chlothar, the father of the Neustrian branch of the Merovingian dynasty. In itself, this was not unusual. After all, everyone has a name, and naming is always an act of social positioning, for both giver and receiver. Here, however, another detail reveals one of the informal niceties of social and political positioning, one not channeled by ritual. The chronicler notes, for the summer of 585, that the boy was "already"—and we know that this had been the case as early as the end of 584—being called Chlothar in public.[127] Naming, however, was an official ritual act which at that time was part of the act of baptism.[128] The boy had not yet been baptized, though, and that must be the reason why Gregory mentions that he had "already" been named before the baptism—that is, unofficially.[129] It did not escape his attention that the powerful men in the kingdom had created reality by informal means, calling the infant by his name before baptism, and a powerful name at that—powerful for the boy and for those around him.

We know that immediately after Chilperic's death the dangerous neighbor Gunthchramn was asked "at the [Chlothar's] mother's request . . . to receive him [Chlothar] from the holy font."[130] This meant not least that the official naming in the act of baptism was also to be incorporated immediately into the strategy. In the sixth century, it was the godfather who carried out the act of naming, for which Gregory provides ample evidence.[131] What other benefits Gunthchramn's sponsorship might (or was intended to) bring with it will be analyzed below; at any rate it was one of the tactical moves undertaken by the people around the infant immediately after Chilperic's death.[132]

Finally, the nobles took further action to secure their position: "They exacted from all the cities which had acknowledged the rule of Chilperic an oath of loyalty to Guntram and his nephew Lothar."[133] This, too, was a clever move, for, apart from the Neustrian motherlands in the far northwest, it was by no means certain who would take possession of the cities that "had acknowledged the rule of Chilperic." What *was* certain was that, at the moment, Gunthchramn was not merely stronger but could also prove his attested rights to many of these cities, whereas Chlothar's party was not only militarily and politically weaker but also had no legitimate claim to most of the cities once ruled by Chlothar's father. Thus they anticipated Gunthchramn's assumption of power in the critical territories and ensured that Chlothar, and with him they themselves, might not be wholly displaced, and that the cities would pay homage not only to Gunthchramn, but to Chlothar as well.

In short, at this moment after the death of the powerful Chilperic, when the Neustrian royal family and their beneficiaries suddenly found themselves in acute danger, a number of tactical measures were taken which, in combination, at least maintained a claim and—for the time being—made whatever concessions necessary to the formidable Burgundian neighbor. The chief men of the kingdom offered Gunthchramn the *potestas* that he sought to exercise. By taking the initiative themselves, they could offer a *potestas* that did not necessarily signify annexation. In addition, when they offered familial forms such as *adoptio* (and, apparently, also sponsorship soon thereafter), they may have been motivated by the hope of keeping this *potestas* tied to the family. Last, but not least, they sought to establish Chlothar's claims by obliging Gunthchramn in the naming of the boy and the homage of the cities.

The Resistance of the Consolidated Neustrians

These were all early reactions. The course of later events gives the impression that the decision makers in Neustria soon rallied and presented a united front against Gunthchramn. This began with the trouble they put Gunthchramn to over the planned baptism—making him travel in vain several times in late 584 and over the course of 585.[134] If Gunthchramn was willing to put up with this, he must not only have had an interest in the sponsorship, but also have seen the limits of his actual power. When, in mid-summer 585, he finally did put up a fight, he adopted extreme methods, casting doubt on Chlothar's legitimacy; the only effect, however, was to arouse a virtually prototypical reaction: the demonstrative solidarity of the Neustrian nobles, three hundred in number, and of the most important bishops along with the king's mother.[135]

If we are to believe the chronicler, a variety of options were debated. Did, or should, Gunthchramn want "to take"[136] or only "to govern"?[137] Was the territory in question "the kingdom of his brother"?[138] The kingdom of his nephew?[139] Or that which "had acknowledged the rule of Chilperic"?[140] Certainly, more had "belonged" to King Chilperic "previously" than Gunthchramn now wished to have regarded as the "kingdom of his brother" and more than he was prepared to count as part of the "kingdom of his nephew." Conversely, the Neustrian nobles, who did not have the same problems of legitimation in all regions, wished to see the kingdom defined as broadly as possible. We catch glimpses of this struggle in the conflicts Gregory considered worth recounting.

Gunthchramn appears to have taken the cities south of the Loire without difficulty after they had temporarily fallen into the hands of Gundovald, a usurper. It may be that here, where Roman culture and Roman consciousness had survived the decline of the Merovingians and where no "Neustrian" consciousness had arisen,[141] people were little interested in which Merovingian happened to be ruling over them at any given moment. We have no evidence here of conflicts with the population or of any attempts to preserve these regions for Neustria. In 585, Gunthchramn had already appointed his own candidate for bishop against the will of the electors in Bordeaux.[142] Gunthchramn also appears to have won Paris without a struggle.[143]

As for the other regions, it is striking for which territories Gunthchramn's interventions are documented. We do not know where the victims he helped lived, nor in which cases he restored testaments; but he banished the king's mother to Rouen and appointed local rulers in Rouen, Angers, and Rennes. It was also at Rennes that he later levied an army. The luckless Promotus, who sought Gunthchramn's aid, presented to him a dispute involving the diocese of Chartres. In short, all these interventions took place in the territory that had once belonged to Charibert; no record of intervention in the Neustrian motherlands themselves has come down to us. This does not mean that Gunthchramn respected Neustrian sovereignty in these territories any more than it means that the Neustrians respected Gunthchramn's sovereignty in Charibert's former territories. Here, too, the parties used various legitimations to secure their positions as best they could.

What the chronicler—who regarded himself as a subject of Childebert's and had only submitted to Gunthchramn's authority under duress—defines as "the kingdom of his nephew Chlothar," in which Gunthchramn desired "to govern on his own account," is striking enough. He is referring to the fact that Gunthchramn "appointed Theodulf count of Angers" and another man *dux* in the territory of Angers and Rennes.¹⁴⁴ Because neither city lay within the Neustrian motherlands, but instead belonged to territory the Neustrians had acquired in 567 from Charibert's kingdom, one might assume that they now belonged to Gunthchramn's kingdom. After the partition treaty, the Neustrians lost their entire inheritance in Charibert's kingdom to Burgundy because of Chilperic's violation of the pact. According to the pact, the Neustrian portions of Charibert's legacy would thus no longer have been "Chlothar's realm." This is no mere academic speculation to the extent that Gunthchramn had laid claim to these territories before Childebert¹⁴⁵ and apparently also enforced his claim in the territories beyond the Loire. Gregory, however, appears to have continued to regard certain cities between the Seine and the Loire, at least Angers and Rennes, as Neustrian, even if Gunthchramn ultimately gained authority over them.¹⁴⁶ Gregory was not alone in this interpretation: he frequently reports that the local population vehemently resisted the neighboring king. Theodulf, who had been chosen as count of Angers, was immediately driven off by the people there. A certain Domigisil, probably a close ally of Chilperic's, played an active role. Gunthchramn then sent Theodulf reinforcement in the form of *dux* Sigulf, who was deposed only a year later.¹⁴⁷ His successor as duke of Rennes and Angers, a turncoat named Beppolen, also met with sharp resistance. First, "the people of Rennes refused to receive him." Not long after Beppolen had asserted his claim with military force and left his son behind as his deputy, "they fell upon the boy, who was slain, together with many [respected] men. . . ."¹⁴⁸ Gunthchramn also tried unsuccessfully to reinstate Bishop Praetextatus, who had been banished by Chilperic, in Rouen. No sooner had the citizens brought him back, and Gunthchramn confirmed him, than he was murdered, and his successor was appointed not by Gunthchramn but by Fredegund.¹⁴⁹

This was an act of legitimate power. Doubtless, Fredegund succeeded only because there was an opportunity to claim the *civitas* as "Neustrian" and to enforce the claim. It is not clear from Gregory's account just how Fredegund asserted herself. She does not seem to have had much support in Rouen, where "all" the citizens were mourning the dead bishop—"above all," in Gregory's words, "the chief men of the Franks in that place."¹⁵⁰ Apparently she had her enemies deliberately liquidated¹⁵¹ and, as Gregory specifically reports, was supported by the nobles who had rallied round her son.

For his part, Gunthchramn attempted to prosecute the bishop's murderers, which would also have been an act of legitimate power, and, to that end, sent a few Burgundian bishops to Chlothar's court, where they confronted his governors (*qui parvolum nutriebant*) with Gunthchramn's claim.¹⁵²

For these courtiers it was not opportune to react, as the people of Rennes and Angers had done, with violence; thus, they tried argument instead: "'But we cannot admit that if the guilty man be found among us, he should be taken before your king, since we are able, with the royal sanction, to put down the crimes of our own folk ourselves.'"[153] Scarcely a year after these very courtiers of Chilperic's had had all the cities swear an oath of loyalty to Gunthchramn and Chlothar, they again declared Gunthchramn a foreign king, a *rex vester*, doing so even though the event in question took place at Rouen, where, we might think, the partition pact offered Gunthchramn quite solid legitimation.[154] Suddenly nobody wanted to be reminded of the fact that Fredegund had called on her brother-in-law to "take the kingdom of his brother [Chilperic]," and that she had said that she would submit to "his governance *(dicio).*"[155] Now the old law was brought forward once more. The royal authority was that of the minor Chlothar, and the nobles well knew that precedents existed to legitimate their claim to guardianship, not least of the Austrasian nephew.

Ancient rights appear to have been a good argument for rejecting Gunthchramn's *regni principatus*. This, at least, is the message conveyed by the chronicler, who does not have the delegation bring forward any opposing argument—no *adoptio* and no partition pact, let alone a senior, agnate, or the like. He simply has them threaten to use force; if the perpetrator were not brought to light, Gunthchramn would lay waste to the land. A year after Chilperic's death, this no longer made much of an impression on the nobles; they refused to give the delegation "any proper answer" and let them depart without having accomplished their mission.[156] Gunthchramn was apparently no longer essential; his opponents had "rallied,"[157] demonstrated solidarity,[158] and were now ready to marshal old legitimations.

Naturally this too was only an attempt, which could not be asserted everywhere. There are, however, other indicators as well. The Neustrians did not succeed in expelling the *dux* Beppolen once and for all, and many years later, in 590, Gunthchramn raised his army against the Bretons in the kingdom of his nephew Chlothar.[159] At this point the bishop of Vannes still considered it advisable, though, to swear oaths of loyalty to both kings, while the Breton Waroch, against whom Gunthchramn had waged war, supposedly even pledged peace only to him.[160]

6
A Failed Attempt

P*ATER* WITHOUT P*OTESTAS*

After the deaths of his brothers, King Gunthchramn sought to secure sovereignty over the entire kingdom, the *regni principatus,* as his father, Chlothar I, had done after the deaths of his own three brothers. Chlothar, however, had achieved his aim only after the deaths of his nephews and their sons as well, and Gunthchramn apparently did not wish to wait that long. The vehicle he chose to help him attain power, bypassing the practice of the previous generation, was *adoptio,* and Gunthchramn made use of it twice, each time after the death of a brother. It seems to have been a flexible vehicle, allowing those who resorted to it to solve the problems, variously, of a change of family, the bestowing of a legacy, paternal authority, and a lack of biological sons. Thus, Gunthchramn's assertion that he had adopted Chlothar appeared to be based on nothing more than the claim to *patria potestas.* He did not intend to make Chlothar his heir.[1] In the Lex Ribuaria, in contrast, it is precisely inheritance that is the focus of attention: Here, a Roman name, *adoptio in hereditate,* was given to an old Frankish inheritance custom *(acfatimire).* As the case of Pippin the Younger several generations later demonstrates, both elements, inheritance and paternal authority, could just as easily be absent. When he took the Langobard king as his pater, Pippin probably was thinking neither of submitting to an outside authority nor of inheriting the Langobard kingdom. What mattered was *naturam imitari,* the fiction of royal blood.[2] *Adoptio* could mean inheritance in one case (Lex Ribuaria), *imitatio naturae* (Pippin) in another, paternal authority (Gunthchramn and Chlothar) in a third, or all of these together (Gunthchramn and Childebert).

In the history of the second generation of Merovingians, King Gunthchramn had to cope politically with the death of a brother three times. Two of these brothers left behind a son, and both times Gunthchramn tackled his political problems by resorting to an action he could not justify by precedent: the *adoptio* of his orphaned nephews. This, at least, is what the chronicler tells us. The conclusion that Gunthchramn must have had two sons after 585 does not, however, do justice to the situation. First, Gunthchramn was the father of these sons only according to his own and the chronicler's account; and second, the king in the chronicler's report did not always describe matters in this way. Sometimes he only defined one of them as his son, and he is said to have referred to the "sons" in question sometimes as "son," and sometimes as "nephew."

Adoptio in this case was nothing more than a weapon Gunthchramn deployed in his struggle to enforce a concrete political line. The chronicler has provided enough indication of how and why he did this. We have clear examples for both Neustria and Austrasia.

After Chilperic's death, a struggle for political terrain began in Neustria. The warring parties juggled with legitimation and claims, conceded the unavoidable as long as necessary and appealed to ancient rights as soon as they could. Gunthchramn deployed military force, while Fredegund resorted to devious violence, and rebellions arose in the cities. In this wrangling over political terrain, *adoptio* was one of the instruments that Gunthchramn marshaled in order to present his interventions as legitimate. It was a legitimation the nobles apparently could tolerate at a time when their position was highly tenuous—after all, an *adoptio* was preferable to annexation—but against which they soon deployed their own instruments: violence or the old law "on behalf of the king," as the occasion dictated.

If we were to ask which party—the nobles around Chlothar, or Gunthchramn—was the stronger, we would be missing an important element of the practice of such conflicts. For one thing, the conflicts apparently were decided differently in each case, with a different outcome in Aquitaine than in the motherlands, and a different outcome there than in the region between the Seine and Loire, and even variations from one *civitas* to the next. Furthermore, the question fails to reflect practice because the desire "to govern on his own account "[3] in Neustria was not Gunthchramn's only interest. His readiness to take action and his choice of weapons emerged from a weighing of all his interests that, on the one hand, permitted him to use harsh means to expand his rule in Neustria but, on the other, called for a more yielding stance or avoidance of confrontation in the name of other interests. For the Neustrians, the situation was life-threatening; for Gunthchramn, it was not. Just because Gunthchramn did not assert himself in certain cases does not mean he was incapable of doing so or that his legitimation was too weak. One can well imagine that immediately following Chilperic's death, Gunthchramn, particularly in conjunction with Childebert, was strong enough to eliminate the Neustrian court. He may have had other priorities, interests not discussed here, or moral scruples that did not allow for certain actions. Thus, in the *History*, Gunthchramn, unlike Fredegund, is never described using murder as a political weapon. The chronicler also attributes to him a reputation for holiness which must at times have been difficult to maintain.[4] Thus, for example, he was not as adventurous as Childebert in regard to expeditions to Italy.

In the end, he rarely got his way. When it came to legislation and ecclesiastical sovereignty, the sections of the kingdom belonging to his two nephews remained largely beyond his grasp. The borders of each constituted the limits of official rule. To be sure, the section that could still be referred to as Chlothar's remained vaguely delineated and, however defined, much smaller than Childebert's territory. The cities north of the Seine, at least, evidently stood up to the Neustrians successfully and managed as early as 585 to reject Gunthchramn's claim to jurisdiction.[5]

Gunthchramn's position in Austrasia was more difficult still. Here, he could not benefit from the weakness of the dynasty, and thus his attempts at intervention were doomed to failure. The Austro-Burgundian synods "summoned" by him did not take place, and he appears to have had no influence to speak of in the marriage between Chlodosvinda, daughter of the Austrasian king, and the Visigoth Recared, to which Brunechildis and Childebert supposedly "dared" to agree without consulting Gunthchramn.[6] As his conduct toward the Goths had already shown, Childebert pursued an independent foreign policy that at times ran counter to Gunthchramn's interests.[7] Only once do we hear of Burgundian troops on Childebert's territory: after Gunthchramn vanquished his insurgent *dux* Mummolus at the Burgundian town of Comminges he also had the rebel's treasures brought to him from Avignon. Avignon lay in an Austrasian corridor close to the frontier separating the kingdoms. He then brought half of the treasure to King Childebert.[8] Another time, in 587, at Andelot, Gunthchramn sat in judgment on a rebel from Childebert's realm whom Childebert had turned over to him for this purpose. We do not know how Childebert justified his action, but we do know why he did it. He wanted to see the conspirator punished, but his own hands were tied—not because he was a minor, or subject to force—but because of an obligation incurred by godparenthood. This will be explained in greater detail below; for the present, suffice it to say that this case cannot be claimed as an example of Gunthchramn's *potestas* in Austrasia.[9]

As for the success of *adoptio*, Gunthchramn ultimately achieved his objective only when it was a matter of influencing political circumstances in the period after his death—that is, only in those cases where his aims were consistent with those of the Austrasian nobles: the regulation of inheritance in Childebert's favor.

The Pact of Andelot: An Exercise in Damage Limitation

When compared to Gunthchramn's claim (and Gregory's assertion) that he now had the *regni principatus* since he had "adopted" both of his nephews as his "sons,"[10] his actual success was thus extremely modest. This also places the pact of Andelot in a rather different light:

Gunthchramn did not succeed in attaining the paternal authority he had laid claim to with the *adoptio,* and with the help of which he had intended to rule in Austrasia. After two luckless run-ups in 577 and 585, a few political mishaps (synods), and dangerous trials of strength with the Austrasian nobility, the pact of Andelot reveals a new politics: Gunthchramn restricted his claims to those he could enforce; he no longer insisted on paternal authority. Once and for all, the agreement put Gunthchramn in his place, and that place was inside the borders of his own kingdom. It was a pact between two sovereign and equal rulers, which did no more than coordinate the measures taken by the two kings and regulate the question of inheritance. Naturally the Austrasian nobility put up no resistance to the latter. Thus the pact did not legitimate what Gunthchramn had sought to legitimate, using the *adoptio*—his opportunity to intervene in Austrasia. The pact was less a parallel to the family law rites (stage-managed twelve years earlier!)[11] than a less ambitious political substitute for the unattainable *potestas* of Roman *adoptio*. To be sure, an attempt was still made here to gain a tactical advantage over the nobility by means of an unusual guardianship agreement for the event that Childebert predeceased Gunthchramn.[12] Since this never occurred, however, it remained a claim not tested in practice. The discussions at Andelot saw Gunthchramn relinquish his farther-reaching claims. When, at the subsequent feast, he continued to refer to Childebert as his *filius*,[13] this may at most have served to justify his preferential treatment in the matter of inheritance.

Viewed from this vantage point, the pact of Andelot hardly seems to have been a "victory for Gunthchramn and Brunechildis."[14] Rather, it appears to demonstrate the successful opposition of the Austro-Burgundian nobility who, before they finally gained the upper hand in the seventh century, were already effectively resisting the expansion of royal power. For the kings, the pact was more an exercise in damage limitation than a victory.

Part III:
Sponsorship

7
Practices in Antiquity

Unlike *adoptio*, baptismal sponsorship was not an invention of antique society. It is only in the fifth century that we begin to find scattered evidence of those practices that were to become so powerful socially in the Middle Ages. They apparently emerged from modifications and combinations of various rites and ideas among Christians in late antiquity.[1] Scholars of the liturgy, but also dogmatists and fundamentalist theologians have long shown great interest in these late antique practices, but scarcely from a social historical perspective.[2] Historians, in contrast, have paid little attention to the topic up until now. Once its political and social functions become apparent, however, sponsorship does become interesting for social historians. Late antique sponsorship practices could contribute substantially to our understanding of the political and social conduct of the Merovingians and their contemporaries, especially since the first appearance in the sources of sponsorship as a social practice coincides with the Merovingian's entry on the political stage. The Merovingians immediately deployed this institution within their own political framework. Thus, they provide us not only with the earliest evidence of this practice in a non-Roman society, but also with the first clearly recognizable examples of sponsorship as a social practice anywhere. Before we proceed to an analysis of these examples, it may be useful to sketch those late antique traditions which were not yet sponsorship but which provided the requisite ritual and normative material. In the interest of brevity, the focus here will be on those aspects (all but ignored in the theological and liturgical literature) that laid the groundwork for the political and social utility of the institution.

Let us begin with the New Testament. In the Acts of the Apostles, baptism appears as a ritual requiring only two persons, the baptizee and the baptist.[3] From the beginning, however, ecclesiastical authors favored a public act—that is, the presence of the congregation at the baptism.[4] The early Christians, whose living conditions were undergoing rapid change, increasingly elaborated on this public act. They began to involve more people beyond the baptizee and the baptist, each with a ritual or pedagogical duty to fulfill. These duties developed at different periods under the pressures of changing necessity. Once introduced, they continued to be practiced long after circumstances had changed. They were adapted to new challenges, reinterpreted and recast, overlaid with other practices and combined with new ones. Such combinations, modifications, and overlappings of various functions in and around the act of baptism led to the emergence around 500 of those participants in the baptismal rite who, from the Carolingian period on, frequently came to be known by the now common name of "godparent" *(patrinus, matrina)*. At first glance, it is not apparent how these sponsors came to develop from certain ancient functionaries. Thus, if we analyze the tasks they undertook, particularly the components that could be functionalized socially, we find that the three main figures who played a role in ancient baptism were the guarantor for candidates for baptism, the assistant at baptism,[5] and the proxy necessary for infant baptism.

Adult Baptism

New "Fathers"

In the third century, for the first time another person appeared who had to vouch for the baptismal candidate.[6] Scholars have called this sponsor a "catechumenate witness" because his work began at the end of the catechumenate, the sometimes years-long trial period preceding baptism.[7] His introduction into the rite is probably connected with the large number of new converts experienced by Christian communities at this time. These communities were increasingly confronted with converts who were not Jews but, rather, people largely, if not wholly, unfamiliar with either the Christian or the Jewish context. Christian ecclesiastical authors—including those of the Middle Ages—claimed faith to be an essential prerequisite to baptism.[8] Apparently the communities were responding to this situation by increasing the period of instruction before baptism, also in order to test the seriousness of each candidate's intentions. Thus, in the second century, more intensive preparation become common practice. This preparatory phase quickly became standardized and took on such firm contours that, from the third century on, it appears as an autonomous, precisely defined and ritually structured phase, "a way of being a Christian before baptism"[9]: the catechumenate. Those who learned and practiced Christianity in this context formed a specific group within the community, known as *catechumeni* or *novicioli*, *audientes* or *auditores*.[10] They were supposed to receive special attention, which became institutionalized over time into the office of the catechumenate witness. Scholars postulate that, by the end of the third century, this practice had become standard throughout the Mediterranean region.[11]

Before the fourth century, however, only Hippolytus' (died after 253) *Apostolic Tradition*, provides anything approaching a full picture of the duties of these catechumenate witnesses. Normally, people were baptized at Easter. Twice, at the beginning and the end of their (according to Hippolytus) three-year probationary period (catechumenate), all those desiring baptism were required to name people who would vouch for them *(dent testimonium)*. At the beginning, the witnesses were supposed to confirm that the candidates were serious in their desire to convert.[12] After three years the witnesses were then supposed to testify that the candidates "lived piously while they were catechumens . . . honored the widows, . . . visited the sick, . . . did every sort of good thing"[13] and, as a (probably) fourth-century source adds, were not drunkards or boasters.[14] The congregation demanded this second testimony at the beginning of Lent, after which the candidates were given a new status; for the period of Lent they were now *electi* or *competentes*,[15] having been found worthy of baptism, thanks to their witnesses.

These early testimonies leave us in the dark about the practical relevance of such regulations. Hippolytus is silent on the matter of how witnesses were to judge worthiness. He says nothing about the role of these witnesses during the three years of the catechumenate and offers no hint as to the seriousness or status of this custom. He says nothing, for example, about whether negligent witnesses were threatened with any consequences, and what these might have been. A remark by his contemporary Origen (died ca. 254), at least, indicates that some provisions were made: "people are assigned" to the catechumens, writes Origen, "who observe the way of life and conduct of those desiring entry."[16]

Fourth-century authors proved more prolix. In one of his many sermons, John Chrysostom (d. 407), an influential preacher whose eventful life as a churchman brought him to the chair of the patriarch of Constantinople, offers an instructive version of the naming of these persons, referred to by Hippolytus simply as "witnesses" and by Origen as "assigned people." He calls them guarantors *(anadechomenoi)*[17] and admonishes them that they are responsible (before God) for the conduct of their catechumens. He cautions them to tend to their charges conscientiously—in the interest of their own salvation.[18] One might be tempted to see this as an anticipation of the medieval situation—the close connection between godparent and baptizee entailing social obligations. A sermon by Bishop

Theodore of Mopsuestia (d. 428), however, shows that this would be a hasty conclusion. While also insisting on the duty of conscientiousness, Theodore adds that the guarantor "does not make himself responsible for them [the baptizees] in connection with future sins, as each one of us answers for his own sins before God. He only bears witness to what the catechumen has done and to the fact that he has prepared himself in the past to be worthy of the city and of its citizenship."[19] Catechumenate witnesses thus bore no responsibility for adult baptizees after baptism. The guarantor was not "answerable" in this world, but at most before God at the Last Judgment. Such a temporary relationship was not yet of any benefit in the sense of medieval and modern practice.

A further linguistic convention shared by fourth-century documents on adult baptism is striking when viewed from the standpoint of later developments. John Chrysostom requires of guarantors "paternal love *(patriken philostorgian),*" calls them "spiritual fathers *(pateras pneumatikous)*" and accordingly sees the catechumen as taking the role of a "spiritual son *(teknou pneumatikou).*"[20] The Aquitainian or Galician nun Egeria, who wrote an account of a pilgrimage in the fourth century, also mentions that in Jerusalem the (adult) baptizees were accompanied by *patres* and *matres.*[21] It is likely that, in her account, Egeria was not necessarily speaking of their natural parents, who may not have been Christians or who may no longer have been alive,[22] although she does not specifically mention this.

Egeria's pilgrimage account contains another noteworthy detail: when the *pater* or *mater* had testified to the good conduct of their charges at the end of the period of catechumenate—at the beginning of Lent—their duties were not yet over. Not only did they participate in the intensive scriptural exegesis for baptizees during Lent, they also accompanied the baptizee at the preparatory rites during Holy Week. Thus, according to Egeria, they were present at the *redditio symboli,* the rite in which the baptizee had to recite the Creed.[23] This is no mere marginal detail, to the extent that the weight in baptismal practice was soon to shift and the emphasis increasingly to be placed on infant baptism. In the course of this shift, a shortening of the long process of preparation for baptism became unavoidable. The three-phase procedure of catechumenate, competentate, and baptism was compressed into a standardized *ordo baptismi,* which occupied only the period around Easter. Little remained of the probationary period, the catechumenate, which could be waived in the case of newborns.[24] What was retained, however, were the prebaptismal rites, such as the recording of the names of the candidates, the renunciation of the devil, and the recitation of the Creed *(redditio symboli).* If, as Egeria maintains, the catechumenate witnesses were still involved, there was no problem in continuing to use these witnesses, the *patres* and *matres*, in the new streamlined *ordo baptismi*.

Assistants

What did the act of baptism itself look like? Here, too, we have scant evidence scattered widely across the Mediterranean region. Not infrequently, the authors mention others besides the person administering baptism who performed various tasks during the ceremony. Thus, third parties appear to have undressed the baptizees and led them to the font, assisted in the immersion, dried them off, and reclothed them in the christening gown. According to Hippolytus' account, it appears that these tasks were performed by deacons and deaconesses.[25] Whatever the practice in individual cases, in the Middle Ages at least some of these duties fell to the godparent.[26] Some writers also inform us that the catechumenate witnesses might have duties to perform at the baptism as well. Thus, Theodore of Mopsuestia states that during the anointing that preceded baptism they stood behind the kneeling candidate, laid a linen cloth over the anointed head, then helped them to their feet.[27] The Ethiopian version of Hippolytus' *Canons* stipulates that the witness is to receive the baptizee after baptism.[28] This is striking, because here the witness performed a task which from the early Middle Ages on was assigned by liturgical instructions to the godparent.[29] We do not have sufficient material to follow with any precision how these late antique practices were slowly and constantly modified in the different regions, finally coming to be performed by godparents in the Middle Ages. We must content ourselves with knowing that in Rome, if only in far-off Mopsuestia and even more distant Ethiopia, late antique writers reported (or only called for) practices that were not so different from what we can observe in Carolingian Europe as the duties of godparents.

The factor that constituted the social utility of godparenthood was still absent in late antiquity. The tasks of the witnesses described up to this point stopped at the baptism itself. After the baptism, the *anadechomenoi*, the *patres* and *matres*—at least, in our texts—had no further role to play. But it was precisely this opportunity to establish lasting ties after baptism that made sponsorship attractive as a social instrument. The only (at least, implicit) reference to such a lasting bond may be that provided by Theodore of Mopsuestia, who denies any such ties and emphasizes that the guarantor was not responsible for the sins of a candidate after baptism.[30] Perhaps, we might conclude, this was not the universal opinion, and the occasional person did hold witnesses responsible for their charges even after baptism. It is certainly not improbable, since, in a practice similar to adult baptism (the baptism of infants), the existence of such a bond after baptism was never questioned.

Infant Baptism

The End of the Age of Innocence

There was only one baptismal rite, and it was designed for adults. The baptism of small children began quite early, however, and to perform this rite upon infants at all, a number of alterations had to be made. Once again, the help of third parties was enlisted, whose duties were clearly related to the tasks later assigned to godparents.

When and under what circumstances the baptism of infants was first undertaken can no longer be ascertained, but by the year 200, it had become common practice in Christian families.[31] When it came to baptismal practice, by the year 200 the demand expressed by early ecclesiastical authors with so much vehemence that Christians make a conscious decision to believe[32] had already succumbed to an apparently much more popular notion which would soon receive the support of nearly all of the famous theologians. Original sin was believed to weigh so heavily even on infants that they faced damnation if they died unbaptized. In a final attack on this practice, Tertullian (died after 220) once again discussed the competition between conscious decision and original sin: "So let them [the children] come, when they are growing up, when they are learning, when they are being taught what they are coming to: let them be made Christians when they have become competent to know Christ. Why should innocent [!] infancy come with haste to the remission of sins?"[33] Tertullian's position did not prevail. Scarcely a generation later, the bishops of North Africa had other concerns. Whereas Tertullian had expressed serious misgivings about infant baptism, his successors argued over how many days old a baptizee should be—which sounds downright medieval. Cyprian, who otherwise owed much to Tertullian,[34] is the source of the *opinio communis* reached by that point; he wrote to a certain Bishop Fidus:

> As far as concerns the case of infants, you expressed your view that they ought not to be baptized within the second or third day of their birth; rather, the ancient law on circumcision ought to be respected and you therefore concluded that the newly-born should not be baptized and sanctified before the eighth day.
>
> Our Council adopted an entirely different conclusion. No one agreed with your opinion on the matter; instead, without exception we all formed

the judgment that it is not right to deny the mercy and grace of God to any man that is born.[35]

It was no longer important to the discussion whether "any man that is born" was capable of having any thoughts on the matter. Cyprian's testimony was no isolated case.[36] Assemblies of bishops[37] and papal circulars[38] now established authoritatively that infants who died unbaptized were damned. Origen supported this teaching,[39] as did Augustine[40] and Ambrose.[41] A dissenting voice such as that raised by Julian of Eclanum "echoed all but unheard in the Church."[42] The majority opinion was then followed by those antique writers who were active on Roman soil under the rule of the new Germanic kingdoms: Gennadius of Marseilles,[43] Caesarius of Arles,[44] Isidore of Seville,[45] and finally—particularly significant for the Middle Ages—Gregory the Great.[46] An "innocent infancy," as propagated by Tertullian,[47] was alien to theologians in East and West alike. Fulgentius of Ruspe, who propagated and radicalized the teachings of Augustine,[48] believed that even infants who died in the womb were damned.[49] They had doubtless lived, if only in the womb, and had thus died unbaptized.

Infants were thus to be baptized without delay, a principle that clearly enjoyed the highest priority among the teachings of bishops from the third century on. The practice for the conversion of adults was no longer of much use here, however. Serious interventions were necessary, and it was these that would largely determine the function of what was to become the godparent.

Ritual Fixation

Despite the rapid establishment of infant baptism, no new rite developed in response to the new situation. Baptism continued to be administered as if infants, like adults, submitted to baptism as a conscious act of faith. Thus, the newborn baptizee had to demonstrate at the *redditio symboli* that he or she was familiar with the canon of faith, had to renounce the devil, even had to speak the essential baptismal phrases.[50] Scholars of the liturgy generally explain that "all ritual is subject to the law of fixation,"[51] and that the baptismal liturgy was no exception. Despite the myriad theoretical problems surrounding rites and the "laws" governing conduct, one may let this stand as a summary of antique practice. Once established, the practice of baptizing adults—and children—clearly not least bolstered the authority of the supposedly apostolic tradition.[52]

Naturally, those who organized the baptism of children, if they wanted to apply the existing baptismal rite to infants, were compelled to devise auxiliary measures. Models already existed for other situations—namely, the baptism of the infirm and the mute. At least one, if rather distant example, the Ethiopian version of Hippolytus' Canons, would seem to suggest that these models were, indeed, consulted. Here, children, the ill, and the mute were treated together in a single rubric: "and for a child who cannot yet speak, or for a mute or sick person, for this child [or for him] who cannot yet speak or for this mute or sick person, the Christian mother or father or close kin who are also believers respond instead, speaking the name of each."[53] The baptizee incapable of speech had to speak "through" (*per*)[54] a third party.[55] From the perspective of religious phenomenology, the procedure is hardly surprising, since, in both antiquity and the Middle Ages, intermediaries and proxies were normal components of religion. One need only think of the role of Jesus and the Old Testament prophets as intermediaries and proxies[56] or of the medieval practice of intercession for the dead, which the actors sometimes expressly wished to see regarded as "lending a voice."[57] Those medieval authors who interpreted social reality using the well-known functional division of society into three parts[58] made proxies a virtual pillar of their definition and legitimation of the social order.

A "Parajuridical" Rite

The way Christian authors of antiquity describe the use of proxies during the initiation suggests that it could have dangerous consequences. The authors portrayed baptism as a promise with contractual character[59] and demanded of those who spoke as proxies that they guarantee the fulfillment of the promise.[60] In order to lend weight to this obligation, the theologians made use of a juridical vocabulary that had been employed in the Roman empire for centuries. In each case, they adapted their language precisely to developments in secular law—a not insignificant detail, indicating that just this "parajuridical" function of proxies was important to the authors. They tried to establish for the period after baptism the same normative force that would later be used for social relationships. Although this is not the place for a semantic field analysis, it may be useful to point out some of the most conspicuous terms used by late antique writers.

Roman law recognized the institution of the so-called stipulation guarantor who "provided surety for a debt."[61] The classical jurists had divided these guarantors into *sponsores, fidepromissores,* and *fideiussores* according to their degree of responsibility and citizenship rights.[62] Western jurists also referred to the *fideiussor* as a *fidedictor*.[63] In the so-called late classical period, when the possession of Roman citizenship had become practically worthless, jurists had already largely removed the distinctions among the three groups.[64] In postclassical legal sources, the words *sponsor* and *fide-*

promissor appear increasingly rarely, and Justinian finally replaced them systematically with *fideiussor*.[65]

Reading theological tracts with this in mind, it appears that the ecclesiastical authors virtually emulated this development in legal writing. Although Tertullian, a contemporary of the classical jurists, still calls the children's proxies *sponsores*,[66] authors of the postclassical phase had reoriented themselves. Like the jurists, they now used the more "modern" terminology. Augustine, for example, employs the term *fidedictores*[67] which was common only in Western legal sources, and Caesarius of Arles the term *fideiussores*.[68] The fact that these influential theologians dispensed with the term *spondere* is significant to the extent that, with its disappearance from the legal sources, *spondere* now referred only to "any kind of promise without any technical significance whatsoever."[69] This apparently was unattractive for theologians. What seems to have been at stake here was the quasi-legally binding nature of the sponsorship role, a standard theme, for example, in the *sermones* of a Caesarius.[70]

In contrast to their Western counterparts, Greek-speaking writers had no access to a unified legal structure with a binding specialist vocabulary. Attempts to install Roman stipulation law, for example, from which Western authors borrowed their vocabulary, in the East only began in earnest under the Emperor Caracalla.[71] This may explain why, in the East, the vocabulary for the infant's proxies at baptism was not standardized in the same way as in the West. When Eastern writers sought to admonish the proxies to remember their promises, they chose words similar in meaning to the legal terms, frequently the Greek *anadechomai*.[72]

At first, those people who raised the child—the parents—were used for the role of proxy, which, at the same time, was supposed to represent a sort of surety God could collect on.[73] Only occasionally—and this was controversial—could outsiders assume the office out of *misericordia*, for example when the parents were dead.[74]

Patterns of Interpretation: Proxies and Compensation

Tertullian, of course, was not the last patristic author to notice that his fundamental expectation and that of his comrades-in-arms was far removed from actual practice.[75] The call for a conscious decision to believe clearly was inconsistent with infant baptism and the practice of proxies, and the theologians had some difficulty justifying the practice. According to a fifth-century source,

> The fact that children not yet able to understand divine things become recipients of the holy rebirth in God and the most sacred symbols of the supremely divine Communion seems . . . to merit the legitimate ridicule

of the profane, for it is as though the bishops teach divine things to those who cannot hear, and in vain hand down the sacred tradition to those who do not understand. Not less worthy of ridicule is the fact that others pronounce the abjuration and sacred promises for them.[76]

Pseudo-Dionysius, who cites the "profane" here, does not accept the objections. The third party does not speak as a proxy, "he himself does not say, 'I abjure,' and make the sacred promises in place of the child," but rather, in Dionysius' preferred interpretation, "I promise to persuade the child by my instruction in godly matters, when he is able to understand holy things, to renounce completely all that is contrary, and profess and realize the divine promises."[77] In his apologia, Dionysius apparently was concerned to portray the act more as a binding agreement on the part of the sponsor to educate the child than as a contract made on the baptizee's behalf. As a consequence, by extension, the spiritual father was to be held responsible only for his own transgressions and not for those of the baptized child. Here, too, the statement of a third party—his agreement to educate the child—is binding,[78] but that third party is at least speaking only for himself, with his promise to educate, and not responding on behalf of another.[79]

Dionysius remained an outsider with this opinion, however.[80] Other theologians who addressed such questions—Augustine[81] or his fellow bishop Boniface of Cataqua,[82] John the Deacon[83] or Fulgentius of Ruspe[84]—supported another solution: if, they argued, the sins of others *(peccata aliena)* could become the undoing of personally innocent children, then at baptism the faith of others *(fides aliena)*, who spoke on their behalf *(respondere pro)*, could be their salvation. Rupert Berger's study of the phrase *offerre pro* in the Roman liturgy may be helpful for understanding what the theologians were propagating here.[85] According to Berger, in antiquity and the Middle Ages, the *offerre pro*, in which *pro* was the translation of the Greek *anti* or *hyper*, could always mean two things at once, "to offer instead of" and "to offer for the benefit of/in the interest of" a dead person, for example. As Berger emphasizes "in the Latin-speaking region . . . the intersection of interest and representation was particularly strong," with "one of the two usually leading, but only rarely exclusively."[86]

It was precisely these variants that the writers were working with in the tracts on baptism and sponsorship, as well. The chief duty of the sponsor was the *respondere pro*, answering for the child,[87] which they did, as in the offertory, on the one hand, *instead* of the child and, on the other, *for the benefit of* the child. Thus, it was claimed that children ultimately answered for themselves, even if it was "through those who brought them forward."[88] This interpretation relieved church leaders of the necessity of designing a separate rite for infant baptism. At the same time, the argument of *fides aliena* brought into play the idea of a retaliatory balance: the *alieni* should be responsible for what they had done to the child through original sin, responding with their faith for the benefit of *(respondere pro)* the innocently defiled. Even Augustine, schooled in the Donatist controversy, who no longer accepted the crass retaliatory thinking of a Boniface of Cataqua,[89] continued to foster this argument of retaliatory compensation. To be sure, he specifically describes baptism as a sacrament, an *opus operatum*, in order that the child's salvation not be endangered by heathen and heretical sponsors.[90] But, as if to meet his fellow bishop Boniface halfway, he adds a further interpretation: the heretics and heathens ultimately merely offered their arms, while it was the church, the community of saints and believers,[91] that actually brought forward the infant—i.e., a sufficient amount of *fides aliena*.

We have no evidence, either for antiquity or the early Middle Ages, about whether parents were actually worried about such issues when they brought their newborns to be baptized. The same argument resurfaces in the Middle Ages in the work of one famous scholar only: Alcuin.[92] In the light of the religious practices of the early Middle Ages, however, we may assume that the utility of *fides aliena* was not a scholarly concept alone. As it is usually interpreted, trust in the faith of others was, along with interest in representation and alliances, a central motive for medieval gift-giving behavior, friendship, and memorial practices, and the concepts and practices of penance substitution (that is, replacing one mode of penance, such as reciting the Lord's Prayer one thousand times, with a less time-consuming one, such as two psalms).[93] The medieval hagiographers also frequently maintain that people had a particular interest in winning holy men as sponsors for their children.[94] Augustine's consolation that, ultimately, the "whole community of saints and believers"[95] always functioned as sponsors, however unworthy a particular sponsor might be, was a truly scholarly consolation. People, on the other hand, had little use for such abstract saints. For everyday use, they preferred in many cases to choose real holy men, hermits and monks, as sponsors, apparently so often that the authors of the monastic rules expressly forbade this in their concern for the welfare of the men of God.[96]

One might add here that the authors did not use the argument of *fides aliena* before Augustine, that is, not until infant baptism was well established. The argument appears, however, already to have been familiar to bishops and authors at the time of Augustine, who no longer called it into question. He turned his attention to one further scholarly problem of detail, which, however, reveals an intervention into antique practice that would have a decisive impact on further developments. Bishop Boniface of Cataqua was of the opinion that these saving others *(alieni)* had, in a reflexive manner, to be the actual culprits—the parents—which, in his day, was usually the case. Augustine rejected this demand. He expressly accepted others, too, in this role while at the same time explaining that, at least in exceptional cases, in his own day other persons were already allowed to act as sponsors.[97] This modification of ancient practice would prove decisive for the development of the office of godparent.

In short, the different requirements of adult and infant baptism led to the parallel development of two practices which scholars had trouble reconciling with each other. In the case of adult baptism, "witnesses" carried out certain actions before and during the baptism. In contrast, in the case of infant baptism, proxies were at work during the baptism whom theologians, at least, wished to see entrusted with the child's subsequent spiritual education. This is more or less well documented for the third and fourth centuries. It is easy to see how few modifications were necessary in order for the institution of godparenthood as it became common in the Middle Ages to develop out of these antique practices: adult baptism incorporated third parties whose responsibility ended with the baptism itself. Infant baptism created a tie that continued after baptism, but this role was normally assumed by the natural parents.

FIFTH-CENTURY MODIFICATIONS

Another century separates the writings of Augustine and his contemporaries from the sources on Frankish history. For the purposes of the present study, this means that we must examine the "imperial history" of sponsorship during those hundred years whose last witness was Caesarius of Arles.[98] At the same time, the sermons of the southern Gallic bishop are already part of the narrower segment of the story, taking us beyond the framework of the Roman Empire and bringing the Merovingian kingdom into view.

How, then, might we describe developments in the fifth and early sixth centuries? Adult baptism became ever less frequent and, in the face of widespread infant baptism, the catechumenate, that long, drawn-out probationary period before baptism, became ritualized and reduced to a compact liturgy performed before Easter.[99] The few fifth-century documents we have show how the previously clearly recognizable differences between the practices of adult and infant baptism, adaptations of the rites to the concrete needs of adult or infant baptism, now disappeared.[100]

Pseudo-Dionysius (late fifth century) was the first writer to document the process of change in infant baptism. He claims that "our godlike instructors, initiated in ancient tradition," had transmitted the order "that the physical parents of the child presented confide the child to someone of the initiated in divine things who is a good teacher. Henceforth, the child will be his care to perfect; he will be like a divine father *(pater divinus, theos pater)* and the sponsor of his holy salvation."[101] The transition is clear; while outsiders to the family had originally been involved only in adult baptism and only for instruction *before* baptism, matters had apparently changed by the time Dionysius was writing. He already believed that the participation of outsiders in infant baptism and postbaptismal educational duties, which fourth-century authors had described as the province of parents, had a long tradition. This was the decisive step. The nonparental proxy at baptism remained connected to the baptizee and was considered—as the guarantor *before* baptism had been to the catechumen—as a *pater* to the child *after* baptism as well. Baptism now created a postbaptismal bond between people who were not (necessarily) related, which, in a continuation of ancient Christian language, was referred to in familial terms. Dionysius was the first to describe—for infant baptism—what is generally understood as godparenthood. What is more, he describes the very same constellation that Gregory of Tours was to present some fifty years later as a socially functionalized relationship.

For the time being, however, the old practice continued to find supporters alongside the new. Thus, in the West, Pope Gelasius (492–96) still expressly accorded sponsorship duties to the parents,[102] while only a short time later, at the beginning of the sixth century, the Roman deacon John offered both possibilities.[103] Around the same time, in one of his many appeals to sponsors, Caesarius of Arles remarked in passing that at Arles the child's sponsors were normally no longer its parents. He writes, "therefore admonish and discipline those whom you have received from the font just as you do those who are born from you."[104] Like Dionysius for the East, Caesarius describes for the West, around the year 500, a practice that, according to the notions of these authors, was supposed to lead to a lasting bond between people not previously tied to one another.

In this Caesarius was not alone in the West. Suddenly, at the beginning of the sixth century, we find several documents in which such spiritual "fathers" and "mothers"—let us now call them godparents—are mentioned. We know of the godparents of Avitus of Vienne, of Abbot Florianus of Romenum who corresponded with Nicetius of Trier,[105] and perhaps also of Saint Genovefa and King Clovis. We know of one godson of Bishop Ennodius of Pavia.[106] Thus a new practice appears to have emerged by the early sixth century. We must ask ourselves what social value these novel relationships possessed—in particular, what moved the authors of our sources to begin mentioning their own and their heroes' spiritual kin all of a sudden in letters, treatises, and *Vitae*.

Let us first take another look at adult baptism. As a part of missionary activity, it continued to be the rule, and thus was no less important than infant baptism for the medieval functionalization of sponsorship. Here, too, we begin to notice a modification of practices around 500, apparently under the influence of rites previously peculiar to infant baptism. Even adult baptizees could now apparently expect from the guarantor, whose role previously would have ended at baptism, a bond that continued after the rite, as if the witness had sponsored a child in need of education. Dionysius does not yet describe this phenomenon,[107] but Caesarius of Arles does. He becomes strikingly concrete in his appeal, cited above, to sponsors to treat their spiritual children as they would their natural offspring: both *before* and *after* baptism, godparents should "admonish [the baptizees] to chastity, humility, sobriety and peace and instruct them therein."[108] The mention of instruction *before* baptism would seem to indicate, here, that Caesarius was not necessarily thinking of infant baptism. Nevertheless, these baptizees too were now supposed to receive instruction after baptism, and from those same people who had once been expected only to vouch for candidates. Here, too, then, we can recognize that modification of the rite which made possible the social and political functionalization of sponsorship.

It made possible a functionalization, as we can say from a retrospective survey, but by no means all constructions that theoretically (or officially) could have been functionalized for social relations were actually so functionalized by the individuals involved. Pierre Bourdieu has an apt image for this:[109] not all red lines on the map are really beaten tracks. Later, to name one example, churchmen derived a number of further ties from baptism which played practically no role in social reality.[110] The actual social applications later described by Gregory of Tours left no trace in Caesarius' *sermones*.[111] Of course, there may well have been a social functionalization of sponsorship in Caesarius' day, and his silence may be related to the textual genre in which he was writing. Caesarius was a preacher. He does not yet provide us with evidence of such a use in the social field, though.

The other writers of the period who suddenly begin to mention spiritual kinship after 500 are scarcely more helpful. And yet these documents are not wholly useless in this regard, offering as they do the only opportunity to learn something about the social significance of sponsorship before Gregory of Tours.

The Earliest Documents

Around 520, Saint Genovefa's hagiographer wrote that after the death of her parents, she went from Nanterre to live with her *mater spiritualis* in

Paris.[112] Was the hagiographer trying to say that this woman from Paris had received Genovefa from the font and was therefore the saint's godmother? If that is the case, the sponsorship—assuming an infant baptism—would have occurred around the year 420,[113] at a time, that is, at which Augustine or Boniface of Cataqua considered parental "sponsors" to be the norm.[114] Was the author perhaps transporting conditions prevailing in his own era backwards into the time of his heroine? The *Life* gives us no grounds to assume such historical unreliability.[115] We would do better to consider whether the *mater spiritalis* might not point to a context other than baptismal sponsorship.

In both non-Christian and Christian antiquity it was common to refer to teachers in matters intellectual and spiritual as "father,"[116] although it is conspicuous that these teachers were often called *pater*, but rarely *pater spiritualis*.[117] For baptismal sponsorship, in contrast, the term *pater/filius spiritualis* was used frequently, particularly from the Carolingian period on.[118] However, Gregory of Tours—a witness of the early period—uses the term *pater/filius spiritualis* only once and then specifically with the addition "from the font" *(ex lavacro)*.[119] This specification already indicates that not every *pater spiritualis* was a sponsor (that is, *ex lavacro*),[120] just as not every sponsor in the sources is called a *pater spiritualis*. Many different appellations occur, including the simple *pater (filius)*[121] or *pater (filius) ex lavacro*,[122] *patrinus/matrina*,[123] *patronus*,[124] *offerens*,[125] or *suscepturus*.[126]

Pater/mater spiritualis is thus not a technical term that, in itself, points to sponsorship. Thus, we should not exclude the possibility, particularly because the testimony on Genovefa would be unusually early for a godparent relationship, that Genovefa's spiritual mother may have been her tutor or teacher. One of the other examples to follow, that of Florianus of Romenum, demonstrates a similar use of terminology.[127]

Nevertheless, as the hagiographer has nothing further to report on this spiritual mother, we cannot say for certain that she was not a baptismal sponsor.[128] There is no indication why she took in the orphaned girl, of whether this *mater* was perhaps a relation of some kind who might have been expected to care for her in any case.[129] To be sure, one could argue that the hagiographer only found the spiritual bond worth mentioning, but here too we should exercise caution. The author was writing the life of a saint and the "outstanding importance of spiritual kinship" in this genre[130] should not be mistaken for its significance within social reality. We should also be cautious because no example of an orphan being taken in by a sponsor, and no injunction to do so, occurs in any of the narrative or normative sources, whether medieval or modern.[131]

The three sources that follow—which, like the life of Genovefa, come from the early sixth century, and in which the authors also recount events from the late fifth century—offer no further insights.[132] They do, however, at least clearly mention sponsorship relationships and reveal some interesting details.

The first example is a sermon by Bishop Avitus of Vienne (490–519). Avitus tells of the activities of one of his predecessors by the name of Mamertus, mentioning in passing that the latter had been his own "spiritual father at baptism *(spiritualis a baptismo pater)*."[133] We know nothing about Mamertus other than that he apparently was quite powerful and that he was succeeded as bishop of Vienne by Avitus' father, Hesychius.[134] These few hints do at least contain some valuable information: Avitus, who was born around 460, had a nonparental sponsor, a fact he considered interesting enough to mention to his audience, even though it was not essential to the narrative. In so doing, he may well have provided the first firm practical example of a nonparental sponsor. And, in passing, he revealed a not insignificant detail about social practice: his father Hesychius, whose family had occupied the highest episcopal see in Burgundy for several generations and thus doubtless belonged to the magnates of Vienne,[135] chose as his son's sponsor a certain Mamertus, who was also one of the most powerful men in the city and clearly had a say in the awarding of episcopal office, which he himself had held for some time.

Another document attributed to a contemporary and fellow bishop mentions sponsorship with the same casualness as Avitus' text. This document is the testament of Remigius of Reims (d. 533), which, however, has only come down to us in Hincmar's (d. 882) version. According to the text recorded by Hincmar, Remigius states therein that he had received Clovis from the font.[136] Assuming that the testimony is reliable,[137] this sponsorship too would have occurred in the fifth century, more precisely at Christmas 496/499.[138] At any rate, this episode in the testament fits in with Avitus' account, as well as with the following example of Ennodius of Pavia, which makes it at least historically possible.

Ennodius is the third witness from the period around 500. Writing before 513,[139] he is somewhat more forthcoming than his fellow bishops Avitus and Remigius. In one of his model orations *(dictiones)*, he mentions a certain Paterius who was born to him from "the body of the holy spring, the virgin and mother"—that is, the baptismal font. He was thus Paterius' father *(genitor)* in his second birth. For this reason, Ennodius concludes, he bore responsibility for Paterius' upbringing.[140]

Here, alongside the sponsor's educational function already familiar to us from Caesarius, Ennodius also elucidates a pattern of interpretation for this new "fatherhood." Unspectacular, it corresponds to the ancient theologians' predilection for enlisting vocabulary taken from the family and antique family law for their interpretations of the *ecclesia*. These terms require explanation, since they were not least a vehicle for conveying the norms of sponsorship. Let us turn first, however, to the last of the early testimonies.

Around 551–52 Abbot Florianus of the monastery of Romenum[141] wrote a letter to Bishop Nicetius of Trier, asking the bishop for his intercession.[142] In the letter he calls the late Bishop Ennodius of Pavia his "father from baptism." This would not be worth mentioning had the abbot not gone on to recount what he expected of his sponsor, "whom I trust *(credo)* will intervene *(intervenire)* for his son [Florianus] with the eternal Father through the Son."[143] Thus what the abbot was asking of Nicetius was something he felt was already assured him by his sponsor. And not only by him: Florianus still refers to himself as the "follower and disciple" of his Latin teacher, Caesarius of Arles, and "son and disciple" of his abbot and predecessor, Theodatus. He also felt secure in his expectation that the latter two would intercede on behalf their "son" before the divine judge.[144]

This last of the early witnesses was especially candid in explaining the social function of the newly developed institution of sponsorship to his correspondent. Florianus considered his sponsor one of his "fathers," that is, one of those from whom he could expect "fatherly" behavior. He had the same expectations of all of them (abbot, teacher, and sponsor): they would pray for him. It might seem noteworthy that he does not mention his biological father here. Was spiritual fatherhood perhaps, as the *Lives* suggest,[145] so much more important than biological fatherhood? This would be a rather hasty conclusion. Florianus, the author, was writing to a bishop he probably did not know personally and to whom he apparently had no close ties. It would hardly have lent much weight to his request if he had mentioned that his natural father was also praying for him. Naturally, his father was doing so (if he was fulfilling his duty); but stating something so obvious was unlikely to make any impression on the famous Bishop Nicetius and therefore move him to assent to Florianus' request. Matters were different in the case of those whom Florianus named instead. With his references to Ennodius of Pavia and Caesarius of Arles, Florianus was displaying personal relationships he considered impressive and efficacious. What better way could there be to inform Nicetius about himself than by mentioning such spiritual kinsmen? A reference to his biological father had no place here.

This letter demonstrates, once again, that the function of baptismal sponsorship in the period around 500 was directly connected with the norms that could be evoked by the word *father*. What did these fathers, whom Florianus does mention, have in common with the biological father, whom he does not? What could one achieve by using the word *father* at a time when people were beginning more and more to admit outsiders as proxies and guarantors in baptism, and to refer to these people henceforth as their "fathers"?

"Fathers" and the "Virgin of the Holy Spring"

The concept of the spiritual father can best be understood by looking at the first context that comes to mind when we hear the term *father*. In Roman society, the "family father" *(pater familias)* was a social role whose parameters were laid down by Roman law *(ius)* and no less by custom, although the latter is far less tangible.

As the term was used by Roman jurists, the *pater (familias)* was not the biological father but the head of household *(dominus)*, and *familia* was a purely legal concept encompassing all those persons who were subject to the authority of the *pater*.[146] To put it another way, the *familia* of the Roman jurists was formed by the idea of authority, and the *pater* was the bearer of that authority.[147] His authority was—according to these norms—all-encompassing and included the right to sell or kill his children.[148]

This *pater* of the Roman jurists, who seems so "unclassical" to us, was only one side of the image of the father revealed in the antique sources. The image of the father and the various manifestations of paternal authority were shaped as much by custom, the *mos maiorum*, as by law *(ius)*. The *mos maiorum* was apparently no less binding, and perhaps even "far more effective" than the law.[149] And this *mos* did not measure fathers against the norm of the wielder of authority, but rather that of the protector and caregiver, who was expected to treat his own family, particularly his son, with care *(cura)* or paternal love *(patrius amor)*—indeed, with *pietas*.[150] Catullus once even placed the father's love for his son over that for his wife.[151] In short, "the extent of power was matched by the extent of responsibilty."[152] The *familia*, for its part, was expected to return this paternal love in the form of obedience *(obsequium)*, love, and respect *(pietas)*.[153]

This paternal responsibility, it should be emphasized, was not codified like the *ius* and did not function by means of institutional threats of punishment. The pressure was for social, not legal conformity.[154] At work here were the unspoken commandments of social morality,[155] of custom, "the opinion of vigilant neighbors and . . . fear of the gods."[156] Neighbors did not judge a man by whether he acted according to rights granted him as a father. Instead, according to their respective values, they reached an opinion about the whole person, his individual characteristics, which were not granted like rights but had to be won individually and by hard work as a sort of social credit, and which determined the degree of respect or contempt that was owed a man. This was the force of custom *(mos)* which committed fathers to act in a certain way and exerted control over them.[157]

When, then, our authors and guarantors around 500 (and earlier as well) used the term *father (pater)*, at first for the "catechumenate witnesses" and then for the earliest recognizable baptismal sponsors, they could expect to tap into two different concepts: on the one hand, "father" as a legal concept, primarily representing and legitimating the authority of the lord *(dominus)*, and, on the other hand, "father" as a term of moral valuation, representing and invoking an all-encompassing caretaker.

In antiquity, this *pater familias* was referred to in many areas of life, with a greater emphasis now on the normative and moral, now on the authoritative aspect, but always with an eye to the dual nature of the concept.[158] To cite a well-known example, in the year 44/45, Caesar received the title *pater patriae*, which founded an entire tradition. This title expressed gratitude for Caesar's paternal leniency toward his vanquished foes after the end of the civil war, while at the same time legitimating the extent of the dictator's power, which was portrayed here as *patria potestas*.[159] This dual function remained a part of the emperor's honorary title. Seneca refers to it directly: the ruler was called the *pater patriae* "in order that he may know that he has been entrusted with a father's power which is most forbearing *(temperatissima)* in its care for the interests of his children and subordinates his own to theirs."[160] Dio Cassius is similarly concerned to place the honorary title within a moral framework: "yet it did not signify this [paternal authority] at first, but betokened honour and served as an admonition both to them, that they should love their subjects as they would their children, and to their subjects, that they should revere them rulers as they would their fathers."[161]

The Romans also called their principal gods *patres*[162]—once again, in a dual sense: as both uncanny powers *(numen)*[163] and protectors.[164] The senators were referred to as *patres*,[165] as were certain priests.[166] As regards the term for sponsors, the fact that in antiquity guides or teachers in spiritual matters were also referred to as *pater* is not without significance.[167]

The father, like the family (or "house") more generally may have been the most familiar of people and may have presented himself, not least "thanks to age and duration, ubiquity and variability" as a model for that which was less familiar—God and the gods or communal orders beyond the family, rulers, priests, spiritual leaders, and teachers.[168] In these and many other areas of life the father, like the family or the "house," was the standard example (or model) with which one created the proper relationships between things.

This applied to Christians as well, who from the beginning used the term *father* and its semantic field, as well as familial ideas more generally, as a way of conceiving of the *ecclesia*.[169] The image of God, as it was sketched by early Christian authors, may serve as a familiar example. Here, paternal authority *(potestas)*, care, and affection *(cura, pietas)* became intertwined and displaced each other: the authors of the New Testament placed most emphasis on the kindly Father-God *(abba)*. They did not, to be sure, wholly eliminate the punitive Lord-God, but pushed him into the background. The classic site of this New Testament image of God is the parable of the wicked servant. This fatherly God forgave him who was deeply in his debt but demanded of him that he show equal leniency to others, punishing him only when he proved wholly intransigent and hard-hearted.[170] The theologians and ecclesiastical writers, however, quickly shifted the emphasis. The *pater familias* of Roman law explicitly entered their concept of God—still, to be sure, a kindly father *(pietas)*, but at the same time also an angry one *(potestas timenda)*.[171] We know how the successors to these specialists further modified the image in the early Middle Ages: they completely reestablished the idea of a vengeful God against which the authors of the New Testament had fought. In their *Sermones*, *Lives*, council resolutions, and particularly in the penitentials, they saw to it that the God of dread, the *tremendum* reigned supreme. Gone was paternal forgiveness. Even the tiniest sin had to be punished, a state of affairs that lasted well into the late Middle Ages.[172]

Christians adopted the practice of referring to spiritual teachers as fathers. Saint Paul made the first and most emphatic claim to the title.[173] From the second century on, *pater* was "a much used if by no means stock appellation ... for the bishop."[174] It demonstrated respect for episcopal authority and was, at the same time, a normative requirement for his exercise of office. The title *father* also had normative implications for catechumenate witnesses whose duties, as we have seen, were virtually juridically defined.[175] The churchmen then firmly emphasized the fatherhood of the abbots *(abbas)*, who could command the strictest obedience,[176] but who also bore the most extensive responsibility for the care *(pietas)* of their monastic "sons."[177] Benedict explicitly likens them to the Roman *paterfamilias*.[178]

This terminology, with its many facets and the entire weight of tradition, was used by our informants at the turn of the sixth century to refer to "sponsors" (as we shall call them here, for the sake of simplicity), those people who represented baptizees during baptism, vouched for them, and apparently, from that moment forward, maintained a relationship with them whose social function is not clear from these few documents. We will not have made good use of the few indications these first witnesses—Florianus and Ennodius, Caesarius, Avitus, and (if we are to believe Hincmar) Remigius—do provide, however, unless we examine how they handle the terminology. They give enough hints of what the term *pater* was intended to express. For Caesarius, it was always moral and religious education and spiritual leadership,[179] and Ennodius took a similar view.[180] Florianus, the youngest witness, went even further: he was certain that his sponsor would intercede for him in Heaven.[181] All these texts refer to the reliable and total concern of the father who was willing to do anything for his son. Clearly, none of these early witnesses wished to portray the *paternitas* arising from baptism as authority *(potestas)*. They emphasized the provider's all-encompassing responsibility *(provisio)*.[182] This is precisely what churchmen had to offer those who included sponsors in their by no means always religious considerations and actions.

Here, too, one could naturally point to the genre of texts in question and—certainly with justification—assert that the accounts we do possess are very one-sided: bishops and abbots for other clerics, mentioning sponsorships in passing but not the situations in which sponsors actually interacted socially with their baptizees. Their sermons *(sermones, homeliae)* and model orations *(dictiones)* have less to say about actual interactions between sponsors and baptizees than about what these authors—learned (Gallo-) Roman clerics—believed they should be, that is, about official norms among churchmen. But the creation of norms in which these orators were engaged is also a form of practice. Knowing about the norms makes it much easier to analyze the social practice Gregory of Tours depicted a short time later, but in quite a different genre.

In order to round out the picture one aspect of *paternitas* from baptism remains to be addressed: Ennodius mentions that it was the "virgin of the holy spring *(virgo sacri fontis)*" from whom his (baptismal) son had been born to him, as *genitor*. The reference to the other parent—the mother—lays the trail to a further, frequently employed metaphor in the ecclesiastical sources: the *ecclesia* as *mater*. She not only completed the "family" consisting of baptismal father and son, but also, in a way that appears peculiarly contradictory to us, built a bridge to *adoptio*.

On the one hand, the baptismal rite obviously was modeled on the real act of conception and birth. If we follow the liturgical evidence, the baptizee stepped into the font "in order that out of the immaculate womb of the divine spring, which is rendered fertile by the sanctification [of the spirit], a heavenly descendant might emerge as a newly reborn creature."[183] The authors of the New Testament texts had already used this concept of the church as bride and *mater* who gave spiritual birth to the faithful in baptism and who, at the end of days, will be led to the marriage supper by Christ the bridegroom.[184] Paul, however, also introduces the image of baptism as the installing of a son *(hyio-thesia)* by God, as adoption.[185] Birth in baptism and adoption in baptism are the two concepts that dominated

Christian treatises on baptism from the New Testament on. If the church fathers used these concepts quite naturally as the basis for explaining other articles of faith, without once offering, for example, a more precise explanation of the image of supernatural adoption,[186] their listeners or readers appear to have understood perfectly well. Clearly, the concepts had entered popular consciousness.

The baptismal liturgy even united the two concepts of spiritual birth and supernatural adoption in a single sentence: "Send the spirit of adoption *(spiritum adoptionis)* so that he may create new peoples *(creandos novos populos)* who will be born *(parturit)* to you from the spring of baptism."[187]

The family and family law were thus omnipresent in the semantics of the early Christian writers, particularly in the liturgical texts surrounding baptism and the institution of sponsorship then emerging.

The Franks found themselves confronted with this semantics when they came in contact with the religion of the old empire. How they processed it depended not least on whether, as listeners or readers, they understood these concepts in the same way the ancient ecclesiastical authors themselves had done. Tailoring the question to the problem of sponsorship: Did the Franks have the same notion of the father? If we are to believe specialized studies on the subject, they did. On the one hand, we have normative documents from the early Middle Ages (for example the penitentials) which, like Roman law, emphasize only the father's *potestas* (or mund).[188] This mund was apparently similar to the paternal authority of Roman law.[189] On the other hand, however, in the Middle Ages, legal obligations coexisted with the social obligations of custom, which demanded parental love. Despite the denials of an entire tradition of scholarship, "an astonishing variety and amount of evidence of parental affection has come down to us" from the Middle Ages.[190] Paternal love also was a frequently invoked image in the Middle Ages.[191] Thus, the Franks may well have "read" those practices which, beginning around 500, assumed the contours of what came to be known as godparenthood in much the same way as late antique writers did.

Some Questions for Gregory of Tours

Notions of the "father" may thus have been similar. Until the Carolingian period, however, the structures and practices of the socially, culturally, ethnically, and religiously very diverse groups living in Gaul and east of the Rhine were so disparate that a practice which some learned Roman bishops were speaking of around 500 would scarcely have had any meaning outside that circle. Between the fifth and eighth centuries, generations of these initially very disparate groups were engaged in a process of constant modification and combination of their own and foreign practices and patterns of perception until at last a relatively coherent society emerged with coherent modes of social interaction, legitimation, stabilization, and perception.

To name a few examples we will encounter later, it took a good two hundred years for late antique diocesan and parish structures to be replaced by a new organizational form, one that apparently served the sociopolitical and religious interests of the aristocracy in particular.[192] Similarly, a new religious topos, such as the image of the saint of noble birth who was active in the world, only emerged in the seventh and eighth centuries.[193] The role of the bishops had undergone a thorough redefinition between the fifth and eighth centuries, and what the documents have to say about sponsorship had changed just as radically. Those who first wrote of sponsors around the year 500 did not, to be sure, report on actual practice, but they did associate a distinct expectation with sponsorship: the all-encompassing care and concern of the sponsor, akin to what custom (*mos maiorum*), from time immemorial, had demanded that fathers offer their sons. The sponsor was a father, but he was less the father of law than that of custom—not the omnipotent (*patria potestas*) but, rather, the caring and devoted (*cura, pietas*) father. This is not to say that such a concept was absent from the Carolingian period; but apparently it was only one of several. In the Carolingian period, the bishops seem to have worried more about all the impediments to marriage that they derived from sponsorship, and kings used sponsorship as an instrument of imperial power.[194]

Gregory of Tours lived and worked between these two epochs. He is the only writer who offers any information about how sponsorship was dealt with in this diverse society between the old Roman empire and the Carolingian one. He recounts a number of cases of sponsorship particularly from the royal dynasty, although it was apparently not his particular intention to inform his readers about the royal family's sponsors.[195]

In most cases, Gregory mentions sponsorship only because it played some role in the other events he describes. This, of course, is of great interest for the study of social groups, since his accounts allow us to ask questions about the social consequences of sponsorship ties. What obligations or constraints on action were encountered by the participants in Gregory's narrative? Exactly what duties did spiritual kin agree to, and how were they held to them? What demands could they make, and how could they do so? For example, did the *pater spiritualis* have *potestas*? What about his duty to educate his godchildren? Were the sponsor's religious duties, of which the earliest witnesses speak, accompanied by secular ones? Is there any evidence of a material side to these ties—for example, in inheritance?

What advantages did the sponsorship tie have over other ties? Finally, what gave this bond its strength?

One qualification is necessary at the outset: the chronicler is miserly with information that could be particularly instructive for understanding this practice's *Sitz im Leben*: why particular parents chose a particular sponsor. Only in one case—and a rather unusual one, at that—did he apparently consider it advisable to inform his readers that a bishop who was just about to become a sponsor to a king's son "was at this time endowed with great power of miracle."[196] Despite the chronicler's silence, political and social motives were probably the primary interests involved in the choice of a sponsor, especially since sponsorships frequently appear at prominent moments in Merovingian politics, and we know how the Carolingians later dealt with sponsorship. On closer examination, this can be demonstrated for practically all of the sponsorships mentioned by the chronicler.

The case studies will be guided by two issues: first, which criteria did parents use in choosing a sponsor, and second, how did baptisms affect the behavior of the participants toward one another?

A note on the organization of the materials is in order here. Rather than retain Gregory's chronology, the examples will be grouped and analyzed thematically. We will begin with the six cases in which bishops appear as sponsors to members of the royal family. They will be followed by the sponsorship relationships between kings or bishops and secular nobles, as well as those within the royal family. The nature of Gregory's narrative dictates that the longest chapter deal with Gunthchramn's sponsorship of Chlothar. Here, in particular, his account permits us to illuminate the action itself and the social and political relevance of the ritual components, as well as the interests and effects being pursued.

8
The Rule of the Merovingians and the Power of the Bishops

Almost all of the baptismal sponsors to royal children whom the chronicler mentions were bishops, and all these connections doubtless served political ends. That may be reason enough to begin by recalling how important bishops were for Merovingian rule.

A "Dualistic" Structure

Friedrich Prinz has suggested that "in the case of the Merovingian kingdom, one should speak of a 'dualistic' structure."[1] His thesis, though perhaps a bit emphatically formulated, has largely been accepted by scholars. The Merovingian rulers drew support from two very different and largely separate groups—the Frankish nobles and the Gallo-Roman upper class.[2] Even if the occasional "mixed marriage" and joint activities at court slowly brought the two groups together, they retained their distinctive characteristics until the end of the seventh century, at which point the traces of the Roman families become lost. The Irish monks, by offering these families a new identity as Christian patrons, apparently played a major role in weakening their Roman identity.[3]

The first group was shaped by its Germanic-Frankish traditions. These Frankish nobles were already powerful and influential by the time the Merovingians first appear in the sources, but their origins and the sources of their legitimation remain obscure and beyond the reach of scholarly reconstruction.[4] In the sixth and seventh centuries these nobles are always to be found in the vicinity of the kings, where they also appear in sponsorship relationships.[5]

The second group, the episcopate, acquired their role as supporters or wielders of political rule in late Roman Gaul and increasingly expanded it, particularly in the fifth century. From the moment at the end of the fourth century when the last emperors left Gaul, the Gallic senatorial aristocracy lost contact with the imperial court and thus increasingly lacked legitimation for their political power and ambitions, which remained strong. This senatorial aristocracy established the episcopate as a new arena of political influence, and quite soon set about distributing sees internally—indeed, virtually passing them on through inheritance.[6] The circumstance that the emperors themselves, beginning with Constantine, had transferred state authority to the bishops may have helped this process along, but it was not a central factor. After all, a similar authority was bestowed on bishops throughout the Roman Empire, but political rule by the bishops was a specifically Gallic phenomenon.[7]

With the disappearance of Roman centralized power in the West, this aristocracy apparently managed (or was compelled) to attach "'overall state' functions"[8] to the bishoprics, to the extent that they were still intact, and to rule over them as a kind of "aristocratic republic with an episcopal leadership."[9] The aristocracy provided the bishops, who were expected to devote less attention to the welfare of souls (increasingly the province of monks)[10] than to the secular sociopolitical needs of the population. On the occasion of an episcopal election at Bourges, Sidonius Apollinaris (d. 480/490), himself bishop of Clermont, described the candidate of his choice as follows: he "can intercede with the secular powers for the bodies of men" and as a *comes* he offered the best prerequisites for serving both the church and the state. He expressly mentions the man's high rank; indeed, even the origins of his wife spoke in his favor.[11] As a member of this aristocracy, Sidonius could scarcely have said more plainly "that, from such a perspective, the episcopal dignity appeared as the crowning achievement of a secular career in state service and was desirable precisely for that reason."[12] It is noteworthy (if not, perhaps, wholly typical)[13] that Sidonius' description of his candidate of choice makes no mention of the ascetic ideal that had still wholly dominated the Vita Martini[14] and indeed expressly relegates such asceticism to the abbots. The late-antique episcopal city had become an arena more for a political than a spiritual elite, even if asceticism remained unforgotten, at least in funerary inscriptions.[15]

Among the bishops, the Merovingians found the administrative apparatus they needed to master the tasks of running an extensive kingdom. And, since Frankish social and political structures had nothing similar to offer, the new rulers adopted the structures already in place.[16]

The Merovingians thus relied on those who, according to their self-image and representation, had, since the time of the late Roman emperors, "rested as securely in the 'friendship of God' as the emperor himself"[17] and who now, under the new barbarian kings "by no means derived [their legitimation] from emperor or king, but rather from their own virtues which were a result of *nobilitas*."[18] The above-cited Sidonius Apollinaris is a clear example. Here, the Merovingians were confronted with an autonomous power factor that they needed, but could, like the Frankish nobles, just as easily turn into an opponent.

The Power of the Bishops

It is widely accepted that the bishops of the early Merovingian era were powerful.[19] Debate remains about whether the bishops of the fifth and sixth centuries were already lords like their seventh and eighth century successors[20] or merely outstanding representatives, *patroni civitatis*, who still lacked "the essential element of political rule more generally—namely, the institutionalized exercise of power" *(dominium)*: exclusive jurisdiction in the city.[21] Which interpretation one prefers depends not least on one's assessment of the condition of the late antique *comitatus* system in the Merovingian era, which potentially provided the only competition to episcopal rule in the cities. Here, too, however, we have too little information. Was the regular presence of *comites* in the cities "very dubious,"[22] and thus extensive episcopal lordships probable, or was the institution of the *comitatus*—at least in the heartland—ubiquitous?[23] Were the bishops of Trier, who managed to displace the *comes* as early as the sixth century, typical or exceptional?[24] To judge by the conclusions of specialized studies, this appears to be as unanswerable a question as that regarding the precise function served by the *comites*. Thus, to cite only a few opinions, Reinhold Kaiser finds the *comes* in the city[25] while, according to Dietrich Claude he "[spent] a good portion of his time in the country."[26] Finally, Rolf Sprandel, distinguishing between a late-Roman urban and a Merovingian rural *comes*, assumes that the two belonged to separate institutional traditions.[27]

All, however, try to fix an official definition of an episcopate whose shape was, in fact, extremely fluid and a matter of permanent controversy at the time. Apart from these discussions, there is no doubt that, in most places, officeholders had substantial de facto political power.[28] In the royal cities *(sedes regiae)*, though, the bishops appear to have been relatively powerless. As early as 511, in Orléans, at the first Gallic council held under Merovingian rule, the bishops consolidated the economic foundations of their power by securing for themselves the spiritual and legal supervision of the monasteries and convents.[29] Apparently, it did not take long for the kings to recognize the danger from this quarter. Chlothar I (d. 561) tried to secure for himself a one-third share in the income of the church,[30] and Chilperic I (d. 584) "ever made it his habit to tear up all wills" in favor of the all-powerful church,[31] which he held responsible for his own weakness: "'See how poor our treasury always is! Look how the churches have drained our riches away! Of a verity, none ruleth at all, save only the bishops. Our royal office is lost and gone; it hath passed to the bishops in their cities.'"[32] This, at least, is the version supplied by the narrator, Gregory.

This state of affairs persisted until Charles Martel broke this power economically by introducing specific exemptions for the suburban monasteries.[33] Under the Merovingians, episcopal power frequently revealed itself in the exercise of politics.[34] It was the bishops who opened the gates of the city to this or that king. Gregory of Tours, for example, warned Bishop Maroveus of the neighboring diocese of Poitiers, not to cast in his lot with Childebert but, rather, with Gunthchramn.[35] When Gunthchramn sent envoys the following year "to discover whether the army would be peacefully admitted or not" it was the bishop, in turn, who received them—"harshly" *(dure)* as the chronicler informs us.[36] It was also Maroveus whom Gunthchramn then accused of disloyalty and who had to ransom himself and the city with gold tributes.[37] Similarly, after Gundovald's revolt, King Gunthchramn attempted to call to account the bishops in whose *civitates* the rebel had taken refuge.[38] Armed and fighting bishops must have been the order of the day, if we are to take the oft-repeated prohibitions at face value.[39]

These allusions may suffice to illustrate that the bishops were "comporting themselves in their cities as de facto rulers."[40] They also had a de facto monopoly over education, which alone would have rendered them politically powerful. Education, essential for the administration of such a large kingdom, may have continued within a lay context at a rudimentary level for a time during the sixth century,[41] but most of the effort was invested in clerical education,[42] which remained centered in the episcopal cities[43] until it moved to the large rural monasteries in the seventh century.

During the sixth-century partitions of the kingdom, the kings made it plain that the role of the episcopal see as "a sort of sub-lordship under Merovingian sovereignty" had not escaped their notice.[44] The partitions were oriented throughout toward the borders of the *civitates* (and not, for example, toward the ecclesiastical provinces).[45] Furthermore, and even more strikingly, in those cases where partition did not follow the boundary of a *civitas*, the kings frequently used the occasion of partition to found new episcopal sees. Thus, the see of Laon was established in 511 after the death of Clovis,[46] and the see of Mâcon during the partition of the Burgundian kingdom in 534.[47] When, in 567, Sigibert received a part of the bishopric of Chartres from the inheritance of his brother, Charibert, while the diocesan town itself fell to Neustria, he appointed a separate bishop for his own segment in the *castrum* of Châteaudun, who managed to maintain his position until Sigibert's death.[48] Childebert I of Paris also tried to separate the diocese of Sens, which belonged to Theudebert of Reims, from his own territory and create a new bishopric of Melun. He was thwarted by the resistance of the bishop of Sens.[49] Apparently, the Merovingians avoided ruling over a region that belonged to the episcopal see of a neighboring kingdom.

The *Sanctitas* of the Merovingians

It was not only their economic and political power as representatives of the cities that made the bishops so indispensable to the Merovingians; it was the bishops who allowed the kings their sacral legitimation and representation in the first place. We need only recall how, in his famous letter to Clovis, Avitus of Vienne supplemented the latter's kingly representation, the *felicitas* of the Merovingians, with a Christian one, *sanctitas*.[50] Clovis, for his part, actively helped shape this new representation of his rule by immediately adopting Martin of Tours as his family's patron saint.[51]

The Merovingians needed the participation of the bishops, for example, in establishing and propagating the new places of worship set up by the early Merovingians. They needed the royal prayer which also constituted public recognition.[52] Even Chlothar I, the most "barbarian" Merovingian with perhaps the harshest policy toward the church,[53] took steps to alleviate the North's lack of centers of worship and saints. In his capital, Soissons, he founded the basilica of St. Médard as his mortuary chapel and, contrary to his usual policy, saw to its furnishing himself.[54]

The New Lords of the Church

At the moment of his baptism, the Gallic bishops granted to Clovis, as the patron of the true faith in the West, those rights that previously had belonged (officially) to the emperor. At the very first Gallic national council, Clovis was acknowledged as the supreme overlord of the church.[55] The kings well knew how to use this power. They immediately appropriated the right to appoint bishops and took every opportunity to reward laymen, faithful followers, and court personnel with this influential office.[56] Thus, for the period after 561 alone, Gregory reports on ten former secular officials in episcopal livings.[57] The episcopal councils resisted in vain: the second and third synods of Orléans (533 and 538) were already emphasizing election by the populace and clergy and opposing various abuses such as simony, lay investiture, last-minute consecrations and the manipulation of electors.[58] A synod held at Clermont in 535 sought to secure at least a right of consent for the metropolitan,[59] but the fourth council of Orléans (549) now, for the first time, formally accorded this right to the king.[60] Finally, the second council of Paris (558–73) at least tried to prevent the king from appointing a bishop against the will of the provincial bishops.[61] Pope Gregory I also repeatedly appealed to the Merovingians, demanding canonical election—with no more success than the bishops.[62] The kings appear to have paid little mind to council resolutions, which were frequently repeated. The "conferring of an episcopal see [appeared] as a capricious sign of royal favor,"[63] and kings were not interested in whether the candidate came from the metropolitan district in which the vacant see lay. What mattered was that the candidate came from the portion of the kingdom belonging to the ruler who was appointing the bishop.[64] If the vacant see belonged to a kingdom other than the ecclesiastical metropolis, the metropolitan could neither use his right of consent nor his rights of consecration. Not even the papal vicar in Arles could reach beyond the kingdom to which he belonged.[65]

The Need for New Ties

This, of course, does not mean that the kings found in the episcopate the willing instruments of their authority. Just as we hear of revolts in court circles, we also hear of revolts from among "the citizens."[66] And the episcopate was still recruited largely from Gallo-Roman families who, even if they were appointed by the king and connected with the court, remained, in the first instance, representatives of their *civitates* and a central autonomous power factor. Their primary source of social responsibilities and loyalties, of kinship, consideration and support, remained the urban Roman aristocracy rather than the court.

The kings had to bind this influential and relatively independent group to themselves, and it was not always sufficient merely to exert influence over appointments. The constellations of rule shifted frequently, for example, as a result of partitions of the kingdom; and a king might find himself confronted in a *civitas* he had just inherited or conquered with a bishop whom he had not appointed and with whom he had had no previous contact. Effective ties were needed here, and it seems that baptismal sponsorship was intended to serve this purpose.

9
Sponsorship Bonds (1): Bishops and Kings

Praetextatus of Rouen as Merovich's Godfather

The first case in which the chronicler Gregory speaks of a sponsorship relationship comes from Neustria at the time of King Chilperic. In the year 577, Bishop Praetextatus of Rouen was called before Chilperic's court in Paris, accused of trying to topple the king and stealing royal property. Chilperic also accused him of performing a marriage that violated canon law between Chilperic's son, Merovich, and his aunt, Brunechildis, mother of the Austrasian king. In the course of these proceedings, Bishop Praetextatus cited the fact that he was Merovich's sponsor as a central argument in his defense against the charge of theft. The allegedly stolen property "'seemed to me in some sort mine, because it belonged to my son Merovech, whom I had received from the font of regeneration.'"[1] As for the role of sponsorship, this episode raises two questions. First, why was Praetextatus, of all people, chosen as Merovich's sponsor? Second, what purpose was this argument intended to serve, and how did the bishop incorporate it in his defense?

An Inherited Metropolitan

We need to take a few detours to grasp what Chilperic hoped to gain by making Praetextatus the godfather of Merovich. We know nothing of the circumstances of Merovich's birth or baptism. Similarly, we have virtually no information about Bishop Praetextatus; there is not even a record of when he took office. All we have for either participant are hints.

Merovich was one of three sons born to Chilperic's first wife, Audovera, who left the king around 566–68.[2] It would be interesting for our purposes here to know when he was born, but we can only be highly approximate:

during an attack on his brother's kingdom in 561 or 562, the Austrasian Sigibert found one of Merovich's brothers, Theudebert, in the capital city of Soissons, carried him off, held him captive for a year, and then released him upon an oath of Chilperic's.[3] The attachment between Chilperic and Audovera thus predated 561. However, the chronicler's first account of Merovich himself concerns the year 576. In that year, Chilperic sent his son out with an army against Poitiers. The son traveled instead via Tours to Rouen, where he married[4] the Austrasian king's widow, Brunechildis, who had been banished there by Chilperic.[5] According to this account Merovich was already capable of leading military campaigns around 576; thus he must have been born between the years 558 and 562, at the latest.

One thing may be safely said of Bishop Praetextatus: he was not appointed bishop by Chilperic. From 511 to 558, Rouen, his diocesan town, belonged to the kingdom of Childebert of Paris (d. 558), then to the united Gallic kingdom of Chlothar I (d. 561) and after 561 once again to the kingdom of Paris, now ruled by Chilperic's brother Charibert (d. 567). Only after Charibert's death did Chilperic inherit the city.[6] Praetextatus must have been bishop by that time. His predecessor, Flavius, is mentioned for the last time in 541,[7] and Praetextatus himself for the first time either at the second synod of Paris,[8] whose date is uncertain (556–73), or at the Council of Tours, in 567.[9] Charibert died during the year of that council, but since the years of his reign were used as dates there, he probably was still alive when it took place. Praetextatus participated in the Council of Tours in 567, so he was certainly already bishop of Rouen when Chilperic inherited the *civitas*. There is much to be said for Odette Pontal's suggestion that the second synod of Paris took place around 561.[10] If she is correct, Praetextatus would have been in office for at least six years when Chilperic took power in Rouen.

In short, when Rouen came under Chilperic's rule in 567 Merovich was a young boy and Praetextatus had been bishop for several years. This means Praetextatus either became Merovich's godfather before 567, indicating that Chilperic chose a bishop from the neighboring kingdom as his son's sponsor, or that Merovich was not baptized until after 567, several years after his birth. The penitentials stipulated that baptism should take place no later than three years after birth, which likely indicates that the inventors of such regulations feared—and, indeed, had often experienced—longer delays.[11] We may well conclude from this that postponing baptism was not unusual. There is no reason to assume that this did not happen to Merovich, especially since we know of only one case in which a king chose a sponsor from outside his own kingdom.[12] Yet it still appears worth asking why Chilperic waited until after 567 to have his son baptized, and why his choice fell on this particular bishop. Chilperic had not appointed

Praetextatus, and we do not have any evidence that the bishop possessed any special qualities or good relations with the king.

It is conspicuous that Chilperic chose the only metropolitan in his kingdom: before 567, there was no metropolitan see under his rule; only later, through his share of Charibert's inheritance, did he gain the metropolises of Rouen and—geographically disconnected from the motherlands—Bordeaux.[13]

What significance did the metropolitans have for kings in the sixth century? Their constant, sometimes quite vigorous, attempts to assert their canonical rights[14] before the kings met with no visible success. They nevertheless probably wielded more clout than normal bishops, since their quasi-lordly power may have been greater than that of other members of the episcopate, given that the metropolises, through their secular tradition as seats of the Roman provincial governors, had generally remained regional centers. Thus, the metropolis of Rouen apparently surpassed the other episcopal cities of the province in economic might. To be sure, we cannot estimate its economic significance in the sixth century, but scholars have noted that in the seventh and eighth centuries, the city was a center on the lower Seine with a market and a mint.[15]

Chilperic thus had good reason to wait until after 567 to baptize his son. In choosing the most distinguished of his bishops as a sponsor, Chilperic also selected the bishop of the most important *civitas* of his kingdom, whose power in the city must have made him a political factor to be reckoned with, a man who evidently enjoyed substantial support among the "citizens of Rouen," as Gregory calls them, and "above all the chief men of the Franks of that place."[16] We will return later to a few anonymous figures who did their best to gain the bishop's favor.

On the whole, it appears that Chilperic's choice fell on the most powerful bishop in his realm, a bishop who had become his subject only in 567 and who could not have been appointed by the king himself. The sponsorship tie does not appear (as we might be tempted to assume) to have been the reflection of a good relationship between the two participants; at any rate, we have no evidence of this. It is more likely that the appointment was set up primarily to establish a relationship between the king and bishop.[17]

A Trial

Matters were to take another course, however. Chilperic became the bishop's bitter enemy. In 577 he convened an "episcopal council"[18]—reportedly attended by forty-five bishops[19]—in order to have judgment passed on the bothersome bishop. The chronicler, who was present at this occasion and involved in the proceedings,[20] provides a detailed and blatantly partisan account of the trial. He records some of the king's individual accusations and the bishop's arguments, but breaks off at a certain point and notes only that the "dispute was being carried farther. . . ."[21] We thus have only a fragmentary picture of what Gregory believed was necessary to present the condemnation of Praetextatus as unjust. In order to do so, the deeply involved chronicler cites and recounts a sharp exchange in which the accused twice refers to baptismal sponsorship and which contains a number of useful details concerning the conduct of this particular godfather.

Chilperic accused the bishop of three activities that formed the basis of the case against him. First, the bishop had given objects belonging to Queen Brunechildis as gifts to certain of Chilperic's subjects. Second, he had demanded that these people swear an oath of loyalty to the king's son, Merovich. Third, he had married Merovich to his Austrasian aunt Brunechildis. The bishop made no attempt to deny any of this. The only point of controversy was whether these deeds deserved punishment, and one by one the participants brought forward different arguments.

A Reciprocal Gift

The king began by reproaching the bishop for performing the uncanonical marriage and called "false witnesses" who were supposed to confirm that the bishop had "given gifts to the people in order that together ye might compass my death." The bishop's reply to these accusations was: "'Ye say true that often ye received rewards from me; but not to drive the king from his dominion. For since ye gave me fine horses and other things, what else could I do but make presents of like worth in return?' The king now returned to his lodging"[22] and had to come up with a new case. The chronicler would have us believe that Praetextatus chose his arguments well.

The events surrounding the gifts were by no means as clear-cut as they seemed. Chilperic had called witnesses whom the accused Praetextatus immediately claimed had offered him gifts first, and very valuable gifts at that. According to Praetextatus' version of the affair, he had reacted to the offers in two ways, first by accepting the gifts and then by giving gifts of his own in return—"often." The chronicler does not name the figures (*populus*)[23] with whom the bishop had dealings, nor does he report exactly what it was they wanted from him. Whoever presented the bishop with "the fine horses" will have known the reason why. It would be all the more interesting to discover their identity, since these men appeared in court on Chilperic's side. It would be equally interesting for our interpretation to know exactly how these actions proceeded, for example, how much time elapsed between the gifts and the bishop's reciprocal gifts. And why did

Praetextatus give them gifts "often"? Did they also often give him gifts? At any rate, nobody claimed that they did. Gregory's description of these witnesses as "false" is hardly impartial, as they were clearly telling the truth (if not the whole truth, since they suppressed the fact that they had given presents first). Was the bishop merely making excuses here, and was the king's accusation perhaps less false than the chronicler would have us believe? Let us take a closer look at how the exchange of words developed.

Chilperic began by attacking two of the bishop's actions: the marriage Praetextatus performed between Merovich and his aunt Brunechildis and his distribution of gifts. The first, as he saw it, violated the canons, while the second was part of an attempt by Praetextatus and Merovich to overthrow and, indeed, kill the king. Praetextatus (or the chronicler) said nothing of the uncanonical marriage; this was wise, since he must have known all too well that, here, Chilperic had right on his side. Praetextatus himself had been involved in the prohibition of such marriages at the second Paris synod.[24] Neither did he deny having distributed gifts, although Praetextatus interpreted his actions differently. He had only been reciprocating, an act he evidently regarded as necessary, as his rhetorical "what else could I do?" indicates.[25] This argument apparently decided the first round, and the king left the room, his attack repelled for the time being.

If we are looking for an interpretation, there is scarcely a handbook on medieval history nowadays that does not offer some explanation of these events. The idea that for "medieval people" a "gift always implies reciprocity," is an integral part of the current image of the Middle Ages. As two protagonists of this discussion have noted, "Gifts were continually being exchanged in barbarian society,"[26] and a "considerable portion of what was produced" entered this "heavy traffic in necessary [!] generosity."[27]

The example of Praetextatus adds to this picture in two ways. First, it shows that, in fact, recognition of the norm of reciprocating gifts was so official that the king could not ignore this reasoning. The duty of reciprocating gifts was the decisive, winning argument in the first round of the trial. On the other hand, though, the example shows the limits of the model of gift exchange as a *scholarly explanation* ("universal cultural model")[28] of that obligation. In a situation where a social norm was as universal as the scholarly model of gift exchange claims the obligation of reciprocity to have been (documenting it with a multitude of examples from every possible era, region, and cultural form), there must have been so many adaptations to each situation, so many ways of dealing with this norm, so many variations, that the term *gift exchange* can scarcely be more than a program for an actual analysis of social practice. If Praetextatus received "fine horses" and gave valuable objects from the royal treasury in return, what use is it for the analysis of these actions and their social and political relevance that

Marcel Mauss studied parties who exchanged "dried fish ... for jellied birds or matting" or that Maori hunters—a key story for Mauss—made a reciprocal gift of some of the birds they had killed to the priests they believed responsible for their successful hunt?[29] Let us recall that, according to Marcel Mauss, "everything—food, women, children, property, talismans, land, labour services, priestly functions, and ranks—is there for passing on, and for balancing accounts. Everything passes to and fro as if there were a constant exchange of a spiritual matter, including things and men, between clans and individuals, distributed between social ranks, the sexes, and the generations."[30]

The function of a gift to the gods (or to their priests) is not the same as that of a gift between political officeholders, nor of those small presents exchanged by neighbors as part of everyday life. The gift-giving activities of a Praetextatus were not predictable, like the donations to the king upon his entry into a city;[31] nor did they recur regularly, like a harvest thanksgiving; nor were they constant, as in neighbor relations. They were special gifts, given for a particular reason, especially valued and, not least because of that, highly conspicuous. Just as there were, ultimately, as many kinds of gift-giving and giving in return as there were practical situations, the chronicler also describes several viewpoints on a single act of giving. What Praetextatus portrayed as compulsory reciprocation is interpreted by Chilperic as leading "astray the people with bribes" *(seducere)*, and "making largess to the people" *(populis munera dare)*.[32]

A Problem of Time

The two parties to the conflict had not yet finished with the topic of gift exchange; they returned to it in the very next round. Chilperic now confronted the bishop with the fact that valuable objects had been found in his possession "'which he hath purloined from us.'" And a bishop caught in larceny could not retain his episcopal office. In fact, objects belonging to Queen Brunechildis had been found among Praetextatus' effects, which he did not deny. Once again, he disputed only the king's interpretation. He had only had the objects for safekeeping, and then successively delivered them up to Brunechildis's envoys. He had consulted Chilperic beforehand each time. This was thus "not a case of theft, but of custody,"[33] and with the king's knowledge at that. It may have been a strategic move on Chilperic's part to describe the objects as "ours," thus suggesting that it was he himself (or the royal family as a collective) who had been robbed. Praetextatus replied with another version, one element of which, that the objects belonged to Queen Brunechildis, remained undisputed.

The king, however, did not allow himself to be swayed by the bishop's assertion that it was only a matter of "custody," and prepared a new attack: if this were true, then he was interested to hear why Praetextatus, who supposedly only had these objects for safekeeping, had cut up "an orphrey woven of gold thread" and distributed the pieces to the men in question. In so doing, the bishop had actually given away royal property, which might be considered a serious charge. It is all the more instructive to hear how the bishop managed to answer such an accusation. He began with the statement that "'I have already told thee that I had received gifts from them, and therefore I borrowed this and gave it to them as a return present, because I had nothing else at hand to give.'"[34]

Now bishops were hardly poor men (we need only recall the testament of Berthchramn of Le Mans),[35] and Praetextatus owed some explanation of why he was reduced to offering royal property in exchange for the "fine horses and other things" he had received. Couldn't he have come up with something else? His argument is more implied than explicit: it was only at that particular moment that he had "nothing else at hand." And this can only mean that he was in a hurry. We are also inclined to assume that he, who had "often" given gifts, only had recourse to royal property once, since Chilperic gave a precise description of the "purloined" object.

Another aspect fundamental to the social effect of many gifts, but which is often ignored in analyses, begins to take shape here: the effect of time.[36] All but unnoticed, it runs through the accounts on which Marcel Mauss based his theories. In the key testimony cited by Mauss, his native informant explains the system of gift exchange by saying that one reciprocated gifts only "after some time"[37] or "at a later time," as another scholar cited by Mauss noted.[38] According to a newer translation of that key document, "a long time" even passed.[39] Bourdieu has explained that the intervening time period, the time of being-in-someone's debt, is what makes this form of gift-giving efficacious and that one needs to have a precise feeling for the customs in a given case, a certain knack, or *sens pratique*, in order neither to wait too long to reciprocate with a gift nor to react hastily and cancel one's debt prematurely.

In other situations, gifts were exchanged directly. The social value of these acts apparently did not reside in the latency period between gift and return gift. Gregory offers some examples of this phenomenon. Gunthchramn and Childebert exchanged gifts *(munera)* when they met at Pompierre in 577,[40] and King Gunthchramn's solemn entry into Orléans included the direct exchange of gifts.[41] When Recared's Visigothic emissaries arrived to ask Childebert for his sister's hand in marriage, the envoys exchanged gifts with him.[42]

In all three cases, Gregory's description gives the impression that we are dealing with firmly entrenched practice and ceremony: "*se muneribus honorantes*" at Pompierre, "*muneratus muneraque ipsis . . . largitus est*" at Orléans and "*acceptisque ac datis muneribus*" in the case of the Gothic envoys.

The account does not tell us which of these two situations—or perhaps another one altogether—Praetextatus found himself in when he believed that he had to reciprocate immediately. It may well be that, when the men arrived with horses, Praetextatus truly was compelled to come up with a gift right away. We do not know, since we are unfamiliar with the nature of the encounter and the course it took. But the tribunal knew, since those who had received the gifts were present as witnesses. And, since Chilperic also lost this round of the trial, the argument seems to hold up; apparently the fact that Praetextatus might actually have been compelled to act on the spot outweighed actual ownership of the objects in question.

Taking into account the time pressures under which actors were operating is, incidentally, a form of methodological discipline that prevents us from viewing gift exchange as a social mechanism that ran like clockwork (or that regularity and predictability often attributed to ritual). Incorporating the factors of time and time pressure as basic aspects of practice enables us to integrate into our analysis the subjective tension of an actor such as Praetextatus, who might be able to calculate the outcome but who could not predict it, as suggested by the explanatory model of gift exchange. Perhaps Praetextatus was forced to decide quickly whether he should refuse the gift, or offer half a belt to each, or perhaps a whole one, properly responding to or even outdoing the gift of "fine horses," whether he should react immediately or wait awhile, give presents "often" or erase his debt with an immediate return gift and then withdraw.

A Calculation

Praetextatus apparently calculated the size of the return gift carefully; he did not choose an object of royal provenience for each of those whom he owed a gift, but rather cut up and distributed a single valuable belt. Here, too, the available information suffices only to indicate the radius of action available to the bishop. Did he cut up the belt because a belt for each man would have been too much in relation to the value of the horses? Did he thus wish to reciprocate "in like manner" (*similiter*), as the chronicler reports for another case?[43] Was this calculation of the proper gift the borderline to "bribery," of which Chilperic accused him?[44] Did he cut up the belt because he had given "often" and fulfilled his obligations? At any rate, it is unlikely that he divided up the gift out of miserliness, for generosity (*largitas*) made particular economic sense in that society.[45] The further development of the story also makes it unlikely that some other motive, perhaps distancing or provocation, led him to give the persons involved less than their due. He had by no means, as he claimed, merely given the return gift required by duty; rather, as he failed to mention here but was soon forced to admit, he was indeed interested in using his return gift to obtain practical services from these men. Therefore, the fact that he cut up the belt may be an example of the calculation of gifts, of the bishop's attempt to arrive at the appropriate value: to give neither too much nor too little.

A Reinterpretation

Nevertheless, the belt was not the bishop's property, and for that reason he presented the court with a further argument. "'It seemed to me in some sort mine, because it belonged to my son Merovech, whom I had received from the font of regeneration.'"[46] The underlying assumption here is that Brunechildis's property, as it had been referred to up to that point, was, because of her marriage, Merovich's property as well. The basis for the assertion that Merovich's property somehow (he is cautious here: *mihi videbatur*) belonged to him is less easy to pinpoint. We have no other document that presents this assertion within the framework of custom or that might elucidate what precisely Praetextatus meant. Perhaps he was using the reciprocity of a gesture arising from *caritas* or *amicitia* ("What is mine is yours") in his defense. At any rate, this would make sense within the context of his deft shift of perspective. Whether Praetextatus had stolen or not was, not least, a matter of representation: where Chilperic depicted him as a subject who had unlawfully helped himself to the king's property, thereby labeling him a thief, Praetextatus claimed a familial relationship, making it far more difficult to accuse him, as a "father" who appropriated his "son's" things in time of need, of theft. Godparenthood imparted a different quality to the relationship and thus, at least according to Praetextatus, to the deeds as well.

The chronicler Gregory also recounts another tale in which baptismal sponsorship recast a relationship. Gregory himself had once stood by while someone stole property from his church. He apparently believed that his inactivity was sufficiently explained by the fact that he had received the thief's son from the font. As his readers, we may ask ourselves whether he was fooling us or himself.[47] Whatever the answer, such explanations for the behavior of spiritual kin and thus also such expectations of their behavior must have been accepted socially. If we are to believe the chronicler, Chilperic, too, had to accept the arguments involving the return gift and sponsorship. "King Chilperic now perceived that he could not get the better of Praetextatus by false charges; he left us, much marvelling and troubled in conscience."[48] He was not prepared to give up just yet, though.

Not Just a Return Gift

Chilperic produced one fresh accusation before achieving the desired result with the help of deception: "'If thou only gavest these men gift for gift, wherefore didst thou demand of them an oath of fidelity to Merovech?'" Once again, Praetextatus was ready with a reply: "I confess that I sought their friendship for him."[49] He had to begin by admitting that his gifts had not been intended solely to settle an "account," as he had at first claimed. Rather, he had bestowed presents (and social anthropologists have made similar observations)[50] in such a way that he could now avail himself of the power of the gift: with his return gifts, he again put those who had given him gifts in his debt, exacting their promise of loyalty to Merovich.

Are we supposed to believe that Praetextatus did all this, as he initially claimed, "'but not to drive the king from his dominion'"?[51] Anyone who has followed the prehistory of the trial in Gregory's chronicle will soon have some doubts about this version. Can the bishop truly have been unaware of the fact that Merovich had long been engaged in open rebellion against his father? The year before the trial, it was Praetextatus who married Merovich to Brunechildis. Is it likely that he did not know at the time that Merovich's father had other plans for him than marrying in Rouen? And did he not know that Brunechildis was Chilperic's archenemy and that she was in Rouen because he had banished her there?[52] The fact that the marriage violated canon law may not have been exceptional, and it may have been of interest only to someone looking for ammunition against the bishop.[53] And, we might be tempted to think, if the bishop had been looking for a reason not to perform the marriage he could easily have found one. It cannot have escaped his attention that the king was incensed at the marriage, immediately setting off for Rouen and separating Merovich and Brunechildis, who had taken refuge in one of the city's churches.

To be sure, what happened next did not take place in Rouen, but since Praetextatus had "given gifts to the people"[54]—or reciprocated them—in order to gain loyal followers for Merovich, he can scarcely have been ignorant of how matters developed thereafter: Chilperic brought his son back to Soissons, kept him captive there, and had him tonsured.[55] Merovich managed to flee to the Church of St. Martin at Tours, however, and there now began an open confrontation replete with all those features that always characterize such conflicts in Gregory's accounts—devastations, violations of asylum, deviousness, and all manner of cruelty.[56] "Merovech made many charges against his father and his step-mother [Fredegund]"; the chronicler leaves no room for doubt that Merovich's objective was to "possess himself of the whole kingdom."[57]

If in this situation Praetextatus made use of gifts—if only return gifts—to assemble followers for Merovich (which he never denied), then Chilperic could only interpret it as open hostility: "Thou hast set a son at enmity with his father; thou hast led astray the people with bribes that no man might keep with me his plighted faith; thou hast sought to betray my kingdom into the hands of another [i.e., Merovich]."[58]

What is interesting is that although his interpretation was apparently not incorrect, Chilperic still did not prevail in court through legitimate means. Why was this? Apparently he could not offer clear enough proof, and could not—officially—permit the use of all available means to remove the bishop. Thus, scarcely had he accused the bishop when "there rose a great murmur from the crowd of Franks without; they wished to break in the doors of the church, drag forth the bishop, and stone him." However underhanded and scheming he would be in his later resolution of the affair, "the king forbade" the stoning.[59] Here, as during the entire trial, he kept up appearances before the assembled bishops. It seems that Praetextatus, who was hardly an innocent, clearly had the better norms on his side.

A Welcome Duty

Praetextatus demonstrated this fact one last time in justifying his search for trusty followers. As he put it, "'had it been permitted, I would have summoned not mortal man, but an angel from heaven to succour him [Merovich]; for, as I have often repeated, he was my spiritual son, from his baptism.'"[60] Whatever his true objectives may have been, once again he successfully cited a norm, in this case, the father's duty to offer his son complete and unconditional protection—even, one might add, if he was planning a revolt.

With this, the king, whose actions were observed and thus controlled by at least forty-five bishops and who had to reach a collective judgment,[61] clearly had exhausted the legitimate means at his disposal. If we are to believe the chronicler, it was only by using a trick that he managed to get the bishop to confess (according to Gregory, falsely) that he had been involved in the son's insurrection after all.[62]

Praetextatus must have believed that all the arguments he brought forward could really defend him. Thus, they appear to have belonged to the canon of what people believed to be the normal and decent thing to do. As far as we can tell, Chilperic had to accept them. The norms cited by Praetextatus did, indeed, possess the power to justify his actions, which, to be sure, is not the same thing as the power to determine actions as well. Why the bishop actually supported his godson is another question altogether. Did he feel that it was his duty as a godfather? Did Merovich possess the means to compel him to act in one way or another? Or did Praetextatus ally himself with the rebel for other, perhaps political, motives, cleverly defending himself once betrayed? Why was it not mentioned in the trial that Praetextatus was also Chilperic's cofather *(compater)*?[63] Could not Chilperic, for his part, have reproached Praetextatus for violating the duties of cofatherhood, which in most cases seem to have been the truly significant ones?[64] He did not do so, and this is a universal phenomenon: not once do we find an actor or the commenting chronicler accusing someone of neglecting his duties as a *compater* or baptismal sponsor. Was it perhaps impossible to demand the fulfillment of these duties after all? When and how securely could one rely on such obligations as Praetextatus refers to here? Could one really not remind one's godson or *compater* of his duty? The story of Praetextatus does not answer these questions, but the cases that follow are clearer.

Ageric of Verdun as Childebert II's Godfather

We have accounts of two sponsorship relationships from the Austrasian dynasty because certain Austrasian nobles relied on sponsorship ties in times of crisis: Ageric of Verdun's sponsorship of Childebert II and Magneric of Trier's sponsorship of Childebert's son Theudebert. Let us begin with Ageric.

King Sigibert I of Austrasia (561–75) chose Bishop Ageric of Verdun as godfather to his son, Childebert (II). Gregory writes of it in his account of Gunthchramn Boso, the ringleader in both the Austrasian "palace revolution" and the rebellion by the usurper Gundovald.[65] This Gunthchramn Boso had taken refuge with Bishop Ageric of Verdun around 586-87 to escape pursuit by King Childebert, and the chronicler claims to know why, remarking that he expected "to obtain pardon through the mediation of Bishop Ageric, who had been sponsor to the king at his baptism."[66] Long negotiations ensued which Gregory describes in detail. He fails to mention, though, what motives drove King Sigibert to chose Ageric, of all people, to sponsor his son, so that, once again, we must make do with some suppositions on the significance and location of Verdun and the bishop.

One of the Citizens of the Town

If Gregory does not tell us why Sigibert chose Ageric, he at least says something about the role of Verdun in that period, as well as shedding light on Ageric's role.

We begin with Verdun, with which city the Merovingians had had ties ever since the days of Clovis. During a revolt by the citizens, a presbyter of the city named Euspicius is said to have negotiated a peace with King Clovis. According to the account, Clovis thereupon tried to appoint this presbyter bishop of Verdun.[67] According to Gregory's *History*, Clovis' son Theuderic I (511–34) "had done many injuries" to Bishop Desideratus and robbed him of his property.[68] His son and successor, Theudebert I (534–48), in contrast, had made the city rich. Bishop Desideratus had borrowed money from him and passed it on to the city's impoverished merchants in order to establish in Verdun such trade "as other cities can show."[69] From this account, we may conclude that Verdun was not exactly a flourishing metropolis at that time. The citizens did achieve a certain measure of wealth, however, "and to this day are held in great consideration," with the very money provided by the king, who did not even want it back, so that it was he who "thus enriched the citizens of Verdun."[70] In Gregory's day, the *civitas* was known for its lively commerce, the bishop appears in the role of *patronus*, and he remained in contact with the kings. Childebert, too, appears to have maintained an interest in Verdun. Not only did he donate lands in the Moselle region and Lorraine to the Verdun church during Ageric's tenure, but more conspicuously yet, he appointed his referendary, Charimer, as Ageric's successor.[71]

As for the role played by Ageric, it would be interesting to know when, and especially by whose appointment, he became bishop. But we can do no more than venture a guess here. We last hear of Ageric's predecessor at a synod held in 549. Of Ageric, we at least know that he was a citizen of Verdun.[72] Gregory mentions his appointment only in passing in connection with events that occurred after 555, so that Ageric may also have been appointed after that date.[73] This is a useful hint, since that is the year when the Austrasian branch of the Merovingians died out with Theudebald. From that time forward, the eastern kingdom was co-ruled by the Neustrian Chlothar I (d. 561), whose reign evidently was plagued by difficulties.[74] At such a time of weakened royal power the appointment of a bishop "from among the citizens,"[75] that is, the city's notables, seems likely.

That he probably belonged to the group of notables opens, if only vaguely, another aspect that might have increased his importance for the king. Ursio and Bertefred, two of the leaders of the nobles who appear later under Childebert's minority and became involved in revolts and conspiracies, also came from the region of Verdun.[76] One of them, Bertefred, like Gunthchramn Boso, had sought protection from Ageric. In both cases, Ageric proved a reliable, if ultimately unsuccessful, ally.[77] A third case has come down to us, in which Ageric is said to have intervened successfully on behalf of a nobleman (*vir valde nobilis*) sentenced to death.[78]

We need to ask why these nobles placed their trust in Ageric and why he intervened on their behalf. This was the sort of help one could reasonably expect from a bishop, and one might argue that these persecuted men facing death were simply turning to the instance responsible for such hopeless cases. The institution, one might conclude, here personified by Ageric, was merely serving its social function.

Social historians, however, cannot simply explain conduct by referring to duties or norms. We need to explain why a given norm was followed in one case and not in another. The decisive question is why, in this specific case, Ageric in particular did what was referred to at the same time as his religious duty, and why an insurgent like Gunthchramn Boso knew in advance that he could count on his help. A comparison between two episodes the chronicler recounts about Gunthchramn Boso helps illuminate his reasoning. The first episode is Gunthchramn Boso's flight to Ageric, on which the chronicler offers the following commentary: "[He hoped] to obtain pardon through the mediation of Bishop Ageric, who had been sponsor to the king at his baptism. The bishop hastened to intercede for him [Gunthchramn Boso] with the king."[79] As a result of a number of circumstances that may be ignored here, Boso soon found himself forced, once again, to seek refuge with a bishop, in this case, Magneric of Trier, who was also godfather to a king. This story reads quite differently from that of his flight to Ageric in Verdun. In the case of Magneric, Gunthchramn Boso was not content to hope. Instead, he appeared before the bishop with his "drawn sword," and the following exchange ensued:

> The bishop was dismayed at this threat, and answered: 'How can I do aught, if I am kept here by thee? Release me, that I may go and entreat the compassion of the king; haply he will have mercy upon thee.' Guntram answered: 'Not so; but send thy abbots and persons in thy confidence to set forth what I have said to thee.'[80]

Apparently Boso felt surer of the one than of the other, and Ageric had, in fact, "interceded," not without effect. Magneric, in contrast, apparently used his vague promises that the king might "haply" have mercy on Boso in order to escape the threatening situation. The chronicler, at any rate, believed that Magneric had no serious intentions of protecting the rebel, adding, "But these things were not told to the king as they were; the messengers only said that the bishop was protecting Guntram [Boso]."[81]

The narrative does not permit any more precise conclusions. It does not explain why the rebel trusted Ageric but not Magneric. It may be that Ageric had simply gained more respect through his fulfillment of Christian obligations. It may also be that loyalties forged in everyday economic and social relations, which we can no longer reconstruct, were operating here. Even without further explanation, the bishop's activities offer some help in explaining Sigibert's choice of sponsor: if Ageric was a reliable ally of the king's enemies, then he might have been dangerous for the king, or at least of dubious loyalty. Sigibert may have hoped that by making Ageric his son's godfather, he could shift the balance in his own favor.

In choosing Ageric as a sponsor, Sigibert thus appears to have been pursuing interests similar to those which moved Chilperic when he selected Praetextatus of Rouen: King Sigibert chose a bishop whom he could scarcely have appointed himself, indeed, one who may have attained the episcopal dignity at a time when royal power in Austrasia was extremely weak (555–61). In Ageric Sigibert selected as sponsor the bishop of one of the most important cities in his realm, a city also on the road linking Metz and Reims, the two main cities of the Austrasian Merovingians. In contrast, nothing points to a close relationship between bishop and royal dynasty before the baptismal sponsorship. It is more a reflection of present-day assumptions than empirical evidence when, as is occasionally the case,[82] scholars cite this sponsorship tie as proof of the good relationship between the bishop of Verdun and the kings. What is likelier is that the sponsorship was intended as a means of creating this good relationship in the first place, and of binding to the king the bishop of a key *civitas*, which was in the domain of powerful and potentially dangerous nobles. There is no indication whether, or how, the king or his son, Childebert, made actual use of this tie. That a certain bond existed is at least documented; some subjects attempted to make use of this relationship.

A Clever Godson

If Gunthchramn Boso fled in great peril from Childebert to Ageric, hoping "to obtain pardon through the mediation of Bishop Ageric, who had been sponsor to the king at his baptism," this meant two things: first, that he actually expected Ageric to intervene on his behalf; and, second, that he expected this intervention to be successful. The first point presents us with the question of Ageric's relationship to Gunthchramn Boso and some other nobles, and offers some clues as to the reasons for Sigibert's choice of sponsor. The second—Boso's faith in the success of the intervention—involves the bishop's relationship to King Childebert and thus a relationship that was (at least additionally) defined by sponsorship. The chronicler devotes a few sentences to the encounter between these two men: "Ageric, who had been sponsor to the king at his baptism. . . . hastened to intercede for him [Gunthchramn Boso] with the king, who, feeling unable to refuse the petition, said: 'Let him first come before us and give sureties; thereafter let him go before our uncle; we will put into execution whatever our uncle will decide.'"[83] And when Ageric brought the insurgent forward the "king

... gave him into the hands of the bishop, saying: 'Let him remain in thy charge, holy bishop, until he appear before King Guntram.'"[84]

The neighboring king, Gunthchramn, was thus supposed to decide matters. Was Childebert "still too young to rule in his own right"?[85] Was he trying to evade the issue,[86] and if so, why? Why was he "unable to refuse"? There is ample evidence that Gunthchramn never ruled in Austrasia.[87] Childebert also had been active often enough as a magistrate, sitting in judgment over the noble Waddo in 590, Theodore of Marseille in 585, and originally also Gunthchramn Boso; at any rate, Ageric turned not to Gunthchramn but to Childebert.[88] A murder in Tours was also tried before Childebert's royal tribunal in 584–85.[89] Thus, Childebert lacked neither the actual power nor the necessary legitimation to summon the insurgent before his own court. The fact that he nevertheless turned the case over to his uncle demands some other explanation.

One interpretation might be that it was fundamentally difficult for the king to ignore the intervention of a bishop.[90] This may have been the case, but it is extremely vague and ignores the fact that, in this case, the chronicler suggested a more concrete solution: the bishop "had been sponsor to the king at his baptism" and for that reason the king's hands were tied. The chronicler, at least, asserts that he felt "unable to refuse the petition" because of the sponsorship bond.

As events developed, it indeed seems that the king could not formally refuse the petition, but at most undermine its effects. Childebert did, in fact, agree to his godfather's request; actually, he, who was under duress, did not punish the rebel Boso. This was of no use to the latter, however, for Childebert took precautions: he did not exact punishment, which he may have felt "unable" to do after the intervention, but he was quite capable of having Boso punished by others. In sharp contrast to his usual politics,[91] Childebert, who was powerful and legitimate enough to take care of matters himself, delegated Boso to the court of his uncle, Gunthchramn. The latter, apparently free of any obligation to Ageric, was just the right judge in this case. As if wanting to lay his cards on the table right away, Childebert immediately built in further insurance: just to be on the safe side, "it had been decided" that the king's godfather, Ageric, should be excluded from Gunthchramn's court in order to prevent him from intervening again.[92]

Other men persecuted by the king also appear to have relied on Ageric. The chronicler reports that another rebel, Bertefred, fled to the church at Verdun, "more especially as Bishop Ageric was living there."[93] He seems to have placed less faith in the asylum than in the person of the bishop. It did not save him, to be sure, but as Gregory emphasizes, he was killed without Childebert's knowledge. The latter even tried to console his spiritual father Ageric with presents.[94] We might also recall the case of that anonymous *vir valde nobilis* who was pardoned upon Ageric's request after being sentenced to death.⁹⁵ All these men clearly trusted in the influence Ageric could exert over his godson, Childebert.

It is Childebert's behavior in particular that sheds light on the quality of this influence. We know of Childebert's obligation, for Bishop Praetextatus had referred to it before Chilperic's royal tribunal: for baptismal kin, he had argued, one would if necessary enlist the aid of the angels in heaven.⁹⁶ Childebert apparently could not afford to ignore the duties of the sponsorship bond. For the time being, the rebel had widened his scope, but he was neither forgiven nor out of danger. We would do better to seek an explanation here in the realm of honor and reputation than that of "conscience" or a "binding of the will," even if such aspects may well need to be considered in other examples. This finding is not insignificant for illuminating social techniques: the rebels placed some hope in this pressure. The example that follows will be even clearer.

MAGNERIC OF TRIER AS THEUDEBERT'S GODFATHER

In 585, "a son was born to King Childebert and received from the sacred font by Magneric, bishop of Trèves. The boy was named Theudebert."⁹⁷ Two years later, because of this sponsorship tie, Magneric, like Ageric of Verdun before him, found himself unwillingly involved in Gunthchramn Boso's conflicts with the kings. Childebert had left it to his uncle, King Gunthchramn, to pass judgment on Boso, who had to appear in court without Ageric's protection. The trial was held in 587 at Andelot and the rebel was sentenced to death.

A Clever "Cofather"

No sooner had he fled to Ageric of Verdun to escape Childebert's wrath than Gunthchramn Boso once again found himself in mortal danger. Yet again, he sought refuge with a protector:

> As soon as news of this reached him, he flew to the dwelling of Bishop Magneric, shut out all the clergy and the servants, fastened the doors, and spoke as follows: 'I know, most blessed bishop, that the kings hold thee in high honour, and now I have fled to thee to escape from them. . . . Therefore know thou, clearly that if thou rescue me not, first will I slay thee, and then go forth to meet my death.'

He went on to explain why he had fled to Magneric: "'. . . holy bishop, I know that thou art father in common with the king [Childebert] of his son

[Theudebert] . . . and that whatsoever thou askest of him shall be granted thee, nor can he refuse thy sanctity anything which thou shalt request.'"[98] The rebel had once again intentionally sought out a godfather, for, as he knew *(novi)*, Childebert could not "refuse . . . [him] anything *(nec negari omnino poterit)*" he asked for. This explanation will sound familiar by now; as the chronicler had commented in the case of Ageric, Childebert felt "unable to refuse" his sponsor's petition. There were, however, differences between the two cases. Ageric was Childebert's own sponsor, while Magneric was his son's godfather. His tie with Magneric was that of a "father in common" *(pater communis)* or—as other documents put it—of a "cofather" *(compater)*.[99] This episode probably is the earliest evidence of cofatherhood as a socially relevant phenomenon.

Compared with the example of Praetextatus, it also reveals a new aspect of social relevance. Praetextatus had tried in court to justify his conduct as deftly as possible, using whatever norms seemed most opportune. Norms were of interest to him for their legitimating power. For Boso, however, only those norms of conduct for baptismal kin that actually had a normative effect, and that were likely to be obeyed, were of any use. If he relied twice on these institutionalized normative sponsorship ties, they must indeed have had a socially regulating effect.

This does not, to be sure, tell us anything about *how* they regulated social behavior. Childebert's reaction to Ageric's intervention indicates one possibility: regulation as social control, and obedience as honorable behavior. Such obedience was, not least, a question of cleverness, and Childebert appears to have been the cleverer party here. He not only protected himself by excluding his sponsor, Ageric, from the trial. After all, Boso could have replaced the latter with Childebert's "father in common" Magneric. Childebert had, however, also withdrawn from the affair and left its resolution to his uncle Gunthchramn, who had nothing to do with Childebert's cofathers. If he believed that Magneric was protecting the accused, he could, without any breach of the rules, also order the killing of his nephew's godfather. What becomes apparent here is that ritual kinship, unlike its biological counterpart, did not function at several removes. There was no defined relationship between the uncle and his nephew's father from the font. Childebert withdrew from his obligations to his spiritual kin without violating them—an action, incidentally, by means of which he publicly bowed to the norms at the same time.

Another Metropolitan

We still need to consider what Childebert stood to gain by making Magneric his son's godfather. Why was Childebert interested in Magneric or the city of Trier? What was Trier's role here, and what was Magneric's?

Like Rouen, Trier was the seat of a metropolitan bishop. We know practically nothing about Trier's economic significance in the sixth century, but at least some traces of bygone splendor remained: there was a market, the city participated in the salt trade and long-distance trade more generally, and coins were minted there.[100] We have a good deal of information about the prominent position held by Magneric's predecessor Nicetius. He corresponded with the Langobard kings[101] and was one of the last clerics in Gaul to participate in theological debates with the East.[102] His Byzantine contacts must have been attractive for both Austrasian dynasties, since both sought good relations with the emperor,[103] and even enforced Byzantine laws.[104] Nicetius often came into conflict with the kings, for example, with Theudebert[105] and the Neustrian Chlothar, who ultimately banished him.[106] Venantius lauds the political achievements of Nicetius[107] who probably was the only bishop who had already managed to displace the *comes* in the sixth century.[108]

During the era of Nicetius, at least, the old imperial city played a significant role in the itinerary of the Merovingians. It is doubtful whether Theuderic I had already sojourned there,[109] but his son Theudebert appears to have held court in Trier on numerous occasions, probably as the first Merovingian to do so.[110] In any case the *civitas* possessed a *palatium* and received gifts from the Merovingians early on.[111]

With the death of Nicetius, the interesting political information ends. The authors report only Magneric's pastoral activities.[112] Gregory is silent on why he considered him a great bishop.[113] Magneric's presence at Andelot is the only indication we have that he enjoyed any political clout in Austrasia. On the other hand, there is no indication that, for example, the *comites* managed to reestablish themselves in the *civitas*; thus it may make the most sense to apply the conditions prevailing in Nicetius' day to Magneric's.

We have no evidence that the bishop maintained particularly good relations with the court and was chosen as a godfather for that reason, as some scholars have assumed.[114] His presence at Andelot is no proof of good relations; despite widespread assumptions about the relations between the nobility and the kings in Austrasia, the participation of nobles and bishops was probably more a reflection of their actual power than a sign of royal favor.[115] Neither does the fact that only Magneric is mentioned by name[116] deserve particular attention, inasmuch as he was only one of several bishops present, as the text of the pact shows ("agreed between them with the concourse of their bishops and chief men").[117] Gregory mentions him only because he became embroiled in the affair against his will. The only other confirmation of Magneric's influence is Gunthchramn Boso's assertion that he could get anything he wanted from Childebert,[118] but this assertion still does not indicate the reason why Magneric became a godfather. On the contrary, it touches only on the duties of a sponsor, doing nothing to shed light on the purpose of such a choice of godfather. On the whole, there is no way to tell whether Magneric was a "loyal supporter" of the Austrasian dynasty[119] and "trusty follower of Queen Brunechildis and her son Childebert"[120] or possessed "great significance at Childebert's court."[121] We also have no serious evidence of the opposite, that Magneric was perhaps in league with the aristocracy.[122]

If, despite the meager documentation, we nevertheless wish to venture a summary conclusion, two aspects should be emphasized. First, the bishops of Trier were particularly successful in expanding their power at the expense of the royally appointed *comites;* second, they did not present themselves as partisans of the kings. Magneric was no protégé of the court, but rather of his predecessor, Nicetius.[123] If Magneric later appeared as godfather to the king's son the value of this sponsorship too should be sought in Childebert's interest in binding a man with local authority more closely to himself.

Let us take another look at the Austrasian context. Assuming that the choice was a political one, who were the potential candidates for sponsor in Austrasia? Apart from the royal seats of Reims and Metz, the only cities in Austrasia of any greater significance were Verdun and Trier and, perhaps, on the outermost frontiers, Cologne and Mainz. The last two are mentioned much less frequently, however.[124] Bishop Aegidius of Reims was a sworn enemy of Brunechildis,[125] and Ageric of Verdun was already Childebert's godfather. This left only Trier and Metz, and here we may be inclined to agree with Reinhold Kaiser's assessment that the bishops of the royal cities were not so dangerous because they had relatively little economic might.[126] As we know absolutely nothing about Bishop Petrus of Metz, however, these speculations cannot take us very far.

Samson's Godfather

The sponsorship bonds analyzed up to now show the political and social functions of baptismal kinship, which we will encounter later in the relationships among laypersons. Among the Merovingians' episcopal sponsors, however, there were two who were obviously chosen for other reasons. They were the godfathers of Samson, one of Chilperic's sons, and Theuderic, a son of Childebert's.

An Emergency

For 577 Gregory reports:

> After this, Samson, younger son of King Chilperic, was attacked by dysentery and fever, and passed from the world of men. He was born at the

time when Chilperic was besieged by his brother in Tournai; and his mother, from fear of death, cast him away from her, and would have let him die. The king chid her, and having failed in her desire, she ordered the child to be baptized. He was christened, the bishop himself receiving him from the water, but he died before he reached five years.[127]

The royal infant Samson was thus born in 575, at a time when Sigibert was besieging Chilperic, then entrenched at Tournai.[128] Two years later, the child fell seriously ill and was baptized. Gregory had not mentioned Samson's birth in his account of the events of 575 and made up for this in his narrative for 577. Here he mentions Tournai as the place of birth but not the *civitas* in which Samson fell ill and was baptized in 577. Thus we cannot identify the sponsor, who was the bishop of that city. But if we choose to speculate, there is at least one important clue: that Chilperic usually held court in Paris and that there is evidence of his presence there during the period in question.[129] Thus, if an ailing son suddenly had to be baptized in 577, with "the bishop himself receiving him from the water," the most likely sponsor was Bishop Ragnemod of Paris, whom, after Samson's death, Chilperic later chose as godfather to another of his sons. This, however, is a mere statistical consideration requiring no further elaboration since, in this case, the choice of sponsor clearly was random, determined solely by the emergency situation. It remains remarkable, however, that in the case of even such a chance baptism, Gregory knew who the sponsor was and that this Merovingian child, like Merovich before him, had remained unbaptized two years after his birth.

To be sure, this bishop was chosen for reasons of convenience. The important thing here was not the sponsor but the baptism itself. Fredegund apparently hoped that the baptism would ensure her son's recovery. This was not a new idea, and by no means a product of the early Middle Ages. Augustine had already warned one of his correspondents against such practices and notions.[130] We begin to encounter such accounts with any frequency only in the early Middle Ages, and the present account is a particularly instructive one for the light it sheds on prevailing ideas.[131] Generally such narratives appeared in the Lives of the Saints, which quite naturally focused on the powers of the saintly sponsor, the man of God. Miraculous cures demonstrated the saint's merits. An emphasis on the efficacy of holy water in such a cure would have been not merely superfluous but even harmful, inasmuch as it would have deflected attention from, or even diminished, the hero's achievements.[132] There was no saint to praise at Samson's baptism. Samson was received from the font by some bishop or other. It was the holy water of baptism, the concrete and actual effect of the water as consecrated matter, that was supposed to save the life of the king's son.[133]

Veranus of Cavaillon as Theuderic's Godfather

The most remarkable tale is that involving Bishop Veranus of Cavaillon. As Gregory recounts: "This year [587] another son was born to King Childebert. He was received from the font by Veranus, bishop of Cavaillon, and was given the name Theuderic."[134] Veranus is the only godfather to a king we know of who came from an episcopate in southern Gaul, a tiny one at that, and the only one whose see was not within the kingdom of the baptizee.[135] He was, finally, also the only saint among them.

The *civitas* of Cavaillon seems to have been insignificant—at least it is mentioned nowhere—and the bishopric was established relatively late, at the end of the fourth century.[136] Its small territory was apparently further reduced by the founding of Carpentras, probably in the fifth century.[137] Apart from Veranus, we find no particular mention of any bishop of the *civitas* during the Merovingian period.[138] Whether the city, which came under Gunthchramn's rule in 561, attained any significance after 561 (because of its location on the border dividing Burgundy from the Austrasian corridor to the Mediterranean) is not documented,[139] unless we choose to take the sponsorship as evidence of this.

We know nothing of the origins and career of the bishop, who was appointed between 554 and 585, except that the sources twice place him in proximity to King Gunthchramn. Veranus was part of Gunthchramn's delegation charged with investigating the murder of Praetextatus of Rouen and he was also present at a meeting between Burgundian bishops and the king in 589.[140]

Scholars have offered several possible motives for King Childebert's choice of this bishop as a sponsor. According to Eugen Ewig, "the succession of Childebert's elder son Theudebert II in Austrasia and of the younger Theuderic II in Franco-Burgundy was probably already resolved during Gunthchramn's lifetime, as the sponsorship of Theudebert by the bishop of Trier, and of Theuderic by the bishop of Chalon [he means Cavaillon] shows."[141] What, then, are we to make of Fredegar's assertion that Theuderic and Theudebert received their subkingdoms by lot?[142] Margarete Weidemann's suggestion that Childebert was seeking to assert himself vis-à-vis Gunthchramn makes more sense. In her interpretation, he chose a sponsor from Gunthchramn's kingdom in order to demonstrate a claim to Burgundy that arose out of the acts of 577 and 585.[143] Childebert himself had been made Gunthchramn's sole heir and had been called on to act as coregent in Burgundy and to undertake a royal progress.[144] Gunthchramn's improved relations with Neustria had, however, aroused Childebert's suspicions, and according to the chronicler he lodged a complaint with Gunthchramn regarding the latter's relations to Neustria soon after this baptism.[145] The complaint was preceded by Neustrian negotiations with Gunthchramn over a date for Chlothar's baptism, at which Gunthchramn was supposed to act as godfather. As we shall see, this was the immediate occasion for Childebert's suspicions.[146] Thus, it is conceivable that Childebert intended to assert his claim to Burgundy by choosing Veranus as a sponsor.

A Friend of God

These attempts at explanation nevertheless remain surprising, since this is one case in which Gregory actually mentions a reason for the choice of godfather: "This bishop [Veranus] was at this time endowed with great power of miracle, and when he made the sign of the Cross over the sick by God's aid they were often restored to health."[147] In these few words the chronicler sketches a social type that we encounter with increasing frequency from late antiquity on: "making the sign of the Cross over the sick" and restoring them to health "by God's aid" was the practice of the holy man, the *vir dei*.[148] Gregory, chronicler and hagiographer, always describes these men's deeds in a similar manner: for the ascetic priest Julian, "it was a simple thing to heal the possessed, give sight to the blind, and drive forth all other infirmities by calling on the name of the Lord and making the sign of the holy Cross."[149] Another man "destroyed the poison of malignant pustules" by making the sign of the Cross, and "by prayer cast out evil spirits from the bodies of the possessed."[150] Yet another "restored [the sick] to health by laying on of hands with the sign of the Cross."[151]

These men evidently[152] enjoyed increasing popularity beginning in late antiquity since their ascetic achievements supposedly enabled them to offer assistance in practically any situation from fires, storms, illnesses, and demonic possession to infertility.[153] What form these beliefs actually took is less interesting here[154] than the fact that people were apparently prepared to grant these men authority and thus power.[155] We have an account concerning Childebert's mother Brunechildis in which she attempted to harness this power for her own interests. After Childebert's death she had to secure her great-grandsons' claims to the succession. Their legitimacy was in question because they had been born to a concubine *(de concubina)*. In this matter Brunechildis turned not to a bishop but to the Irish ascetic monk Columbanus, saying: "They are the king's children, lend thou them strength with *thy* blessing."[156] She apparently regarded less the blessing itself than the holy man Columbanus *(... tu ... tua ...)* as the guarantor of success. That she believed in the certain efficacy of this supernatural fortification is likely, although we cannot demonstrate it. What is clearer is that the boys would doubtless have been the stronger with the holy man's worldly authority on their side. Let us recall the pope's famous 751 dictum on behalf of the Carolingians. When Columbanus could not be won over to the queen's side, and refused to give his blessing, she had him expelled from the kingdom.[157]

If, in sharp contrast to all that we have observed up to now, King Childebert chose such a holy man as godfather to his son, it was no less of a practical political action than any other Merovingian sponsorship tie. He secured for his son those supernatural powers which the friend of God could invoke with the sign of the Cross, as well as access to the authority of the holy man, whose fame henceforth would be linked with the royal child's name. In exchange for this, he apparently was willing to accept a bishop who ruled over an insignificant see, far from the center of Austrasian power.[158]

Ragnemod of Paris as Theuderic's Godfather

Let us turn now to the last recorded sponsorship of a king's son by a bishop. In 582, a son was born to Chilperic and the name Theuderic chosen for him.[159] At Easter the following year, Bishop Ragnemod of Paris became the infant's godfather. "He [Chilperic] kept the Easter feast with great cheer, and caused his son to be baptized. The boy was received from the font by Ragnemod, bishop of Paris, and by the king's will was named Theuderic."[160] Ragnemod's situation must have been quite different from that of Praetextatus, whom Chilperic had selected to sponsor an earlier son. In choosing Ragnemod, we may assume that he had other interests in mind.

A "Sycophant"

Although Paris had been rendered neutral in the partition pact of 567, the Neustrian Chilperic had resided there since the death of King Sigibert (in 576), who probably had already violated the pact.[161] In the very "first year of his [Childebert's] reign King Chilperic came to Paris, seized Brunhild and banished her to Rouen."[162] In 577, he sat in judgment on Bishop Praetextatus in Paris,[163] and in his account of the year 579 Gregory mentions Parisian citizens who were "among the first at the court of Chilperic."[164] In 580 the king interred a son in St. Denis[165] and he apparently also stayed in Paris on numerous other occasions.[166] Thus when Chilperic entered Paris at Easter 583 for Theuderic's baptism, with relics carried on before him, purportedly because he feared punishment for breaching the pact,[167] he had already reigned there for seven years.

Ragnemod had been bishop of Paris for seven years. His predecessor, Germanus, had died on May 28, 576, about six months after Sigibert's death.[168] Chilperic must already have been reigning in Paris at that time.[169] Thus, just a few months later, he could appoint the new bishop, Ragnemod, whom we know only as an ally of Chilperic's.[170] The situation, then, was not comparable to those we have treated thus far: Rouen, Verdun, and Trier. Paris was not an ecclesiastical metropolitan city, but rather belonged to Sens,[171] and the king did not need to gain the bishop's support since he had already seen to his appointment. What's more, the bishop of Paris can scarcely have been a threat to the king's power. To be sure, as everywhere he had property rights over the suburbican places of worship,[172] but the ruler's extensive personal land holdings[173] and the presence in Paris of the king, who probably had also appointed a *comes*,[174] make it unlikely that Ragnemod was among the most powerful bishops. At any rate, he evidently showed more obsequiousness toward Chilperic than other bishops did, leading Gregory of Tours to immortalize him in the *History* as a sycophant *(adolator)*.[175]

A Political Display

If the choice of Ragnemod cannot be explained in terms of his political power, the action nonetheless lends itself to a political explanation. Ragnemod was, after all, the bishop of the old royal capital, possession of which the subkings could not decide peacefully. By choosing this old capital as the site of the baptism, and its fairly harmless bishop as the sponsor, Chilperic, could, as he had done in interring a son at St. Denis, emphasize his ties and claims to Paris. In this case, the sponsorship bond may have been interesting less as a means of creating an alliance than as an instrument of political display. This aspect, which has been less prominent in previous examples, was to play a major role in the baptism of Chlothar II. Just as the missionizing Carolingians would later use baptism and sponsorship for their imperial self-representation,[176] these rituals already served as instruments of political prestige among the Merovingians. Chilperic had celebrated the baptism of his son lavishly and "with great cheer" and had made a solemn entry into the city accompanied by the "the relics of many saints" for this very purpose.[177]

The question remains why a royal infant born in 582 was not baptized until 583. The most likely reason is that the king wanted to wait until the next Easter, as suggested by the ecclesiastical regulations prevailing in Gaul.

They stipulated the feasts of Epiphany, Easter and Whit Sunday as dates for baptism.[178] Chilperic's preference for Paris as the location and Ragnemod as sponsor, at any rate, does not seem to have been the reason for the delay. All of Book IV of the *History* places King Chilperic in Paris.[179] The ceremony thus followed a very logical order: the king's son was received from the font in the city where the king was residing at the appointed time by the local bishop.

10
Sponsorship Bonds (2): Nobles and Bishops, Kings and Outsiders

The chronicler Gregory tells us not only of bishops who were the sponsors of kings, but also of kings who acted as godfathers to their subjects and other royal persons. Finally, he also mentions that he himself was a baptismal kinsman to the king's treasurer. Three of the four episodes with which he was familiar occurred in his own immediate environment. The fourth, in contrast, which occurred more than half a century before, was one he can only have heard about through various mediators, which clearly left a mark in his account. All of these episodes refer to persons who took a practical view of their sponsorship ties, referring to the norms and duties when it was convenient and appearing to ignore them altogether when it was not.

KING THEUDEBERT I AS SIGIVALD'S GODFATHER

These events, which occurred more than forty years before they were recorded, at a time when the chronicler Gregory (born 538 or 539) was six or seven years old, took place in the Austrasia of the second generation of Merovingians. King Theuderic reigned there until 534, and like the other early Merovingians he tended to get rid of his inconvenient kinsmen. It is in connection with such an action that Gregory mentions sponsorship for the first time. In the year 532, Theuderic undertook a punitive expedition against Clermont, subsequently leaving behind a kinsman *(parentem suum)* named Sigivald "as a sort of guard" *(quasi pro custodia)*.[1] Shortly thereafter, however, he killed this kinsman, confiscated his property and was on the point of having the kinsman's son, also called Sigivald, killed as well.[2] The chronicler does not give more precise details,[3] but does inform us that Theuderic's plans for the son were not carried out.

A Dangerous Kinsman

According to the chronicler, the assault failed because the younger Sigivald had the right godfather at the right moment. King Theuderic had sent "word secretly to [his son] Theudebert that he should put to death Sigivald's son [Sigivald], who was with him at the time. But Theudebert, who had received him from the sacred font, would not so destroy him. . . ."[4] Instead, Theudebert apparently ordered him to flee and to return after Theuderic's death, which actually followed soon thereafter. Gregory then recounts how Theudebert at first successfully defended his inheritance against his fellow kings from the other sub-kingdoms, and how one of these kings, the childless Childebert I, agreed to name him as heir and showered him with gifts. Childebert "gave him [Theudebert] three pairs of all things meet for a king's possession."[5] Then we hear once again of Sigivald, the godson, who returned from exile as planned. Gregory relates that "Theudebert received him with joy, and embraced him, presenting him with a third part of his uncle's gifts. . . ." Theudebert also restored to his godson the goods belonging to Sigivald's slain father.[6] At this point Sigivald disappears from the written record.[7]

On the whole, the story raises more questions than it answers. If we begin by asking what were the elder Sigivald's interests in choosing a godfather, and what value the king's son Theudebert might have had for the two Sigivalds, the answer—in analogy to the previous stories (Praetextatus, Ageric)—might be the neutralization of potential opponents. The two Sigivalds were kinsmen of the Merovingians who somehow had been spared in Clovis's removal campaigns. They continued to live dangerously under the Merovingians of the second generation, who were hard at work expanding and stabilizing Clovis's rule.[8] Following the lines of our previous conclusions, it would have made good sense for the elder Sigivald to try to bind his potentially dangerous kinsman through sponsorship. He would not have been unique in placing his trust in sponsorship; we need only recall the cases of Bertefred and Gunthchramn Boso. And, if we take the later episodes as a yardstick, the elder Sigivald could have created a bond of obligation, not only between his son and the godfather but also between the sponsor, Theudebert, and himself—that is, the boy's cofathers. To be sure, this did not help him in the end, since his murderer, Theuderic, had no part in the bond which the baptism was intended to create. Gregory, however, had no trouble attributing the deliverance of the younger Sigivald to the sponsorship tie: "But Theudebert, who had received him from the sacred font, would not so destroy him. . . ."

We will have to make do with the chronicler's interpretation; his account does not allow us to weigh all the advantages and disadvantages that this act brought Theudebert, the emotional and rational "arguments" that spoke for or against dutiful conduct. We do not know what relationships the two Merovingians maintained with the two Sigivalds, nor the circumstances under which the elder Sigivald was able to invite the king's son to sponsor his son. We also do not know why, as the chronicler claims, the younger Sigivald was staying with his godfather when his father was murdered.

Gregory does, however, provide us with a (for him) rare detail in this case, namely, that "Theudebert received him with joy" and kissed his godson. Although his other accounts emphasize the duties of sponsorship in order to explain actions which not infrequently seemed to be motivated by something else altogether,[9] here he takes a different approach. He has the sponsor feel and act as an ideal godfather; he has Theudebert kiss and embrace *(congaudens ac deosculans)* his godson, just as the presbyter Agnellus would later do with his two merchants *(dilectionem habuerunt in invicem in Spiritu sancto et obsculo pacis)*.[10] This is not surprising: the farther back in time the story lies, and the more people relate it, the more idealized it becomes.

CHILPERIC AS GODFATHER TO THE JEW PATHIR

There is one instance in which Gregory describes a deed by King Chilperic, whom he was otherwise pleased to refer to as the "Nero and Herod of our time," in a favorable light[11]—favorable, to be sure, only because Gregory deemed a detail he mentions in passing to have been both uninteresting and anything but a blot on the king's character:

> In this year [582] King Chilperic ordered the baptism of a number of Jews; he himself received many of them from the sacred font. . . . Priscus, however, could by no argument whatsoever be induced to receive the truth. . . . But in the meantime a dispute arose between him [Priscus] and Phatyr, one of the converted Jews who had become godsons of the king; and on the Sabbath, when Priscus, bound with a kerchief, and carrying naught made of iron, was proceeding to a place apart, to fulfill the laws of Moses, Phatyr came upon him and slew him with the sword, with all those in his company. After they were slain, this man took sanctuary, together with his servants, in the church of the holy Julian, which was in a street hard by. While they remained there, the men heard that the king intended to spare their lord, but that they themselves were to be dragged from the church and put to death. . . . Phatyr received permission to return to the kingdom of Guntram, whence he had come. . . .[12]

For Pathir, the Merovingian king thus proved a useful sponsor, indeed, but it is highly unlikely that he chose him personally. In this case, it was Chilperic, the sponsor, who did the choosing, meaning that in this exceptional case it was the sponsorship's implications for the social or political interests of the godfather that were in the forefront.

A Friend of the Byzantine Emperor

What Gregory's account makes it easy to overlook is the forced nature of the baptisms of the Jews that took place in Neustria in 582.[13] Suddenly in the sixth century, the Frankish kings adopted these measures, which were without any precedent in antique Gaul, and they would continue them until the twelfth or thirteenth century.[14] The Frankish king Chilperic had ordered them himself *(multos Iudaeorum baptizare praecepit)* and even took active part in them by receiving the "converts" from the font *(ex quibus pluris excipit a sancto lavacro)*. Compulsory baptisms of Jews are reported from Clermont as early as 576; the chronicle of Pseudo-Fredegar contains a short note that the last important Merovingian, Dagobert I (d. 638) had carried out forced baptisms. This note of Fredegar's on the measures taken by Dagobert is significant, inasmuch as it provides the necessary context to help us understand these sudden measures. The Byzantine emperor Heraclius had asked Dagobert "to have all the Jews of his kingdom baptized—which Dagobert promptly carried out."[15] Dagobert thus forced the Jews to undergo baptism because he was following the wishes of the emperor of Byzantium. Michel Rouche has shown that we can make a similar assumption about Chilperic. The Neustrian king undertook the baptism of the Jews in 582, the same year the Byzantine emperor adopted similar measures. In the previous year, a Neustrian delegation had returned from Byzantium, and, according to Rouche, they may have learned of the emperor's plans at that time.[16] Thus, in 582, Chilperic appears to have acted in accordance with a Byzantine edict, just as Dagobert was to do later.[17] The fact that one can point to a number of similar practices under Chilperic's reign, which reveal him, on the whole, as an emulator of all things "Roman" and of the emperor, would seem to favor this interpretation. "He wrote two books in verse, taking Sedulius as his model. . . . He wrote other short pieces, hymns and chants for the Mass. . . ."[18] His hymn to Médard,[19] the patron saint of the Neustrian Merovingians—composed in the classical manner on antique models—has survived.[20] Chilperic tried to emulate the emperor as much in his theological essays on the Trinity as in his circus buildings in Paris and Soissons.[21] The letters invented by Chilperic clearly are based on the Greek alphabet; the Emperor Claudius may even have been a model for his expansion of the alphabet.[22] Finally, Gregory relates the king's pride at displaying his Byzantine gifts.[23]

Chilperic's style was not unusual; he is only a particularly clear example of a general tendency among the Germanic kings: *imitatio imperii* and subordination to the emperor at the same time. Theoderic had practiced this, as did Clovis and his successors.[24]

We have good reason to regard the Byzantine emperor as a model not only for Chilperic's campaign of forced baptism but also for sponsorship. The Byzantine emperors had been practicing since the beginning of the sixth century what became common in the West only under the Carolingians. The emperors themselves frequently received from the font those rulers whom their missionaries had converted.[25] To be sure, there is no evidence of a connection between this practice and Chilperic's sponsorship of converted Jews. Since he frequently adopted "Roman" practices, however, which evidently included the Byzantine forced baptisms, it would at least provide a plausible explanation for this unusual measure if he had been emulating the emperor in sponsorship as well.

A Pardon

Chilperic pardoned his murderous godson but had the godson's servants driven from the church and slain. Under whatever law Pathir might normally have been tried, he would surely have been punished for murder,[26] especially because the slain Priscus was probably under the king's protection.[27] The only visible reason for pardoning Pathir, but punishing his servants, was the sponsorship tie. This is all the more remarkable since the king is said to have received "a number of" *(plures)* Jews from the font, and since the events took place in public. The people *(populus)* stood before the church; it was also they who "cruelly" executed the sentence on the servants. Before the eyes of the populace the king proved himself a Christian king, pardoning and shielding his "son" with a *licentia*[28] and acting as befitted a godfather.

If we were tempted to see the powerful force of the sponsorship tie and its obligations at work here, which extended even to breaking the law, we should recall the deceitfulness with which the same Chilperic treated his cofather Praetextatus, that Praetextatus who apparently had had some part in the rebellion of the king's son, Merovich.[29] In the case of Praetextatus, proving a true cofather would not have been without its dangers for Chilperic. In the case of Pathir, there was no risk in acting as duty dictated; on the contrary, it may have been conducive to the self-representation of a legitimate Christian king.

Gregory of Tours as the *Compater* of the Treasurer Eberulf

A Schemer

As if the fact had escaped the notice of his contemporaries, the chronicler once again relates the following about his relationship to a certain Eberulf: "But God. . . . knoweth that I gave him [Eberulf] aid in singleness of heart and to the utmost of my power."[30] Eberulf was a Frankish nobleman from the region of Tours, treasurer to King Chilperic, and, if Gregory is to be believed, a true scoundrel. He had frequently helped himself to the property of the diocesan church of Tours, confiscating a house here, taking land there, and holding banquets in the diocesan church where he also committed murders, tyrannized the populace, and, not least, hatched a number of intrigues *(multas insidias)* against Gregory. This by no means prevented him from taking asylum in the very same church he previously had plundered. He is described as a godless man *(numquam in Deum ullum timorem)* of the worst type,[31] yet this is the man of whom Gregory claims "that I gave him aid in singleness of heart and to the utmost of my power" and "I always bestirred myself right loyally in his affairs. . . ."[32] He even reports a dream in which he physically defended this scoundrel, who had taken refuge in the bishop's church, against an attack by King Gunthchramn.[33]

Whatever Gregory actually did in the concrete situation, apparently it was his intention to present himself to his readers as a reliable ally of the godless Eberulf. He had his reasons: "And though he [Eberulf] had often in time previous dealt treacherously with me in the matter of things belonging to the holy Martin, yet, as I had received his son from the sacred water at his baptism, I had ever a reason to overlook his misdeeds."[34] Put another way, Eberulf could get away with all this scandalous behavior because he was the bishop's cofather, and he could even rely on Gregory's defense in an emergency. It looks as though Gregory was giving himself a testimonial for posterity here—all the more so, considering his portrayal of Eberulf as a *compater* innocent of any idea of obligation.

The fact that Eberulf was apparently unaware of the conscientious assistance of his episcopal cofather should give us cause to examine Gregory's self-representation a bit more closely. Gregory may have portrayed himself as the soul of loyalty, but his cofather Eberulf clearly viewed him as highly perfidious. When King Gunthchramn was preparing to have Eberulf killed and his property confiscated, Eberulf held Gregory responsible ("The blame for this he chiefly threw on me"), "reviling me in every possible way." He swore to take revenge on Gregory if the occasion presented itself.[35] Clearly, he viewed the bishop more as an enemy than the reliable partner whom Gregory presented himself as to his readers.

A little incident that took place in St. Martin's church reveals how little Eberulf trusted his cofather, Gregory. It also shows that Gregory was by no means as solicitous of Eberulf's welfare as he pretended. Eberulf, who had taken asylum in the church, was in the sacristy one evening when Gregory and his priests were singing psalms in the church. Beforehand, one of the priests had nailed up and bolted the door between the church and the sacristy.[36] Gregory provides two interpretations of the episode, his own and Eberulf's. He relates that Eberulf burst into the church and "began to attack me with curses and abuse, reproaching me amid his railings with having sought to keep him from the cloth on the holy bishop's tomb."[37] This would have been a serious threat for Eberulf. It was precisely touching the cover that was considered the actual guarantee of freedom from injury, and Gregory knew this. In the dream in which he defended Eberulf, he had called on the persecuted man to do just what Eberulf accused him of trying to prevent him from doing in real life. In his dream, Gregory claims, he spoke to Eberulf, saying, "'Lay hold, unhappy wretch, of the cloth upon the altar . . . lest thou be cast out hence.'"[38] Thus, he knew the value of the cover; nevertheless, he cut his cofather, Eberulf, off from the possibility of rescue. Eberulf did not allow himself to be appeased "with soothing words" nor his fury "to be overcome . . . by gentle speech."[39]

Gregory, however, goes on to label this fury "madness" (*insania*) and his cofather, Eberulf, as, if not exactly possessed, "so to speak driven of devils."[40] He provides a far more innocent explanation for bolting the door, noting that "girls and other servants of Eberulf would come in by this sacristy door, admire the paintings on the walls, and pry into the ornaments of the blessed tomb, which was a crime against religious feeling"[41] and apparently reason enough for the bishop to forget, whether deliberately (as Eberulf believed) or not, his cofather's life-or-death situation.

In sharp contrast to his dream, on the critical day when Eberulf was killed in his church asylum, Gregory was "staying at a country estate some thirty miles out of the city."[42] He places this information quite skillfully in his narrative. Gregory gives a detailed description of the prolonged preparations for the murder, describing how the murderer first pocketed gifts from the king, then mustered 300 soldiers, took notice of omens, inquired after the holy Martin's favored punishments, took an interest in the speed of divine vengeance and finally set to work in Tours, where he prepared to commit the deed. Then, just as the bishop and chronicler is about to describe the murder itself, he adds, as an aside, that he himself was far away at the time.[43] "Let no reader therefore ask," runs the subtext, "why I did not warn or aid my *compater*."

It is unlikely, though, that these elaborate preparations should have gone unnoticed by the bishop and de facto lord of the city, who could later report them in such precise detail. To be sure, Gregory's mere absence is no proof that he took off to avoid events in town; his journey may have belonged to his everyday duties. It was useful, at any rate, and helped the chronicler provide his readers with a skillfully deployed justification, one that could scarcely be refuted. After all, the readers know only what Gregory chose to tell them. And he does not choose to tell us when he found out about the murder plot. Perhaps Eberulf, in his suspiciousness of his *compater*, was not as "mad" or "driven of devils," as Gregory would have us believe.

Feigned Powerlessness

Something else is odd. However much Eberulf had "dealt treacherously with me in the matter of things belonging to the holy Martin," Gregory "had ever a reason to overlook his misdeeds" because he "had received his son from the sacred water at his baptism."[44] Without questioning the chronicler's sincerity here, we may still ask what he would have done had he *not* received this son from the font—or more properly, what he *could* have done. If we scan Gregory's work for information on the fate of other scoundrels and thieves, we might conclude that there was nothing he could have done.

In almost every case in which a church was robbed (and Gregory recounts numerous such incidents), contemporaries (at least the authors of the texts that have come down to us) interpreted some event that occurred soon thereafter as a punitive miracle. Such crimes were rarely punished by the earthly authorities. What this means here is that the secular authorities usually could not punish theft from churches, not least because it was often the most powerful men closest to the king who were behind such deeds. Eberulf is an example. Thus, those who lacked the power to intervene viewed the injured saints themselves as miraculous avengers. These saints caused some grave robbers to be apprehended by corpses, while others quarreled among themselves and slaughtered each other, or lost their way, fell asleep, simply died, or—a favorite punishment of saints in those days—fell ill.[45] If the scoundrels saw the error of their ways, they were shown mercy and delivered from their suffering—either through cure or death. Gregory's interpretation of the fate of Eberulf fits this pattern.[46]

In short, Gregory attributed to sponsorship what initially was a problem of power relations, using *compaternitas* to explain an inactivity that was no less forced on him: sponsorship as a more palatable reading, a veil over actual power relations.

Brunechildis as Godmother to Bertefred's Daughter

For the year 587, Gregory tells of an apparently dangerous, large-scale uprising of Austrasian nobles. In the course of this rebellion, he has Queen Brunechildis say to one of the rebels, a certain Bertefred, "'Separate thyself from this our enemy [a certain Ursio], and thou shalt have thy life; if not, thou shalt perish with him.'" The chronicler elucidates: "For the queen had received his daughter from the water of baptism, and for this reason was fain to have compassion with him."[47] Once again, Gregory describes someone turning a blind eye because of baptismal kinship.

A Tactic of War

On closer examination, we can find the sociological logic behind Gregory's reference to the duties of godparenthood. Even assuming for a moment that we know nothing of this sponsorship relationship, Gregory's account could still explain why the royal family turned to Bertefred. He was harmless, and "Ursio was the head and fount of all the mischief."[48] This was the assessment of the chronicler, and Childebert's general, Godegisil, appears to have shared it. His feeling, after slaying Ursio, was "'Let there now be peace, for behold the greatest foe of our lords is fallen; let Bertefred have his life.'"[49] If Godegisil did not need a sponsorship tie to save Bertefred's life, then we should think twice before believing, with the chronicler, that Brunechildis' "compassion" owed anything to sponsorship. We need not deny its usefulness in order to bring to the surface what Gregory's rhetoric conceals: the fact that this cofather of Brunechildis was, in relative terms, the least dangerous of the rebels.[50] To be sure, the utility of sponsorship needs to be defined differently—or at least more precisely—than the chronicler does, and the following observation can take us in that direction.

Ursio and Bertefred had barricaded themselves, together with their women and entourage, in a well-fortified place, where they prepared to defend their lives with force of arms.[51] If we were unfamiliar with the chronicler's commentary and had only Brunechildis' offer to Bertefred to go on, the matter would not be difficult to interpret. This offer, which at once threatened death and beckoned with life, has the appearance of a tactic of war with a simple objective: to drive a wedge between the enemy allies.

Such a reading by no means contradicts the chronicler's interpretation: one of the allied rebels was to be promised mercy, and it had to be one with whom it was easy to establish contact and where the prospect of success was good. The idea of reactivating an old relationship now fallen into disuse doubtless seemed a logical one to the royal family. The sponsorship tie between Bertefred and Brunechildis was just such a relationship.

Brunechildis may well have been a pious woman who took her godmotherly duties seriously; but this cannot be inferred from the sources. All that is clear is that, in the given situation, her action, whether taken out of piety or tactical considerations or both, had a social logic beyond Brunechildis' sponsorship obligations: it was the "familial" relationship that the queen activated when it was necessary.

Competing Loyalties

Brunechildis had miscalculated, however. Bertefred is said to have declared, "'I will never forsake him [Ursio], until death rend us asunder.'"[52] Thus he remained loyal to Ursio, not to his comother, a loyalty which can be explained from the chronicler's accounts. On three occasions, Gregory reports that Ursio and Bertefred had made a pact with each other and with other nobles (*coniunctus, conventio, consilium*).[53] He does not, to be sure, tell us how they sealed this pact, whether with an oath or a handshake; but he does report the proclaimed purpose: "under the pretext that he acted on behalf of peace, and wished to prevent quarrels and raids across the frontiers of the two kingdoms"—in actual fact, to murder the king and grab power for himself.[54] What the allies proclaimed (if only as a "pretext") as the purpose of their pact is familiar to us in similar form from the *coniurationes* or guilds of the Carolingian period.[55] These Merovingian noblemen portrayed their coalition as a self-help organization dedicated to the maintenance of peace and security. Doubtless, this was not all that unusual even in the sixth century, for it was precisely in this period that the clergy in many towns apparently founded self-help organizations, much to the displeasure of the bishops, who opposed them energetically and, in the long term, successfully.[56]

As in the case of the clerics' guilds and most self-help organizations of the Carolingian period, the chronicler tells us nothing more precise about the practices and functioning, ties and loyalties of this alliance. The little information we have helps us understand Bertefred's behavior, as well as to grasp the sponsorship tie as an instrument that could, at times, be useless in social practice. Bertefred belonged to an alliance to which he had already sworn allegiance when the queen menacingly presented him with an alternative—one Gregory believed was the sponsorship alliance. The rebel, who had long "murmured" against his *commater*, "and longed once more to humiliate her" was not tempted to accept her offer.[57]

11
An Exemplary Case: Gunthchramn as Chlothar's Godfather

As a sort of conclusion to his accounts of the Merovingians, the chronicler relates the story of how King Gunthchramn became the sponsor of his Neustrian nephew, Chlothar. This is the only baptism Gregory describes using a wealth of politically as well as ritually instructive detail. It took place in the year 591, after much long and "diplomatically" explosive wrangling over the date[1] and evoked vehement protest from the Austrasian Childebert: "'It was no part of thy recent promise to thy nephew Childebert that thou shouldst make his enemies thy friends. But so far as we see, thou keepest nothing of thy pledge, but rather disregardest thy promise and settest this boy on the royal throne in the city of Paris.'"[2] Up until this point, Gunthchramn's activities of 577 (at Pompierre) and 585 and 587 (at Andelot) clearly favored Childebert over his Neustrian cousin Chlothar.[3] Childebert's vehement protest against the baptism, however, gives the impression that the sponsorship had dire consequences for him, threatening his claims as an *adoptivus* who, as the sole surviving male of Gunthchramn's *stirps*, had a contractually guaranteed right to inherit.[4]

Eugen Ewig probably is referring to such a possibility when he remarks that Gunthchramn "as the senior member of the royal dynasty and *presumptive* godfather [filled] the position of father in relation to the Neustrian dynasty."[5] What is at stake here is the complicated issue of contemporaries' concrete intentions when they referred to a sponsor as "father." *How* was such a sponsor "to fill the position of father"? Was he to acquire the rights of paternity or only the duties? Or perhaps only certain rights or duties? In Neustria, we have no evidence pointing to any of these options. Gunthchramn could scarcely have intervened unimpeded there. Soon after Chilperic's death, the nobles insisted on their own rights, although Gunthchramn was still the *presumptive* godfather (and senior).[6] We also should not ignore the circumstance that, when addressing the Parisian population, Gunthchramn himself invoked (as Gregory had done before the people of Poitiers) a concrete legitimation for his interventions: not sponsorship, but *adoptio*.

Doubtless, sponsorship was a tactical tool used by the Neustrian party to pursue their interests after the death of Chilperic. With respect to the function of sponsorship, the most interesting questions here are what concrete success the Neustrians were pursuing, why the ritual act was postponed several times, and what Childebert feared. What purpose was sponsorship supposed to serve, and what was its relationship to *adoptio*? Could it even replace it?

Thus, there is little reason to believe that Gunthchramn could have justified his actions in Neustria with the (planned!) sponsorship. He referred to the *adoptio* of 584 and the inheritance pact of 567. He was, not least, simply all-powerful for a time.[7] Nevertheless, he apparently maintained an interest in the sponsorship; at least, he was willing to tolerate a number of provocations (witness his several fruitless journeys to Paris) along the way to realizing his goal.[8] The Neustrians, too, when they offered Gunthchramn the sponsorship, must have been pursuing some end, if scarcely that of seeing Gunthchramn "in the position of father" (Ewig). The value of sponsorship in this test of strength remains to be revealed; the best way to do so would seem to be an analysis of Gregory's account of the baptism and Fredegar's commentary on it.

Ritual as Political Strategy

Whatever the sponsorship was intended to achieve was ritually constructed in baptism, and the baptism of a king's son was a meticulously planned public spectacle. When Fredegund and the Neustrian nobles offered just this opportunity to their Burgundian neighbor they could count on this rite and its "public" effect. At any rate, the chronicler devotes two sentences of his extensive account to the ritual, which tell us a good deal about the usefulness of this particular sponsorship relationship.

Preparations and Presentation

The chronicler begins by recounting how, in 591, Fredegund asked her dangerous brother-in-law, Gunthchramn, to act as godfather to Chlothar, then nearly seven years old. "'Let my lord the king come to Paris; let him send for my son, his nephew, and bid him receive the consecration of holy baptism; let him with his own hands receive the child from the sacred font. . . .'"[9] According to this invitation, Gunthchramn, the godfather, was supposed to be the active party *(iubeat consecrare)*, and, according to Gregory's account, he was precisely that. Gunthchramn "caused the child to be brought" and "bade preparation for the baptism to be made...." Furthermore, "the king, approaching the sacred font, presented the boy for baptism."[10] The godfather acted, but the mother, Fredegund, took no role in the baptism.

That it was Gunthchramn who initiated preparations should not be interpreted in terms of the office of sponsor. The fact that the baptism was performed in Paris, where Gunthchramn was then reigning king, is explanation enough.

That he "presented the boy for baptism" *(obtulit puerum ad baptizandum)*, however, was part of the rite, and, in light of the liturgical instructions, one that is not without interest here. To the extent that they mention the matter at all,[11] the great majority of the surviving liturgical instructions expressly declare the presentation of the candidate for baptism to be the duty not of the sponsors but of the parents.[12] The compiler of one tenth-century manuscript even made the addendum: "as it is proper *(sicut justum est)*."[13] This means that sponsors and parents must have alternated. The sponsor was supposed to hold the baptizee in his arms at those times when he had to answer as a proxy—that is, during the renunciation of the devil and the recitation of the Creed. Then the parents had to present the child for baptism.

Those liturgical texts that give such unanimous instructions have something else in common: they are all oriented toward the liturgy exported from Rome beginning in the seventh century. If, then, it was the godfather who "presented the boy for baptism" at Chlothar's 591 christening, does this indicate that Gallic practice deviated from Roman practice? Did sponsors in Gaul also take over presentation of children for baptism?

Only a few sacramentaries have survived from Gaul during that period, which, though compiling the texts of prayers, do not—in contrast to the Roman *Ordines* —describe the acts involved. We can, however, compare Gregory's account with the Spanish rite which has many features in common with the Gallic one.[14] Apart from the priest, records of the Spanish liturgy mention only the sponsor as participating in all parts of the rite (renunciation of the devil, the Creed, baptism, enclothing, and anointing).[15] The Frankish "imperial abbot" Benedict of Aniane later compiled the same rite when he was commissioned by Charlemagne with improving a virtually unusable "authentic" Roman sacramentary,[16] which Pope Hadrian had sent the emperor as a model.[17] As in the Spanish example (and in Gregory's account) this abbot, who was able to incorporate autochthonous Frankish practices into his work on the papal codex,[18] mentions only the sponsor apart from the priest. And it does not appear that he was merely leaving out the obvious—namely, the active parents of the Roman liturgy. The so-called *Pontificale Romano-Germanicum*, that grand Ottonian compilation of Roman and autochthonous elements, is even less ambiguous on this point. Here, just before the baptism and after the renunciation of the devil and the Creed, the text explicitly states that the sponsor should present the child for baptism. Some uncertainty persisted, however, for another group of manuscripts of this *Pontificale* offers both possibilities, noting that "when the priests have received the children from the sponsors or the parents, they baptize them."[19]

We must thus consider the possibility that Gunthchramn's presentation of his godchild, Chlothar, in 591 represented a native Gallic baptismal practice, a practice that ritually increased the value of the sponsor—in this case, Gunthchramn. The ritual actions discussed in what follows will confirm this interpretation. It was precisely this strong participation of the sponsor that must have been quite useful for the Neustrians, if, as I maintain, the baptismal events were to be used for purposes of 'interstate' relations.

Receiving from the Font: Ritual Assistance or Familial Association?

How could the Neustrians use sponsorship for their sociopolitical purposes? Is there any evidence for Arnold Angenendt's suggestion that this sponsorship "included a politically significant adoption" and thus represented serious competition to Gunthchramn's bond with Childebert?[20] Let us see how the chronicler continues: "And lifting him from the holy font . . . he desired him to be named Chlothar."[21] Here, too, we recognize another piece of ritual: Gunthchramn's assistance as the person who both presented the boy *(obtulit puerum ad baptizandum)* and lifted *(excipiens")* him from the font.

It is at this point in the rite that Angenendt inserts his argument, positing "that baptismal sponsorship was brought together with . . . acts of 'lifting' which were of relevance in family law."[22] According to Angenendt, such "acts of 'lifting' . . . of relevance in family law" existed among the Romans as well as the Germanic peoples. Among the Germanic peoples, fathers supposedly acknowledged newborns as their own by lifting them off the ground. Similarly, in classical Roman law, the lifting up of the child *(tollere liberum)* was considered an act of acknowledgment.[23] This also left traces in the Vulgate: Jerome translated Ps. 138:13 as "*Suscepisti me de utero matris meae.*" To be sure, it does not appear that the rite of lifting up continued to be practiced in the "post-classical" phase of Roman law, but jurists retained the term *suscipere* in situations involving "begetting," "conception," and "childbearing."[24]

At first glance, three observations would seem to confirm the postulate that sponsorship was associated with these secular rites. First, the term *suscipere* came to be used with increasing frequency to describe the ritual duties of baptismal sponsors. Gregory of Tours had used the words *excipere* and *suscipere* with nearly equal frequency in describing such procedures.[25] Other sixth-century authors tended to use the two words interchangeably: for example, Caesarius in his *sermones* and *Rule for Nuns*, his successor Aurelian, or Bishop Ferreolus of Uzès. Fredegar and Ildephonsus of Toledo also use the word *excipere*.[26] Thereafter, however, the term *excipere* disappears from descriptions of the act of sponsorship. In the *Lives*, written from the seventh and eighth centuries on, we encounter only *suscipere*[27] or, more rarely, *levare*.[28]

Second, the instructions in the liturgical texts are striking. Some eighth-century compilers evidently considered neither the presentation nor the lifting of baptizees from the font to be the duty of the godparent. Instead, they stipulate that deacons or presbyters should baptize and lift up *(levare)* the children, then hand them to another presbyter for anointing. Only then should the godparent stand prepared to receive the children and dress them again. These instructions do not, however, stop the compilers from speaking of sponsors as "those who must lift" *(qui eos suscipere debeant)*.[29] The sponsors are thus referred to in a way that has nothing to do with their ritual activities. Third, during the same period in which these *Ordines* or sacramentaries were being compiled and the use of the term *suscipere* became established practice, we also find the first reference to a godson as an *adoptivus*.

This all seems to fit together: If the act of sponsorship was increasingly being described as "lifting" *(suscipere)*, but the sponsor did not actually do this, other associations may have been behind the standard use of the term *suscipere*. We may be inclined to think of family law here, especially since sponsors had been declared spiritual fathers from the beginning. Sponsorship could then be described as a ritual replete with family law associations, duties, and consequences, in which case it was entirely possible that it "included a politically significant adoption."[30] This would have been a good reason for Fredegund to choose Gunthchramn as a godfather.

This is not as straightforward as it might seem, however. If we limit ourselves to the Gallican sacramentaries, there is no evidence whatsoever of who was supposed to lift children from the font.[31] Gregory of Tours and some authors of *Lives*, in contrast, are more definite here. In several cases, it was clearly the sponsors who lifted the children from the font.[32] As for the Roman liturgy, according to which sponsors seem to have played a role only after the deacon had lifted the child from the "sacred font" and passed him or her on for anointing, later instructions from the tenth century exhibit a curious interpretation of this rite. By that time, compilers had expanded the liturgical *Ordines* with additional commentaries and segments from the sacramentaries, thus creating a sort of reference manual which described the ritual more precisely.[33] Without instituting any great changes, the compilers succeeded here in making the sponsors actual "lifters" once again. This was accomplished in the following way: the deacons continued to receive children from their parents before baptism and to raise them from the font, but they did not lift them out completely. They left the feet in the water and in this complicated posture passed the small baptizee on to the godparent. The sponsor then lifted the child's feet from the font *(extrahere)*[34] and presented the child for anointing.[35]

Of what use are these tenth-century regulations? We would be ill advised to use these detailed and annotated compilations as aids for interpreting the less precise seventh- and eighth-century instructions, or to attribute the technique of successive liftings from the font to the earlier regulations.[36] It seems more plausible that learned specialists set out to correct the rite in the tenth century. Did it bother them that "those who are supposed to lift" (as any priest could read in any liturgy) did not actually lift baptizees from the font? Were the actors concerned here, too, to proceed "as it is proper"?[37] This seems likely. The very convolutedness of the ritual solution, the fact that the deacons continued to raise baptizees from the font and that the sponsors were only additional "lifters," makes it likely this was an intervention intended for corrective purposes. Normally, such interventions sought to avoid destroying the existing rite, whose antiquity made it appear sacrosanct. This may have led to the idea of leaving the infant's feet in the water *(pedibus infantum adhuc in aqua)*.

These are not unimportant findings in this context, since they indicate that, in the tenth century, experts still believed that the sponsor had the task of actually lifting the child from the font. They derived the designation "lifter" *(susceptores)* from ritual assistance and sought to reestablish it. It is possible, nonetheless, that, in contrast to the logic of the compilers, this "lifting" was interpreted within the framework of the acknowledgment of newborns, thus intensifying the familial representation of sponsorship. In order to demonstrate this, however, it is not sufficient for scholars to locate similarities among Germanic, ancient Roman, and Christian rites of initiation. Scholars may or may not be able to demonstrate the existence of a ritual of receiving among the "Teutons,"[38] but at least they no longer attribute this custom to the period since the "adoption of Christianity"[39] (or: "the Middle Ages").[40] And, by late antiquity, the Roman "lifting up of the child" *(tollere liberum)* had already disappeared from the sources. Why, then, should anyone in the Middle Ages have associated lifting from the font, *suscipere*, with such a profane practice? If we are to believe the dictionaries *suscipere*, in both the Roman legal texts and the so-called *leges*, seems to have been the general term for the acceptance of a newborn or outsider into a community.[41] Apart from the acceptance of an outsider—or, for example, the king—the term *suscipere* apparently was scarcely used in the Middle Ages to express anything but sponsorship.[42]

This does not, of course, mean that Gunthchramn's sponsorship of Chlothar could not have been dangerous for Childebert. It may well have been dangerous, indeed; but we cannot use the ritual of "lifting" to prove that this danger proceeded from echoes of rites or terms from family law.

Naming

Politically speaking, the most attractive element of the rite probably was the Gallic practice of naming. If we follow Gregory, who is the earliest witness, naming was tied up with baptism as an act for which the sponsor was responsible. It was Gunthchramn who received his nephew from the font and "had him named Chlothar," or, more literally, who "desired him to be named Chlothar."[43] If the chronicler still has the godfather "desiring" that the boy should be "named Chlothar" in 591, at a time when he was already seven years old, and after having referred to him by this name many times in the *History*,[44] then he must have been transmitting a bit of ritual with this "desire." As early as 585, he used a conspicuous phrase when he had Gunthchramn travel to Paris "to receive from the sacred font of regeneration the son of Chilperic. . . ." Here, he expressly adds, "whom men *already* called Chlothar."[45] Is this supposed to indicate that such use of a name before baptism was unusual? That can hardly have been the case, since Chlothar was not the only boy who was not baptized until he was several years old,[46] and such children were surely not nameless before baptism. Gregory may well have been referring here to the fact that this use of the name was an unofficial one, that nobody had yet given this boy his name officially, that is, in baptism.[47]

Like presentation and receiving, this practice, too, deviated from the Roman baptismal rite, which did not include naming. In the Roman liturgy, the names of candidates for baptism were already recorded without any ritual act during the preparatory rites (the *scrutinium*):[48] one already had a name before baptism.

The chronicler Gregory, however, associates baptism with naming in his accounts. The deacon Waldo, for example, had "received in baptism the name of [his bishop] Bertram."[49] And the chronicler has the king's son, Herminigild, a convert from Arianism, take the name John "when he received the chrism" (*dum chrismaretur*").[50] In cases of adult baptism and conversion, though, naming appears to have had no practical function. Gregory himself continues to refer to the newly named by their old names,[51] or he does not mention any change of name at all, as in the conversions of Pathir, Gundobad, Brunechildis, Galswintha, and Clovis.[52]

Naming could be deployed to greater social and political effect in the baptism of infants and toddlers since they needed to be named anyway. Thus, Gregory writes of Chrodechild, the wife of Clovis: "Afterwards she bore another son, who was baptized with the name of Chlodomer."[53] The grammar of some of Gregory's accounts shows even more clearly that naming was a ritual act during baptism. "And Chilperic presented his son for baptism, who was lifted from the font by Ragnemod, bishop of Paris, and by the king's will was named Theuderic."[54] Another example is: "After these events a son was born to King Childebert, who, received from the sacred font by Magneric, bishop of Trier, was named Theudebert."[55]

Theuderic and Theudebert thus received their names at baptism. What Gregory does not tell us in these two cases is who ritually bestowed these names on them. Was it their fathers (Chilperic and Childebert) or their sponsors (Ragnemod and Magneric)? The following example is less ambiguous: "This year another son was born to King Childebert. Lifting him from the font, Veranus, bishop of Cavaillon, gave him the name of Theuderic."[56] Here, it was the godfather, Veranus, who gave the baptizee his name when he received *(suscipiens)* him, as had been the case with Gunthchramn who, "lifting him [his nephew] . . . desired him to be named Chlothar" *(excipiens Chlotharium vocitare voluit)*.

Other writers present a similar picture. Jonas of Bobbio, for example, remarks in his account of the baptism of Donatus, the future bishop of Besançon, that the "holy man" Columbanus "himself received the purified one from the sacred font and gave him the name Donatus *(suscepit Donatumque nomen imponet)*."[57]

If we check this observation against the Gallican liturgies, we find a corresponding naming rite placed between the renunciation of the devil and the Creed and immediately before the act of baptism itself: "Question: What is his name? Answer: So and so."[58] Benedict of Aniane used the same form to improve the "authentic" sacramentary of Pope Hadrian: "While taking the child from the one who is to lift him [from the font], the priest asks: What is thy name? Answer [of the sponsor speaking on the baptizee's behalf]: So and so."[59] The tenth-century scholars who created that successful new compilation of the liturgical material we now know as the *Pontificale Romano-Germanicum*[60] retained naming, an element wholly absent from the "Roman" liturgies, as part of the baptismal liturgy.[61] Apart from these normative texts, the christening of Louis the Child (d. 911) is one of the few examples from Frankish practice. The case of Louis illustrates the very practice stipulated in the sacramentaries. An annalist noted that at his christening the young prince "was given his grandfather's name, Louis, by Archbishop Hatto of Mainz and Bishop Adalbero of Augsburg...."[62] The annalist does not state positively that the two were Louis' sponsors, but both Louis' father and Louis himself did so. Arnulf once addressed Hatto as his *compater*, and Louis referred to both Hatto and Adalbero as his *pater spiritualis*.[63]

We also have examples of naming at baptism from outside the Frankish realm, although the individual practices were not always identical. For example, the Irish scribes who recorded the deeds and miracles of their saints in the early Middle Ages not infrequently mention naming. The saints do not appear as godparents here, but rather as baptists, and in this capacity they were the bestowers of names at baptism, as the sponsors were in Gaul.[64] In the Spanish (Mozarabic) liturgy, which bears a strong similarity to the Gallic and deviates markedly from the Roman, naming was also part of the baptismal rite.[65] In short, in the era and environment in which Gregory of Tours lived, ritual naming, like the presentation and receiving of the baptizee, was (in contrast to the Roman liturgy) most likely the duty of the godparents.

The baptism of Chlothar and the activities of his sponsor, Gunthchramn, however, leave no doubt that the latter, in his capacity as godfather, was merely completing ritually (or officially) what others had already decided. Obviously, this too was the case in the *Life* of Geremar, a nobleman at the court of Dagobert I: First, we hear of Geremar that a son was born to him "whom he"—that is, the father—"christened under the name of Amalbert."[66] Only then does the author provide the details that Geremar sent a messenger to his friend Audoin (d. 684) to ask him to act as godfather, that the latter consented and then "came to the baptismal font and lifted the little son from the water, named, blessed, and released him."[67] The hagiographer thus relates the naming twice, attributing it once to the father and once to the sponsor. Apparently, in the first case, he was less concerned with formal bestowal than with the choice of name. The second time, however, when the correct ritual is at stake, the hagiographer states only *that* the saint gave the boy a name, without mentioning *which* name he gave him.

It was precisely this ritual naming by the godparent that Fredegund must have found particularly useful. She and her nobles had chosen this mighty name and with it furthered her own and her son's social and political positioning.[68] They left the official bestowal of the name up to the boy's powerful uncle, however. After the many interventions and encroachments, the dangerous doubts cast on Chlothar's legitimacy and repeated stalling, it was the *senior* and most dangerous neighbor himself who, acting as godfather, ritually bestowed this potent name on the Neustrian boy-king.

Baptism as a Political Action

As instructive as we may find these liturgical details, for the chronicler they represented mere commonplaces deserving no more than two lines in a lengthy text. He devotes considerably more attention to the political goings-on that surrounded the act of baptism—the preparations, the intervention of the other nephew, and actions that accompanied the christening. Not surprisingly, it was a thoroughly political affair, a circumstance apparent in every line of Gregory's account.

A Foster Son?

In her invitation to Gunthchramn to sponsor Chlothar, Fredegund had added a provision: Gunthchramn was to raise his nephew Chlothar "with his own hands ... from the sacred font, and deign to treat *(habere)* him like *(tamquam)* his own foster son *(alumnus)*."[69] Now the same boy whom Gunthchramn had already called his *adoptivus* years before—also, so it seems, at Fredegund's express invitation[70]—was to become his *alumnus*. How were these two circumstances to be reconciled? How, and to what end, did Fredegund bring fosterage into the equation? Why associate sponsorship and fosterage *(exceptum tamquam alumnum proprium habere)*—apparently as a simile *(tamquam)*?

We know virtually nothing about such fostering relationships in Francia, and can at most regard Fredegund's offer as evidence that it cannot have been wholly uncommon in the Frankish kingdoms. Documents from the Franks' Visigothic, Irish, and Norse neighbors indicate that fosterage apparently was a widespread practice there,[71] albeit—and this does not make the matter any simpler—not always with the same emphasis everywhere. Thus, one Norse saga states: "It is said that it is the lesser man who raises another man's child."[72] A curious affinity between Gregory's narrative and this Norse saga makes it appear likely that a similar argument might have been made in Gaul. King Gunthchramn appears to have anticipated the accusation that he was demeaning himself by participating in the baptism. At any rate, he felt it necessary to utter the following self-defense to Childebert's envoys, before anyone had had the chance to make such an accusation: "No indignity is done to our race if I take up this child [Chlothar]." He then expanded on the theme, adding that "lords [even] lift their servants from the sacred font,"[73] which probably was true.[74] He thus did not wish to be viewed as a "lesser man," but at the same time reckoned with the possibility of such an interpretation. What we need to know here is whether this fear of "indignity" reveals a conceivable association among sponsorship, fosterage, and humiliation. Was Fredegund subtly insulting Gunthchramn when she brought up fosterage?

As tempting as this explanation may be, the Norse document alone is insufficient to link Gunthchramn's concern for his dignity with Fredegund's comparison with fosterage. Other arguments would seem to contradict this. Irish sources on fosterage, for instance, indicate that people of higher rank were preferred as foster fathers.[75] It is also likely that when Fredegund summoned Gunthchramn to Paris in 591, she did so by using an inviting, rather than an insulting, comparison. If Gunthchramn was to become Chlothar's godfather, then, as the chronicler specifically mentions in regard to one of the earlier planned dates, it was as an "invited" one *(invitatus)*.[76]

It would scarcely do justice to the speech situation if we were to pit *fosterage* against *adoptio* and analyze just why Fredegund offered her son *like* an *alumnus* to the same man who had claimed him years before *as* an *adoptivus*. When Fredegund and her coactors made use of similes or analogies, they were content to stick to broad similarities, similarities that remained vague in detail and which referred only to certain aspects of the things being compared. Which aspects the simile was supposed to apply to was not made explicit; depending on the situation, the aspects emphasized might well change gradually and imperceptibly, with hidden aspects coming to the fore and those no longer relevant receding into the background. Fredegund *somehow* compared sponsorship to fosterage, and it does justice to the vagueness of this comparison if we assume that a foster father, in whatever relative social position he might find himself, was expected to be an affectionate caretaker, that Fredegund invoked the image of the loving caretaker—that is, the *nutritor* and *amator*,[77] those very virtues of the sponsor that usually were expressed in the terminology of an affectionate father.

A "State Occasion"

Upon receiving the invitation, Gunthchramn sent a few bishops "and others" to Paris, and "many from his kingdom, both officers of the household and counts" appeared.[78] This was not unusual for a royal baptism. Gregory also reports of Chilperic that he had had his son christened at Eastertide "with great cheer."[79] And, when Dagobert I had his son, Sigibert (III), baptized, the godfather—Saint Amandus—is said to have "filled the king and the entire army with joy" on this occasion.[80] A baptism was part of royal representation before the eyes of the nobility, the bishops, and the army. It was a kind of "state occasion," a political performance. As we can see from his reaction, this was precisely what worried the Austrasian Childebert, who (like some modern scholars) regarded it as competition to his own status as an *adoptivus* and partner in the pact of Andelot.

The Baptismal Site

As to where the baptism took place, the chroniclers Gregory and Fredegar contradict each other, albeit in a manner that appears at first scarcely worth mentioning. According to Gregory, Gunthchramn first traveled to Paris, then continued to the royal court at Rueil. It was not there in the palace that he made preparations for the baptism but, rather, in the nearby village of Nanterre.[81] Fredegar, in contrast, who was not privy to better information than Gregory, transferred the entire action to the palace at Rueil.[82] What might be behind this discrepancy?

Gregory's assertion fits in well with our general assumptions about ecclesiastical organization in the sixth century. It seems that in the Gaul of Gregory of Tours, the diocesan system that had been developed in late antiquity persisted for some time. This means that the central villages *(vici)* possessed parish churches *(ecclesiae baptismales)* in which priests licensed by the bishop could undertake baptisms. In contrast, the estates *(villae)* and small villages had basilicas or oratories in which the priests were allowed only to preach or celebrate mass.[83] Chlothar's baptism appears to have been organized according to this system. Gunthchramn set forth from his *villa*, where christenings could not be performed, for the nearest *vicus*, with a priest authorized to perform baptisms.

In the few generations separating Gregory from Fredegar,[84] there appear to have been some changes in this organization. Ever since the appearance of Irish monks on the Continent around the year 600, the powerful nobles had suddenly begun to take a strong interest in religious life. As some scholars believe,[85] they immediately and instinctively knew how to make use of the social and political possibilities Celtic Christianity offered them. The religious practices of the Irish now enabled the nobility to take advantage of the sacral legitimation of their power, something that previously had fallen into the laps of kings as a gift from the Gallic bishops. Where these bishops had built up an organization of episcopal sees, *vici*, and *villae*, the powerful nobles now established places of worship on their family estates. Privatizing religious sites as well as the administration of the sacraments, they confronted the late-antique "public" *(publicus)*[86] church organized around the metropolitan sees with an aristocratic church—complete with private churches [*Eigenkirchen*] and priests, centers of worship on noble estates, and private baptistries.[87] Up to that time, ordination had been a commission tied to a particular office and particular place; now it was considered an absolute gift of divine grace to an individual person. Thus, the

Neustrian *maior domus* Erchinoald invited the Irish holy man Furseus (d. ca. 650), whom he wished to sponsor his son, to his *palatium* for the baptism.[88] The bishops later tried to intervene and regain control of this area. In contrast to the practices of the aristocracy, they demanded that "all priests in a *parochia* be subject to the authority of the bishop . . . and that no priest in any *parochia* should perform baptisms or celebrate mass unless the bishop of that *parochia* has given him license [*licentia*] to do so."[89] By no means should aristocrats protect their clerics against the bishop.[90] With Charlemagne's support, the bishops proceeded, at least verbally, against the practice of absolute ordination.[91] Even Charlemagne, however, had the vanquished Saxon, Widukind, christened not in the relevant *parochia* but, rather, in his palace at Attigny.[92]

Matters were different in Gunthchramn's day. He seems to have acted according to the regulations of the bishops. Like all believers, he had to proceed to the "public baptistry" *(publicum baptisterium)* in the nearest *vicus*. By the time of Fredegar, this had apparently become inconceivable.

Childebert's Attack

Before the baptism, Austrasian envoys came to Gunthchramn to present Childebert's interpretation of the affair: Gunthchramn had, they said, violated the pact, made friends with Chlothar, and was even setting "this boy on the royal throne in the city of Paris."[93] Childebert thus had his emissaries portray the proceedings as competition to the agreements reached at Andelot. And since, according to the pact of Andelot, Childebert already had a claim to Gunthchramn's entire legacy, had he truly set "this boy on the royal throne in the city of Paris," Gunthchramn's conduct would indeed have constituted a breach of contract.

How did Childebert arrive at this accusation? As far as we can tell from the sources, Gunthchramn had done nothing more than organize a solemn christening. Might his actions have been intended to give his godson, Chlothar, a claim on the capital, Paris? We have no evidence (not even for the period that followed) that baptism bestowed inheritance rights on either godparents or godchildren,[94] just as there is no mention of Chlothar assuming power in Paris after Gunthchramn's death. Childebert assumed power over the entire Burgundian kingdom, including Paris, just as the pact of Andelot stipulated; in addition, his claim was strengthened by the *adoptio*.[95]

Why all the protest, then? In 588, three years before the baptism, Childebert had complained that, as "often perceived," Gunthchramn had received Fredegund's "embassies with greater honour *(dignius)* than ours."[96] His envoys had specifically asked Gunthchramn to be "less kindly disposed (*caritas*) towards that queen [Fredegund]."⁹⁷ Now that Gunthchramn was organizing a sponsorship relationship, rather than being "less kindly disposed," Childebert naturally thought that he knew what function it was intended to serve. He knew that it was good for at least one thing, and that was to give this inconvenient *caritas* an official form, officially establishing a bond of friendship (*amicitias conlegare*). At the very last minute before the christening, this was what he sent his envoys to protest against.⁹⁸

This *amicitia* did not suffice to set Chlothar "on the royal throne in the city of Paris." Gunthchramn had laid claim to Paris in 584, sent Fredegund to the vicinity of Rouen, and finally secured the city of Paris for himself at Andelot—"in perpetuity."⁹⁹ Nevertheless, and this is at least striking, it does not seem that Fredegund restricted herself to her widow's estate near Rouen. If Fredegund repeatedly invited her uncle Gunthchramn to Paris for the planned baptism, then one must consider the possibility that she herself traveled there each time as well. Other episodes give the impression that Fredegund stayed in Paris with Gunthchramn's consent, whatever the officially declared property arrangements. The chronicler relates an earlier episode from 585, involving the reckless Claudius, who failed to fulfill one of Gunthchramn's commissions, then "flew to Paris" and "turned the question over in his mind, whether he should see Queen Fredegund" in order to receive some reward from her for the same commission.¹⁰⁰ Fredegund thus appears to have been back in Paris a year after Chilperic's death. A second episode, which Gregory relates for the year 587, suggests that her presence there was not an exception, let alone a misinterpretation of the sources. In that year, Gunthchramn had a wrongdoer sent from Chalon to Paris. "The king said: 'If Fredegund by the help of men of good repute, can clear him of the charge brought against him, let him go free. . . .' "But," Gregory continues, "when Baddo came to Paris, no one was sent by Fredegund able to maintain his innocence. He was then brought back . . . to Chalon. . . ."¹⁰¹ Fredegund was thus in Paris once again. Finally, in a third story from 590, the chronicler relates that "Lothar . . . fell grievously ill; he was so far given up that his death was announced to King Guntram, who [set] out from Chalon for Paris. . . ."¹⁰² Would it have made sense to travel to Paris if Chlothar had died somewhere else, for example, in Rouen? It might have, if Gunthchramn had been worried about securing Paris for himself. But, since Gunthchramn was the undisputed ruler in Paris by 590, and since the ailing boy's mother sometimes sojourned in that city, the assumption that it was there that Chlothar fell ill in 590 is not far-fetched.

Fredegund's frequent presence in Paris (although we occasionally find her elsewhere)¹⁰³ may well have been the cause of Childebert's suspicion. Gunthchramn tolerated the Neustrian rulers in the old capital city. Officially, Gunthchramn had stipulated where Fredegund was to have her widow's estate, and he had pacts and undisputed claims on his side; but, in reality, Fredegund and Chlothar were in the capital and were treated in a "fitting" *(dignus)* manner. Now, it may have appeared to Childebert, there also was to be a formal bond between these two parties, a bond from which no one could derive any territorial or inheritance rights but which might, in practical political terms, have weakened Childebert's clear position of privilege. As Childebert had found on a previous occasion, Gunthchramn was not inclined to take the pact of Andelot literally. In 588, the year after the pact, Gunthchramn had repeated the pact's contents correctly to Childebert's envoys: ". . . all that I have is his [Childebert's]." He had gone on, however, to provide his own rather eccentric interpretation of it: "I shall give Lothar . . . two or three cities in some part *(in parte aliqua)* of my dominions, that he may not feel himself disinherited; thus may Childebert be easy as to the inheritance which his cousin shall receive."[104]

In short, Childebert had reason to be suspicious. At the same time, it is impossible to tell what exactly he could have deemed a violation of the pact or even as setting Chlothar on the throne. The sponsorship? The *amicitia*? Neither is likely. Was the attack by his envoys, therefore, simply wrong? The question itself seems misplaced. After all, the violation of "international" treaties must have been a hackneyed accusation even in those days, but one that was no more than an instrument of practical politics. It was less important that it be correct than that it produce the desired effect. Whether Childebert assessed the situation correctly is another matter. At any rate, his attack produced results, and Gunthchramn's answer had to as well.

Gunthchramn's Pretext

Gunthchramn, for his part, immediately produced a bundle of arguments and innuendoes with which to counter the attack of the Austrasian envoys and justify his action. They included the following:

> He ought not to take offence if I receive from the sacred font his cousin, my own brother's son; the call to perform this office is one that no Christian should refuse. As for me, God best knoweth that I seek to act without any subtlety, but in the singleness of a pure heart, for if I do not so, I dread to incur the divine anger.

He continued, remarking that "No indignity is done to our race if I take up this child. For if lords lift their servants from the sacred font, how should it be unlawful for me to raise a close relative, and make him my son by the spiritual grace of baptism?"[105]

Although he does not specifically marshal them as an argument, in his reply, Gunthchramn does cite the norms of kinship. It was, after all, a matter of "your cousin" and "my own brother's son," "a close relative." Gunthchramn used designations of familial relationship as terms expressing moral values, defending himself by their mere use and invoking the entire system of rules and duties associated with kinship. Then he referred to Christian duty, noting that "the call to perform this office is one that no Christian should refuse." In his interpretation of this passage Joseph Lynch warns us against being "too quick in believing what is said"; in this case, however, he decided that Gunthchramn's defense was credible, since "in Frankish society refusal to serve as a sponsor was not something to be done lightly."[106] He also is able to cite another enticing example from the same period. The authors of the *Regula Tarnatensis* (551–73), which prohibited monks from serving as sponsors, appear to have made explicit allowances for such social constraints. To make the strict regulation more practicable, they stipulated that if a monk "could not escape from the prohibited act, then for *caritas* sake he should be spared the punishment intended for the disobedient."[107]

Was Gunthchramn thus actually "credible," was "the call to perform this office" truly "one that no Christian should refuse"? It is not difficult to find a counterexample in Gregory's chronicle. Gunthchramn himself had shown a few years earlier just how well he knew how to refuse. After repeatedly traveling to Paris in vain for the baptism of his nephew, he finally threatened to refuse to sponsor him after all.[108] A "Christian" who wished to do so could refuse if he knew how to handle the situation and understood the rules. We have evidence of such an act on the part of Amandus, one of the seventh-century holy men. He had dared to accuse King Dagobert I, who apparently was given to sexual escapades,[109] of "capital crimes" and was thus driven from the kingdom by the king—"not without injustice," as his hagiographer believed. When the king subsequently had a son, he wanted this very same Amandus to stand as his godfather. He proceeded in an exceedingly regal manner, sending out *ministri* to look for him and admonish him *(admonere)* "that he must come to the king." Amandus did come, but when the king, after a few conciliatory words, asked him to sponsor his son, the holy man managed to get out of doing so. He referred the king to a well-known rule: God's *militia* must not become entangled in the affairs of the world *(saecularibus negotiis)*, but rather seek solitude and shun the palaces. Then he departed, and only consented to act as sponsor after the king made him a good offer.[110]

To return to Gunthchramn: according to the norm, a "Christian" might not refuse the office of sponsor, but it remained practically possible if he were only clever enough. And, thus, Gunthchramn argued that he was not acting out of "subtlety," but—in the chronicler's Pauline phrasing—"in the singleness of a pure heart."[111]

To be sure, even if there were ways of refusing such an official request, it remained an affront to do so. One could refuse, but it was—Lynch rightly chooses a vague formulation here—"not something to be done lightly."[112] Gunthchramn's argument was thus, at first glance, not wholly false; it remains, on closer scrutiny, a mere pretext. Naturally, Gunthchramn could hardly have refused when Fredegund addressed him in the following manner: "Let the lord my king . . . with his own hands lift the child from the sacred font. . . ."[113] Fredegund would scarcely have made such a request in such a politically important affair unless she was already sure of Gunthchramn's answer.[114] Historical scholarship on the matrimonial politics of the European royal families, as well as anthropological studies of marriage practices, have shown how, at every stage of the negotiations, the parties involved used complicated social techniques to preserve the honor of the participants whatever the outcome might be. In most cases, the danger of an official request being refused could be circumvented in advance. Those officially responsible went into action only when the matter had already been decided. At that point, it was no longer dangerous to request someone's hand in marriage, for, by then, it could no longer be refused without causing a scandal.[115]

The organization of political sponsorships must have proceeded in a similar manner, since the threat to the honor of those doing the asking was scarcely less serious than in matrimonial politics. It is hardly surprising that the negotiations carried out by subordinate persons are well-nigh impossible to grasp, using the available sources. If, as in the case of Dagobert's courting of Amandus, we hear that this was done through his *ministri*, we do not know how they negotiated or what they did or did not settle in advance. Nor do we not know who went to a Magneric, Veranus, Praetextatus, or Ragnemod to convey the king's wish that he sponsor his son, nor what constraints the bishops were subject to, how many bishops refused, or how they did so. We see only the results—or, at most, the official requests. Someone must have been working behind the scenes, though, setting the stage, obtaining consent.[116] And, at this stage, long before the invitation, a "Christian" could prevent what he did not wish to happen. That, however, was a matter of practical diplomacy, not of official "rules."

Gunthchramn's Answer

Gunthchramn, too, replied; he by no means restricted himself to "avoidance," nor did he offer "basically no answer to the Austrasians' actual accusation."[117] The "Austrasians' actual accusation" must have been that of violating the pact of Andelot, and to this Gunthchramn provided quite an unambiguous answer: "'To the promise which I made to my nephew Childebert I shall not be false.... Depart therefore, and tell your lord this, that the pact which I made with him I am minded to keep intact, and if it be not annulled by any fault on his side, it shall never be annulled by me.'"[118] This reply left little room for interpretation. To "keep intact" the pact of Andelot meant leaving his entire kingdom, including Paris, to Childebert.[119] Some scholars believe that, in reality, Gunthchramn did not keep the pact but, rather, gave Chlothar the "two or three cities" *(duas aut tres civitates)* he intended for him,[120] one of which was Paris, in 591.[121] Roderich Schmidt goes even further in his assertion "that Gunthchramn, by receiving Fredegund's son from the font at Paris strengthened his rule there and thereby secured this capital for him."[122] Apparently, Schmidt assumes that Chlothar already ruled over Paris, that the "capital" only needed to be "secured." Margret Wielers also views the sponsorship as a "legal act to regulate the succession."[123]

There is some evidence, however, that these scholars were reconstructing events from the perspective of Austrasian protest. Thus, Fredegar, the most important source for the period after Gregory, notes laconically on the death of Gunthchramn: "Childebert succeeded him."[124] Chlothar apparently reached Paris only after the death of Childebert (596), then he took the city by force. Fredegar reports on the succession of Childebert's sons as if it were a matter of course.[125] The boys were still in their minority, aged eight and nine years; so their grandmother, Brunechildis, ruled in their stead.[126] Austrasia had also just been through wars against the Warni and the Bretons.[127] It was only under these circumstances, after the rulers in Austrasia were forced to go through a regency and several wars, that Chlothar and Fredegund took Paris "after the barbarian fashion."[128] If we are to credit Fredegar's account, Chlothar did not receive the "two or three cities" Gunthchramn supposedly had once intended for him, let alone the capital at Paris.

Margarete Weidemann has correctly pointed out that this fact alone tells us nothing about Gunthchramn's politics. It is conceivable that Chlothar simply was unable to assert the succession Gunthchramn had planned after the latter's death. Weidemann's broadly convincing reconstruction of the history of the Neustrian territories under the reign of Chlothar II proceeds from this possibility.[129] She is the first scholar to have attempted to use the sources to verify the dominant view that Chlothar inherited two or three *civitates*. According to her study, it was Gunthchramn's wish that Chlothar inherit the *civitates* of Séez, Chartres, and Paris and the *pagi* of Ressons-sur-Matz (diocese of Beauvais) and Etampes (diocese of Sens), a wish, however, that the powerful Childebert managed to thwart after

Gunthchramn's death.[130] This assessment, then, also assumes that Gunthchramn lied to Childebert's envoys at the baptism in 592—that he never intended, as he claimed, to keep the pact of Andelot intact.

We are still faced with the question whether this sponsorship could have had a tangible effect on the succession. Weidemann's reconstruction illustrates the dilemma for the Île-de-France. While for the Neustrian territories between the Seine and the Loire Weidemann has successfully consulted the testament of Berthchramn of Le Mans, a useful and, in this context, hitherto little-noticed document,[131] when it comes to the Île-de-France she, too, must rely on the meager references provided by Gregory of Tours. In order to follow her reasoning, we must take a closer look at some details of the pact of Andelot.

A Legacy for Chlothar?

Two agreements from the pact of Andelot have convinced Margarete Weidemann to embrace the generally accepted, but hitherto never expressly substantiated, opinion that Chlothar was made an heir—on the one hand, the arrangements regarding Paris, Chartres, and Etampes, and, on the other, those concerning the *pagus* of Ressons-sur-Matz in the diocese of Beauvais. All these places had something in common: they had all been divided into three parts or neutralized in the partition of 567.[132]

Let us begin with Paris, Chartres, and the *pagus* of Etampes. It was decided at Andelot that Gunthchramn should retain these places "in perpetuity." In exchange, Childebert got back the Austrasian city of Meaux, which Gunthchramn had occupied.[133] In Weidemann's view, this strict division of territories would "scarcely have been necessary" if Childebert was supposed to inherit everything anyway. Their purpose can only have been to keep Childebert away from the territories Chlothar was supposed to inherit.[134] This thesis rests on the implicit premise that in making the territorial arrangements at Andelot, Gunthchramn and Childebert were chiefly interested in regulating the succession in Gunthchramn's kingdom. This cannot have been their only interest, though, as the text of the pact reveals.

They had come together—as the pact's very first sentence states—"that they might take full counsel to end whatsoever causes of offence might arise between them...."[135] The first matters of dispute they discussed were territorial disagreements, "since King Guntram, in accordance with the treaty which he made with King Sigibert of good memory, claimed all the portion of the said Lord Sigibert in the kingdom of Charibert"; furthermore, "since King Childebert sought to recover the whole part which his father had possessed ."[136]

This contested territory, authority over which was negotiated at Andelot, by no means encompassed only those cities in the Île-de-France which Weidemann considers Chlothar's potential legacy. The participants also fought over places Childebert was later to inherit without dispute. Thus the kings finally determined who would rule over Tours, Poitiers, and Meaux, even if they were merely lending official approval to matters that had already been regulated before.[137] There also had been conflicts between Gunthchramn and Childebert over Marseilles, which had already been settled in 584.[138]

Clearly, Childebert did not consider the efforts to recover cities Gunthchramn had taken from him "scarcely necessary," just because he would someday come into his inheritance. Conversely, wherever disputes arose, Gunthchramn showed no interest during his lifetime in giving the Austrasians what was due to them or what they would someday inherit. Thus, after his brother Chilperic's death, he not only conquered his territories in Aquitaine but also those belonging to Brunechildis, the mother of the Austrasian king; he did not give them back. He made sure that the pact of Andelot documented his right to keep Brunechildis' Aquitainian holdings under his authority for the remainder of his lifetime.[139]

All of these arrangements apparently were necessary to maintain peace between Gunthchramn and Childebert—quite apart from any questions of succession. When the chaotic 567 regulation of the frontier in the Île-de-France was rectified by means of an exchange of lands, the process reveals a logic familiar to us from the Merovingian partitions. To all appearances, the Merovingians did their best in their partitions to avoid dividing the *civitates*. Apparently, nobody wanted to rule over portions of a *civitas* whose bishop was subject to another king.[140] Thus, instead of ruling over only parts of several dioceses (Paris, Chartres, Senlis, and Sens), Gunthchramn and Childebert secured undivided bishoprics for themselves[141]—Gunthchramn taking Paris, Chartres, and (through the acquisition of Etampes) Sens, and Childebert Senlis and (at an earlier period) Marseilles.

The measure thus need not have been a strategy of Gunthchramn's to separate out territory as Chlothar's legacy.[142] If we choose to interpret it thus, we must find an additional explanation for all territories outside the Île-de-France about which the parties negotiated at Andelot. It would be simpler to interpret all these agreements—whether in the Île-de-France, Aquitaine, or the Novempopulana—as settling constant sources of tension, which affected Gunthchramn more than they did his legacies. This interpretation makes all the more sense, since the two kings addressed issues of inheritance—incidentally, quite unambiguously—in the second part of the pact.

Whether the treaty partners' treatment of the *pagus* of Ressons-sur-

Matz offers any useful clues to the planned succession remains to be investigated. This *pagus*, located in the Neustrian diocese of Beauvais, had also been divided into three parts in 567. Like the once divided *civitates* it, too, was once again brought under the authority of a single ruler at Andelot, in this case Gunthchramn.[143] In return for his third of this *pagus*, Childebert received Gunthchramn's third of Senlis. Gunthchramn gained a small exclave in this exchange, and Margarete Weidemann sees therein a further argument for the idea that Chlothar was also supposed to inherit something: "This exchange only makes sense if we proceed from the assumption that Gunthchramn wished to give Ressons-sur-Matz to Chlothar II."[144]

Other features of the pact will show that the exchange may have served other ends as well. First, the exclave of Ressons was surrounded by Austrasia and Neustria, so that its site alone did not necessarily mark it as a legacy of the Neustrian Chlothar. We might also ask whether the fact that the pact created an exclave for Gunthchramn requires special explanation. Exclaves were a not uncommon result of the Merovingian partitions. Around 567, Gunthchramn acquired several small exclaves (Séez, Nantes, and Oloron), in addition to a large one, as had the Austrasian Sigibert (Avranches and Couserans, alongside Tours and Poitiers). Although from our present-day perspective some of the exclaves appear to make sense—for example, Avranches as a port town,[145] or Tours and Poitiers as dynastic shrines—this does not apply to all of them. For this reason, Eugen Ewig, writing of the partition of 567, preferred not to seek the particular "meaning" behind the exclaves, but instead decided "not to think too highly of the political talent of their creators."[146]

One may explain the kings' acceptance of the exclave of Ressons-sur-Matz within the context of all the pact's agreements without assuming that it was part of the planned legacy for Chlothar, provided the pact of Andelot was intended, in the interest of peace, to resolve the question of the frontier (that is, that in the territories that had been partitioned into thirds, the political and diocesan borders were to be made to coincide once again), at the price, however, of denying Gunthchramn any access to the little *pagus* of Ressons. In all previous partitions, the diocesan borders had always been a central criterion and exclaves had apparently been accepted. Why should the pact of Andelot have made other arrangements?

It does not, on the whole, seem plausible that Gunthchramn officially and unambiguously left his entire legacy (*in integritate*)[147] to Childebert in the second half of the pact, while at the same time secretly preparing, in the territorial arrangements of the first part, to leave an inheritance to Chlothar. It would be simpler to interpret the territorial arrangements as the kings described them: as a resolution of their conflicts in the name of peace.

We still need to ask how the widespread assumption that Gunthchramn meant to leave a legacy for Chlothar came about. The answer probably lies in a statement made by Gunthchramn in 588 to Childebert's envoys.

> Heaven grant that my nephew [Childebert] keep his promises, for all that I have is his.... I shall give Lothar ... two or three cities in some part *(in parte aliqua)* of my dominions, that he may not feel himself disinherited; thus may Childebert be easy as to the inheritance which his cousin shall receive.[148]

One cannot help but read this as a threat to violate the pact. But was the old capital, Paris,[149] of all places, the suitable object "in some part" *(in parte aliqua)* of Gunthchramn's dominions which Childebert should "be easy" about Chlothar's inheriting? It may have been, but we have no further evidence, and thus need not favor this interpretation, however widely accepted it may be among scholars. It is unique on precisely this point: in no other situation does Gunthchramn (or the chronicler) say anything about a legacy for Chlothar—not even at his christening! And the king (or the chronicler) spoke often enough of his own legacy, after these soothing words as well. As early as 577, he had vowed to settle his kingdom on his nephew and "son" Childebert, and he expressly repeated his intentions in 585, asserting that he had "shut out all others from the succession." In 587, at Andelot, he once again promised him his kingdom "in its entirety and forever"; finally, as his last word on the succession, Gunthchramn confirmed just before the baptism that he intended "to keep intact" the pact he had made with Childebert.[150] This last statement was no less unequivocal than the pact of Andelot.

Gunthchramn thus expressed his intentions plainly and on several occasions. Only once is he said to have mentioned a small inheritance for Chlothar. It may be that in 588, he wanted to put something aside for Chlothar. We would not be doing justice to the sources, however, if we were to view all of Gunthchramn's other assertions and agreements in the light of this one statement. Why should the chronicler have Gunthchramn declare something in 577, 585, 587, and 591 that he had no intention of doing? And why should he have him announce only in 588 what he was already planning in 587, and was still planning at the baptism in 591? This question is all the more important, since Childebert, in fact, inherited everything.[151] Gunthchramn had, after all, taken some trouble to justify his plan to bestow his legacy on Childebert alone. It was for him alone that he had arranged the prayer for the king as a form of spiritual aid, publicly declared him alone a member of his line *(stirps)*, and played diplomatically with doubts about Chlothar's legitimacy on more than one occasion.[152] His only official tie to Chlothar, apart from the uncle-nephew relationship, was sponsorship. Apparently, neither Gunthchramn nor his successors used sponsorship to legitimate the bestowal of a legacy.[153] Because the pact of Andelot provides no new clues, Gunthchramn's statement of 588 remains a lone voice in Gregory's chronicle, amid numerous contrary assertions and in contrast to the actual course of events. We have no reason to believe that the utterances Gregory records for July 588 can help us interpret the rest of what he relates in his chronicle.

Let us turn once again to the occasion for scrutinizing the succession: Gunthchramn's interpretation of his sponsorship of Chlothar. He had maintained that he did not thereby violate the pact of Andelot, nor make Chlothar his heir. The chronicler gives us no reason to doubt this. There is no evidence to support Childebert's accusation that Gunthchramn was using the sponsorship to set "this boy [Chlothar] on the royal throne in the city of Paris."[154]

This is not to say that Gunthchramn did not strengthen his nephew Chlothar's position in his Neustrian realm. That will be the subject of the following section. The assumption that he put him on the throne in Paris, and thus used sponsorship to manipulate the succession is, however, rather implausible.

Practical Effects

It was not the succession that was at stake here. Gregory has the king speak the following words immediately after the naming ritual: "'Let the boy grow and fulfill the meaning of this name; may he one day enjoy a power equal to that of the former Lothar whose name he hath received.'"[155] The boy did fulfill the meaning of his name, solidifying, as Fredegar put it "the entire Frankish kingdom" so that it "was united as it had once been under the first Chlothar. . . ."[156] His ability to accomplish this was, however, unconnected to any transfer of a claim on Gunthchramn's part. The very exaggeration, the comparison with Chlothar I who had ruled the entire kingdom on his own, makes it clear that this was not the speech situation in which claims were transferred. Gunthchramn's words were good wishes which clearly indicate the purpose of the occasion: if the aristocrats had already (before baptism) bestowed on the boy that name which demonstrated a claim to legitimate succession in Neustria,[157] Gunthchramn now explicitly took up and recognized this claim. It was Gunthchramn who officially named the boy in the ritual act —the same Gunthchramn who had banished the queen in 584, repeatedly tried to interfere in Neustrian affairs, and officially cast doubt on the boy's legitimacy.[158] Now the Neustrians around the young Chlothar had succeeded, with the help of sponsorship, in domesticating their powerful neighbor and providing the boy with a recognized legitimation. This is precisely what Fredegar relates as the heart of the proceedings: "He [Gunthchramn] had Chlothar baptized at his villa of Rueil, himself standing godfather to him: and he established him over [his father] Chilperic's kingdom."[159]

His father's kingdom *(regnum patris)* was Neustria, not Paris. In the version which Gunthchramn had proclaimed elsewhere, Paris belonged not to Chilperic's kingdom, but to his own.[160] Sponsorship here did not incorporate "a politically significant adoption,"[161] it permitted no claim to the succession, and did not secure for Chlothar the *sedes* of Paris. It represented recognition of the Neustrian king. Sponsorship served here as a familial instrument for resuming and stabilizing good relations. It was no more and no less valuable than the feast *(convivium)* and exchange of gifts that followed the baptism.

Feasts and Gifts

The story ends in a shared meal and the reciprocal giving of presents: "The ceremony ended he invited the boy to his table, and loaded him with many gifts [*muneribus*]. He was invited by his nephew in return [*similiter*] and departed enriched with numerous presents [*donis refertur*]. . . ."[162] The chronicler describes these events immediately following the christening as a series of connected reciprocal activities. He reveals no differences between the actions of the two parties, no latent period between the individual acts. Gift exchange and the reciprocal offering of food were components of a single ceremonial event.

If we ignore the fact that these events were part of a christening ceremony, we can find numerous parallel examples for this practice. At Pompierre, in 577, for example, after the *adoptio* Gunthchramn and Childebert ate and drank "together, honouring each other with worthy gifts [*se muneribus honorantes*] and so parted in peace."[163] In Andelot, in 587, these same partners "concluded peace . . . ; they exchanged gifts, and . . . sat down together at a banquet."[164] A few centuries later, Flodoard portrayed the encounter between King Henry I and King Robert of France on the River Roer (923) in similar terms: "There they fed each other *(invicem paverunt)* and after they had formed a friendship *(amicitia)* and exchanged gifts *(datis ab alterutro muneribus)* they parted."[165]

One could cite any number of similar stories.[166] Finding parallels becomes more difficult when we view such reciprocal acts in connection with baptismal ceremonies and compare them with other political baptisms. To be sure, we possess detailed accounts of a few more episodes in which one king sponsored another, but in none of these examples were the ceremonies surrounding the christening organized in a reciprocal manner. When, for example, King Aethelwalh of Sussex was baptized in 661, his godfather, Wulfhere of Mercia, bestowed two of his "provinces" on him. Aethelwalh apparently gave him nothing in return.[167] At the baptism of Widukind, leader of the Saxons, in 785, only one person "honored" another with "wondrous gifts," and that one person was the sponsor, Charlemagne.[168] The same was true of the baptism of Harald of Denmark, in 826, which Ermoldus Nigellus has described in meticulous detail: only the godfather, Louis the Pious, gave gifts to his godson. And he alone hosted a feast.[169] Finally, when Charles III made peace with the Norman leader Godefrid through an act of baptism and received him from the font, according to all accounts, it was the sponsor alone who gave generous gifts.[170]

Gunthchramn and Chlothar thus combined the repertoire of symbolic, imposing ceremonies differently than Wulfhere, Charlemagne, Louis the Pious, or Charles III had done at the political christenings at which they stood as sponsors. We need to ask how Gunthchramn and Chlothar influenced the political value of the ceremony through the reciprocity of their actions and what ends were served by this reciprocal organization.

Let us begin with the feast. Gregory explains the social value of official banquets in an episode in which he himself participated. In 577, Gregory was summoned into the presence of King Chilperic because he had publicly supported the accused Praetextatus at his trial. A war of words between the king and Gregory ensued. When Gregory appeared to be gaining the upper hand, the king, if we are to credit Gregory's account, changed his tactics in order to bend the bishop to his will. He invited him to eat,[171] as Gregory reports, "as if to propitiate me, deeming that I did not see through his crafty dealing."[172] Gregory saw through this, however, "knowing his insinuating arts," and said he would only eat if certain conditions were met: "promise first thyself to keep the law and the canons."[173] Only after the king swore to do so did he eat "some bread and even drank wine before I went away."[174]

Gregory himself (and many other authors of the early Middle Ages) repeatedly describe why Gregory had to exercise caution. Had he eaten right away, he would have been compelled to maintain peace with the king, at least officially or publicly (for example, in court). By taking food together, the participants demonstrated publicly (and reciprocally requested) peace (*pax*), friendship (*amicitia*), love (*caritas, diligentia*), and familiarity (*familiaritas*)[175] or, in more theoretical terms, "inclusion in a single moral and social community among whose members there is trust."[176] Gregory knew this and took appropriate precautions.

These general remarks, however, tell us little about the reciprocal hospitality of 591. At the banquet, in particular, an "event of physiological primitiveness and unavoidable generality in the sphere of social interactions,"[177] the potential social uses were extremely numerous. The official banquet assembled the most diverse groups—relatives, friends, kings, monks, merchants, guild members, and people of equal and differing social and political ranks.[178] The relationships aspired to and demonstrated in a given case were exceedingly diverse, whether they were referred to in terms of "love," "friendship" or the vocabulary of kinship. It is less important *that* Gunthchramn and Chlothar demonstrated "inclusion in a single moral and social community" than *what kind of* membership in a group that functioned in *what way* Gunthchramn and Chlothar displayed publicly in 591. What kind of bond, entailing what consequences, was the feast supposed to represent?

It was less the banquet itself than the way in which it was organized[179] that made a public statement. This question brings us to the limits of the sources; Gregory has almost nothing to say here. He tells us nothing about the participants, for example about the role of Fredegund and Chlothar in the order of seating, nothing about how long the feast proceeded in comparison with others, about the many signs with which such a banquet (and with it, the guests) was positioned socially and politically, the variety and use of which later descriptions of courtly culture give us some impression.[180] The few details Gregory does relate always apply at the same time to the exchange of gifts, so that it will be practical to examine these first.

The chronicler limits himself to a single sentence here. Gunthchramn "honored him [Chlothar] with many gifts [*muneribus honoravit*] . . . and departed enriched with numerous presents [*donis refertur*]. . . ." There is little more to interpret in these few words on gift exchange than the stereotypical quality of the description, which the chronicler expresses even more formulaically elsewhere: on one occasion he writes *"muneratus muneraque ipsis . . . largitus est"*[181] and on another *"acceptisque ac datis muneribus."*[182] This formulaic language is simply another version of that general maxim Praetextatus had already referred to in court: a gift always implies reciprocity.[183] With these conventional turns of phrase, Gregory cites the "rule"; he maintains that the figures in his account have done what was required in such a situation. How exactly this was handled in 591, and to what end the protocol of gift exchange was used practically, is something Gregory does not even hint at. When the Neustrians "gave gifts in return" (*dona referre*), was the value of their presents calculated to pacify or to challenge? Were the gifts "equal" (*similiter referre*), as Gregory claims, or did they outshine Gunthchramn's presents—a not uncommon form of aggression?[184] We know nothing about these aspects, which would tell us far more about the practical relationships between the participants than the general and formulaic account Gregory provides. Gregory's phrases describe gift exchange as a social mechanism and conceal the participants' aims, they conceal the techniques actors used to represent themselves within this framework, the "controlled challenge"[185] that each of these solemnly bestowed gifts represented for the receiver, the various possible means of meeting the challenge in a given case.

Other documents provide a better idea of such practices, which Gregory's report tends to obscure. John the Deacon, for example, relates an event that occurred in 1001: In that year Otto III became godfather to a daughter of Petrus Orseolo, the doge of Venice. The accompanying exchange of gifts began with Otto's release of the doge and his successors from the yearly tribute of a *pallium*, which had been levied on the doges since 967. Then the emperor refused to accept return gifts, arguing that he did not wish anyone to believe that he had come out of greed, when he had come for the sake of Saint Mark and the doge. Afterward, he allowed himself to be coaxed for some time *(coartatus precibus)*, and finally accepted the gifts "reluctantly" *(licet invitus)*.[186]

Just as Otto used the exchange as an occasion to deploy the rhetoric of modesty and to display his imperial virtue—without even denying that it was a matter of prestige *(ne quis asserat . . .)*—the doge, too, placed the exchange in the service of his reputation. The benefit the doge drew from the exchange, of which the chronicler was aware but which he does not mention in the chronicle, is evident in the emperor's deed of gift. The deed shows that Petrus Orseolo had previously sent the chronicler John to the emperor as an emissary to ask for the very thing that Otto later gave him.[187] In the Venetian envoy's chronicle, the doge's request that the emperor release him from an obligation to pay tribute becomes an exchange of gifts between cofathers—a form of debt remission acceptable to the doge.

Gregory of Tours does not touch on such aspects of the issue. Only two details give some impression of the value of the events of 591: the fact that the actions of the parties were reciprocal and that the actions were part of a single ceremonial.

In 585, at a time when Gunthchramn still had the upper hand, when, in the eyes of the chronicler, he held the reigns of power in the whole kingdom *(regni principatus)*,[188] it was he alone who invited Fredegund, which, as the chronicler interprets it, was at once a sign of protection *(patrocinio suo fovebat)*, and—which Gregory does not say—of rule.[189] Those imperial sponsorships involving Charlemagne and Louis the Pious, Wulfhere or Charles III in which only the imperial godfather bestowed gifts and hosted a banquet were at the same time demonstrations of subjugation.[190] If things were different in 591, in Paris, if the "son" acted like the "father" *(similiter)*, the possibility of any demonstration of Gunthchramn's superiority was removed here. The protocol did emphasize Chlothar's "sonship" and put it on display in the way that the emperors would later do. What was at stake here was not subordination but acknowledgment—"international" relations. The reciprocal ritual of 591 demonstrated what Fredegar understood: Gunthchramn was establishing *(firmavit)* his nephew's rule over his father's kingdom.[191] He officially recognized him as the king of the neighboring territory. In this case the asymmetrical father-son metaphor was impractical. It would have better represented a time the participants preferred to forget in 591—a time when Gunthchramn had claimed paternal authority *(esse pater)* in Neustria, desiring "to govern on his own account the kingdom of his nephew Lothar," when he had appointed counts, disposed of church property and offices, and raised armies.[192] Now he was using the reciprocity of ritual practice to demonstrate something else altogether: his amicable *(amicitia)*, peaceful *(pax)*, and affirming *(firmare)* attitude.

What is striking is that Gunthchramn did not act otherwise in his meetings with Childebert, not even in 577, when he declared himself Childebert's adoptive father. Gregory does not tell us how (or even whether) such a protocol was arrived at, but he shows all the more clearly that Gunthchramn's striving for power in Austrasia had met with little success and, for example, that he repeatedly lost the diplomatic conflicts over synods. These fruitless efforts may have found further expression in the reciprocity of Gunthchramn's encounters with Childebert, whom he frequently claimed as a "son."[193]

Finally, knowing that the reciprocal actions followed immediately upon each other may help to explain something of the social and political function of this 591 action. Gift-giving particularly within the context of everyday social relations—for example, in a village—will have developed its value precisely in the latency period between the presentation of the gift and the return gift—in that period in which the receiver was in the giver's "debt." Only the return gift *(referre)* signaled release from obligation.[194] In the imperial sponsorships, too, the godfather's unilateral gifts created an obligation to that gratitude and obedience which is evoked by the image of the baptizee as "son."[195] Those cases in which no release from obligation, no *dona referre*, was intended, shed light on the harsh side of the son status of the baptizee, who was generally expected at the same time to take an oath of vassalage to his spiritual father. At the baptism of 591, however, neither participant owed a debt of gratitude to the other, and there was no advantage to be gained by playing out the latency period between gift and return gift. Gunthchramn's and Chlothar's gifts were instruments of representation, ones that were particularly well suited in this case to redefining Gunthchramn's politics by ritual means—demonstrating mutual recognition in a reciprocal rite where previously Gunthchramn had laid claim to protection and power by means of unilateral hospitality, *adoptio* and interventions.

The feast and the gift, forms of social relations far more common and older than sponsorship, thus did not merely intensify the sponsorship relationship, which was, after all, predated by a relationship of biological kinship. With the help of the banquet and gift exchange, Gunthchramn and Chlothar modified the way in which their relationship was represented. A variety of different attributes were now available to portray Chlothar's relationship to Gunthchramn. He was a nephew, a spiritual son, an *adoptivus*, an *alumnus*, and, finally, a man acting as an equal partner *(similiter)* in hospitality and gift exchange.

12
Sponsorship as a Social Practice

Gregory's account of the exchange of gifts in 591 is particularly revealing of the way in which such reports (not unlike official declarations) frequently mention only one aspect of social reality—namely, the rules—and present them as the whole reality. For the interpretation of such a case, other, more concrete examples can scarcely replace the information the narrator withholds, since, when it comes to interpreting social practice, there are as many possible actions as there are practical situations. Parallel examples can only furnish hints to the conceivable options. The individual instances studied here have presented the conceivable options, provided a glimpse of the work of creating and enforcing norms, and revealed the different ways in which sponsorships and their norms were used for the purposes of social or political positioning. Like marriages, baptisms and sponsorships were mass practices that played a significant role in both social and political life. With a combination of conventional allusions and a wealth of individual pieces of information, the medieval authors indicate, at least in outline form, the care and caution that were devoted to constructing and maintaining such relationships.

THE SEARCH

A hagiographer wrote of King Dagobert that he began, after the birth of his son, "to consider whom he should entrust with his son, to give him new birth in holy baptism."[1] It is a fair assumption that all parents engaged in such reflections, unless, of course, an angel in human form happened by to take the decision out of their hands.[2] The choice of a godparent is important to us in explaining the value of sponsorship for social relations, although the early medieval parents for whom we have any information largely selected their children's sponsors from among kings and aristocrats.

We know nothing about the circles of people from whom members of the lower strata chose sponsors for their children. As Hartmut Zwahr's study suggests for the early modern period,[3] such parents may have chosen their lords as godparents. At least we hear that, in the sixth century, such "lords lift their servants from the sacred font *(domini proprios famulos de sacro fonte suscipiunt)*."[4] It is also conceivable, as examples from the late Middle Ages show, that village parents chose sponsors from among their social peers. To take a famous example: Joan of Arc, the daughter of respected farmers from the parish of Domremy/Greux, was christened there, and all the godfathers and godmothers about whom we know anything were, like her parents, esteemed members of the village community.[5]

This example also reveals an option not available in the early Middle Ages: the choice of several sponsors, both male and female. All the early medieval examples recounted both by Gregory of Tours and by later chroniclers and hagiographers feature only one sponsor. By the sixth century, the sponsor's sex apparently was no longer of any great importance, although we know of few instances in which godparent and godchild were of different sexes. Saint Fridolin (sixth century) received a girl child from the font, Saint Tigernach (sixth century) had a godmother, and Saint Odilia (born ca. 660) a godfather.[6]

In some cases, it is evident that parents took a good deal of time searching for just the right sponsor, and perhaps for the right moment as well. We know that Chilperic's sons, Merovich and Samson, remained unbaptized for several years—in one case, two years, and in the other, probably even longer.[7] Ordered by the child's father to kill their blind daughter, the mother of Saint Odilia nevertheless did not make haste to baptize and thus save her from eternal damnation. Such worries seem to have been the province more of churchmen than of the laity.[8] Instead, she secretly gave the girl to a foster mother with whom she remained "for almost a year *(fere per annum integrum)*" before curiosity got the better of the neighbors. The foster mother then fled with the child to a convent and only there did a holy man, allegedly sent by God for this purpose, receive the girl from the font and give her the gift of sight.[9] Finally, Chlothar II reached the age of six before he was baptized.

Barring an acute emergency, such as Samson's illness,[10] parents would have taken care in choosing a godparent, whether they emphasized healing powers, as in the case of Odilia, or the sponsor's potential value for the family's social connections. The kinds of discussions that may have gone on between parents are among the private matters scarcely, if ever, alluded to in the sources. Let us take the argument between a certain Warache and his wife over the right sponsor for their child. The details are calculated less to "prove" the earnestness of such a search for godparents than to inform us about the social role of the person whose choice brought down upon Warache the "mighty wrath of his wife." According to the *Life* of Saint Fridolin, Warache chose Fridolin, who happened to be passing by, evidently without knowing him. His wife was so angry, the hagiographer reports, because Warache "had chosen such a wholly unknown and ragged man as his *compater*," one who was also not content to wander the roads on his own, but rather drifted around *(circumquaque vagare)* in the company of a number of others *(aliorum congregata multitudine)*.[11] Was it the hagiographer's intention here to present the typology of a woman who would not accept a holy man as a sponsor, or that of a woman who did not recognize the wandering Fridolin as a holy man? Either version is possible. Another set of parents, at least, who are mentioned in the *Life* of Trudo, were more cautious than Warache and waited until the holy man had performed a miracle before inviting him to sponsor their child. One evening, Trudo arrived at their home, shared a meal with them, and asked to spend the night. The pious host assented, but in the night his wife, plagued by curiosity, got up to watch the saintly guest while he slept. Naturally, and it is for this reason that the *Life* relates the story, she witnessed a miraculous sign which she immediately showed to her husband. The following day, the hosts pressed the holy man to stay, and, now that he had proven himself, asked him to stand as godfather to their son.[12]

In the case of Trudo, we also know of a second sponsorship.[13] This was not uncommon, since holy men were by no means averse to sponsoring children. To be sure, as early as the sixth century monks repeatedly were forbidden to enter into the "familiarity" *(familiaritas)* of sponsorship ties,[14] but the heroes of the early medieval *Lives* (who, of course, were not always monks) "gladly" *(libenter)* entered such relationships,[15] or at least had "nothing against them" *(nihil denegans)*[16] and did not refuse *(non rennuens)*;[17] indeed, they occasionally even asked to serve as sponsors.[18]

It is extremely likely, however, that not everybody could afford a saint as a godparent. The hosts described in the *Lives* were in a position to offer the holy men food and drink[19] and if they happened to be walking by, or returned later,[20] a bed for the night.[21] In some cases they erected a chapel if the *compater* had just performed a miracle on the site.[22] Some holy men even received large amounts of the hosts' property in conjunction with such sponsorships.[23] In short, the people described in the *Lives* were generally well-off.

To be sure, much remains hidden here. There may have been holy men who followed the rules and refused to serve as sponsors; and, with time, people may have learned whom they could turn to and whom not. Those who refused—perhaps, like Saint Amandus, citing the Apostle Paul's prohibition—lost social contacts and thus publicity. Potential hosts and donors had less interest in commemorating him, and a holy man who did not consent *libenter* to undertake such duties must have had far fewer chances of finding a hagiographer. We also do not know how high the proportion of holy men and churchmen, of monks, itinerant ascetics, or secular clergy was among godparents.

Among the known sponsors of the Merovingians, at least, very few are identified as holy men. Childebert II asked the miracle-working Veranus of Cavaillon to sponsor one of his sons and Dagobert I turned to Saint Amandus. Otherwise, the Merovingians, like the aristocrats of that era for whom we possess such information,[24] and the early Carolingians[25] seem to have chosen from among those in political power, some of them[26] preferring sponsors who were already kin, and others[27] men who possessed worldly power but who as bishops had the benefit of spiritual prestige as well. The great variety of sponsors who were chosen points to the diversity of social aims sponsorship could be expected to serve in the daily business of building and maintaining social relationships, and protecting oneself and one's family from harm in this life and the next.

Social Aims

The "Privatization" of the Holy Men

The aforementioned Warache, who invited the holy man Fridolin to serve as godfather to his daughter, did not stop there. He presented this "unknown and ragged man" with "a large part of his legacy and property," which apparently made his wife "even more furious."[28] If we are to credit the accounts in the *Lives*, Warache's actions were not all that unusual. The Neustrian *maior domus* Erchinoald treated the Irishman Furseus with equal generosity. First, he invited him to his farm, asked him to sponsor one of his children, and shared a meal with him; then he instructed three of his servants to show him all of his property so the holy man might select an appropriate site on which to establish his monastery.[29] Pirmin was also permitted to choose the island of Reichenau for the foundation of a monastery after serving as godfather.[30]

If a well-to-do man wanted to persuade a renowned holy man, whose *fama* had reached his ears,[31] to found a monastery on his land, he had first to establish social contact and create an appropriate atmosphere. The most common opportunity was the invitation to a meal. If we generalize the examples of the holy men Furseus, Trudo, and Pirmin, however, sponsorship also appears to have been a useful (and, correspondingly, widespread) means of creating the kind of bonds that might move a holy man to stay. In short, sponsorship was one of the methods aristocrats used to convince holy men to settle on their estates, and part of their efforts to "privatize" holy men and the places of worship they founded. In this way, the aristocrats also did something for the good of their own eternal souls and associated the holy men's prestige with their own names.[32]

Flexible Ties

In their accounts of sponsorship by holy men, as well as by political rulers, early medieval narratives contain several different expressions used by their authors to suggest that sponsorship was generally associated with the hope of social connections. Childebert II accused his fictive father, Gunthchramn, of using his sponsorship of Chlothar II to create "friendship" between himself and Chlothar.[33] A later hagiographer, who attributed the same sponsorship to Bishop Faro of Meaux (died ca. 672), also believed that it was a "friendship pact" *(pactum amicitiae)*.[34] The baptist Colmanus made a vow of "fraternity" *(fraternitas)* to his godson, Declanus, after the baptism,[35] while Fredegund wished the godfather, Gunthchramn, to regard her son Chlothar "as his own foster son" *(tamquam alumnum proprium)*.[36] According to a ninth-century hagiographer, a certain Count Waltbert set up a relationship of *compaternitas* with the holy man Bertinus (d. 698), "according to the laudable rite which is sanctified to create bonds of brotherly love *(fraternae caritatis foedera)*" among Christians. Similarly, according to an early-ninth-century source, two merchants of Ravenna "who wanted to create a bond between them" *(cupientes foedus inter se iungi)* used sponsorship as the means to do so.[37] Finally, we should not forget the standard terms for sponsors and baptizees, and occasionally the baptists as well, who were referred to as "fathers" (or "cofathers") and "sons."

For social historians, the type of bond sought in a given case is more interesting than the mere fact that sponsorship was used to create social ties. In the examples cited here, a sponsor could be referred to not only as a "friend" of the father but also as a "friend" of the baptizee,[38] and the godfather could promise "fraternity" to his spiritual son, but could just as easily refer to him as a "foster child" or "adoptive son." Such statements about sponsorship seem contradictory only if we assume that all these elements can be distilled into an institution with an ever-certain and unchanging meaning, regardless of context.[39] In reality, however—and here the difficulties disappear—a godchild was never "brother," "friend," "foster child," and "adoptive son" all at the same time. In each situation, the speaker emphasized whichever aspect seemed most appropriate. The stock of available terms did not follow a logic that always strove for consistency, but rather a practical logic, which emphasized a coherence sufficient to the goals at hand. One situation could require a "fraternal" relationship between sponsor and godson, and another that of (adoptive) father and son—just as one type of relationship between sponsor and baptizee might be represented by the reciprocal exchange of gifts[40] and another by a bond of vassalage.[41] The structure of such a sponsorship relationship depended not on the "character" or "nature" of the institution of sponsorship, but on the purpose for which the relationship had been set up in a given case. Sponsorship had a clearly defined field of application in ritual terms, but not in social terms. It was well suited to representing the imperial subjugations of the eighth to tenth centuries as father-son relationships, thus making them appear friendlier than they sometimes were. It was also well suited to creating a more or less symmetrical relationship between the "father" Gunthchramn and "son" Chlothar or, in the case of Colmanus and Declanus, even a relationship in which the father "commended" himself to the holiness of his spiritual son *(commendo me sanctitate tue)*.

However much the rite itself and perhaps the elaborations of the churchmen (such as the *sermones* of Caesarius) may have offered the semantics of "father" and "son" for the relationship between sponsor and baptizee, for the purposes of concrete social relationships this symbolism was set aside when not needed. None of the sixth- or seventh-century examples indicate any interest in a bond explicitly representing an asymmetrical relationship such as we find later in the imperial sponsorships. They follow the same ritual but do not use father-son imagery to define the relationship. To judge from the sixth- and seventh-century evidence, a sponsor did not use his or her relationship to a godchild any differently from that to the child's parents. Thus, it appears to have made no practical difference to Childebert that Bishop Ageric of Verdun could refer to him as his son, while Bishop Magneric of Trier was the king's cofather. Unlike the emperors of a later era, the Merovingians apparently placed little value on the status-conscious differentiation between subordinate sons from the font and equal cofathers. To put it another way, as in the guilds *(coniurationes)* or the Frankish institution of oath brotherhood, sponsorship created a relationship whose practical value was rendered as broad as possible by the vocabulary of kinship or words such as "friendship" and "love," and which, in concrete situations, was subject only to rather vague norms. The baptismal ceremony played the same role in cementing the relationship that the oath and the common meal played for the guilds and oath brotherhoods.

The ties were also flexible to the extent that they appear usually to have resulted from parents' momentary interest in a sponsor, and only later may also have become attractive as a connection between the sponsor and the child.[42] This is not as obvious a statement as it might seem for the sixth century, since the works of the late antique theologians and the earliest examples from social practice[43] have nothing to say about what was soon to be called *compaternitas*. Only in the sixth century was the sponsor's relationship to the godchild's natural parents provided with a nomenclature and a system of norms, i.e., institutionalized. When did the practice itself begin? Joseph Lynch has postulated that in the Arles of Caesarius[44] "many children [already] had a third parent . . . who had strong secular bonds to the child and to the child's parents." According to Lynch, Caesarius attempted to use this "social reality" for pastoral ends by encouraging sponsors to participate with parents in the child's religious education.[45] This interpretation is not improbable, although we have no sources to substantiate Lynch's assumption for Arles or for the era of Bishop Caesarius. No author before the second half of the sixth century mentions the formalized relationship between a sponsor and the baptizee's natural parents, that is, "coparenthood" as it would later come to be called.[46] Gregory's account of his own relationship to Eberulf, Magneric's relationship to Childebert, and Brunechildis' to Bertefred are the earliest evidence of *compaternitas* or *commaternitas*,[47] while nonetheless presenting it as a practice already common. Of the authors of the early Gallican rules for monks and nuns, which forbade them to act as sponsors, only Ferreolus, who was writing at the end of the sixth century, used *compaternitas*[48] as an argument for the prohibition, while Aurelian and the *Regula Tarnatensis*[49] give no grounds, and Caesarius still argues that those who voluntarily relinquished their freedom for the love of God should seek no other ties.[50]

One may follow Lynch in interpreting these pieces of evidence from the second half of the century to mean that in his pastoral admonitions Caesarius was already reacting to a widespread "popular practice" of setting up "strong secular ties" between parents and godparents. Caesarius did not go that far, however, writing only that the sponsors bore equal responsibility with the parents for the child's upbringing.[51] The existence of "coparenthood" as a social practice in Caesarius' Arles is thus an unprovable if not improbable hypothesis. The behavior of one of Caesarius' contemporaries, at least, may offer support for Lynch's interpretation. The man in question is Sigivald, who chose as a sponsor the son of King Theuderic, who represented a danger for him. This behavior is scarcely explicable unless we take into account the benefit this sponsorship tie would have a generation later—that is, creating *compaternitas* together with *paternitas*.[52]

We may follow Lynch this far, but there is no evidence to support one of his further, and initially tempting, assumptions. Lynch asserts that this popular practice of *compaternitas* was established by the laity without the approval of the church. He remarks that: "Only with difficulty over a fairly long period of time was coparenthood accepted and domesticated by the official church, and this relative freedom from ecclesiastical control probably enhanced its appeal."[53] The fact that churchmen gave this practice no place in the baptismal liturgy may support Lynch's assumption, since the liturgy was an official matter. But the idea that *compaternitas* should have enjoyed popularity among the laity specifically because the "official" Church had not integrated it (for example into the rite) is one for which Gregory's *History* or Caesarius' *sermones* offer no evidence. Gregory in particular, himself a bishop, invokes "cofatherhood" to explain to his readers why he stood idly by while his *compater* Eberulf plundered the churches.[54] And Gunthchramn Boso relied upon Bishop Magneric's ability to convince his "cofather" Childebert to spare the rebels.[55] In Gregory's *History* members of the laity do not use the institution of *compaternitas* any more frequently than kings and bishops. Sixth-century popular practice remains largely obscure among both the Franks and Caesarius' Gallo-Roman audience.

We may concede that the new types of ties did represent popular practice. The attitude of the "official church" at the time of Gregory of Tours, however, had already approached popular practice in many areas. According to Gregory's account, the "official church"—Lynch is doubtless thinking of the episcopate here—was by no means hostile to this development. The bishops were involved from the beginning. We would have difficulty distinguishing these bishops from the "people." Under the rule of Gunthchramn's godson Chlothar a number of these bishops had already emerged from this very same people.[56] We find no ecclesiastical resistance to this practice and thus need not read Caesarius' exhortations to sponsors to involve themselves in their godchildren's moral education as natural parents would as an attempt at domestication. There is no evidence that the "people" were taking advantage of a niche that had initially gone unnoticed by the church. This also applies to the rules for nuns and monks. In these rules Caesarius and his successors forbade those who had taken vows to renounce the world to return to that world. According to the regulations, those who had left their families to serve God should not enter into a new *familiaritas* nor seek any pretext for leaving the monastery or convent. This was a general objective of the authors of monastic rules. There is thus a perfectly good explanation for these prohibitions which need not have been associated with a general rejection of *compaternitas* on the part of the "official" church. As there is no evidence for such a rejection apart, perhaps, from the absence of coparenthood from ritual, we also have no grounds for claiming that the church had "great difficulties" with *compaternitas*.

Formalizing, Establishing, and Intensifying Relationships

In some cases, the participants evidently had no relations with each other before the establishment of the sponsorship tie. Thus, for example, Chilperic "inherited" Bishop Praetextatus in 567 along with the city of Rouen and found himself suddenly confronted with a powerful metropolitan bishop whom he perhaps did not know and certainly had not appointed.[57] King Sigibert doubtless had a similar experience with Bishop Ageric when he inherited Austrasia in 561.[58] The authors of some *Lives* also give the impression that their heroes were chosen as godfathers by people with whom they had had no previous contact. Furseus' hagiographer would have us believe that Erchinoald had only heard of Furseus' *fama*[59] when he summoned him. Fridolin is said to have been selected as a godfather by a man whose angry wife had no idea where he and his companions came from.[60] It seems that in these cases the parents used sponsorship to create a binding social relationship in the first place. This probably also applies to the imperial sponsorships, which were often preceded by military conflicts. They were intended to establish political ties between rulers who had not previously maintained such relations.

This was apparently not the case with the two merchants of Ravenna of whom the ninth-century presbyter Agnellus writes. It makes sense (although one could also make a case for the opposite situation) that two merchants who sought to "form an alliance with each other,"[61] should already have had a functioning and useful relationship with each other. An Austrasian aristocrat like Bertefred could probably only have chosen Queen Brunechildis to sponsor his daughter if he already belonged to the circle around the queen.[62] In such cases, which one may assume occurred more frequently in village contexts, it was less a matter of *establishing* a binding relationship than of *formalizing* a preexisting and useful relationship. People used the "laudable rite" of baptism to lend an existing informal relationship the status of a formal, publicly visible and presentable "alliance *(foedus)* of fraternal love," a formal *pactum*.[63]

Sponsorship was only one of a number of options for establishing a relationship or formalizing one that already existed. In all of the examples that are described in any detail we find a combination of several techniques for forming an official alliance. Chlothar and Gunthchramn were already bound by kinship ties when they entered into a sponsorship relationship, and they formally demonstrated their bond with banquets and gifts.[64] In the case of Charlemagne and Widukind, as in other, similar, examples the oath of vassalage was an additional official technique for creating bonds.[65] Aristocrats took a similar approach when they sought to win over one of the holy men, such as Fridolin, Furseus, or Pirmin: the holy man stayed on as a guest, ate with his host, was invited to stand as a sponsor and offered gifts.[66] Dudo of St. Quentin (d. 1026) captured the moment of intensification, of the accumulation of techniques for creating bonds: "may the bond of *greater* esteem and the tie of *greater* love unite them."[67]

These usually ritual techniques for creating formal ties had their value for social relations in the norms which, through ritual performance, became recognized as officially binding for future interactions between the parties. There were numerous overlaps among the rather broadly and vaguely defined norms, referred to by such words as *fides* or *caritas*, which governed the rituals of gift exchange and hospitality, vassalage, the oath brotherhood or guild, the sponsorship tie or kinship, but each emphasized a different aspect. With the accumulation of various ritual acts, official relations became intensified and alternative means of representation were created, means with whose aid certain aspects could be nuanced or toned down, expressed more vaguely or harmonized.

Harmonization

Imperial godparenthood is an example of how power relations were harmonized by means of sponsorship: the fathers were usually the victors, the sons the vanquished. Take the case of Charlemagne and the Saxon leader Widukind. At the time when Charlemagne instituted peace negotiations he had not managed fully to subjugate the Saxons with the efforts he was willing (or able) to make. Thus the Saxon leader was also in a position to dictate conditions. Charlemagne offered Widukind a form of treaty that preserved his honor and status: at Attigny he raised *(suscepit)* the Saxon leader "from the font and honored *(honoravit)* him with wondrous gifts."[68] Widukind was, of course, Charlemagne's vassal,[69] and he was clearly the vanquished party. But this fact was masked by an additional bond, whose prestige value lay precisely in its capacity to disguise the element of defeat and emphasize the honor *(rex honoravit)* of the vanquished. The spiritual sonship/adoption could be interpreted as an honor, and the act of subjugation was presented as a familial celebration, so that the conquered leader could return home an honored man, a "son" laden with gifts.

At times this form of harmonization might simply serve to conceal actual power relations. Charles III, for example, bought peace with the Norman leader Godefrid in 882 by means of a substantial contribution and the conferral of a powerful *dux*, but clothed his action as sponsorship: thus he ritually demonstrated his supremacy as Godefrid's "father" and could also present the contributions as christening gifts.[70] Regino of Prüm, however, tore the veil off the proceedings: according to his account, "the Norman leader Godefrid promised to become a Christian on the condition that the king bestow on him the province of *Fresia* as a gift *(munus)* and that he be given Chlothar's daughter Gisela in marriage."[71] Godefrid set the conditions for peace. The fact that here, unlike in other cases, there is no evidence of a *commendatio*, but only of a relationship by marriage, also makes clear that the sponsorship was intended to salvage the prestige of an emperor who was otherwise incapable of gaining the upper hand over the Normans. Sponsorship made it possible to compromise elegantly, without subjecting either side to humiliation.

Modifications and Ambiguities

What Regino of Prüm so baldly relates of this obvious case of euphemistic misrepresentation could easily be misleading if generalized. Charlemagne's imperial sponsorship of Widukind should not be read simply as the more attractive packaging of an 'objectively' none the less harsh subjugation. The combination of the two rituals—vassalage and sponsorship—actually changed the representation and definition of the bond of vassalage, interpreting it through the lens of filial status. In a similar way Gunthchramn and the Neustrians had limited the prestige effect of the asymmetrical sponsorship relationship at Chlothar's baptism by means of the accompanying rituals, the reciprocal exchange of gifts and hospitality. The same technique of accumulation was deployed at the christenings of Widukind and Harald of Denmark with the opposite objective. In these cases, the emperor's unilateral gift giving and hospitality intensified the public representation of vassalage and the father-son relationship in such a way that the receiver, who could not give in return, became "indebted" to the giver by the logic of gift exchange.[72]

This accumulation of various ritual actions which were, in their the normative and representative value, never wholly congruent, made these very representations and norms appear vague at the same time. [73] When combined into a single ritual ceremony, gifts, hospitality, vassalage, and sponsorship—each of which, when applied practically, opened up a wealth of nuances—produced a picture puzzle that could later be contemplated and displayed in various ways, depending on the situation. The accounts of Gregory of Tours reveal some of the possible ways of representing sponsorship relationships. Fredegund wished to have sponsorship interpreted as foster parenthood,[74] while Childebert associated it with his inheritance.[75] It could be read as humiliation, or as a universal Christian duty which lords even fulfilled for their servants.[76] In one case one could act as if a godfather disposed of his godson's property just as he would that of his blood offspring, while in another sponsorship could be imbedded in a ceremony emphasizing the equality of the participants.[77] Using the example of a letter from Charlemagne to Pope Hadrian, Arnold Angenendt has shown us the kind of fine-tuned "diplomatic" options for shifts of meaning that this very vagueness made possible.[78] Following Pope Hadrian's sponsorship of Charlemagne's son Carloman in 781, the emperor was able to refer to himself not only, as was traditional, as a "son" of the church and of the pope, but also as the *compater* of the pope. Charlemagne used the ambiguity that arose out of the juxtaposition of the two words to assert his version of the relationship between monarch and pope. He emphasized equality over subordination, mentioning first the *compaternitas* and then his filial status. According to his version he was "*compater* and son *(compater idemque filius)*," the pope "*compater* and father in Christ *(compater in Christoque pater)*." Ever since the days of Stephan and Pippin the popes had always interpreted the relationship in the reverse order.[79]

It appears that it was precisely this vagueness that was an important aspect of the sponsorship tie. Sponsorship was not as risky as marriage (however interpreted), which ultimately entailed certain relatively irreversible consequences, for example as regards inheritance. Sponsorship could be shaped quite freely and flexibly, and one had little to lose but a child "available" for such a bond. If the bond functioned properly, all was well, and if it did not, which was not infrequently the case in the instances discussed here,[80] the potential damage was rather limited in contrast to marriage.

Taking the Initiative

Parents faced with choosing a godparent lived in a social world which must have burdened the selection with all manner of constraints and considerations. We must proceed from the assumption that parents were expected to choose certain sponsors, just as social anthropologists and historians studying marital behavior have observed certain "expected" marriages (such as those with female parallel cousins), which were difficult to avoid. Scholars who wish to study such social "rules" governing marriage or the choice of a godparent need a mass of material that is unavailable for the early Middle Ages. A representative study of the expectations placed on parents, of the necessary considerations and constraints they faced, which we must take into account particularly in the case of small social formations such as villages, is impossible for the period in question. Only in exceptional cases do we possess any description, or even mention, of the interests not only of parents but of others active in the same social world.

Knowing who took the initiative for a given sponsorship tie might provide a clue to such interests. Normally the initiative would have come from the parents, as was usually the case in Gregory's examples[81] and as the *Lives* frequently relate.[82] Occasionally, however, we find instances of persons approaching the parents of a newborn and asking, or even demanding, to become the child's godparent and the parents' *compater*. One of these persons was Columbanus. When he was asked to intercede with his prayers and help *dux* Waldelenus and his wife Flavia to have a child he was quite prepared to do so but only, he is reported to have said, on the condition that "you dedicate this gift of the Eternal Donor to His name and give it to me to receive from the font." Columbanus was a socially powerful figure thanks to his contemporaries' high opinion of his piety *(virtus)* and in this case—at least according to his hagiographer—he used this reputation to recruit new blood for the monastic life. To be sure he promised the childless couple that he would pray for them to conceive another child so that they might have an heir, but he also warned them not to violate the pact *(pacti foedus violare)*.[83] The parents agreed to the conditions and events proceeded according to plan: Flavia bore a son whom Columbanus received from the font and then returned to her to raise *(nutrire)*, later accepting him into the monastery at Luxeuil.[84]

Columbanus was thus asked to help and negotiated the price in advance. If he demanded sponsorship in return, it must have appeared to him a significant and promising means of binding the boy and his wealthy parents to the monastery. Other, similar, stories substantiate this assumption. The Irish holy man Fregius is said to have asked his sister, who had just given birth to a son, to let him baptize the boy.[85] The sister agreed and when she wanted to take the child back after the christening in order to nurse him "the holy man would not permit this, saying: ... In God's name the boy will remain with me."[86] This holy man also had his way. In other cases the hagiographers and chroniclers do not, to be sure, relate that holy men took the initiative in order to gain novices for the monasteries, but they do occasionally report that children who had a holy man as a godfather (or in Ireland as a baptist) were destined for the ascetic life with that same holy man. The Irish holy man Colmanus baptized a boy by the name of Declanus, returned him to his natural parents to be raised and then took him back at the age of seven.[87] When he himself became a holy man this same Declanus made a similar request of the parents of a certain Ciaran, whom he had baptized.[88] Saint Fridolin was the godfather of a girl whose parents later turned her over to him *(commendare)*.[89] Saint Gamalbert, who received a boy from the font during a journey to Rome, imposed on his parents the condition *(indicere)* that they educate the boy and then, when he had reached manhood *(virum factum)*, send him to Gamalbert to take possession of his holy legacy *(hereditatem post se possessurum)*.[90] The father of a blind boy seems to have made clever use of this practice. He first ordered that the boy be killed, then came to fear for his soul and took him back. When Saint Colmanus came and claimed that the boy was a "servant of God" and more valuable than any of the man's other offspring, "the father loved him and gave him to the holy Colmanus so that he might raise him for God. And the holy Colmanus immediately baptized the child and gave him the name of Chellanus."[91] Sponsoring (or in the case of Ireland, baptizing) a child thus seems to have been one of the means by which holy men could recruit novices, and in the cases of Saint Columbanus and Saint Fregius it is clear that they themselves took the initiative and asked to sponsor, or in Ireland to baptize, a child.

This imperious behavior was, to be sure, the behavior of the stronger party. Not everyone who wanted to be a godparent could afford to be so bold. In the twelfth century Petrus Cantor related the story of a godfather whose godson had died. The godfather became "afraid that the goodwill (*gratia*) of his cofather (*compater*) might soon cool,"[92] and thus asked his cofather to give him his youngest child as a godson. This man had to negotiate from a weak position, since he was unsure of the "goodwill" of his "cofather." He then had to accept a rejection.[93] The fact that this story remains an isolated incident in the sources naturally does not mean that the situation itself was unique. All it tells us is that such failed efforts to form social ties did not find their way into the sources. Petrus Cantor also did not relate this story because he was interested in the practice of social relations; he was interested only in the norm which thwarted the father's effort.

It is unlikely, however, that people placed themselves in such situations frequently, since they represented a potential threat to the reputation of the participants, particularly the supplicants. Studies of how people deal with socially risky situations (such as arranging a marriage) demonstrate the existence of normally rather routine activities that enable participants to recognize a collision of interests in time, thus avoiding situations damaging to their reputations, such as the refusal of a request.[94]

NEGOTIATIONS

People usually avoid threats to their reputations by shunning the dangerous contact and sending a mediator to lay the groundwork for them.[95] We find only vague hints of such preparations in the organization of sponsorships, not least because the chroniclers and hagiographers generally report only the participants' formal requests and not the informal contacts that were so important in everyday political and social relations, and whose very nature it was to remain hidden. An account of events that reportedly took place at court in Paris at the time of Dagobert I paints a very clear picture. At that time a certain Geremar and his friend Audoenus *(amicus eius nomine Audoenus)* were sojourning in Paris as "advisers" *(consiliarii)*[96] to the king. Geremar asked his friend's advice on all matters *(omnia quae agebat per consilium eius exercebat)*. The two thus doubtless not only knew each other well, but also saw each other frequently. In spite of this, when Geremar had a son he did not personally ask his friend and constant interlocutor to sponsor his child; he sent a messenger to do so. According to the *Life* of Geremar the messenger prostrated himself and bade Audoenus to become the boy's godfather.[97]

It would not have been equally dangerous for all petitioners to ask another to be a sponsor. All other factors being equal, the petitioner was always in the more precarious position. The dangers and options the participants faced also depended upon a number of external factors, including the petitioner's social status relative to that of the potential sponsor, any preexisting relationship between the two, the religious prestige of the participants, and the means of enforcement available to the petitioner. The nature of the early medieval sources makes it well-nigh impossible to uncover and weigh the various social dangers and constraints that might have played a role in setting up an individual sponsorship relationship.

In the case of Geremar and Audoenus, the social position of the parties involved, to the extent that it was very similar, probably played a rather minor role, but the good friendship attributed to them by the *Life* was doubtless one of the constraints that would have made it difficult for Audoenus to refuse the request. We also need to ask what opportunities an Irish *peregrinus* like Furseus had to refuse if the Neustrian *maior domus* asked him to stand as sponsor. Did Furseus perhaps not refuse *(non rennuens)*[98] because he could not do so and remain in the country? In case of conflict it was the holy men who had to step aside, as Columbanus and Furseus later discovered. What of the other holy men who "gladly" fulfilled such requests[99] or had "nothing against it" *(nihil denegans)*?[100] Were they not obliged to create a network of at once well-disposed and well-heeled men whom they could call upon from time to time, requesting favors and property? What might the chronicler and bishop Gregory have had to fear had he refused to sponsor the son of the treasurer Eberulf, the same man who had ruthlessly and violently plundered and ravaged the region of Tours? What options were available to the "sycophant" Ragnemod, whom Chilperic had appointed bishop of his capital at Paris, when that same Chilperic wanted him to stand as godfather to his son?

We will have to settle for the hypothetical answers hinted at in these questions, since we lack the material for more concrete replies. Where one father might have to send out a mediator to test the waters another, perhaps because he had the right social position, could make his request straightforwardly without any risk of losing face. In order to grasp this in any detail, we would need far more information than we have in most cases. The available evidence offers no more than snippets of information on certain aspects, which can scarcely be generalized.

An interesting case is recounted by the holy man Amandus, who apparently managed to negotiate a sponsorship with King Dagobert from a position of strength. He had once done "what none of the bishops dared to do": he had criticized the king's sexual license and found himself driven from the kingdom by Dagobert. This measure was surely not calculated to further the king's reputation, and when the king, after extensive apologies, asked this same holy man to return to sponsor his son it certainly had the appearance of a peace offering. First, however, he had to send out a party of *ministri* to search for the man he had banished. We do not know whether they explained matters to the holy man; the *Life*, at least, maintains that Amandus returned with them rather reluctantly. The *ministri* told him "that he must go to the king," and he is said to have accompanied them in recollection of the Pauline dictum (Rom. 13:1) "Let every person be subject to the governing authorities."[101] The "diplomatic" situation was not a favorable one for the king. In banishing Amandus he had already deployed some of his heaviest artillery, and even now, when he had a request to make of the holy man, he had arranged the meeting in a most imperious manner, summoning him to his court through *ministri*. Thus when Dagobert formally asked his forgiveness and then requested that he sponsor his son, the holy man refused at first because "it is written" (2 Tim. 2:4) that the *militia* of God should not become entangled in secular pursuits *(saecularibus negotiis)*, but rather must seek solitude and shun the palaces. Then, it is reported, he left.[102]

As subsequent events revealed, this was nothing more than a move in a game that was by no means over. By adhering to the biblical norm Amandus raised his price substantially. The king persisted in his efforts, now no longer sending mere *ministri* after the holy man,[103] but rather two "illustrious men" with substantial religious cachet, as we know from other sources: Dado/Audoenus, the future bishop of Rouen, and Eligius, the future bishop of Noyon. The two no longer "summoned" *(admonere)* him to appear before the king, as the *ministri* had done, but rather negotiated *(petierunt)* with him. If he agreed to the sponsorship, they argued, he would have "more freedom in the kingdom because of this familial bond *(familiaritas)*" and "permission to preach wherever he wished." Amandus agreed to these conditions and the hagiographer could find only a flimsy excuse for this rapid lapse of scriptural memory, namely, that his hero was "wearied by the entreaties" of these illustrious men.[104]

There are at least some indications in other stories that Amandus was not alone in turning such a situation to his advantage. Columbanus demanded sponsorship as the price for his prayers on behalf of a childless couple who were trying to conceive.[105] When the Neustrians provoked him, Gunthchramn threatened not to fulfill his promise to sponsor Chlothar after all.[106] And in the sponsorship of sons of aristocrats by the holy men Furseus, Fridolin, and Pirmin, donations of land were always made *after* the christenings, but they were recounted as part of the same event. It is highly unlikely that these donations of land were surprising post-baptismal offerings that had not been negotiated beforehand. The fact that a father did not have an unlimited number of sons with whom to forge sponsorship ties with a holy man makes it probable that an agreement was reached on the proceedings as a whole, including the sponsorship and the present of land. And if the father's wish was to establish a monastery on his land, then he had to ascertain in time whether the saintly godfather fully intended to do his part.

It should be emphasized once again that if these examples reveal certain aspects of negotiation, this only proves that under certain circumstances it was possible to discuss the terms of such a sponsorship, but not that such negotiations were common. Relations of dependency and status inequalities, and not least the social arena in which the participants moved must have had an effect here. A Merovingian who offered a sponsorship tie to one of his bishops will have behaved differently and anticipated different reactions than a subject like Bertefred when he made his request to the queen. And a holy man will have responded differently to the request of a king or a *maior domus* than to that of an aristocrat. To ask a friend, as Geremar did, was quite another matter from what Eberulf had in mind when he made his request to the politically unavoidable Bishop Gregory. And a man such as Eberulf who had a high office at court doubtless asked differently from a man without such an office. Finally, these examples have about as much relevance to social arenas beyond the realm of the "great" and politically active, for example to the village context, as the marriage negotiations of the ruling dynasties have to the marital strategies of "normal" people.[107]

The Official Request

The careful testing of the waters through mediators, which anthropologists have sometimes observed among parents looking for a sponsor for their child, aims to safeguard the reputation of the petitioners. In other words, by the time they make a formal request the answer is already fairly certain[108] The very point of such preliminary discussions is that they are informal and inconspicuous, and therefore perhaps subject to observation by anthropologists, though we would be very lucky to happen upon them in the early medieval sources. King Gunthchramn used one of the two complementary social techniques for limiting the potential conflicts and risks involved in setting up a sponsorship tie as an argument when compelled to justify his sponsorship before his Austrasian nephew. He noted that "the call to perform this office is one that no Christian should refuse."[109] He was doubtless citing a generally accepted norm here, but he was nonetheless not telling the whole truth. He suppressed the fact that, in order to avoid imperiling one's own reputation, one never asked someone to become a sponsor who intended to refuse. Thus when Fredegund formally asked her brother-in-law Gunthchramn to sponsor her son, she must have been sure of his assent. What opportunities Fredegund had to test his willingness, and what opportunities Gunthchramn had to prevent Fredegund from making her request, however, belong to the realm of informal practices whose existence we must assume without being able to prove it.

It was precisely because they were informal that Gunthchramn could suppress them in his argument. He argued in terms of the norm and not its practical application. In fact, once a formal request had been made it was indeed something no Christian could refuse, at least not without provoking a conflict and perhaps even losing face, since humiliating others rarely boosts one's own social prestige. Such a loss of prestige, however, is just as difficult to demonstrate in the early medieval sources[110] as the informal explorations which doubtless occurred particularly in political sponsorships. There is only rarely any evidence in the sources of a risk to the parents' prestige, a risk dependent on the exploratory discussions that had gone before and on the status of the relationship.

An account by Agnellus concerning the two merchants of Ravenna who wished to form an alliance with the help of a sponsorship tie at least provides some hints. Agnellus imagined the following dialogue:

> Two men desired to form an alliance *(foedus)* with each other. One of them said to the other, who had [just] had a child: 'I ask a small favor of thee and hope that my entreaty *(obsecratio)* will not go unheeded.' The other then replied: 'I shall not make difficulties for thee. Thou shalt have thy wish.' And [the other one] spoke: 'Give me thy son, that I may be his father in holy baptism. . . . Let us be fathers in common, thou his bodily and I his spiritual *(spiritualis)* father.' And the other said: 'In the name of our Lord Jesus Christ let it be so.' And thus did they act.[111]

In the story as told by Agnellus, the two men were of one mind about the alliance and chose a tried and true method for cementing it. Since they were in agreement, the petitioner took no social risk. The fact that the other man had already offered him a sort of carte blanche ("I shall not make difficulties for thee. Thou shalt have thy wish") before he had even uttered his request also indicates that this request situation was a ritualized game whose possible outcome had already been explored.

The chronicler Gregory also begins his account of the baptism of Chlothar II with an official request by Fredegund: "'Let my lord the king come to Paris; let him send for my son, his nephew, and bid him receive the consecration of holy baptism; let him with his own hands lift the child from the sacred font, and deign to treat him as his own son.'"[112] At this point Fredegund had already known for some time that Gunthchramn would "deign" to undertake the sponsorship, since it had been arranged years before and Gunthchramn had long demonstrated his great interest in doing so.[113]

To this extent the encounter between Dagobert and Amandus represents a striking departure: it was precisely not an "avoidance process,"[114] not a tentative exploration, but rather a continuation of the conflict. Amandus had provoked the conflict with his criticism of the king's excesses, which had led to his banishment, and then, when the king had used up his heaviest artillery and gone down on his knees *(prostratus)*[115] to offer peace—as the hagiographer claims—he provoked him once again. What Amandus wanted was not to arrive at a conflict-free solution, but rather to have it out with the king.

Prestige through Ritual

The ritual act through which sponsorship was established was, not least, an act of prestige. When Chilperic staged the christening of his son Theuderic in Paris in 582 it was just as elaborate a celebration as Chlothar's baptism in 591 and that of Dagobert I's son Sigibert, whose godfather was Saint Amandus.[116] The occasions were "grand festivities" attended by "the entire army," "many nobles . . . , court officials and counts," and naturally also by that unmentioned backdrop of people who watched the king enter the city for his son's baptism, "preceded by the relics of many saints."[117] Such descriptions give us some sense of the elaborate preparations Chilperic may have made when, in emulation of the Byzantine emperor, he became godfather to converted Jews, or of the celebration of the christening of Clovis at which Remigius reportedly stood as sponsor.[118]

As for the imperial sponsorships, Arnold Angenendt has explained the prestige value for the imperial godfather in terms of monarchical self-display. He believes that the striving of rulers to occupy not merely a secular but also a priestly office *(rex et sacerdos)* was, in the reality of mission, ritually demonstrated in one place only: in sponsorship. It was only here that the ruler performed a liturgical service, only here that his priestly pretensions took visible form in the mission.[119] It is, to be sure, difficult to grasp this increase in prestige, but the fact that the chroniclers occasionally "improved" upon the story, if necessary inventing an imperial sponsorship of a converted king is, at least, a clear indicator.[120] The sponsorship act as the visible expression of active and successful missionary activities "demonstrated" that the emperor conformed to the western Christian ideal of a ruler, i.e., that he was an ideal ruler.[121]

Having the right godfather also boosted the prestige of baptizees. Harald of Denmark for example, whose sponsor was Louis the Pious, was doubtless one of the baptizees who himself took the initiative. At a time when he needed strong support against his rivals in Denmark he turned to his mighty neighbor Louis and had himself made into his "son."[122] There are also examples of proselytes themselves expressly requesting a particular godfather. Thus in 864/66 Boris, khan of the Bulgars, who had been conquered by Byzantium, asked to be baptized with the emperor's name, which probably means that he had asked the emperor to sponsor him.[123] In a letter to the Byzantine emperor Leon III, Pope Gregory II (715–31) spoke of western princes to whom he had "already sent out bishops and priests of our holy church" noting that "the rulers of those people, however, did not want to bow their heads before them and accept baptism, but rather requested us personally as a godfather."[124] And according to the hagiographer Rodulph, Robert, the father of William of Dijon, was able to "convince" *(suggessit)* Emperor Otto to become his son's catechumenate sponsor—a sign for Rodulph that Robert was "wise and resolute."[125]

The Practical Relationship

Cultivating the Relationship

Whether or not sponsorship actually established a lasting relationship in social practice depended less on sponsorship as a ritual and normative system than on its regular cultivation in concrete individual cases, which was the only guarantee that it would be there to fall back on when necessary.

The sources occasionally hint that a particular sponsorship affected social relations over a long period of time. For example, more than fifteen years after the birth of King Childebert the rebels Berthefred and Gunthchramn Boso still knew who his godfather was and relied upon this sponsorship tie. And the last of our "late-antique" witnesses, Caesarius and

Florianus, describe the sponsorship tie as having an existence that survived even death. Florianus wrote to Nicetius of Trier that when he atoned for his sins he relied upon the intercession of his dead sponsor,[126] and in his sermons Caesarius declared the godfather responsible before the divine judge for the sins of his godchild.[127] We must leap ahead several centuries before finding further evidence to support this argument. In her *Liber manualis,* Dhuoda admonished her son William not to omit from his prayers the now dead man "who adopted you as a son in Christ through the font of regeneration."[128] Finally, Petrus Cantor ends the story in which a man asked a father for a new godson after his first had died with the father's answer: "For *caritas* sake we entered the bond of cofatherhood and thou art tied to me by cofatherhood as I am to thee. . . . If thy godson has died, I need not enter into cofatherhood with thee again [through a second son]."[129]

According to these texts, the dead were as present in the cultivation of sponsorship relationships as they were in other familiar social formations of the early Middle Ages, such as monasteries and guilds.[130] The cases cited refer to the norm, however. Caesarius and Dhuoda were both admonishing others, and the father in Petrus Cantor's account needed a reason to reject a sponsorship. We have no practical evidence of this presence of the dead and of the cultivation of relationships with them such as exists for the monastic custom of the necrologies.

We nonetheless possess a number of examples of the cultivation of sponsorship relations with living allies. Sigivald lived with his godfather while his father was elsewhere.[131] A "cofather" of Saint Trudo's demanded *(postulare)* that the latter visit him.[132] Saint Fidolus received a similar request and found that the wine flowed freely in his cofather's house.[133] The hagiographer of Saint Richarius (Riquier) mentions in passing that whilst on a journey he visited a woman whose son he had sponsored, and enjoyed a cheerful meal there.[134] The *Life* of the Irish holy man Abbanus recounts that he had undertaken the baptism of a "*heros* and tyrant, who was always killing and robbing" and of his son who then remained in contact *(in conversacione felici)* with Abbanus "until his death."[135] And a man who had forged a "bond of love" *(foedus caritatis)* with the abbot Bertinus through sponsorship "often visited Bertinus."[136] Since this practice was not merely expressly forbidden by many monastic Rules, but also, as Saint Amandus is reputed to have said, because this prohibition could be justified by Scripture, the hagiographers generally omitted any mention of wine and convivial feasts at such meetings, relating instead behavior better befitting a holy man: parents and sponsors met to discourse on holy matters.[137] And when people met for such pious colloquies or to drink wine or dine sociably,[138] the hagiographers also sometimes mention the bestowing of gifts upon visiting spiritual kin. Saint Trudo, for example, is said to have received a wild boar[139] while Remigius of Reims received a silver vase from King Clovis.[140] Finally, the reciprocal forms of address also contributed to the constant cultivation of relationships. Whatever other kin or formal relationships might have connected a father or mother with a child's godparent, it was now possible, for example for Fredegund, to speak of Gunthchramn as her *compater* as well as her brother-in-law. This is how the popes and the Carolingians spoke to each other, and this is how Agnellus imagined the two merchants of Ravenna addressing each other in his story.[141] Each time they used these forms of address, the participants evoked the sponsorship relationship with its normative value, thereby renewing and stabilizing it.

Activating Relationships

The social value of such a carefully cultivated relationship lay in the opportunity to activate it when it was needed. Thus the holy man Tigernach went to see his godmother, Saint Brigid, one day. During this visit she decided that he was worthy of the episcopal dignity and "after having called together the episcopate, she made him a bishop."[142] When the holy man Berchar wanted to found a monastery with several "brothers" he turned to his godfather, Nivard of Reims, so that he might give him a suitable piece of land. Nivard fulfilled his wish and made his godson an abbot.[143] In the case of Brunechildis it appears that during an uprising she attempted to activate a sponsorship tie to one of her enemies in order to neutralize him.[144] Finally, it is striking that Gregory recounts in several cases how third parties relied on the possibility of successfully activating a sponsorship bond. Both Gunthchramn Boso (twice) and Bertefred counted on the ability of the godparents and cofathers of kings to activate these ties on their behalf.[145]

The Value of the Rules

Forms of Address—Valuation and Prestige

When medieval authors interpret sponsorship ties or describe someone else's interpretation of them, they use the words *amicitia* or *pactum amicitiae*, *fraternitas, amor, caritas, dilectionis vinculum*, or *foedus*.[146] When, however, the text focuses not on the interpretation of this social and religious apparatus but rather on a description of how the participants dealt with each other, then the form of address itself is used to express the relationship. Baptismal sponsors, or occasionally (in Ireland always) baptists, and quite rarely confirmation sponsors on the one side, and the child and his or her parents on the other, referred to each other using words that were either borrowed from the terminology of biological kinship or easily distinguishable modifications thereof: *compater, commater, filius/filia spiritualis/ex lavacro, filiolus, filiola, patrinus, matrina*. This vocabulary recalled the morality of kinship without however creating any confusion or ambiguity between spiritual and carnal kinship. In the comparatively rare examples that simply used the terms *pater* or *filius*[147] to refer to spiritual kinship, the context itself prevents any confusion ("my son Merovech, whom I had received from the font of regeneration").[148]

In social intercourse, these modes of address using kinship terms had less descriptive than normative or prestige value. By referring to someone as "father" or "mother," "cofather" or "comother," "son," or "daughter" one evoked the norms of conduct that applied to the parent-child relationship and thus expected a certain mode of behavior from an addressee. The nephew Chlothar, for example, could call his uncle Gunthchramn *pater* or *pater spiritualis* (*patrinus* was not yet in use) if he wished.

Apart from their value for making demands, familial forms of address when used between those linked by baptism had prestige value both internally, in regard to their self-perception as allies, and externally, in regard to one or both participants' presentation to the outside world. Florianus of Romenum for example, mentioned his "father in baptism," Ennodius of Pavia, by name in a letter to Nicetius of Trier, who was probably a stranger to him, using this relationship with his sponsor as a recommendation.

Fulfilling the Duties of a Sponsor—Honorable Behavior, Emotions, and Morality

Chilperic pardoned Pathir, at whose forced baptism he had stood as sponsor, protecting him with a *licentia*.[149] Theudebert saved the life of his godson and kinsman Sigivald and reportedly "received him with joy" and "embraced him" when they were reunited.[150] Chlothar II allowed his godson Merovich—who was also the grandson of his cousin Childebert—to live when he had all other members of this branch of his family killed, and he too is said to have "felt a godfather's affection" for him.[151] The chronicler also explains Brunechildis' offer of amnesty to Bertefred in terms of sponsorship.[152] Louis the Pious is said to have given his godson Harald gifts "in love," and Dhuoda calls the godfather of William of Aquitaine his *amator*.[153] The two merchants whose sponsorship relationship Agnellus mentions "loved each other in the Holy Spirit and in the kiss of peace, as is fitting for those who have such dealings with each other"[154]—a stock story which expresses the norm of godparently behavior without therefore necessarily rendering the account unrealistic.[155] It appears that Agnellus and the authors of the other examples cited here were trying to say the same thing as the author of the *Vita Bertini* who remarked that the "sanctified and laudable rite" of baptism created "the bond of fraternal love between Christians."[156]

We may wish to refer to emotions when speaking of "love," and to "morality" when speaking of the fulfillment of the obligations of "love." These are, however, ciphers at best which are of no use to social historians until we interpret them. Emotions as a category applicable within social history are not fragile "mere automatic responses," but rather "a sort of *institution* controlled in the same way as a ritual,"[157] possessing a "grammar" of its own,[158] which was "known" within a given social space. In other words, this emotional grammar was transmitted socially, at least in part. This is all the truer (and doubtless undisputed) as it applies to "morality," which might be defined for the work of the social historian as "the totality of the conditions . . . according to which decisions about respect and disrespect are made in this system."[159] If the norms of sponsorship could regulate behavior, the fulfillment of the norms must have had a corresponding place within the matrix of respect and disrespect.

To this extent emotions and "morality" guarantee relatively similar and thus relatively predictable reactions in a social field,[160] and it was only for this reason that it made sense for legal texts to invoke the duties of "love."[161] It was also for this reason that Chilperic, Theudebert or Chlothar II, acting in concrete contexts, gave a similarly material form to the "love" of spiritual kinship. The actors, Chilperic, Theudebert or Chlothar II shared a similar morality and relatively similar emotional reactions with other people from their social world, so that their moral conduct, where they acted publicly, was at the same time honorable conduct, a mode of behavior that heightened their prestige. When, for example, Chilperic allowed his godson Pathir to live, this was also an act of royal prestige for, as the chronicler reports, "the people" were standing before the church in which Pathir had taken refuge.[162] This naturally does not mean that Chilperic only acted as he did to gain public approbation, but such actions following the norm (or morality) had that consequence nevertheless, as Chilperic well knew.

Calling in the Obligations of Sponsorship—The Use of Gentle Force

When making requests of their spiritual kin, those who cultivated their sponsorship ties carefully and kept them alive always used the same implicit argument: that familial obligation demanded the fulfillment of their petitions. What was formulated as a request became, to all intents and purposes, a demand, as the language of the authors reveals. According to the chronicler, King Childebert felt "unable" to refuse his godfather Ageric's request to spare the life of Gunthchramn Boso.[163] It is precisely this argument that the chronicler had the rebel make when he fled for the second time to the godfather of a king: "'. . . holy bishop, I know that thou art as a father to the king's [Childebert's] son [Theudebert] . . . and that whatsoever thou askest of him shall be granted thee, nor *can* he refuse thy sanctity anything which thou shalt *request (poscere)*.'"[164] The hagiographers of the holy men Trudo and Fidolus relate similar stories. Their "cofathers" did not *ask* the two holy men for a blessing, or *invite* them to visit; they demanded *(postulare)* their blessings and visits—which also entailed a shared meal, that is, the cultivation of the relationship.[165] This was the central social value of a sponsorship bond: a request to a spiritual kinsman was in practice a demand which could be avoided only at the cost of social tensions or a loss of reputation (trustworthiness, credit).

This does not, however, help us in our analysis of individual cases, since in social practice a sponsorship was only a *potential* bond, whatever the norms may have dictated. In the case of each individual sponsorship, the bond and thus its social value depended upon the cultivation of the relationship, upon gifts and hospitality, upon constant reminders, in the form of representation and demands, of the sponsorship tie and its norms.

We must assume that in their practical dealings with each other spiritual kin were linked by the informal force of trust and piety, personal obligation and loyalty, indebtedness and gratitude (for example for hospitality or gifts), which arose from such bonds more frequently than we can demonstrate in an individual case. The rather sparse descriptions typical of the medieval documents in particular make it well-nigh impossible to see these socially quite effective forms of force at work in a concrete case. When, for example, we hear that Saint Brigid received a visit from her godson, found him worthy to become a bishop, and then immediately "made" *(facere)* him one with the help of an assembly of bishops,[166] the author leaves out precisely how her godson managed this, how he had previously cultivated his sponsorship relationship to Brigid, why he went to her, how she presented her decision to the bishops or what role she played among them so that she was able simply to "make" her godson a bishop. Similar unanswered questions remain when, for example, we read that the holy man Gamalbert made his godson, who apparently had traveled far to see him, his heir and successor.[167] There are also many open questions in all those instances in which someone fulfilled his duties as a sponsor without our knowing who or what inspired him to do so, what "belief," interests or social pressure from what quarter determined his actions.

Citing Norms—Legitimating Practice

We have several examples in which one of the actors used the norms of sponsorship to justify his conduct. Gregory of Tours allowed the treasurer Eberulf to steal church property and then explained to his readers that, as his "cofather," he was obliged to "overlook such deeds."[168] And when King Gunthchramn became godfather to his nephew Chlothar he had to justify this action to his other nephew, Childebert, also invoking a norm: that no one may refuse a request for sponsorship.[169] But this is precisely what the holy Amandus did (at least initially) when King Dagobert wished him to sponsor his child, and Amandus also cited a norm in justification of his behavior: namely, that a man of God may not become entangled in familial matters.[170] Petrus Cantor tells of another man in a different situation who also rejected such a request and invoked a rule: the man making the request was already the godfather of a now dead child from the same family, and it was as forbidden to sponsor two children from the same family *(cognatio)* as it was to have (consecutively) two wives from the same family.[171] Praetextatus, who had taken Merovich's side even when he rebelled against his father, Chilperic, declared in court that he would have done anything, even "summoned . . . an angel from heaven to succour him [Merovich]; for . . . he was my spiritual son, from his baptism.'"[172] He too justified his behavior by citing a norm.

Doubtless at least some of those who justified their actions by referring to the rules were also subjectively convinced by their own arguments. When Fredegar, for example, states that Chlothar II had mercy on the Austrasian Merovich because of the sponsorship tie, and when Gregory informs us that Brunechildis wished to spare the rebel Bertefred because he was her *compater*, the chroniclers may well have believed what they were writing. It was not incorrect as such, and we can imagine some good reasons why Brunechildis, for example, should have turned to her *compater* of all people. The chronicler, however, by no means mentions all of her motivations, and perhaps not even the most important of them.[173] The same could be said for other cases. Praetextatus does not appear to have fulfilled his godfatherly duties as innocently as the speech he made in his own defense would have us believe.[174] King Gunthchramn, although mentioning the "rules of the game," also fails to specify the concrete application of these rules: normally, no one was asked to stand as sponsor whose consent was not a foregone conclusion.[175] Was Amandus genuinely interested primarily in remaining faithful to the norm when he rejected Dagobert's request? At any rate, he forgot the norm soon enough when he was offered better conditions.[176] And the man whom Petrus Cantor cites referred to a prohibition which the scholastic believed was unknown to the church in many regions.[177] Certainly this does not mean that the man simply invented this curious analogy which he referred to as a prohibition. However, it does mean, had he placed much value on his relationship with the petitioner, that he could easily have found arguments against his "misgivings."

In short, the rules governing the sponsorship bond at once legitimated practices and (through the making of implicit or explicit demands) regulated them. Since this regulated behavior was not merely honorable conduct but also "moral" conduct, with less emphasis on the element of utility, people in the examples cited here also did not use the legitimating function simply as a trick. The apparently devious application of the rules destroyed their practical utility. Churchmen soon found new rules to try to thwart such parents as those who "cunningly *(callide)*"[178] received their own child from the font "by mistake" in order to separate from their spouses, citing the rules on incest.

Avoidance and Disrespect—The Limits of the Rules

Some of the examples cited here have also allowed us to observe the value of the rules governing sponsorship in competition with other factors that determined practice. When Childebert, the Austrasian king and godson of Bishop Ageric, was asked by his godfather to spare the life of the insurgent Gunthchramn Boso, the chronicler tells us that he "could not" afford to refuse. Gunthchramn Boso was not, however, just any criminal, but rather a rebel and the king could not simply let him off scot-free. He fulfilled the letter of the "kinship" rules, but in fact continued to pursue his own interests by turning the matter over to his uncle Gunthchramn.

Implicitly, though, he at least acknowledged a rule, which he dared to circumvent, but not to break. The social utility of such a ruse is not easy to pinpoint. On the one hand, as the trial of Praetextatus had shown,[179] it was advantageous to have the rules of sponsorship on one's side at least formally. On the other hand, such merely formal or deceitful behavior was damaging to one's social position. In this case no criticisms of Childebert's behavior have come down to us, but in other cases of crafty conduct the chroniclers stated their opinions quite plainly. According to Gregory of Tours the actions of the devious Rauching were "villainous" *(nequissimus)* and "evil" *(perversus)*, while Widukind of Corvey found the crafty deeds of Bishop Hatto of Mainz "treacherous" *(perfidus)*. Finally, the compiler of an Irish penitential wished to see the penance for deceit made equal to that for murder and incest.[180] The public judgment of a person was "a total judgment on the total man, which like such judgments in all societies, involves the ultimate values and takes into account—at least as much as wealth and solvency—the qualities strictly attached to the person, those which 'can neither be borrowed nor lent.'"[181] Deceit might render one's position legally unassailable—we may recall Praetextatus here—but it could also be deleterious to the reputation, the public "total judgment of the total man." A man who voluntarily risked acquiring such a negative reputation as Hatto or Rauching, however, must have felt the benefits outweighed the potential perils. Childebert, for example, was faced with a conflict between two interests when he pursued the rebel Gunthchramn Boso: he could follow the rules with honor and prestige by pardoning the rebel, or he could circumvent the rules with craft, condemning the rebel via the detour of his uncle. He chose what was more important to him, namely the removal of the dangerous insurgent, over the prestige that following the rules would have gained him.

In other examples the participants paid far less attention to the duties of the sponsorship tie. Chilperic apparently was not at all worried (neither was Praetextatus, incidentally) by the fact that Praetextatus was his "cofather."[182] Eberulf's material interests and his actual military might were sufficient to render the obligations of sponsorship a completely useless weapon against him.[183] Charles Martel deposed and banished his godfather (whom his father, not he, had chosen).[184] Finally, there is the case of Berthefred: he entered into several competing alliances, a coalition of rebels and one of baptismal kin. He chose the alliance of rebels, although we may suspect that the man who had "murmured against Queen Brunhild, and longed once more to humiliate her"[185] had not cultivated his cofatherly relationship to the queen for some time, so that the bond he sacrificed was scarcely socially efficacious anymore.[186]

Not even in the case of this rebel, however, does it seem promising to draw any inferences about "morality" from his actions. Even here we are hard-pressed to make it plausible that he did not take the rules of sponsorship seriously or view them as an obligation. Our analysis of the multiple purposes and benefits, and our insights into the dependency of the various possible readings on specific situations, cannot hide the fact that the actors doubtless often believed what they said: that subjectively speaking they acted out of piety, frequently loved their spiritual kin, and were convinced that they were doing their best for them. However, even if more abundant sources occasionally allow us to show this concretely for a later period, we can only make general assumptions about the early Middle Ages. All that the sources permit us to reconstruct with any certainty is the social functioning of relationships: the value of the rules governing sponsorship in concrete situations in which they were invoked to justify actions, explicitly or implicitly called in, deftly circumvented, or followed in a mundane or sometimes more demonstrative and elaborate manner. Viewed in this way—leaving aside all questions of the actors' subjective feelings—these rules proved themselves to be exceedingly open and flexible instruments of social practice and regulation, or of individual positioning.

Notes

*Chapter 1. Examining Sponsorship and Adoption
in the Realm of Kinship Studies*

1. Saint Boniface, *Die Briefe des heiligen Bonifatius und Lullus*, ed. M. Tangl, MGH, Epp. sel. I (Berlin, 1916), Letter 32, 56: "Quod peccati genus, si verum est, actenus ignorabam et nec in antiquis canonibus nec in decretis pontificum patres nec in calculo peccatorum apostolos usquam enumerasse cognovi." Saint Boniface, *The Letters of Saint Boniface*, trans. Ephraim Everton (New York, 1940; repr. New York, 1976), 61–62 (with some modifications).

2. Boniface, *Briefe*, nos. 33, 58: "Ut si hoc in catholicorum patrum decretis vel canonibus vel etiam in sacro eloquio pro tam magno peccato conputatum esse inveniretis, indicare mihi curetis"; *Letters of Boniface*, 63.

3. *Briefe*, 56: "Adfirmant sacerdotes per totam Franciam et per Gallias nec non et pro his maximi criminis reum esse hominem, qui in matrimonium acciperit illam viduam, cuius antea filium in baptismo adoptivum suscipiebat"; *Letters of Boniface*, 61.

4. *Briefe*, 58: "ut et ego intellegendo cognoscam, cuius auctoritas sit in illo iudicio, quia nullatenus intellegere possum, quare in uno loco spiritalis propinquitas in coniunctione carnalis copulae tam grande peccatum sit, quando omnes in sacro baptismate Christi et ecclesiae filii et filiae fratres et sorores esse comprobemur." *Letters of Boniface*, 63.

5. See Josef Freisen, *Geschichte des canonischen Eherechts bis zum Verfall der Glossenliteratur*, 2d ed. (Paderborn, 1893), 507–55; and Joseph H. Lynch, *Godparents and Kinship in Early Medieval Europe* (Princeton, 1986), 219–81.

6. See, among Arnold Angenendt's works, *Kaiserherrschaft und Königstaufe: Kaiser, Könige und Päpste als geistliche Patrone in der abendländischen Missionsgeschichte*, Arbeiten zur Frühmittlalterforschung 15 (1984); and "The Conversion of the Anglo-Saxons Considered Against the Background of the Early Medieval Mission," *Angli e Sassoni al di qua e al di là del mare. Settimane di studio del Centro Italiano di studi sull'alto medioevo*, 32 (1986): 747–92. Among Joseph Lynch's works, see *Godparents*, as well as his "Hugh I of Cluny's Sponsorship of Henry IV: Its Context and Consequences," *Speculum* 60 (1985): 800–826. For a discussion of social anthropological research, see Lynch, *Godparents*, 57–74; for research by modern historians on sponsorship, see esp. David Sabean, *Kinship in Neckarhausen 1700–1870* (Cambridge, 1997); and, for a comparison, Jürgen Schlumbohm, *Lebensläufe, Familien, Höfe. Die Bauern und Heuerleute des Osnabrückischen Kirchspiels Belm in proto-industrieller Zeit, 1650–1860* (Göttingen, 1994), esp. 595–606.

7. Lynch, *Godparents*, 337.

8. Rimbert, Vita Anskarii auctore Rimberto, ed. Georg Waitz, *MGH SS rer. Germ.* 55 (Hanover, 1884), 26: "ipse de sacro fonte suscepit sibique in filium adoptavit"; The Venerable Bede, *Vererabilis Bedae historia ecclesiastica gentis Anglorum*, IV, 34, 2 vols., ed. G. Spitzbart (Darmstadt, 1982), 356: "a quo etiam egressus de fonte loco filii susceptus est; in cuius signum adoptionis duas illi provincias donauit, Uectam uidelicet insulam et Meanuarorum prouinciam in gente Occidentalium Saxonum."

9. See, for example, the contributions in *Memoria. Der geschichtliche Zeugniswert des liturgischen Gedenkens im Mittelalter*, ed. Karl Schmid and Joachim Wollasch (Munich, 1984) and *Gedächtnis, das Gemeinschaft stiftet*, ed. Karl Schmid (Munich and Zurich, 1985).

10. David Kronenfeld, "Kinship Terminology," in *Encyclopedia of Cultural Anthropology* 2, 1996, 682–85; here, 684.

11. Ernst Wilhelm Müller, *Der Begriff der "Verwandtschaft" in der modernen Ethnosoziologie* Mainzer Ethnologica 2 (Berlin, 1981), 40; Müller introduces the development of theory since the 1930s. The quotation comes from the chapter on Needham, whom Müller defends against Ernest Gellner.

12. Kronenfeld, "Kinship," 684.

13. Charlotte Seymour-Smith, "Kinship" (157–58) and "Affinity" (5–6), in *Macmillan Dictionary of Anthropology* (London, 1986). In many other articles (compadrazgo, fictive kinship, kinship, kinship terminology, marriage, ritual kinship), she states that kin ultimately are constituted through biology and that ties such as godparenthood are "kin like relationships" ("Compadrazgo," 47); she does not explain the inconsistency between this view and her own definition of kinship as "social and cultural constructions which do not necessarily refer to biological facts"; ibid., 158.

14. "Kinship," in *International Encyclopedia of the Social Sciences* 8, 1968, here, Jack Goody, "Kinship II: Descent Groups," cols. 401–408; Julian Pitt-Rivers, "Kinship III: Pseudo-kinship," cols. 408–413; all quotations are found on p. 408.

15. Sabean, *Kinship*; in a similar vein, see also Schlumbohm, *Lebensläufe*.

16. See note 4.

17. Otto Gerhard Oexle, "Peace Through Conspiracy," in *Ordering Medieval Society: Intellectual and Practical Modes of Shaping Social Order*, ed. Bernhard Jussen (Philadelphia, 2000); "Die mittelalterlichen Gilden. Ihre Selbstdeutung und ihr Beitrag zur Formung sozialer Strukturen," in Albert Zimmermann, ed., *Soziale Ordnungen im Selbstverständnis des Mittelalters*, vol. 1 (Berlin and New York, 1979), 203–26; here, 215–16. See also, his "Coniuratio und Gilde im frühen Mittelalter. Ein Beitrag zum Problem der sozialgeschichtlichen Kontinuität zwischen Antike und Mittelalter," in Berent Schwineköper, ed., *Gilden und Zünfte. Kaufmännische und gewerbliche Genossenschaften im frühen und hohen Mittelalter* (Sigmaringen, 1985), 151–214. Of the older research see, in particular, Wolfgang H. Fritze, "Die fränkische Schwurfreundschaft der Merowingerzeit. Ihr Wesen und ihre politische Funktion," *ZRG Germ.* 71 (1954): 74–125; and Reinhard Schneider, *Brüdergemeine und Schwurfreundschaft. Der Auflösungsprozess des Karolingerreiches im Spiegel der caritas-Terminologie in den Verträgen der karlingischen Teilkönige des 9. Jahrhunderts.* Historische Studien, vol. 388 (Lübeck and Hamburg, 1964).

18. Cf. Gerd Althoff, *Amicitiae et pacta. Bündnis Einung Politik und Gebetsgedenken im beginnenden 10. Jahrhundert*, Hanover 1995; the classic work is Marc Bloch, *Feudal Society*, trans. L. A. Manyon, 2 vols. (Chicago, 1961), 1:123–25.

19. Josef Fleckenstein, *Early Medieval Germany* (Amsterdam, 1978), 9.

20. Cf. Joseph Lynch: "Spirituale vinculum: The Vocabulary of Spiritual Kinship in Early Medieval Europe," in *Religion, Culture and Society in the Early Middle Ages: Studies in Honour of R. A. Sullivan*, ed. Thomas F. X. Noble and John J. Contreni (Kalamazoo, Mich., 1987), 181–204; especially important here is Anita Guerreau-Jalabert, "La designation des relations et des groupes de parenté en latin médiéval," *Archivum latinitatis medii aevi* 46–47 (1986/87): 65–108; on the earliest evidence of sponsorship, see below chap. 7, pp. 128–32.

21. Cf. Pitt-Rivers, Kinship III: Pseudo-kinship, cols. 408–13, where he divides "pseudo-kinship" into "fictive or artificial" and "ritual" kinship; on godparenthood see Karl Hauck, "Formes de parenté artificielle dans le haute moyen âge," in Georges Duby and Jacques Le Goff, eds., *Famille et parenté dans l'occident médiéval* (Rome, 1977), 43–47.

22. Robert Vivelo, *Cultural Anthropology* (New York, 1978), 38, 158.

23. See, among others, Hugo G. Nutini and Betty Bell, *Ritual Kinship: The Structure and Historical Development of the Compadrazgo System in Rural Tlaxcala* (Princeton, 1980); Hugo G. Nutini, *Ritual Kinship: Ideological and Structural Integration of the Compadrazgo System in Rural Tlaxcala* (Princeton, 1984).

24. Charlotte Seymour-Smith "Compadrazgo," in *Macmillan Dictionary of Anthropology*, 47.

25. The only studies I am aware of are Anita Guerreau-Jalabert, "Spiritus et caritas," in Françoise Héritier-Augé and Élisabeth Copet-Rougier, eds., *La parenté spirituelle*, 1996, 133–203; and Joseph Morsel, "Geschlecht und Repräsentation. Beobachtungen zur Verwandtschaftskonstruktion im fränkischen Adel des späten Mittelalters," in Otto Gerhard Oexle and Andrea von Hülsen, eds., *Die Repräsentation der Gruppen* (Göttingen, 1998), 259–325.

26. Cf. Henry Sumner Maine, *Ancient Law: Its Connection with the Early History of Society and its Relation to Modern Ideas* (1861), 20–41 and 125–28; on fiction, cf. Jürgen Mittelstrass, "Fiktion," in *Enzyklopädie Philosophie und Wissenschaftstheorie*, vol. 1, 1980, 648.

27. Cf. Pitt-Rivers, Pseudo-kinship, 408–9, and esp. Esther Goody, *Parenthood and Social Reproduction. Fostering and Occupational Roles in West Africa*, Cambridge, 1982, esp. 28–34; for more on adoption, see chapter 3 of this work.

28. John Boswell, *The Kindness of Strangers: The Abandonment of Children in Western Europe from Late Antiquity to the Renaissance* (New York, 1988); on the *tollere liberum* see below pp. 184–87.

29. See *Collectio canonum in V libris*, 1:57, ed. M. Fornasari, CCCM 6 (Turnhout, 1970), 47. "et quod neque uxorem, neque liberos eorum qui habet, neque concubinam uel liberos naturales cognoscunt eum habuisse uel habere"; ibid. 1:120:87. "Et neque concubinam uel quae naturales liberos habet uel habuit; sed uel castitate praeditum uel uxorem legitimam et ipsam unam et primam habentem uel suam habuerit"; cf. *Juliani Epitome latina Novellarum Iustiniani* 115:2:424 and 151:18:444; ed. G. Haenel (Leipzig, 1873), 147, 152.

30. On the views of priests, see Bernhard Jussen, "Le parrainage à la fin du moyen âge: Savoir public, attentes théologiques et usages sociaux," *Annales E.S.C.* 47 (1992): 467–502.

31. Cf. Otto Gerhard Oexle, "Deutungsschemata der sozialen Wirklichkeit im frühen und hohen Mittelalter. Ein Beitrag zur Geschichte des Wissens," in Frantisek Graus, ed., *Mentalitäten im Mittelalter. Methodische und inhaltliche Probleme* (Sigmaringen, 1987), 80–82, with theoretical remarks particularly on pp. 69–76; and "Die 'Wirklichkeit' und das 'Wissen': Ein Blick in das sozialgeschichtliche Oeuvre von

Georges Duby," *Historische Zeitschrift* 232 (1981): 61–91, 78–80; and Pierre Bourdieu, *The Logic of Practice*, trans. Richard Nice (Cambridge, 1990), 86–88, 97.

32. Cf. Goody, *Parenthood*, 6–34, quotations on pp. 6–7, 17–19.

33. Goody, *Parenthood*, 17.

34. See p. 56f.

35. See Jean Gaudemet, "Familie," in *RAC* 7, 1969, col. 324.

36. For but one example of a formulation that would become widespread particularly among authors of the High Middle Ages, see the definition in Augustine's *De trinitate* 15,7,11, ed. W. Mountain, CCSL 50 A (Turnhout, 1968), 474: "homo est substantia rationalis constans ex anima et corpore"; I refer here to the important article by Guerreau-Jalabert, *"Spiritus"* (on *corpus* et *anima* pp. 155–60) and, following Guerreau-Jalabert, Morsel, "Geschlecht."

37. On this, see Morsel, "Geschlecht," note 106.

38. This perspective was made popular by Jack Goody's *The Development of Family and Marriage in Europe* (Cambridge, 1983); Anita Guerreau-Jalabert has honed and elaborated on Goody's theses in several articles and accepts his basic ideas on adoption. See, for example, Guerreau-Jalabert, "Spiritus," and esp. "La parenté dans l'Europe médiévale et moderne: à propos d'une syntèse récente," *L'homme* 29 (1989): 69–93; for the transitional period, the studies in chapters 4 to 6 can be viewed as supporting Goody's theses. We still lack detailed discussions for later periods.

39. Take, for instance, the example cited in chapter 2, note 9, wherein King Gunthchramn refers to his adopted nephew Childebert as *de stirpe mea*.

40. Cf. note 38.

41. E. P. Thompson, *The Making of the English Working Class* (Harmondsworth, 1968), 9–10, 937–39. Thomas Sokoll has rightly praised Sabean's study on Neckarhausen as a fine example of kinship research that takes seriously the idea that "family happens"; see Thomas Sokoll, "Familien hausen. Überlegungen zu David Sabeans Studie über Eigentum, Produktion und Familie in Neckarhausen 1700–1870," *Historische Anthropologie* 3 (1995): 335–48, quotation on page 339.

42. On the Welfs see, in particular, Otto Gerhard Oexle, "Das Evangeliar Heinrich des Löwen als geschichtliches Denkmal," in D. Kötzsche, ed., *Das Evangeliar Heinrich des Löwen. Kommentar zum Faksimile* (Frankfurt, 1989); see also, K. Schmid, "Welfisches Selbstverständnis," in *Adel und Kirche: Festschrift Gerd Tellenbach* (Freiburg, Basel, and Vienna, 1968), 389–416. On the Staufers, see K. Schmid, "De regia stirpe Waiblingensium: Bemerkungen zum Selbstverständnis der Staufer," *Zeitschrift für die Geschichte des Oberrheins* 124 (1976): 63–73.

43. This is a significant difference between blood brotherhood and baptismal sponsorship; for example, David Sabean in *Kinship in Neckarhausen*, which is based on broad statistical material, notes that sponsorship ties were "heritable," that is, that a family chose its children's godparents from a particular other family over many generations, taking first the father as a sponsor, and then his son.

44. An example is the use of adoption to legitimize illegitimate children.

45. Cf. Herwig Wolfram, *Geschichte der Goten. Von den Anfängen bis zur Mitte des sechsten Jahrhunderts. Entwurf einer historischen Ethnographie*, 2d ed. (Munich, 1980), 381–96 with source materials.

46. Wolfram, *Geschichte der Goten*, 329–30, 394.

47. On the history of the names of the Frankish kingdoms, see Eugen Ewig, "Das merowingische Frankenreich, 567–687," in Theodor Schieffer, ed., *Europa im Wandel von der Antike zum Mittelalter* (Stuttgart, 1976), 396–433, here, 405–6.

48. L.H. V,17, p. 521[14–16]: "Nam illum non opportet scandalizare, si consubrinum eius, filium fratris mei, de sancto suscipiam lavacro, quia hanc petitionem nullus

christianorum debet abnuere"; for more detail see pp. 195–98. English translation from Gregory of Tours, *History of the Franks*, trans. O. M. Dalton, Oxford: Clarendon, 1927, vol. II, X 29, p. 465. This edition will be referred to henceforth as HF. Occasional modifications to the text of the translation are in square brackets.

49. On this see pp. 197–99.

50. This is referred to, with varying degrees of theoretical acuity, as habituation *(Gewöhnung)*, in Max Weber, "Stammlers 'Überwindung' der materialistischen Geschichtsauffassung," in Weber, *Gesammelte Aufsätze zur Wissenschaftslehre*, ed. J. Winckelmann, 6th ed., Tübingen, 1985, 291–359, here, 331; P. L. Berger and T. Luckmann, *The Social Construction of Reality* (New York, 1966), institutionalization (53–67), "sedimentation" (67–72), or "incorporation" (Bourdieu, *Logic of Practice*, 66–79).

51. For a rare case see below, pp. 166ff.

52. See the example of Magneric of Trier's sponsorship of Theuderic II in Reinhard Schneider, *Königswahl und Königserhebung im Frühmittelalter* (Stuttgart, 1972), 131.

53. Cf., for example, Stephen D. White, *Custom, Kinship and Gifts to Saints: The laudatio parentum in Western France 1050–1150* (Chapel Hill and London, 1988), 55, 71, and 120.

54. On the Welf example, see Oexle, *Evangeliar*; Schmid, "Welfisches Selbstverständnis"; on the Staufers, see Schmid, "De regia stirpe"; for Anglo-Saxon examples, see D. N. Dumville, "Kingship, Genealogies and Regnal Lists," in P. H. Sawyer and Ian N. Wood, eds., *Early Medieval Kingship* (Leeds, 1979), 72–104.

55. "Iordanis de origine actibusque Getarum," in *Iordanis Romana et Getica*, ed. Theodor Mommsen (Berlin, 1882), 53–138, 134[21]: "comperit Eutharicum Veterici filium Beretmodi et Thorismodi nepotem"; cf. Wolfram, *Geschichte der Goten*, 384–85.

56. See Roger Sablonier, "The Aragonese Royal Family Around 1300," in Sabean and Medick, eds., *Interest and Emotion*, 210–39.

57. See White, *Custom, Kinship and Gifts to Saints*, esp. 55–62, and, on the ambiguous rights of kin, 63–76.

58. See K. Schmid, "Zur Problematik von Familie, Sippe und Geschlecht, Haus und Dynastie beim mittelalterlichen Adel: Vorfragen zum Thema 'Adel und Herrschaft im Mittelalter'," in Schmid, *Gebetsgedenken und adliges Selbstverständnis im Mittelalter. Ausgewählte Beiträge* (Sigmaringen, 1983), 183–244, 211.

59. For an example of sudden doubts, see below, pp. 76–79 (Gunthchramn), for a "discovery" see above, p. 32 (Theoderic), for cunning, see below p. 159f. (Childebert), for dodging, p. 32f. (the example from Petrus Cantor).

60. See Angenendt, "Kaiserherrschaft und Königstaufe," 156; one cannot quantify the proportion of women and girls in the social use of sponsorship in the Middle Ages; the earliest statistical material that does exist, however, shows the eminent significance of female baptizees and sponsors for social alliances. For a detailed account, see Sabean, *Kinship in Neckarhausen*.

61. Angenendt, "Kaiserherrschaft und Königstaufe," 111–26; Lynch, *Godparents and Kinship*, 163–204; on ties involving the spouse of the godparent, see Lynch, 252 and 228; Freisen, *Geschichte des canonischen Eherechts*, 549–55.

62. See the examples in Lynch, *Godparents and Kinship*, 209–10.

63. Cf. Arnold Angenendt, "Bonifatius und das Sacramentum initiationis: Zugleich ein Beitrag zur Geschichte der Firmung," *Römische Quartalschrift für christliche Altertumskunde und Kirchengeschichte*, 72 (1977): 133–83, here 142–58; and "Kaiserherrschaft und Königstaufe," 75–91.

64. Cf. the stipulations of King Ine of Wessex (688–725), who demanded only half as much weregild for the killing of a confirmation sponsor as for that of a "blood" kinsman or baptismal sponsor. "Institutiones Ine regis," 76, 1–3, in F. Liebermann, ed., *Die Gesetze der Angelsachsen: Text und Übersetzung*, vol. I (Halle, 1903), 88–123, here 122–23; see also, Lynch, *Godparents and Kinship*, 212; more generally, Pitt-Rivers, "Pseudo-kinship," 411.

65. See the detailed interpretation in Angenendt, *Kaiserherrschaft und Königstaufe*, 124, 155 and 269; also Lynch, *Godparents and Kinship*, 210–12.

66. That, as Lynch suggests, it was easier to keep children "in reserve" for confirmation than for baptism, because the time point was less precisely fixed, is more of a theoretical consideration, since baptism, however precisely churchmen may have set the proper time for it, was often put off for years. *Godparents and Kinship*, p. 212; cf. below, pp. 146 and 164.

67. There is as yet no satisfactory term for the written law that arose in the new kingdoms; for a summary of the *leges* scholarship, see Gabriele von Olberg, *Freie, Nachbarn und Gefolgsleute: Volkssprachige Bezeichnungen aus dem sozialen Bereich in den frühmittelalterlichen Leges* (Frankfurt, Berne, New York, 1983), 37–69, here 37; C. Schott, "Der Stand der Legesforschung," *Frühmittelalterliche Studien* (FMSt), 13 (1979): 29–55.

68. See n. 50.

69. Pippin subjected baptismal and confirmation sponsors to the same incest prohibitions; cf. Pippin's capitulary of 754–755 (*Capitularia regum Francorum* 1, ed. Alfred Boretius, MGH Leges Abt. 2, Hanover 1881–83, 31[18-26]): "Si homo incestum commiserit de istis causis, de Deo sacrata, aut commatre sua, aut cum matrina sua spiritali de fonte et confirmatione episcopi [!] aut cum matre et filia . . . de istis capitulis pecuniam suam perdat, si habet. . . . Et si pecuniam non habet, si liber est, mittatur in carcere usque ad satisfactionem. Si servus aut libertus est, vapuletur plagis multis"; see also, Council of Mainz 813, can. 55, (*Concilia aevi Karolini* 1.1, ed. A. Werminghoff, MGH Conc. 2.1 and 2.2, Hanover and Leipzig, 1906 and 1908, 273); and *Norwegisches Recht: Das Rechtsbuch des Gulathings*, ed. R. Meissner (Weimar, 1935), I, 26, p. 25; *Norwegisches Recht. Das Rechtsbuch des Frostothings* ed. R. Meissner (Weimar, 1939), III, 8, pp. 48–49.

70. Among the more recent literature, see, for example, G. Fehring, "Beitragsmöglichkeiten der Archäologie zu Fragen der Bevölkerungsentwicklung und ihren Voraussetzungen im Mittelalter," in B. Herrmann and Rolf Sprandel, eds., *Determinanten der Bevölkerungsentwicklung im Mittelalter* (Weinheim, 1987), 73–90, esp. 85–86; H. Jäger, "Determinanten mittelalterlicher Bevölkerungsentwicklung aus historisch-geographischer Sicht," in *Determinanten der Bevölkerungsentwicklung*, 91–108, esp. 92–93; and Martin Heinzelmann, "Beobachtungen zur Bevölkerungsstruktur einiger grundherrschaftlicher Siedlungen im karolingischen Bayern, *Frühmittelalterliche Studien* 11 (1977): 202–17, esp. 209.

71. Cf. *Die Canones Theodori Cantuariensis und ihre Überlieferung. Untersuchungen zu den Bußbüchern des 7., 8. und 9. Jahrhunderts*, ed. P. Finsterwalder, vol. 1 (Weimar, 1929), 2,4,8, p. 317: "In catechumino et baptismate et confirmatione unus potest esse pater si necesse est non est tamen consuetudo sed per singula singuli suscipiunt"; see Lynch, *Godparents and Kinship*, pp. 213–14; further church documents in Freisen, *Geschichte des canonischen Eherechts*, 534–36.

72. Cf. *Rodulphus Glabers Vita domni Wilhelmi abbatis: Neue Edition nach einer Handschrift des 11. Jahrhunderts* (Paris, Bibliothèque nationale, lat. 5390), ed. N. Bulst, DA 30, 1974, 450–487, 464: "Tunc quoque isdem Rotbertus, ut erat vir prudens ac strenuus, suggessit imperatori, ut filium, quem ei uxor sua . . . peperat, catecuminum fieri per manum imperialem preciperet. Quod ille libenter annuens. . . ."

NOTES TO CHAPTER ONE

73. Burchard of Worms, *Burchardi Wormaciensis ecclesiae episcopi decretorum libri XX*, in J. P. Migne, ed., *Burchardi Vormatiensis episcopi opera omnia* [PL 140] (Paris, 1888), cols. 537–1084, Book XVII,44, col. 928D: "Scitis quia quomodo sunt septem dona sancti Spiritus, ita sunt septem dona baptismi. A primopabulo sacrati salis, et ingressu sanctae Ecclesiae usque ad confirmationem Spiritus sancti per Chrisma. Ab hoc primo Spiritus sancti dono usque ad septimum, nullus Christianus suam commatrem in coniugium recipere debet, et qui praesumpserit, anathemis vinculo religetur in perpetuo, nisi poenitentiam egerit digne."

74. Ibid., and *Decretum Magistri Gratiani*, ed. A. Friedberg (Leipzig, 1879), C. XXX q. I.c.I., col. 1096.

75. Six for the mother and five each for father and son.

76. *Norwegisches Recht. Rechtsbuch des Gulathings* I, 26, p. 25; similarly, *Norwegisches Recht. Rechtsbuch des Frostothings* III,8, 48–49; on these laws, see F. Merzbacher, article "Nordisches Recht" in *Handwörterbuch der deutschen Rechtsgeschichte*, 3, 1984, cols. 1032–38.

77. Figures are provided in Jäger, "Determinanten mittelalterlicher Bevölkerungsentwicklung."

78. Agnellus, *Agnelli qui et Andreas liber ponitificalis ecclesiae Ravennatis*, ed. O. Holder-Egger (Hanover, 1878), 30, p. 294$^{4-7.10-12}$: "Duo viri cupientes foedus inter se iungi, dixit unus ad alterum habentem sobolem: . . . Da mihi filium tuum, ut sim ei pater de sancto baptismo. . . . Et ex illa die, postquam baptizatus est infans, fuerunt communiter patres, et dilectionem habuerunt in invicem in Spiritu sancto et obsculo pacis, quia et sic cundecet fieri, qui inter se talia faciunt."

79. On this see H. Gerndt, "Zur kulturwissenschaftlichen Stereotypenforschung," in Gerndt, ed., *Stereotypvorstellungen im Alltagsleben. Beiträge zum Themenkreis Fremdbilder—Selbstbilder—Identität. Festschrift für G. R. Schroubek* (Munich, 1988), 9–12; H. Bausinger, Name und Stereotyp in *Stereotypvorstellungen im Alltagsleben*, 13–19; for a detailed account, see A. Schaff, *Stereotypen und das menschliche Handeln* (Vienna, Munich, Zurich, 1980).

80. According to Sabean, *Kinship in Neckarhausen*.

81. In the case of this village, these priorities changed fundamentally within the space of a century, to the extent that socially less well placed parents initially tended to choose better-off ones, occasionally the local lord of the manor, and later, with growing industrialization sought godparents within their own social group. Hartmut Zwahr encountered the same phenomenon in early modern Leipzig; see his *Zur Konstituierung des Proletariats*, 163–89.

82. See note 66.

83. See note 57.

84. See pp. 15.

85. According to Paul Mikat, these prohibitions can all be explained without recourse to Byzantine models; cf. his "Die Inzestverbote des Konzils von Epaon. Ein Beitrag zur Geschichte des fränkischen Eherechts," in Mikat, *Religionsrechtliche Schriften: Abhandlungen zum Staatskirchenrecht und Eherecht*, vol. 2, ed. J. Listl (Berlin, 1974), 869–88.

86. Cf. Lynch, *Godparents and Kinship*, 236; Concilium Romanum I, ch. 4, in *Sacrorum conciliorum nova et amplissima collectio*, ed. J. D. Mansi (Florence, 1766), vol. 12, col. 263.

87. Cf. Lynch, *Godparents and Kinship*, 234–57; see notes 55, 84, and 103–6.

88. See note 3.

89. On the whole, Lynch has something of a tendency to locate these notions very generally in "the people" ("among the Christian peoples" [260], "popular

attitudes" [231–32], "popular aversion toward the products of incest" [241]). Even if one assumes, along with Lynch (260) that written royal or canon law is more a reaction to corresponding ideas than a reason for them (at least initially), and that the idea must thus have been there first, the problem remains of whose ideas written law was reacting to. In addition, research in social anthropology now no longer views incest taboos as such a universal phenomenon as they were long assumed to be (see , for example, the summary in Vivelo, *Cultural Anthropology Handbook*, 169, 214–30).

90. Angenendt, *Kaiserherrschaft und Königstaufe*, 104.
91. See note 57.
92. See p. 33f.
93. Lynch makes a similar point in *Godparents and Kinship*, 214.
94. See Liutprandi leges anni XI, ch. 34, *Leges Langobardorum 643–866*, ed. F. Beyerle, 2d ed. (Witzenhausen, 1962), 99–176, here 118.
95. Cf. Zachary's letter to Pippin, *Codex Carolinus*, ed. W. Gundlach (Berlin, 1892), MGH Epp. 3, 485$^{31/32}$; Pippin's capitulary of 754–55, *Capitularia regum Francorum* 1, ed. A. Boretius, MGH Leges Abt. 2 (Hanover, 1881–83), 31^{19}.
96. See note 62.
97. Citations in Lynch, *Godparents*, 237 and notes 44–46.
98. Cf. Ghaerbald of Liège II, in *Capitula episcoporum* 1, ed. P. Brommer (Hanover, 1980), 16–17, p. 31$^{11-18}$.
99. Cf. *Liber historiae Francorum*, ed. Bruno Krusch, MGH SS rer. Merov. 2 (Hanover, 1888), 31A, pp. 292^{27}–93^{31}; a concrete case was treated in ch. 18 of a Council in Metz in 888 (Mansi 18a, col. 69); on this, see Lynch, *Godparents and Kinship*, 271.
100. Cf. Council of Chalons (813), ch. 31, in *Concilia aevi Karolini* 1,1, ed. A. Werminghoff, MGH Conc. 2.1 (Hanover and Leipzig, 1906–8), 279: "Dictum etiam nobis est quasdam feminas desidiose, quasdam vero fraudulenter, ut a viris suis separentur, proprios filios coram episcopis ad confirmandum tenuisse. Unde nos dignum duxit, ut, si qua mulier filium suum desidia aut fraude aliqua coram episcopo ad confirmandum tenuerit, propter fallatiam suam paenitentiam agat, a viro tamen suo non separetur"; similarly, on confirmation: Pippin's capitulary of 757, ch. 15 (*Capitularia regum Francorum* 1, 38$^{39-41}$): "Si quis filiastram aut filiastrum ante episcopum ad confirmationem tenuerit, separetur ab uxore sua et alteram non accipiat. Similiter et femina alterum non accipiat."
101. Cf. *Decretum Magistri Gratiani*, ed. A. Friedberg (Leipzig, 1879), ch. XXX, col. 1095.
102. Petrus Cantor, *Summa de sacramentis et animae consiliis* 3.2, ed. J.-A. Dugauquier, (Leuven and Lille, 1963), Summa § 334, p. 404$^{1-15}$: "modo timet ne langueat gratia compatris sui und: Compaternitas fuit instituta causa dilatande caritatis, tu autem astrictus es michi compaternitate una et ego tibi."
103. See note 102.
104. Petrus Cantor, *Summa de sacramentis et animae consiliis*, p. 404$^{8-13}$: "Si enim haberem uxorem de cognatione aliqua, illa mortua, non possem aliam accipere de illa cognatione. . . . A simili, ex quo filiolus tuus mortuus est, non debeo te iterum recipere ad compaternitatem."
105. It is difficult to decide in individual cases whether someone actually acted under the subjective pressure of marital norms or merely referred to this pressure; Hincmar was once called upon to decide a case in which a nobleman named Stephan was accused of refusing to consummate his marriage; Stephan defended himself by saying that he had previously had a kinswoman of his wife's as a concubine and

thus feared that he would be committing incest (cf. *Hincmari archiepiscopi Remensis epistolae*, ed. E. Perels, MGH Epp. 8 (Berlin, 1939), ep. 136, 87–107); although Stephan may indeed have been moved by such fears, it is also possible that he was trying to get out of a marriage he may have contracted against his will, as Hincmar then suggested; on this, see Jean Devisse, *Hincmar, archevêque de Reims 845–882*, vol. 1 (Geneva, 1975), 432–36; and H. Schroers, *Hinkmar, Erzbischof von Reims. Sein Leben und seine Schriften* (Freiburg, 1884), 211–20.

106. The information offered here is based on Inquisition records. *Procès en nullité de la condamnation de Jeanne d'Arc*, vol. 1, ed. P. Duparc (Paris, 1977), 244ff. and *Procès de condamnation de Jeanne d'Arc*, vol. 1, ed. P. Tisset (Pai, 1960), 66 and 198. For more detail see the present author's essay, "Le parrainage à la fin du moyen âge. Savoir public, attentes théologiques et usages sociaux," *Annales E.S.C.* (1992): 467–502.

107. Cf. Lynch, *Godparents*, 219–281.

108. Cf. Lynch, *Godparents*, 229, and note 25 of this chapter.

109. For an overview, see Vivelo, *Cultural Anthropology Handbook*, 169 and 214–230; see also note 110.

110. Paul Mikat has described in detail "how difficult it was for the Church to enforce its notion of marriage and its marriage law among the Germanic peoples . . . during the Merovingian-Frankish period and the centuries that followed as well." "Dotierte Ehe—rechte Ehe. Zur Entwicklung des Eheschließungsrechts in fränkischer Zeit," *Rheinisch-Westfälische Akademie der Wissenschaften. Vorträge*, G 227 (Opladen, 1978), 76. See also, his essay "Zu den Voraussetzungen der Begegnung von fränkischer und kirchlicher Eheauffassung in Gallien" in his *Religionsrechtliche Studien. Abhandlungen zum Staatskirchenrecht und Eherecht*, vol. 2, ed. J. Listl (Berlin, 1974), 889–913.

111. See Mikat, "Dotierte Ehe" and "Voraussetzungen," for more details.

112. See the examples in Mikat, "Die Inzestverbote," 879–80.

113. On research in this area, see pp. 59ff.

114. Cf. *Capitula episcoporum*, Haito of Basel, ch. 13, 218$^{3-5}$: "Plura sunt, quae ad incesti crimen scribi poterant, sicut in matre et filia et noverca, et paene innumera, quae menti ad scribendum non occurrunt."

115. See the letter from Pope Zachary to Theodore of Pavia. Cf. Theodore, *Epistolae Langobardicae collectae*, ed. W. Gundlach. MGH Epp. 3 (Berlin, 1892), 18, 710$^{3-6}$: "per quod nos sciscitari curasti, si liceat filium, cuius pater alterius filiam ex sacro baptismate suscepit id est spiritalem eiusdem patris filiam, quod dici crudele est, in matrimonio suscipere, quod apud te enormiter disseruisti contigisse."

116. Ibid, 711$^{3/4}$: "De filiis autem, qui ex eis nati esse probantur, retulisti, si liceat eos coniugio copulari. Sed hi cur prohibeantur a coniugio aut pro huiusmodi poenitentiam agere compellantur?"

117. Council of Tribur 895, c. 48 (*Capitularia regum Francorum* 1, p. 240$^{21-25}$): "Illud etiam nec canonica institutione diffinimus nec introductione aliqua refutamus, sed propter eos, qui diverse de eo setiunt, hoc loco aliquid commemoramus: Si quis suae spiritualis commatris filiam fortuito et ita contingente rerum casu in coniugium duxerit, consilio maturiori servato habeat atque honeste legitimo coniugio operam det."

118. Cf. Zachary's letter to Pippin, *Codex Carolinus* 3, p. 485$^{33-36}$): "In tantum enim grave est, ut nullus sanctorum patrum atque sacrarum sinodorum adsertiones vel etiam in imperialibus legibus quippiam iudicatum sit; sed, terribile dei iudicium metuentes, siluerunt sententiam dare."

119. Quoted in note 101.

120. Cf. Council of Epaon, ch. 30, *Concilia Galliae 2, A.511– A.695*, ed. C. De Clercq (Turnhout, 1963), 32$^{1/2}$): "praeter illos, quos uel nominare funestum est."

121. Pope Zachary decided differently, however (in a letter to Theodore of Pavia; see note 101), as did King Liutprand (Liutprandi leges anni XI, cap. 34, p. 118).

122. At least it is not mentioned anywhere.

123. Petrus Cantor, *Summa* § 334, p. 404[14/15]: "ecclesia non reprobat talem iteratam compaternitatem in multis locis, nescio tamen qua de causa."

124. Cf. the examples in Freisen, *Geschichte*, 516/517; a clear example is Tancred of Bologna (died ca. 1236), who did not doubt the kinship between godparent and godchild, but wanted to consult the pope on the question of impediments to marriage. *Tancredi summa de sponsalibus et matrimonio*, ed. A. Wunderlich (Göttingen, 1841), I.5, ch. 2, 36.

125. See note 86.

126. See the detailed account in Freisen, *Geschichte*, 507–55, esp. 539–55.

127. Letter from Zachary to Theodore of Pavia, in *Epistolae Langobardicae collectae*, 710[6].

128. See above notes 59 and 62.

129. Cf. Pitt-Rivers, "Pseudo-kinship," 412; Lynch, *Godparents*, 207; Donn V. Hart, *Compadrinazgo: Ritual Kinship in the Philippines* (DeKalb, Ill., 1977), 73–74.

130. Cf. the example recounted by Petrus Cantor, note 88 in this chapter.

131. Eight names were mentioned during the rehabilitation proceedings for Joan of Arc (see above, note 92); according to the records studied and described by Peter Becker in his *Leben und Lieben in einem kalten Land: Sexualität zwischen Ökonomie und Demographie. Das Beispiel St. Lambrecht, Steiermark 1600–1850* (Frankfurt a.M. and New York, 1990), 33 and 66–69, example on p. 69; in early modern Styria, it was still the rule to have only one godparent.

132. Cf. pp. 39ff.

133. Cf. Angenendt, *Kaiserherrschaft*, 1–17 and 165–315.

134. See note 10.

135. Angenendt, *Kaiserherrschaft*, 201–2.

136. See ibid., esp. pp. 181–86 (Anglo-Saxons), 207–12 (Widukind) and 215–23 (Heriold of Denmark).

137. See Angenendt, *Kaiserherrschaft*, 4–5 and 311.

138. Since the work of Franz Josef Dölger, this imperial strategy from Byzantium has been referred to as "the family of kings"; see Dölger, "Die 'Familie der Könige' im Mittelalter." *Historisches Jahrbuch* 60 (1940): 397–420.

139. As, for example, in the missions of Otto I, for which we have no evidence of sponsorship and which apparently made do with vassalage; the Magyar leader Bulscu, who was proselytized by the Byzantine competition, was executed after the battle of Lechfeld and the mission from the West could begin soon thereafter; see Angenendt, *Kaiserherrschaft*, 274–300 (on Otto I), and 305–6 (on Bulscu).

140. We know, for example, of no imperial sponsorship in the conversion of the Bohemian *duces* by Louis the German (see Angenendt, *Kaiserherrschaft*, 237) or by the Moravian Svyatopluk (ibid., 243), of the Norman Weland by Charles the Bald (ibid., 260), of the Danish ruler Ragnovald by Ethelstan (ibid., 269–70), of the tribes converted under Otto I (ibid., 276ff.) and of Waik/Stephan of Hungary under Otto III (ibid., 306–10).

141. Cf., for example, the privileges accorded to the Danish bishoprics by Otto I in Diploma No. 294, in *Ottonis I. imperatoris diplomata*, ed. Theodor Sickel, MGH Diplomata regum et imperatorum Germaniae 1:3 (Hanover, 1884), 411.

142. Cf. the detailed account of the baptism of Heriold of Denmark in Ermoldus Nigellus, *Carmen in honorem Hludowici christianissimi caesaris augusti*, ed. E. Faral,

Les classiques de l'histoire de France au moyen age, 14 (Paris, 1932), 1–201, here 170–91; sponsorship is mentioned on p. 170, verse 2239 and commendation on p. 188, verses 2481–82; on this, see Angenendt, *Kaiserherrschaft*, pp. 215–23.

143. This list follows the chapter divisions in Angenendt, *Kaiserherrschaft*, 106–20.

144. See Angenendt, *Kaiserherrschaft*, 114; on the case of King Gunthchramn's sponsorship of King Chlothar II, which is the focus of attention here.

145. See pp. 31.

146. See M. Verdon, "Virgins and Widows: European Kinship and Early Christianity," *Man*, 23 (1988): 488–505, here 497–98; see also, Jack Goody, *Development*.

147. See, for example, Eduard Hlawitschka, "Adoptionen im mittelalterlichen Königshaus," in *Beiträge zur Wirtschafts- und Sozialgeschichte des Mittelalters. Festschrift für H. Helbig*, ed. K. Schulz (Cologne and Vienna, 1976), 1–32; for more detail, see chapter 3 of this book.

Chapter 2. Kinship Strategies: The Example of King Gunthchramn

1. [Fredegar] *Chronicarum quae dicuntur Fredegarii scholastici libri IV*, ed. Bruno Krusch, in Fredegarii et aliorum chronica. Vitae sanctorum, MGH SS rer. Merov. 2 (Hanover, 1888), 1–193, here14, 127[17]: "Regnum eiusdem Childebertus adsumsit."

2. On the political history of this third generation of Merovingians see Ian Wood, *The Merovingian Kingdoms 450–751* (London and New York, 1994), 55–155; Patrick J. Geary, *Before France and Germany* (New York and Oxford, 1988), 117–50.

3. This had been the practice in the earlier partitions of the Frankish kingdom in 511, 534, 561, and 567. See Eugen Ewig, "Die fränkischen Teilungen und Teilreiche 511–613," *Akademie der Wissenschaften und der Literatur Mainz. Abhandlungen der sozialwissenschaftlichen Klasse* 9 (Wiesbaden, 1953), 651–715.

4. On the widespread assumption that he received a few cities after all, see below, pp. 197–204.

5. See in particular the studies by Karl A. Eckhardt, Eugen Ewig, Eduard Hlawitschka, Roderich Schmidt, and Reinhard Schneider, which have been consulted for the following and can be found in the bibliography.

6. Cf. L.H. V,17, p. 216[45]: "Gunthchramnus rex ait: Evenit impulso peccatorum meorum, ut absque liberis remanerem, et ideo peto ut hic nepus meus mihi sit filius. Et imponens eum super cathedram suam, cunctum ei regnum tradedit."

7. Cf. L.H. VI,3, p. 267[7–9]: "ait Chilpericus rex: Filii mihi, peccatis increscentibus, non remanserunt, nec mihi nunc alius superest heres nisi fratris mei Sigyberthi filius, id est Childeberthus rex, ideoque in omnibus quae laborare potuero hic heres existat"; L.H. VI,31, p. 299[10]: "filius meus Childebertus."

8. L.H. VII,8, p. 331[5–7]: "Rex conversus ad populum dicerit: . . . liceatque mihi vel tribus annis nepotis meus, qui mihi adoptivi facti sunt filii, enutrire"; the same statement out of Gregory's mouth to the citizens of Poitiers in L.H. VII,13, p. 334[3–7]: "Nos [Gregorius] vero . . . remisimus . . . , hunc [Gunthchramnus] esse nunc patrem super duos filios, Sigyberthi scilicet et Chilperici, qui ei fuerant adoptati."

9. Cf. L.H. VII,33, p. 353[16–18]: "Nihil enim, facientibus peccatis, de stirpe mea remansit nisi tu tantum, qui mei fratris es filius. Tu enim heres in omni regno meo succede, ceteris exheredibus factis."

10. L.H. IX,20, p. 436[1–3]: "quem Deus de ipsis regibus suprestitem esse praeciperit, regnum illius, qui absque filiis de praesentis saeculi luce migraverit, ad se ad se in integritate perpetuo debeat revocare."

11. Cf. L.H. IX,11, p. 426[10/11]: "ut videre merear filios de filio meo Childebertho."

12. L.H. IX,20, p. 441$^{9/10}$: "Dabo enim Chlothario . . . aut duas aut tres in parte aliqua civitatis, ut nec hic videatur exheredari de regno meo"; Engl. translation, Gregory of Tours, *History of the Franks,* trans. O. M. Dalton, 2 vols. (Oxford, 1927), vol. 2, p. 394. This edition will be referred to as HF.
13. Cf. note 9. HF 2, 311.
14. Cf. below, pp. 76f.
15. Cf. L.H. X,28, p. 520$^{22/3}$: "[Fredegunde] dicens: . . . ipsumque de sancto lavacro exceptum, tamquam alumnum proprium habere dignetur."
16. Cf. L.H. X,28, p. 521$^{8-12}$: "Non enim ista nuper nepote tuo Childebertho pollicitus eras, ut cum inimici eius amicitias conlegaris. Sed in quantum cernimus, nihil de promissione tua custodis, sed potius quae promiseras praetermittis et puerum istum in urbis Parisiacae cathedram regem statues."
17. On the last extensive controversy see Karl A. Eckhardt, *Studia Merovingica* (Aalen, 1975), 235–61; Eduard Hlawitschka, "Studien zur Genealogie und Geschichte der Merowinger und der frühen Karolinger. Eine kritische Auseinandersetzung mit K. A. Eckhardts Buch Studia Merovingica, *Rheinische Vierteljahrsblätter* 43 (1979): 1–99, 96–99; see also, Reinhard Schneider, *Königswahl und Königserhebung im Frühmittelalter* (Stuttgart, 1972), for example, p. 113; on critiques of this method, see pp. 53–56 and 62–64.
18. This is the position adopted by Eckhardt, *Studia Merovingica,* 235–39.
19. Schneider, who treats Childebert and Chlothar as Gunthchramn's adoptive sons, and Childebert as having been adopted by Chilperic, leans towards this position; he relieves himself of worries about greater precision, which may make sense for his purposes, by generally setting the word "adoption" in quotation marks. See Schneider, *Königswahl. und Königserhebung.*
20. This is the tack taken by Hlawitschka in "Studien zur Genealogie und Geschichte," 99.
21. This is Hlawitschka's answer to the contradictions in the case, "Studien zur Genealogie und Geschichte, 99.
22. Cf. L.H. VII, 7, p. 330$^{2/3}$: "Nam Fredegunde patrocinio suo fovebat, ipsamque sepius ad convivium evocans, promittens, se ei fieri maximum defensorem"; in the second passage quoted in Hlawitschka's "Studien," 99 n. 413 (L.H. VII,5), though, he is speaking of a request by Fredegund.
23. See note 15; emphasis added.
24. Arnold Angenendt's interpretation of the *adoptio* of 584, is similar to Hlawitschka's in his "Studien." Angenendt, *Kaiserherrschaft und Königstaufe. Kaiser, Könige und Päpste als geistliche Patrone in der abendländischen Missionsgeschichte* (Berlin and New York, 1984), 113.

Chapter 3. Adoption Contextualized: Legal Culture

1. Eduard Hlawitschka, "Adoptionen im mittelalterlichen Königshaus," in *Beiträge zur Wirtschafts- und Sozialgeschichte des Mittelalters. Festschrift für H. Helbig,* ed. K. Schulz (Cologne and Vienna, 1976), 1–32, 8 note 30 and 11 with note 48.
2. See chapter 2 note 7.
3. Hlawitschka, "Adoptionen im mittelalterlichen Königshaus," p. 11 note 48; emphasis added.
4. Hlawitschka orients himself towards these concepts; see the quotation in note 13 of this chapter.
5. See pp. 58f.
6. For this period, at least, there is no question of "Frankish" adoption regu-

lations, and even if there were any we would have to ask who could have stopped the king and how concrete and firmly anchored such regulations were.

7. See note 3.

8. Hlawitschka, "Adoptionen," p. 11 note 48.

9. In late antiquity, adoptions were supposed to be contracted before the *curia;* see Max Kaser, *Das römische Privatrecht*, 2 vols., 2d ed. (Munich, 1971–75), vol. 2, 210 and 208 note 13.

10. Cf. the letter from Paul I to Pippin in *Codex Carolinus*, ed. W. Gundlach, MGH Epp. 3 (Berlin, 1892), 469–657, 512^{19-28}.

11. On this see Arnold Angenendt, *Kaiserherrschaft und Königstaufe. Kaiser, Könige und Päpste als geistliche Patrone in der abendländischen Missionsgeschichte* (Berlin and New York, 1984), 249.

12. Cf. below pp. 58f.

13. Hlawitschka, "Adoptionen," 7.

14. Historians are always pointing to "misunderstandings" of classical tradition; for a few examples from scholarship in legal history see H. Brunner, *Deutsche Rechtsgeschichte*, 2 vols., 2d ed. (Leipzig, 1906, and Munich, 1928), 265: "alarming misunderstandings of the Roman form that has come down to us"; K. Jordan, "Die Entstehung der römischen Kurie. Ein Versuch," ZRG Kan., 28 (1939), 97–152, 114: "without having understood the Roman forms that have been handed down"; Kaser, *Das römische Privatrecht*, vol. 2, 210 ("misinterpretation") and 212 ("degenerate"); also in the usually very circumspect Hermann Nehlsen's article "Zur Aktualität und Effektivität germanischer Rechtsaufzeichnungen," in *Recht und Schrift im Mittelalter*, ed. P. Classen (Sigmaringen, 1977), 449–502, 473: "no longer understood"; Hlawitschka, for example speaks of "actual" ("true") adoptions, "Adoptionen," 8 note 30, 12 with note 48; the astonishing thing about all of these examples is not the assumption that misunderstandings occurred, although one would, to be sure, need to show in each individual case that they were indeed misunderstandings and not useful modifications. What is surprising are the sometimes flagrant judgments ("alarming," "degenerate"), which reveal the extent to which scholars have tacitly granted classical legal attitudes the status of norms; In *Privatrechtsgeschichte der Neuzeit unter besonderer Berücksichtigung der deutschen Entwicklung*, 2d ed. (Göttingen, 1967), esp. 128, F. Wieacker emphatically highlights the dangers of the notion of reception (more pointedly in the first edition [1952], p. 64).

15. For instances of misinterpretations of literature and visual arts, see, for example, Ernst Robert Curtius, *Europäische Literatur und lateinisches Mittelalter*, 2d ed. (Berne, 1954), 407–9.

16. As in chapter 2 note 20.

17. Alf Lüdtke's concept of *Eigensinn* is outlined in his essay, "What is the History of Everyday Life and Who Are Its Practitioners?" in *The History of Everyday Life: Reconstructing Historical Experiences and Ways of Life*," ed. Alf Lüdtke (Princeton, 1995); the type of research of which Lüdtke is one of the proponents opposes the widespread notion that everyday life is the eternally same practice of the masses, which changes only under the influence of "great" personalities, as well as the covert hypostatization of abstractions to the detriment of active subjects ("division of labor," "class," etc.) as it can be found in the historical social sciences; for further conceptual contributions, as well as concrete applications, see ibid.; the problem is also referred to in P. M. Spangenberg, "Pragmatische Konzepte als Horizonte von Stilreflexionen im Mittelalter," in *Stil. Geschichten und Funktionen eines kulturwissenschaftlichen Diskurselements*, ed. H. U. Gumbrecht and K. L. Pfeiffer, Frankfurt a.M., 1986), 68–92.

18. Cf. pp. 59ff.
19. Cf. the examples on p. 61.
20. As in chap. 2 note 6.
21. It is striking that practically no historians have taken Gunthchramn's statements literally in the "Roman" sense of *adoptio*; Hlawitschka, for example, calls them a "regulation of inheritance" and "political coalition" ("Adoptionen," 10) and, in another work (*Studien* p. 99), "*adoptio in hereditatem*"; Franz Irsigler uses the phrase: "A pact of friendship and succession" in his "Untersuchungen zur Geschichte des frühfränkischen Adels," *Rheinisches Archiv*, no. 70, 2d ed. (Bonn, 1981), 113; Reinhard Schneider speaks of "a heightened entitlement to inherit" (p. 120) and an "act of adoption motivated by and conceived in relation to inheritance law" (p. 121) in *Königswahl und Königserhebung im Frühmittelalter* (Stuttgart, 1972).
22. For an extensive account, see Ludwig Mitteis, *Reichsrecht und Volksrecht in den östlichen Provinzen des Römischen Kaiserreiches* (Leipzig, 1891, repr. 1963). It is of no significance here that the Roman jurists distinguished adoption from adrogation depending upon the status of the adoptee; on this topic see the literature listed in note 23.
23. Hlawitschka, "Adoptionen," 2–3; for an extensive account, see Kaser, *Das römische Privatrecht*, vol. 1, 65–68 and 347–350, vol. 2, 207–11; E. Weiss, *Institutionen des römischen Privatrechts*, vol. 2, 2d ed. (Stuttgart, 1949), 470–73; L. Wenger, article, "Adoption" in *Reallexikon für Antike und Christentum (RAC)*, vol. 1, 1950, 99–103); H. Honsell, *Römisches Recht* (Berlin and Heidelberg, 1988), 122–23.
24. Cf. Wenger, "Adoption," 100; H. Kuhn, article, "Adoption" in *Reallexikon der germanischen Altertumskunde*, vol. 1 (Berlin and New York, 1973), 83–85, 83.
25. See Kaser, *Das römische Privatrecht*, vols. 1 and 2, under *paterfamilias* and *patria potestas*; see also, on this and what follows, A. Wlosok, "Vater und Vatervorstellungen in der römischen Kultur," in *Das Vaterbild im Abendland*, vol. 1, *Rom, frühes Christentum, Mittelalter, Neuzeit, Gegenwart*, ed. H. Tellenbach (Stuttgart, Berlin, Cologne, Mainz, 1978), 18–54, esp. 21; see also, pp. 132f. on the *patria potestas*.
26. Cf. Ulpian, in *Corpus Iuris Civilis*, vol. 1: *Institutiones. Digesta*, ed. Paul Krueger and Theodor Mommsen (Berlin, 1911), 50,16,195,2, p. 917: "Pater autem familias appellatur, qui in domo dominium habet, recteque hoc nomine appellatur, quamvis filium non habeat."
27. Ibid.
28. Ibid. "familiam dicimus plures personas, quae sunt sub unius potestate aut natura aut iure subiecta"; see also, E. Sachers article "Pater familias" in *Paulys Real-Encyclopädie der classischen Altertumswissenschaft*, vol. 18.4 (Berlin, 1949), cols. 2121–57, 2134 (no VI, 2a); Jean Gaudemet, "Familie I. Familienrecht," in *RAC*, vol. 7, 1969, cols. 286–358, 320–22 on the various meanings of *familia*; see also, Ernst Dassmann and Gregor Schöllgen, article "Haus II," in *RAC*, vol. 13, 1986, cols. 801–905, 805.
29. "Mosaicarum et Romanarum legum collatio," in *Fontes iuris Romani antejustiniani*, ed. J. Baviera and J. Furlani, vol. 2 (Florence, 1968), 16, 6, 588 (Ulpian); the idea of the *naturam imitari* is also considered a product of "classical" jurisprudence; see Kaser, *Das römische Privatrecht*, vol. 2, 208.
30. Ibid., pp. 202–3; on the extra-legal counterbalances see pp. 132f.
31. Cf. Kaser, *Das römische Privatrecht*, vol. 2, 465–66.
32. Most recently, for example in Michael Verdon, "Virgins and Widows: European Kinship and Early Christianity," *Man*, 23 (1988): 488–505, 497–98.
33. Kaser, *Das römische Privatrecht*, vol. 2, 208 and 209 note 18.
34. Kaser, *Das römische Privatrecht*, vol. 2, 210–11; quotation on 211.

35. For details, see Ludwig Mitteis, *Reichsrecht*.

36. Documents in Heinrich Mitteis, "Adoptionsurkunde vom Jahre 381 n. Chr.," *Archiv für Papyruskunde*, 3 (1906): 171–84; Leopold Wenger, *Die Quellen des römischen Rechts* (Vienna, 1953), 815.

37. On this see Kaser, *Das römische Privatrecht*, vol. 2, 207–11.

38. Ian N. Wood, "Disputes in Late Fifth- and Sixth-Century Gaul: Some Problems," in *The Settlement of Disputes in Early Medieval Europe*, ed. Wendy Davies and Paul Fouracre (Cambridge, 1986), 7–22, 8; on the sources concerning Roman vulgar law, see H. Nehlsen, *Sklavenrecht zwischen Antike und Mittelalter. Germanisches und römisches Recht in den germanischen Rechtsaufzeichnungen*, vol. 1: *Ostgoten, Westgoten, Franken, Langobarden* (Göttingen, 1972), 62–67.

39. See, for example, Wood, "Disputes," 22; Karl Kroeschell, *Deutsche Rechtsgeschichte*, vol. 1 (up until 1255), 5th ed. (Opladen, 1982), 55–56; fundamental here are Ernst Levy's *West Roman Vulgar Law: The Law of Property* (Philadelphia, 1951); and *Weströmisches Vulgarrecht: Das Obligationenrecht* (Weimar, 1956).

40. Wood, "Disputes," 17 (on the oath) and 19 (on trial by ordeal); the same holds true for the *placita*; see Paul Fouracre, "'Placita' and the Settlement of Disputes in Later Merovingian Francia," in *The Settlement of Disputes in Early Medieval Europe*, 23–43, 34; and R. Collins, Paul Fouracre and Chris Wickham, "Conclusion," in ibid., 207–40, 220–23.

41. Cf. Kaser, *Das römische Privatrecht*, vol. 1, 349; Mitteis, *Reichsrecht*, 339–40; A. Lefas, "L'adoption testamentaire a Rome," *Nouvelle revue historique de droit français et étranger*, 21 (1897): 721–63.

42. The problem of the term "Germanic peoples" has doubtless been sufficiently addressed in the meantime, so that any further elucidation is unnecessary; for an introduction, see the extensive treatment in Arnold Angenendt, *Kirchengeschichte des frühen Mittelalters* (Stuttgart, 1990), §3–§6.

43. Cf. Hlawitschka, "Adoptionen," 4–5; W. D. Wackernagel, "Die rechtliche Stellung der Nachkommen des Adoptivkindes nach schweizerischem Recht. Der Ursprung der Adoption," Ph.D. diss., Univ. of Basel, 1953, 69; for a summary of the preceding controversy, see Wackernagel, 64 and Hlawitschka, "Adoption"; *adoption* here always refers to classic Roman adoption.

44. "Research [on *Affatomie*] has not progressed since the middle of the last century." W. Sellert, article, "Erbvertrag" in *Handwörterbuch der deutschen Rechtsgeschichte* (HRG), vol. 1, 1971, cols. 981–85, 981; for the currently most common interpretation see Sellert; also Mitteis, *Privatrecht*, 32, 77–78 and 172; for more detail, see A. Heusler, *Institutionen des deutschen Privatrechts*, vol. 2 (Leipzig, 1886), 621–23; also R. Schröder, *Lehrbuch der deutschen Rechtsgeschichte*, revised by E. Freiherr v. Künßberg, 7th ed. (Berlin and Leipzig, 1932), 367–68; Schröder brought together the source materials in his articles on *adfatimire* and *adfatimus* in *Deutsches Rechtswörterbuch*, vol. 1 (Weimar, 1914–1932), cols. 441–43 and 443–44, resp.

45. On foster fatherhood, see Max Pappenheim, "Die Pflegekindschaft in der Graugans," in *Festschrift Heinrich Brunner zum siebzigsten Geburtstag* (Weimar, 1910), 1–15; François Kerlouegan, "Essai sur la mise en nourriture et l'éducation dans les pays celtiques d'après le témoignage des textes hagiographiques latin," *Études celtiques* 12 (1968–69), 101–46; K. Arnold, "Kindheit im europäischen Mittelalter," in *Zur Sozialgeschichte der Kindheit*, ed. J. Martin and A. Nitschke (Freiburg and Munich, 1986), 443–67, 455; see pp. 190ff.

46. *Lex Ribvaria*, ed. F. Beyerle and R. Buchner, MGH LL nat. Germ. 3,2 (Hanover, 1954), Tit. 50,1, 101[6]; it was compiled under Chlothar II and Dagobert I (see Kroeschell, *Rechtsgeschichte* 1, 31).

47. Cf. *Pactus legis Salicae*, ed. K. A. Eckhardt, MGH Leg. nat. Germ. 4,1 (Hanover, 1962), 46, pp. 176–77, which was compiled under Clovis (cf. Kroeschell, *Rechtsgeschichte* 1 31 and 41) or in the subsequent period "up until the first third of the seventh century" (Nehlsen, *Sklavenrecht*, 357 and "Zur Aktualität," 453–55); similarly the "Capitula legi Salicae addita," 101 (*Pactus legis Salicae*, 258); *Lex Salica*, ed. K. A. Eckhardt, MGH LL nat. Germ. 4,2 (Hanover, 1969), D 81,1 and E 80, 134–35; text class D arose around 763–64, text class E shortly after 798 (according to R. Schmidt-Wiegandt, article "Lex Salica," in *HRG* 2, 1978, cols. 1949–1962, 1951.

48. According to R. Schmidt-Wiegandt, it was precisely in such cases that vernacular words were used. "Die volkssprachigen Wörter der Leges barbarorum als Ausdruck sprachlicher Interferenz," *Frühmittelalterliche Studien* (FMSt) 13 (1979), 56–87, 60.

49. Thus, it would be equally possible "to assume a linguistic conservatism" which expressed itself in the fact "that the expressive side of vernacular words . . . had changed little, while the actual context had been reshaped by altered living conditions. . . ." (G. v. Olberg, "Zum Freiheitsbegriff im Spiegel volkssprachiger Bezeichnungen in den frühmittelalterlichen Leges," Akten des 26. Deutschen Rechtshistorikertages, ed. D. Simon, *Ius commune*, Sonderheft 30 (1987), 411–26, 415; the same could be said, of course, of many terms adopted from Roman law which survived long after their original meanings had changed; see the example of the word *curia*, pp. 60f.

50. This was the initial question in the discussion as formulated by Peter Classen; quotation in Nehlsen, "Zur Aktualität," 451.

51. Cf. Nehlsen, "Zur Aktualität," esp. 465–67; see also, the literature cited below; for a different view, see Schmidt-Wiegandt, "Lex Salica"; in contrast, greater practical relevance is attributed to Langobard and Visigothic written law, which, however, does not concern us here (cf. Nehlsen, "Zur Aktualität," 483–95).

52. On this see Alexander C. Murray, *Germanic Kinship Structure: Studies in Law and Society in Antiquity and the Early Middle Ages* (Toronto, 1983), 127–29 (in which he distinguishes among symbolic, ideological, and antiquarian uses); Patrick Wormald, "*Lex scripta* and *verbum regis*: Legislation and Germanic Kingship, from Euric to Cnut," in *Early Medieval Kingship*, ed. P. H. Sawyer and Ian N. Wood (Leeds, 1979), 105–38, 106, 115, 119–25, 127–28, 133 and 135; Nehlsen, "Zur Aktualität," 468; E. Wadle, "Über Entstehung, Funktion und Geltungsgrund normativer Rechtsaufzeichnungen im Mittelalter. Notizen zu einem Durchblick," in *Recht und Schrift im Mittelalter*, ed. P. Classen (Sigmaringen, 1977), 503–18, 508.

53. Wormald, "*Lex scripta* and *verbum regis*," 115–16.

54. See Nehlsen, "Zur Aktualität," 469–70; and Wormald, "*Lex scripta* and *verbum regis*," 113–14.

55. See Nehlsen, "Zur Aktualität," 455–56; and Wormald, "*Lex scripta* and *verbum regis*," 122–23.

56. Cf. K. Nehlsen-von Stryk, "Die Freien im Frankenreich als ungelöstes Problem der Rechts-, Sozial- und Verfassungsgeschichte," *Ius commune*, Sonderheft 30 (1987), 427–41, esp. 434–41; Wood, "Disputes," 9.

57. *Marculfi Formulae*, ed. K. Zeumer, MGH Formulae Merowingici et Karolini aevi (Hanover, 1886) II, 13, 83–84; on this see Nehlsen-von Stryk, "Die Freien im Frankenreich," 438; Hlawitschka, "Adoptionen," 6–7; the dating follows H. J. Becker, article "Formel, Formular, Formelsammlung," in *HRG* 1, 1971, cols. 1157–63, 1158.

58. *Formulae Turonenses vulgo Sirmondicae dictae*, ed. K. Zeumer, MGH Formulae Merowingici et Karolini aevi (Hanover, 1886), 128–65, 23, 147^{25}–148^{1}.

59. See Kaser, *Das römische Privatrecht* 2, 210.

60. Cf. for example Jordan, "Die Entstehung der römischen Kurie," 108 and 114; the Tours collection of formulas has been dated to the mid-eighth century; see Kroeschell, *Deutsche Rechtsgeschichte*, 69.
61. Jordan, "Die Entstehung der römischen Kurie," 114, and more extensively, Brunner, *Deutsche Rechtsgeschichte* 2, 263–66.
62. Nehlsen, "Zur Aktualität," 449.
63. Such a case is mentioned in Jordan, "Die Entstehung der römischen Kurie," 114.
64. Nehlsen-von Stryk, "Die Freien," 440.
65. This is particularly striking in the Lex Salica, which remained practically unchanged into the Carolingian period; on this see Nehlsen, "Zur Aktualität," 470–72 and 481; for a summary of the phenomena surrounding literacy and illiteracy in the law see A. M. Hespanha, "Savants et rustiques: La violence douce de la raison juridique," *Ius commune* 10 (1983): 1–48, esp. 11–14; see also, M. T. Clanchy, "Remembering the Past and the Good Old Law," *History* 55 (1970): 165–76; and Olberg, "Zum Freiheitsbegriff," 415–16; Olberg also discusses the difficulty of drawing conclusions about practice from legal texts in "Ein sozialgeschichtliches Schlüsselzeugnis im Licht der Textsortenforschung," *FMSt* 20 (1986): 123–36.
66. Beda, *Historia ecclesiastica* V,19, p. 492: "ut, si uellet, partem Galliarum non minimam illi regendam committeret, ac filiam fratris sui uirginem illi coniugem daret, eumque ipse loco adoptiui semper haberet"; similarly, *Vita Wilfridi* 4, p. 197$^{12-14}$: "dabo ... virginem ... filiam fratris mei in uxorem et te ipsum adoptivum filium habebo et tu me patrem, in omnibus fideliter adiuvantem."
67. [Thule 10] "Die Geschichte von den Leuten aus dem Seetal (Fünf Geschichten aus dem westlichen Nordland)," trans. W. H. Vogt and F. Fischer, in *Thule. Altnordische Dichtung und Prosa* , vol. 10 (Düsseldorf and Cologne, 1964), 21–125, chap. 5, 32.
68. *Decretum Magistri Gratiani*, ed. A. Friedberg, Corpus iuris canonici, vol.1 (Leipzig, 1879), chap. XXX, q. III, col. 1095: "quem uir adoptauit sibi in filium, et ex uxore sibi filia nascitur, quam filio suo adoptiuo ... tradedit. ... Quaeritur ... an spirituales uel adoptiui filii naturalibus copulari ualeant"; the case becomes more complicated because the son adopted by the father was at the same time the mother's godson, a fact unknown, however, to the participants; this is dealt with in a separate *quaestio*.
69. Cf. *Decretum Magistri Gratiani*, chap. XXX, q. III, cols. 1100–2; *Nicolai I: papae epistolae*, ed. E. Perels, MGH Epp. 6 (Berlin, 1952), 257–690, ep. 99, c. 2, p. 596$^{9-36}$; *Corpus Iuris Civilis* 1. *Institutiones. Digesta*, ed. P. Krueger and Theodor Mommsen (Berlin, 1911), I,10.1, 4; the "classical" jurist Gaius was more generous here; cf. ibid., *Digesta*, 23, 2, 17, 331.
70. According to an observation in Pierre Bourdieu, *The Logic of Practice* (Cambridge, 1992), 178–79.
71. Thus, the definition of Roman adoption; as in note 23; Hlawitschka, for example, interprets Markulf's formula in this way, "Adoptionen," 6.
72. On these techniques, which are very difficult to grasp systematically, see Pierre Bourdieu, *Distinction: A Social Critique of the Judgement of Taste* (London and Cambridge, Mass., 1984).
73. Cf. for example, chapter 1 note 43 and the example on p. 63 and the various forms of appropriation, p. 61.
74. On this, see Bourdieu, *Logic of Practice*, 81–83, 112–21.
75. In 585, Gregory, as a partisan of Childebert's, reminded Gunthchramn's legates of a statement made by Gunthchram in that same year; cf. L.H. VIII, 13,

379[21]: "iuxta id quod eum anno praesenti audivimus loqui"; in 591 Childebert reminded his uncle of the pact of Andelot (cf. chapter 2 note 16); in 588 the dangers and uses of the written became evident when, in the dispute between Gunthchramn and Childebert's legates, very different "recollections" of the pact of Andelot clashed and Gunthchramn had the text of the pact read aloud for purposes of clarification; see L.H. IX, 20, 434–41.

76. See, for example, L.H. VIII, 4, 373[10/11] (in 585): "Unum vos tantummodo, sacerdotes domini, deprecor, ut pro filio meo Childebertho Domini misericoriam exoretis."

77. Cf. L.H. X, 28, 521[12-14] (in 591): "Promissionem, quam in nepotem meum Childeberthum regem statutam habeo, non obmitto."

78. Cf. L.H. IX, 33, 451–54 and X, 12, 495; on this, see Murray, *Germanic Kinship Structure*, 197–200.

79. Cf. L.H. X,12, 495[15]: "Rex vero oblitus iudicii, quod matri eius fecerat."

80. One thinks of the many posthumous contestations of pious donations by relatives which one finds in the eleventh and twelfth centuries; cf. chapter 1 note 43.

Chapter 4. King Gunthchramn: Interventions in Kinship

1. We now know more about the structure of the work through Martin Heinzelmann, *Gregor von Tours: Zehn Bücher Geschichte*, and Adriaan Breukelaar, *Historiography*.

2. Cf., for example, Eugen Ewig, *Die Merowinger und das Imperium* (Opladen, 1983), 39; see also Franz Irsigler, *Untersuchungen zur Geschichte des frühfränkischen Adels*, 2d ed. (Bonn, 1981), 139–42; H. Grahn-Hoeck, *Die fränkische Oberschicht im sechsten Jahrhundert: Studien zu ihrer rechtlichen und politischen Stellung* (Sigmaringen, 1976), 250–63.

3. They had originally belonged to the kingdom of Charibert of Paris, Gunthchramn's brother. When, after Charibert's death in 567, the remaining brothers—Gunthchramn, Sigibert, and Chilperic—wanted to divide his legacy, the towns were promised to the Austrasian Sigibert, the father of Childebert II. The Neustrian Chilperic, however, soon occupied them, and after his death, both the Burgundian Gunthchramn and the Austrasian Childebert laid claim to the towns.

4. L.H. VII, 13, 334[5/6]: "Nos [Gregorius] vero . . . remisimus . . . hunc [Guntchramnus] esse nunc patrem super duos filios, Sigyberthi scilicet et Chilperici, qui ei fuerant adoptati; et sic tenere regni principatum, ut quondam Chlotharius rex fecerat, pater eius"; HF 2, 294.

5. L.H. V, 17, 216[1-14].

6. L.H. VII, 8, 331[5-9].

7. L.H. VII,8, 331[6/7]; quoted in chapter 2 note 8. HF 2, 292.

8. On the various possible options, as suggested in the literature, see p. 70f.; the "presumptive godfather" is brought up by Eugen Ewig, "Studien zur merowingischen Dynastie," *FMSt* 8 (1974), 15–59, 20.

9. On Gregory's references to the *nutritores* at the royal courts, see Margarete Weidemann, *Kulturgeschichte der Merowingerzeit nach den Werken Gregors von Tours*, 2 vols. (Mainz, 1982), 1:99–100.

10. L.H. VII, 8, 331[79]: "ne forte contingat, quod Divinitas aeterna non patiatur, ut illis parvolis, me defuncto, simul pereatis, cum de genere nostro robustus non fuerit qui defensit."

11. See note 3.

12. L.H. VII, 5, p. 328$^{15-17}$: "Fredegundis . . . dicens: Veniat dominus meus et suscipiat regnum fratris sui. Est, inquid, mihi infans parvolus, quem in eius ulnis ponere desiderans, me ipsam eius humilio dicione"; HF 2, 289–90.

13. See p. 67; on the journey, see L.H. VII, 5, 328^{18}.

14. Cf. pp. 103f. and 184f.

15. In "Studien zur Genealogie und Geschichte der Merowinger und der frühen Karolinger. Eine kritische Auseinandersetzung mit K. A. Eckhardts Buch Studia Merovingica (*Rheinische Vierteljahrsblätter* 43, 1979, 1–99, 99), Eduard Hlawitschka denies that such an action occurred, arguing that in 585 Gunthchramn had "still never set eyes on Chlothar." He bases his conclusion on the fact that in the summer of 585 Gunthchramn had cast doubt on the boy's legitimacy. See L.H. VIII, 9, 376$^{10-17}$ and L.H. IX, 20, 441$^{9-10}$. Later doubts about Chlothar's legitimacy had nothing to do with the earlier encounter, however, if we abandon the idea that the legal institutions brought in by Gunthchramn must have been followed with logical stringency. If, in 584, all participants, including Fredegund, broached the subject of paternal authority, this still tells us nothing about how people viewed this years later or how long they claimed to know something about such actions and claims; on the doubts, see pp. 76–79; on Fredegund's tactics and her unfavorable situation in 584, see, for example, pp. 103ff.

16. If we are to believe Gregory, he—like his coactors—by no means always did this; on Gunthchramn, for example, see chapter 3 note 77; for others, see chapter 2 note 16, chapter 4 note 35, chapter 5 note 49, and chapter 11 note 9.

17. That seniority carried no weight remains to be demonstrated; see p. 70f.; on the role of the nearest agnate (*Schwertmage*), cf., for example, H. Conrad, *Deutsche Rechtsgeschichte*, vol. 1: *Frühzeit und Mittelalter: Ein Lehrbuch*, 2d ed. (Karlsruhe, 1962), 158–59.

18. See W. Ogris, "Munt, Muntwalt," in HRG 3, 1984, cols. 750–61, 752; for a description of the paternal *mundiburdium*, see ibid., 756–57; on the *patria potestas*, see p. 56f.

19. This appears to be the drift of Hlawitschka, "Studien zur Genealogie und Geschichte," 99.

20. See esp. Conrad, *Deutsche Rechtsgeschichte*, 159; R. Schröder, *Lehrbuch der deutschen Rechtsgeschichte*, revised by E. Freiherr v. Künßberg, 7th ed. (Berlin and Leipzig, 1932), 353–56.

21. This is made particularly clear on p. 70f. (a parallel case) and p. 107f. (the nobles formulate their claim).

22. L.H. V,17, 216^2: "pacem petens ac deprecans eum videre"; HF 2, 185.

23. This meeting bore "the typical 'international law' traits of a number of similar early medieval royal encounters in the borderlands between two kingdoms"; Reinhard Schneider, *Königswahl und Königserhebung im Frühmittelalter* (Stuttgart, 1972), 118). For an extensive account, see W. Kolb, *Herrscherbegegnungen im Mittelalter* (Berne, Frankfurt a.M., New York, and Paris, 1988).

24. See L.H. V,17, 216$^{1-11}$; quoted in chapter 2 note 6.

25. L.H. VII,33,353$^{7/8}$: "rex arcessire nepotem suum Childeberthum iubet"; HF 2, 311.

26. According to this account, the legates of the usurper Gundovald were captured on their way to King Gunthchramn and brought before the king, who interrogated and imprisoned them; he summoned Childebert to this location in order to interrogate the emissaries again; cf. L. H. VII,32/33, 352–53. Kolb assumes that the location was Paris; *Herrscherbegegnungen im Mittelalter*, 161.

27. L.H. IX,10, 424^{10}: "morae omnes abscedant, et veni, ut te videam." HF 2,

379; Andelot apparently lay on the common frontier; A. Longnon, *Géographie de la Gaule au 6ᵉ siècle* (Paris, 1878), 372.

28. See pp. 96f.
29. L.H. VIII,13, 379¹⁶: "quod simul decreveratis"; HF 2, 338.
30. Weidemann, *Kulturgeschichte* 1, 356, no. 22.
31. As in n. 24. HF 2, 311.
32. L.H. VII, 33, 353¹⁸–54¹: "Tunc relictis omnibus, adsumpto seursum puero, clam locutus est. . . . Tunc indicavit ei, quos in consilio haberet aut spernerit a conloquio, quibus se crederit, quos vitarit, quos honorarit muneribus, quos ab honore depellerit." HF 2, 311.
33. Cf. L.H. VII, 33, 354²⁻³: "interea interdicens, ut Egidium episcopum . . . nullo modo . . . haberet."
34. Cf. L.H. VIII, 13, 379¹⁰⁻²², quotation on 379¹⁸: "rege tacente." On Gregory's answer, see p. 96f.
35. Ibid., 379¹³; evidence in Longnon, *Géographie*, 333.
36. L.H. IX, 20, 440¹²/³: "indecastis enim nepoti vestro, ut omnes regni sui episcopi in unum convenerint"; the list of topics shows that Gunthchramn's bishops also were supposed to take part; cf. L.H. IX, 20, 440¹⁹⁻²⁴; on the postponement, see L.H. IX, 20, 440²⁴/⁵: "Tunc iussit, ut in calendis mensis IIII. haec sinodus prolongaretur."
37. Cf. L.H. IX, 32, 451¹¹/¹²: "unde etiam synodum episcoporum . . . praecepit."
38. L.H. IX,32, 451¹⁴/¹⁵.
39. Cf. L.H. V, 17 (Pompierre, as in chapter 2 note 6); L.H. VII, 8 (Paris, as in chapter 2 note 8); L.H. VII, 33 (meeting of 585, as in chapter 2 note 9; on this, see p. 78f.); L.H. VIII, 3, 373⁶/⁷: "non ego, quod peius est, alium filium praeter Childeberthum habeo"; L.H. IX, 11, 426¹¹: "Gunthchramnus rex, dicens [in Andelot]: Refero tibi maximas gratias, omnipotens Deus, qui mihi praestetisti, ut videre merear filios de filio meo Childebertho"; from Gregory's mouth: L.H. VII, 13 (to the citizens of Poitiers, as in chapter 2 note 8) and L.H. VIII, 13, 379¹⁹⁻²²: [to Gunthchramn:] "Nulli enim latet, quod Childeberthus rex alium patrem nisi patruum non habet, neque ille alium filium nisi hunc habere disponit, iuxta id quod eum anno praesenti audivimus loqui."
40. See, for example, IX,20, 441⁶: "Omnia enim quae habeo eius sunt" (in reference to Andelot, where the adoption was recalled. See chapter 2 note 11).
41. See chapter 5.
42. L.H. VIII, 18, 385¹³⁻¹⁴: "Guntchramnus vero rex volens regnum nepotis sui Chlotchari, fili scilicet Chilperici, regere"; HF 2, 343.
43. Ibid. 385¹⁴: "Theodulfum Andegavit comitem esse decrevit"; on Beppolen, see L.H. VIII, 42, 408; see also p. 107.
44. L.H. VII, 16, 337–38.
45. L.H. VII, 7, 330²⁻³: "Nam Fredegunde patrocinio suo fovebat"; HF 2, 291.
46. L.H. VII, 19, p. 339²⁻³: "Fredegundem quoque reginam ad villam Rodoialensim, quae in Rhodomagensi termino sita est, abire praecepit."
47. L.H. VII, 7, 330¹⁴/¹⁵: "Gunthchramnus vero rex omnia, quae fidelis regis Chilperici non recte diversis abstulerant, iustitia intercedente, restituit, multa et ipsi ecclesiis conferens."
48. L.H. VII,7, p. 330¹⁵/¹⁶: "testamenta quoque defunctorum, qui eclesias heredis instituerant et ad Chilperico conpressa fuerant, restauravit"; HF 2, 291; quotation in L.H. VI, 46, 320¹⁶/¹⁷: "testamenta, quae in eclesias conscripta erant, plerumque disripuit."
49. As in note 46.

50. That is, from areas that had fallen to Neustria from Charibert's legacy; see L.H. X, 9, 491–94. Another campaign against the Bretons is mentioned in L.H. IX, 18, 431–32, after the Bretons had attacked Nantes; since Nantes belonged to Burgundy, this campaign may be ignored here.

51. This was the case according to Ewig, *Studien*, 20.

52. Cf. L.H. IV, 6, 139[6]: "rex vero parvulus est"; Agathias Scholasticus Myrinensis, *Historiarum libri quinque*, in *Sancti patris nostri Johannis Scholastici . . . Agathiae Myrinaei . . . scripta quae extant*, ed. J. P. Migne (Paris, 1860), cols. 1268–1612, 1, 4, col. 1290, no. 23 (here, the Latin text that Migne printed parallel to the Greek original): "Theodibaldus . . . qui quidem tametsi juvenis admodum atque adhuc sub magistri cura institutioneque esset." Apparently, the accounts are not dependent on each other; Agathias died in 582 and appears to have drawn his knowledge from "oral accounts and eyewitness reports." K. Krumbacher, *Geschichte der byzantinischen Literatur von Justinian bis zum Ende des oströmischen Reiches (527–1453)*, 2d ed. (Munich, 1897), 241; see also, H. Gärtner, "Agathias," in *Reallexikon der germanischen Altertumskunde* 1, 1973, 93–94, 93.

53. As in note 7.

54. Cf. pp. 107f; on Theudebald, see p. 70f.; on Childebert, see pp. 92f.

55. See chapter 5.

56. L.H. VI, 46, 319[13/14]: "Chilpericus, Nero nostri temporis et Herodis."

57. Eugen Ewig, "Die fränkischen Teilungen und Teilreiche 511–613," *Akademie der Wissenschaften und der Literatur Mainz. Abhandlungen der sozialwissenschaftlichen Klasse* 9 (Wiesbaden, 1953), 651–715, here 679–80.

58. For a detailed account of the *duces*, see Weidemann, *Kulturgeschichte* 1, 34–40.

59. On Cambrai and Soissons, see Ewig, "Die fränkischen Teilungen," 142; on Soissons in Childebert's hands, see L.H. X, 36, 457; on Paris, see L.H. VII, 5, 328[18/19].

60. L.H. VII, 19, 338[20]–39[1]: "Cum autem magnus clamor fierit adversus eos qui potentes cum rege fuerant Chilperico, scilicet ut abstulissent vel villas vel res reliquas de rebus alienis, omnia, quae iniuste ablata fuerant, rex reddi praecepit"; HF 2, 298.

61. Gregory clearly makes this connection; cf. the quotation in note 59.

62. Cf. L.H. VII, 17, 338[5–12]; earlier, in 573, there had already been an attempt at a synod in Paris to depose Promotus, but this apparently failed because of the opposition of Sigibert; for details, see O. Pontal, *Die Synoden im Merowingerreich* (Paderborn, Munich, Vienna, Zurich, 1986), 140–42.

63. This practice was not uncommon among the Merovingians (cf. p. 142f.).

64. Cf. L.H. VII, 16, 337–38, quotation, 337[15/16]: "Praetextatum vero episcopum egre suscoepit, quem cives Rhodomaginsis post excessum regis de exilio expetentes, cum grande laude civitati suae restituerunt. Post reditum . . . se Gunthchramno regi repraesentavit."

65. See chapter 5.

66. L.H. VII, 6, 329[15–18]: "Per has ergo transgressiones amiserunt partes suas. Ideoque, quia illi iuxta Dei iudicium et maledictionibus pactionum defecerunt, omnem regnum Chariberthi cum thesauris eius meis ditionibus, lege opitulante, subiciam nec exinde alicui quicquam nisi spontanea voluntate indulgeam"; HF 2, 290–91.

67. See above, notes 42, 43, and 61.

68. As in note 45.

69. L.H. V, 1, 194[15]–95[1].

70. L.H. VII, 8, 331[6/7]; quoted in chapter 2 note 8; HF 2, 292.

71. As in note 3; HF 2, 294.

72. See pp. 105–8, 199f.
73. As in note 65.
74. As in note 65.
75. As in note 3.
76. As in notes 6 and 9.
77. Cf. L.H. VII, 12 and 13, 333–34.
78. On this, see pp. 76–79.
79. On this, see pp. 57ff.
80. On this, pp. 105–8.
81. L.H. VIII, 9, 376[10-11]: "Germanus meus Chilpericus moriens dicitur filium reliquisse"; HF 2, 334; the chronicler himself adopts this expression in L.H. VIII,31, 399[19]–400[1].
82. Ibid., 376[11-16]: "cuius nutritores, matre deprecante, petierunt, ut eum de sancto lavacro in dominici natalis solemnitate deberem excipere, et non venerunt. Rogaverunt deinceps, ut ad sanctum pascha baptizaretur, sed nec tunc adlatus est infans. Depraecati sunt autem tertio, ut ad festivitatem sancti Iohannis exhiberetur, sed nec tunc venit. Moverunt itaque me per tempus sterile de loco ubi abitabam. Veni igitur, et ecce! Absconditur nec ostenditur mihi puer"; HF 2, 334–35.
83. L.H. VIII, 9, 376[16-19]: "Unde, quantum intellego, nihil est quod promittitur, sed, ut credo, alicuius ex leudibus nostris sit filius. [. . .] Ideoque noveritis, quia a me non suscipitur, nisi certa de eo cognuscam indicia"; HF 2, 335 (revised here, see below. Buchner translates *suscipere* as "acknowledge" (in German, *anerkennen*) which may come to the same thing in the end (on this, see chapter 11, pp. 184–87) but renders invisible an important aspect—namely, that it was the baptismal sponsorship that brought the boy acknowledgment. Translator's note: O. M. Dalton, like Buchner, translates *suscipere* as "acknowledge," which has been changed here to "receive him from the font."
84. See chapter 11.
85. As we will see, the baptism was not the only point on which the Neustrians acted in an uncooperative manner; cf. p. 107.
86. This is Hlawitschka's supposition (see n. 14).
87. See p. 31.
88. Cf. ibid.
89. L.H. VIII, 9, 376[19-21]: "Haec audiens Fredegundis regina, coniunctis prioribus regni sui, id est cum tribus episcopis et tricentis viris optimis, sacramenta dederunt, hunc ab Chilperico rege generatum fuisse"; HF 2, 335.
90. L.H. VIII, 9, 376[21/22]: "et sic suspicio ab animis regis ablata est"; HF 2, 335.
91. Cf., for example, Childebert's decision, pp. 63–64; cf. R. Collins, Paul Fouracre, and C. Wickham, "Conclusion," in *The Settlement of Disputes in Early Medieval Europe*, ed. W. Davies and Paul Fouracre (Cambridge, 1986), 207–40, esp. 220–22.
92. This is the theme of chapter 11.
93. On this see pp. 198–204.
94. L.H. VII, 8, 331[79].
95. HF 2, 311; L.H. VII, 33, 353[16-18]; quoted in chapter 2 note 9; the expression *ceteris exheredibus* is a Roman testamentary formula; see U. Nonn, "Merowingische Testamente. Studien zum Fortleben einer römischen Urkundenform im Frankenreich," *Archiv für Diplomatik* 18 (1972): 1–129, esp. 13.
96. See, for example, L.H. V, 17, 204[2]: "Fuit enim genere Theifalus."
97. Gregory uses the following terms: "royal family" (L.H. II, 28, 126[17]: *de genere regio*); senatorial family (L.H. V, 45, 245[8]–56[1]: "fuitque homo valde elegans ac prudens, genere senaturio"); see also L.H. VI, 11, 281[4].

NOTES TO CHAPTER FOUR   261

98. L.H. VII, 8, 331[9]: "cum de genere nostro robustus non fuerit qui defensit"; on the Latin usage, see *Oxford Latin Dictionary*, fasc. 3, ed. P. W. G. Glare (Oxford, 1971), cols. 760–61: including descent, origin, implication of high and noble descent, a family, offspring, nationality, race, generation.

99. According to G. Koebler, *Lateinisch-Althochdeutsches Wörterbuch* (Göttingen, Frankfurt a.M., Zurich, 1971); the translations into New High German follow R. Schuetzeichel, *Althochdeutsches Wörterbuch*, 4th ed. (Tübingen, 1974).

100. Cf. L.H. II, 42, 93[5]: "Fuerunt autem supradicti regis propinqui huius."

101. L.H. II, 42, 92[15/16]. HF 2, 80.

102. Cf. L.H. II, 27, 71[14]: "Chlodovechus cum Ragnechario, parente suo, quia et ipse regnum tenebat."

103. Cf. L.H. VII, 27, 346[2]: "nullus de stirpe regum Francorum"; L.H. VII, 36, 358[4/5]: "[Gundovaldus:] nec superesse de stirpe nostra nisi Childeberthum et Gunthramnum"; L.H. VIII,9, 376[18]: "[Gunthramus:] Nam si de stirpe nostra fuisset"; see also K. E. Georges, *Ausführliches lateinisch-deutsches Handwörterbuch*, 2 vols., 14th ed. (Hanover, 1976), vol. 2, 2806 on *stirps*: "Stamm, Wurzel, Ursprung, Abkunft, Stammhalter, Geschlecht, Familie, Nachkommenschaft, Sprößling"; *Oxford Latin Dictionary*, fasc. 8, cols. 1822–23: "applied to an individual, from whom a family is sprung."

104. [Fredegar] *Chronicarum quae dicuntur Fredegarii scholastici libri IV*, ed. B. Krusch, in *Fredegarii et aliorum chronica. Vitae sanctorum*, MGH SS rer. Merov. 2, (Hanover, 1888), 1–193, III, 5, 94[11]: "Dehinc extinctis ducibus, in Francis dinuo regis creantur ex eodem stirpe, qua prius fuerant."

105. Cf. *Der althochdeutsche Isidor* XI, p. 67[605/607]; cf. Koebler, *Lateinisch-Althochdeutsches Wörterbuch* , 193.

106. L.H. VIII, 9, 376[18].

107. Cf. note 94.

108. As in chapter 3 note 29; on the fiction, see p. 21.

109. Cf. L.H. V, 17, 216[5]; HF 2, 185, translation modified from Dalton's "be to me as a son"; quoted in chapter 2 note 6; similarly in the *Vita Amandi episcopi*, ed. Bruno Krusch, in *Passiones vitaeque sanctorum aevi Merovingici*, MGH SS. rer. Merov. 5 (Hanover and Leipzig, 1910), 395–485, 17, 441[9/10], King Dagobert offers Saint Amandus his son as a godson: "ut tibi sit filius spiritalis."

110. Cf. L.H. III, 24, 123[6/7]: "te tamquam filium habere desidero." HF 2, 105.

111. Cf. below notes 134 and 136.

112. What is being referred to here is baptismal sponsorship (cf. p. 190).

113. The fact that Gunthchramn said exactly the opposite in the very next sentence requires special elucidation; on this, see pp. 81–85.

114. L.H. VIII, 13, 379[20–22]: "neque ille alium filium nisi hunc habere disponit, iuxta id quod eum anno praesenti audivimus loqui."

115. L.H. VIII, 4, 373[10–11, 21–22]: "Unum vos tantummodo, sacerdotes domini, deprecor, ut pro filio meo Childebertho Domini misericoriam exoretis. . . . Unde, si oratio vestra prosequitur, poterit hic, Domino annuente, regnare." HF 2, 331–32.

116. And one which can scarcely be adequately explained in terms of any "sentimentality" on Gunthchramn's part, as Weidemann does in *Kulturgeschichte* 1, 364.

117. On this, see below, chapter 8.

118. Cf. pp. 96–103.

119. L.H. VIII, 4, 373[22–23]: "omnes orationem fuderunt ad dominum, ut utrumque regem eius misericordia conservaret."

120. On the royal prayer see, for example, K. H. Krüger, *Königsgrabkirchen der Franken, Angelsachsen und Langobarden bis zur Mitte des 8. Jahrhunderts. Ein historischer Katalog* (Munich, 1971), 476–81.

121. L.H. VIII, 13, 379$^{20-22}$; quotation in note 113. HF 2, 338.

122. In 584, too, when Gunthchramn sought recognition in Paris after Chilperic's death (see p. 67), Gregory portrays the citizens' acknowledgment of him by having them pray for Gunthchramn; cf. L.H. VII, 8, 331$^{9/10}$.

123. Cf. L.H. VIII, 4, 373$^{15-21}$: "unaque vox fuit pronunciantes lectionem euangelicam ac nuntii dicentis: Filius natus est tibi. Unde factum est, ut omnis populus in utraque adnuntiatione pariter proclamaret: Gloria Deo omnipotenti."

124. Cf. p. 79f.

125. See Julian Pitt-Rivers, article "Kinship III. Pseudo-Kinship," in *International Encyclopedia of the Social Sciences*, 8, 1968, cols. 408–13, 408–9.

126. As in chapter 2 note 7.

127. Cf. Schneider, *Königswahl und Königserhebung*, 121.

128. The examples would also seem to substantiate this. See pp. 87f.

129. This is the position taken by Schneider, *Königswahl und Königserhebung*, p. 121; similarly Heinz Thomas, "Die Namenliste des Diptychon Barberini und der Sturz des Hausmeiers Grimoald," *Deutsches Archiv*, 25 (1969), 17–63, 41, note 100; in *Thronsturz und Herrscherabsetzung im Frühmittelalter* (Bonn, 1979), 297 with note 235, K. Bund interprets the solution of Pompierre exactly as Schneider does, but considers it to not be the exception but the rule.

130. L.H. V, 17, 216^{79}: "quod si filius habuero, te nihilominus tamquam unum ex his reputabo, ut illa cum eis tecumque permaneat caretas, quam tibi hodie ego pollicitur, teste deo." HF 2, 185–86.

131. According to Reinhard Schneider, *Brüdergemeine und Schwurfreundschaft. Der Auflösungsprozess des Karolingerreiches im Spiegel der caritas-Terminologie in den Verträgen der karlingischen Teilkönige des 9. Jahrhunderts* (Lübeck and Hamburg, 1964), 81.

132. Schneider, *Brüdergemeine und Schwurfreundschaft*, 83; a brief glance at the follow-up projects to Du Cange also shows this.

133. L.H. IX, 20, 436$^{1/2}$; quoted in chapter 2 note 10. HF 2, 389.

134. Wolfgang Fritze, "Die fränkische Schwurfreundschaft der Merowingerzeit. Ihr Wesen und ihre politische Funktion," *ZRG Germ.*, 71 (1954): 74–125; according to Fritze (97) even outside of the phrase *fides et caritas, caritas* is "a term used to refer to an objective socio-legal relationship"; alongside the oath *(iurare)*, the promise *(promittere)*, or, in the example used here *(pollicere)*, it is also constitutive (cf. ibid., 95–96); Schneider, *Brüdergemeine und Schwurfreundschaft*, 91, also refers to *caritas* as "the significant content of oath brotherhood together with *fides* " (Schneider, *Brüdergemeine und Schwurfreundschaft*, 91).

135. L.H. IX, 20, 436$^{13-16}$: "si contigerit domnum Childeberthum . . . migrari, filius suas Theodeberthum et Theodoricum reges . . . ut pius pater sub sua tuitione et defensione recipiat, ita ut regnum patris eorum sub omni soliditate possedeant."

136. Cf. chap. 4 n. 38. HF 2, 381.

137. L.H. IX, 20, 436^{19}–37^{1}: "tamquam sororem bonam et filias in sua tuitione et defensione spiritali dilectione recipiat"; in his edition of the *History*, Buchner 263, translates it as "als seine liebe Schwester" [as his dear sister]. *Gregorii Episcopi Turonensis historiarum libri decem*, ed. R. Buchner (Darmstadt, 1955). Engl. trans., HF 2, 390.

138. See also Grahn-Hoeck, *Die fränkische Oberschicht*, 262.

139. As in note 19.

140. Cf. pp. 107f.; on Theudebald see pp. 70f.; on Childebert see pp. 92f.

141. For a detailed account, see Bund, *Thronsturz und Herrscherabsetzung*, 297, 308 and 355–60; also Thomas, "Namenliste," 17–63; Hlawitschka, "Adoptionen," 16–19.

142. On the chronology, see Thomas, "Namenliste," esp. 23–33 and 44–48.

143. "Chronologica regum Francorum stirpis Merowingicae," ed. B. Krusch, in *Passiones vitaeque sanctorum aevi Merovingici*, MGH SS rer. Merov. 7 (Hanover and Leipzig, 1920), 468–516, lists 2 and 3, 480[15-17] and 481[7-9]; a third list on the so-called Barberini diptych is problematic; on the whole, the solution proposed by Thomas in "Namenliste" appears to me less conclusive than that of Karl A. Eckhardt in *Studia Merovingica* (Aalen, 1975), 262–79; according to Eckhardt's interpretation the diptych does not contain a regnal list, so that the list is of no interest here.

144. Introduction to *Vita Boniti epsicopi Arverni*, ed. B. Krusch, in *Passiones vitaeque sanctorum aevi Merovingici*, MGH SS rer. Merov. 6 (Hanover and Leipzig, 1913), 110–39, 112.

145. Ibid, 120[23]: *Post cuius obitum, filiisque defunctis, pronepos eius suscepit sceptra.*

146. Cf. ibid. chapters 1–5, 120–122; quotation in chapter 5, 121[17-19]: "Eodem tempore sub Theoderico principe Pippinus regni primatum tenens atque curam palacii gerens, cunctaque gubernacula suo disponebantur arbitrio."

147. Cf. ibid. chapter 16, 127[20/21].

148. On this see Bund, *Thronsturz und Herrscherabsetzung*, 299 with note 240.

149. Cf. *Vita s. Sigeberti regis Austrasiae auctore Sigeberto monacho Gemblacensi*, Recueil des historiens des Gaules et de la France, vol. 2, ed. M. Bouquet (Paris, 1869), 597–602, 15, 602: "non erat ei haeres legitimus. Quia vero Grimoaldum Majorem-domus sibi in omnibus fidelem, morigerum et cooperatorem eatenus expertus erat, filium ejus Childebertum regni Austrasiorum haeredem delegat: hoc tamen proposito conditionis tenore, si ipsum contigeret sine liberis obire. Rex quidem, utpote futurorum nescius, quod tunc sibi videbatur, ex temporis convenientia fecit: postea vero filium genuit, quem nomine patris sui Dagobertum vocavit: et priori testamento ad irritum redacto, hunc nutriendum commisit Majori-domus Grimoaldo, ut ejus potentia contra omnes tutus sublimaretur in Austrasiorum regno."

150. Some scholars, such as Eugen Ewig, have also interpreted Grimoald's coup d'état in this manner. Ewig, "Die fränkischen Teilreiche im 7. Jahrhundert (613–714)," *Trierer Zeitschrift für Geschichte und Kunst des Trierer Landes und seiner Nachbargebiete*, 22 (1953), 85–144, 121: "The inheritance right of the king's son naturally took precedence over that of the adoptive son."

151. L.H. III, 24, 123[6/7]: "dicens: filios non habeo, te tamquam filium habere desidero." HF 2, 105.

152. L.H. V, 17, 216[4/5]; quoted in chapter 2 note 6. HF 2, 185. Translation modified.

153. L.H. VI, 3, 267[7/8]: Filii mei, peccatis increscentibus, non remanserunt, nec mihi nunc alius superest heres nisi fratris mei Sygiberthi filius, id est Childeberthus rex." HF 2, 234.

154. L.H. VI, 24, 291[7/8]: "Quem ille, eo quod ei fili non essent, accipiens, retinebat secum." HF 2, 254. Translation modified.

155. L.H. VI, 24, 291[11/12]: "Igitur post Chlothari regis obitum a Charibertho rege susceptus est"; on Sigibert III, see Ewig, "Die fränkischen Teilreiche," 120–21.

156. Cf. *Marculfi Formulae*, ed. K. Zeumer, MGH Formulae Merowingici et Karolini aevi (Hanover, 1886), 32–112, II,13, 83[24,30]; similarly the *Formulae Turonenses vulgo Sirmondicae dictae*, MGH Formulae Merowingici et Karolini aevi, 128–65, 23, 147[24-25]; *Formulae Salicae Lindenbrogianae*, MGH Formulae Merowingici et Karolini aevi, 265–84, 18, 279[13-14].

157. *Lex Ribuaria*, ed. F. Beyerle and R. Buchner, MGH LL nat. Germ. 3,2 (Hanover, 1954), Tit. 50, 1, 101[4-8]; even if this condition is not mentioned in the Lex Salica under *Affatomie* this aspect was not necessarily new; we know very little

about *Affatomie* and what recorded law does give us is—at best—only a very coded message about social reality; on this, see chapter 3; cf. *Pactus legis Salicae*, ed. K. A. Eckhardt, MGH Leg. nat. Germ. 4,1 (Hanover, 1962), 46, 176–77; *Lex Salica*, ed. K. A. Eckhardt, MGH LL nat. Germ. 4,2 (Hanover, 1969), D 81, 1 and E 80, 134–35.

158. See p. 61.
159. This is the term used in the collection of Markulf's formulae, II,13, 83^{23}.
160. Arnold Angenendt, *Kaiserherrschaft und Königstaufe. Kaiser, Könige und Päpste als geistliche Patrone in der abendländischen Missionsgeschichte* (Berlin and New York, 1984), 114.
161. L.H. VIII, 18, 385$^{13/14}$: "Guntchramnus vero rex volens regnum nepotis sui Chlothari, fili scilicet Chilperici, regere"; HF 2, 343.

Chapter 5. Counterstrategies: Gunthchramn's Nephews and Their Nobles

1. L.H. IX,16,431$^{8-11}$: "Promissio nostra ex hoc habile dabitur, sed sine patrui nostri Gunthchramni regis consilio haec facere non audemus. Promissum enim habemus de maioribus causis nihil sine eius consilio agere"; HF 2, 385.
2. See L.H. IX, 16,431–32, quotation on 431$^{4-5}$: "promiserunt Childeberthus rex et mater eius pacem et caritatem cum ipso se integre custodituros"; HF 2, 385.
3. See L.H. IX,20, 440$^{1-3}$.
4. L.H. IX,20,440$^{5-6}$: "Rex ait: Si enim nepus meus implet, quae in pactionibus conscribi voluit, et ego de his facio voluntatem eius"; HF 2, 393.
5. See L.H. IX,20,435$^{4-5}$: "fidem et caritatem puram et simplicem," and ibid. (438^{17}): "pura et simplex est in Dei nomen concordia inligata"; on this see Wolfgang Fritze, "Die fränkische Schwurfreundschaft der Merowingerzeit. Ihr Wesen und ihre politische Funktion," *ZRG Germ.* 71 (1954): 74–125, 96–97.
6. See pp. 29f.
7. See L.H. IX,20, 434$^{13-16}$.
8. Gregory noted: "quem [Gunthchramnum] apud urbem Cavillonensim repperimus, dicentes . . ."; see L.H. IX,20, 434^7; in the course of the discussion, two of the emissaries appear as speakers, a certain Felix and Gregory himself.
9. L.H. IX,20, 434$^{8-10}$: "Childebertus . . . immensas referens gratias pietate tuae, quod a te iugiter commonetur, ut ea agat, quae et deo placeant et tibi sint accepta et populo congrua"; HF 2, 388.
10. See L.H. VII,8, 331^7; quoted p. 67.
11. "The specifically paternal right was paternal authority . . . , which however chiefly differed from that of the guardian in that it served the unilateral interests of the possessor of power"; K. v. Amira, *Germanisches Recht*, 2 vols., ed. K. A. Eckhardt, 4th ed. (Berlin, 1960–67), 2:79.
12. Cf. chapter 4 note 3.
13. Quotation note 46, on the synods see the pages that follow, 96ff. HF 2, 338.
14. See L.H. IX, 20, 440.
15. Gunthchramn had complained that the Austrasians did not respect the pact, did not give him his portion of Senlis and also "homines, quos pro utilitate mea, quia mihi infensi erant, migrare volui, non permiserunt"; (L.H. IX,20, 434$^{18-19}$); the envoys promised that Senlis would be partitioned immediately if he so desired, and that those Gunthchramn wished to see emigrate would do so as soon as Gunthchramn had their names written down; ibid.
16. See chapter 4, note 3.
17. See note 1.

18. L.H. VIII, 18, 385[6-8]: "uxorem in regno regis antedicti relinquens. Cui obtestaverat rex, ne virum videre praesumeret, nisi prius ille regali gratiae reconciliaretur"; HF 2, 343.
19. See p. 100f.
20. On the first and second arrests, see L.H. VI, 11, 280–82; on the third see L.H. VI, 24, 292[79]; on the partition of Marseilles, see L.H. VI, 24, 280[24]–81[1] and VI,33, 304[3-4].
21. L.H. VIII,12, 378[1-6]: "Denique cum rex maxima intentione Theodorum episcopum iterum persequi conaretur et Massilia iam in Childeberthi regis dominatione revocata fuisset, ad discutiendas causas Ratharius illuc quasi dux a parte regis Childeberthi dirigetur"; HF 2, 336.
22. This emerges from L.H. VI, 11, 282 and L.H. VIII, 13, 379[23]–80[1]: "Childeberthus rex rogavit, dicens: Deprecor dominum et patrem meum, ut Theodoro episcopo nihil iniuriae inferat; quod si fecerit, confestim inter nos scandalum germinavit, erimusque, discordia impediente, disiuncti, qui debemus amorem tuendo esse pacifici."
23. L.H. VIII,12, 378[3-5]: "Sed postposita actione, quae ei a rege [Childebertho] iniuncta *d*fuerant, episcopum vallat, fideiussores requirit et ad praesentiam regis Gunthchramni irexit"; HF 2, 336.
24. See L.H. VIII,13, 379[23]–80[1]; quoted in note 22; on the salutation *dominus et pater meus*, see Margret Wielers, "Zwischenstaatliche Beziehungsformen im frühen Mittelalter (pax, foedus, amicitia, fraternitas)," Ph.D. diss., University of Münster, 1959, 51. She infers, from the same form of address for the Byzantine emperor, that it was not a formal legal title.
25. See the compilation of evidence in Margarete Weidemann, *Kulturgeschichte der Merowingerzeit nach den Werken Gregors von Tours*, 2 vols. (Mainz, 1982), 1:61–62.
26. On this and what follows, see L.H. VI, 7, 276–77; quotation on 276[18-19]: "Post cuius obitum Albinus ex praefecto per Dinamium rectorem Provinciae extra regis consilium suscepit episcopatum"; HF 2, 242.
27. Ibid., 277[1-2]: "Iovinus iterum, qui quondam Proviciae rector fuerat, regium de episcopatum praeceptum accipit"; HF 2, 242.
28. See L.H. VI, 11, 280[16-18]: "[Theodorus] cum Iovino ex praefectum a Gunthramno rege deteneri iubetur."
29. See L.H. VII, 33, 354[2-3]: "interea interdicens, ut Egidium episcopum . . . nullo modo . . . haberet."
30. Ewig speaks of a "temporary unification of the two kingdoms" from 584 to 595. Eugen Ewig, *Trier im Merowingerreich: Civitas, Stadt, Bistum* (Trier, 1954), 85; see also, Ewig, "Das merowingische Frankenreich. 561–687," in *Europa im Wandel von der Antike zum Mittelalter*, ed. Theodor Schieffer (Stuttgart, 1976), 396–433, 405.
31. See L.H. VIII,13, 379[16]: "quod simul decreveratis"; HF 2, 338.
32. L.H. VII,33, 353[14-16]: "Hoc est indicium, quod tibi omne regnum meum tradedi. Ex hoc nunc vade et omnes civitates meas tamquam tuas proprias sub tui iuris dominatione subice"; HF 2, 311.
33. L.H. V,17, 216[5-6]: "Et imponens eum super cathedram suam, cunctum ei regnum tradedit"; HF 2, 185.
34. This is the view of Karl Hauck, "Von einer spätantiken Randkultur zum karolinischen Europa," *FMSt* 1 (1967): 3–93, 70.
35. This is Schmidt's standpoint in his reply to Hauck, R. Schmidt, "Zur Geschichte des fränkischen Königsthrons," *FMSt*, 2 (1968): 45–66, esp. 54–55.
36. Reinhard Schneider, *Königswahl und Königserhebung im Frühmittelalter* (Stuttgart, 1972), 119.

37. As for the progress, Reinhard Schneider speaks both of "pre-homage" and a "form of co-rule"; ibid., 122.
38. This is the case, although Karl Hauck clearly emphasizes this in his oft-cited essay (Hauck, "Von einer spätantiken Randkultur," 70).
39. Wielers, *Zwischenstaatliche Beziehungsformen im frühen Mittelalter*, 49.
40. Quoted in note 32.
41. See pp. 62ff.
42. See note 30.
43. Cf. L.H. VII, 33, 353^{18}–54^1. For the quotation, see chapter 4 note 31.
44. See p. 69f. with notes 35 and 36.
45. L.H. VIII,13, 379$^{13-4}$: "sacerdotibusque de regno Childeberthi congruum non fuit"; HF 2, 337–38; on Gunthchramn's summons, see pp. 69f.
46. See L.H. VIII,13, 379$^{18-23}$: "Tunc ego, rege tacente, respondi: . . . nulli enim latet, quod Childeberthus rex alium patrem nisi patruum non habet, neque ille alium filium nisi hunc habere disponit, iuxta id quod eum anno praesenti audivimus loqui. Absit ergo, ut inter eos radix discordiae germinet, cum se pariter et tuere debeant et amare"; HF 2, 338.
47. On Gunthchramn's protest, see L.H. VIII, 13, 279$^{15-17}$: "Patruus tuus, o rex, diligenter interrogat, quis te ab hac promissione retraxit, ut sacerdotes regni vestri ad concilium, quod simul decreveratis, venire different"; the rump synod was then moved to Mâcon (see L.H. VIII, 20, 386^6–87^{13}); on this, see Weidemann, *Kulturgeschichte der Merowingerzeit* 1, 361–62; on the Austrasian representatives present at Mâcon, see p. 99.
48. See chapter 4 note 35.
49. L.H. IX,20, 440$^{12-18}$: "Et ego [Gregorius]: . . . Sed iuxta consuetudinem canonum placebat gloriosissimo nepoti vestro, ut unusquisque metropolis cum provincialibus suis coniungeret et tunc, quae inrationabiliter in regione propria fiebant, sanctione sacerdotali emendaretur. Quae enim causa extat, ut in unum tanta multitudo conveniat? Aeclesiae fides periculo ullo non quatitur; heresis nova non surgit. Quae erit ista necessitas, ut tanti debeant in unum coniungi domni sacerdotes?"; HF 2, 393.
50. See chapter 4 note 35.
51. See L.H. X,15–16, 501–9, quotation, 503$^{7-12}$:"Childebertus . . . legationem ad Gunthramno regem direxit, ut scilicet episcopi, coniuncti de utroque regno, haec quae gerebantur sanctione canonica emendarent. Ob hanc causam Childebertus rex mediocritatis nostrae personam cum Eberegiselum Agripinensim et ipsum urbis Pectavae Maroveum episcopum iussit adesse; Gunthramnus vero rex Gundigisilum Burdegalensim cum provincialibus suis, eo quod ipse metropolis huic urbi esset."
52. See note 49.
53. L.H. X,15, 503$^{9-12}$.
54. Compare the list of themes in Pontal, *Synoden*.
55. See note 45.
56. See note 49.
57. L.H. X,19, 510$^{13-15}$: [Childebertus] dirigens epistulas . . . ut medio mense nono ad discutiendum in urbe supradicta adesse deberent. Erant enim pluviae validae, aquae immensae, rigor intolerabilis, dissolutae luto viae, amnis litora excidentes; sed praeceptione regiae obsistere nequiverunt"; HF 2, 455.
58. See note 49.
59. Ibid.
60. See the relevant passages in L. Duchesne, *Fastes épiscopaux de l'ancienne Gaule*, 3 vols., vol. 1, 2d ed. (Paris, 1907), vol. 2, 2d ed. (Paris, 1919), vol. 3 (Paris, 1915).

61. According to Weidemann (*Kulturgeschichte* 1, 136), it no longer existed; A. Longnon, in contrast, refers to an Emmo Aresetensi, who was at the council of Reims in 625. Longnon, *Geographie de la Gaule au 6ᵉ siécle* (Paris, 1878), 538–39; see Flodoard, *Historia Remensis ecclesiae*, ed. J. Heller and G. Waitz, MGH SS 13 (Hanover, 1881), 405–599, II,5, 452¹⁰.

62. See L.H. V,5, 201¹²: "nunc vero Dalmatius Rutenensis episcopus iudicat."

63. Weidemann, *Kulturgeschichte* 1, 137.

64. L. Falck, *Mainz im frühen und hohen Mittelalter (Mitte 5. Jahrhundert bis 1244)* (Düsseldorf, 1972), 8; F. Jürgensmeier, *Das Bistum Mainz. Von der Römerzeit bis zum II. Vatikanischen Konzil* (Frankfurt a.M., 1988), 20–22.

65. Compiled in Weidemann, *Kulturgeschichte* 1, 156 (Clermont) and 188 (Rodez).

66. It had come to the Neustrian Chilperic from the inheritance of Charibert, and then went to his second wife Galsvintha as a wedding gift [*Morgengabe*]. After she was murdered, it was granted to her sister, Brunechildis, by a judgment of Gunthchramn's but remained in Chilperic's possession and was in Gunthchramn's hands in 587, as it was to remain until his death under the stipulations of the pact of Andelot, at which point it was to be returned to Brunechildis; see L.H. IX,20, 437⁸⁻¹⁹; Longnon, *Géographie*, 598; Weidemann, *Kulturgeschichte* 1, 158; Eugen Ewig, "Die fränkischen Teilungen und Teilreiche 511–613," *Akademie der Wissenschaften und der Literatur Mainz: Abhandlungen der sozialwissenschaftlichen Klasse* 9 (Wiesbaden, 1953), 651–715, 676 and 680.

67. See Concilium Matisconense a. 585, in *Concilia Galliae 2, A.511–A.695*, ed. C. De Clercq, CCSL 148a (Turnhout, 1963), 249³⁶¹.

68. See Michel Rouche, *L'Aquitaine des Wisigoths aux Arabes. 418–781: naissance d'une région* (Paris, 1979), 500, note 168; see also, Longnon, *Géographie*, 591.

69. The assertion that Aix was Burgundian (made by R. Buchner in *Die Provence in merowingischer Zeit. Verfassung – Wirtschaft – Kultur*, Stuttgart, 1933, 10) because Pientius' representative was in Mâcon, is already contradicted by the fact that Pientius' predecessor Franco is attested before the royal tribunal of the Austrasian Sigibert; see Gregory of Tours, *Liber in gloria confessorum* 70, 339⁴⁻¹⁶. English: *Glory of the Confessors*, trans. and ed. Raymond van Dam (Liverpool, 1988), 74.

70. According to Gallia Christiana 1, 301–2; A. Rastoul, article "Aix en Provence," in *Dictionnaire d'histoire et de géographie ecclesiastiques*, vol. 1 (Paris, 1912), cols. 1235–41.

71. See L.H. VI,11, 282⁶⁻⁸.

72. Cf. Gunthchramn's edict of November 10, 585. *Capitularia regum Francorum* 1, ed. A. Boretius, MGH Leges Abt. 2 (Hanover, 1881–83), 10–12.

73. Rouche, *L'Aquitaine des Wisigoths*, 78–79.

74. See Duchesne, *Fastes*, 268; *Gallia Christiana* 1, 798; Concilium Matisconense a. 585, *Concilia Galliae*, 150³⁸⁷.

75. This is Buchner's suggestion in *Die Provence in merowingischer Zeit* (10), citing L.H. IV, 44, 178¹⁶–79³.

76. Concilium Matisconense a. 585, in *Concilia Galliae*, 248³³⁷); on Marseilles, see J. R. Palanque, "L'époque mérovingienne," in *Le diocèse de Marseille*, ed. Palanque (Paris, n.d.), 29–33.

77. On Gunthchramn's occupation of the city and the dispute with Childebert, see L.H. VI, 11, 280²⁴–81¹ and L.H. VI,31, 299⁶⁻⁸.

78. The date here is that given by Duchesne, *Fastes*, 275; see [Venantius Fortunatus], *Venanti Honori Clementiani Fortunati carminum epistularum expositionum libri undecim*, ed. F. Leo, MGH AA 4,1 (Berlin, 1881) 1–292, IV,10, 152⁶⁷⁻⁷⁰.

79. Compiled by Weidemann in *Kulturgeschichte* 1, 172–74; see also p. 93; when Theodorus was once led to Childebert "under careful guard *(sub ardua custodia)*" (see L. H. VIII,12, 378–79, quotation 378[16]), Gunthchramn was probably also behind it; see N. Gauthier, *L'évangélisation des pays de la Moselle* (Paris, 1980), 192–93.

80. L.H. VI,11, 281; quotation 281[8]: "qui iam tunc cum Gundulfo iunxerat"; on Dynamius, see pp. 93f.

81. L.H. VI,24, 291–92, quotation, 378[16]: "a Theodoro episcopo susceptus est" and VIII, 5, 374.

82. See p. 93.

83. L.H. IX,40, 464[5-6]: "Tempore vero Sygiberthi, postquam Maroveus episcopatum urbis adeptus est"; on the partition, see Ewig, "Die fränkischen Teilungen," 680.

84. See L.H. V, 24, 230[14-15]; Ewig, "Die fränkischen Teilungen," 681; Weidemann, *Kulturgeschichte* 1, 143.

85. For all of these events see L.H. VII, 13, 333–34.

86. L.H. VII, 24, 344; quotations lines 10 and 19; HF 2, 303.

87. L.H. VII, 30, 354[9-10].

88. L.H. IX, 20, 435[16].

89. L.H. VII, 33, 354[2]: "Egidium episcopum, qui ei [Gunthchramno] semper inimicus exteterat"; HF 2, 311.

90. L.H. VII, 14, 364[15-17]: "Tunc rex his verbis succensus, iussit per capita euntium proici aequorum stercora, putrefactas astulas, paleas ac faenum putridine dissolutum ipsumque foetidum urbis lutum"; HF 2, 296. See also the account in Weidemann, *Kulturgeschichte* 1, 182–86.

91. According to Gregory, Gunthchramn saved the citizens of Marseilles from a glandular plague by constant prayer, the fringe of his mantle had healing powers, and his *virtus* (442[8]) could tame evil spirits. L.H. IX, 21, 441–42; HF 2, 394–95.

92. Gregory of Tours, *Liber de virtutibus sancti Martini* II, 1, 158[32]–59[3] and Venantius Fortunatus, *Carminum liber* V,3, 106[15-16]; see L. Pietri, "Gregor von Tours," in *Theologische Realenzyklopädie* (TRE), vol. 14 (Berlin and New York, 1985): 184–88, 188.

93. See L.H. VII, 12, 333[8-18] on the first raid on the city; see ibid., VII,13 p. 334[3-7], on Gregory's attitude; and VII,24, 344[12] on the second raid.

94. See note 87.

95. For an account of Gregory's actions and sojourn at Childebert's court, see Weidemann, *Kulturgeschichte* 1, 207–20.

96. On both, see L.H. IX, 20, 439–40.

97. See above, pp. 91ff.

98. According to Gregory's account a possessed woman rebuked Bishop Magneric with the words: "O sceleste . . . , qui pro inimico nostro Theodoro orationem fundis" (L.H. VIII,12, 379[3-5]); Childebert, however, did not regard Theodore as an *inimicus* and strongly criticized Gunthchramn's actions against the bishop (see note 22); the possessed woman must thus be the chronicler's vehicle for reflecting Gunthchramn's attitude; this also is Gauthier's position in *L'Évangélisation*, 192–93.

99. See L.H. IX, 10, 425[15-17]: "ait rex Gunthchramnus: Incite ignem in domo, et si exire nequiverit episcopus, pariter concrementur"; for a more detailed account, see below, pp. 161ff.

100. See L.H. IX,23, 443: "in meo vos odio orfani relicti estis"; HF 2, 396.

101. See L.H. IX,12, 427; quotation lines 23–24: "ut a merore revocaretur"; HF 2, 382. On this case, see pp. 156f.

102. See pp. 159ff.

103. See L.H. IX,10, 424[16]: "convenerat, ut absque ullius defensione regi praesentaretur" HF 2, 379; on the initiative for the meeting at Andelot, see chapter 4 note 26.

104. See note 49.

105. On the uprising in Uzès, see p. 93ff.; cf. L.H. VI,7, 277[3-4]: "Qui, convocatis conprovincialibus, per consilium Dinami episcopus ordinatus est."

106. On Arisitum see note 61, on Toulouse see Weidemann, *Kulturgeschichte* 1, 175 (Narbonne province); on the province's other bishoprics, see ibid., 233 (on Marcellus).

107. See p. 70f.

108. See chapter 4 note 11. HF 2, 289.

109. See chapter 4.

110. Gregory tells us nothing further of the fate of Bobo, the only dux who ruled at least in part over the Neustrian motherland (see p. 72).

111. See L.H. VII,28, 346[15-16]; and VIII,6, 375[8-9].

112. See L.H. VII,9, 331[19-22]; VII,10, 332[1-3]; VII,34, 354[13-15]; and VIII,27, 390[12-17]; cf. Weidemann, *Kulturgeschichte* 1, 37–8.

113. L.H. VIII,26, 390[4-11].

114. Gregory notes that the unpopular Chilperic was abandoned by all after his death: "a nullo dilectus est, ideoque, cum spiritum exalasset, omnes'eum reliquerunt sui"; L.H. VI,46, 321[6].

115. L.H. VII,4, 328[10-13]: "Reliquos vero thesauros, qui apud villam Calam remanserant, in quibus erat missurium illud aureum quod nuper fecerat, thesaurii levaverant et ad Childeberthum regem, qui tunc apud Meldensem conmorabatur urbem, velociter transierunt"; HF 2, 289.

116. L.H. VII,21, 340[1-2]: "rogatus enim fuerat ab ea, ut post mortem regis cum ipsa resederet, sed obtenere non potuit"; HF 2, 299.

117. See chapter 4 note 59; HF 2, 298.

118. On the war between the cities, see L.H. VII, 2, 327[8-17]; on Meaux, see L.H. VII, 4, 328; and on Paris, L.H. VII,5, 328[18-19]; on Soissons in Childebert's hands, see L.H. X, 36, 457; on Cambrai and Soissons, see Ewig, "Die fränkischen Teilungen," 683.

119. See L.H. VIII,42, 408[6-19]; and Weidemann, *Kulturgeschichte* 1, 34–35.

120. See chapter 4 notes 44 and 11; and on Gunthchramn's claims, chapter 4 note 65.

121. L.H. VII,5, 328[15-17]. HF 2, 289–90; quoted in chapter 4 note 11.

122. L.H. VII,8, 331[6-7]; quoted in chapter 2 note 8; HF 2, 292.

123. It is, however, doubtful that this action had anything to do with the Germanic and early Roman practice of "receiving" or "lifting up" by which fathers signalized their acknowledgment of a child; only baptizees continued to be "received" or "raised up" by their sponsors; we might also think here of the familial meanings of the word *suscipere* ('to beget', 'to conceive') in late antique legal texts. On all of this see p. 184f.

124. L.H. VIII,18, 385[13-14]; quoted in chapter 4 note 41. HF 2, 343.

125. L.H. VII,7, 330[9-11]: "Prioribus quoque de regno Chilperici, ut erat Ansovaldus, et reliqui ad filium eius . . . se colligerunt, quem Chlotharium vocitaverunt"; and note 127 below.

126. See note 125. HF 2, 291.
127. Gunthchramn traveled to Paris in 585, "ut Chilperici filium, quem iam Chlothacharium vocitabant, a sacro regenerationes fonte deberet excipere." L.H. VIII,1, 370[8-9]; HF 2, 329; on the end of 584, see note 125.
128. See pp. 187–90.
129. See p. 187.
130. See chapter 4 note 81. HF 2, 334.
131. For a detailed account, see pp. 187f.
132. See chap. 11.
133. L.H. VII,7, 330[11-13]: "Prioribus quoque de regno Chilperici, ut erat Ansovaldus, et reliqui ... exegentes sacramenta per civitates, quae ad Chilpericum prius aspexerant, ut scilicet fideles esse debeant Gunthchramno rege ac nepote suo Chlothario"; HF 2, 291.
134. See p. 76.
135. See chapter 4 n. 88.
136. This was the offer made immediately after Chilperic's death; see chapter 4 note 11.
137. Gregory believed this to be Gunthchramn's objective; see chapter 4 note 41.
138. This was the offer after Chilperic's death; see chapter 4 note 11.
139. According to the chronicler's commentary, this was the case; see chap. 4, note 41.
140. The nobles exacted oaths of loyalty to both kings from all these cities; see note 133.
141. See Rouche, *L'Aquitaine des Wisigoths*, part 2: *Les structures romaines de l'Aquitaine*, 133–466.
142. L.H. VIII,22, 388–89.
143. For a detailed account, see p. 194.
144. See p. 70.
145. See chapter 4, note 65.
146. Margarete Weidemann has provided a largely convincing reconstruction of the succession in the Neustrian cities between the Seine and the Loire on the basis of a thorough study of the testament of Bertram of Le Mans; see her *Das Testament des Bischofs Berthramn von Le Mans vom 27. März 616: Untersuchungen zu Besitz und Geschichte einer fränkischen Familie im 6. und 7. Jahrhundert* (Mainz, 1986), 148–60.
147. See L.H. VIII,18, 385[13-15]; on Domigisel, see Weidemann, *Kulturgeschichte* 1, 104; on Sigulf, ibid., 45–46.
148. L.H. VIII, 42, 408[9] and 408[18-19]: "sed a Rhedonis non receptus est. [. . .] filium suum in hoc loco reliquit. Qui non multum intercedente tempus, in reventibus Rhedonicis, interremptus est cum multis honoratis viris"; HF 2, 362–63.
149. On the murder of Praetextatus, see L.H. VIII, 31, 397–400; on the appointment of Melantius by Fredegund, see L.H. VIII, 41, 408[5].
150. L.H. VIII, 31, 398[18-19]: "Magnus tunc omnes Rothomagensis cives et praesertim seniores loci illius Francos meror obsedit"; HF 2, 354.
151. See ibid., 399.
152. Ibid., 400.
153. Ibid., 400[5-7]: "Nam non potest fieri, ut, si quis inter nos culpabilis invenitur, in conspectu regis vestri deducatur, cum nos possimus nostrorum facinora regale sanctione compraemere"; HF 2, 356.

154. L.H. VII, 7, 330[11–13].
155. See chapter 4, note 11.
156. See L.H. VIII, 31, 400[7–11]: "Tunc sacerdotes dixerunt: Noveritis enim, quia, si persona, quae haec perpetravit, in medio posita non fuerit, rex noster cum exercitu hic veniens, omnem hanc regionem gladio incendioque vastavit. . . . Et his dictis discesserunt, nullum rationabilem responsum accipientes."
157. See note 125.
158. See chapter 4, note 88.
159. L.H. X, 9, 491[8–10]; Beppolen led the army.
160. See L.H. VII, 7, 330[11–13]: "exegentes sacramenta per civitates, quae ad Chilpericum prius aspexerant, ut scilicet fidelis esse debeant Gunthchramno rege ac nepote suo Chlothario"; see also L.H. X, 9, 492[18]: "Regalis episcopus dicens. . . : Nihil nos dominis nostris regibus culpabelis sumus"; also ibid., 492[15–16]: "[Warocus] promittens, se numquam contra utilitatem Gunthchramni regis esse venturum."

Chapter 6. A Failed Attempt

1. See p. 198–204.
2. See [Paul the Deacon] *Pauli historia Langobardorum*, ed. G. Waitz, MGH SS rer. Germ. 48 (Hanover, 1887), VI,53, 237[6]: "[Liutprand] eio pater effectus est"; on this, see Eduard Hlawitschka, "Adoptionen im mittelalterlichen Königshaus," in *Beiträge zur Wirtschafts- und Sozialgeschichte des Mittelalters. Festschrift für H. Helbig*, ed. K. Schulz (Cologne and Vienna, 1976), 1–32, 19–20.
3. L.H. VIII, 18, 385[13/14]: "Gunthchramnus vero rex volens regnum nepotis sui Chlotchari, fili scilicet Chilperici, regere"; HF 2, 343.
4. Cf. L.H. IX, 21, 441–42.
5. See chapter 5 note 153; we know of no conflicts over the cities of Coutence, Bayeux, Lizieux and Evreux to the south, which, according to Weidemann, were also apparently still in Chlothar's hands. Margarete Weidemann, *Das Testament des Bischofs Berthramn von Le Mans vom 27. März 616. Untersuchungen zu Besitz und Geschichte einer fränkischen Familie im 6. und 7. Jahrhundert* (Mainz, 1986), 152–53.
6. He expressed clear opposition before finally agreeing (see L.H. IX, 20, 440[1–3]), retained the negative stance he had already demonstrated and continued to wage war on the Visigoths; on the Visigoths' unsuccessful peacemaking attempts before the marriage negotiations, see L.H. VIII, 35, 404; VIII, 45, 411; IX, 1, 413–14; and IX, 16, 430–31; on Gunthchramn's military campaigns, see L.H. VIII, 30, 393–94 and VIII,45, 411; Gunthchramn is named as the initiator of the war in IX,1, 420; see also L.H. IX, 31, 450.
7. See Eugen Ewig, *Die Merowinger und das Imperium* (Opladen, 1983), 43 and 45–47.
8. Cf L.H. VII, 40, 363[16]; on Comminges see chapter 5, note 68; on Avignon, see Eugen Ewig, "Die fränkischen Teilungen und Teilreiche 511–613," *Akademie der Wissenschaften und der Literatur Mainz. Abhandlungen der sozialwissenschaftlichen Klasse*, 9 (Wiesbaden, 1953): 651–715, 678.
9. For a more extensive account see pp. 159ff.
10. See chapter 4, note 3.
11. This is the interpretation offered by Reinhard Schneider, *Königswahl und Königserhebung im Frühmittelalter* (Stuttgart, 1972), 125.
12. See pp. 84f.
13. See chapter 2, note 11.

14. This is the position taken, for example, by Eugen Ewig, in "Das merowingische Frankenreich, 561–687," in *Europa im Wandel von der Antike zum Mittelalter*, ed. Theodor Schieffer (Stuttgart, 1976), 396–433, 399.

Chapter 7. Practices in Antiquity

1. There are various useful collections of documents on the early history of baptism; for sources up to the Tridentine Council, see *Le baptême des enfants dans la tradition de l'église*, ed. J. C. Didier (Tournai, Paris, Rome, New York, 1959); for documents up until the early Middle Ages in English translation see *Documents of the Baptismal Liturgy*, ed. E. C. Whitaker (London, 1960); for antique documents in French translation, see *L'initiation chrétienne*, ed. A. Hamman and J. Danielou (n.p., 1980).

2. In addition to the above-mentioned studies by Arnold Angenendt (*Kaiserherrschaft und Königstaufe. Kaiser, Könige und Päpste als geistliche Patrone in der abendländischen Missionsgeschichte*, Berlin and New York, 1984); and Joseph H. Lynch (*Godparents and Kinship in Early Medieval Europe*, Princeton, 1986). See also, V. Saxer, "L'initiation chrétienne du IIe au VIe siècle: Esquisse historique des rites et de leur signification," in *Segni e riti nella chiesa altomedievale occidentale*, 1, Settimane di studio del centro italiano di studi sull'alto medioevo, 33 (Spoleto, 1987), 173–205; among the older literature, see Michel Dujarier, *Le parrainage des adultes aux trois premiers siècles de l'église. Recherche historique sur l'évolution des garanties et des étapes catéchuménales avant 313* (Paris, 1962), and *A History of the Catechumenate: The First Six Centuries* (New York, 1979); M. Van Molle, "Les fonctions du parrainage des enfants en occident. Leur apogée et leur degradation (du VIe au Xe siecle)," *Paroisse et Liturgie*, 46 (1964), 121–46.

3. See the account in Acts 8:26–40 of the baptism of the Ethiopian eunuch by the deacon Philip.

4. O. Heggelbacher, *Die christliche Taufe als Rechtsakt nach dem Zeugnis der frühen Christenheit* (Fribourg, 1953), 72–75, 96.

5. According to Angenendt (*Kaiserherrschaft und Königstaufe*, 91); Lynch takes another view, rejecting the idea that the assistants at baptism were the forerunners to godparents; *Godparents and Kinship*, 113; see p. 119.

6. See the sources in Dujarier, *Parrainage*, 177–379.

7. See Ernst Dick, "Das Pateninstitut im altchristlichen Katechumenat," *Zeitschrift für katholische Theologie* 63 (1939): 1–49, here 3–36.

8. See, for example, Dujarier, *Parrainage*, 199–202 (Hippolytus) and 220–23 (Tertullian); on the Middle Ages, cf., for example, Alcuin's influence on Carolingian missionary policy. Let us also recall that the central texts of Christian faith (the Lord's Prayer, the Creed, and the baptismal vow) are among the oldest German linguistic monuments, the translation of which was intended to ensure at least some measure of comprehension; see Hans Eggers, *Deutsche Sprachgeschichte*, 1: *Das Althochdeutsche* (Reinbek bei Hamburg, 1963), (on the earliest period), 169–70 and 270–71 (on usage), 256–58 (early translations of the Lord's Prayer); see also the Old Saxon creed: "Interrogationes et responsiones baptismales," in *Capitularia regum Francorum*, 1, ed. A. Boretius, MGH Leges Abt. 2 (Hanover, 1881–83), 222; on this, see Arnold Angenendt, "Bonifatius und das Sacramentum initiationis: Zugleich ein Beitrag zur Geschichte der Firmung," *Römische Quartalschrift für christliche Altertumskunde und Kirchengeschichte* 72 (1977): 133–83, 139–40.

9. G. Kretschmar, "Die Geschichte des Taufgottesdienstes in der alten Kirche," in *Leiturgia: Handbuch des evangelischen Gottesdienstes*, vol. 5, ed. K. F. Müller and W. Blankenburg (Kassel, 1970), 1–348, 66.

10. See Dujarier, *Parrainage*, 230 and 238.
11. Dujarier, *A History of the Catechumenate*, 68.
12. [Hippolytus, *Traditio apostolica*], *Hippolyte de Rome, La Tradition apostolique d'après les anciennes versions*, ed. B. Botte, SC 11bis, 2d ed. (Paris, 1984), 15, 68: "Et dent testimonium super eos illi qui adduxerunt eos an sit eis virtus ad audiendum verbum."
13. Hippolytus, *Traditio apostolica*, 20, 78: "Cum autem eliguntur qui accepturi sunt baptismum, examinatur vita eorum: an vixerint in honestate dum essent catechumeni, an honoraverint viduas, an visitaverint infirmos, an fecerint omnem rem bonam. Et cum illi qui adduxerunt eos testantur super eum. . . ." English, in Lynch, *Godparents and Kinship*, 92.
14. *Itinerarium Egeriae*, ed. A. Franceschini and R. Weber, in *Itineraria et alia Geographica*, CCSL 175 (Turnhout, 1965), 29–103; XLV, 3, 87[14]: "si ebriacus non est aut uanus"; on the dating, see p. 30.
15. See, for example, Hippolytus, *Traditio apostolica*, 20; quoted in note 13 *(eliguntur)*; on the *competentes* in Augustine, see Robert de Latte, "Saint Augustin et le baptême. Etude liturgico-historique du rituel baptismal des adultes chez saint Augustin," *Questions liturgiques et paroissiales* 56 (1975): 175–223, 191–203.
16. [Origen] *Contre Celse* 2, ed. M. Borret, SC 136 (Paris, 1968), III, 51, 122; Kretschmar incorrectly invokes Tertullian as a third authority alongside Hippolytus and Origen; see "Geschichte des Taufgottesdienstes," 70; when Tertullian mentions *sponsores* he is speaking of infant baptism; these *sponsores* fulfilled a different function (see note 60).
17. See John Chrysostom, *Huit Catéchèses baptismales inédites*, ed. Antoine Wenger, SC 50, 2d ed. (Paris, 1970), II,15, 141[14]; if Lynch (*Godparents and Kinship*, 105) believes that *anadechomenoi* is "basically a financial term," he should supply evidence for this; the term *spondere*, which was used for financial actions in Roman imperial law, appears to have been adopted in the East not as *anadechomai*, but as *homologein*; see L. Mitteis, *Reichsrecht und Volksrecht in den östlichen Provinzen des Römischen Kaiserreiches* (Leipzig, 1891, reprint 1963), 468–98, esp. 486–90; L. Wenger, *Die Stellvertretung im Rechte der Papyri* (Leipzig, 1909), 193–217; later, too, in the basilics, the Greek translations of Justinian's *Code*, *fideiussio* was rendered not as *anadechomai* but as *engyein*; see, for example, Basilics 20, 1, 53, 994[26] (= *Corpus Iuris Civilis* 1: *Institutiones. Digesta*, ed. P. Krueger and Theodor Mommsen, Berlin, 1911, Digesta 19, 2, 54, 290[35]) or 26, Tit 1a, 1241[4] (=Digesta 46,1 Titel, 788[3]). Lynch may have had in mind the western development, where the adoption of legal terminology by theologians is, indeed, apparent (see pp. 122ff.); Tertullian's use in the early third century of the term *spondere* belongs in another context, that of infant baptism (see note 60).
18. See John Chrysostom, *Huit catéchèses*, II, 15, 141–42.
19. Theodore of Mopsuestia, *Les homélies catéchétiques de Théodore de Mopsueste*, ed. Raymond Tonneau and Robert Devreesse (Rome, 1949), XII, 14–15 [Syriac facsimile text with French translation]: "Ce n'est pas, certes, pour les péchés à venir qu'il est garant, puisque chaqun de nous répond pour soi-même à Dieu. Mais, pour celui qui se présente, il rend témoignage de ce qu'il a fait et qu'il s'est préparé, durant le temps passé, à devenir digne de cette cité et de la vie qu'on y mène"; English in Lynch, *Godparents and Kinship*, 107–8.
20. John Chrysostom, *Huit Catéchèses*, II,15, 142[15/16] and II,16, 142[6/11].
21. *Itinerarium Egeriae*, XLV, 2, 87[10/11]: "si uiri sunt, cum patribus suis ueniunt, si autem feminae, cum matribus suis"; on the dating, see p. 30.
22. This is the position taken by most authors, for example, by Lynch in *Godparents and Kinship*, 97–101.

23. *Itinerarium Egeriae* XLVI, 1, 87[6-8]: "et sedent omnes in giro prope episcopo, qui baptidiandi sunt, tam uiri quam mulieres, stant etiam loco patres uel matres"; ibid., XLVI, 5, 88[37-39]: "et ibi unus et unus uadet, uiri cum patre suo aut mulier cum matre sua, et reddet simbolum episcopo."

24. See J. A. Jungmann, "Katechumenat," in *Lexikon für Theologie und Kirche*, vol. 6, 1961, cols. 51–54, col. 53; Saxer, "L'initiation chrétienne," 194–95.

25. Hippolytus, *Traditio Apostolica*, 21 (S) [=Coptic text], 84[1]: diaconus descendat cum eo in aquam et dicat ei adiuvans eum ut dicat: Credo; for a further example, see note 27.

26. Opinions differ on whether elements of this tradition were integrated into the godparent role. Arnold Angenendt (*Kaiserherrschaft und Königstaufe* 91) and Ernst Dick ("Das Pateninstitut," 48) argue that such integration did take place; Joseph Lynch (*Godparents and Kinship*, 113) and Derrick S. Bailey (*Sponsors at Baptism and Confirmation: An Historical Introduction to Anglican Practice*, New York, 1951, 13–14) argue that it did not.

27. Theodore of Mopsuestia, *Les homélies catéchétiques*, XIII, 19, 399–400: "Aussitôt ton garant qui se tient derrière toi, à la fois étend aussitôt un orarium de lin sur ta tête et te relève, il te fait te tenir droit. Et en te relevant de ton agenouillement, tu fais voir que tu as laissé ton antique chute et que tu n'as aucune part avec la terre et les affaires terrestres."

28. See Hippolytus, *Der äthiopische Text der Kirchenordnung des Hippolyt*, ed. H. Duensing (Göttingen, 1946), 95: "And when he rises, he shall be received by him who vouched for him."

29. For documents, see chapter 11, note 29.

30. See chapter 11, note 29.

31. On the discussion surrounding the first two centuries, see H. Hubert, *Der Streit um die Kindertaufe: Eine Darstellung der von Karl Barth 1943 ausgelösten Diskussion um die Kindertaufe und ihre Bedeutung für die heutige Tauffrage* (Berne, 1972); for the subsequent period see the detailed account in E. Nagel, *Kindertaufe und Taufaufschub: Die Praxis vom 3.–5. Jahrhundert in Nordafrika und ihre theologische Einordnung bei Tertullian, Cyprian und Augustinus* (Frankfurt, Berne, Cirencester, 1980).

32. See note 8.

33. [Tertullian], "Q.S.Fl. Tertulliani de baptismo," ed. J. G. Ph. Borleffs, in *Quinti Septimi Florentis Tertulliani opera* vol. 1, CCSL 1 (Turnhout, 1954), 275–95, 18,5, 293[29-32]: "Ueniant ergo dum adolescunt, dum discunt, dum quo ueniant docentur; fiant Christiani cum Christum nosse potuerint! Quid festinat innocens aetas ad remissionem peccatorum?"; translation in Lynch, *Godparents and Kinship*, 124; on this text, see Nagel, *Kindertaufe und Taufaufschub*, 41–76.

34. See M. Bénevot, "Cyprian von Karthago", in *TRE* 8 (1981), 246–54, 250–52.

35. [Cyprian] *Thasci Caecili Cypriani Epistulae, S. Thasci Caecili Cypriani opera omnia*, vol. 2, ed. W. Hartel, CSEL 3.2 (Vienna, 1871), Ep. 64, 2, 718: "Quantum uero ad causam infantium pertinet, quos dixisti intra secundum vel tertium diem quam nati sint constitutos baptizari non opportere et considerandam esse legem circumcisionis antiquae, ut intra octauum diem eum qui natus est baptizandum et sanctificandum non putares: longe aliud in concilio nostro uisum est. In hoc enim quod tu putabas esse faciendum nemo consensit, sed uniuersi potius iudicauimus nulli hominum nato misericordiam Dei et gratiam denegandam"; English from *The Letters of St. Cyprian of Carthage*, trans. and ed. G. W. Clarke, 4 vols. (New York and Mahwah, N.J., 1986), vol. 3, p. 110; on Cyprian's ideas about baptism, see Nagel, *Kindertaufe und Taufaufschub*, 92–96.

36. For extensive source materials on the doctrine of original sin see E. Gaudel,

"Péché originel," in *Dictionnaire de théologie catholique* 12.1 (n.p., 1933), cols. 275–606. See also, Julius Gross, *Entstehungsgeschichte des Erbsündendogmas von der Bibel bis Augustinus* (Munich and Basel, 1960); and *Entwicklungsgeschichte des Erbsündendogmas im nachaugustinischen Altertum und in der Vorscholastik: 5.–11. Jahrhundert* (Munich and Basel, 1963).

37. Cf. note 35; see also, Council of Carthage, 418, in *Concilia Africae 345–525*, ed. C. Munier, CCSL 149 (Turnhout, 1974), 74^7–75^{12}: "Item placuit ut quicumque paruulos recentes ab uteris matrum baptizandos negat aut dicit in remissionem quidem peccatorum eos baptizari sed nihil ex Adam trahere originalis peccati quod lauacro regenerationis expietur, unde sit consequens ut in eis forma baptismatis in remissionem peccatorum non uera sed falsa intelligatur, anathema sit"; on this, see Gross, *Entstehungsgeschichte*, 285–89.

38. Ep. VII, ad omnes episcopos per Picenum, Gelasius I, Epistolae et Decreta, in *SS. Gelasii I Papae, Aviti, Faustiani . . . opera omnia . . .* , ed. J. P. Migne, PL 59 (Paris, 1862), cols. 13–140, 37^D–38^A): "De parvulis autem, quod asserit sine sacro baptismate pro solo originali peccato non posse damnari, satis impia, satis profana propositio est; quamvis enim recentes ab utero matrum in remissionem peccatorum baptizari nullus Christianus ignorat, quod utique non fallaciter, sed veraciter catholica celebrat Ecclesia, ne in sacramentis caelestibus (quod absit) mentita videatur; proinde quia propria non habeant ulla peccata, constat eius [eis] sola prorsus originalia relaxari. Itaque omnibus etiam solis remissis vitam per baptismum consequuntur aeternam; consequens est, ut solis etiam non remissis, ad aeternam vitam pervenire non possint."

39. See Origen, In Lucam homelia XIV, 5, *Homélies sur S. Luc*, ed. H. Crouzel, F. Fournier, and P. Périchon, SC 87 (Paris, 1962), 222: "Parvuli baptizantur in remissionem peccatorum. Quorum peccatorum? vel quo tempore peccaverunt? aut quomodo potest illa lavacri in parvulis ratio subsistere, ni iuxta illum sensum, de quo paulo ante diximus: nullus mundus a sorde, nec si unius quidem diei fuerit vita eius super terram? Et quia per baptismi sacramentum nativitatis sordes deponuntur, propterea baptizantur et parvuli: nisi enim quis renatus fuerit ex aqua et spiritu, non poterit intrare in regnum caelorum."

40. See Augustine, "Contra Julianum haresis Pelagianae defensorem libri VI," in *Sancti Aurelii Augustini Hipponensis episcopi opera omnia* 10,1, ed. J. P. Migne, PL 44 (Paris, 1841), cols. 641–874, I, 3, 6, col. 644 (Augustine cites Cyprian, in Ep. 64, 720–21); Ep. 157,11, vol. 3, 457^7–58^7; Ep. 157, 18, vol. 3, 466^{13-21}; Ep. 175,6, vol. 3, 662^{8-10}; Ep. 186,11, vol. 4, 54^{4-11}; see also, *De peccatorum meritis et remissione et de baptismo paruulorum ad Marcellinum libri tres* in *Sancti Aureli Augustini opera* 8, 1, ed. C. F. Urba and J. Zycha, CSEL 60 (Vienna and Leipzig, 1913), 1–152, I,16,21, $20^{20/21}$; on Augustine's ideas concerning baptism see P. Cramer, *Baptism and Change in the Early Middle Ages, c. 200–c. 1200* (Cambridge and New York, 1993).

41. Ambrose, *De Abraham* in *Sancti Ambrosii opera* 1, ed. K. Schenkl, CSEL 32,1 (Prague, Vienna, Leipzig, 1897), 499–638, II,11,81, 632^{25}–633^{11}: "egregie autem infantiae in primis uagitibus circumcidi mares lex iubet, etiam vernaculos, quia sicut ab infantia peccatum ita ab infantia circumcisio. nullum tempus vacuum debet esse tutelae, quia nullum est culpae uacuum. . . . nec senex ergo proselytus, nec infans uernaculus excipitur, quia omnis aetas peccato obnoxia et ideo omnis aetas sactamento idonea"; see also, "Explanatio psalmorum XII," in *Sancti Ambrosii opera* 6, ed. M. Petschenig, CSEL 64 (Vienna and Leipzig, 1919), XXXVIII,29, 205^{22-27}.

42. Gross, *Entstehungsgeschichte*, 366.

43. See Gennadius of Marseilles, *Liber de ecclesiasticis dogmatibus* in *Sanctorum Hilari, . . . Gennadii, presbyteri Massiliensis opera omnia*, ed. J. P. Migne, PL 58 (Paris,

1862), cols. 979–1054, 989; Gennadius quotes the Council of Carthage here (see note 35); the canon may have been interpolated at a later date. It is, at any rate, absent from the later edition by C. H. Turner, which he described as preliminary without, however, offering any explanation. See C. H. Turner, "The 'Liber ecclesiasticorum dogmatum,'" *Journal of Theological Studies*, 7 (1906): 78–99.

44. See Caesarius of Arles, *Opusculum de Gratia*, in *Sancti Caesarii Arelatensis opera omnia*, vol. 2, ed. Germain Morin (Maredsous, 1942), 159–64, 162$^{26/27}$: "Tamen cum sine dei gratia [infantes] moriantur, quod etiam et tu credis, propter originale peccatum pereunt in aeternum."

45. See Isidore of Seville, *De ecclesiasticis officiis*, ed. Christopher Lawson, CCSL 113 (Turnhout, 1989), II, 25, 7, 105: "Qui si priusquam regenerentur transierint, procul dubio a regno Christi alieni sunt, ipso saluatore testante: Nisi quis renatus fuerit ex aqua et spiritu sancto, non intrabit in regnum Caelorum."

46. See Gregory I, *Moralia in Iob*, in *S. Gregorii Magni moralia in Iob libri I–X*, ed. M. Adriaen, CCSL 143 (Turnhout, 1979), IX,21,32, 479$^{4-6}$: "Quos quia a culpa originis salutis sacramenta non liberant, et hic ex proprio nil egerunt, et illuc ad tormenta perueniunt."

47. See note 33.

48. See P. Langlois, "Fulgentius," in RAC 8 (n.p., 1972), cols. 632–61, 651–52; the parallels to Augustine are developed with particular cogency in J. J. Gavigan, "Fulgentius of Ruspe on Baptism," *Traditio* 5 (1947): 313–22.

49. See Fulgentius of Ruspe, *De fide ad Petrum*, in *Fulgentii episcopi Ruspensis opera*, ed. J. Fraipont, CCSL 91A (Turnhout, 1968), 709–60, 735$^{1247-53}$: "Firmisse tene et nullatenus dubites . . . parvulos, qui siue in uteris matrum uiuere incipiunt et ibi moriuntur . . . , ignis aeterni sempiterno supplicio puniendos."

50. This is sometimes contested by historians of the liturgy. E. Nagel (*Kindertaufe und Taufaufschub*, 163) and Robert de Latte ("Saint Augustin et le baptême. Étude liturgico-historique du rituel baptismal des enfants chez Saint Augustin," *Questions liturgiques et paroissiales*, 57, 1976: 41–55, here 45) assume that the prebaptismal catechism, renunciation of the devil, and *redditio symboli* were dropped in the case of infant baptism. From the fourth century on, however, there is clear and sufficient evidence to the contrary. Cf. Augustine's remarks in note 54 and the quotations in note 55; see also *Ordo romanus*, ed. Michel Andrieu, *Les ordines Romani du haut moyen âge*, vol. 5 (Louvain, 1961) XI,82, 443^2: "catecizantur et reddunt symbolum et baptizantur"; and [Sacramentarium Gelasianum vetus] *Liber sacramentorum Romanae ecclesiae ordinis anni circuli*, Cod. Vat. lat. 316, ed. L. C. Mohlberg (Rome, 1960), 67^{21}: "reddunt infantes symbolum."

51. This is the formulation used in de Latte, "Rituel baptismal des enfants chez Saint Augustin," 44.

52. See Origen, *Commentaria in epistolam b. Pauli ad Romanos*, in *Originis opera omnia*, ed. J. P. Migne, vol. 4, PG 16 (Paris, 1862), 837–1292, V,9, col. 1047^B: "Pro hoc et Ecclesia ab apostolis traditionem suscepit etiam parvulis baptismum dare". This, however, is a highly dubious text. See Berthold Altaner and Alfred Stuiber, *Patrologie*, 8th ed. (Freiburg, 1978) 202; recourse to the apostolic tradition as a virtual program is revealed in the very name of Hippolytus' text *(Traditio apostolica)* and in Pseudo-Dionysius' chosen pseudonym; see also, Augustine, *De peccatorum meritis et remissione*, I,27,40, 38^{79}: "porro quia paruulos baptizandos esse concedunt, qui contra auctoritatem uniuersae ecclesiae procul dubio per dominum et apostolos traditam uenire non possunt."

53. [Hippolytus], *Der äthiopische Text der Kirchenordnung des Hippolyt*, ed. H. Duensing (Göttingen, 1946), Ethiopian text , 113$^{7-13}$.

54. Augustine, Ep. 194,43 ad Sixtum, in *S. Aureli Augustini Hipponiensis episcopi epistulae*, ed. A. Goldbacher, vol. 4 (Prague, Vienna, Leipzig, 1911), 210[16]: "et cum ei [infantes] se per eos, a quibus gestantur, renuntiare respondent."

55. In addition to Augustine, see also Caesarius of Arles, Sermo 200 in *Sancti Caesarii Arelatensis sermones*, 2 vols., ed. G. Morin, CCSL 103/103A (Turnhout, 1953), 6, 811: "[fideiussores] pro ipsis enim respondent, quod abrenuntient diabolo pompis et operibus eius"; Pseudo-Dionysius' apologetic against the ridicule of the "profane" shows, on the one hand, that this practice was the norm and, on the other, that Dionysius considered it problematic and sought to create a theological superstructure for it. See [Dionysius the Areopagite] *De hierarchia ecclesiastica* in *Dionysiaca*, vol. 2, ed. P. Chevallier, n.p., 1950, 1069–1476, 7, sect. 92, 1471–73; quoted pp. 123f.

56. On the Old Testament see especially, J. Scharbert, *Heilsmittler im Alten Testament und im alten Orient* (Freiburg, Basel, Vienna, 1964); on the interpretation of the death of Jesus as a surrogate sacrifice, see the collection of essays *Der Tod Jesu*, ed. K. Kertelge, 2d ed. (Freiburg, 1976), particularly the articles by Gnilka and Vögtle.

57. See R. Berger, *Die Wendung "offerre pro" in der römischen Liturgie* (Münster, 1965), 31–32 and 210–23; to be sure, Berger emphasizes the lesser role of the proxy in comparison to the intermediary (pages 164 and 222), but he does cite a number of documents that clearly mention proxies; see, for example, page 33 (penance by proxy in Cyprian), pages 202 and 203 (baptismal proxies in the Ordo Romanus 11), page 213 (proxies for the dead in Jacob of Batnae).

58. On this, see the following essays by Otto Gerhard Oexle: "Peace through Conjuration," in *Ordering Medieval Society*, ed. Jussen; and "Die funktionale Dreiteilung als Deutungsschema der sozialen Wirklichkeit in der ständischen Gesellschaft des Mittelalters," in *Ständische Gesellschaft und soziale Mobilität*, ed. W. Schulze (Munich, 1988), 19–51.

59. See E. Herrmann, *Ecclesia in re publica* (Frankfurt, Berne, Cirencester, 1980), 150–62; O. Heggelbacher, *Die christliche Taufe als Rechtsakt nach dem Zeugnis der frühen Christenheit* (Fribourg, 1953), 96–99; on Tertullian, see Nagel, *Kindertaufe und Taufaufschub*, 74–76.

60. This is particularly apparent in Tertullian, who saw therein a great danger for the sponsor; Tertullian, *De baptismo*, XVIII,4, S. 293[25-27]: "Quid enim necesse, si non tam necesse est, sponsores etiam periculo ingeri qui et ipsi per mortalitatem destituere promissiones suas possunt et prouentu malae indolis falli?"; Caesarius von Arles, Sermo 200,6, 811: "Et ideo tam illi qui excipiunt, quam qui excipiuntur, id est, tam patres quam filii, pactum quod cum Christo in baptismi sacramento conscribunt custodire contendant."

61. M. Kaser, *Das römische Privatrecht*, 2 vols., 2d ed. (Munich, 1971–75), 1:661.

62. Kaser, *Das römische Privatrecht*, 1:660–63.

63. Ibid, vol. 2, 457 note 3.

64. Ibid., vol. 1, 661.

65. Ibid., vol. 2, 457 and 458 with note 2.

66. See note 60.

67. See Augustine, Ep. 98,7, vol. 2, 528[16/17]: "quando [parvuli] ad baptismum offeruntur, pro eis parentes tamquam fidedictores respondent."

68. See Caesarius of Arles, Sermo 200,6, 811[24/25]: "Et agnoscant se fideiussores esse ipsorum"; see also, Sermo 12,3, 58[24], Sermo 13,2, 64[3], Sermo 130,5, 821[12], Sermo 229,6, 910[23/4].

69. Kaser, *Das römische Privatrecht* 2, 377; for the sources, see E. Levy, *Weströmisches Vulgarrecht: Das Obligationenrecht* (Weimar, 1956), 50–52.

70. See the references in note 68; see also, Caesarius of Arles, Sermo 204,3,

777–78; see also, John Chrysostom (notes 18 and 20); for a detailed account, see Henry G. J. Beck, *The Pastoral Care of Souls in South-East France During the Sixth Century* (Rome, 1950).

71. See L. Mitteis, *Reichsrecht und Volksrecht in den östlichen Provinzen des Römischen Kaiserreiches* (Leipzig, 1891, repr. 1963), 486–88; Mitteis cites a Greek example, dating back to 235, of the stipulation formula adopted from the Romans as the earliest evidence of its use. The next mention is not until 354.

72. See Pseudo-Dionysius, *De ecclesiastica hierarchia* 7, sec. 92, S. 1470; see also John Chrysostom (note 17); on the Greek terminology for stipulation guarantors see note 17; Pseudo-Dionysius also uses the term *homologein* (see note 76).

73. See Hippolytus, *Traditio apostolica* 21, 80: "Omnes autem qui possunt loqui pro se, loquantur. Qui autem non possunt loqui pro se, parentes eorum loquantur pro eis, vel aliquis ex eorum genere."

74. See Augustine, Ep. 98,6 ad Bonifatium, vol. 2, 527^{13}–28^{7}.

75. See note 33.

76. Dionysius the Areopagite, *De hierarchia ecclesiastica*, sec. 92, 1465–66; *The Ecclesiastical Hierarchy*, trans. and ed. Thomas L. Campbell (Lanham, Md., 1981), 89.

77. *De hierarchia ecclesiastica*, 1471–72; English, *The Ecclesiastical Hierarchy*, 90.

78. Pseudo-Dionysius uses the term *homologein*; on this, see note 17.

79. In "Les fonctions du parrainage des enfants en occident. Leur apogée et leur degradation (du VIe au Xe siecle)." *Paroisse et Liturgie* 46 (1964): 121–46, 132–33, Marie-Madeleine van Molle cites this passage from Pseudo-Dionysius as an example of a juridical understanding of sponsorship as acting as a proxy, which had already been opposed by Tertullian since it was too risky for the sponsor; in fact, this passage is better suited to demonstrating that Pseudo-Dionysius also opposed the notion of proxies.

80. Even scholars of liturgical history have failed to acknowledge his interpretation.

81. See Augustine, *De libero arbitrio*, in *S. Aurelii Augustini opera* 2,2, ed. W. M. Green and K. Dauer, CCSL 29 (Turnhout, 1970), 207–321, III,23,67, 314^{20}–15^{28}: "Qua in re satis pie recteque creditur prodesse paruulo eorum fidem a quibus consecrandus offertur.... Quanto ergo potius fides aliena potest consulere paruulo, cui sua perfidia non potest imputari!"

82. This has come down to us in Augustine's letter replying to Boniface; see Augustine, Ep. 98, 6 ad Bonifatium, Bd 2 S. 527$^{13/14}$): "sic enim scribens dicis" [=Boniface]: "Ut, sicut parentes fuerunt auctores ad eorum poenam, per fidem parentum identidem iustificentur."

83. See John the Deacon, *Epistola Johanni Diaconi ad Senarium*, in *Analecta Reginensia. Extraits des manuscrits latins da la reine Christine conservés au Vatican*, ed. A. Wilmart (Rome, 1933), 170–79, 175$^{3-5}$: "Unde scire debetis quia, dum a parentibus aut a quibus libet aliis offeruntur, aliena eos professione saluari necesse est qui fuerant alieno errore dampnati."

84. See Fulgentius of Ruspe, Ep. XII,17 ad Ferrandum, in *Fulgentii episcopi Ruspensis opera*, ed. J. Fraipont, CCSL 91A (Turnhout, 1968), 372$^{348-51}$: "In cuius ablutione si quando illa aetas est, cui propria non possit inesse confessio, aliis credentibus et confitentibus, datur paruulis salus, quibus, aliis peccantibus, est reatus ascriptus."

85. See Berger, *Die Wendung "offerre pro"*.

86. Ibid., 3–12; quotations on 10–11.

87. See Hippolytus (quoted in note 73); Augustine (quoted in note 54), Caesarius

of Arles (quoted in note 55) or the defense of Pseudo-Dionysius, who has the "unholy" ridicule just this practice (see p. 123f.).

88. According to Augustine (quoted in note 54); for further examples, see notes 50 and 55.

89. See notes 82 and 97; the letter is from 408.

90. See Augustinus, Ep. 98,5 ad Bonifatium, vol. 2, 526$^{9-11}$: "celebrantur enim per eos necessaria ministeria et uerba sacramentorum, sine quibus consecrari paruulus non potest"; the term *opus operatum* is not, to be sure, Augustinian, but it is a technical term that aptly describes Augustine's line of argument; see K. Flasch, *Augustin. Einführung in sein Denken* (Stuttgart, 1980), 160–63; J. Finkenzeller, *Die Lehre von den Sakramenten im allgemeinen. Von der Schrift bis zur Scholastik* (Freiburg, Basel, Vienna, 1980), 43; Burkhard Neunheuser, *Taufe und Firmung* (Freiburg, Basel, Vienna, 1983), 67–69.

91. See Augustine, Ep. 98,5 ad Bonifatium, vol. 2, 526$^{14-18}$: "offeruntur quippe paruuli ad percipiendam spiritalem gratiam non tam ab eis, quorum gestantur manibus . . . quam ab universa societate sanctorum atque fidelium"; if present-day dogmatists find in Augustine's writings less the argument of *fides aliena* than a complicated theology of the sacraments (an example is Neunheuser), this is of no great significance for the social historical question of the effects his argument had on Boniface of Cataqua, for example.

92. See Alcuin, *Alcvini sive Albini epistolae*, ed. E. Duemmler, Epp. Karolini aevi 2, MGH Epp. IV (Hanover, 1895), 1–481, Ep. 110, 158$^{31/32}$: "Igitur infantes—ratione non utentes, aliorum peccatis abnoxii—aliorum fide et confessione per baptismi sacramentum salvari possunt"; on this tradition, see Angenendt, *Kaiserherrschaft und Königstaufe*, 99.

93. On penance substitution see Arnold Angenendt et al., "Counting Piety in the Early and High Middle Ages," in *Ordering Medieval Society*, ed. Jussen.

94. For examples, see pp. 166ff. and 213f.

95. Quoted in note 91.

96. See [Ferreolus of Uzès], *Ferreoli Ucetiensis episcopi regula ad monachos*, in *Codex regularum monasticarum et canonicarum* 1, ed. L. Holstenius and M. Brockie (Augsburg, 1759), 155–66, 15, 159: "neque Monacho ullo loco lavacro filios cujuslibet excipere: ne parentibus illius, ut fieri solet, illicita paulatim vel turpi familiaritate jungatur"; [Aurelian of Arles], *Aureliani Arelatensis episcopi regula ad monachos* in *Codex regularum monasticarum et canonicarum* 1, 147–54, 20, 151: "Nullus infantem de baptismo excipiat"; [Caesarius von Arles] *Sancti Caesarii Arelatensis Statuta Sanctorum Virginum*, in *S. Caesarii Arelatensis episcopi regula sanctarum virginum aliaque opuscula ad sanctimoniales directa*, ed. C. Morin (Bonn, 1933), 6–17, 11, 7$^{26/27}$: "Nulla cuiuslibet filiam in baptismo, neque divitis neque pauperis, praesumat excipere"; see also, [Regula Tarnatensis], "La 'Regula monasterii Tarnatensis'. Texte, sources et datation," ed. F. Villegas, *Revue Benedictine*, 84 (1974): 7–653, 19–20: "Nulla cuiuslibet filiam in baptismo abbatis imperio nullatenus adquiescat"; on the social role of the holy man in late antiquity, see Peter Brown, "The Rise and Function of the Holy Man in Late Antiquity," *Journal of Roman Studies* 61 (1971): 80–101, esp. 97–101; see also pp. 166ff.

97. For Boniface's views, see note 82; Augustine answered "cum uideas moltos non offerri a parentibus sed a quibuslibet extraneis, sicut a dominis seruuli aliquando offeruntur. et nonnumquam mortuis parentibus suis paruuli baptizantur ab eis oblati, qui in illis huius modi misericordiam praebere potuerunt."

98. His stance is described in detail in Lynch, *Godparents and Kinship*, 143–62.

99. See, for example, the abbreviated ceremony in Pseudo-Dionysius, *De ecclesiastica hierarchia* 7, sec. 92, 1470–73; see also note 24 in this chapter.

100. This is also the interpretation of Lynch, *Godparents and Kinship*, 134.

101. Pseudo-Dionysius, *De ecclesiastica hierarchia* 7, sec. 92, 1470; English trans. (slightly modified here) quoted in Lynch, *Godparents and Kinship*, 138; see also, Angenendt, *Kaiserherrschaft und Königstaufe*, 97.

102. See Gelasius I, *Dicta adversus Pelagianam haeresim*, in *Epistulae imperatorum pontificum aliorum*, ed. O. Guenther, CSEL, 35.1 (Prague, Vienna, Leipzig, 1895), 400–36, 425[4].

103. Quoted in note 83; the dating follows Cyrille Vogel, *Medieval Liturgy: An Introduction to the Sources* (Washington, D.C., 1986), 11.

104. Caesarius of Arles, Sermo 13,2, vol. 1, p. 65: Filios, quos in baptismo excepistitis, scitote vos fideiussores pro ipsis apud deum extitisse: et ideo tam illos qui de vobis nati sunt, quam illos quos de fonte excepistitis, semper castigate atque corripite, ut caste et iuste et sobrie vivant"; for a detailed discussion of sponsorship in Caesarius' writings, see Lynch, *Godparents and Kinship*, 143–62.

105. Since M. Coens' article "Les vies de S. Cunibert de Cologne et la tradition manuscrite," (*Analecta Bollandiana* 47, 1929, 338–67, 357), most authors—with the exception of the editor Wilhelm Gundlach (who argues in favor of Romenum in the diocese of Milan; *Epistolae austresicae*, ed. W. Gundlach, MGH Epis, vol. 3, Berlin, 1892), p. 116, A.1)—have located Florianus in Romain-Moutiers; see also, Lynch, *Godparents and Kinship*, 167; and H. H. Anton, *Trier im frühen Mittelalter* (Paderborn, Munich, Vienna, Zurich, 1987), 131, A. 111.

106. On all of the above figures see pp. 128–32.

107. Lynch (*Godparents and Kinship*, 138) believes that it was Pseudo-Dionysius who made the decisive break here, for whom the guarantor, once the guide through the catechumenate, now also becomes the baptizee's guide after baptism. Dionysius, however, merely explains, after describing the act of baptism: "Then the priests take him [the candidate for baptism] in charge and confide him to his guarantor [*to anadocho*], the one in charge of his introduction [*taes prosagogaes kai haegemoni*]" (Dionysius, *De ecclesiastica hierarchia* 3, 78, 1127; English *The Ecclesiastical Hierarchy*, 26–27; translation slightly modified). The fact that, according to the account of the baptism, the catechumen's "guarantor and guide" was still referred to as "guarantor and guide", is not sufficient grounds for Lynch's assertion that there existed no special term for catechumenate witnesses. It appears likely that "guarantor and guide" was a substitute for such a term, which is supported by a glance at Theodore of Mopsuestia, who describes the witness as follows: "a special appointed person . . . conducts him to the registrar and *testifies* for him to the effect that he is worthy of the city and of its citizenship and that . . . he himself would be willing to act as a *guide* to his inexperience" (Theodore of Mopsuestia, Homelie 12,14, f. 86v. and 343; English translation according to Mingana, 25); in using the term *guarantor and guide* Pseudo-Dionysius probably only wanted to say that the catechumenate witness still played a role in the ceremony of baptism; this is precisely what the Ethiopian version of the Canons of Hippolytus, which arose at the same time in the same region, reports.

108. Caesarius of Arles, Sermo 200,6, vol. 2, 811: "praecipue tamen, qui filios aut filias excipere religioso amore desiderant, et ante quam baptizentur, et postea quam baptizati fuerint, de castitate, de humilitate, de sobrietate vel pace eos ammonere vel docere non desinant."

109. Bourdieu, *The Logic of Practice*, trans. Richard Nice (Cambridge, 1990), 35.

110. See chapter 1.

111. Lynch is less reticent when it comes to practice at the time of Caesarius; see *Godparents and Kinship*, 144–62.

112. See *Vita Genovefae virginis Parisiensis*, ed. B. Krusch, *Passiones vitaeque sanctorum aevi Merovingici et antiquiorum aliquot*, MGH SS rer. Merov. 3 (Hanover, 1896), 204–38, 9, 218[13/14]: "Parentibus defunctis, arcessita a matre sua spiritalem, in Parisius urbem migravit."

113. On Genovefa's dates, see Martin Heinzelmann, "Vita sanctae Genovefae. Recherches sur les critères de datation d'un texte hagiographique," in M. Heinzelmann and J. C. Poulin, eds., *Les vies anciennes de sainte Geneviève de Paris. Etudes critiques* (Paris, 1986), 1–111, 80–81; for a summary of the results, see also Heinzelmann, "Zum Stand der Genovefa-Forschung," *DA*, 41 (1985): 532–48.

114. See pp. 123f. and 125f.

115. See Heinzelmannn, "Vita sanctae Genovefae," 71–80.

116. For a detailed account, see P. Gutierrez, *La paternité spirituelle selon saint Paul* (Paris, 1968), 119–211; Irénée Hausherr, "Direction spirituelle II. Chez les chrétiens orientaux," in *Dictionnaire de spiritualité* vol. 3 (1957), cols. 1008–60, esp. 1009; within Christianity, Paul was the first to emphasize this idea strongly; see A. Schindler, "Geistliche Väter und Hausväter in der christlichen Antike," in *Das Vaterbild im Abendland*, vol. I, ed. H. Tellenbach (Stuttgart, Berlin, Cologne, Mainz, 1978), 70–82, 71–72; see also, G. Schrenk, article *"pater,"* in *Theologisches Wörterbuch zum Neuen Testament* 5 (1954), 5:946–59 and 974–1024, 1006–7.

117. The Benedictine rule, for example, uses the term *pater spiritualis*. [Benedict of Nursia], *La règle de saint Benoît*, I and II, ed. A. de Vogüé and J. Neufville, SC 181–82 (Paris, 1972), II,49,7, 606; cf. *Vita sanctae Segolenae viduae*, Acta Sanctorum (Paris and Rome, 1868), 5:628–37, 632 A–B: Quodam tempore adveniente quodam Fratre in urbe jam dicta, religiosa gratulatione Beatissima cum reverentia, ut patrem suscepit spiritualem . . . dicens: Animam meam servare (salvare) volo; doce me, obsecro, viam justitiae. . . . ait: Scio, pater, quia a Deo continentiae virtus datur; zu pater/filius." Cf. note 144 below.

118. For example in the *Capitula e canonibus excerpta a. 813*, c. 18, in *Capitularia regum Francorum*, vol. 1, ed. A. Boretius, MGH Leges Abt. 2 (Hanover, 1881–83), 78, 174[25/6]); *Walafridi Strabonis libellus de exordiis et incrementis quarundam in observationibus ecclesiasticis rerum*, ed. A. Boretius and B. Krause, in *Capitularia regum Francorum* 2, 471–516, 27, 512[14]; *Amalarii episcopi opera liturgica omnia*, vol. 2, *Liber officialis*, ed. J. M. Hanssens (Rome, 1948) I,29,10, 156[40/41]; letter from Pope Zachary to Pippin in *Codex Carolinus*, ed. W. Gundlach, Epistolae Merowingici et Karolini aevi 1, MGH Epp. 3, Berlin, 1892), 469–657, 3, 485[31].

119. See L.H. V,18, 222[16] (on Praetextatus of Rouen); Avitus of Vienne uses the same expression in "Homilia in rogationibus," in *Alcimi Ecdicii Aviti Viennensis episcopi opera quae supersunt*, ed. R. Peiper, MGH AA 6.2 (Berlin, 1883), 108–12, 110[20].

120. See, for example, *Vita Trudonis confessoris Hasbaniensis auctore Donato*, ed. W. Levison, Passiones vitaeque sanctorum aevi Merovingici, MGH SS rer. Merov. 6 (Hanover and Leipzig, 1913), 264–98, 287[29/30]: "baptizavit illum et a sacro fonte suscepit; in utroque [sic] pater illi spiritalis effectus est [i.e., also as a baptist]"; Amalar, *Liber officialis* I,29,10, 156[36–41]: "Illi qui baptizant, patres sunt baptizatorum . . . Quoniam plures sunt baptizatorum . . . commendantur ceteris [sic] patribus spiritualibus"; see also Vita Segolenae (see note 117); the *Vita Nivardi* specifically explains the term: "beatus Bercharius . . . , spiritualis eius [Nivardi] filius, quoniam eum a sacris fontibus susceperat." *Vita Nivardi episcopi Remensis auctore Almanno monacho Altivillarensi*, ed. W. Levison, Passiones vitaeque sanctorum aevi Merovingici, MGH SS rer. Merov. 5 (Hanover and Leipzig, 1910) 157–71, 7, 165[1/2].

121. Council of Metz, 888 c. 6 (Mansi 18, col. 79); [Bede], *Venerabilis Bedae historia ecclesiastica gentis Anglorum*, 2 vols., ed. G. Spitzbart (Darmstadt, 1982), IV,13, 356; Adam of Bremen, *Hamburgische Kirchengeschichte*, ed. B. Schmeidler, MGH SS rer. Germ. 2, 3rd ed. (Hanover and Leipzig, 1917), I,20, 26[18]; see also L.H. IX,10, 425[6] (on Magneric of Trier) and note 119 above (on Praetextatus of Rouen).

122. L.H. IX,8, 421[9] (on Ageric of Verdun).

123. *Ordo Romanus*, XI,12, 420[11/12]; Walafrid Strabo, *Libellus de exordiis et incrementis* 27, 512[12]; [Pontificale Romano-Germanicum], *Le pontifical Romano-germanique du dixième siècle*, 2, *Le texte*, ed. C. Vogel and R. Elze (Rome, 1963), no. 375, vol. 2, 106[20].

124. Amalar, *Liber officialis*, I,29,9, 156[34]; Council of Paris, 829 c. 54, in *Concilia aevi Karolini*, vol. 1.2, ed. A. Werminghoff, MGH Conc. 2.2 (Hanover and Leipzig, 1908), 648[39].

125. Amalar, *Liber officialis*, I,24,13, 132[13].

126. *Ordo Romanus*, XI,32, 425[11].

127. Cf. p. 131.

128. For example, one of those nonparental guarantors whose existence Augustine had, at least, already accepted; see note 97 above.

129. Other considerations, such as whether Genovefa might have inherited something from this *mater spiritualis*, are so vague and without substantiation in the sources that they are of no use to us; on this, see Heinzelmann, "Vita sanctae Genovefae" (91) with cautious hints and, even more tentatively, "Zum Stand der Genovefa-Forschung," 546.

130. See L. v. Padberg, "Heilige und Familie. Studien zur Bedeutung familiengebundener Aspekte in den Viten des Verwandten- und Schülerkreises um Willibrord, Bonifatius und Liudger," Ph.D. diss., University of Münster, 1981, 91–123; quotation on page 91.

131. Despite a large data pool for early modern Neckarhausen, David Sabean found not a single case over a 150-year period there; see his *Kinship in Neckarhausen, 1700–1870* (Cambridge, 1997).

132. The information contained in a ninth-century *Passio* on two fifth-century saints, Desiderius und Reginfridus, is of no use for our present purpose. Chapter 2 of this *Passio* claims that the Reginfrid was the *filius de baptismo* of Bishop Desiderius. *Passio Desiderii episcopi et Reginfridi diaconi martyrum Alsegaudiensium*, ed. W. Levison, Passiones vitaeque sanctorum aevi Merovingici, MGH SS rer. Merov. 6, 51–63, 56[19].

133. Avitus of Vienne, "Homilia in rogationibus," 110[20].

134. See Martin Heinzelmann, *Bischofsherrschaft in Gallien: Zur Kontinuität römischer Führungsschichten vom 4. bis zum 7. Jahrhundert. Soziale, prosopographische und bildungsgeschichtliche Aspekte* (Munich, 1976), 222 and 225–26.

135. Heinzelmann, *Bischofsherrschaft*.

136. See Hincmar, *Vita Remigii episcopi Remensis auctore Hincmaro*, ed. Krusch, Passiones vitaeque sanctorum aevi Merovingici et antiquiorum aliquot, MGH SS rer. Merov. 3 (Hanover, 1896), 239–341, 32, 337[8-10]: "Aliud argenteum vas, quod mihi domnus illustris memoriae Hludowicus rex, quem de sacro baptismatis fonte suscepi, donare dignatus est, ut de eo facerem, quod ipse voluissem, tibi, heredi meae aecclesiae supra memoratae, iubeo turibulum et imaginatum calicem fabricari."

137. The testament as a whole is considered to be authentic at present, but not the specific wording; we would thus do better not to attribute evidential value to the document; see U. Nonn, "Merowingische Testamente. Studien zum Fortleben einer römischen Urkundenform im Frankenreich," *Archiv für Diplomatik*, 18 (1972):

1–129, 26–27; A. H. M. Jones, Philip Grierson, and J. A. Crook, "The Authenticity of the 'Testamentum S. Remigii," *Revue belge de philologie et d'histoire* 35 (1957): 356–73.

138. For an overview of the literature on the baptism of Clovis, see Angenendt, *Kaiserherrschaft und Königstaufe*, 166.

139. See J. Fontaine, article "Ennodius", in *RAC*, vol. 5 (1962), cols. 398–421, col. 399.

140. Ennodius of Pavia, Dictio 13, in *Magni Felicis Ennodi opera*, ed. L. Vogel, MGH AA 7 (Berlin, 1885), 309$^{28-30}$: "ego sum, cui Paterium filium mater et virgo sacri fontis alvus effudit: ego in animae eius secunda nativitate aut recreatione sum genitor. ergo peculiaris eruditionis eius me provisio respicit, cuius pater et inter caelestia sum vocatus."

141. See note 105 on the question of the location of Romenum.

142. Cf. the letter from Florianus of *Romenum* to Nicetius (*Epistolae Austrasicae* 5, 116–17, esp. 116^{26}): "quaeso, ut pro me . . . oretis."

143. Ibid., 116$^{34-35}$: "Ipse [Ennodius] ergo meus est pater ex lavacro, quem credo apud eternum patrem per filium intervenire pro filio."

144. Ibid, 117$^{4.9/10}$ to Caesarius: "pro famulo discipulo suo impetrare confido, und zu Theodatus: qui pro filio et discipulo successoreque suo, licet indigno, non ambigo, quod laus exoret."

145. See note 130.

146. On this see Kaser, *Das römische Privatrecht*, vols. 1 and 2, s.v. *paterfamilias* and *patria potestas*; on this and what follows see also A. Wlosok, "Vater und Vatervorstellungen in der römischen Kultur," in *Das Vaterbild im Abendland*, vol. 1, 18–54, esp. 21; see also pp. 56f.

147. See Jean Gaudemet, "Familie I. Familienrecht," in *RAC*, vol. 7 (1969), cols. 286–358, 324.

148. See, for example, Kaser, *Das römische Privatrecht*, vols. 1 and 2, s.v., *patria potestas*.

149. Gaudemet, "Familie," 331; see also Wlosok, "Vater und Vatervorstellungen," 23–25; C. Meier, *Caesar* (Berlin, 1982), 82.

150. Wlosok, "Vater und Vatervorstellungen," 24 and 44.

151. See Catullus, Liber 72,2, in *C. Valerius Catullus*, ed. W. Kroll (Berlin and Leipzig, 1923), 244$^{2/3}$: "Dilexi tum te non tantum ut volgus amicam,/Sed pater ut gnatos diliget et generos."

152. Meier, *Caesar*, 82.

153. Wlosok, "Vater und Vatervorstellungen," 28.

154. See Heinrich Fichtenau, *Lebensordnungen des 10. Jahrhunderts. Studien über Denkart und Existenz im einstigen Karolingerreich*, vol. 1 (Stuttgart, 1984), 48.

155. For more on the term "morality," a cipher which only interpretation can render useful for social history, see pp. 232f.

156. Gaudemet, "Familie," col. 331.

157. Under the heading "symbolic capital," Pierre Bourdieu has treated these mechanisms in several analyses which have been very helpful for work in social history (among others in *The Logic of Practice*, 112–21; the aspect mentioned here is treated particularly on pp. 119–20); the distinction, introduced by the anthropologist Ruth Benedict, between *shame cultures* and *guilt cultures*, seems heuristically fruitful. See her *The Chrysanthemum and the Sword: Patterns of Japanese Culture* (London, 1967), 222ff.; E. R. Dodds applies this idea convincingly in a historical context in his *The Greeks and the Irrational* (Berkeley and Los Angeles, 1950), 17–18, 28–49.

158. See the summary in A. Demandt, *Metaphern für Geschichte: Sprachbilder und Gleichnisse im historisch-politischen Denken* (Munich, 1978), 28–30.

159. See A. Alföldi, *Der Vater des Vaterlandes im römischen Denken* (Darmstadt, 1971), 86–87 on *clementia*; see also, S. Weinstock, *Divus Iulius* (Oxford, 1971), 200–27, esp. 204 on the *patria potestas*.

160. Seneca, *De clementia*, in *L. Annaei Senecae opera quae supersunt*, ed. F. Haase (Leipzig, 1852), 276–304, I,14,2/3, 290: "Patrem quidem patriae adpellavimus, ut sciret datam sibi potestatem patriam, quae est temperatissima, liberis consulens suaque post illos reponens." English, "On Mercy," in Seneca, *Moral Essays*, with an English trans. by John W. Basore, 3 vols. (London and Cambridge, Mass., 1963), 1:350–447, 399.

161. *Dio's Roman History*, trans. Earnest Cary, 9 vols. (London and New York, 1917), vol. 6, LIII,18,3, 240–43.

162. G. Kruse, article "Pater", in *Paulys Real-Encyclopädie der classischen Altertumswissenschaft*, vol. 18.4 (1949), cols. 2120–21; A. Wlosok, *Laktanz und die philosophische Gnosis* (Heidelberg, 1961), 236.

163. See A. Wlosok, "Römischer Religions- und Gottesbegriff in heidnischer und christlicher Zeit," *Antike und Abendland*, 16 (1970), 39–53, 39–46; see also, W. Pörtschner, "Numen," *Gymnasium*, 66 (1959), 353–74.

164. The philosophers emphasized only this aspect; see W. Burkert, "Gott I. Antike," in *Historisches Wörterbuch der Philosophie* 3, cols. 721–25, 722–23; Seneca, for example, writes: "Deos nemo sanus timet." Seneca, *De beneficiis*, in *L. Annaei Senecae opera quae supersunt* I, 1–154, 4,19,1, 71; see Wlosok, "Römischer Religions- und Gottesbegriff," 46–48.

165. Wlosok, "Vater und Vatervorstellungen," 38.

166. See Kurt Latte, "Römische Religionsgeschichte," in *Handbuch der Altertumswissenschaften* V, 4 (Munich, 1960, repr. 1970), 121 on the *pater patratus* ("appointed father"), and 110, on the *pontifex maximus* as the *pater familias* of the vestal virgins.

167. See Gutierrez, *La paternité spirituelle*, 49–78.

168. On the metaphor of the house, see F. Ohly, "Haus III (Metapher)," in *RAC*, vol. 13 (1986), cols. 905–1063, 906–7.

169. See J. Bellamy, "Adoption surnaturelle de l'homme par Dieu dans la justification," in *Dictionnaire de théologie catholique*, vol. 1 (1930), cols. 425–37, 425.

170. Matthew 18:23–35; see, more generally, Arnold Angenendt, "Theologie und Liturgie der mittelalterlichen Toten-Memoria," in *Memoria: Der geschichtliche Zeugniswert des liturgischen Gedenkens im Mittelalter*, ed. K. Schmid and J. Wollasch (Munich, 1984), 79–199, 120–21, 123.

171. See, for example, *Q.S.Fl. Tertulliani adversus Marcionem*, ed. A. Kroymann in *Quinti Septimi Florentis Tertulliani opera*, vol. 1, CCSL, 1 (Turnhout, 1954), 437–726, I,27,3, 471[23-26]: "Plane nec pater tuus est, in quem competat et amor propter pietatem et timor propter potestatem, nec legitimus dominus, ut diligas propter humanitatem et timeas propter disciplinam"; we find a similar view in the works of Lactantius; for a detailed account, see Wlosok, "Vater und Vatervorstellungen," 48–54; on the shift of accent in Tertullian, see Angenendt, "Theologie und Liturgie," 121–22.

172. See Angenendt et al., "Counting Piety in the Early and High Middle Ages"; and Thomas Lentes, "Counting Piety in the Later Middle Ages," in *Ordering Medieval Society*, ed. Jussen.

173. See Schindler, "Geistliche Väter," 70–71; Schrenk, "*pater*," 946–59 and 974–1016; for a more extensive account, see Gutierrez, *La paternité spirituelle*, 119–211.

174. O. Bardenhewer, *Geschichte der altkirchlichen Literatur*, I, 2d ed. (Freiburg, 1913): 37–46, quotation on page 38; see also Heinzelmann, *Bischofsherrschaft in Gallien*, 154–59.

175. See pp. 122f.

176. See, for example, *Regula sancti Benedicti*, I. Prol. 1, vol. 1, 412: "admonitionem pii patris libenter excipe"; cf. vol. 2, index, s.v., *pater* and *oboedientia* (785–94).

177. Ibid. c. 2,24, 446: "[Abbas] pium patris ostendat affectum"; see also the quotation in note 176.

178. Ibid., I, cap. 2,7, 442; see U.K. Jacobs, *Die Regula Benedicti als Rechtsbuch. Eine rechtshistorische und rechtstheologische Untersuchung* (Cologne and Vienna, 1987), 17–18; if Jacobs comes to the conclusion that the abbot did not have the power of the *paterfamilias*, since it was not comparable to the abbot's pastoral responsibility, this may reflect his concentration on issues of legal history; as historical anthropology has shown, the *paterfamilias* also had an extra-legally defined responsibility similar to that of the pastor; see pp. 132f. In contrast to Jacobs, H. Emonds (article "Abt," in RAC 1 (1950), cols. 45–55, 54–55) emphasizes the parallels between the office of abbot under the Benedictine rule and Roman family law.

179. See notes 68 and 70.

180. See note 140.

181. See note 143.

182. See, for example, Ennodius, as quoted in note 140.

183. [Sacramentarium Gregorianum = Hadrianum] *Le sacramentaire Grégorien. Ses principales formes d'après les plus anciens manuscrits* 1, ed. J. Deshusses, 2d ed. (Fribourg, 1979), no. 374b, 186: "ut sanctificatione concepta ab immaculato divini fontis utero, in novam renatam creaturam progenies caelestis emergat"; see also, *Sacramentarium Gelasianum vetus*, 445, 73^{2-4}; [Sacramentarium Gellonense], Liber sacramentorum Gellonense, ed. A. Dumas, CCSL 159a (Turnhout, 1981), 2, 704a, 98^{17}–99^{19}; Ildephonsus of Toledo makes the point explicitly in *De cognitione baptismi*, in *Sanctorum Hildefonsi, Leodegarii . . . opera omnia . . .*, ed. Jacques Paul Migne (Paris, 1862), 111–72, 159^B: "Illi sane, qui ex utero matris Ecclesiae, id est ex lavacri fonte per Spiritum sanctum genitos in adoptionem filiorum religioso amore excipiunt."

184. Revelation 19:7–9 and 22:17; Matthew 25:1–13; 2 Corinthians 11:2; see Kretschmar, "Die Geschichte des Taufgottesdienstes," 31.

185. See Galatians 4:5; Romans 8:15; Kretschmar, "Die Geschichte des Taufgottesdienstes," 16.

186. See Bellamy, "Adoption surnaturelle," col. 426.

187. *Sacramentarium Hadrianum* no. 373, 185^{314}: "ad creandos nouos populos quos tibi fons baptismatis parturit spiritum adoptionis emitte"; auch: *Sacramentarium Gelasianum vetus*, no. 444, $72^{18/19}$; *Sacramentarium Gellonense*, no. 703, 98^{315}; *Sacramentarium Bergomense. Manoscritto del secolo IX*, ed. A. Paredi (Bergamo, 1962), no. 531, 164; *The Bobbio Missal: A Gallican Mass-Book*, ed. E. A. Lowe (London, 1920), no. 235, 72^{17-19}; *Missale Gallicanum vetus*, ed. L. C. Mohlberg (Rome, 1958), no. 164, 40^{9-11}; one finds the same combination in Ildephonsus of Toledo (quoted in note 183).

188. Raoul Manselli, "Vie familiale et éthique sexuelle dans les pénitentiels," in *Famille et parenté dans l'occident médiéval*, ed. Georges Duby and Jacques Le Goff (Rome, 1977), 363–78, 366.

189. See W. Ogris, "Munt, Muntwalt," in *HRG*, vol. 3 (1984), cols. 750–61, 756–57.

190. Klaus Arnold, *Kind und Gesellschaft in Mittelalter und Renaissance*, Beiträge und Texte zur Geschichte der Kindheit (Paderborn, 1980), 82 with sources.

191. To cite one example, the popes not infrequently addressed their secular audience as "beloved sons" or "most beloved sons"; see, for example, *Liber Diurnius Romanorum Pontificum*, ed. H. Foerster (Berne, 1958), C 1 (=V 1), $182^{3/7}$ (p. 78): *Dilectissimo filio*; see also C 65 (p. 224^9), C 65 (p. 230^{34}); the modes of address have

been compiled by T. Frenz, *Papsturkunden des Mittelalters und der Neuzeit* (Stuttgart, 1986), 35 and, for the period before 1000, 13.

192. See pp. 191ff.

193. For the role of the bishops, see Bernhard Jussen, "Liturgy and Legitimation, or How the Gallo-Romans Ended the Roman Empire," in *Ordering Medieval Society*, ed. Jussen; for the saints, see Friedrich Prinz, *Frühes Mönchtum im Frankenreich. Kultur und Gesellschaft in Gallien, den Rheinlanden und Bayern am Beispiel der monastischen Entwicklung (4.–8. Jahrhundert)* (Munich, 1965), 496–501; for a partial corrective, see Frantisek Graus, "Sozialgeschichtliche Aspekte der Hagiographie der Merowinger- und Karolingerzeit: Die Viten der Heiligen des südalemannischen Raumes und die sogenannten Adelsheiligen," in *Mönchtum, Episkopat und Adel zur Gründungszeit des Klosters Reichenau*, ed. Arno Borst (Sigmaringen, 1974), 131–76; and H. Keller, "Mönchtum und Adel in den Vitae patrum Jurensium und in der Vita Germani abbatis Grandivallensis. Beobachtungen zum frühmittelalterlichen Kulturwandel im alemannisch-burgundischen Grenzraum," in *Landesgeschichte und Geistesgeschichte. Festschrift für Otto Herding* (Stuttgart, 1977), 1–23.

194. See pp. 32–35 and 43–45.

195. He mentions a godfather only four times when reporting the birth or baptism of a king's son; see chapter 9 note 97 (Magneric), note 134 (Veranus), note 127 (Samson's godfather), note 160 (Ragnemod); he also tells of baptisms without naming the sponsor; see L.H. V,34, 239[12/13], regarding one of Chilperic's sons; the sponsor at the baptism of the deacon Waldo is also not named, but the baptismal name Bertram makes it likely that it was the baptist, Bishop Bertram of Bordeaux, himself; we have no further evidence from this period, however, that baptizees took the names of their godparents (cf. L.H. VIII,22, 388–89); Gregory also does not name Clovis' sponsor.

196. L.H. IX, 4, 416[8–10]; HF 2, 372. See pp. 166f.

Chapter 8. The Rule of the Merovingians and the Power of the Bishops

1. Friedrich Prinz, "Die Rolle der Iren beim Aufbau der merowingischen Klosterkultur," in *Die Iren und Europa im frühen Mittelalter*, vol. 1, ed. H. Löwe (Stuttgart, 1982), 202–18, 205; see also his "Die bischöfliche Stadtherrschaft im Frankenreich vom 5. bis zum 7. Jahrhundert," *Historische Zeitschrift*, 217 (1975), 1–35, 21.

2. See, for example, Josef Fleckenstein, *Early Medieval Germany* (Amsterdam and New York, 1978); Ian N. Wood, "Disputes in Late Fifth- and Sixth-century Gaul: Some Problems," in *The Settlement of Disputes in Early Medieval Europe*, ed. Wendy Davies and Paul Fouracre (Cambridge, 1986): 7–22.

3. On this, see Friedrich Prinz, *Frühes Mönchtum im Frankenreich. Kultur und Gesellschaft in Gallien, den Rheinlanden und Bayern am Beispiel der monastischen Entwicklung (4.–8. Jahrhundert)* (Munich, 1965), 488–89.

4. See the summary of the discussion in Karl Ferdinand Werner, "Adel A. Fränkisches Reich, Imperium, Frankreich," in *Lexikon des Mittelalters*, vol. 1 (1980), cols. 118–28, 120–21, with bibliography.

5. For a prosopography of the nobles in royal service, see Margarete Weidemann, *Kulturgeschichte der Merowingerzeit nach den Werken Gregors von Tours*, 2 vols. (Mainz, 1982), vol. 1, 24–106; on their sponsorship ties see chapter 10.

6. For an extensive discussion, see Bernhard Jussen, "Liturgy and Legitimation, or How the Gallo-Romans Ended the Roman Empire," in *Ordering Medieval*

Society, ed. Jussen; and B. Jussen, "Über 'Bischofsherrschaften' und die Prozeduren politisch-sozialer Umordnung in Gallien zwischen 'Antike' und 'Mittelalter,'" *Historische Zeitschrift* 260 (1995): 673–718.

7. For a concise and well-organized account of the function of bishops in late antiquity, see W. Gessel, "Die spätantike Stadt und ihr Bischof," in *Stadt und Bischof*, ed. B. Kirchgässner and W. Baer (Sigmaringen, 1988), 9–28.

8. Friedrich Prinz, *Klerus und Krieg. Untersuchungen zur Rolle der Kirche beim Aufbau der Königsherrschaft* (Stuttgart, 1971), 53.

9. Eugen Ewig, "Milo et eius modi similes", in *S. Bonifatius. Gedenkgabe zum Zwölfhundertsten Todestag*, 2d ed. (Fulda, 1954), 412–40, 434.

10. The division of labor between monks and bishops is stated clearly by Sidonius Apollinaris: "Si quempiam nominauero monachorum, . . . murmur euerberat. . . . Hic qui nominatur, inquiunt, non episcopi, sed potius abbatis complet officium et intercedere magis pro animabus apud caelestem quam pro corporibus apud terrenum iudicem potest." *Sidoine Apollinaire 3. Lettres, livres VI–IX*, ed. A. Loyen (Paris, 1970), Ep. 7,9,9, 55.

11. Ibid.; see also, ibid., Ep. 7,9,16, 57: "habendus ordinis comes, ita utrique parti uel actu uel professione respondet, ut et res publica in eo quod admiretur et ecclesia possit inuenire quod diligat"; Ep. 7,9,17, 58: "parentes ipsius aut cathedris aut tribunalibus praesederunt"; Ep. 7,9,24, 60: "Uxor illi de Palladiorum stirpe descendit, qui aut litterarum aut altarium cathedras cum sui ordinis laude tenuerunt."

12. R. Schieffer, "Der Bischof zwischen Civitas und Königshof (4. bis 9. Jahrhundert)," in *Bischofstypus und Bischofsideal im Spiegel der Kölner Kirche. Festgabe für Joseph Kardinal Höffner zum 80. Geburtstag*, ed. P. Berglar and O. Engels (Cologne, 1986), 17–39, 21.

13. According to Martin Heinzelmann, there is no epitaph that does not show at least traces of ascetic stylization. See his *Bischofsherrschaft in Gallien: Zur Kontinuität römischer Führungsschichten vom 4. bis zum 7. Jahrhundert. Soziale, prosopographische und bildungsgeschichtliche Aspekte*, Beihefte der *Francia* 5 (Munich, 1976), 234.

14. See Fontaine, "Introduction," in Sulpice Severe, *Vie de Saint Martin*, vol. 1, SC 133 (Paris, 1967), S. 17–243 and "Commentaire," in ibid., vol. 3, SC 135 (Paris, 1969), 76–80. According to Fontaine, Sulpicius wanted to compose "une réplique occidentale à l'oeuvre d'Athanase" (p. 78); see also Fontaine, "Commentaire," 1077–80; "c'est l'idéale de sainteté de l'ascétisme gallo-romain primitif, qui se trouve ici esquissé" (1078).

15. See note 14.

16. This varied regionally; see Eugen Ewig, "Das merowingische Frankenreich. 561–687," in *Europa im Wandel von der Antike zum Mittelalter*, ed. Theodor Schieffer (Stuttgart, 1976), 396–433, 419–21, and 424–27; Ewig, "Das Fortleben römischer Institutionen in Gallien und Germanien," in X. Congresso internazionale di scienze storiche, *Relationi* 6 (Florence, 1955), 561–98; Reinhold Kaiser, *Untersuchungen zur Geschichte der Civitas und Diözese Soissons in römischer und merowingischer Zeit* (Bonn, 1973), 158–59.

17. Peter Brown, *Die letzten Heiden. Eine kleine Geschichte der Spätantike* (Berlin, 1986), 28.

18. This is the quintessence of Heinzelmann, *Bischofsherrschaft in Gallien*, 246.

19. See, for example, the works of Dietrich Claude, Martin Heinzelmann, Reinhold Kaiser, and Friedrich Prinz which are cited below.

20. So Prinz, "Die bischöfliche Stadtherrschaft," 2–3; fundamental for the seventh and eighth centuries is R. Kaiser, *Bischofsherrschaft zwischen Königtum und*

Fürstenmacht. Studien zur bischöflichen Stadtherrschaft im westfränkisch-französischen Reich im frühen und hohen Mittelalter (Bonn, 1981), esp. 55–74.

21. Kaiser (ibid., 67–68; quotation p. 55); see also D. Claude, *Topographie und Verfassung der Städte Bourges und Poitiers bis in das 11. Jahrhundert* (Lübeck and Hamburg, 1960), 60 (on Poitiers) and 73 (on Bourges); Paul Fouracre, notes, however, that "Of the episcopal courts we know almost nothing."; Fouracre, "'Placita' and the Settlement of Disputes in Later Merovingian Francia," in *The Settlement of Disputes in Early Medieval Europe*, ed. Wendy Davies and Paul Fouracre (Cambridge, 1986), 23–43, 37.

22. According to Friedrich Prinz, *Klerus und Krieg. Untersuchungen zur Rolle der Kirche beim Aufbau der Königsherrschaft* (Stuttgart, 1971), 53; he cites D. Claude ("Untersuchungen zum frühfränkischen Comitat," *ZRG Germ.*, 81, 1964, 1–79, 22 ff.), who, however, concludes that "in the interior of the Frankish kingdom there were probably always *comites*" (29).

23. This is the position of Kaiser, *Bischofsherrschaft*, 69–70; for a similar view, see Claude, "Untersuchungen zum frühfränkischen Comitat."

24. They are, at any rate, the only known example; see Claude, "Untersuchungen zum frühfränkischen Comitat," 29.

25. Kaiser, *Bischofsherrschaft*, 69.

26. Claude, "Untersuchungen zum frühfränkischen Comitat," 22.

27. See Sprandel, "Dux und comes in der Merowingerzeit," in *ZRG. Germ.*, 74 (1957), 41–84, 67–79. For a different view, see M. Borgolte, "Comes II. Vorkarolingische Zeit," in *Lexikon des Mittelalters*, vol. 3 (1986), cols. 71–75, 72.

28. These discussions seem to me to miss the point, as I discuss at greater length in my essay "Liturgy and Legitimation, or How the Gallo-Romans Ended the Roman Empire."

29. The bishops in the royal cities lacked the economic power base because they resided in the midst of extensive royal property; see Kaiser, *Bischofsherrschaft*, 69, and, on the example of Paris, 476. See also his *Untersuchungen zur Geschichte der Civitas* (p. 228), on Soissons. See Council of Orléans, 511, can. 7 and can. 19.22.23 (*Concilia Galliae 2, A.511–A.695*, ed. C. De Clercq, CCSL 148a, Turnhout, 1963, 7 and 10–11); see also, Kaiser, *Bischofsherrschaft*, 474.

30. See L.H. IV,2, 136[1/2]: "Denique Chlothacharius rex indixerat, ut omnes eclesiae regni sui tertiam partem fructuum fisco dissolverent"; this plan was thwarted by the resistance of the bishops (see ibid., 136[19]).

31. L.H. VI,46, 320[16/17]: "adsiduae testamenta, quae in eclesias conscripta erant, plerumque disripuit"; HF 2, 279.

32. L.H. VI,46, 320[13–16]: "Ecce pauper remansit fiscus noster, ecce divitiae nostrae ad eclesias sunt translatae; nulli penitus nisi soli episcopi regnant; periet honor noster et translatus est ad episcopus civitatum"; HF 2, 279.

33. On this, see Kaiser, *Bischofsherrschaft*, 60 (on Tours and Le Mans), 62–63 (on Chur and Trier) and *passim*, see, more generally, 74 and 401; for a detailed account, see Josef Semmler, "Episcopi potestas und karolingische Klosterpolitik," in *Mönchtum, Episkopat und Adel zur Gründungszeit des Klosters Reichenau*, ed. A. Borst (Sigmaringen, 1974), 305–95.

34. On the examples frequently cited in the literature, see Venantius Fortunatus, Carminum liber III,12 with the title "Item de castello eiusdem [Nicetii] super Mosella" in *Venanti Honori Clementiani Fortunati carminum epistularum expositionum libri undecim*, ed. F. Leo, MGH AA 4,1 (Berlin, 1881), 1–292 (pp. 64–65); liber VIII,9 on the building of dams on the Rhine by Sidonius of Mainz (p. 216[27/28]); liber III,10 on the straightening of rivers by Felix of Nantes (pp. 62–63).

35. L.H. VII,13, 334³⁻⁴: "Nos [Gregorius] vero haec rursum episcopo et civibus mandata remisimus, quod, nisi se ad tempus Gunthchramno rege subderent, similia paterentur."

36. L.H. VII,24, 344⁸⁻¹⁰: "Miseruntque prius legationem, ut scirent, utrum susceperuntur ab his an non. Sed episcopus loci Maroveus dure suscepit hos nuntios"; HF 2, 303.

37. L.H. VII,24, 344.

38. See L.H. VIII,20, 386¹¹⁻¹³ on the synod of Mâcon: "Ursicinus Cardureinsis episcopus excommunicatur, pro eo quod Gundovaldum excipisse publice est confessus"; Faustianus of Dax had the same experience (ibid., 433⁷/⁸), as did those in attendance at Orléans (L.H. VIII,2, 371–72), where Gunthchramn attacked Palladius of Saintes and Bertram of Bordeaux.

39. For an extensive account, see Prinz, *Klerus und Krieg*, 58.

40. Schieffer, "Der Bischof," 21.

41. See Pierre Riché, article "Bildung IV. Alte Kirche und Mittelalter," in TRE, vol. 6 (1980), 595–611, 598–99 and, in more detail, *Éducation et culture dans l'occident barbare. VIᵉ–VIIIᵉ siècle* (Paris, 1962), 220-91 and 311-20; not until 663, in a document of Chlothar III's for Saint Bénigne in Dijon do we have evidence of the first referendarius who was definitely a cleric (see *Diplomata regum Francorum e stirpe Merowingica*, ed. K. A. F. Pertz, MGH DD I (Hanover, 1872), 1–88, 41, 39³⁸); on this, see Josef Fleckenstein, *Die Hofkapelle der deutschen Könige, I: Grundlegung. Die karolingische Hofkapelle* (Stuttgart, 1959), 9.

42. See, for example, Boehm, article "Erziehungs- und Bildungswesen A. Westliches Europa," in *Lexikon des Mittelalters*, vol. 3 (1986), cols. 2196–2203, 2198.

43. See Riché, *Éducation et culture*, 324–31.

44. Prinz, "Die Rolle der Iren," 205.

45. Eugen Ewig, "Die fränkischen Teilungen und Teilreiche 511–613," in *Akademie der Wissenschaften und der Literatur Mainz. Abhandlungen der sozialwissenschaftlichen Klasse*, 9 (Wiesbaden, 1953), 651–715, 654.

46. See Kaiser, *Untersuchungen zur Geschichte*, 159; and *Bischofsherrschaft*, 580–81.

47. Kaiser, *Bischofsherrschaft*, 342.

48. See L.H. VII,17, 338⁵/⁶; and L. Duchesne, *Fastes épiscopaux de l'ancienne Gaule*, vol. 2, 2d ed. (Paris, 1919), 426–27.

49. See the letter from Leo of Sens to Childebert I in *Epistolae aevi Merowingici collectae*, ed. W. Gundlach, Epp. Merowingici et Karolini aevi 1, MGH Epp. 3 (Berlin, 1892), 434–68, 437–38.

50. See the letter from Avitus von Vienne to Clovis in *Alcimi Ecdicii Aviti Viennensis episcopi opera quae supersunt*, ed. R. Peiper, MGH AA 6.2 (Berlin, 1883), 76²/³; treated in detail in N. Staubach, "Germanisches Königtum und lateinische Literatur vom fünften bis zum siebten Jahrhundert. Bemerkungen zum Buch von Marc Reydellet, La royauté dans la littérature latine de Sidoine Apollinaire à Isidore de Séville," in *FMSt*, 17 (1983), 1–54, 17–38; Angenendt, *Kaiserherrschaft und Königstaufe. Kaiser, Könige und Päpste als geistliche Patrone in der abendländischen Missionsgeschichte* (Berlin and New York, 1984), 166–70.

51. Eugen Ewig emphasizes the important role of the episcopate in the propagation of the cult of St. Martin in "Der Martinskult im Frühmittelalter," *Archiv für mittelrheinische Kirchengeschichte*, 14 (1962): 11–30, 16–19; in the course of the Iro-Frankish monastic movement, the means of stabilizing authority already demonstrated by Clovis became the favored means of the nobility, as well as the Carolingians; see, for example, Friedrich Prinz, *Askese und Kultur: Vor- und Frühbenediktinisches Mönchtum an der Wiege Europas* (Munich, 1980), 76–82.

52. See pp. 80ff.

53. According to Dietrich Claude, "Die Bestellung der Bischöfe im merowingischen Reiche," in *ZRG Kan.*, 49 (1963), 1–75, 42; quotation in Ewig, "Die fränkischen Teilungen," 675 note 5.

54. Documents in Kaiser, *Untersuchungen zur Geschichte*, 246–47; see K.H. Krüger, *Königsgrabkirchen der Franken, Angelsachsen und Langobarden bis zur Mitte des 8. Jahrhunderts. Ein historischer Katalog* (Munich, 1971), 126–27.

55. See Council of Orléans, 511, can. 4, in *Concilia Galliae*, 649/650): "ut nullus saecularium ad clericatus officium praesumatur nisi aut cum regis iussone aut cum iudicis uoluntate"; see O. Pontal, *Die Synoden im Merowingerreich* (Paderborn, Munich, Vienna, Zurich, 1986), 26–34.

56. Thus, Theuderic I made his court chaplain bishop of Clermont (see Gregory von Tours, *Liber vitae patrum* VI,3, 232); Chlothar first appointed the loyal abbot Domnulus to one episcopal see, which he did not like, and then to another, more suitable one (L.H. VI,9 279$^{1-12}$); Chilperic made his *maior domus* Badegisil bishop of Le Mans (ibid., 279$^{16/17}$), and Childebert named his referendary Charimer bishop of Verdun (L.H. IX,23, 443$^{8/9}$).

57. See Weidemann, *Kulturgeschichte der Merowingerzeit* 1, 108 (laymen), 107 (officials), 90 (referendaries); on the development of royal appointments of bishops, see Georg Scheibelreiter, *Der Bischof in merowingischer Zeit* (Vienna, Cologne, Graz, 1983), 128–71.

58. See Council of Orléans 533, can. 3.4.7 (*Concilia Galliae*, 99–100) and 538, can. 3.6 (115–17); see Weidemann, *Kulturgeschichte der Merowingerzeit* 1, 115–16; Pontal, *Die Synoden im Merowingerreich*, 74 and 81–82.

59. See Council of Clermont 535, can. 2, in *Concilia Galliae*, 106; Pontal, *Die Synoden im Merowingerreich*, 78.

60. Council of Orléans 549, can. 10, in *Concilia Galliae*, 151–52.

61. Council of Paris 556–573, can. 8, in *Concilia Galliae*, 208–9; on the dating of the synods, see chapter 9 note 10.

62. See Gregory I, Ep. V,60, to Childebert, in *S. Gregorii Magni. Registrum epistularum*, ed. D. Norberg, CCSL, 140/140A (Turnhout, 1982), 360–62; ep. VIII,4, to Brunechildis (ibid., 518–21); ep. IX,214, to Brunechildis (ibid., 772–75); ep. IX,216, to Theuderic and Theudebert (ibid., 776–77); ep. XI,47, to Theuderic (ibid., 945–46); ep. XI,49, to Brunechildis (ibid., 948–49); ep. IX,50, to Theudebert (ibid., 949–50); ep. XI,51, to Chlothar (ibid., 950–51); ep. XIII,5, to Brunechildis (ibid., 997–1000).

63. A. Hauck, *Kirchengeschichte Deutschlands*, vol. 1, 4th ed. (Leipzig, 1904), 144; in agreement with his assessment are Schieffer, "Der Bischof zwischen Civitas und Königshof" (23); and Scheibelreiter, *Der Bischof in merowingischer Zeit* (149–71); in *Kulturgeschichte der Merowingerzeit* (vol. 1, 116) Weidemann reaches a different conclusion, namely "that canon law was generally followed"; the letters of Gregory the Great might be cited as counterexamples; see note 63 and Gregory I, Ep. IX,219, Suagrio [etc.] episcopis a paribus Galliarum, in *Registrum epistularum*, 782–90.

64. Weidemann, *Kulturgeschichte der Merowingerzeit* 1, 110 and the table on 112–13.

65. G. Langgärtner, *Die Gallienpolitik der Päpste im 5. und 6. Jahrhundert. Eine Studie über den apostolischen Vikariat von Arles* (Bonn, 1964), 140.

66. On Ageric of Verdun, see L.H. III,35, S. 130^{12}: "quidam e civibus"; HF 2, 110. For more on Ageric, see pp. 157ff.

Chapter 9. Sponsorship Bonds (1): Bishops and Kings

1. L.H. V,18, 222$^{3/4}$, HF 2, 190–91; quoted in note 46.
2. See L.H. IV,28, 161$^{13/14}$: "Habebat autem tunc Chilpericus tres filius de Audovera priore regina sua, id est Theudoberthum, cui supra meminimus, Merovechum atque Chodovechum."
3. L.H. IV,23, 155^{16}–56^2.
4. L.H. V,2, 195$^{5-9}$.
5. L.H. V,1, 194^{15}–95^1.
6. A. Longnon, *Géographie de la Gaule au 6ᵉ siécle* (Paris, 1878), 117, 122–23, 142, 236.
7. See L. Duchesne, *Fastes épiscopaux de l'ancienne Gaule*, vol. 2, 2d ed. (Paris, 1919), 207; Council of Orléans 541, *Concilia Galliae 2, A.511.–A.695*, ed. C. De Clercq, CCSL 148a (Turnhout, 1963), 142^7.
8. See Council of Paris, 556–573, *Concilia Galliae*, 209^{146}.
9. See Council of Tours, 567, *Concilia Galliae*, 194^{555}.
10. See O. Pontal, *Die Synoden im Merowingerreich* (Paderborn, Munich, Vienna, Zurich, 1986), 122–26.
11. Documents in M. Rubellin, "Entrée dans la vie, entrée dans la chrétienté, entrée dans la société: Autour du baptême à l'époque carolingienne," in *Les entrées dans la vie: Initiation et apprentissages. XIIᵉ Congrès de la Société des historiens médiévistes de l'Enseignement supérieur public* (Nancy, 1981–82), 31–51, 38/39 with notes 26–27.
12. This choice is also the only one for which Gregory gives a specific reason; see pp. 166ff.
13. Leontius of Bordeaux, who, according to Duchesne, probably did not die before 570 (*Fastes épiscopaux* 2, 61) apparently had no contact with Chilperic. His successor, Bertram, first mentioned in 577 (see ibid., 62), was a faithful follower of the king (Weidemann, *Kulturgeschichte der Merowingerzeit* 1, 143–44), and a sycophant *(adolator)* in Gregory's eyes (L.H. V,18, 219^1).
14. A provincial synod in Saintes (561/567) attempted to depose a bishop whom the king had appointed without the approval of the metropolitan; see L.H. IV,26, 157–58; Pontal, *Die Synoden im Merowingerreich,* 127; at the second Parisian synod the already traditional demands for a canonical election were accompanied for the first time by a catalog of penalties.
15. S. Deck assumes that there was already a mint in the sixth century but dates the first evidence of trade in Rouen to 629. "Les marchands de Rouen sous les ducs," *Annales de Normandie* 6 (1956), 245–54, 245. See also, Reinhold Kaiser, *Bischofsherrschaft zwischen Königtum und Fürstenmacht. Studien zur bischöflichen Stadtherrschaft im westfränkisch-französischen Reich im frühen und hohen Mittelalter* (Bonn, 1981), 152.
16. L.H. VIII,31, 398$^{18/9}$: "Ad quem sepeliendum ... magnus tunc omnes Rothomagensis cives et praesertim seniores loci illius Francos meror obsedit"; HF 2, 354.
17. This interpretation will doubtless not be undermined by the knowledge that in Bishop Raganfried, the *compater* of Pippin the Younger, this very *civitas* also possessed a spiritual kinsman of the first Carolingians; see *Gesta sanctorum patrum Fontanellensis coenobii*, ed. F. Lohier and J. Laporte (Rouen and Paris, 1936), 59: "Compater etiam spiritalis regenerationis Pippini magni regis."
18. L.H. V,18, S. 216^{18}: "eum in exilium usque sacerdotalem audientiam retenere praecepit"; this, most likely, was a royal tribunal; see W. Bergmann, "Untersuchungen

zu den Gerichtsurkunden der Merowingerzeit," *Archiv für Diplomatik* 22 (1976), 1–186, 16–22, esp. 21.

19. L.H. VII,16, 337[19].
20. L.H. V,18, 219–20.
21. L.H. V,18, 222[19]: "haec altercatio altius tolleretur"; HF 2, 191.
22. L.H. V,18, 217[5-14]: "[Chilpericus:] datis muneribus, ut ego interficerer.... Advenerunt falsi testis, qui ostendendebant species aliquas.... Ad haec ille dicebat: Verum enim dicitis vos et me saepius muneratus; sed non haec causa extetit, ut rex eieceretur a regno. Nam et cum vos mihi et equos optimos et res alias praeberetis, numquid poteram aliud facere, nisi et ego vos simile sorte remunerarem. Recedente vero regem..."; HF 2, 186–87; on the uncanonical marriage see L.H. V,18, 217[1-4].
23. Ibid., 216[16]: "Praetextatus... populis munera daret."
24. See Council of Paris 556–573, can. 4. (*Concilia Galliae*, 207) and the list of names 209[146]); the council most likely took place in 561–62 (see note 10).
25. See note 22.
26. Aron Iakovlevich Gurevich, *Categories of Medieval Culture*, trans. George L. Campbell (London and Boston, 1985), 223.
27. Georges Duby, *The Early Growth of the European Economy*, trans. Howard B. Clarke (London, 1974), 51.
28. Claude Lévi-Strauss, *The Elementary Structures of Kinship*, trans. James Harle Bell, John Richard von Sturmer, and Rodney Needham (Boston, 1969), 113–14.
29. Marcel Mauss, *The Gift: The Form and Reason for Exchange in Archaic Societies*, trans. W. D. Halls (London, 1990), 10. Mauss' interpretation of this story has since been criticized from several quarters. For a brief sketch of the critiques (by Lévi-Strauss, Firth, and Johansen) and a plausible interpretation with a new translation of the key text, see Marshall Sahlins, *Stone Age Economics* (Chicago and New York, 1972), 149–83.
30. See Mauss, *The Gift*, 14.
31. See, for example, King Gunthchramn's entry into Orleans, which the chronicler describes; L.H. VIII,1, 370; quoted in note 41 of this chapter.
32. See L.H. V, 18, 217[5] and note 23.
33. See L.H. V,18, 221[1-19]; quotations on 221[4] ("Vidistis enim species, quas nobis furtu abstulit") and 221[18/19] ("cum haec causa non ad furtum, sed ad custodiam debeat deputare"); HF 2, 190; see also 217[17]: "Reperrit cum eodem res Brunichildis reginae conmendatas."
34. Ibid., 221[19]–22[3]: "Ad haec rex: Si hoc depositum penes te habebatur ad custodiendum, cur solvisti unum ex his et lymbum aureis contextum filis in partibus desecasti et dedisti per virus, qui me a regno deicerent? Praetextatus episcopus respondit: Iam dixi tibi superius, quia munera eorum acciperam, ideoque haec, cum non haberem de praesenti quid darem, hinc praesumpsi et eis vicissitudinem munerum tribui"; HF 2, 190.
35. See the reconstruction of his property in Margarete Weidemann, *Das Testament des Bischofs Berthramn von Le Mans vom 27. März 616. Untersuchungen zu Besitz und Geschichte einer fränkischen Familie im 6. und 7. Jahrhundert* (Mainz, 1986).
36. Pierre Bourdieu emphasizes this factor in *The Logic of Practice*, 98–111.
37. According to the translation by Best, which Mauss uses in *The Gift* (quoted in Sahlins, *Stone Age Economics*, 151): "après qu'un certain temps (after some time)".
38. See Mauss, *The Gift*, 10.
39. New translation in Sahlins, *Stone Age Economics*, 152.
40. See L.H. V,17, 216[10/11]: "Et manducantes simul atque bibentes dignisque se muneribus honorantes, pacifici discesserunt."
41. See L.H. VIII,1, 370[11/12]: "Nam per domibus eorum [civium Aurelianensis

urbis] invitatus abibat et prandia data libabat; multum ab his muneratus muneraque ipsis proflua benignitate largitus est."

42. L.H. IX,16, 431$^{5/6}$: "acceptisque ac datis muneribus."

43. See p. 204 (refers to L.H. X, 28, 522 $^{4/5}$).

44. See note 43.

45. See J. Hannig, "Ars donandi. Zur Ökonomie des Schenkens im früheren Mittelalter," in *Armut, Liebe, Ehre. Studien zur historischen Kulturforschung*, ed. Richard van Dülmen (Frankfurt a.M., 1988), 11–37 and 275–78.

46. L.H. V,18, 222$^{3-4}$: "Proprium mihi esse videbatur, quod filio meo Merovecho erat, quem de lavacro regenerationis excipi"; HF2, 190–91.

47. For more detail see pp. 177ff.

48. L.H. V,18, 222$^{5/6}$: "Videns autem rex Chilpericus, quod eum his calumniis superare nequiret, adtonitus valde ac conscientia confusus"; HF 2, 191.

49. L.H. V,18, 222$^{14-17}$: "adveniensque et rex, ait ad episcopum: Si munera pro muneribus his hominibus es largitus, quur sacramenta postulasti, ut fidem Merovecho servant? Respondit episcopus: Petii, fateor, amicitias eorum habere cum eo"; HF 2, 191.

50. See, for example, the summarizing description of this system in Claude Lévi-Strauss, *The Elementary Structures of Kinship*, trans. Bell, von Sturmer, and Needham (Boston, 1969), 113–14.

51. See note 22; HF 2, 187.

52. See note 5.

53. The example of the chronicler himself shows how canon law could be treated when it was opportune. Gregory relates that King Chilperic once demanded that he speak an oath to clear himself of an accusation and "though these conditions were contrary to the canons, they were fulfilled out of consideration for the king" (L. H. V,49, 261$^{8/9}$; HF 2, 225). Or were they perhaps fulfilled more out of consideration for the author? It might have been unwise, indeed, dangerous for Gregory to cite canon law against the order of "the Nero and Herod of our time" (L.H. VI, 46, 319$^{13/14}$; HF 2, 278)—and so he refrained from doing so.

54. See note 23. HF , 186.

55. L.H. V,3, 195 *(valde amarus)* and V,11.

56. L.H. V,11–14, 205–13 and V,48, 258.

57. L.H. V,14, 209$^{8/9}$: "orans [. . .] ut regnum accepere possit"; ibid., 209^{17}: "Merovechus de patre atque novercam multa crimina loquebatur," ibid., 212$^{7/8}$: "possit regnum accepere"; HF 2, 181.

58. L.H. V,18, 217$^{4-7}$: "cum illo egisti, datis muneribus, ut ego interficerer. . . . seduxisti paecuniam plebem, ut nullus mecum fidem habitam custodiret, voluistique regnum meum in manu alterius tradere"; HF 2, 186.

59. L.H. V,18, 217$^{7-9}$: "Haec eo dicente, infremuit multitudo Francorum voluitque ostea basilicae rumpere, quasi ut extractum sacerdotem lapidibus urgueret; sed rex prohibuit fieri"; HF 2, 186.

60. L.H. V,18, 222$^{17-19}$: "et non solum hominem, sed, si fas fuisset, angelum de caelo evocaveram, qui esset adiutor eius; filius enim mihi erat, ut saepe dixi, spiritalis ex lavacro"; HF 2, 191.

61. See J. Weitzel, *Dinggenossenschaft und Recht. Untersuchungen zum Rechtsverständnis im fränkisch-deutschen Mittelalter* 1 (Cologne and Vienna, 1985), 274–81; Gregory gives a similar account; see L.H. V,18, 222^{21}–23^{2}.

62. Ibid., 222^{19}–23^{11}.

63. A formula such as "godparenthood negates *compaternitas*" would be an unwarranted conclusion here.

64. The *pactum* or *vinculum compaternitatis* is mentioned frequently; see, for example, *Vita Bertini*, ed. W. Levison, in *Passiones vitaeque sanctorum aevi Merovingici*, MGH SS rer. Merov. 5 (Hanover and Leipzig, 1910), 765–69, 19, 765[19/20]: "compater fuit secundem laudabilem ritum, inter christianos ad coniugenda fraternae caritatis foedera consecratum"; compare the account by Agnellus, cited in chapter 1, note 64; or by Petrus Cantor in chapter 1, note 88.

65. For a compilation of the accounts from Gregory's *History*, see Weidemann, *Kulturgeschichte der Merowingerzeit*, 1, 47–52.

66. L. H. IX, 421[8-10]. Quoted in note 79; HF 2, 376.

67. Berthar, *Gesta episcoporum Virdunensium*, ed. G. Waitz, MGH SS 4 (Hanover, 1841), 38–45, 4, 41[1-6]; Euspicius refused.

68. See L.H. III,34, 129[14/15]: "multas iurogavit iniurias", and III,35, 130[14/15]: "non solum spoliatus, verum etiam suppliciis adfectus fuisset."

69. L.H. III,34, 130[2/3]: "cumque hi negutium exercentes responsum in civitate nostra sicut reliquae habent, praestiterint."

70. See L.H. III,34, 129[20]–30[10]; quotation, p. 130[5/6] and [9/10]: "At illi negutia exercentes divites per hoc effecti sunt et usque hodie magni habentur. . . . Et nihil exigens, antedictus cives divites fecit"; HF 2, 110

71. On these donations see Berthar, Gesta episcoporum Virdunesium, 6, 41[34-39]; see also P. E. Hübinger, *Die weltlichen Beziehungen der Kirche von Verdun zu den Rheinlanden* (Bonn, 1935), 6–11; the distant possessions in Rodez probably cannot be connected with the Merovingians; on the referendary Charimer as the successor, see L.H. IX,23, 443[8/9].

72. See chapter 8 note 67; Duchesne, *Fastes épiscopaux*, 3, 70; the precise date is unknown; Gregory reports the appointment in connection with events that took place in 539 (L.H. III,32, 128) and 548 (L.H. III,36, S. 131/132), that is, chronologically incorrectly; on Ageric's installation, see L.H. III,35, 130–31.

73. According to an observation by R. Buchner in his edition of *Gregorii Episcopi Turonensis historiarum libri decem* (Darmstadt, 1955) 1, 189 note 4.

74. On the difficulties, see E. Freise, "Das Frühmittelalter bis zum Vertrag von Verdun (843)," in *Westfälische Geschichte*, 1: *Von den Anfängen bis zum Ende des alten Reiches*, ed. W. Kohl (Düsseldorf, 1983), 276–335, 277.

75. See chapter 8 note 66; on Ageric, see N. Gauthier, *L'évangélisation des pays de la Moselle* (Paris, 1980), 223–29.

76. At any rate they had entrenched themselves there with their families and servants; see L.H. IX,12, 426–27; cf. Eugen Ewig, "Das Trierer Land im Merowinger- und Karolingerreich," in *Geschichte des Trierer Landes*, vol. 1, ed. R. Laufner (Trier, 1964), 222–302, 229.

77. See notes 83 and 93.

78. See note 95.

79. L.H. IX,8, 421[8-10]: "Ille vero cum se cerneret positum in discrimine, Veredunensem eclesiam petiit, per Agericum prorsus episcopum, qui erat regis pater ex lavacro, veniam impetrare confidens"; HF 2, 376.

80. L.H. IX,10, 425[9-12]: "Haec autem evaginato aiebat gladio. Turbatus auditu episcopus ait: Et quid faciam, si hic a te tenior. Demitte me, ut eam et deprecer misericordiam regis, et fortassis miserebitur tui. Et ille: Nequaquam, sed transmitte abbates et creditus tuos, ut haec quae loquor exponat"; HF 2, 380.

81. L.H. IX,10, 425[12-13]: "Verumtamen non haec rege, ut erant, nuntiata sunt; sed dixerunt, quod hic ab episcopo defensaretur"; HF 2, 380.

82. See, for example, Weidemann, *Kulturgeschichte der Merowingerzeit* 1, 225; Hübinger, *Die weltlichen Beziehungen*, 6.

83. L.H. IX,8, 421[8–12]: "[Gunthchramn Boso] per Agericum prorsus episcopum, qui erat regis pater ex lavacro, veniam impetrare confidens. Tunc pontifex ad regem properat deprecaturque pro eo; cui rex cum negare nequiret quae petebat, ait: Veniat coram nobis, et datis fideiussoribus in praesentia patrui mei, quicquid illius iudicium decreverit, exsequamur"; HF 2, 376.

84. L.H. IX,8, 421[16–18]: "Rex . . . eum . . . posuit in manu episcopi, dicens: Sit penes te, sanctae sacerdos, donec in praesentia Gunthchramni regis adveniat"; HF 2, 377.

85. Arnold Angenendt, *Kaiserherrschaft und Königstaufe. Kaiser, Könige und Päpste als geistliche Patrone in der abendländischen Missionsgeschichte* (Berlin and New York, 1984), 107.

86. This is the view of Hübinger, *Die weltlichen Beziehungen*, 6.

87. See chapter 5.

88. On Waddo, see L.H. X,21, 512–14 (on the year 590); the episode involving Theodorus took place in 585 (cf. chapter 5 note 21), that involving Gunthchramn Boso in 587.

89. L.H. VII,23, 343–44.

90. This is the interpretation of the episode in Edward James, "'Beati pacifici': Bishops and the Law in Sixth century Gaul," in *Disputes and Settlements: Law and Human Relations in the West*, ed. J. Bossy (Cambridge, 1983), 25–47, 35–36; it is probably an oversight that James refers to both Gunthchramn Boso and Childebert as Ageric's godsons.

91. See p. 111 and chapter 5.

92. L.H. IX,10, 424[16–18]: "quia convenerat, ut absque ullius defensione regi praesentaretur, scilicet ut, si ipse decerneret eum morte debere, non excusaretur a sacerdote"; HF 2, 379.

93. L.H. IX,12, 427[13]: "praesertim cum et ipse pontifex Agericus in hac domo resederet"; HF 2, 382.

94. L.H. IX,12, 427[16–24]; quotation in chapter 5 note 101.

95. See Berthar, *Gesta episcoporum Virdunensium* 6, 41[27/8]: "Quidam autem vir valde nobilis cum pro suis sceleribus a rege vita debuiset privari, petitione praefati [Agerici] antistitis salvatus est"; Berthar's account (p. 41[25–27]), according to which the 590 synod was transferred from Verdun to Metz for Ageric's sake is incorrect, since Ageric had already died in 588; see, instead, L.H. IX,23, 443 (on Ageric's death) and X,19, 510[8–16] (on the synod); see also Hübinger, *Die weltlichen Beziehungen*, 7.

96. See pp. 155f.

97. L.H. VIII,37, 405[1/2]: "Post haec Childebertho regi filius natus est, qui a Magnerico Treverorum episcopo de sacro fonte susceptus, Theudeberthus est vocitatus"; HF 2, 360.

98. L.H. IX,10, 424[19]–25[8]: "Quod cum ille comperisset, ad mansionem Magnerici episcopi convolavit et, clausis osteis, segregatis ab eo clericis vel famulis, ait: 'Scio te, beatissime sacerdos, magnum cum regibus honorem habere. Et nunc ad te confugio, ut evadem . . . , unde manifeste scias, quod si a te non eruor, interfectu te, egrediar foris et moriar. . . . O sanctus sacerdos, scio enim, te patrem communem cum rege esse filio eius, et novi, quoniam quaecumque petieris ad eo obtenebis, nec negari omnino poterit sanctitate tuae quaecumque poposceris'"; HF 2, 379–80; translation modified.

99. See, for example, the Council of Auxerre 561–605, can. 25 (*Concilia Galliae*, 268[78/79]): "Non licet abbate filios de baptismo habere nec monachus commatres habere."

100. See H. H. Anton, *Trier im frühen Mittelalter* (Paderborn, Munich, Vienna, Zurich, 1987), 119–21.

101. See the letter from Nicetius to Chlodosuinda in *Epistolae Austrasicae*, ed. W. Gundlach , Epistolae Merowingici et Karolini aevi 1, MGH Epp. 3 (Berlin, 1892), 110–53, 8, 119–20.

102. See the letter from Nicetius to Emperor Justinian (*Epistolae Austrasiacae* 7, 118–19), in which he displays a striking lack of judgment.

103. See Eugen Ewig, *Die Merowinger und das Imperium* (Opladen, 1983), 16–38.

104. See Michel Rouche, "Les baptêmes forcés de juifs en Gaule mérovingienne et dans l'Empire d'Orient," in *De l'antijudaisme antique à l'antisémitisme contemporain*, ed. V. Nikiprowetzky (Lille, 1979), 105–24, 113–18; on this see pp. 174f.

105. See [Vita Magnerici], *De s. Magnerico confessore archiepiscopo Trevirensi*, AA SS Juli 6 (Paris and Rome, 1868), 168–92, 184; Gregory of Tours, *Libri octo miraculorum*, ed. B. Krusch, in *Gregorii episcopi Turonensis miracula et opera minora*, MGH SS rer Merov. 1,2 (Hanover, 1885),1–370, 7: Liber vitae patrum, XVII,2, 279$^{14-36}$; on this, see Anton, *Trier*, 134 with note 119; on Nicetius, see Anton, 131–38, as well as Ewig, *Das Trierer Land*, 97–106; and E. Winheller, *Die Lebensbeschreibungen der vorkarolingischen Bischöfe von Trier* (Bonn, 1935), 3–9.

106. See Gregory of Tours, *Libri octo miraculorum*, 7, *Liber vitae patrum* XVII,2/3, 280$^{8-22}$; Anton, *Trier*, 134 with note 120.

107. See chapter 8 note 34.

108. According to D. Claude, "Untersuchungen zum frühfränkischen Comitat," ZRG Germ., 81 (1964): 1–79, 29; on Trier, see, similarly, Anton, *Trier*, 127 and 130.

109. Weidemann, *Kulturgeschichte der Merowingerzeit* 1, 154, Gauthier, *L'évangélisation des pays*, 173, and Anton, *Trier*, 98, base their assumption that Theuderic was in Trier on Gregory of Tours, *Libri octo miraculorum*, 231$^{11-14}$; but their interpretation is dubious on this point. See Arnold Angenendt and Bernhard Jussen, review of Margarete Weidemann, *Kulturgeschichte der Merowingerzeit nach den Werken Gregors von Tours*, Theologische Revue, 83 (1987):34–37, 36–37.

110. C. Brühl, "Königspfalz und Bischofsstadt in fränkischer Zeit," *Rheinische Vierteljahresblätter* 23 (1958), 161–274, 254; King Theudebert accepted Aredius of Limoges as one "of the noble youths", whom Nicetius later discovered *in regis palatio* (L.H. X,29, 522$^{10.13}$; HF 2, 465); from the context the palace appears to have been in Trier; Gregory reports on Theudebert's dispute with Nicetius during the king's visit to a fair, apparently in Trier (see Gregory of Tours, *Libri octo miraculorum* , 279–80); in Trier Theudebert visited *loca sancta . . . causa orationis* (*Libri octo miraculorum*, 356$^{19/20}$); finally, Theudebert's tax collector Parthenius was killed in Trier after the king's death; see L.H. III,36, 131–32.

111. On the *palatium*, see Brühl, "Königspfalz und Bischofsstadt," 256: "Gregory of Tours speaks of Theudebert I's *palatium regis*, which can only be the *palatium* in Trier"; according to Brühl, the kings had palaces everywhere they traveled because they only lived on their own property; see *Fodrum, gistum, servitium regis. Studien zu den wirtschaftlichen Grundlagen des Königtums im Frankenreich und in den fränkischen Nachfolgestaaten Deutschland, Frankreich und Italien vom 6. bis zur Mitte des 14. Jahrhunderts*, 2 vols. (Cologne and Graz, 1968), 16; according to Ewig the distant land holdings of the Trier church went back to royal donations from the period before 555 (Ewig, *Das Trierer Land*, 98 and 100).

112. These are brought together in Anton, *Trier*, 139–41.

113. See L.H. VIII,12, 379^8: "tamen qualis esset sacerdus."

114. See notes 119–21.

115. After the death of Sigibert, the Austrasian nobles were involved in a constant struggle with Brunechildis to gain influence over the young king; for an overview, see Eugen Ewig, "Die fränkischen Teilungen und Teilreiche 511–613," in

Akademie der Wissenschaften und der Literatur Mainz. Abhandlungen der sozialwissenschaftlichen Klasse 9 (Wiesbaden, 1953), 651–715, 681–82 and 687–88.

116. L.H. IX,10, 424[13/14].

117. See L.H. IX,20, 435[2/3]: "mediantibus sacerdotibus atque proceribus"; HF 2, 389.

118. See note 98.

119. According to Ewig, *Das Trierer Land*, 108.

120. Anton, *Trier*, 100 and 139.

121. Weidemann, *Kulturgeschichte der Merowingerzeit* 1,222; see also, Eugen Ewig, "Zur Geschichte von Contrua-Gondorf," in *Von der Spätantike zum frühen Mittelalter. Aktuelle Probleme in historischer und archäologischer Sicht*, ed. J. Werner and E. Ewig (Sigmaringen, 1979), 371–77, 376; as evidence Ewig cites Magneric's mediation between Bishop Theodulf of Marseilles and King Gunthchramn; "The fact that he was successful demonstrates that his high reputation extended to the ruler of Franco-Burgundy"; Gregory mentions no such mediation (see L.H. VIII,12, 378–79); Anton (*Trier*, 100 and 132) points to Magneric's efforts on behalf of Theodore alongside his participation at Andelot, his role as sponsor, and his intervention on behalf of Gunthchramn Boso.

122. Gauthier, *L'évangélisation des pays*, 191.

123. See ibid., 190.

124. See the index to Gregory's *History of the Franks*; later, at least, Childebert entrusted the bishop of Cologne with various duties, so that he may have already entertained connections to the royal court; see chapter 5 note 53.

125. For an account of their conflict, see G. Schenk von Schweinsberg, "Reims in merowingischer Zeit: Stadt, Civitas, Bistum. Anhang: Die Geschichte der Reimser Bischöfe in karolingischer Zeit bis zur Bischofserhebung Hincmars (845)," Ph.D. diss., University of Bonn, 1971, 99–109.

126. See chapter 8 note 28.

127. L.H. V,22, 229[15]–30[1]: "His ita gestis, Samson, filius Chilperici regis iunior, a desenteria et febre compraehensus, a rebus humanis excessit. Hic vero, cum Chilpericus rex Tornacum a fratre obsederetur, natus est; quem mater ob metum mortis a se abiecit et perdere voluit. Sed cum non potuisset, obiurgata a rege, eum baptizare praecepit. Qui baptizatus et ab ipso episcopo susceptus, lustro uno nec perfuncto, defunctus est"; HF 2, 198.

128. L.H. IV,50, 187[14/15].

129. See L.H. V,18, 217; see also the evidence from book 6 cited in note 179 below; in naming the Bishop of Tournai as the sponsor, Duchesne ignores the account's two temporal levels: Samson was born, but not baptized, at Tournai. *Fastes épiscopaux*, 3, 115, no. 3. Joseph H. Lynch also names the bishop of Tournai as Samson's godfather; *Godparents and Kinship in Early Medieval Europe* (Princeton, 1986), 185 note 88.

130. See Augustine, ep. 98,5, letter to Bishop Boniface, in *S. Aureli Augustini Hipponiensis episcopi epistulae*, ed. A. Goldbacher, vol. 2 (Prague, Vienna, Leipzig, 1898), 526[4-7]: "Nec illud te moueat, quod quidam non ea fide ad baptismum percipiendum paruulos ferunt, ut gratia spiritali ad uitam regenerentur aeternam, sed quod eos putant hoc remedio temporalem retinere vel recipere sanitatem"; see also *Vita Magnerici*, 186[A]: "a quo statim baptizatus, et a sancto diacono de fonte susceptus, lepra carnis et animae deinceps caruit"; see also note 132.

131. See the examples in Angenendt, *Kaiserherrschaft und Königstaufe*, 57 note 4.

132. See, for example, the *Vita Magnerici* (quoted in note 130); among the seven examples of the efficacy of baptismal water cited by Angenendt in *Kaiserherrschaft und Königstaufe* (p. 57 note 4), for example, the baptismal font possesses definite

healing powers only in the *Vita Odiliae*, since no attention is paid to the baptist, "cuidam episcopo nomine Erhardo." *Vita Odiliae abbatissae Hohenburgensis*, ed. W. Levison, in *Passiones vitaeque sanctorum aevi Merovingici*, MGH SS rer. Merov. 6, (Hanover and Leipzig, 1913), 24–50, 4, 40[3-4].

133. For a detailed discussion of the notion of "consecrated matter", see Arnold Angenendt, "Bonifatius und das Sacramentum initiationis. Zugleich ein Beitrag zur Geschichte der Firmung," *Römische Quartalschrift für christliche Altertumskunde und Kirchengeschichte* 72 (1977): 133–83, 159–61.

134. L.H. IX,4, 416[7/8]: "Eo anno Childebertho rege alius filius natus est, quem Veranus Cavelonensis episcopus sucipiens a lavacro, Theodorici nomen imposuit"; HF 2, 372.

135. This is assuming that Merovech was baptized after 567 (see above, pp. 146f.); that Cavaillon belonged to Burgundy is clear from L.H. VIII,31, 400[1-4]: Veranus and two Burgundian bishops are mentioned as Gunthchramn's envoys; see also L.H. IX,41, 468[1-5], which mentions a meeting of Burgundian bishops, including Veranus, with Gunthchramn; on Veranus, see "Saint Vrain" in *Vies des Saintes et des Bienheureux selon l'ordre du calendrier avec l'historique des fêtes*, vol. 10 (Paris, 1952), 629–31.

136. M. H. Laurent, "Cavaillon," in *Dictionnaire d'histoire et de géographie ecclésiastiques*, vol. 12 (1953), cols. 25–26; according to this article, the first evidence of a bishop is for 396.

137. According to the article "Saint Vrain," in *Vies des Saintes* 10, 629); on Carpentras, see M. H. Laurent, article "Carpentras," in *Dictionnaire d'histoire et de géographie ecclésiastiques*, vol. 11 (1949), cols. 1112–14.

138. See the summary of what is known in *Gallia Christiana in provincias ecclesiasticas distributa* (Paris, 1715) 1, 940–42, which however bases its information on Veranus on his unusable anonymous *Vita*.

139. On the corridor see Ewig, "Die fränkischen Teilungen," 678.

140. On his accession to power see Duchesne, *Fastes épiscopaux* 1, 271; on his relations with Gunthchramn cf. note 135.

141. Eugen Ewig, "Das merowingische Frankenreich. 561–687," in *Europa im Wandel von der Antike zum Mittelalter*, ed. Theodor Schieffer (Stuttgart, 1976), 396–433, 400.

142. See Fredegar, *Chronicarum quae dicuntur Fredegarii scholastici libri IV*, ed. B. Krusch, Fredegarii et aliorum chronica. Vitae sanctorum, MGH SS rer. Merov. 2 (Hanover, 1888), 1–193,16, 127[26-27]: "Teudebertus sortitus est Auster, sedem habens Mittensem, Teudericus accipit regnum Gunthramni in Burgundia."

143. Weidemann, *Kulturgeschichte der Merowingerzeit* 1, 148; Weidemann is also in accord with Ewig's interpretation.

144. On Pompierre see L.H. V,17, 216[5-9], on the meeting of 585 see L.H. VII,33, 353[13-16].

145. See L.H. IX,20, 439[21-23]: "Utinam tu, o rex gloriosissime, minus cum eam [Fredegundem] caritatem haberes! Nam ut saepe cognovimus, dignius eius legationem quam nostram excepis."

146. See pp. 193–96.

147. L.H. IX,4, 416[8-10]: "Erat enim eo tempore ipsi pontifex magnis virtutibus praeditus, ita ut plerumque infirmis signum crucis inponens, statim sanitate, tribuenti Domino, restauraret"; HF 2, 372.

148. See Angenendt, *Kaiserherrschaft und Königstaufe*, 139–40; on the *vir dei* see Angenendt, "Bonifatius und das Sacramentum initiationis," 164–69; Peter Brown, *The Making of Late Antiquity* (Cambridge, Mass., 1978), and "The Rise and Function

of the Holy Man in Late Antiquity," *Journal of Roman Studies* 61 (1971): 80–101; Basilius Steidle, "Homo Dei Antonius. Zum Bild des 'Mannes Gottes' im alten Mönchtum," in *Antonius magnus eremita 356–1956. Studia ad antiquam monachismum spectantia*, ed. B. Steidle (Rome, 1956), 148–200.

149. L.H. IV,32, 166[12-14]: "cui inerguminos curare, caecos illuminare vel reliquas infirmitates depellere per invocationem dominici nominis et signaculum sanctae crucis facile erat"; HF 2, 142.

150. L.H. VI,8, 278[3-5]: "pusularum malarum venenum crucis signum saepe compressit, daemonas de obsessis corporibus oratione abegit"; HF 2, 242.

151. L.H. X,29, 523[16/17]: "quos [Aredius], manus singulis cum crucis vexillo imponens, sanitati reddebat"; HF 2, 466. Aredius is called a *vir Dei* (ibid., 523[3]); Weidemann counts 16 such cures in Gregory's works; *Kulturgeschichte der Merowingerzeit* 2, 195; see also, Gregory of Tours, *Libri octo miraculorum* 7, 282[19] (Nicetius calms a storm by making the sign of the Cross); *Libri octo miraculorum* 8, 330[9] (overcoming a fire with the sign of the Cross); similarly, Gregory of Tours, *Libri octo miraculorum* 1, 45[28].

152. According to the research in, among others, Brown, "Rise of the Holy Man" and *The Making of Late Antiquity*; Angenendt, "Bonifatius und das Sacramentum initiationis," or K. Schäferdiek, "Columbans Wirken im Frankenreich 591–612," in *Die Iren und Europa im frühen Mittelalter* 1, ed. H. Löwe (Stuttgart, 1982), 171–201, esp. 186–88.

153. For example, Columbanus helped the Austrasian noble Waldelenus and his wife, who was suffering from infertility. See Jonas of Bobbio, *Vitae Columbani abbatis discipulorumque eius libri II*, ed. B. Krusch, MGH SS rer. Germ. 37 (Hanover and Leipzig, 1905), 1–294, I,14, 174[10]–75[13]; on the other ailments, see notes 149–52.

154. Compare the reflections of Paul Veyne who, although using mainly antique examples, provides a broader analysis; Veyne, *Did the Greeks Believe in the Myths? An Essay on the Constitutive Imagination*, trans. Paula Wissing (Chicago, 1988).

155. Brown, *The Making of Late Antiquity*, for example, p. 58f.

156. See Jonas, *Vita Columbani* I,19, 188[5]: "Regis sunt filii, tu eos tua benedictione robora"; on the children's descent *de concubina* see ibid., I,18 187[4-9]; see also, Fredegar IV,21.24.29.42, 129[1], 130[1.7/8], 132[17/18], 141[18/19].

157. Jonas, *Vita Columbani* 19–20, 187–98.

158. The monastic rules of the sixth century, which not infrequently prohibited monks from serving as sponsors, would seem to indicate that Childebert was not alone in desiring a holy godfather; see the evidence in chapter 7 note 96.

159. L.H. VI,23, 290[20].

160. L.H. VI,27, 295[4-6]: "reliquas sanctorum multorum praecidentibus, urbem ingressus est diesque paschae multa iocundate tenuit filiumque suum baptismo tradedit, quem Ragnemodus ipsius urbis sacerdus de lavacro sancto suscepit ipsumque Theodoricum vocitare praecepit"; HF 2, 257.

161. See L.H. IV,51, 187[17]–88[2]; L.H. VII,5, 329[13-19].

162. L.H. V,1, 194[15/16]: "Anno igitur primo regni eius Chilpericus rex Parisius venit adpraehensamque Brunichildam apud Rodomaginsem civitatem in exilio trusit thesaurisque eius, quos Parisius detulerat, abstulitque"; HF 2, 168.

163. L.H. V,18, 216–23.

164. L.H. V,32, 237[11/12]: "primi apud Chilpericum regem"; HF 2, 203.

165. L.H. V,34, 240[15/16].

166. See the examples from book 6 in note 179.

167. This is the chronicler's interpretation; L.H. VI,27, 295[14].

168. Sigibert was murdered before December 25, 575; see Weidemann, "Zur Chronologie der Merowinger im 6. Jahrhundert," *Francia* 10 (1982): 471–513, 485; on the date of Germanus' death see Duchesne, *Fastes épiscopaux* 2, 471.

169. The time given for his arrival in Paris, "in the first year of Childebert's reign" does permit us to date the event to December 25, 576 (see Weidemann, "Zur Chronologie der Merowinger," 485), but after Sigibert's death, there was a rush to move Childebert out of Paris; his mother Brunechildis and her possessions fell into Chilperic's hands (L.H. V,1, S. 194^{15}195^{1}; quoted in note 162); thus, he must have arrived in Paris fairly soon, while Bishop Germanus was still alive.

170. See the account in Weidemann, *Kulturgeschichte der Merowingerzeit* 1, 178.

171. Duchesne, *Fastes épiscopaux* 2, 393–95.

172. Kaiser, *Bischofsherrschaft zwischen Königtum und Fürstenmacht*, 474.

173. According to M. Roblin, this accounted for three-quarters of the *civitas*. *Le terroir de Paris aux époques galloromaine et franque*, 2d ed. (Paris, 1971), 342.

174. Audo, the tax collector for Chilperic whom Gregory calls *iudex*, fled to Paris after Chilperic's death; see L.H. VII,15, 337$^{9-14}$; cf. Weidemann, *Kulturgeschichte der Merowingerzeit* 1, 75–76.

175. L.H. V,18, 219^{1}.

176. See pp. 43f.

177. See note 160.

178. Angenendt, *Kaiserherrschaft und Königstaufe*, 31; the planned christening dates for Chlothar II show that this was not strictly observed; see L.H. IX,9, 376$^{13-16}$.

179. The following chapters deal with Chilperic: L.H. VI,2 and VI,3 in Nogent sur Marne (Dep. Seine); VI,5, 272^{2}: "Rex vero . . . Parisius est regressus"; VI,9.10.12 at an unnamed location; VI,17 in Paris; VI,18 unnamed; VI,19 in Paris; VI,22 unnamed; VI,23, the birth of a son at an unnamed location; VI,27 baptism in Paris; VI,31 in Paris; VI,32 Melun near Paris; VI,34 Paris; VI,35 Paris and Compiègne; VI,36.40 unnamed; VI,41 Cambrai; VI,45 Paris; VI,46 Chelles near Paris.

Chapter 10. Sponsorship Bonds (2):
Nobles and Bishops, Kings and Outsiders

1. See L.H. III,13, 110$^{2/3}$: "Theudoricus autem ab Arverno discendens, Sigivaldum, parentem suum, in ea quasi pro custodia dereliquid."

2. On the killing see L.H. III,23, 122^{8} and on the confiscation L.H. III,24, 123$^{13/14}$; on the killing of the kinsman's son, see note 4.

3. Some scholars assume that Sigivald was a member of the Cologne royal family which Clovis removed around 508–11, and that Theuderic was satisfying the claims of the kinsman when he ceded the territory to him. This is the view of Reinhard Wenskus, "Bemerkungen zum Thunginus der Lex Salica," in *Festschrift Percy Ernst Schramm*, 1 (Wiesbaden, 1964), 217–36, 225; and Franz Irsigler, "Untersuchungen zur Geschichte des frühfränkischen Adels," *Rheinisches Archiv*, 70, 2d ed. (Bonn, 1981): 117–18; the dating of Clovis' actions follows that in Eugen Ewig, "Das merowingische Frankenreich. 561–687," in *Europa im Wandel von der Antike zum Mittelalter*, ed. Theodor Schieffer (Stuttgart, 1976), 396–433, 259.

4. L.H. III,23, 122$^{8-10}$: "Theudoricus . . . mittens occulte ad Theudobertum, ut et ille Sigivaldum, filium eius, neci daret, quem tunc secum habebat. Sed quia eum de sacro fonte exciperat, perdere noluit"; HF 2, 104.

5. L.H. III,24, 123$^{8/9}$: "Nam de rebus bonis, tam de armis quam de vestibus vel reliquis ornamentis, quod regem habere decet, terna ei paria condonavit"; HF 2, 105; on the preceding events, see III,23/24, 122–23.

6. L.H. III,24, 123[11/12]: "Quem ille congaudens ac deosculans, tertiam partem ei de muneribus, quae a patruo acceperat, est largitus"; on the goods see ibid., 123[12/13].

7. The fact that Sigivald was given "things meet for a king's possession" may support the thesis of his descent from the Cologne royal family.

8. On this, see Ewig, "Das merowingische Frankenreich," 260–64.

9. This is particularly apparent in the examples, which will follow, of Gregory himself, Queen Brunechildis and King Gunthchramn.

10. See chapter 1, note 64; Fredegar relates a similar story about Chlothar II, who, when he had the Austrasian Merovingians eliminated in 613, is said to have secretly saved one of them, for whom "he felt a godfather's affection"; here, too, the information is so sparse that we have no evidence of any interest Chlothar may have had in saving a kinsman (for example, because he did not yet have any sons and wanted to prevent his *stirps* from dying out); *Fredegarii Chronicorum Liber Quartus/The Fourth Book of Fredegar*, trans. and ed. J. M. Wallace-Hadrill (London, 1960), pp. 34–35: "Captis filiis Theuderici tres, Sigiberto, Corbo et Meroeo, quem ipse de fontes excipit, Childebertus fugaciter ascendens. . . . Sigybertus et Corbus, filius Theuderici, iusso Chlothariae interfecti sunt. Meroeus secrecius iusso Chlothariae in Neptrico perducetur; eodem amplectens amore, quod ipso de sancto excepisset lavacrum, Ingobode graffione commendatur, ubi plures post annos vixit."

11. See chapter 4 note 55.

12. L.H. VI,17, 286[5]–87[3]: "Rex vero Chilpericus multos Iudaeorum eo anno baptizare praecepit, ex quibus pluris excipit a sancto lavacro. . . . Priscus vero ad cognuscendam veritatem nulla penitus potuit ratione deflecti. . . . Interea oritur intentio inter illum et Pathirem ex Iudaeo conversum, qui iam regis filius erat ex lavacro. Cumque die sabbati Priscus praecinctus oratio, nullum in manu ferens impleturus, secretiora competiret, subito Pathir adveniens, ipsumque gladio cum sociis qui aderant iugulavit. Quibus interfectis, ad basilecam sancti Iuliani cum pueris suis, qui ad propinquam plateam erat, confugit. Cumque ibidem resederent, audiunt, quod rex, dominum vitae cessum, famolos tamquam malefactores a basilica tractos iuberet interfici. . . . Pathir autem, accepta licentia, ad regnum Gunthchramni, unde venerat, est regressus"; HF 2, 250–51.

13. Michel Rouche has documented this in detail in "Les baptêmes forcés de juifs en Gaule mérovingienne et dans l'Empire d'Orient," in *De l'antijudaisme antique à l'antisémitisme contemporain*, ed. V. Nikiprowetzky (Lille, 1979), 105–24, esp. 111–13.

14. On the Merovingians, see Rouche, "Les baptêmes forcés"; more generally, see B. Blumenkranz, "Die Entwicklung im Westen zwischen 200 und 1200," in *Kirche und Synagoge. Handbuch zur Geschichte von Christen und Juden* 1, ed. K. H. Rengstorf and S. v. Korzfleisch (Stuttgart, 1968), 84–135, 104–32; and W. P. Eckert, "Hoch- und Spätmittelter. Katholischer Humanismus," in ibid., 215–20.

15. *Chronicle of Fredegar*, 54: "[Aeraglius] legationem ad Dagobertum regem Francorum dirigens, petens, ut omnes Iudeos regni sui ad fidem catolecam baptizandum praeciperit. Quod protenus Dagobertus emplevit." This account is repeated in *Gesta Dagoberti I regis Francorum*, ed. B. Krusch, in *Fredegarii et aliorum chronica. Vitae sanctorum*, MGH SS rer. Merov. 2 (Hanover, 1888), 396–425, 409[26–31]; on the Byzantine roots of Merovingian forced baptisms see Rouche, "Les baptêmes forcés," esp. 107 and 113.

16. On both, see Rouche, "Les baptêmes forcés," 113 (with sources).

17. There is also a temporal connection between the baptisms of Jews in the Austrasian city of Clermont in 576, and the return of a legation of Sigibert's in the

same year from Byzantium, where forced baptisms of pagans (not, however, of Jews) are documented from 574 on; according to Rouche, however, no connection can be proven; see "Les baptêmes forcés," 114–15.

18. L.H. VI,46, 320[69]: "Conficitque duos libros, quasi Sidulium meditatus... et alia opuscula vel ymnus sive missas"; HF 2, 279.

19. See *Ymnus in solemnitate sancti Medardi episcopi*, ed. K. Strecker, MGH poetae latini aevi Carolini 4,2 (Berlin, 1896), 455–57.

20. Dag Norberg believes that the model was a particular epitaph, the text of which has survived; see his *La poésie latine rythmique du haut moyen âge* (Stockholm, 1954), 33; Pierre Riché agrees with this view, *Éducation et culture dans l'occident barbare. VI*^{e}–*VIII*^{e} *siècle* (Paris, 1962), 268, note 328.

21. According to Riché, *Éducation et culture*, 269; see L.H. V,17, 216[13/14]: "apud Sessionas atque Parisius circus aedificare praecepit, eosque populis spectaculum praebens"; L.H. V,44, 252[16]–53[6]: "Per idem tempus Chilpericus rex scripsit indicolum, ut sancta Trinitas non in personarum distinctione, sed tantum Deus nominaritur, adserens indignum esse, ut Deus persona sicut homo carneus nominetur; adfirmans etiam, ipsum esse Patrem, qui est Filius, idemque ipsum esse Spiritum sanctum, qui Pater et Filius. Sic, inquid, prophetis ac patriarchis apparuit, sic eum ipsa lex nuntiavit. Cumque haec mihi recitare iussisset, ait: Sic, inquid, volo, ut tu vel reliqui doctores eclesiarum credatis."

22. See L.H. V,44, 254[4-6]; Riché, *Éducation et culture*, 269.

23. L.H. VI,2, 266[17]–67[3].

24. See Karl Hauck, "Von einer spätantiken Randkultur zum karolinischen Europa," *FMSt* 1 (1967): 3–93, esp. 50–57; Eugen Ewig, *Die Merowinger und das Imperium* (Opladen, 1983), esp. 60–62; and Georges Duby, *The Early Growth of the European Economy: Warriors and Peasants from the Seventh to the Twelfth Century*, trans. Howard B. Clarke (London, 1974).

25. See Arnold Angenendt, *Kaiserherrschaft und Königstaufe. Kaiser, Könige und Päpste als geistliche Patrone in der abendländischen Missionsgeschichte* (Berlin and New York, 1984), 5–11.

26. Rouche's reflections refer to Roman law ("Les baptêmes forcés," 112), as does Margarete Weidemann, *Kulturgeschichte der Merowingerzeit nach den Werken Gregors von Tours*, 2 vols. (Mainz, 1982), 2, 304–5; according to H. Brunner, Pathir normally would have been dealt with according to the *lex loci*, that is, Frankish law; *Deutsche Rechtsgeschichte*, vol. 1, 2d ed. (Munich, 1928), 402–3; the *Codex Theodosianus* (16,8,5, S. 888) punishes crimes by baptized Jews against unbaptized Jews; *Theodosiani libri XVI. Cum constitutionibus Sirmondianis*, 2 vols., ed. Theodor Mommsen (Dublin and Zürich, 1904, 4th ed., 1971), 16,8,5, 888; Gregory says nothing about the servants; Weidemann (*Kulturgeschichte der Merowingerzeit* 2, 289) suspects that, contrary to Roman law, they were Christian bondmen; the *Codex Theodosianus* (16,9, 895–97) prohibited Jews from owning Christian slaves; for a general account see R. C. v. Caenegem, "Das Recht im Mittelalter," in *Entstehung und Wandel rechtlicher Traditionen*, ed. W. Fikentscher, H. Franke, and O. Köhler (Freiburg and Munich, 1980), 609–67, 611–13; on the law of asylum, which Chilperic broke at least according to the stipulations of the synods, see P. Landau, "Asylrecht III. Alte Kirche und Mittelalter," in TRE 4, 1979, 319–27, 320–21.

27. D. Claude, "Hofkaufleute im Frühmittelalter," in *Akten des 26. Deutschen Rechtshistorikertages*, ed. D. Simon, *Ius commune*, Sonderheft 30 (Frankfurt, 1987), 403–9, 406.

28. L.H. VI,17, 287[23]; quoted in note 12.

29. See pp. 148ff.

30. L.H. VII,22, 340[25]–41[1]: "Deus enim novit, [...] quia de puro corde in quantum potuemus, solatium ministravimus"; HF 2, 300.
31. On all this, see L.H. VII,22, 340[17]–43[8]; quotation on 342[22]; see the account in Weidemann, *Kulturgeschichte der Merowingerzeit*, 1, 94.
32. For the first quotation, see note 30; for the second quotation, L.H. VII,22, 340[23]: "qui in causis eius fideliter currebamus"; HF 2, 300.
33. See L.H. VIII,22, 342[1–15].
34. L.H. VII,22, 341[1-3]: "Et quamquam multas nobis insidias prius de rebus sancti Martini fecisset, extabat tamen causa, ut eadem obliviscerem, eo quod filium eius de sancto lavacro suscipissem"; HF 2, 300.
35. See L.H. VII,21/22, 339[18]–40[24]; quotation on 340[22-24]: "Ex hoc nos maxime suspectus habebat ... promittens plerumque, quod, si umquam ad regis gratiam perveniret, in nobis haec quae perferebat ulcisceretur"; ibid., 341[21]: "me diversis obpropriis inpugnabat"; HF 2, 300-1.
36. L.H. VII,22, 341[9-24].
37. Ibid., 341[15-17]: "furibundus ingreditur meque convitiis ac maledictionibus urguere coepit, illud inter iurgia exprobans, quod ego eum vellim a sancti antestitis fimbriis separare"; HF 2, 300–1. Translation slightly modified.
38. L.H. VII,22, 342[6/7]: "Appraehende palleum altaris, infelix, ... ne hinc abiciaris"; HF 2, 301.
39. L.H. VII,22, 341[17-19]: "sed ego ... blandis sermonibus mulcire, conatus sum. Sed cum eius furias verbis lenibus superare non possim"; HF 2, 301.
40. L.H. VII,22, 341[18] *(insania)* and 341[22]: "eum, ut ita dicam, agi a daemone"; HF 2, 301.
41. L.H. VII,22, 341[11/12]: "per illum salutaturii osteum introeuntes puellae cum reliquis pueris eius, suspiciebant picturas parietum rimabantque ornamenta beati sepulchri; quod valde facinorosum relegiosis erat"; HF 2, 300.
42. L.H. VII,29, 348[1]: "Die autem altero, cum nos in villam quasi milia triginta ab urbe commoraremur"; HF 2, 306.
43. See L.H. VII,29, 347–48.
44. See note 34. HF 2, 300.
45. See the examples from the works of Gregory of Tours in Weidemann, *Kulturgeschichte der Merowingerzeit*, vol. 1, 299–301 and 310–11, and vol. 2, 200; in most of the examples assembled by Weidemann, the miscreants fell ill.
46. See L.H. VII, 22, 341[4/5]: "Sed credo, infilici ea res maximum fuit inpedimentum, quod nullam reverentiam sancto praestabat antestiti."
47. L.H. IX,9, 424[5-7]: "dicens: Disiungere ab homine inimoco, et habebis vitam. Alioquin cum eodem interibis. Filia enim eius ex lavacro regina susciperat et ob hoc misericordiam de eo habere voluit"; HF 2, 379; on the rebellion, see L.H. IX,9, 421–24 and IX,12, 425–27.
48. L.H. IX,9, 424[4]: "Caput enim horum et causa malorum Ursio erat"; HF 2, 379.
49. L.H. IX,12, 427[9/10]: "'Fiat nunc pax! Ecce maximus inimicus domnorum nostrorum ruit; hic vero Bertefredus vitam habeat'"; HF 2, 382.
50. Needless to say, his relative harmlessness *cannot* be explained in terms of his duties as a cofather.
51. See L.H. IX,9, 422[9-21] and 423[19]–24[4].
52. L.H. IX,9, 424[7/8]: "Nisi morte devellar ad eo, numquam a me relinquitur"; HF 2, 379.
53. See L.H. VI,4, 267[16]–68[1]: "conventione facta"; L.H. IX,9, 421[19/20]: "coniunctus confingens"; L.H. X,19, 510[5/6]: "Egidium Remensim episcopum socium fuisse in illo Rauchingi, Ursionis ac Berthefredi consilio."

54. See L.H. IX,9, 421[20/21]: "confingens se quasi tractaturus de pace, ut inter terminum utriusque regni nulla intentio aut dereptio gereretur"; HF 2, 377.
55. See Otto Gerhard Oexle, "Gilden als soziale Gruppen in der Karolingerzeit," in *Das Handwerk in vor- und frühgeschichtlicher Zeit*, 1: *Historische und rechtshistorische Beiträge und Untersuchungen zur Frühgeschichte der Gilde*, ed. H. Jankuhn, W. Janssen, R. Schmidt-Wiegandt and H. Tiefenbach (Göttingen, 1981), 284–354, 305–7.
56. See Oexle, "Gilden als soziale Gruppen," 341–48. Clerics' organizations were constituted in writing and by oath; we know nothing about the organization of the conspiracy by Austrasian noblemen.
57. L.H. IX,9, 422[2/3]: "multa etiam contra Brunechilde reginam frementes, ut eam in contuniliam redigerent, sicut prius fecerant in viduetate sua"; HF 2, 377.

Chapter 11. An Exemplary Case: Gunthchramn as Chlothar's Godfather

1. See above, pp. 76–79.
2. L.H. X,28, 521[8-12]; quoted in chapter 2 note 16. HF 2, 464.
3. On this, see above chapter 2 notes 6, 9, and 10.
4. For the baptism, see L.H. X,28, S. 520–522; for the dates, see L.H. VIII,9, 376[12-16]; on his protest and Gunthchramn's reply see below pp. 193–99; on his claims deriving from the pact, see chapter 2 note 10; on *stirps* see above, pp. 78f.
5. Eugen Ewig, "Studien zur merowingischen Dynastie," *FMSt* 8 (1974), 15–59, 20.
6. See above, pp. 105–8.
7. See above chapter 4 notes 3, 6 *(adoptio)*, 65 (claims derving from the pact).
8. See pp. 76–79.
9. L.H. X,28, 520[20-23]: "Profiscatur dominus meus rex usque Parisius, et arcessitu filio meo, nepote suo, iubeat eum baptismatis gratia consecrare; ipsumque de sancto lavacro exceptum, tamquam alumnum proprium habere dignetur"; HF 2, 464.
10. L.H. X,28, 521[6/7]–522[1/2]: "evocato puero, iussit baptisterium praeparari in vico Nemptudoro; rex accedens ad lavacrum sanctum, obtulit puerum ad baptizandum"; HF 2, 464–65.
11. No detailed instructions are provided in the *Ordo Romanus*, ed. Michel Andrieu. *Les Ordines Romani du haut moyen âge*, vols. 2,3,5 (Louvain, 1948–61), XI,96, vol. 2, 445; *Ordo Romanus* XXXb,50, vol. 3, 473; *Sacr. Gelasianum vetus. Liber sacramentorum Romanae ecclesiae ordinis anni circuli* (Cod. Vat. lat. 316), ed. L. C. Mohlberg (Rome, 1960), no. 449, 74; *Sacr. Hadrianum, Le sacramentaire Grégorien. Ses principales formes d'après les plus anciens manuscrits* 1, ed. J. Deshusses, 2d ed. (Fribourg, 1979), nos. 374–75, 188–89.
12. See, for example, *Ordo Romanus* XV,74, vol. 3, 112[3-5]: "Deinde discalciati presbiteri aut diaconi [...] ingrediuntur in fontes et acceptis infantibus de parentibus baptizantur eos"; we find similar wording in *Ordo Romanus* XXVIII,75, vol. 3, 407[6]; *Ordo Romanus* XXXI,84, vol. 3, 502[26]; also *Liber sacramentorum Gellonense* 2, ed. A. Dumas, CCSL 159a (Turnhout, 1981), no. 707, 100 (a Roman-style sacramentary produced in Gaul, the so-called eighth-century Gelasianum); see Cyrille Vogel, *Medieval Liturgy: An Introduction to the Sources* (Washington, D.C., 1986), 71.
13. Ordo baptismatis [=Vienna cod.lat. 1888], Appendix ad saeculum X, ed. Jacques Paul Migne, PL 138, cols. 949–60, 955: "presbyter accipiens infantes a parentibus eorum sicut justum est."
14. On relations of exchange with Gaul, see J. Krinke, "Der spanische Taufritus im frühen Mittelalter," in *Gesammelte Aufsätze zur Kulturgeschichte Spaniens* 9 (Mün-

ster, 1954), 33–112, 112; Krinke concludes that the "kinship [of the old Spanish baptismal rite] with [that practiced in] Gaul . . . is to a large extent the natural result of a political union in which both countries were long connected under the Visigothic kings and in which Spain was by no means only on the receiving end"; Krinke continues with a long list of common elements (112–13), followed by a list of the numerous deviations from the Roman liturgy (114), and notes that "the Roman influence is unexpectedly slight."

15. See *Liber mozarabicus, Le liber ordinum en usage dans l'église wisigothique et mozarabe d'Espagne du cinquième au onzième siècle*, ed. M. Férotin (Paris, 1904, repr. 1969), cols. 31[27]–33[6]; according to Vogel (*Medieval Liturgy*, 36), the rite appears to go back to the first half of the fifth century.

16. It also contains no useful information on the baptismal rite; see *Sacr. Gregorianum* nos. 374–75, 188–89.

17. On this, see *Sacr. Gregorianum*, Introduction, 85–90; Vogel, *Medieval Liturgy*, 85–92.

18. For example, the specific feast days or prayers for the Frankish kings (see Vogel, *Liturgy*, 89).

19. See Pontificale Romano-Germanicum, *Le pontifical Romano-germanique du dixième siècle*, vol. 2, *Le texte*, ed. Cyrille Vogel and R. Elze (Rome, 1963) 375 Ms K, 106[19-21]: "Deinde accipiat infantes a patrinis vel matrinis, baptizat"; the (according to ibid., vol. 3, 39 and 41) most authentic manuscript of this Pontifical mentions both possibilities: *Pontificale Romano-Germanicum* 375 ms C, vol. 2, 106[20-22] (manuscript of 1022–35): "Et acceptis infantibus a parentibus vel patrinis eorum, baptizant eos"; on the influences taken up by this Pontifical, see the stemma in ibid., vol. 3, 57.

20. Arnold Angenendt, *Kaiserherrschaft und Königstaufe. Kaiser, Könige und Päpste als geistliche Patrone in der abendländischen Missionsgeschichte* (Berlin and New York, 1984), 114.

21. L.H. X,28, 522[2/3]: "Rex accedens ad lavacrum sanctum, obtulit puerum ad baptizandum. Quem excipiens, Chlotharium vocitare voluit."

22. Angenendt, *Kaiserherrschaft und Königstaufe*, 94.

23. For a summary of the literature, see W. Ogris, article "Aufnehmen des Kindes," in HRG 1, 1971, 253–54; on Roman law see M. Kaser, *Das römische Privatrecht*, 2 vols., 2d ed. (Munich, 1971–75), vol. 1, 345–46.

24. There are numerous examples in *Vocabularium iurisprudentiae Romanae auspiciis Savigniani institutum* 5, ed. Preußische Akademie der Wissenschaften (Berlin, 1939), cols. 894–95.

25. On *excipere* see notes 9, 69 and 73 (Gunthchramn), chapter 9 note 47 (Praetextatus), chapter 10 notes 4 (Theudebert) and 12 (Chilperic), on *suscipere* note 73 (Gunthchramn), chapter 9 notes 98 (Magneric), 128 (Samson's godfather), 135 (Veranus), 161 (Ragnemod), chapter 10 notes 34 (Gregory), and 47 (Brunechildis).

26. See Ferreolus of Uzès, *Regula ad monachos*, in *Codex regularum monasticarum et canonicarum* 1, ed. L. Holstenius and M. Brockie (Augsburg, 1759), 155–66, 15, 159 (quoted in chapter 7 note 96); Aurelian, *Regula ad monachos*, in ibid., 20, 151 (quoted in chapter 7 note 96); Caesarius of Arles, *Regula sanctarum virginum aliaque opuscula ad sanctimoniales directa*, ed. C. Morin (Bonn, 1933), 6–17, 11, 7[26/27] (quoted in chapter 7 note 96); Caesarius of Arles, *Sermones*, ed. G. Morin, CCSL 103/103A, 2 vols. (Turnhout, 1953), Sermo 13,2, 65 (quoted in chapter 7 note 104); Sermo 200,6, 811 (quoted in chapter 7 note 60); Sermo 50,3, 226: "Filios, quos in baptismo suscipitis," and passim; *The Fourth Book of the Chronicle of Fredegar with Its Continuations*, ed. and trans. J. M. Wallace-Hadrill (London, 1960), 35: "quod ipso de sancto excepisset lavacrum" and 5; on Ildephonsus see chapter 7 note 183.

27. See, for example, *Vita Fridolini confessoris Seckingensis auctore Balthero*, ed. B. Krusch in *Passiones vitaeque sanctorum aevi Merovingici et antiquiorum aliquot*, MGH SS rer. Merov. 3 (Hanover, 1896), 351–69, 24, 365[29.33]; *Vita Geremari abbatis Flaviacensis*, ed. B. Krusch, in *Passiones vitaeque sanctorum aevi Merovingici*, MGH SS rer. Merov. 4 (Hanover and Leipzig, 1910), 626–33, 5, 629[15]; *Vita virtutesque Fursei abbatis Latiniacensis et de Fuilano additamentum Nivialense*, ed. B. Krusch, in *Passiones vitaeque sanctorum aevi Merovingici*, MGH SS rer. Merov. 4 (Hanover and Leipzig, 1902), 423–51, 10, 443[24]; *Vita Nivardi episcopi Remensis auctore Almanno monacho Altivillarensi*, ed. W. Levison, in *Passiones vitaeque sanctorum aevi Merovingici*, MGH SS rer. Merov. 5 (Hanover and Leipzig, 1910), 157–71, 7, 165[3]; *Vita Faronis episcopi Meldensis*, ed. B. Krusch, in *Passiones vitaeque sanctorum aevi Merovingici*, MGH SS rer. Merov. 5 (Hanover and Leipzig, 1910), 171–206, 22, 185[29]; Vita Trudonis confessoris Hasbaniensis auctore Donato, ed. W. Levison, in *Passiones vitaeque sanctorum aevi Merovingici*, MGH SS rer. Merov. 6 (Hanover and Leipzig, 1913), 264–98, 15 and 19, 287[29] and 290[11]; *Vita Pardulfi abbatis Waractensis*, ed. W. Levison, in *Passiones vitaeque sanctorum aevi Merovingici*, MGH SS rer. Merov. 7 (Hanover and Leipzig, 1920), 19–40, 20, 37[12]; *Vita Rigoberti*, in ibid., 8, 59[21]; *Vita Heriberti archiepiscopi Coloniensis auctore Lantberto*, ed. G.H. Pertz, MGH SS 4 (Hanover, 1841), 739–53, 9, 748[6]; Jonas of Bobbio, *Vitae Columbani abbatis discipulorumque eius libri II*, ed. B. Krusch, Ionae vitae sanctorum Columbani, Vedastis, Iohannis, MGH SS rer. Germ. 37 (Hanover and Leipzig, 1905), 1–294, I,14, 175[4.17/18]; and, finally, Henry III's sponsorship request to Hugo of Cluny in Diploma 263, *Heinrici III. diplomata*, ed. H. Bresslau and P. Kehr, MGH DD regum et imperatorum Germaniae 5 (Berlin, 1931), 351[31].

28. On *levare*, see *Vita et miracula sancti Pirminii*, ed. O. Holder-Egger, MGH SS 15,1 (Hanover, 1887), 17–35, 5, 24[16]; *Vita sancti Tigernaci episcopi de Cluain Eois*, Vitae sanctorum Hiberniae 2, ed. C. Plummer (Oxford, 1910), 262–69, 266.

29. See *Ordo Romanus* XV (late eighth century) nos. 74–76, vol. 3, 112[3–12]: "(74) Deinde discalciati presbiteri aut diaconi . . . ingrediuntur in fontes et acceptis infantibus . . . baptizantur eos. . . . (75) Levatis ipsis infantibus, offerrunt eos in manibus suis uni presbitero. Ipse vero presbiter facit de crisma crucem. . . . (76) Deinde sunt parati, qui eos suscipere debeant, cum lenteis in manibus eorum et traduntur eis a presbyteris vel diaconibus qui eos baptizantur"; the same rite in *Ordo Romanus* XXVIII (ca. 800) nos. 75–77, vol. 3, 407[6–18] and *Ordo Romanus* XXXB (ca. 770–90) nos. 50–54, vol. 3, 473[5–16]; *Ordo Romanus* XXXI (ca. 850–900) nos. 84–86, vol. 3, 502[26]–503[5]; similarly, *Sacr. Gellonense* nos. 707–9, 100; in light of these clear instructions, we might consider interpreting the less unambiguous text in the Ordo Romanus XI ([ca. 650–700] nos. 96–98, 445[15]–46[8]) in the same manner as well; in the latter, it is not the *diaconi* who receive the baptizees and present them for anointing, but rather *levantes*; although after anointing a similar formulation appears as in the other Ordines: "et sunt parati, qui eos suscepturi sunt"; the dating here follows Vogel, *Medieval Liturgy*, 152–53, 165, 172–73.

30. This is the approximate line of argumentation in Angenendt, *Kaiserherrschaft und Königstaufe*, 94, 109–10, 114.

31. See *Missale Gallicanum vetus*, ed. L. C. Mohlberg (Rome, 1958), nos. 170–76, 41–42; [Missale Bobbiense] *The Bobbio Missal: A Gallican Mass-book*, ed. E. A. Lowe (London, 1920), nos. 245–49, 74–75; *Missale Gothicum*, ed. L. C. Mohlberg (Rome, 1961), nos. 259–61, 67.

32. This is particularly clear in the cases of Gunthchramn (see note 21: *excipiens*) and Veranus (chap. 9 note 56: *suscipiens*); see, similarly, Columbanus (note 57) and Audoin (note 67).

33. See Vogel, *Medieval Liturgy*, 230; the insertion "sicut justum est" in the quotation in note 13 will suffice as an example.
34. Ordo baptismatis Vienna cod. lat. 1888, col. 956.
35. *Pontificale Romano-Germanicum C* [i.e., the most authentic version] no. 377, 106[36]–7[5]: "Cum autem infantes elevati fuerint a fonte, patrini vel matrinae singulorum accipientes eos habeant intra baptismum pedibus infantum adhuc in aqua consistentibus donec episcopus vel presbyter chrisma requirens faciat crucem cum pollice in vertice eorum"; on this, see the edition of the *Ordo Romanus L*, 285[1–12] (middle column) with the same text; on the relationship of the *Ordo Romanus L* to the *Pontificale Romano-Germanicum*, see Vogel, *Medieval Liturgy*, 232; on this, see Ordo baptismatis Vienna cod. lat. 1888, col. 955; on this manuscript, see Vogel, *Medieval Liturgy*, 233.
36. This is already doomed to fail because, in the early instructions, the sponsors only came in after the anointing, when any "lifting" was already finished, while in tenth-century instructions their work began before the anointing.
37. As expressly noted in regard to presentation by the parents by one of the compilers; see note 13.
38. The standard works on the subject are strikingly identical in their descriptions and dispense with examples; see R. Schröder, *Lehrbuch der deutschen Rechtsgeschichte*, ed. E. v. Künßberg, 7th ed. (Berlin and Leipzig, 1932), 71–72; H. Conrad, *Deutsche Rechtsgeschichte 1: Frühzeit und Mittelalter. Ein Lehrbuch*, 2d ed. (Karlsruhe, 1962), 152; H. Brunner, *Deutsche Rechtsgeschichte*, 2 vols., vol. 1, 2d ed. (Leipzig, 1906), 101–2; W. Ogris, "Aufnehmen des Kindes."
39. Conrad, *Deutsche Rechtsgeschichte*, 152.
40. Ogris, "Aufnehmen des Kindes," 254.
41. See H. Heumann and E. Seckel, *Handlexikon zu den Quellen des römischen Rechts*, 9th ed. (1907), cols. 574 s.v. *Suscipere*; esp. nos. 5–8 on the custom cited here: to save *(servum, fugitivum alienum, desertorem agro tectove)*, to protect *(plebem)*, to pick a newborn child up off the ground and conceive, beget, get *(liberos, filium, filiam)*, to take in place of one's own child *(filium alienum, in adoptiva familia susceptus)*; see also note 24; see the so-called *leges*: the *Pactus legis Salicae*, ed. K.A. Eckhardt, MGH Leg. nat. Germ. 4,1 (Hanover, 1962), 45,1. 46,2. 46,5, S. 173[5].178[2].180[3]; and *Lex Ribvaria*, ed. F. Beyerle and R. Buchner, MGH LL nat. Germ. 3,2 (Hanover, 1954), 68,3, 119[8].
42. See A. Blaise, *Dictionnaire latin-français des auteurs du moyen-age. Lexicon latinitatis medii aevi* (Turnhout, 1975), 895–96 (s.v. *susceptor/suscipio*) and C. Du Cange, *Glossarium mediae et infimae latinitatis*, ed. L. Favre (repr. Graz, 1954), vol. 7, 680–81 (s.v. *susceptores/suscipio*).
43. L.H. X,28, 522[2]: "Chlotharium vocitare voluit"; HF 2, 465.
44. See L.H. VII,7, 330[11.13]; VIII,18, 385[13]; VIII,42, 408[8]; VIII,43, 409[9] and passim.
45. L.H. VIII,1, 370[8/9]: "ut Chilperici filium, quem iam Chlothacharium vocitabant, a sacro regenerationes fonte deberet excipere"; HF 2, 329. Emphasis added. In Dalton's translation, Chlothar is called Lothar.
46. This was also the case with Merovich and Samson (see pp. 146f. and 165f.).
47. One finds the same phrase in the *Vita sancti Declani episcopi de Ard Mor* in *Vitae sanctorum Hiberniae* 2, ed. C. Plummer (Oxford, 1910), 32–59, 14, 41: "Illi iam [*sic*] filii Colmanus et Eochu uocabantur. Colmanus utique... ad sanctum Ailbeum episcopum perrexit; et baptizatus est."
48. See *Sacr. Gelasianum vetus* no. 197, 33, on the third scrutinium before Easter: "recitantur numina electorum"; ibid., no 284 (p. 42) in the *Hanc igitur*: "Ut autem

venerint ad ecclesiam, scribuntur nomina infantum ab a[c]colyto, et vocantur in ecclesia per nomina, sicut scripte sunt"; similarly, see *Sacr. Gellonense* no. 2216, 312; no. 2226, 314; no. 2258, 319; see also: *Ordo Romanus* XI,2, 418$^{1/2}$: "ut autem ad ecclesiam venerint, [...] scribantur nomina infantum"; *Ordo Romanus* XI,35, 426$^{1/2}$ on the *Hanc igitur*: "haec expleta, recitantur nomina electorum."

49. L.H. VIII,22, 388$^{17/18}$: "Bertchramnus ... a febre corripitur; arcessitumque Waldonem diaconum, qui et ipse in baptismo Berthchramnus vocitatus est"; HF 2, 346.

50. L.H. V,38, 245^5: "[Herminigildus] conversus est ad legem catholicam ac, dum chrismaretur, Johanni est vocitatus"; converted Arians only had to go through anointing; HF 2, 547n. Dalton's translation (HF 2, 210): "by his baptism," misses this point.

51. Hermenegild as John: L.H. V,38, 244$^{17/18}$ and again as Hermenegild, ibid., 245^5 and VI,18, 310^{13} and passim.

52. On Pathir see L.H. VI,17, 286; on Gundobad II,34, 81; on Brunechildis IV,27, 160; on Galswintha IV,28, 160–61; on Clovis II,31, 76–78.

53. L.H. II,29, 75$^{8/9}$: "Post hunc vero genuit alium filium, quem baptizatum Chlodomere vocitavit"; HF 2, 68. In his edition of the *History, Gregorii Episcopi Turonensis historiarum libri decem* (Darmstadt 1955) R. Buchner translates: "whom she called Chlodomer in [*sic*] baptism" (117); in this case, Gregory says nothing of such simultaneity which might lead one to assume that the mother gave the boy his name.

54. HF 2, 257; translation slightly modified. "[Chilpericus] filiumque suum baptismo tradedit quem Ragnemodus ipsius sacerdus de lavacro sancto suscepit ipsumque Theodoricum vocitare praecepit"; L.H. VI,27, 295$^{5/6}$.

55. HF 2, 360; translation slightly modified. "Post haec Childeberetho regi filius natus est qui a Magnerico Treverorum episcopo de sacro fonte susceptus Theodoberthus est vocitatus"; L.H. VIII,37, 405$^{1/2}$.

56. HF 2, 372; translation modified. "Eo anno Childeberetho rege alius filius natus est quem Veranus Cavelonensis episcopus suscipiens a lavacro Theodorici nomen imposuit"; L.H. IX,4, 416$^{7/8}$.

57. Jonas of Bobbio, *Vita Columbani* I,14, 175$^{16-18}$: "Quem vir sanctus suis manibus receptum sacravit sacroque lavacro ablutum ipse suscepit Donatumque nomen imponet."

58. *Missale Gallicanum vetus* 170, 41^{35}: "Interrogatio: Quis dicitur? Responsio: Illi"; *Missale Bobbiense* 245, 74^{21}.

59. [Supplementum Anianense] *Hadrianum revisum Anianense cum supplemento (Le sacramentaire Grégorien. Ses principales formes d'après les plus anciens manuscrits,* vol. 1., ed. J. Deshusses, 2d ed. (Fribourg, 1979), 349–605, no. 1084, 378: "Benedicto fonte tenente infantem a quo suscipiendus est, interroget sacerdos ita: Quis vocaris. R.[=Responsio] Ille."

60. See the detailed account in Vogel, *Medieval Liturgy*, 230–39.

61. See Pontificale Romano-Germanicum version K no. 370 and versions C and K no. 372, 105$^{2.28/9}$; one might object that Gregory of Tours describes naming at a different moment in the ritual, namely the lifting from the baptismal font *(excipiens)*, but not between the renunciation of the devil and the Creed; here, too, a look at the work of the tenth-century compilers might be helpful; they use the word *baptize* twice, once to describe the entire rite (naming, the declaration of faith, the baptismal act) and once to designate only the act of baptism proper (immersion or affusion) (version K, 105^{25}–107^1): (371) "et baptizantur [*sic*] primo masculini deinde femininae

sub hac interrogatione": (372) "Quis vocaris? Resp.: Ille vel Illa." (373) "Credis in Deum omnipotentemtem semel invocantes ita dicendo: Ego te baptizo in nomine patris, et mergit semel, [etc.]" (377) "Ut autem surrexerint a fonte, illi qui eos suscipiunt, levantes ipsos infantes in manibus suis, offerunt eos uni presbitero. Ipse vero presbiter facit de chrismate crucem"; we thus might consider that Gregory's statement may be read not merely as: "receiving (*suscipiens*) him, he named him" but also as: "whilst performing the act of godfather (*suscipiens*) he named the child."

62. See *Annalium Fuldensium continuatio Ratisbonensis a.882–897*, ed. G. H. Pertz and F. Kurze, MGH SS rer. Germ. 7 (Hanover, 1891), 107–31, a. 893, 122: "De qua ei non multum post filius nascebatur, quem Haddo Magonciacensis archiepiscopus et Adalpero Augustae Vindelicae episcopus sacro fonte baptismatis chrismantes nomine avi sui Hludowicum appellaverunt."

63. *Compater* in *Arnolfi diplomata*, ed. P. Kehr, MGH DD regum Germaniae ex stirpe Karolinorum 3 (Berlin, 1940), diploma no. 135, 203^4: "Hathonis venerabilis archiepiscopi et carissimi compatris nostri"; and *pater spiritualis* in *Ludowici infantis diplomata*, nos. 60, 66, 71, 72, ed. Theodor Schieffer, MGH DD regum Germaniae ex stirpe Karolinorum 4 (Berlin, 1960), 73–238, 190^7, 197^{30}, 207^{32}, 209^{27}.

64. *Vita sancti Colmani de Land Elo* in *Vitae sanctorum Hiberniae* 1, ed. C. Plummer (Oxford, 1910), 258–73, 26, 269: "Et statim baptizauit sanctus Colmanus illum infantem, dans ei nomen Cheallanum"; *Vita sancti Boecii* in *Vitae sanctorum Hiberniae*, 87–97, 2, 87: "Denique uir ille sanctus, paruulum aqua perfundens, totum baptismatis ordinem compleuit, eumque Boecium nominauit"; *Vita Declani* 5, 37: "Tunc sanctus Colmanus baptizauit sanctissimum infantulum, Declanum nomen ei imponenes"; *Vita Declani* 31, 54: "sanctus Declanus antistes ibi illum infantem baptizauit, et dedit ei nomen Chiaranum."

65. See the *Liber mozarabicus* (32^5) where, as in the Gallican rite, naming took place between the renunciation of the devil and the Credo: "quis vocaris"; see also 26^{9-10} (preparatory exorcisms): "Et signans eum in fronte imponit ei nomen in hunc exorcimum"; on the Mozarabic liturgy and its relationship to the Gallican liturgy, see note 14.

66. *Vita Geremari* 5, $629^{10/11}$: "Filius ei autem fuit superstes, cui nomen imposuit in baptismo Amalbertus."

67. *Vita Geremari* 5, 629^{15-17}: "ivit ad fontem et suscepit eum ab ipsis aquis vocitavitque illum filiolum benedixitque eum atque dimisit."

68. On this see pp. 103f.

69. L.H. X,28, $520^{22/3}$: "ipsumque de sancto lavacro exceptum, tamquam alumnum proprium habere dignetur"; HF 2, 464; trans. slightly modified.

70. See above chapter 4 note 11.

71. See François Kerlouegan, "Essai sur la mise en nourriture et l'éducation dans les pays celtiques d'après le témoignage des textes hagiographiques latin," *Études celtiques* 12 (1968–69): 101–46 (on Irish practice); on Visigothic law, see P. D. King, *Law and Society in the Visigothic Kingdom* (Cambridge, 1972), 239–40; for a Norse example, see note 72; anthropological studies suggest a connection between the practices of foster fatherhood and the complexity of a society; in West African tribal societies with a "simple" structure, for example, anthropologists have observed that children are generally raised by kin, while in societies with a "complex and hierarchical" structure, they are also raised by non-kin; see Esther Goody, "Parental Strategies: Calculation or Sentiment? Fostering Practices among West Africans," in *Interest and Emotion: Essays on the Study of Family and Kinship*, ed. Hans Medick and David Sabean (Cambridge and Paris, 1984), 268–70 (examples) and

271–75 (interpretation); for a more extensive account, see Goody's "Parenthood and Social Reproduction: Fostering and Occupational Roles in West Africa," *Cambridge Studies in Social Anthropology* 35 (1982), 250–81 (summary).

72. [*Thule 8*] *Die Geschichte von Hörd dem Geächteten*, in *Fünf Geschichten von Ächtern und Blutrache*, ed. A. Heusler and F. Ranke (Düsseldorf and Cologne, 1964), 189–256, 9, 201; see also Max Pappenheim, "Die Pflegekindschaft in der Graugans," in *Festschrift Heinrich Brunner zum siebzigsten Geburtstag* (Weimar, 1910) 1–15, 11.

73. L.H. X,28, 521[17-19]: "'Non est enim humilitas genti nostrae, si hic a me excipiatur. Si enim domini proprios famulos de sacro fonte suscipiunt, cur et mihi non liceat, propinquum parentem excipere'"; HF 2, 465; trans. slightly modified.

74. Let us recall that King Chilperic as well as the queen mother Brunechildis served as godparents to their subjects; see chapter 10 notes 12 and 47.

75. See K. Arnold, "Kindheit im europäischen Mittelalter," in *Zur Sozialgeschichte der Kindheit*, ed. J. Martin and A. Nitschke (Freiburg and Munich, 1986), 443–67, 455; Kerlouegan, "Essai sur la mise en nourriture et l'éducation"; Angenendt gives an example in *Kaiserherrschaft und Königstaufe*, 273.

76. In 585 Gunthchramn traveled as an *invitatus* to Paris to the christening that was then postponed (L.H. VIII,1, 370[8]); HF 2, 329.

77. As Dhuoda later said of her son William's godfather; Dhuoda, *Manuel pour mon fils*, ed. Pierre Riché (Paris, 1975), 320[6]: "nutritor et amator tuus fuerat."

78. See L.H. X,28, 520[23]–21[4]; quotation, 522[3/4]: "Haec audiens rex, commotis episcopis . . . vel reliquis, quos voluit, Parisius accedere voluit. . . . Fuerant etiam ad hoc placitum multi de regno eius tam domestici quam comites"; HF 2, 464.

79. See chapter 9 note 161.

80. *Vita Amandi episcopi*, ed. B. Krusch, in *Passiones vitaeque sanctorum aevi Merovingici*, MGH SS. rer. Merov. 5 (Hanover and Leipzig, 1910), 395–481, 17, 442[7-9]: "Statimque eo regenerans sacro baptismate, impositoque nomine Sygiberto, regem atque omnem eius exercitum tunc sanctus Amandus magno replevit gaudio."

81. L.H. X,28 522[5-7]: "accessit Parisius, exinde ad Rotoialinsium villam ipsius urbis properans, evocato puero, iussit baptisterium praeparari in vico Nemptudoro."

82. See *Chronicle of Fredegar*, 5: "Quem Rioilo baptizare iobet, et eum de sancto lavacro excipiens, in regnum patris firmavit."

83. H.E. Feine, *Kirchliche Rechtsgeschichte: Die katholische Kirche*, 5th ed. (Cologne and Graz, 1972), 99–100.

84. The chronicle of the authors known as Fredegar was probably written around 658–60; see the introduction to the German translation by A. Kusternig, ed., *Quellen zur Geschichte des 7. und 8. Jahrhunderts*, Ausgewählte Quellen zur deutschen Geschichte des Mittelalters. Freiherr von Stein Gedächtnisausgabe 4a (Darmstadt, 1982), 12.

85. Starting with Friedrich Prinz (see, for example, his *Frühes Mönchtum im Frankenreich: Kultur und Gesellschaft in Gallien, den Rheinlanden und Bayern am Beispiel der monastischen Entwicklung (4.–8. Jahrhundert)* (Munich, 1965), 492–93; Georg Scheibelreiter agrees with him; see his *Der Bischof in merowingischer Zeit* (Vienna, Cologne, Graz, 1983), 26.

86. See note 89.

87. On this and what follows, see Arnold Angenendt, "Pirmin und Bonifatius: Ihr Verhältnis zu Mönchtum, Bischofsamt und Adel," in *Mönchtum, Episkopat und Adel zur Gründungszeit des Klosters Reichenau*, ed. Arno Borst (Sigmaringen, 1974), 251–304, 290–99; for a detailed account, see Wilfried Hartmann, "Der rechtliche Zustand der Kirchen auf dem Lande: Die Eigenkirche in der fränkischen Gesetz-

gebung des 7. bis 9. Jahrhunderts," in *Christianizzazione ed organizzazione ecclesiastica delle campagne nell'alto medioevo: espansione e resistenze* 1 (Spoleto, 1982), 397–444; on the preconditions in late antiquity, see Peter Brown, "The Rise and Function of the Holy Man in Late Antiquity," *Journal of Roman Studies* 61 (1971): 80–101.

88. See chapter 12 note 29.

89. Council of Ver 755, c. 8, in *Capitularia regum Francorum* 1, ed. A. Boretius, MGH Leges Abt. 2 (Hanover, 1881–83), 34^{42}–35^2: "Ut omnes presbyteri qui in parochia sunt sub potestate episcopi esse de eorum ordine, et ut nullus presbiter non praesumat in illa parrochia nec baptizare, nec missas celebrare sine iussione episcopi in cuius parrochia est"; ibid., c. 7, 34^{37}: "Ut publicum [sic] baptisterium in ulla parrochia esse non debeat, nisi ibi ubi episcopus constituerit cuius parrochia est; nisi tantum si necessitas evenerit pro infirmitate aut pro necessitate, illi presbyteri, quos episcopus in ipsa parochia constituerit, in qualecumque loco evenerit, licentiam [sic] habeat baptizandi."

90. Apart from the Council of Ver, c. 13 (*Capitularia regum Francorum* 1, 36^{4-6}), see also Pope Zachary in a letter sent in 748 to a number of aristocratic Franks; *Die Briefe des heiligen Bonifatius und Lullus*, ed. M. Tangl, MGH Epp. sel. I (Berlin, 1916), no. 83, $186^{11/12}$: "ut nullus saecularis clericum in suum obsequium habeat."

91. See Admonitio generalis a. 789, c. 25 in *Capitularia regum Francorum* 1, 55^{39}: "ut nullus absolute ordinetur sine pronuntiatione et stabilitate loci ad quem ordinatur."

92. *Annales Mosellani*, ed. J. M. Lappenberg, MGH SS 16 (Hanover, 1859), 491–99, a. 785, 497^{38}; see Angenendt, "Pirmin und Bonifatius," 298.

93. L.H. X,28, 521^{8-12}; HF 2, 464; for the full quotation, see chapter 2 note 16.

94. Some remarks on Bertram's testament are in order here: in disposition 63, Bertram made a *compater* by the name of Ghiso, who was a brother of Bertram's sister-in-law his heir (*Das Testament des Bischofs Berthramn von Le Mans vom 27. März 616. Untersuchungen zu Besitz und Geschichte einer fränkischen Familie im 6. und 7. Jahrhundert*, ed. Margarete Weidemann, Mainz, 1986, 42, 127); Bertram must thus have been the godfather of an unnamed son of Ghiso's (the assumption that their common nephew Thoringus, who is also named in the will, was the godson of both Bertram and Ghiso [ibid., 42, 60, 68, 128] rests on the misinterpretation of *compater* as cosponsor rather than cofather [ibid., 42]); what is important here is whether *compaternitas* was significant for Ghiso's designation as an heir; within the context of the testament as a whole this does not seem to have been the case: Ghiso appears only once and receives no substantial legacies. In two cases, Bertram left him his half share of properties of which Ghiso already possessed the other share and in two other cases one half share each in a property; these he received unconditionally; Ghiso was, however, neither the most distant relative mentioned in the will (disposition 14 mentions "the offspring of a sibling of Bertram's mother" [ibid., 17]), nor was he the only legatee not expected to provide any quid pro quo; his nephew, Thoringus, and his *parens*, Sigelenus, also received their legacies unconditionally (ibid., 77–78), and no legatee was expected to fulfill any major conditions; thus, Ghiso does not stand out among Bertram's kin in any way, so that *compaternitas* did not have any visible effect on the inheritance process; Dhuoda's note in her *Liber manualis* VIII, 15 (*Manuel pour mon fils*, 320) of 841–4/3 (according to the editor Riché, 11) that her son William's godfather, Theodericus, had turned over his property to the "lord and senior" (according to Riché, this was William's father, Bernard of Septimania, 322–323) for William's benefit, cannot be used to illuminate questions of inheritance law, since we know nothing about Theodericus (according to J. Wollasch, "Eine adlige Familie des frühen Mittelalters: Ihr Selbstverständnis und

ihre Wirklichkeit," *Archiv für Kulturgeschichte* 39, 1957, 150–88, 187–88), for example, whether he was childless or a kinsman; Riché (19) believes that he was an uncle; for the Anglo-Saxon and Scandinavian regions, see Ursula Perkow, "Wasserweihe, Taufe und Patenschaft bei den Nordgermanen" (Ph.D. diss., Hamburg, 1972); R. Staudt, "Studien zum Patenbrauch in Hessen" (diss. Frankfurt a.M., 1958), to which Perkow refers for German examples, discusses only modern cases.

95. See 198–204.

96. L.H. IX,20, 439[22/23]: "Nam, ut saepe cognovimus, dignius eius legationem quam nostram excepis"; HF 2, 393.

97. L.H. IX,20, 439[21/22]: "Utinam tu, o rex gloriosissime, minus cum eam caritatem haberes"; HF 2, 392.

98. See L.H. X,28, 521[8/9]: "Non enim ista nuper nepote tuo Childebertho pollicitus eras, ut cum inimici eius amicitias conlegaris."

99. See L.H. IX,20, 435[9–18]: "constat . . . , ut illam tertiam portionem de Parisius civitatem . . . quae ad domnum Sigyberthum de regno Chariberthi conscripta pactione pervenerat . . . in iure et dominatione domni Gunthchramni . . . debeant perpetualiter permanere. Pari conditione civitatis Meldus . . . Childebertus rex cum terminibus a prasesenti die suae vindicit potestate"; HF 2, 389. On his claim of 584, see chapter 4 note 65; on Fredegund's widow's estate, see chapter 4, note 45.

100. See L.H. VII,29, 346[19]–47[6]: "misit rex Gunthchramnus Claudium, quendam. . . . Ille vero, ut erat vanitate adque avaritiae deditus, velociter Parisius advolavit. . . . Volvere animo coepit, utrum Fredegundem reginam videret, dicens: Si eam videro, elicere ab ea aliquid muneris possum. . . . Tunc accedens ad eam. . . ."; HF 2, 305.

101. L.H. IX,13, 427[27]–28[4]: "Guntchramnus vero Baddonem, quem pro crimine maiestates superius vinctum diximus, in praesentia sua venire iussit, et transmissum usque Parisius, ait: Si eum cum idoneis hominibus Fredegundis ab hac actione, qua inpetitur inmunem fecerit, abscedat liber et quo voluerit eat. Sed veniens Parisius, nullus de parte memoratae mulieris adfuit, qui eum idoneum reddere possit. Tunc . . . ad urbem Cavillonensim reductus est"; HF 2, 382–83.

102. L.H. X,11, 494[20–22]: "Chlotharius vero, Chilperici quondam regis filius, graviter aegrotavit et in tantum disperatus est habitus, ut rege Gunthchramno obitus eius fuisset nuntiatus. Unde factum est, ut egrediens de Cavillonno, quasi Parisius accedere cupiens"; HF 2, 439.

103. In Rouen, in 585, for example; see L.H. VIII,31, 397[3].

104. L.H. IX,20, 441[5-11]: "Dicebat enim et haec verba: Utinam mihi nepus meus promissa custodiat! Omnia enim quae habeo eius sunt. . . . Dabo enim Chlothario . . . aut duas aut tres in parte aliqua civitatis, ut nec hic videatur exheredario de regno meo, nec huic inquietudinem praeparent, quae isti relinquero"; HF 2, 394.

105. L.H. X,28, 521[14-22]: "Nam illum non opportet scandalizare, si consubrinum eius, filium fratris mei, de sancto suscipiam lavacro, quia hanc petitionem nullus christianorum debet abnuere. Eamque ego, ut Deus manifeste novit, non calliditate, sed in simplicititate puri cordis agere cupio, quia offensam Divinitatis incurrere formido. Non est enim humilitas genti nostrae, si hic a me excipiatur. Si enim domini proprios famulos de sacro fonte suscipiunt, cur et mihi non liceat, propinquum parentem excipere ac filium facere per baptismi gratiam spiritalem"; HF 2, 465; trans. modified.

106. Joseph H. Lynch, *Godparents and Kinship in Early Medieval Europe* (Princeton, 1986), 175; see also, 173–74.

107. Regula Tarnatensis, "La 'Regula monasterii Tarnatensis'. Texte, sources et datation," ed. Fernando Villegas, *Revue Bénédictine* 84 (1974): 7–65, 3, 20: "sed si causa tantae necessitatis extiterit, aut cuiuscumque fidelis personae precibus

inclinatus interdicta non ualet effugere, quod contradicenti cognoscitur impositum, caritatis intuitu est omnimodis omittendum; the dating follows the editor F. Villegas, 62.

108. See chapter 4 note 82.

109. *Vita Amandi* 17, 440$^{8-9}$: "Dagobertus rex, amore mulierum plus quam oportebat deditus omnique spurcitia libidinis inflammatus."

110. For more detail on this conflict see pp. 224ff.

111. See note 105; the text is based on Colossians 3:22.

112. Lynch, *Godparents and Kinship*, 175.

113. See note 9.

114. In a footnote, Lynch cites an anthropological study by Hugo G. Nutini and Betty Bell (*Godparents and Kinship*, 173 note 41), emphasizing not only the element of social pressure contained in a direct request, but also the social compulsion to sound out the answer in advance. In his historical analysis, however, (esp. p. 175) Lynch takes up only the first aspect; for this reason he is inclined to consider Gunthchramn's reply to be "credible" (175).

115. A vivid example is analyzed in Roger Sablonier, "The Aragonese Royal Family," in David Sabean and Hans Medick, eds., *Interest and Emotion: Essays on the Study of Family and Kinship* (Cambridge and Paris, 1984), 210–39; for a discussion drawing on the anthropological literature, see Bourdieu, *Logic of Practice*, esp. 168–69.

116. For more on this see pp. 210–13.

117. As Eugen Ewig maintains in "Studien zur merowingischen Dynastie" (18); Ewig refers to a passage in Fredegar which will be discussed, pp. 203f.

118. L.H. X,28, 521$^{12-22}$: "Promissionem, quam in nepotem meum Childeberthum regem statutam habeo, non obmitto.... Abscedite nunc et nuntiate domino vestro: 'Pactionem quam tecum pepigi, custodire cupio inlibatam; quam si tuae conditionis noxa non obmiserit, a me prorsus omitti non queit"; HF 2, 465.

119. See the text of the pact in L.H. IX,20, 436 $^{1-3}$.

120. See L.H. IX,20, 441$^{9/10}$.

121. According to Eugen Ewig, "Die fränkischen Teilungen und Teilreiche 511–613," in *Akademie der Wissenschaften und der Literatur Mainz. Abhandlungen der sozialwissenschaftlichen Klasse* 9 (Wiesbaden, 1953), 651–715, 689 note 3; he cites L. Levillain's "Les comptes de Paris à l'époque franque," *Le Moyen age* 41, 3e série 12 (1941), 137–205, 138, which, however, only paraphrases Childebert's complaint (see chapter 2 note 16); according to Ewig, ("Die fränkischen Teilungen," 709), Chlothar occupied the *civitas* immediately after Gunthchramn's death; Ewig points to the installation of Berthar as bishop of Chartres, but this event cannot be dated; L. Duchesne (*Fastes épiscopaux de l'ancienne Gaule*, 3 vols., vol. 2, 2d ed., Paris, 1919, 427) asserts that it did not take place until sometime between Childebert's death in 596 and Chlothar's defeat at the hands of Childebert's sons in 599; Chlothar only reigned in Chartres during this period (according to Fredegar; see note 128); Ewig retains this dating, so that the installation of the bishop does not support his thesis.

122. R. Schmidt, "Zur Geschichte des fränkischen Königsthrons," *FMSt* 2 (1968), 45–66, 53. In the German text, Schmidt writes: "daß Gunthram den Sohn der Fredegunde dadurch, daß er ihn zu Paris aus der Taufe hob, in seiner dortigen Herrschaft befestigte, daß er ihm diesen Reichssitz sicherte."

123. See Margret Wielers, "Zwischenstaatliche Beziehungsformen im frühen Mittelalter: pax, foedus, amicitia, fraternitas" (Ph.D. diss., Münster, 1959), 55.

124. *Chronicle of Fredegar*, IV,14, 10: "Regnum eius Childebertus sumsit."

125. Ibid., IV,16, 10: "regnumque eius filii sui Teudebertus et Teudericus adsumunt."

126. See Ewig, "Die fränkischen Teilungen," 689–90.
127. See *Chronicle of Fredegar*, 11.
128. *Chronicle of Fredegar*, 12: "Eo anno Fredegundis cum filio Chlothario regi Parisius vel reliquas civitates rito barbaro occupavit."
129. See chapter 5, above.
130. Weidemann, *Das Testament des Bischofs Berthramn*, 154–55.
131. See ibid., 153.
132. On the partition of 567, see Ewig, "Die fränkischen Teilungen," 679–80; on what follows, see Weidemann, *Das Testament des Bischofs Berthramn*, 154–55.
133. Quoted in note 99; see Weidemann, *Das Testament des Bischofs Berthramn*, 155.
134. See ibid.
135. L.H. XI,20, 435$^{1-2}$: "ut omnia, quae undecumque inter ipsis scandalum poterat generare, pleniori consilio definirent."
136. Ibid, 435$^{6-9}$: "Similiter, quia domnus Gunthchramnus iuxta pactionem, quam cum bonae memoriae domno Sigybertho inierat, integram portionem, quae de rigno Chariberthi ille fuerat consecutus, sibi diceret in integrum redebere et pars domni Childeberthi ea quae pater suus possiderat ad se vellit ex omnibus revocare"; HF 2, 389.
137. See L.H. XI,20, 435^{16}; on the conflict over Tours and Poitiers see chapter 5 note 87; on Meaux see L.H. VIII,18, 385$^{17-19}$ and Margarete Weidemann, *Kulturgeschichte der Merowingerzeit nach den Werken Gregors von Tours*, 2 vols. (Mainz, 1982) 1, 75.
138. See chapter 5 note 77.
139. See L.H. IX,20, 437$^{8-16}$; the cities involved were Bordeaux, Limoges, Béarn, and Cieutat; Gunthchramn returned only Cahors to Brunechildis.
140. See pp. 142f.
141. See note 99.
142. This purported plan would have been contrary to the wording of the pact (see note 135) and, as Childebert's protest at the christening suggests (see chapter 2 note 16), could scarcely have been carried out with his knowledge. One might cite the fact that after Childebert's death Chlothar conquered the very *civitates* in question but then stopped (according to Weidemann, *Das Testament des Bischofs Berthramn*, 159) to support the argument that he had inherited these cities; two things speak against this, however; first, it is not unlikely that he also conquered the clearly Austrasian cities of Avranches, Senlis and Meaux (see ibid., 159–60), and second, other factors, such as Fredegund's death in 597, may have stopped the Neustrian's expansion.
143. See L.H. IX,20, 437^{20}–38^2.
144. Weidemann, *Das Testament des Bischofs Berthramn*, 155, and map on p. 154; that Ressons-sur-Matz was an exclave is suggested by evidence of an adjoining *pagus* of Chambly to the south, which probably abutted on the *civitas* of Senlis and thus precluded a connection between the *pagus* of Ressons and the *civitas* of Paris; on this, see M. Roblin, *Le terroir de l'oise aux époques galloromaine et franque: Peuplement, défrichement, environnement* (Paris, 1978).
145. See Weidemann, *Das Testament des Bischofs Berthramn*, 155.
146. Ewig, "Die fränkischen Teilungen," 680.
147. L.H. IX,20, 436$^{1-3}$: "quem Deus de ipsis regibus suprestitem esse praeciperit, regnum illius, qui absque filiis de praesentis saeculi luce migraverit, ad se ad se in integritate perpetuo debeat revocare."
148. L.H. IX,20, 441$^{5-11}$: "Dicebat enim et haec verba: Utinam mihi nepus meus

promissa custodiat! Omnia enim quae habeo eius sunt. . . . Dabo enim Chlothario . . . aut duas aut tres in parte aliqua civitatis, ut nec hic videatur exheredario de regno meo, nec huic inquietudinem praeparent, quae isti relinquero"; HF 2, 394.

149. On the significance of Paris in the Merovingian period see L. Pietri, "Le premier millénaire," in *Le diocèse de Paris* 1: *Des origines à la Revolution*, ed. B. Plongeron (Paris 1987), 28–57, 27–28; see also Reinhold Kaiser, *Bischofsherrschaft zwischen Königtum und Fürstenmacht. Studien zur bischöflichen Stadtherrschaft im westfränkisch-französischen Reich im frühen und hohen Mittelalter* (Bonn, 1981), 472–73.

150. On the baptism of 591, see note 118; on the meeting of 577, see chapter 2, note 6; on the meeting of 585, chapter 2, note 9; and on the pact of Andelot, chapter 2, note 10. Quotations in HF 2, 311 and 389, respectively.

151. See note 124.

152. See pp. 76–82.

153. See notes 94, 118, and 159.

154. See chapter 2, note 16. HF 2, 464.

155. L.H. X,28 522$^{2-4}$: "[Gunthchramnus] dicens: Crescat puer et huius sit nominis exsecutur ac tale potentia polleat, sicut ille quondam, cuius nomen indeptus est."

156. *Chronicle of Fredegar*, 35: "Firmatum est omnem regnum Francorum, sicut a priorem Chlotharium fuerat dominatum."

157. See above pp. 103f.

158. On Gunthchramn's doubts, see pp. 76–79; on his banishment of Fredegund, see chapter 4 note 45; and on his interference, see pp. 70f.

159. *Chronicle of Fredegar*, 5: "et eum de sancto lavacro excipiens in regnum patris firmavit."

160. See L.H. VII,6, 329$^{11-15}$.

161. Angenendt, *Kaiserherrschaft und Königstaufe*, 114.

162. L.H. X,28, 522$^{4/5}$: "Quod misterium celebratum, invitatum ad epulum parvolum multis muneribus honoravit. Similiter et rex ab eodem invitatus, plerisque donis refertus abscessit"; HF 2, 465.

163. L.H. V,17, 216$^{10/11}$: "Et manducantes simul atque bibentes dignisque se muneribus honorantes, pacifici discesserunt"; HF 2, 186.

164. L.H. IX,11, 426$^{8/9}$: "Rex vero Gunthchramnus cum nepote suo ac reginis pacem firmavit, datis sibi invicem muneribus ac stabilitatis causis publicis, epulati sunt pariter"; HF 2, 381.

165. Flodoard of Rheims, *Annales* ad a. 923, ed. Philippe Lauer (Paris, 1905), 12: "ubi se invicem paverunt et, pacta amicitia datisque ab alterutro muneribus, discesserunt."

166. For example L.H. II,35, 84$^{9/10}$: Alaric and Clovis "comedentes pariter ac bibentes, promissa sibi amicitia, pacifici discesserunt"; for an example without the participation of kings, see L.H. IX,19, 432$^{20/21}$: "Sicharius . . . magnam cum eo [Chramnesindo] amicitiam patravisset et in tantum se caritate mutua diligerent ut plerumque simul cibum caperent"; *Annales Fuldenses sive annales regni Francorum orientalis*, ed. G. H. Pertz and F. Kurze, MGH SS rer. Germ. 7 (Hanover, 1891), 1–107, a. 847, 36: "Hic annus a bellis quievit, quem Hlutharius et Hludowicus mutua familiaritate transegerunt; nam uterque eorum ad domum alterius invitatus conviviis et muneribus regiis honoratus est"; *Nithardi historiarum libri*, ed. E. Müller, MGH SS rer. Germ. 44, 3rd ed. (Hanover, 1907), III,6, 38$^{2-4}$ (to Louis the German and Charles the Bald): "Nam convivia erant illis poene assidua, et, quodcumque precium habebant, hoc alter alteri perhumane dabat"; on these examples see also, G. Althoff, "Der frieden-, bündnis- und gemeinschaftstiftende Charakter des Mahles im

früheren Mittelalter," in *Essen und Trinken in Mittelalter und Neuzeit,* ed. I. Bitsch, T. Ehlert, and X. v. Ertzdorff (Sigmaringen, 1987), 13–25.

167. See Bede, *Historia ecclesiastica gentis Anglorum—Beda der Ehrwürdige, Kirchengeschichte des englischen Volkes,* 2 vols., ed. G. Spitzbart (Darmstadt, 1982), IV,13, 357: "Aedilualch . . . baptizatus . . . suggerente rege Uulfhere, a quo etiam egressus de fonte loco filii susceptus est; in cuius signum adoptionis duas illi prouincias donauit."

168. *Annales Mosellani* ad. a. 785, 497[38–40]: "Widuchind . . . baptizatus est, et domnus rex suscepit eum a fonte ac donis magnificis honoravit."

169. See Ermoldus Nigellus, *Carmen in honorem Hludowici christianissimi caesaris augusti , Ermold le Noir, Poème sur Luis le pieux et épitres au roi Pépin,* ed. E. Faral, in *Les classiques de l'histoire de France au moyen age,* 14 (Paris, 1932), 1–201, v. 2252–77 (gifts) and 2338–61 (banquet), 172–74 and 178–80.

170. See chapter 12 note 70.

171. See L.H. V,18, 219–20.

172. Ibid., 220[3/4]: "Quod dolorose faciens me non intellegere"; HF 2, 189.

173. L.H. V,18, 220[6]: "Ad haec ego, cognuscens adulationes eius, dixi: . . . Tu vero . . . pollicire prius, quod legem et canones non omittas."

174. See ibid., 220[6–20]; quotation 220[11–12]: "Post haec, accepto pane, hausto etiam vino, discessi."

175. See notes 163–66.

176. Esther N. Goody, *Contexts of Kinship: An Essay in the Family Sociology of the Gonja of Northern Ghana* (Cambridge, 1973), 128.

177. Georg Simmel, "Soziologie der Mahlzeit," in *Das Individuum und die Freiheit. Essais* (Berlin, 1984), 205–11, 206.

178. On people of unequal rank, see, for example, L.H. VIII,1, 370[11]: "Nam [Gunthramnus] per domibus eorum [civium Aurelianensis urbis] invitatus abibat et prandia data libabat"; L.H. VIII,2, 371[13/14]: "[Gregory of Tours:] deprecor, ut in mansione mea eulogias beati Martini dignaretur accipere. Quod ille [Guntchramnus] non respuens, benigno animo ingressus, hausto poculo, admonitis nobis ad convivium, laetus abscessit"; Otto Gerhard Oexle, "Mahl und Spende im mittelalterlichen Totenkult," *FMSt* 18 (1984), 401–20, "Gilden als soziale Gruppen in der Karolingerzeit," in *Das Handwerk in vor- und frühgeschichtlicher Zeit 1: Historische und rechtshistorische Beiträge und Untersuchungen zur Frühgeschichte der Gilde,* ed. H. Jankuhn, W. Janssen, R. Schmidt-Wiegandt, and H. Tiefenbach, (Göttingen, 1981), 284–354, esp. 309–28; on the banquet, with more bibliography, see Althoff, "Der frieden-, bündnis- und gemeinschaftstiftende Charakter des Mahles"; and K. S. Kramer, article "Mahl und Trunk," in *HRG* 3, 1984, cols. 154–56.

179. See the exemplary account in Erdmann Weyrauch, "Mahl-Zeiten. Beobachtungen zur sozialen Kultur des Essens in der Ständegesellschaft," in *Leib und Leben in der Geschichte der Neuzeit,* ed. A. Imhof (Berlin, 1983), 103–18, 106–10, which analyzes the modern princely banquet, the bourgeois formal dinner and the peasant meal as semiotic systems; for a systematizing approach see U. Tolksdorf, "Strukturalistische Nahrungsforschung. Versuch eines generellen Ansatzes," *Ethnologica Europea* 9 (1976): 64–85, 66–68.

180. For an example, see the description in J. Bumke, *Höfische Kultur: Literatur und Gesellschaft im hohen Mittelalter* 1 (Munich, 1986), 240–75.

181. L.H. VIII,1, 370[11/12]: "[Gunthchramnus] multum ab his [civibus Aurelianensis urbis] muneratus muneraque ipsis proflua benignitate largitus est."

182. L.H. IX,16, 431[5/6] (between Gothic envoys and Childebert in 587).

183. See pp. 148–51.

184. Examples in Althoff, "Der frieden-, bündnis- und gemeinschaftstiftende Charakter des Mahles," 16 and J. Hannig, "Ars donandi. Zur Ökonomie des Schenkens im früheren Mittelalter," in *Armut, Liebe, Ehre. Studien zur historischen Kulturforschung*, ed. Richard van Dülmen (Frankfurt a.M., 1988), 11–37 and 275–78, 19–21.

185. To borrow Bourdieu's phrase; see *Logic of Practice*, 99.

186. John the Deacon, *La cronaca veneziana del diacono Giovanni* in *Cronache veneziane antichissime* 1, ed. G. Monticolo (Rome, 1890), 57–171, 163$^{10/11}$ and 164$^{6-9}$: "ad perfecte namque fidei vinculum confirmandum, filiam ducis adhuc caticumina de sacro baptismatis lavacro cesar suscepit; pallium quidem, quod pro pacti federe a Veneticis supra quinquaginta libras persolvebatur, eidem suo compatri duci perpetua scriptione donabat.... Altero autem die, cum iam redeundi licitum habere volebat, diversarum generum fortunis dux eum munerare voluit, qui nichil orum continere cupiebat dicens: illud mihi crimen inducere nolo, ne quis cupiditatis et non sancti Marci tueque dilectionis causa me huc venisse asserat. tamen importunis coartatus precibus, eburneum sedile cum suo subsellio, nec non argenteum siphum et urceum raro peractum opere dono, licet invitus, recepit, datoque obsculo, lacrimantibus utrisque separati sunt."

187. See *Ottonis III. diplomata*, ed. Theodor Sickel, MGH DD regum et imperatorum Germaniae 2,2 (Hanover, 1893), 397 a. 1001, 830$^{20-24}$: "Petrus dux Veneticorum et noster compater per suum nuncium, Iohannem videlicet diaconum, nostram humiliter deprecando adiit celsitudinem, quatinus pallium et que camerarii nostri sibi annualiter pro censu exigebant, eidem suisque successoribus perdonare ac concedere omnia, exceptis quinquaginta libris, dignaremus."

188. See chapter 4 note 3.

189. See L.H. VII,7, 330$^{2/3}$: "Nam Fredegunde patrocinio suo fovebat, ipsamque sepius ad convivium evocans, promittens, se ei fieri maximum defensorem."

190. Even if this was at times only an apparent subjugation, as in the case of Charles III (see pp. 219f.). On the entire complex of issues, see Angenendt, *Kaiserherrschaft und Königstaufe*.

191. *Chronicle of Fredegar*, 5.

192. See pp. 70f. and chapter 4 note 3.

193. See pp. 90–103 and 109–12.

194. In *The Logic of Practice*, Bourdieu deals almost exclusively with the type of gift exchange that acquires its value in the game played with that time that elapses between gift and countergift; in *The Gift Economy* (London and New York, 1988), 20–39, David Cheal points out that the most significant gift exchange by far in our societies, that at Christmas, must be explained differently; he argues for the use of Goffman's "tie-sign" model; see Erving Goffman, *Relations in Public: Microstudies of the Public Order* (New York, 1971), 194–99.

195. See, for example, pp. 204f.

Chapter 12. Sponsorship as a Social Practice

1. *Vita Amandi episcopi*, ed. Bruno Krusch, *Passiones vitaeque sanctorum aevi Merovingici*, MGH SS. rer. Merov. 5 (Hanover and Leipzig, 1910), 395–485, 17, 440$^{13/14}$: "cogitare coepit, cui ipsum puerum traderet, qui eum sacro baptismate regenerare deberet."

2. This was the solution chosen by the hagiographer of Saint Moling for his hero. See *Vita sancti Moling episcopi de Tech Moling*, in *Vitae sanctorum Hiberniae* 2, ed. C. Plummer (Oxford 1910), 190–205, 190.

3. Hartmut Zwahr, *Zur Konstituierung des Proletariats als Klasse: Strukturuntersuchung über das Leipziger Proletariat während der industriellen Revolution* (Berlin, 1978), esp. 167–70; Zwahr's findings are substantiated by David Sabean in *Kinship in Neckarhausen 1700–1870* (Cambridge, 1997).

4. As the chronicler Gregory has the Burgundian king Gunthchramn say; see chapter 11 note 73.

5. See chapter 1 note 92.

6. On Tigernach, see note 142; on Fridolin, note 11 (the *Vita* was, however, not written until the ninth century); *Vita Odiliae abbatissae Hohenburgensis*, ed. W. Levison, in *Passiones vitaeque sanctorum aevi Merovingici*, MGH SS rer. Merov. 6 (Hanover and Leipzig, 1913), 24–50, 4, 40$^{3/4.11}$: "[quidam episcopus nomine Erhardus] eam a sancto fonte elevaret"; Joseph H. Lynch's assumption that cross-gender sponsorship began only in the eighth century requires correction on this point; *Godparents and Kinship in Early Medieval Europe* (Princeton, 1986), 223.

7. See pp. 146f. and 164f.

8. See chapter 7 notes 35–49.

9. See *Vita Odiliae* 2–4, 38–40.

10. See pp. 164ff.

11. *Vita Fridolini confessoris Seckingensis auctore Balthero*, ed. B. Krusch, in *Passiones vitaeque sanctorum aevi Merovingici et antiquiorum aliquot*, MGH SS rer. Merov. 3 (Hanover, 1896), 351–69, 24, 365$^{17-32}$: "Inde dum egens hospitio una cum discipulis suis intraret cuiusdam bone qualitatis viri domum Wachere nuncupati, obviam ei venit ipsius predicti hominis uxor, non solum interrogans, quid vellet, sed furibunda nimium mente eum increpando sic alloquitur: Miror, frater, cur . . . me tantummodo aggrederis . . . nec in hoc contentus es, ut solus pergas, sed aliorum,—unde tu vel illi sint, nescio,—congregata multitudine, vagaris circumquaque, minime sciens, que famis angustia nos hoc anno constringit. Illa huiusmodi sermocinante illoque pacienter hoc ausculante, venit eius predictus maritus, et aliquid levigata sue uxoris iracundia, pio eum recepit amore, quia nimie dignitatem sanctitatis in eo florere cognoverat, atque in tantum eum statim dilexit, quatinus suam filiam, quam eadem nocte sua coniux peperit, in crastinum rogaret baptizare et de eiusdem sacri baptismatis fonte levare. Hoc facto cum sua coniux multum irasceretur, eo quod talis vir peregrinus ac pannosus sibi in compatrem eligeretur, ampliavit adhuc eius iracundiam, condonans huic sancto viro magnam hereditatis possessionisque partem. Sed tamen postea [femina . . .] commendavit ei suam quam de sacro levaverat baptismate filiam, ut . . . in Dei permaneret servitio."

12. *Vita Trudonis confessoris Hasbaniensis auctore Donato*, ed. W. Levison in *Passiones vitaeque sanctorum aevi Merovingici*, MGH SS rer. Merov. 6 (Hanover and Leipzig, 1913), 264–98, 15, 286^{34}–87^{30}: "Venerabilis igitur Trudo, dum in ipsius itineris calle consisteret, ad cuiusdam fidelis viri domum, vesperescente iam die, declinavit. . . . Cum autem refecti essent et hora iam requiescendi spatium postulasset, vir dei ab hospite suo petiit, ut in pomerio suo sibi ad requiescendum locus prepararetur. . . . Consensit autem hospes. . . . Uxor eiusdem fidelis viri intempesta noctis silentio a somno expergefacta surrexit, apertoque hostis domus suae, in pomerium respexit, et ecce! Illi magnae admirationis apparuit signum. . . . Conterrita autem mulier reversa est cum festinatione ad virum suum; nuntiavit ei illam mirabilem visionem. . . . Surgentes vero hospites illius prostraverunt se ad pedes eius, postulantes ab eo, ut saltim illius unius diei spatium praesentiae sanctitatis ipsius meruissent habere consortium. Adquievit vir Dei petitioni eorum eosque toto illo die caelestibus monitus salutisque aeternae remediis instanter erudivit. Petivit quoque ab illo isdem fidelis vir, ut filium suum sanro lavacri fonte baptizaret. Ille vero petitionibus eius

libenter obtemperans, statim baptizavit illum et a sacro fonte suscepit; in utroque pater illi spiritalis effectus est."

13. Ibid, 19, 290[10/11].

14. See chapter 7 note 96.

15. *Vita Trudonis* 15, 287[29], quoted in note 12; see also, ibid., 19, 290[13]: "libenter oboediens."

16. *Vita Pardulfi abbatis Waractensis*, ed. W. Levison, in *Passiones vitaeque sanctorum aevi Merovingici*, MGH SS rer. Merov. 7 (Hanover and Leipzig, 1920), 19–40, 20, 37[13].

17. *Vita virtutesque Fursei abbatis Latiniacensis et de Fuilano additamentum Nivialense*, ed. B. Krusch, in *Passiones vitaeque sanctorum aevi Merovingici*, MGH SS rer. Merov. 4 (Hanover and Leipzig 1902), 423–51, 10, 443[25].

18. See the example of Columbanus, p. 225f., and of the holy man Fregius (*Vita sancti Berachi*, in *Vitae sanctorum Hiberniae* 1, ed. C. Plummer [Oxford, 1910], 75–864, 76): "Vir sanctus ... quodam de suis ad se accersito, ait: Ad domum Uendali generi mei progredere, et si forte soror mea partum edidit masculum, ad me cum partu eueniat. ... Mox infans ad sanctum Fregium ducitur. ... [Vir sanctus] ait: Hunc, inquid, infantem ad ecclesiam perducite, ut a lauacro salutis abluatur. ... Infantem in Christo regeneratum mater secum conabatur detinere. ... Sed sanctus uir Dei hoc non permisit dicens: ... Mecum enim in Christi nomine remanebit."

19. *Vita Richarii confessoris Centulensis auctore Alcuino*, ed. B. Krusch, in *Passiones vitaeque sanctorum aevi Merovingici*, MGH SS rer. Merov. 4 (Hanover, 1902), 381–401, 10, 394[20–26]: "Visitavit enim ... feminam Richthrudam nomine, et iam post dulces vitae epulas et post conloquia salubria ipse vir Dei, ascenso equo, ad propria remeare disposuisset ... habens in ulnis filiolum suum, ... quem ipse ante sacro baptismate Deo regeneravit"; *Vita Trudonis* 19, 290[10-16]: "Quadam quoque die quidam religiosus vir nomine Godmundus, cuius etiam filium vir Dei a sacro fonte susceperat, postulavit ab eo, ut domum suam visitaret, ut sua etiam benedictione consecraret. Ille autem piissimus pater petitionibus eius libenter oboediens, ad domum illius perrexit. ... Duxerunt igitur pariter in sancta laetitia illius diei spatium."

20. See *Vita Trudonis* 15, 287[33/34] (immediately follows the text quoted in note 11): "Recedente autem viro dei, praedictus hospes illius surrexit oratoriumque in loco, quo venerandus pater requieverat, ob memoriam admirandae visionis construxit."

21. See notes 11 and 12 for examples.

22. See note 20.

23. For example, Fridolin (see note 11), Furseus (see pp. 213f.), or Pirmin (ibid.).

24. Bertefred (pp. 178f.), Eberulf (pp. 176f.), and Sigivald (pp. 171f.); apparently also, Hesychius, the father of Avitus of Vienne (p. 29f.).

25. Pippin II chose Rigobert of Reims to be the godfather of his son Charles (Martell) (see *Vita Rigoberti episcopi Remensis*, ed. W. Levison, in *Passiones vitaeque sanctorum aevi Merovingici*, MGH SS rer. Merov. 7, Hanover and Leipzig 1920, 54–80, 8, 59[20–23]); Pippin III chose Raganfried of Rouen as a *compater* (see chapter 9 note 17), he also chose Pope Stephan II as the confirmation sponsor for his sons Charles and Carloman and Pope Paul I as godfather to his daughter Gisela. On this, see Arnold Angenendt, *Kaiserherrschaft und Königstaufe. Kaiser, Könige und Päpste als geistliche Patrone in der abendländischen Missionsgeschichte* (Berlin and New York, 1984), 155–56.

26. Sigivald (see pp. 171f.), Chlothar II or the Neustrian rulers (chapter 11), Theuderic II (chapter 10 note 10).

27. Chilperic, Sigibert, Childebert II (see chapter 9 on all three), Pippin II and Pippin III (see note 25 on both).

28. See note 11.

29. See Vita Fursei 10/11, 443^{22}–44^{13}: "[10] Vir Domini memoratus Erchenaldus audiens eius famam, obviam ei perrexit, orans et postulans, ut veniret ad domum eius ad palatium Peronensis vici et in sacrum baptisma filium suum poneret et a fonte susciperet. Qui sanctus non rennuens. . . . Accedens ad epulas. . . . [11] Tunc electus Domini Erchenaldus constituit tres domesticos suos, qui virum iustum per diversa loca deducerent, et ubicumque sua propria fuissent, ei monstrassent, ut, qualis ei locus amabilior fuisset, ad habitandum daretur; qui et fecerunt."

30. *Vita et miracula sancti Pirminii*, ed. O. Holder-Egger, MGH SS 15,1 (Hanover, 1887), 17–35, 5, 24^{10}–25^{15}.

31. See note 29.

32. See pp. 191ff. Elements of the theses (mainly developed by Friedrich Prinz) concerning "noble saints" (*Adelsheiligen*), "family saints" (*Sippenheiligen*), and the "self-sanctification" (*Selbstheiligung*) of the "nobility" have been convincingly refuted (Frantisek Graus, "Sozialgeschichtliche Aspekte der Hagiographie der Merowinger- und Karolingerzeit: Die Viten der Heiligen des südalemannischen Raumes und die sogenannten Adelsheiligen," in *Mönchtum, Episkopat und Adel zur Gründungszeit des Klosters Reichenau*, ed. Arno Borst (Sigmaringen, 1974), 131–76; H. Keller, "Mönchtum und Adel in den Vitae patrum Jurensium und in der Vita Germani abbatis Grandivallensis. Beobachtungen zum frühmittelalterlichen Kulturwandel im alemannisch-burgundischen Grenzraum," in *Landesgeschichte und Geistesgeschichte. Festschrift für Otto Herding* (Stuttgart, 1977), 1–23, but not the influence of nobles over their own foundations, nor the gain in prestige that such foundations brought the donor, particularly when he was related to the respected holy men who lived there (see Graus, "Sozialgeschichtliche Aspekte der Hagiographie," 171–72).

33. Quoted in chapter 2 note 16; for a later example, see *Chronica S. Petri Erfordensis moderna a. 1072–1355*, in *Monumenta Erphesfurtensia saec. XII. XIII. XIV*, ed. O. Holder-Egger, MGH SS rer. Germ. 42 (Hanover, 1899) 153–206, 165$^{18/19}$: "Rex Lotharius apud Marseburg penthecosten celebrans Udalricum ducem Boemorum in amiciciam recepit et filium eius de sacro fonte baptismatis suscepit."

34. *Vita Faronis episcopi meldensis*, ed. J. Mabillon, in *Acta sanctorum Ordinis sancti Benedicti* 2 (Paris, 1669, repr. 1938), 606–25, 22, 613: "pro pacto amicitiae filium Chilperici Regis a sacro fonte suscipiens, Baptismatis novus regenerator efficeretur."

35. *Vita sancti Declani episcopi de Ard Mor*, in *Vitae sanctorum Hiberniae* vol. 2, 32–59, 5, 37: "Colmanus baptizauit sanctissimum infantulum, Declanum nomen ei imponens. Et post baptismum ait. . . . Et ilicito fraternitatem tecum habebo, et commendo me sanctitate tue; post talia iam dicta et facta beatus Colmanus ad locum suum in gaudio recessit, commendans ut diligenter nutriretur sanctus infans, et septimo anno ad legendum traderetur, si Christianus literatus prope inveniretur."

36. See chapter 11 note 69.

37. See the sources cited in chapter 1 note 88 and chapter 9 note 64.

38. Chlothar II in chapter 2 note 16.

39. See pp. 53–64 on the same phenomenon in Merovingian *adoptiones*.

40. As in the case of Gunthchramn and Chlothar; see pp. 204–9.

41. As in the cases of Charlemagne and the Saxon leader Widukind (see chapter 1 note 68) or Louis the Pious and Harald of Denmark (see chapter 1 note 128).

42. As in the cases of Praetextatus and Merovich (pp. 154ff.), Ageric and Childebert (pp. 159ff.), and Chlothar II and Merovich, son of the Austrasian king (chap. 10 note 10).

43. See above pp. 128–32.

44. Lynch, *Godparents and Kinship*, 155–56.
45. Ibid., 157.
46. See the statements of Avitus, Ennodius and Florianus (pp. 129–32), Gregory's account on Theudebert and Sigivald (pp. 171ff.), perhaps the *Vita Genovefae* (see pp. 128ff.), and, finally, the Rule for Nuns of Caesarius of Arles (see chapter 7 note 96).
47. See chapter 9 note 98 and chapter 10 notes 34 and 47.
48. See chapter 7 note 96.
49. Ibid.
50. See Caesarius of Arles, *Statuta Sanctorum Virginum*, in *S. Caesarii Arelatensis episcopi regula sanctarum virginum aliaque opuscula ad sanctimoniales directa*, ed. C. Morin (Bonn, 1933), 6–17, 7: "quia quae suorum libertatem pro dei amore contempsit, aliorum expetere vel habere non debet; ut sine aliquo impedimento deo vacare iugiter possit."
51. See above chapter 7 note 104.
52. See above pp. 171ff.
53. Lynch, *Godparents and Kinship*, 155–56.
54. See chapter 10 note 34.
55. See chapter 9 note 167.
56. See, for example, Friedrich Prinz, *Frühes Mönchtum im Frankenreich. Kultur und Gesellschaft in Gallien, den Rheinlanden und Bayern am Beispiel der monastischen Entwicklung (4.–8. Jahrhundert)* (Munich, 1965), 124–41 and 488.
57. See pp. 145–48.
58. See pp. 156–59.
59. See note 29.
60. See *Vita Fridolini* 24, 365[23]: "unde tu vel illi [discipuli] sint, nescio"; similarly, *Vita Trudonis* 15, 286[34]–87[1]: "Venerabilis igitur Trudo, dum in ipsius itineris calle consisteret, ad cuiusdam fidelis viri domum, vesperescente iam die, declinavit. At ille vir cernens in eo sapientiae spiritum et sanctae religionis habitum recognoscens."
61. See chapter 9 note 64; for the full account see note 111 in this chapter.
62. The case is discussed on pp. 178ff.
63. See chapter 9 note 64; on the *pactum* see note 34 in this chapter.
64. See above chapter 11.
65. See pp. 43ff. and 219f.
66. See pp. 213f.
67. Dudo of St. Quentin, *De moribus et actis primorum Normanniae ducum*, ed. J. Lair (Caen and Paris, 1865), III,55, 199: "quatenus majoris copula dilectionis ampliorisque nexibus amoris colligati."
68. Angenendt, *Kaiserherrschaft und Königstaufe*, 207; see *Annales Mosellani a. 758*, ed. J. M. Lappenberg, MGH SS 16 (Hanover, 1859), 491–99, 497[39/40]: "et domnus rex suscepit eum a fonte ac donis magnificis honoravit."
69. Just as Harald of Denmark would later be the vassal and godson of Louis the Pious (cf. chapter 1 note 128); vassalage was not normally accompanied by gifts from the vassal's lord.
70. *Annales Fuldenses sive annales regni Francorum orientalis*, ed. G. H. Pertz and F. Kurze, MGH SS rer. Germ. 7 (Hanover, 1891), 1–107, 99: "Sed imperator . . . Gotafridum de fonte baptismatis levavit et, quem maximum inimicum de desertorem regni sui habuerat, consortem regni constituit. Nam comitatus et beneficia, quae Rorich Nordmannus Francorum regibus fidelis in Kinnin tenuerat, eidem hosti suisque hominibus ad inhabitandum delegavit"; *Annalium Fuldensium continuatio*

Ratisbonensis a. 882–897, ed. G. H. Pertz and F. Kurze, MGH SS rer. Germ. 7, 107–31, 108: "Duos ibi dies laeti insimul versabant, tum remissis nostris obsidibus de munitione ipse e contrario cum maximis muneribus remissus ad sua. Munera autem talia erant: in auro et argento duo mille libras et LXXX vel paulo plus; quam libram XX solidos computamus expletam"; on this, see Angenendt, *Kaiserherrschaft und Königstaufe*, 260–62.

71. Regino of Prüm, *Chronicon cum continuatione Treverensi*, ed. F. Kurze, MGH SS rer. Germ. 50 (Hanover, 1890), 119–20: "Godefridus rex Nortmannorum ea conditione christianum se fieri pollicetur, si ei munere regis Fresia provincia concederetur, et Gisla filia Lotharii in uxorem daretur."

72. See pp. 204f.
73. See pp. 205–9.
74. See chapter 11 note 69.
75. See chapter 2 note 16.
76. See chapter 11 note 105.
77. See chapter 9 note 46 and chapter 11 note 162.
78. Angenendt, *Kaiserherrschaft und Königstaufe*, 158.
79. See Pope Stephan to Pippin: *Codex Carolinus*, ed. W. Gundlach, in *Epistolae Merowingici et Karolini aevi*, 1, MGH Epp. 3 (Berlin, 1892), 469–657, no. 6, 488$^{34/5}$, no. 7, 491$^{1/2}$, no. 8, 494$^{8/9}$, no. 11, 504$^{12/13}$; Paul I to Pippin: no. 14, 511$^{9/10}$, no. 16, 513$^{8/9}$, 17–22, 24–25, 27–32, 34, 36–38, 40–42; Hadrian to Charlemagne: no. 66, 59^{41}, no. 67, 594^{34}, no. 68, 597^{16}, nos. 70–94.

80. Bertefred and Brunechildis, Eberulf and Gregory, Chilperic and Praetextatus; in a later example, the emperor Lothar, son of Louis the Pious, waged war on his godson, Godefrid, the son of Harald of Denmark (see Angenendt, *Kaiserherrschaft und Königstaufe*, 260).

81. Except in the case of the baptism of Pathir (see pp. 173–76); in all the other examples, sponsorships appear to have followed a concrete and recognizable interest on the part of the parents.

82. See, for example, the *Vita Fridolini* (note 11); *Vita Fursei* (note 29); *Vita Geremari* (note 97); *Vita Pardulfi* 20, 37: "Homo quidam ex pago Biturico, Leodulfus nomine, ad eum veniens poposcerat, ut filium suum ad baptismum fontis susciperet"; *Vita Trudonis* (note 12); an Irish example with a baptist: *Vita sancti Fintani abbatis de Cluain Ednech*, in *Vitae sanctorum Hiberniae* 1, 96–106, 96: "Duxit [pater eius] eum die octauo ad quendam virum sanctum . . . et ipse baptissauit."

83. Jonas of Bobbio, *Vitae Columbani abbatis discipulorumque eius libri II*, ed. B. Krusch in *Ionae vitae sanctorum Columbani, Vedastis, Iohannis*, MGH SS rer. Germ. 37 (Hanover and Leipzig, 1905), 1–294, I,14, 174^{12}–75^{11}: "Eratque enim tunc temporis dux quidam nomine Waldelenus. . . . Hic cum coniuge sua Flaviam nomine et genere et prudentia nobilem ad beatum Columbanum ex Vesontionense oppido pergit, precantes simul, ut pro eis Dominum deprecaretur: se multorum opum esse ditatos, sed, cui hereditatem post obitum linquerent, heredem non habebant. Quibus vir sanctus: Si, inquid, voti vestri est, ut largitoris donum eius nomini consecretis mihique ex lavacro suscipiendum tradatis, pro vobis ego Domini clementiam implorabo, ut non solum eum, quem Domino vovetis habeatis, verum etiam quantum volueritis, post pignora suscipiatis. At illi laeto animo promittunt se eius imperiis parituros, tantum pro ipsis Domini misericordiam non desinat implorare. Spondet vir Dei muneribus plenus se in promptum habere, tantum ne pacti foedus studeant violare."

84. Ibid, 175$^{11-21}$: "Quem vir sanctus suis manibus receptum sacravit sacroque lavacro ablutum ipse suscepit Donatumque nomen imponet."

85. In Ireland the holy baptist played the same social role as the holy godfather on the Continent.
86. *Vita Berachi* 4, 76 (quoted in note 18).
87. See *Vita Declani* 5, 37 (quoted in note 35).
88. *Vita Declani* 21, 54: "[Declanus] illum infantem baptizauit, et dedit ei nomen Chiaranum. Et ait sanctus episcopus illis post baptismum: Hunc meum spiritalem filium diligenter nutrite; et apto tempore ad docendum viris tradite eum catholicis."
89. See *Vita Fridolini* 24, 365 (quoted in note 11).
90. *Vita Gamalberti presbyteri Michaelsbuchensis*, ed. W. Levison, in *Passiones vitaeque sanctorum aevi Merovingici*, MGH SS rer. Merov. 7, 183–91, 4, 188: "Et praevidens, eum in spiritu magnum esse futurum et suam hereditatem post se possessurum, indixit parentibus, ut eum sanctitatis studio nutrirent et virum factum ad se domum transmitterent. Indicavit patriam, nominavit provinciam, vicum et locum indiciis patentibus premonstravit."
91. *Vita sancti Colmani de Land Elo*, in *Vitae sanctorum Hiberniae* 1, 258–73, 26, 269: "Erat quidam uir nobilis et diues de genere Neill, cui aliquando cecus filius natus est; et ille homo, nolens suum filium habere secum propter superbiam, uni seruo de pueris suis precepit, ut illum infantem occideret . . . Deinde uenit sanctus Colmanus ad illum, et illico dixit patri illius: Male et stulte egisti, dampnando seruum Dei innocentem ad mortem; ipse enim melior est tota prole tua. Tunc pater amans illum, obtulit eum sancto Colmano nutriendum Deo. Et statim baptizauit sanctus Colmanus illum infantem, dans ei nomen Chellanum. Postea docuit eum sacris scripturis et bonis moribus. Et ipse erat vir sanctus et sapiens . . . qui uocatur Chellanus caecus."
92. Petrus Cantor, *Summa de sacramentis et animae consiliis* 3.2, ed. J.-A. Dugauquier (Louvain and Lille, 1963), Summa § 334, 404[3/4]: "modo timet ne langueat gratia compatris sui."
93. See chapter 1 notes 88 and 90.
94. Erving Goffman refers to such processes as "avoidance processes." *Interaction Ritual: Essays on Face-to-Face Behavior* (New York, 1967), 15. See also note 95.
95. Goffman, *Interaction Ritual*, 15; Pierre Bourdieu has shown that, for example, in the difficult negotiations accompanying marriage there also is a hierarchy among intermediaries such that the first people to be sent are those possessing little prestige for the families involved and subsequent negotiators have successively higher status; see his *Logic of Practice*, 168–69; in their research on co- and godparenthood in Mexico, Hugo G. Nutini und Betty Bell have observed a similar testing of the waters. See their *Ritual Kinship: The Structure and Historical Development of the Compadrazgo System in Rural Tlaxcala*, 2 vols. (Princeton, 1980–84), 1, 56–57, 2, 72.
96. *Vita Geremari* 3, 628[28].
97. *Vita Geremari* 5, 629[12–15]: "Erat enim in illis diebus in palatio regis quidam amicus eius nomine Audoenus, vir sanctus Dei vocatus, et omnia que agebat per consilium eius exercebat. Direxit itaque nuncium ad eum narravitque ei, quod filius illi successerat; prostratus ergo petivit ab eo, ut a sancto fonte susciperet filium eius."
98. *Vita Fursei* 10, 443[25].
99. *Vita Trudonis* 15, 287[29], and 19, 290[13]: "libenter oboediens."
100. *Vita Pardulfi* 20, 37[13].
101. *Vita Amandi* 17, 440[12–21]: "Cumque ei nuntiatum fuisset, videlicet, quod ei Dominus filium dare dignatus est, magno repletus est gaudio; cogitare coepit, cui ipsum puerum traderet, qui eum sacro baptismate regenerare deberet. Statimque arcessitis ministris, ut sanctum perquirerent Amandum, sagaci intentione praecepit.

Nam dudum ipse pontifex, dum pro capitalibus criminibus, quod nullus ex sacerdotibus facere ausus est, ipsum redargueret regem, in furore accensus, iubente eo, non absque iniuria de regno eius fuerat expulsus, atque remotiora perquirens loca, verbum Dei gentibus praedicabat. Cumque a ministris tandem fuisset repertus est, ut ad regem ire deberet, admonitus, memorans illud apostoli praeceptum, potestatibus sublimioribus se subdi debere."

102. Ibid., 441$^{1-13}$; quotation 441$^{10-13}$: "Quod vir Domini vehementer rennuens, scilicet sciens esse scriptum, militanti Deo non oportere inplicare saecularibus negotiis et quietum atque remotum palatia non debere frequentare regia, e conspectu regis abscessit."

103. In the Merovingian period, the title of "minister" did not designate a specific social rank; on *ministri* in the Merovingian period see Karl Bosl, "Vorstufen der deutschen Königsdienstmannschaft," in his *Frühformen der Gesellschaft im mittelalterlichen Europa. Ausgewählte Beiträge zu einer Strukturanalyse der mittelalterlichen Welt* (Munich and Vienna, 1964), 228–76, 244–45.

104. *Vita Amandi* 17, 441^{13}–42^{1}: "Tunc demum rex misit ad eum virum illustrem Dadonem atque cum eo venerabilem virum Eligium, qui tunc in palatio regis subsaeculare degebantur habitu. . . . Hi humiliter ad virum Dei petierunt, ut praecibus regis daret adsensum, atque filium ipsius sacro dignaretur dilui fonte, et ut eum enutriret atque legem inbueret divinam, quantotius adsentiret, dicentesque, quod si hoc vir Dei non rennueret, per hanc afmiliaritatem liberius in regno ipsius, vel ubicumque eligeret, haberet licentiam praedicandi, seu et nationes quam plures per hanc gratiam se posse conquiri fatebantur. Tandem igitur fatigatus praecibus amborim, facturum se esse promisit."

105. See note 83.

106. See chapter 4 note 82.

107. In the literature by social anthropologists on godparenthood and compadrazgo, at least, such negotiating strategies play no role in the organization of godparent ties. It is not until the late Middle Ages, at the earliest, that we are likely to find evidence regarding the sponsorship strategies of the lower social strata, for example in the records of the Inquisition. See the present author's study "Le parrainage à la fin du moyen âge: Savoir public, attentes théologiques et usages sociaux," *Annales E.S.C.* 47 (1992), 467–502.

108. See note 95.

109. See chapter 11 note 105.

110. We might reflect on the fact that recourse to ruses which allowed actors at once to keep and break their promises were frequently condemned by commentators; on this see p. 236; anthropologists have an easier time of it here; on the complex mechanisms of the conduct of honor, see Bourdieu, *Logic of Practice*, 100.

111. *Agnelli qui et Andreas liber ponitificalis ecclesiae Ravennatis*, ed. O. Holder-Egger, in *MGH SS rer. Lang.* (Hanover, 1878), 265–391, 294$^{4-10}$:" Duo viri cupientes foedus inter se iungi, dixit unus ad alterum habentem sobolem: Petitionem parvam deprecor tibi, rogo, ut non in vacuum revertatur obsecratio mea. Cui ille alter: Non gravabo te; quod tibi placet, fiat. Dixitque: Da mihi filium tuum, ut sim ei pater de sancto baptismo et suscipiam ego eum de fonte sanctificato. Simus cummuniter patres, tu carnalis, ego autem spiritualis. At ille ait: In nomine domini nostri Iesu Christi fiat sic. Factumque est ita."

112. See chapter 11 notes 9 and 69. HF 2, 464.

113. See pp. 76–79.

114. To use Erving Goffmann's phrase; *Interaction Ritual*, 15.

115. *Vita Amandi* 17, 441^{2}; see also *Vita Geremari* 5 (as in note 97).

116. On Merovich see pp. 169f.; on Chlothar II and Sigibert see pp. 191f.
117. See quotations in chapter 9 note 160 and chapter 11 notes 78 and 80.
118. See pp 129f. on Clovis and 173; the later sponsorship of Harald of Denmark by Louis the Pious was described in minute detail by the poet Ermoldus Nigellus; see chapter 1 note 128.
119. Angenendt, *Kaiserherrschaft und Königstaufe*, 5–4 and 311.
120. Adam of Bremen credits Otto I with sponsoring the Dane Sven Fork-Beard (Adam of Bremen, *Hamburgische Kirchengeschichte*, ed. B. Schmeidler, MGH SS rer. Germ. 2, 3d ed. [Hanover and Leipzig, 1917], II, 13, 63) and Ademar of Chabannes claims Otto III as the godfather of the Hungarian Waik/Stephan (*Ademari historiarum*, ed. G. Waitz, MGH SS 4 [Hanover, 1841], 106–48, III,31, S. 129^{50}–130^{15}); the twelfth-century *Liber Eliensis* elaborates on Bede's account of the baptism of King Cenwalh at the East Anglian court, adding the detail that the East Anglian king Ænna stood as sponsor (*Liber Eliensis*, ed. E. O. Blake [London, 1962], 18); on this, see Angenendt, *Kaiserherrschaft und Königstaufe*, 184, 277, 308.
121. On the ideal of the ruler see Angenendt, *Kaiserherrschaft und Königstaufe*, 2–5.
122. Angenendt, *Kaiserherrschaft und Königstaufe*, 215–23.
123. *Iosephi Genesii regum libri quattuor*, ed. A. Lesmüller-Werner and I. Thurn (Berlin and New York, 1978), IV, 16, 69^{50}; on this, see Angenendt, *Kaiserherrschaft und Königstaufe*, 249.
124. Gregory II, letter 2 to Leon III, $305^{390/1}$; on this, see Angenendt, *Kaiserherrschaft und Königstaufe*, 154–55.
125. See chapter 1 note 58.
126. See above chapter 7 note 143.
127. See chapter 7 note 68.
128. Dhuoda, *Liber manualis/ Manuel pour mon fils*, ed. Pierre Riché, trans. B. de Vregille and Claude Mondésert (Paris, 1975), VIII, 15, 320^{2-6}: "Nec hoc praetereundum est, fili, de illo qui te, ex meis suscipiens brachiis, per lauacrum regenerationis filium adoptauit in Christo. Nomen autem eius apellatus est, dum uixit, domnus Teodericus, nunc vero condam."
129. Petrus Cantor, Summa §334, 404^{5-13}: "Compaternitatis fuit instituta causa dilatande caritatis, tu autem astrictus es michi compaternitate una et ego tibi.... ex quo filiolus tuus mortuus est, non debeo te iterum recipere ad compaternitatem."
130. See, for example, Otto Gerhard Oexle, "Die Gegenwart der Toten," in *Death in the Middle Ages*, ed. H. Braet and W. Verbeke (Louvain, 1983), 19–77.
131. See chapter 10 note 4.
132. *Vita Trudonis* 19, S. 290: "quidam vir religiosus nomine Godmundus, cuius etia filium vir Dei a sacro fonte susceperat, postulavit ab eo, ut domum suum visitaret, ut sua etiam benedictione consecraret."
133. *Vita Fidoli abbatis Trecensis*, ed. B. Krusch, in *Passiones vitaeque sanctorum aevi Merovingici et antiquiorum aliquot*, MGH SS rer. Merov. 3 (Hanover, 1896), 427–32, 10, 430^{31-33}: "praemissa postulatione, ut domum ipsius visitaret unici obtinuit caritas. In cuius nomine fides integra lagenam meri vini uberius servaverat plena."
134. Vita Richarii 10, 394^{19-26}: "Visitavit [Richarius] enim equitando quandam Deo devotam feminam Richthrudam nomine, et iam post dulces vitae epulas et post conloquia salubria ipse vir Dei, ascenso equo, ad propria remeare disposuisset, et femina praedicta iuxta morem equitantis vestigia pariter secuta est, habens in ulnis filiolum suum, ut parvulus quoque benedictione hominis Dei roboraretur, quem ipse ante sacro baptismate Deo regeneravit."
135. *Vita sancti Abbani*, in *Vitae sanctorum Hiberniae* 1, 1–32, 26, 20: ". . . quidam ex regali genere istius terre adhuc est incredulus et infidelis, qui est heros et tyrannus,

qui semper occidit et rapit. . . . Tunc vir sanctus baptizauit eum cum suis. Et ille uir unicum habebat filium, et adduxit eum, et baptizatus est. Ille siquidem vir habitum sanctum accepit, et mansit cum sancto Abbano usque ad obitum suum in conversacione felici."

136. *Vita Bertini* 19, 765[22]: "ad Bertinum saepe venire solebat."

137. *Vita Bertini* 19, 765[22-23]: "ut a beato viro divina praecepta audiret"; similarly, in the *Vita Trudonis* 15, 287[26/7]: "Adquievit vir Dei petitioni eorum eosque toto illo die caelestibus monitus salutisque aeterna remediis instanter erudivit"; see also, ibid., 18, 289[29-32].

138. See notes 133 and 134.

139. *Vita Trudonis* 19, 290[17/18]: "[Godmundus], dixit: Unum verrem habeo, pater, quem tibi devoveram"; Trudo was Gudmundus' *compater* (see note 132).

140. According to Hincmar; see chapter 7 note 136.

141. Agnellus, Liber Ponificalis 30, 294[24-30] and 295[3].

142. *Vita sancti Tigernaci episcopi de Cluain Eois*, in *Vitae sanctorum Hiberniae* 2, 262–69, 11, 266: "ad matrem suam spiritalem, que eum olim de fonte baptismatis leuauit, sanctam . . . Brigidam . . . profectus est. Que misticis commonita signis, ac Spiritu ei reuelante quod filius suus spiritualis episcopali dignus esset honore, conuocatis episcopis, eum ad ponitificalis ordinis apicem prouehi fecit."

143. *Vita Nivardi episcopi Remensis auctore Almanno monacho Altivillarensi*, ed. W. Levison, in *Passiones vitaeque sanctorum aevi Merovingici*, MGH SS rer. Merov. 5 (Hanover and Leipzig, 1910), 157–71, 7, 165[1-5]: "beatus Bercharius tunc abbas, nunc martyr, vir magnificus et spiritualis eius [Nivardi] filius, quoniam eum a sacris fontibus susceperat, hoc idem devote a beato presule petierat, scilicet sibi et fratribus suis locum dari pro eterne remunerationis mercede, ubi sub regula sancti patris Benedicti et Columbani vivere posset"; ibid., 10, 168[12]: "Bercharium filiolum, suum abbatem prefecit."

144. See pp. 179f.

145. See pp. 159–63.

146. See notes 33–37; Johannes Diaconus, *Cronica Veneziana*, 116[11]: "ad dilectionis seu pacis vinculum corroborandum."

147. See the examples in chapter 7 note 121.

148. See chapter 9 note 46. HF 2, 190–91.

149. See pp. 175f.

150. See pp. 171f.

151. See chapter 10 note 10.

152. See pp. 179f.

153. *Ermoldus Nigellus in honorem Hludowici christianissimi caesaris augusti/ Ermold le Noir, Poème sur Luis le pieux et épitres au roi Pépin*, ed. E. Faral (Paris, 1932), 1–201, Carmen 4, v. 2275–76, 174: "Nec minus interea Hluttarius ornat amore Heroldi natum vestibus aurigeris"; on Dhuoda see chapter 11 note 77.

154. See chapter 1 note 64.

155. See pp. 34f.

156. See chapter 9 note 64.

157. Lucien Febvre, "Sensibility and History: How to Reconstitute the Emotional Life of the Past" (1941), in *A New Kind of History: From the Writings of Febvre*, ed. Peter Burke, trans. K. Folca (London, 1973), 12–26, 14–15.

158. See Hans Medick and David Sabean's introduction to the volume of essays *Interest and Emotion: Essays on the Study of Family and Kinship* (Cambridge and Paris, 1984), esp. 3.

159. Niklas Luhmann, *Soziale Systeme. Grundriß einer allgemeinen Theorie* (Frank-

furt a.M., 1984), 319. Luhmann's definition also seems to be applicable within the context of other sociological methods than those he himself propagates.

160. According to Febvre, "Sensibility and History," 14–15, or Luhmann, *Soziale Systeme*, 253.

161. *Formulae Turonenses vulgo Sirmondicae dictae*, ed. K. Zeumer, in *MGH Formulae Merowingici et Karolini aevi* (Hanover, 1886), 128–65, no. 25, 149[6/7]: "Pactum inter parentes. Caritatis studio et dilectionis affectu inter propinquos decet"; according to this reflection, it is unnecessary to pronounce *caritas* "less emotional" because it is an "objective behavioral norm" (as Reinhard Schneider does in *Brüdergemeine und Schwurfreundschaft. Der Auflösungsprozess des Karolingerreiches im Spiegel der caritas-Terminologie in den Verträgen der karlingischen Teilkönige des 9. Jahrhunderts* [Lübeck and Hamburg, 1964], 119); it can be both at once.

162. See chapter 10 note 12.

163. See chapter 9 note 83.

164. See chapter 9 note 98; on this story see above pp. 161–64; Bertefred, too, appears to have counted on this when he fled to Bishop Ageric (see above pp. 159f.).

165. See notes 132 and 133.

166. See note 142.

167. See note 90.

168. See pp. 177f.

169. See pp. 195f.

170. See pp. 224f.

171. See pp. 38f.

172. See chapter 9 note 60.

173. On this see p. 179f.

174. See pp. 154ff.

175. See pp. 127ff.

176. See p. 225.

177. See note 109 and chapter 1 note 90.

178. *Decretum Magistri Gratiani*, ed. A. Friedberg (Leipzig, 1879), C. XXX, col. 1095.

179. See pp. 147–56.

180. Gregory of Tours' commentary on the behavior of Rauching, who "fulfilled" an oath promising not to separate a couple of serfs by having both of them buried alive (L.H. V, 3, 198[10/11]); see also Widukind of Corvey's commentary on Hatto of Mainz, who deceitfully turned a nobleman over to the royal tribunal and thus certain death; *Die Sachsengeschichte des Widukind von Corvey*, ed. P. Hirsch and H.E. Lohmann, MGH SS rer. Germ. 60 (Hanover, 1935), I,22, 33[1/2]: "Hac igitur perfidia quid nequius?"; "Excerpta quedam de libro Dauidis," in *The Irish Penitentials*, ed. L. Bieler (Dublin, 1963), 70–73, 7, 70[15-18]: "Episcopus homicidium uoluntate faciens uel quamlibet fornicationem dolumue .xiii. annis peniteat."

181. Bourdieu, *Logic of Practice*, 119–20.

182. See pp. 147–56.

183. See pp. 175f.

184. See Josef Semmler, "Episcopi potestas und karolingische Klosterpolitik," in *Mönchtum, Episkopat und Adel zur Gründungszeit des Klosters Reichenau*, 305–95, 318–19, with documents; on the sponsorship, see *Vita Rigoberti* 8, 59[20-23].

185. L.H. IX,9, 422[2/3]: "multa etiam contra Brunechilde reginam frementes, ut eam in contuniliam redigerent, sicut prius fecerant in viduetate sua"; HF 2, 377.

186. See p. 180.

Bibliography

Primary Sources

Adam of Bremen. *Hamburgische Kirchengeschichte*. Edited by B. Schmeidler. Monumenta Germaniae Historica, Scriptores rerum Germanicarum 2. 3rd edition. Hanover and Leipzig, 1917.

Ademari historiarum libri III. Edited by Georg Waitz, 106–48. Monumenta Germaniae Historica, Scriptores 4. Hanover, 1841.

Agathias Scholasticus Myrinensis. *Historiarum libri quinque*. In *Sancti patris nostri Johannis Scholastici... Agathiae Myrinaei... scripta quae extant*, edited by Jacques Paul Migne, 1268–612. Migne Patrologiae cursus completus, Series graeca 88. Paris, 1860.

Agnelli qui et Andreas liber ponitificalis ecclesiae Ravennatis, edited by O. Holder-Egger, 265–391. Monumenta Germaniae Historica, Scriptores rerum Langobardicarum. Hanover, 1878.

Alcuin. *Epistolae*. Edited by Ernst Duemmler, 1–481. Monumenta Germaniae Historica. Epistolae 4. Hanover, 1895.

Amalar. *Liber officialis*. Edited by J. M. Hanssens. In *Amalarii episcopi opera liturgica omnia*. Vol. 2. Studi e testi, vol. 139. Vatican City, 1948.

Ambrose. *De Abraham*. In *Sancti Ambrosii opera* 1, edited by K. Schenkl, 499–638. Corpus scriptorum ecclesiasticorum latinorum 32,1. Prague, 1897.

———. *Explanatio psalmorum XII*. In *Sancti Ambrosii opera* 6, edited by M. Petschenig. Corpus scriptorum ecclesiasticorum latinorum 64. Vienna and Leipzig, 1919

Annales Fuldenses sive annales regni Francorum orientalis. Edited by G. H. Pertz and F. Kurze, 1–107. Monumenta Germaniae Historica, Scriptores rerum Germanicarum in usum scholarum 7. Hanover, 1891.

Annalium Fuldensium continuatio Ratisbonensis a. 882–897. Edited by G. H. Pertz and F. Kurze, 107–31. Monumenta Germaniae Historica, Scriptores rerum Germanicarum in usum scholarum 7. Hanover, 1891.

Annales Mosellani. Edited by J. M. Lappenberg, 491–99. Monumenta Germaniae Historica, Scriptores 16. Hanover, 1859.

Annales regni Francorum. Edited by G. H. Pertz and F. Kurze. Monumenta Germaniae Historica, Scriptores rerum Germanicarum in usum scholarum 6. Hanover, 1895.

Arnolfi diplomata. Edited by P. Kehr. Monumenta Germaniae Historica, Diplomata regum Germaniae ex stirpe Karolinorum 3. Berlin, 1940.

Augustine. *De libero arbitrio*. Edited by W. M. Green. In *S. Aurelii Augustini opera* 2,2, edited by W. M. Green and K. Dauer, 207–321. Corpus Christianorum, Series Latina 29. Turnhout, 1970.

———. *S. Aureli Augustini Hipponiensis episcopi epistulae* tom. 670,2, 643,3, 643,4. Edited by A. Goldbacher. Corpus scriptorum ecclesiasticorum latinorum 34.2, 44, 57. Prague, 1898 (vol. 2), Vienna and Leipzig, 1904 (vol. 3) and 1911 (vol. 4).

———. *Contra Julianum haresis Pelagianae defensorem libri VI.* In *Sancti Aurelii Augustini Hipponensis episcopi opera omnia* 10,1, edited by Jacques Paul Migne, 641–874. Migne Patrologiae cursus completus, Series latina 44]. Paris, 1841.

———. *De peccatorum meritis et remissione et de baptismo paruulorum ad Marcellinum libri tres* In *Sancti Aureli Augustini opera* 8,1, edited by C. F. Urba and J. Zycha, 1–152. Corpus scriptorum ecclesiasticorum latinorum 60. Vienna and Leipzig, 1913.

Aureliani Arelatensis episcopi regula ad monachos. In *Codex regularum monasticarum et canonicarum* 1, edited by L. Holstenius and M. Brockie, 147–54. Augsburg, 1759.

Avitus of Vienne. *Alcimi Edicii Aviti Viennensis episcopi opera quae supersunt*. Edited by R. Peiper, 108–12. Monumenta Germaniae Historica, Auctores antiquissimi 6.2. Berlin, 1883.

Basilicorum libri LX. Edited by H. J. Scheltema and N. Van Der Wal. Scripta Universitatis Groninganae. Groningen, 1960.

Bede. *Venerabilis Bedae historia ecclesiastica gentis Anglorum—Beda der Ehrwürdige, Kirchengeschichte des englischen Volkes*. 2 vols. Edited by G. Spitzbart. Texte der Forschung 34. Darmstadt, 1982.

Benedict of Nursia. *La règle de saint Benoît* I/II. Edited by A. de Vogüé and J. Neufville. Sources Chrétiennes 181–82. Paris, 1972.

Berthar. *Gesta episcoporum Virdunensium auctore Berthario*, edited by Georg Waitz, 38–45. Monumenta Germaniae Historica Scriptores 4. Hanover, 1841.

Bertram of Le Mans. *Testament*. In M. Weidemann. *Das Testament des Bischofs Berthram von Le Mans vom 27. März 616: Untersuchungen zu Besitz und Geschichte einer fränkischen Familie im 6. und 7. Jahrhundert*, 7–49. Römisch-Germanisches Zentralmuseum. Monographien 9. Mainz, 1986.

Boniface. *Die Briefe des heiligen Bonifatius und Lullus*. Edited by M. Tangl. Monumenta Germaniae Historica, Epistolae sel. I. Berlin 1916.

———. *The Letters of Saint Boniface*. Translated by Ephraim Everton. 1940. Reprint, New York, 1976.

Burchard of Worms. *Decretorum libri XX*. In *Burchardi Vormatiensis episcopi opera omnia*, edited by Jacques Paul Migne, 537–1084. Migne Patrologiae cursus completus, Series latina 140. Paris, 1888.

Caesarius of Arles. *Opusculum de Gratia*. In *Sancti Caesarii Arelatensis opera omnia nunc primum in unum collecta* 2: *Opera varia*, edited by G. Morin, 159–64. Maredsous, 1942.

———. *Statuta Sanctorum Virginum*. In *S. Caesarii Arelatensis episcopi regula sanctarum virginum aliaque opuscula ad sanctimoniales directa*, edited by C. Morin, 6–17. Florilegium Patristicum 34. Bonn, 1933.

———. *Sancti Caesarii Arelatensis sermones*. 2 vols. Edited by G. Morin. Corpus Christianorum. Series Latina 103/103A. Turnhout, 1953.

Die Canones Theodori Cantuariensis und ihre Überlieferung. Untersuchungen zu den Bußbüchern des 7., 8. und 9. Jahrhunderts 1. Edited by P. Finsterwalder. Weimar, 1929.

Capitula episcoporum 1. Edited by P. Brommer. Monumenta Germaniae Historica. Hanover, 1984.

Capitularia regum Francorum 1. Edited by A. Boretius. Monumenta Germaniae Historica Leges Abt. 2. Hanover, 1881–83.

[Cassius] *Dio's Roman History*. Translated by Earnest Cary. The Loeb Classical Library. 9 vols. Vol. 6. London and New York, 1917.

C. *Valerius Catullus*. Edited by W. Kroll. Berlin and Leipzig, 1923.

Chronologica regum Francorum stirpis Merowingicae. Edited by Bruno Krusch, 468–516. Passiones vitaeque sanctorum aevi Merovingici. Monumenta Germaniae Historica Scriptores rerumMerovingicarum 7. Hanover and Leipzig, 1920.

Chronica S. Petri Erfordensis moderna a. 1072–1355. In *Monumenta Erphesfurtensia saec. XII. XIII. XIV*, edited by O. Holder-Egger, 153–206. Monumenta Germaniae Historica, Scriptores rerum Germanicarum in usum scholarum. 42. Hanover, 1899.

Codex Carolinus. Edited by W. Gundlach, 469–657. Epistolae Merowingici et Karolini aevi 1. Monumenta Germaniae Historica Epistolae 3. Berlin, 1892.

[Codex Theodosianus]. *Theodosiani libri XVI: Cum constitutionibus Sirmondianis*. 2 vols. Edited by Theodor Mommsen. 1904. 4th ed. Dublin and Zürich, 1971.

Concilia Africae 345–525. Edited by C. Munier. Corpus Christianorum, Series Latina 149. Turnhout, 1974.

Concilia Galliae 2, A.511–A.695. Edited by C. De Clercq. Corpus Christianorum, Series Latina 148a. Turnhout, 1963.

Concilia aevi Karolini 1.1 and 1.2. Edited by A. Werminghoff. Monumenta Germaniae Historica Concilia 2.1 and 2.2. Hanover and Leipzig, 1906–8.

Corpus Iuris Civilis 1: *Institutiones: Digesta*. Edited by Paul Krueger and Theodor Mommsen. Berlin, 1911.

Cyprian of Carthage. *Thasci Caecili Cypriani Epistulae*. Vol. 2 of *S. Thasci Caecili Cypriani opera omnia*. Edited by W. Hartel. Corpus scriptorum ecclesiasticorum latinorum 3.2. Vienna, 1871.

———. *Letters*. Translated by Rose B. Donna. Fathers of the Church, vol. 51. Washington, D.C., 1964.

Decretum Magistri Gratiani. Edited by A. Friedberg. Corpus iuris canonici 1. Leipzig, 1879.

Dhuoda. *Manuel pour mon fils*. Translated by B. de Vregille and Claude Mondésert and edited by Pierre Riché. Sources chrétiennes 225. Paris, 1975.

Didier, J. C., ed. *Le baptême des enfants dans la tradition de l'église*. Monumenta christiana selecta 7. Tournai, 1959.

Digesta. See *Corpus Juris Civilis*

Dionysius the Areopagite. *De la hiérarchie de l'église*. Edited by P. Chevallier. In *Dionysiaca* 2, 1069–1476. Bruges, 1950.

———. *The Ecclesiastical Hierarchy*. Translated by Thomas L. Campbell. Lanham, Md., 1981.

Diplomata regum Francorum e stirpe Merowingica. Edited by K. A. F. Pertz, 1–88. Monumenta Germaniae Historica, Diplomata I. Hanover, 1872.

[Barberini Diptych] *Inscription mérovingiennes de l'ivoire Barberini*. Edited by H. Omont. Bibliothèque de l'école des Chartes 57 (1901): 152–55.

Dudo of St. Quentin. *De moribus et actis primorum Normanniae ducum*. Edited by J. Lair. Mémoires de la société des antiquaires de Normandie 23/2. Caen and Paris, 1865.

Ennodius of Pavia. *Opera*. Edited by L. Vogel. Monumenta Germaniae Historica, Auctores antiquissimi 7. Berlin, 1885.

Epistolae Austrasicae. Edited by W. Gundlach, 110–53. Epistolae Merowingici et Karolini aevi 1. Monumenta Germaniae Historica, Epistolae 3. Berlin, 1892.

Epistolae aevi Merowingici collectae. Edited by W. Gundlach, 434–68. Epistolae Merowingici et Karolini aevi 1. Monumenta Germaniae Historica Epistolae 3. Berlin, 1892.

Epistolae Langobardicae collectae. Edited by W. Gundlach, 691–715. Epistolae Merowingici et Karolini aevi 1. Monumenta Germaniae Historica Epistolae 3. Berlin, 1892.

Ermoldus Nigellus. *Carmen in honorem Hludowici christianissimi caesaris augusti*. In *Ermold le Noir, Poème sur Luis le pieux et épitres au roi Pépin*. Edited by E. Faral, 1–201. Les classiques de l'histoire de France au moyen age 14. Paris, 1932.

Excerpta quedam de libro Dauidis. In *The Irish Penitentials*, edited by L. Bieler, 70–73. Scriptores latini Hiberniae 5. Dublin, 1963.

Ferreolus of Uzès. *Regula ad monachos*. In *Codex regularum monasticarum et canonicarum* 1, edited by L. Holstenius and M. Brockie, 155–66. Augsburg, 1759.

Flodoard. *Annales*. Edited by Philippe Lauer. Collections des Textes 397. Paris, 1905.

———. *Historia Remensis ecclesiae*. Edited by J. Heller and Georg Waitz, 405–599. Monumenta Germaniae Historica Scriptores 13. Hanover, 1881.

Formulae Salicae Lindenbrogianae. Edited by K. Zeumer, 265–84. Monumenta Germaniae Historica, Formulae Merowingici et Karolini aevi. Hanover, 1886.

Formulae Turonenses vulgo Sirmondicae dictae. Edited by K. Zeumer, 128–65. Monumenta Germaniae Historica, Formulae Merowingici et Karolini aevi. Hanover, 1886.

Fredegar. *Chronicarum quae dicuntur Fredegarii scholastici libri IV*. In *Fredegarii et aliorum chronica: Vitae sanctorum*, edited by Bruno Krusch, 1–193. Monumenta Germaniae Historica Scriptores rerum Merovingicarum 2. Hanover, 1888.

———. *The Fourth Book of the Chronicle of Fredegar with its Continuations*. Edited and translated by J. M. Wallace-Hadrill. London, 1960.

Fulgentius of Ruspe. *De fide ad Petrum*. In *Fulgentii episcopi Ruspensis opera*, edited by J. Fraipont, 709–60. Corpus Christianorum, Series Latina 91A. Turnhout, 1968.

Gelasius I. *Dicta adversus Pelagianam haeresim*. In *Epistulae imperatorum pontificum aliorum*, edited by O. Guenther, 400–36. Corpus scriptorum ecclesiasticorum latinorum 35.1. Prague, 1895.

———. *Epistolae et Decreta*. In *SS. Gelasii I Papae, Aviti, Faustiani . . . opera omnia . . .*, edited by Jacques Paul Migne, 13–140. Migne Patrologiae cursus completus, Series latina 59. Paris, 1862.

Genesius. *Iosephi Genesii regum libri quattuor*. Edited by A. Lesmüller-Werner and I. Thurn. Corpus fontium historiae Byzantinae 14. Berlin and New York, 1978.

Gennadius of Marseilles. *Liber de ecclesiasticis dogmatibus*. In *Sanctorum Hilari, . . . Gennadii, presbyteri Massiliensis opera omnia*, edited by Jacques Paul Migne, 979–1054. Migne Patrologiae cursus completus, Series latina 58. Paris, 1862. A later edition is C. H. Turner, ed. "The 'Liber ecclesiasticorum dogmatum'." *Journal of Theological Studies* 7 (1906): 78–99.

Gesta Dagoberti I regis Francorum. Edited by Bruno Krusch, 396–425. In *Fredegarii et aliorum chronica: Vitae sanctorum.* Monumenta Germaniae Historica, Scriptores rerum Merovingicarum 2. Hanover, 1888.

Gesta sanctorum patrum Fontanellensis coenobii. Edited by F. Lohier and J. Laporte. Rouen and Paris, 1936.

Ghaerbald of Liège. *Capitula episcoporum: Ghärbald von Lüttich.* Edited by P. Brommer, 3–42. Monumenta Germaniae Historica, Capitula episcoporum 1. Hanover, 1984.

Gregory I. *S. Gregorii Magni moralia in Iob libri I–X.* Edited by M. Adriaen. Corpus Christianorum, Series Latina 143. Turnhout, 1979.

———. *S. Gregorii Magni. Registrum epistularum.* Edited by D. Norberg. Corpus Christianorum, Series Latina 140–140A. Turnhout, 1982.

Gregory II, letter to Leon III. Edited by J. Gouillard. In "Aux origines de l'iconoclasme: Le témoignage de Grégoire II." Traveaux et mémoires 3 (1968): 243–307.

Gregory of Tours. *Gregorii episcopi Turonensis libri historiarum X.* Edited by Bruno Krusch und W. Levison. Monumenta Germaniae Historica Scriptores rerum Merovingicarum 1,1. 2d ed. Hanover, 1951.

———. *History of the Franks.* Translated by O. M. Dalton. 2 vols. Oxford, 1927.

———. *Zehn Bücher Geschichte Gregorii Episcopi Turonensis historiarum libri decem.* Translated and edited by R. Buchner. Ausgewählte Quellen zur deutschen Geschichte des Mittelalters 2. Freiherr von Stein-Gedächtnisausgabe. Darmstadt, 1955.

———. *Libri octo miraculorum.* Edited by Bruno Krusch, 1–370. In *Gregorii episcopi Turonensis miracula et opera minora.* Monumenta Germaniae Historica, Scriptores rerum Merovingicarum 1,2. Hanover, 1885.

Haito of Basel. *Capitula episcoporum: Haito von Basel.* Edited by P. Brommer, 203–19. Monumenta Germaniae Historica, Capitula episcoporum 1. Hanover, 1984.

Hamman, A., and J. Danielou, eds. *L'initiation chrétienne.* N.p., 1980.

Heinrici III. diplomata. Edited by H. Bresslau and P. Kehr. Monumenta Germaniae Historica, Diplomata regum et imperatorum Germaniae 5. Berlin, 1931.

[Hincmar]. See *Vita Remigii*

Hincmari archiepiscopi Remensis epistolae. Edited by E. Perels. Monumenta Germaniae Historica Epistolae 8. Berlin, 1939.

Hippolytus. *Der äthiopische Text der Kirchenordnung des Hippolyt.* Edited by H. Duensing. Abhandlungen der Akademie der Wissenschaften in Göttingen. Philologisch-historische Klasse, Dritte Folge 32. Göttingen, 1946.

———. *La Tradition apostolique d'après les anciennes versions.* Edited by B. Botte. Sources Chrétiennes 11bis. 2d ed. Paris, 1984.

Ildephonsus of Toledo. *S. Hildefonsi episcopi Toletani annotationum de cognitione baptismi liber unus.* In *Sanctorum Hildefonsi, Leodegarii ... opera omnia ...,* edited by Jacques Paul Migne, 111–72. Migne Patrologiae cursus completus, Series latina 96. Paris, 1862.

Ine, King of Wessex. *Institutiones Ine regis.* In *Die Gesetze der Angelsachsen: Text und Übersetzung* 1, edited by F. Liebermann, 88–123. Halle, 1903.

Institutiones. See *Corpus Juris Civilis*

Iordanis de origine actibusque Getarum. Edited by Theodor Mommsen. In *Iordanis Romana et Getica,* 53–138. Monumenta Germaniae Historica, Auctores antiquissimi 5,1. Berlin, 1882.

Isidor, the Old High German. *Der althochdeutsche Isidor. Nach der Pariser Handschrift und den Mondseer Fragmenten.* Edited by H. Eggers. Althochdeutsche Textbibliothek 63. Tübingen, 1964.

Isidore of Seville. *De ecclesiasticis officiis.* Edited by Christopher M. Lawson. CCSL 113. Turnhout, 1993.

Egeria. *Itinerarium Egeriae.* Edited by A. Franceschini and R. Weber. In *Itineraria et alia Geographica*, various eds, 29–103. Corpus Christianorum, Series Latina 175. Turnhout, 1965.

[John the Deacon] *La cronaca veneziana del diacono Giovanni.* In *Cronache veneziane antichissime* 1, edited by G. Monticolo, 57–171. Fonti per la storia d'Italia 9. Rome, 1890.

———. *Epistola Johanni Diaconi ad Senarium.* In *Analecta Reginensia: Extraits des manuscrits latins da la reine Christine conservés au Vatican*, edited by A. Wilmart, 170–79. Studi e testi 59. Rome, 1933.

John Chrysostom. *Huit Catéchèses baptismales inédites.* Edited by Antoine Wenger. Sources Chrétiennes 50. 2d ed. Paris, 1970.

Jonas of Bobbio. *Vitae Columbani abbatis discipulorumque eius libri II.* Edited by Bruno Krusch. In *Ionae vitae sanctorum Columbani, Vedastis, Iohannis*, 1–294. Monumenta Germaniae Historica Scriptores rerum Germanicarum in usum scholarum 37. Hanover and Leipzig, 1905.

Lex Ribvaria. Edited by F. Beyerle and R. Buchner. Monumenta Germaniae Historica, Leges nationum Germanicarum 3,2. Hanover, 1954.

Lex Salica. Edited by K. A. Eckhardt. Monumenta Germaniae Historica, Leges nationum Germanicarum 4,2. Hanover, 1969.

Liber Diurnius Romanorum Pontificum. Edited by H. Foerster. Berne, 1958.

Liber Eliensis. Edited by E. O. Blake. Camden third series 92. London, 1962.

Liber historiae Francorum. Edited by Bruno Krusch. In *Fredegarii et aliorum chronica. Vitae sanctorum*, 215–328. Monumenta Germaniae Historica, Scriptores rerum Merovingicarum 2. Hanover, 1888.

[Liber mozarabicus]. *Le liber ordinum en usage dans l'église wisigothique et mozarabe d'Espagne du cinquième au onzième siècle.* Edited by M. Férotin. Monumenta ecclesiae liturgica 5. 1904. Reprint, Paris, 1969.

Liutprandi leges. In *Leges Langobardorum 643–866.* Edited by F. Beyerle, 99–176. Germanenrechte Neue Folge, Westgermanisches Recht 8. 2d ed. Witzenhausen, 1962.

Ludowici infantis diplomata. Edited by Theodor Schieffer, 73–238. Monumenta Germaniae Historica, Diplomata regum Germaniae ex stirpe Karolinorum 4. Berlin, 1960.

Marculfi Formulae. Edited by K. Zeumer, 32–112. Monumenta Germaniae Historica Formulae Merowingici et Karolini aevi. Hanover, 1886.

[Missale Bobbiense] *The Bobbio Missal: A Gallican Mass-book.* Edited by E. A. Lowe. Henry Bradshaw Society 63. London, 1920.

Missale Gallicanum vetus. Edited by L. C. Mohlberg. Rerum ecclesiasticarum documenta, Series maior, Fontes 3. Rome, 1958.

Missale Gothicum. Edited by L. C. Mohlberg. Rerum ecclesiasticarum documenta, Series maior, Fontes 5. Rome, 1961.

Mosaicarum et Romanarum legum collatio. In *Fontes iuris Romani antejustiniani* 2, edited by J. Baviera and J. Furlani, 514–89. Florence, 1968.

Nicholas I. *Nicolai I papae epistolae*, edited by E. Perels, 257–690. Epistolae Karolini aevi 4. Monumenta Germaniae Historica, Epistolae 6. Berlin, 1952.

Nithardi historiarum libri IIII. Edited by E. Müller. Monumenta Germaniae Historica, Scriptores rerum Germanicarum in usum scholarum 44. 3rd ed. Hanover, 1907.

Norwegisches Recht: Das Rechtsbuch des Frostothings. Edited by R. Meissner. Germanenrechte 4. Weimar, 1939.

Norwegisches Recht: Das Rechtsbuch des Gulathings. Edited by R. Meissner. Germanenrechte 6. Weimar, 1935.

Ordo baptismatis [=Vienna cod.lat. 1888]. In *Appendix ad saeculum X*, edited by Jacques Paul Migne, 949–60. Migne Patrologiae cursus completus, Series latina 138.

Ordo Romanus. Edited by Michel Andrieu. Vols. 2, 3 and 5 of *Les Ordines Romani du haut moyen âge*. Spicilegium sacrum lovaniense. Études et documents vols. 23, 24, and 29. Louvain, 1948–61.

Origen. *Contre Celse* 2. Edited by M. Borret. Sources Chrétiennes 136. Paris, 1968.

———. *Commentaria in epistolam b. Pauli ad Romanos*. In *Originis opera omnia* 4, edited by Jacques Paul Migne, 837–1292. Migne Patrologiae cursus completus, Series graeca 16. Paris, 1862.

———. *Homélies sur S. Luc*. Edited by H. Crouzel, F. Fournier, and P. Périchon. Sources Chrétiennes 87. Paris, 1962.

Ottonis I. imperatoris diplomata. Edited by Theodor Sickel. Monumenta Germaniae Historica, Diplomata regum et imperatorum Germaniae 1,3. Hanover, 1884.

Ottonis III. diplomata. Edited by Theodor Sickel. Monumenta Germaniae Historica, Diplomata regum et imperatorum Germaniae 2,2. Hanover, 1893.

Pactus legis Salicae. Edited by K. A. Eckhardt. Monumenta Germaniae Historica, Leges nationum Germanicarum 4,1. Hanover, 1962.

Passio Desiderii episcopi et Reginfridi diaconi martyrum Alsegaudiensium. Edited by W. Levison, 51–63. Passiones vitaeque sanctorum aevi Merovingici. Monumenta Germaniae Historica,Scriptores rerum Merovingicarum 6. Hanover and Leipzig, 1913.

Paul the Deacon. *Pauli historia Langobardorum*. Edited by Georg Waitz. Monumenta Germaniae Historica, Scriptores rerum Germanicarum in usum scholarum 48. Hanover, 1887.

———. *Pauli Warnefridi liber de episcopis Mettensibus*. Edited by H. Pertz, 260–68. Monumenta Germaniae Historica, Scriptores 2. Hanover, 1829.

Petrus Cantor. *Summa de sacramentis et animae consiliis* 3.2. Edited by J.-A. Dugauquier. Analecta mediaevalia Namurcensia 16. Louvain and Lille, 1963

[Pontificale Romano-Germanicum] *Le pontifical Romano-germanique du dixième siècle* 2: *Le texte*. Edited by C. Vogel and R. Elz. Rome, 1963.

Procès de condamnation de Jeanne d'Arc 1. Edited by P. Tisset. Paris, 1960.

Procès en nullité de la condammnation de Jeanne d'Arc 1. Edited by P. Duparc. Paris, 1977.

Regino of Prüm. *Reginonis abbatis Prumiensis chronicon cum continuatione Treverensi*. Edited by F. Kurze. Monumenta Germaniae Historica, Scriptores rerum Germanicarum in usum scholarum 50. Hanover, 1890.

[Regula Tarnatensis] Fernando Villegas, ed. "La 'Regula monasterii Tarnatensis': Texte, sources et datation." *Revue Benedictine* 84 (1974): 7–65.

[Rimbert] *Vita Anskarii auctore Rimberto.* Edited by Georg Waitz, 3–79. Monumenta Germaniae Historica, Scriptores rerum Germanicarum in usum scholarum 55. Hanover, 1884.

"Rodulphus Glabers Vita domni Wilhelmi abbatis. Neue Edition nach einer Handschrift des 11. Jahrhunderts (Paris, Bibliothèque nationale, lat. 5390)." Edited by N. Bulst. *Deutsches Archiv für Erforschung des Mittelalters* 30 (1974): 450–87.

Sacramentarium Bergomense. Manoscritto del secolo IX. Edited by A. Paredi. Monumenta Bergomensia 6. Bergamo, 1962.

[Sacramentarium Gelasianum vetus] *Liber sacramentorum Romanae ecclesiae ordinis anni circuli (Cod. Vat. lat. 316).* Edited by L. C. Mohlberg. Rerum ecclesiasticarum documenta, Series maior, Fontes 4. Rome, 1960.

[Sacramentarium Gellonense] *Liber sacramentorum Gellonense* 2. Edited by A. Dumas. Corpus Christianorum, Series Latina 159a. Turnhout, 1981.

[Sacramentarium Gregorianum = Hadrianum] *Le sacramentaire Grégorien: Ses principales formes d'après les plus anciens manuscrits* 1. Edited by J. Deshusses. Spicilegium Friburgense 16. 2d ed. Fribourg, 1979.

Sacrorum conciliorum nova et amplissima collectio. Edited by J. D. Mansi. Vols. 12 and 18. Florence, 1766 and 1773.

Seneca. *De beneficiis.* In *L. Annaei Senecae opera quae supersunt* I, edited by F. Haase, 1–154. Leipzig, 1852.

———. *De clementia.* In *L. Annaei Senecae opera quae supersunt,* 276–304.

———. *On Mercy.* In Seneca. *Moral Essays,* with an English translation by by John W. Basore. 3 vols. London and Cambridge, Mass., 1963.

Sidonius Apollinaris. *Lettres, livres VI–IX.* Edited by A. Loyen. Paris, 1970.

Sigebert of Gembloux. See *Vita s. Sigeberti*

[Supplementum Anianense] *Hadrianum revisum Anianense cum supplemento.* In *Le sacramentaire Grégorien: Ses principales formes d'après les plus anciens manuscrits* 1, edited by J. Deshusses, 349–605. Spicilegium Friburgense 16. 2d ed. Fribourg, 1979.

Tancredi summa de sponsalibus et matrimonio. Edited by A. Wunderlich. Göttingen, 1841.

[Tertullian] *Q.S.Fl. Tertulliani adversus Marcionem.* Edited by A. Kroymann. In *Quinti Septimi Florentis Tertulliani opera* 1, 437–726. Corpus Christianorum, Series Latina 1. Turnhout, 1954.

———. *De baptismo.* Edited by J. G. Ph. Borleffs. In *Quinti Septimi Florentis Tertulliani opera* 1, 275–95.

Theodore of Mopsuestia. *Les homélies catéchétiques de Théodore de Mopsueste.* Edited and translated by Raymond Tonneau and Robert Devreesse. Studi e testi, vol. 145. Vatican City, 1949.

———. *Commentary of Theodore of Mopsuestia on the Lord's Prayer and on the Sacraments of Baptism and the Eucharist.* Translated by Alphonse Mingana. Woodbrooke Studies, vol. 6. Cambridge, 1933.

[Thule 8] *Die Geschichte von Hörd dem Geächteten.* In *Fünf Geschichten von Ächtern und Blutrache,* edited by A. Heusler and F. Ranke, 189–256. Thule: Altnordische Dichtung und Prosa 8. Düsseldorf and Cologne, 1964.

[Thule 10] *Die Geschichte von den Leuten aus dem Seetal.* In *Fünf Geschichten aus dem westlichen Nordland,* translated by W. H. Vogt and F. Fischer, 21–125. Thule: Altnordische Dichtung und Prosa 10. New edition. Düsseldorf and Cologne, 1964.

[Venantius Fortunatus] *Venanti Honori Clementiani Fortunati carminum epistularum expositionum libri undecim,* edited by F. Leo, 1–292. Monumenta Germaniae Historica Auctores antiquissimi 4,1. Berlin, 1881.

Visio Barontí monachi Longoretensis. Edited by W. Levison, 368–94. Passiones vitaeque sanctorum aevi Merovingici. Monumenta Germaniae Historica, Scriptores rerum Merovingicarum 5. Hanover and Leipzig, 1910.

Vita sancti Abbani. In *Vitae sanctorum Hiberniae* 1, edited by C. Plummer, 1–32. Oxford, 1910.

Vita Amandi episcopi. Edited by Bruno Krusch, 393–485. Passiones vitaeque sanctorum aevi Merovingici. Monumenta Germaniae Historica, Scriptores rerum Merovingicarum 5. Hanover and Leipzig, 1910.

Vita Audemari. Edited by W. Levison, 753–64. Passiones vitaeque sanctorum aevi Merovingici. Monumenta Germaniae Historica, Scriptores rerum Merovingicarum 5. Hanover and Leipzig, 1910.

Vita sancti Berachi. In *Vitae sanctorum Hiberniae* 1, 75–86.

Vita Bertini. Edited by W. Levison, 765–69. Passiones vitaeque sanctorum aevi Merovingici. Monumenta Germaniae Historica, Scriptores rerum Merovingicarum 5. Hanover and Leipzig, 1910.

Vita sancti Boecii. In *Vitae sanctorum Hiberniae* 1, 87–97.

Vita Boniti epsicopi Arverni. Edited by Bruno Krusch, 110–39. Passiones vitaeque sanctorum aevi Merovingici. Monumenta Germaniae Historica, Scriptores rerum Merovingicarum 6. Hanover and Leipzig, 1913.

Vita sancti Carthagi sive Mochutu. In *Vitae sanctorum Hiberniae* 1, 170–99.

Vita sancti Colmani de Land Elo. In *Vitae sanctorum Hiberniae* 1, 258–73.

Vita Columbani. See Jonas of Bobbio.

Vita sancti Declani episcopi de Ard Mor. In *Vitae sanctorum Hiberniae* 2, 32–59.

[Vita Faronis 1] *Vita Faronis episcopi Meldensis.* Edited by Bruno Krusch, 171–206. Passiones vitaeque sanctorum aevi Merovingici. Monumenta Germaniae Historica Scriptores rerum Merovingicarum 5. Hanover and Leipzig, 1910.

[Vita Faronis 2] *Vita Faronis episcopi meldensis.* Edited by J. Mabillon, 606–25. Acta sanctorum Ordinis sancti Benedicti 2. Paris, 1669. Reprint, 1938.

Vita Fidoli abbatis Trecensis. Edited by Bruno Krusch, 427–32. Passiones vitaeque sanctorum aevi Merovingici et antiquiorum aliquot. Monumenta Germaniae Historica, Scriptores rerum Merovingicarum 3. Hanover, 1896.

Vita sancti Fintani abbatis de Cluain Ednech. In *Vitae sanctorum Hiberniae* 1, 96–106.

Vita Fridolini confessoris Seckingensis auctore Balthero. Edited by Bruno Krusch, 351–69. Passiones vitaeque sanctorum aevi Merovingici et antiquiorum aliquot. Monumenta Germaniae Historica Scriptores rerum Merovingicarum 3. Hanover, 1896.

Vita virtutesque Fursei abbatis Latiniacensis et de Fuilano additamentum Nivialense. Edited by Bruno Krusch, 423–51. Passiones vitaeque sanctorum aevi Merovingici. Monumenta Germaniae Historica, Scriptores rerum Merovingicarum 4. Hanover and Leipzig, 1902.

Vita Gamalberti presbyteri Michaelsbuchensis. Edited by W. Levison, 183–91. Passiones vitaeque sanctorum aevi Merovingici. Monumenta Germaniae Historica, Scriptores rerum Merovingicarum 7. Hanover, 1920.

Vita Genovefae virginis Parisiensis. Edited by Bruno Krusch, 204–38. Passiones vitaeque sanctorum aevi Merovingici et antiquiorum aliquot. Monumenta Germaniae Historica, Scriptores rerum Merovingicarum 3. Hanover, 1896.

Vita Geremari abbatis Flaviacensis. Edited by Bruno Krusch, 626–33. Passiones vitaeque sanctorum aevi Merovingici. Monumenta Germaniae Historica, Scriptores rerum Merovingicarum 4. Hanover and Leipzig, 1910.

Vita Heriberti archiepiscopi Coloniensis auctore Lantberto. Edited by G. H. Pertz, 739–53. Monumenta Germaniae Historica, Scriptores 4. Hanover, 1841.

[Vita Magnerici] *De s. Magnerico confessore archiepiscopo Trevirensi.* In *Acta sanctorum,* July 6. Paris and Rome, 1868: 168–92.

Vita sancti Moling episcopi de Tech Moling. In *Vitae sanctorum Hiberniae* 2, 190–205.

Vita Nivardi episcopi Remensis auctore Almanno monacho Altivillarensi. Edited by W. Levison, 157–71. Passiones vitaeque sanctorum aevi Merovingici. Monumenta Germaniae Historica, Scriptores rerum Merovingicarum 5. Hanover and Leipzig, 1910.

Vita Odiliae abbatissae Hohenburgensis. Edited by W. Levison, 24–50. Passiones vitaeque sanctorum aevi Merovingici. Monumenta Germaniae Historica, Scriptores rerum Merovingicarum 6. Hanover and Leipzig, 1913.

Vita Pardulfi abbatis Waractensis. Edited by W. Levison, 19–40. Passiones vitaeque sanctorum aevi Merovingici. Monumenta Germaniae Historica Scriptores rerum Merovingicarum 7. Hanover and Leipzig, 1920.

Vita et miracula sancti Pirminii. Edited by O. Holder-Egger, 17–35. Monumenta Germaniae Historica, Scriptores 15,1. Hanover, 1887.

Vita Remigii episcopi Remensis auctore Hincmaro. Edited by Bruno Krusch, 239–341. Passiones vitaeque sanctorum aevi Merovingici et antiquiorum aliquot. Monumenta Germaniae Historica, Scriptores rerum Merovingicarum 3. Hanover, 1896.

Vita Richarii confessoris Centulensis auctore Alcuino. Edited by Bruno Krusch, 381–401. Passiones vitaeque sanctorum aevi Merovingici. Monumenta Germaniae Historica, Scriptores rerum Merovingicarum 4. Hanover, 1902.

Vita Rigoberti episcopi Remensis. Edited by W. Levison, 54–80. Passiones vitaeque sanctorum aevi Merovingici. Monumenta Germaniae Historica, Scriptores rerum Merovingicarum 7. Hanover and Leipzig, 1920.

[Vita Segolenae] *De s. Segolena vidua.* In *Acta sanctorum,* July 5, Paris and Rome, 1868: 628–37.

Vita s. Sigeberti regis Austrasiae auctore Sigeberto monacho Gemblacens. In *Recueil des historiens des Gaules et de la France* 2, edited by M. Bouquet, 597–602. Paris, 1869.

Vita sancti Tigernaci episcopi de Cluain Eois. In *Vitae sanctorum Hiberniae* 2, 262–69.

Vita Trudonis confessoris Hasbaniensis auctore Donato. Edited by W. Levison, 264–98. Passiones vitaeque sanctorum aevi Merovingici. Monumenta Germaniae Historica, Scriptores rerum Merovingicarum 6. Hanover and Leipzig, 1913.

[Vita Verani] *De sancto Verano confessore et episcopo Cavellicensi in Gallia.* In *Acta sanctorum,* October 8, Paris and Rome, 1869: 452–74.

Vita Wilfridi I episcopi Eboracensis auctore Stephano. Edited by W. Levison, 163–263.

Passiones vitaeque sanctorum aevi Merovingici. Monumenta Germaniae Historica, Scriptores rerum Merovingicarum 6. Hanover and Leipzig, 1913.

Vitae sanctorum Hiberniae. 2 vols. Edited by C. Plummer. Oxford, 1910. Reprint, Oxford, 1968.

Walafridi Strabonis libellus de exordiis et incrementis quarundam in observationibus ecclesiasticis rerum. Edited by A. Boretius and B. Kraus, 471–516. Capitularia regum Francorum 2. Monumenta Germaniae Historica Capit. 2. Hanover, 1897.

Whitaker, E. C., ed. *Documents of the Baptismal Liturgy.* London, 1960.

Widukindi Monachi Corbeiensis rerum gestarum Saxonicarum libri III—Die Sachsengeschichte des Widukind von Corvey. Edited by P. Hirsch and H. E. Lohmann. Monumenta Germaniae Historica, Scriptores rerum Germanicarum in usum scholarum 60. Hanover, 1935.

Ymnus in solemnitate sancti Medardi episcopi. Edited by K. Strecker, 455–57. Monumenta Germaniae Historica, poetae latini aevi Carolini 4,2. Berlin, 1896.

Secondary Sources

Alföldi, A. *Der Vater des Vaterlandes im römischen Denken.* Darmstadt, 1971.

Altaner, Berthold and Alfred Stuiber. *Patrologie,* 8th ed. Freiburg, 1978.

Althoff, Gerd. *Amicitiae et pacta. Bündnis Einung Politik und Gebetsgedenken im beginnenden 10. Jahrhundert.* Hanover, 1995.

———. "Der frieden-, bündnis- und gemeinschaftstiftende Charakter des Mahles im früheren Mittelalter." In *Essen und Trinken in Mittelalter und Neuzeit,* edited by I. Bitsch, T. Ehlert, and X. v. Ertzdorff, 13–25. Sigmaringen, 1987.

Amira, K. v. *Germanisches Recht.* 4th ed., revised by K. A. Eckhardt. 2 vols. *Grundriss der germanischen Philologie* 5.1, 5.2. Berlin, 1960–67.

Angenendt, Arnold. "Bonifatius und das Sacramentum initiationis: Zugleich ein Beitrag zur Geschichte der Firmung." *Römische Quartalschrift für christliche Altertumskunde und Kirchengeschichte* 72 (1977): 133–83.

———. "Das geistliche Bündnis der Päpste mit den Karolingern: 754–796." *Historisches Jahrbuch* 100 (1980): 1–94.

———. "The Conversion of the Anglo-Saxons Considered Against the Background of the Early Medieval Mission." In *Angli e Sassoni al di qua e al di là del mare,* 747–92. Settimane di studio del Centro italiano di studi sull'alto medioevo, 32. Spoleto, 1986.

———. *Kaiserherrschaft und Königstaufe. Kaiser, Könige und Päpste als geistliche Patrone in der abendländischen Missionsgeschichte.* Arbeiten zur Frühmittelalterforschung 15. Berlin and New York, 1984.

———. *Kirchengeschichte des frühen Mittelalters.* Stuttgart, 1990

———. "Pirmin und Bonifatius: Ihr Verhältnis zu Mönchtum, Bischofsamt und Adel." In *Mönchtum, Episkopat und Adel zur Gründungszeit des Klosters Reichenau,* edited by Arno Borst, 251–304. Vorträge und Forschungen 20. Sigmaringen, 1974.

———. "Religiosität und Theologie: Ein spannungsreiches Verhältnis im Mittelalter." *Archiv für Liturgiewissenschaft* 20/21 (1978–79): 28–55.

———. "Theologie und Liturgie der mittelalterlichen Toten-Memoria." In *Memoria: Der geschichtliche Zeugniswert des liturgischen Gedenkens im Mittelalter*, edited by Karl Schmid and Joachim Wollasch, 79–199. Münstersche Mittelalter-Schriften 48. Munich, 1984.

———. "Taufe und Politik im frühen Mittelalter." *Frühmittelalterliche Studien* 7 (1973): 143–68.

Angenendt, Arnold, and Bernhard Jussen. Review of *Kulturgeschichte der Merowingerzeit nach den Werken Gregors von Tours*, by Margarete Weidemann. *Theologische Revue* 83 (1987): 34–37.

Angenendt, Arnold, et al. "Counting Piety in the Early and High Middle Ages." In *Ordering Medieval Society: Intellectual and Practical Modes of Shaping Social Relations*, edited by Bernhard Jussen. Philadelphia, 2000 (in print).

Anton, H. H. *Trier im frühen Mittelalter*. Quellen und Forschungen aus dem Gebiet der Geschichte, n.s., 9. Paderborn, 1987.

Arnold, K. "Kindheit im europäischen Mittelalter." In *Zur Sozialgeschichte der Kindheit*, edited by J. Martin and A. Nitschke, 443–67. Veröffentlichungen des Instituts für historische Anthropologie 4. Freiburg, 1986.

Bailey, Derrick S. *Sponsors at Baptism and Confirmation: An Historical Introduction to Anglican Practice*. New York, 1951.

Bardenhewer, O. *Geschichte der altkirchlichen Literatur*, vol. I. 2d ed. Freiburg, 1913.

Bausinger, H. "Name und Stereotyp." In *Stereotypvorstellungen im Alltagsleben: Beiträge zum Themenkreis Fremdbilder - Selbstbilder - Identität. Festschrift for G. R. Schroubek*, edited by H. Gerndt, 13–19. Münchner Beiträge zur Volkskunde 8. Munich, 1988.

Beck, Henry G. J. *The Pastoral Care of Souls in South-East France during the Sixth Century*. Analecta Gregoriana 51. Rome, 1950.

Becker, H. J. "Formel, Formular, Formelsammlung." In *Handwörterbuch der deutschen Rechtsgeschichte* 1, 1971: 1157–63.

Becker, Peter. *Leben und Lieben in einem kalten Land: Sexualität zwischen Ökonomie und Demographie: Das Beispiel St. Lambrecht, Steiermark 1600–1850*. Studien zur historischen Sozialwissenschaft 15. Frankfurt am Main and New York, 1990.

———. *Leben, Lieben, Sterben. Die Analyse von Kirchenbücher*. Halbgraue Reihe zur historischen Fachinformatik, series A 5. St. Katharinen, 1989.

Bellamy, J. "Adoption surnaturelle de l'homme par Dieu dans la justification." In *Dictionnaire de théologie catholique* 1, 1930.

Benedict, Ruth. *The Chrysanthemum and the Sword: Patterns of Japanese Culture*. London, 1967.

Bénevot, M. "Cyprian von Karthago." In *Theologische Realenzyklopädie*, 8, 1981.

Berger, R. *Die Wendung "offerre pro" in der römischen Liturgie*. Liturgiewissenschaftliche Quellen und Forschungen 41. Münster, 1965.

Berger, P. L., and T. Luckmann. *The Social Construction of Reality* (New York, 1966).

Bergmann, W. "Untersuchungen zu den Gerichtsurkunden der Merowingerzeit." *Archiv für Diplomatik* 22 (1976): 1–186.

Blaise, A. *Dictionnaire latin-français des auteurs du moyen-age. Lexicon latinitatis medii aevi*. CC. continuatio mediaeualis. Turnhout, 1975.

Bloch, Marc. *Feudal Society*. Translated by L. A. Manyon. 2 vols. Chicago, 1961.

Blumenkranz, B. "Die Entwicklung im Westen zwischen 200 und 1200." In *Kirche und Synagoge: Handbuch zur Geschichte von Christen und Juden* 1, edited by K. H. Rengstorf and S. v. Korzfleisch, 84–135. Stuttgart, 1968.
Boehm, L. "Erziehungs- und Bildungswesen A: Westliches Europa." In *Lexikon des Mittelalters* 3, 1986: 2196–203.
Borgolte, M.: "Comes II: Vorkarolingische Zeit." In *Lexikon des Mittelalters* 3: 71–75.
Bosl, Karl. "Vorstufen der deutschen Königsdienstmannschaft." In *Frühformen der Gesellschaft im mittelalterlichen Europa: Ausgewählte Beiträge zu einer Strukturanalyse der mittelalterlichen Welt*. Munich, 1964.
Boswell, John. *The Kindness of Strangers: The Abandonment of Children in Western Europe from Late Antiquity to the Renaissance*. New York, 1988.
Bourdieu, Pierre. *The Logic of Practice*. Translated by Richard Nice. Cambridge, 1990.
———. *Distinction: A Social Critique of the Judgement of Taste*. London and Cambridge, Mass., 1984.
Brown, Peter. *The Making of Late Antiquity*. Cambridge, Mass., 1978.
———. "The Rise and Function of the Holy Man in Late Antiquity." *Journal of Roman Studies* 61, (1971): 80–101.
———. *The World of Late Antiquity, AD 150–750*. London, 1971.
Brühl, C. "Königspfalz und Bischofsstadt in fränkischer Zeit." *Rheinische Vierteljahrsblätter* 23 (1958): 161–274.
———. *Fodrum, gistum, servitium regis: Studien zu den wirtschaftlichen Grundlagen des Königtums im Frankenreich und in den fränkischen Nachfolgestaaten Deutschland, Frankreich und Italien vom 6. bis zur Mitte des 14. Jahrhunderts*. 2 vols. Kölner historische Abhandlungen 14. Cologne, 1968
Brunner, H. *Deutsche Rechtsgeschichte*. 2 vols. Vol. 1, 2d ed. Leipzig, 1906. Vol. 2. 2d ed. rev. by C. Freiherr von Schwerin. Munich, 1928.
Buchner, R. *Die Provence in merowingischer Zeit. Verfassung - Wirtschaft - Kultur*. Arbeiten zur deutschen Rechts- und Verfassungsgeschichte 9. Stuttgart, 1933.
Buisson, Ludwig. "Formen normannischer Staatsbildung." In *Studien zum mittelalterlichen Lehenswesen*. Vorträge und Forschungen 5. Sigmaringen, 1960.
Bumke, J. *Höfische Kultur. Literatur und Gesellschaft im hohen Mittelalter*. Vol. 1. Munich, 1986.
Bund, K. *Thronsturz und Herrscherabsetzung im Frühmittelalter*. Bonner historische Forschungen 44. Bonn, 1979.
Burkert, W. "Gott I: Antike." In *Historisches Wörterbuch der Philosophie* 3.
Caenegem, R. C. v. "Das Recht im Mittelalter." In *Entstehung und Wandel rechtlicher Traditionen*, ed. W. Fikentscher, H. Franke, and O. Köhler, 609–67. Veröffentlichungen des Instituts für historische Anthropologie 2. Freiburg, 1980.
Cheal, David. *The Gift Economy*. London and New York, 1988.
Clanchy, M. T. "Remembering the Past and the Good Old Law." *History* 55 (1970): 165–76.
Classen, P. "Fortleben und Wandel spätrömischen Urkundenwesens im frühen Mittelalter." In *Recht und Schrift im Mittelalter*. Vorträge und Forschungen 23. Sigmaringen, 1977.
Claude, D. "Die Bestellung der Bischöfe im merowingischen Reiche." *Zeitschrift der Savigny-Stiftung für Rechtsgeschichte: Kanonistische Abteilung* 49 (1963): 1–75.

———. "Hofkaufleute im Frühmittelalter." In *Akten des 26. Deutschen Rechtshistorikertages*, ed. D. Simon, 403–9. *Ius commune*. Sonderheft 30. Frankfurt, 1987.

———. *Topographie und Verfassung der Städte Bourges und Poitiers bis in das 11. Jahrhundert*. Historische Studien 380. Lübeck and Hamburg, 1960.

———. "Untersuchungen zum frühfränkischen Comitat." *Zeitschrift der Savigny-Stiftung für Rechtsgeschichte: Germanistische Abteilung* 81 (1964): 1–79.

Collins, R., Paul Fouracre, and C. Wickham. Conclusion to *The Settlement of Disputes in Early Medieval Europe*, ed. W. Davies and P. Fouracre. Cambridge, 1986.

Coens, M. "Les vies de S. Cunibert de Cologne et la tradition manuscrite." *Analecta Bollandiana* 47 (1929): 338–67.

Conrad, H. *Deutsche Rechtsgeschichte* 1: *Frühzeit und Mittelalter. Ein Lehrbuch*. 2d ed. Karlsruhe, 1962.

Cramer, P. *Baptism and Change in the Early Middle Ages, c. 200–c. 1200*. Cambridge Studies in Medieval Life and Thought, ser. 4, 20. Cambridge and New York, 1993.

Curtius, Ernst R. *Europäische Literatur und lateinisches Mittelalter*. 2d ed. Berne, 1954.

Dassmann, Ernst, and Georg Schöllgen. "Haus II: Hausgemeinschaft." In *Reallexikon für Antike und Christentum* 13, 1986.

Deck, S. "Les marchands de Rouen sous les ducs." *Annales de Normandie* 6 (1956): 245–54.

Demandt, A. *Metaphern für Geschichte: Sprachbilder und Gleichnisse im historisch-politischen Denken*. Munich, 1978.

Devisse, Jean. *Hincmar, archevêque de Reims 845–882*. Vol. 1. Geneva, 1975.

Dick, Ernst. "Das Pateninstitut im altchristlichen Katechumenat." *Zeitschrift für katholische Theologie* 63 (1939): 1–49.

Dodds, Eric R. *The Greeks and the Irrational*. Berkeley and Los Angeles, 1950.

Dölger, Franz Josef. "Die 'Familie der Könige' im Mittelalter." *Historisches Jahrbuch* 60 (1940): 397–420.

Drabek, Anna M. "Der Merowingervertrag von Andelot aus dem Jahr 587." *Mitteilungen des Instituts für österreichische Geschichtsforschung* 78 (1970): 34–41.

Duby, Georges. *The Early Growth of the European Economy: Warriors and Peasants from the Seventh to the Twelfth Century*. Translated by Howard B. Clarke. London, 1974.

Du Cange, C. *Glossarium mediae et infimae latinitatis* 7, ed. L. Favre. Reprint, Graz, 1954.

Duchesne, L. *Fastes épiscopaux de l'ancienne Gaule*. 2d ed. 3 vols. Paris 1907–19.

Dujarier, Michel. *Le parrainage des adultes aux trois premiers siècles de l'église: Recherche historique sur l'évolution des garanties et des étapes catéchuménales avant 313*. Paris, 1962.

———. *A History of the Catechumenate: The First Six Centuries*. New York, 1979.

Dumville, D. N. "Kingship, Genealogies and Regnal Lists." In *Early Medieval Kingship*, edited by P. H. Sawyer and Ian N. Wood, 72–104. Leeds, 1979.

Durkheim, Emile. *Die Regeln der soziologischen Methode*. Edited by R. König. Frankfurt am Main, 1884.

Eckert, W. P. "Hoch- und Spätmittelter. Katholischer Humanismus." In *Kirche und Synagoge: Handbuch zur Geschichte von Christen und Juden* 1, ed. K. H. Rengstorf and S. v. Korzfleisch, 84–135. Stuttgart, 1968.

Eckhardt, Karl A. *Studia Merovingica*. Bibliotheca rerum historicarum. Studia 11. Aalen, 1975.

Eggers, Hans. *Deutsche Sprachgeschichte* 1: *Das Althochdeutsche*. Rowohlts deutsche Enzyklopädie 185/186. Reinbek bei Hamburg, 1963.

Emonds, H. "Abt." *Reallexikon für Antike und Christentum* 1, 1950.

Enright, Michael J., and Tara Iona. *Soissons: The Origin of the Royal Anointing Ritual*. Arbeiten zur Frühmittelalterforschung 17. Berlin and New York, 1985.

Ewig, Eugen. "Christliche Expansion im Merowingerreich." In *Die Kirche des frühen Mittelalters* 1, ed. K. Schäferdiek, 116–19 and 127–45. *Kirchengeschichte als Missionsgeschichte* 2.1, ed. H. Frohnes, H. W. Gensichen and G. Kretschmar. Munich, 1978.

———. "Das Fortleben römischer Institutionen in Gallien und Germanien." In *X. Congresso internazionale di scienze storiche: Relationi* 6, 561–98. Florence, 1955.

———. "Das merowingische Frankenreich. 561–687." In *Europa im Wandel von der Antike zum Mittelalter*, ed. Theodor Schieffer, 396–433. Handbuch der europäischen Geschichte 1, ed. Theodor Schieder. Stuttgart, 1976.

———. "Zur Geschichte von Contrua-Gondorf." In *Von der Spätantike zum frühen Mittelalter. Aktuelle Probleme in historischer und archäologischer Sicht*, ed. J. Werner and E. Ewig, 371–77. Vorträge und Forschungen 25. Sigmaringen, 1979.

———. "Die lateinische Kirche im Übergang zum Frühmittelalter." In *Handbuch der Kirchengeschichte* 2,2, ed. H. Jedin, 95–179. Freiburg, 1975.

———. "Der Martinskult im Frühmittelalter." *Archiv für mittelrheinische Kirchengeschichte* 14 (1962): 11–30.

———. *Die Merowinger und das Imperium*. Rheinisch Westfälische Akademie der Wissenschaften. Vorträge G 261. Opladen, 1983.

———. "Milo et eius modi similes." In *S. Bonifatius: Gedenkgabe zum Zwölfhundertsten Todestag*, 412–40. 2d ed. Fulda, 1954.

———. "Studien zur merowingischen Dynastie." *FMSt* 8 (1974): 15–59.

———. "Die fränkischen Teilreiche im 7. Jahrhundert (613–714)." *Trierer Zeitschrift für Geschichte und Kunst des Trierer Landes und seiner Nachbargebiete* 22 (1953): 85–144.

———. "Die fränkischen Teilungen und Teilreiche, 511–613." *Akademie der Wissenschaften und der Literatur Mainz: Abhandlungen der sozialwissenschaftlichen Klasse* 9, 651–715. Wiesbaden, 1953.

———. *Trier im Merowingerreich: Civitas, Stadt, Bistum*. Trier, 1954.

———. "Das Trierer Land im Merowinger- und Karolingerreich." In *Geschichte des Trierer Landes* 1, ed. R. Laufner, 222–302. Schriftenreihe zur Trierischen Landesgeschichte und Volkskunde 10. Trier, 1964.

Falck, L. *Mainz im frühen und hohen Mittelalter (Mitte 5. Jahrhundert bis 1244)*. Geschichte der Stadt Mainz 2, ed. A. P. Brück and L. Falck. Düsseldorf, 1972.

Febvre, Lucien. "Sensibility and History: How to Reconstitute the Emotional Life of the Past." [1941]. In *A New Kind of History: From the Writings of Febvre*. Translated by K. Folca and edited by Peter Burke, 12–26. London, 1973.

Fehring, G. "Beitragsmöglichkeiten der Archäologie zu Fragen der Bevölkerungsentwicklung und ihren Voraussetzungen im Mittelalter." In *Determinanten der Bevölkerungsentwicklung im Mittelalter*, ed. B. Herrmann and Rolf Sprandel, 73–90. Weinheim, 1987.

Feine, H. E. *Kirchliche Rechtsgeschichte: Die katholische Kirche*, 5th ed. Cologne and Graz, 1972.

Fichtenau, Heinrich. *Lebensordnungen des 10. Jahrhunderts. Studien über Denkart und Existenz im einstigen Karolingerreich* 1. Monographien zur Geschichte des Mittelalters 30,1. Stuttgart, 1984.

Finkenzeller, J. *Die Lehre von den Sakramenten im allgemeinen. Von der Schrift bis zur Scholastik*. Handbuch der Dogmengeschichte 4.1a, ed. M. Schmaus, A. Grillmeier, L. Scheffczyk, and M. Seybold. Freiburg, 1980.

Flasch, K. *Augustin. Einführung in sein Denken*. Stuttgart, 1980.

Fleckenstein, Josef. *Early Medieval Germany*. Amsterdam and New York, 1978.

———. *Grundlagen und Beginn der Deutschen Geschichte*. Deutsche Geschichte 1, ed. J. Leuschner. 3rd ed. Göttingen, 1988.

———. *Die Hofkapelle der deutschen Könige* 1: *Grundlegung. Die karolingische Hofkapelle*. Schriften der MGH 16. Stuttgart, 1959.

Fontaine, J. "Ennodius." In *Reallexikon für Antike und Christentum* 5, 1962.

———. Introduction to *Vie de Saint Martin* by Sulpicius Severus, vol. 1. Sources Chrétiennes 133. Paris, 1967.

———. Commentaire to *Vie de Saint Martin* , vol. 3. Sources Chrétiennes 135. Paris, 1969.

Fortes, M. *Kinship and the Social Order: The Legacy of Lewis Henry Morgan*. London, 1969.

Fouracre, Paul. "'Placita' and the Settlement of Disputes in Later Merovingian Francia." In *The Settlement of Disputes in Early Medieval Europe*, ed. Wendy Davies and P. Fouracre, 23–43. Cambridge, 1986.

Freise, E. "Das Frühmittelalter bis zum Vertrag von Verdun (843)." In *Westfälische Geschichte* 1: *Von den Anfängen bis zum Ende des alten Reiches*, ed. W. Kohl, 276–335. Düsseldorf, 1983.

Freisen, Josef. *Geschichte des canonischen Eherechts bis zum Verfall der Glossenlitteratur*. 2d ed. Paderborn, 1893, reprint 1963.

Frenz, T. *Papsturkunden des Mittelalters und der Neuzeit*. Historische Grundwissenschaften in Einzeldarstellungen 2, ed. T. Frenz and P. J. Schuler. Stuttgart, 1986.

Fritze, Wolfgang. *Papst und Frankenkönig. Studien zu den päpstlich-fränkischen Rechtsbeziehungen von 754 bis 824*. Vorträge und Forschungen. Sonderband 10. Sigmaringen, 1973.

———. "Die fränkische Schwurfreundschaft der Merowingerzeit. Ihr Wesen und ihre politische Funktion." *Zeitschrift der Savigny-Stiftung für Rechtsgeschichte: Germanistische Abteilung* 71 (1954): 74–125.

Gärtner, H. "Agathias." In *Reallexikon der germanischen Altertumskunde* 1, 1973.

Gallia Christiana in provincias ecclesiasticas distributa 1, Paris, 1715.

Ganzer, B. "Verwandtschaft." In *Wörterbuch der Ethnologie*, ed. B. Streck. Cologne, 1987.

Gaudel, A."Péché originel." In *Dictionnaire de théologie catholique* 12.1, 275–606, 1933.

Gaudemet, Jean. "Familie I: Familienrecht." In *Reallexikon für Antike und Christentum* 7, 1969.

Gauthier, N. *L'évangélisation des pays de la Moselle*. Paris, 1980.

Gavigan, J. J. "Fulgentius of Ruspe on Baptism." *Traditio* 5 (1947): 313–22.

Gedächtnis, das Gemeinschaft stiftet. Edited by Karl Schmid. Munich and Zurich, 1985.

Das geistige Leben. Edited by B. Bischoff. Vol. 2 of *Karl der Große: Lebenswerk und Nachleben,* edited by W. Braunfels. Düsseldorf, 1965.

Georges, K. E. *Ausführliches lateinisch-deutsches Handwörterbuch.* 14th ed. 2 vols. Hanover, 1976.

Gerndt, H. "Zur kulturwissenschaftlichen Stereotypenforschung." In *Stereotypvorstellungen im Alltagsleben: Beiträge zum Themenkreis Fremdbilder - Selbstbilder - Identität: Festschrift für G. R. Schroubek,* ed. H. Gerndt, 9–12. Münchner Beiträge zur Volkskunde 8. Munich, 1988.

Gessel, W. "Die spätantike Stadt und ihr Bischof." In *Stadt und Bischof,* edited by B. Kirchgässner and W. Baer, 9–28. Stadt in der Geschichte 14. Sigmaringen, 1988.

Goffman, Erving. *Relations in Public: Microstudies of the Public Order.* New York, 1971.

———. *Interaction Rituals: Essays on Face-to-Face Behavior.* Garden City, N.Y., 1967.

Goody, Esther N. *Contexts of Kinship. An Essay in the Family Sociology of the Gonja of Northern Ghana.* Cambridge Studies in Social Anthropology 7. Cambridge, 1973.

———. "Parental Strategies: Calculation or Sentiment?: Fostering Practices Among West Africans." In *Interest and Emotion: Essays on the Study of Family and Kinship,* ed. Hans Medick and David Sabean, 266–77. Cambridge, 1984.

———. *Parenthood and Social Reproduction. Fostering and Occupational Roles in West Africa.* Cambridge Studies in Social Anthropology 35. Cambridge, 1982.

Goody, Jack. *The Development of Family and Marriage in Europe.* Cambridge, 1983.

———. "Kinship II: Descent Groups." In *International Encyclopedia of the Social Sciences* 8, 1968.

Goody, Jack, and Ian Watt. "The Consequences of Literacy." In *Literacy in Traditional Societies,* ed. J. Goody, 27–68. Cambridge, 1968.

Grahn-Hoeck, H. *Die fränkische Oberschicht im sechsten Jahrhundert. Studien zu ihrer rechtlichen und politischen Stellung* Vorträge und Forschungen. Sonderband 21. Sigmaringen, 1976.

Graus, Frantisek. *Volk, Herrscher und Heiliger im Reich der Merowinger: Studien zur Hagiographie der Merowingerzeit.* Prague, 1965.

———. "Sozialgeschichtliche Aspekte der Hagiographie der Merowinger- und Karolingerzeit: Die Viten der Heiligen des südalemannischen Raumes und die sogenannten Adelsheiligen." In *Mönchtum, Episkopat und Adel zur Gründungszeit des Klosters Reichenau,* edited by Arno Borst, 131–76. Vorträge und Forschungen 20. Sigmaringen, 1974.

Gross, Julius. *Entstehungsgeschichte des Erbsündendogmas von der Bibel bis Augustinus.* Vol. 1 of *Geschichte des Erbsündendogmas. Ein Beitrag zur Geschichte des Problems vom Ursprung des Übels.* Munich and Basel, 1960.

———. *Entwicklungsgeschichte des Erbsündendogmas im nachaugustinischen Altertum und in der Vorscholastik (5.–11. Jahrhundert).* Vol. 2 of *Geschichte des Erbsündendogmas.* Munich and Basel, 1963.

Guerreau-Jalabert, Anita. "La designation des relations et des groupes de parenté en et des groupes de parenté en latin médiéval." *Archivum latinitatis medii aevi* 46/47 (1986–87): 65–108.

———. "Spiritus et caritas." In *La parenté spirituelle,* edited by Françoise Héritier-Augé and Élisabeth Copet-Rougier, 33–203. Paris, 1995.

Gurevich, Aron Iakovlevich. *Categories of Medieval Culture*. Translated by George L. Campbell. London, 1985.

Gutierrez, P. *La paternité spirituelle selon saint Paul*. Paris, 1968.

Hannig, J. "Ars donandi: Zur Ökonomie des Schenkens im früheren Mittelalter." In *Armut, Liebe, Ehre: Studien zur historischen Kulturforschung*, edited by Richard van Dülmen, 11–37 and 275–78. Frankfurt am Main, 1988.

Hart, Donn V. *Compadrinazgo: Ritual Kinship in the Philippines*. DeKalb, Ill., 1977

Hartmann, Wilfried. "Der rechtliche Zustand der Kirchen auf dem Lande: Die Eigenkirche in der fränkischen Gesetzgebung des 7. bis 9. Jahrhunderts." In *Christianizzazione ed organizzazione ecclesiastica delle campagne nell'alto medioevo: espansione e resistenz*e 1, 397–444. Settimane di studio del centro Italiano di studi sull'alto medioevo 28. Spoleto, 1982.

Haubrichs, W. "Christentum der Bekehrungszeit: B. Frömmigkeitsgeschichte (Kontinent)." In *Reallexikon der germanischen Altertumskunde* 4, 1981.

Hauck, A. *Kirchengeschichte Deutschlands* 1. 4th ed. Leipzig, 1904.

Hauck, Karl. "Formes de parenté artificielle dans le haute moyen âge." In *Famille et parenté dans l'occident médiéval*, ed. Georges Duby and Jacques Le Goff, 43–47. Rome, 1977.

———. "Von einer spätantiken Randkultur zum karolinischen Europa." *Frühmittelalterliche Studien* 1 (1967): 3–93.

Hausherr, Irénée. "Direction spirituelle II: Chez les chrétiens orientaux." In *Dictionnaire de spiritualité* 3, 1957.

Heggelbacher, O. *Die christliche Taufe als Rechtsakt nach dem Zeugnis der frühen Christenheit*. Paradosis 8. Fribourg, 1953.

Heinzelmann, Martin. "Beobachtungen zur Bevölkerungsstruktur einiger grundherrschaftlicher Siedlungen im karolingischen Bayern." *Frühmittelalterliche Studien* 11 (1977): 202–17.

———. "Bischof und Herrschaft vom spätantiken Gallien bis zu den karolingischen Hausmeiern: Die institutionellen Grundlagen." In *Herrschaft und Kirche. Beiträge zur Entstehung und Wirkungsweise episkopaler und monastischer Organisationsformen*, edited by Friedrich Prinz, 23–82. Monographien zur Geschichte des Mittelalters 33. Stuttgart, 1988.

———. *Bischofsherrschaft in Gallien: Zur Kontinuität römischer Führungsschichten vom 4. bis zum 7. Jahrhundert: Soziale, prosopographische und bildungsgeschichtliche Aspekte*. Beihefte zu Francia 5. Munich, 1976.

———. "Zum Stand der Genovefa-Forschung." *Deutsches Archiv für Erforschung des Mittelalters* 41 (1985): 532–48.

———. "Vita sanctae Genovefae: Recherches sur les critères de datation d'un texte hagiographique." In M. Heinzelmann and J.C. Poulin. *Les vies anciennes de sainte Geneviève de Paris. Etudes critiques*, 1–111. Bibliothèque de l'école des hautes études. 4e section 329. Paris, 1986.

Herrmann, E. "Ecclesia in re publica." In *Europäisches Forum* 2. Frankfurt am Main, 1980.

Hespanha, A. M. "Savants et rustiques: La violence douce de la raison juridique." *Ius commune* 10 (1983): 1–48.

Heumann, H., and H. Seckel. *Handlexikon zu den Quellen des römischen Rechts*. 9th ed., 1907.

Heusler, A. *Institutionen des deutschen Privatrechts* 2. Systematisches Handbuch der deutschen Rechtswissenschaft 2.2.2., ed. K. Binding. Leipzig, 1886.

Heuss, A. "Das spätantike römische Reich kein 'Zwangsstaat'?: Von der Herkunft eines historischen Begriffs." *Geschichte in Wissenschaft und Unterricht* 37 (1986): 603–18.

Hlawitschka, Eduard. "Adoptionen im mittelalterlichen Königshaus." In *Beiträge zur Wirtschafts- und Sozialgeschichte des Mittelalters. Festschrift für H. Helbig*, ed. K. Schulz, 1–32. Cologne and Vienna, 1976.

―――. "Studien zur Genealogie und Geschichte der Merowinger und der frühen Karolinger. Eine kritische Auseinandersetzung mit K. A. Eckhardts Buch Studia Merovingica." *Rheinische Vierteljahrsblätter* 43 (1979): 1–99.

Holzhauer, H. "Meineid." In *Handwörterbuch der deutschen Rechtsgeschichte* 3, 1984.

Honsell, H. *Römisches Recht*. Berlin, 1988.

Hubert, H. *Der Streit um die Kindertaufe. Eine Darstellung der von Karl Barth 1943 ausgelösten Diskussion um die Kindertaufe und ihre Bedeutung für die heutige Tauffrage*. Europäische Hochschulschriften, Reihe 23, Theologie 10. Berne, 1972.

Hübinger, P. E. *Die weltlichen Beziehungen der Kirche von Verdun zu den Rheinlanden*. Rheinisches Archiv 28. Bonn, 1935.

Illmer, D. "Zum Problem der Emanzipationsgewohnheiten im merowingischen Frankenreich." In *L'enfant* 2: *Europe médiévale et moderne*, 127–68. Recueils de la société Jean Bodin pour l'histoire comparative des institutions 36. Brussels, 1976.

Interest and Emotion: Essays on the Study of Family and Kinship. Edited by Hans Medick and David Sabean. Cambridge, 1984.

Irsigler, Franz. *Untersuchungen zur Geschichte des frühfränkischen Adels*. Rheinisches Archiv 70. 2d ed. Bonn, 1981.

Jäger, H. "Determinanten mittelalterlicher Bevölkerungsentwicklung aus historisch-geographischer Sicht." In *Determinanten der Bevölkerungsentwicklung im Mittelalter*, ed. B. Herrmann and Rolf Sprandel, 91–108. Weinheim, 1987.

Jacobs, U. K. *Die Regula Benedicti als Rechtsbuch. Eine rechtshistorische und rechtstheologische Untersuchung*. Forschungen zur kirchlichen Rechtsgeschichte und zum Kirchenrecht 16. Cologne and Vienna, 1987.

James, Edward. "'Beati pacifici': Bishops and the Law in Sixth-century Gaul." In *Disputes and Settlements. Law and Human Relations in the West*, ed. J. Bossy, 25–47. Cambridge, 1983.

Jarnut, J. *Agilolfingerstudien. Untersuchungen zur Geschichte einer adeligen Familie im 6. und 7. Jahrhundert*. Monographien zur Geschichte des Mittelalters 32. Stuttgart, 1986.

Jones, A. H. M, Philip Grierson, and J. A. Crook. "The Authenticity of the 'Testamentum S. Remigii'." *Revue belge de philologie et d'histoire* 35 (1957): 356–73.

Jordan, K. "Die Entstehung der römischen Kurie. Ein Versuch." *Zeitschrift der Savigny-Stiftung für Rechtsgeschichte: Kanonistische Abteilung* 28 (1939): 97–152.

Jürgensmeier, F. *Das Bistum Mainz. Von der Römerzeit bis zum II. Vatikanischen Konzil*. Beiträge zur Mainzer Kirchengeschichte 2. Frankfurt am Main, 1988.

Jungmann, J. A. "Katechumenat." In *Lexikon für Theologie und Kirche* 6, 1961.

Jussen, Bernhard. "Le parrainage à la fin du moyen âge: Savoir public, attentes théologiques et usages sociaux." *Annales E.S.C.* 47 (1992): 467–502.

―――. "Liturgy and Legitimation, or How the Gallo-Romans Ended the Roman

Empire." In *Ordering Medieval Society: Perspectives on Intellectual and Practical Modes of Shaping Social Relations*, edited by B. Jussen. Philadelphia, 2000 (in print).

———. "Über 'Bischofsherrschaften' und die Prozeduren politisch-sozialer Umordnung in Gallien zwischen 'Antike' und 'Mittelalter'." *Historische Zeitschrift* 260 (1995): 673–718.

Kaiser, Reinhold. *Bischofsherrschaft zwischen Königtum und Fürstenmacht. Studien zur bischöflichen Stadtherrschaft im westfränkisch-französischen Reich im frühen und hohen Mittelalter.* Pariser historische Studien 17. Bonn, 1981.

———. "Königtum und Bischofsherrschaft im frühmittelalterlichen Neustrien." In *Herrschaft und Kirche: Beiträge zur Entstehung und Wirkungsweise episkopaler und monastischer Organisationsformen*, ed. Friedrich Prinz, 83–108. Monographien zur Geschichte des Mittelalters 33. Stuttgart, 1988.

———. *Untersuchungen zur Geschichte der Civitas und Diözese Soissons in römischer und merowingischer Zeit.* Rheinisches Archiv 89. Bonn, 1973.

Kaser, Max *Das römische Privatrecht.* Handbuch der Altertumswissenschaften X,3,3,1. 2 vols. 2d ed. Munich, 1971–75.

Keller, H. "Mönchtum und Adel in den Vitae patrum Jurensium und in der Vita Germani abbatis Grandivallensis: Beobachtungen zum frühmittelalterlichen Kulturwandel im alemannisch-burgundischen Grenzraum." In *Landesgeschichte und Geistesgeschichte. Festschrift für Otto Herding*, 1–23. Stuttgart, 1977.

Kerlouegan, François. "Essai sur la mise en nourriture et l'éducation dans les pays celtiques d'après le témoignage des textes hagiographiques latin." *Études celtiques* 12 (1968–69): 101–46.

King, P. D. *Law and Society in the Visigothic Kingdom.* Cambridge Studies in Medieval Life and Thought, 3rd ser., vol. 5. Cambridge, 1972.

Koebler, G. *Lateinisch-Althochdeutsches Wörterbuch.* Göttinger Studien zur Rechtsgeschichte. Sonderband 12. Göttingen, 1971.

Kolb, W. *Herrscherbegegnungen im Mittelalter.* Europäische Hochschulschriften. Reihe III. Geschichte und ihre Hilfswissenschaften, vol. 359. Berne, 1988.

Kramer, K. S. "Mahl und Trunk." In *Handwörterbuch der deutschen Rechtsgeschichte* 3, 1984.

Kretschmar, G. "Die Geschichte des Taufgottesdienstes in der alten Kirche. In *Leiturgia: Handbuch des evangelischen Gottesdienstes* 5, ed. K. F. Müller and W. Blankenburg, 1–348. Kassel, 1970.

Krinke, J. "Der spanische Taufritus im frühen Mittelalter. In *Gesammelte Aufsätze zur Kulturgeschichte Spaniens* 9, 33–112. Spanische Forschungen der Görresgesellschaft 1/9. Münster, 1954.

Kroeschell, Karl. *Deutsche Rechtsgeschichte* 1 (bis 1255). 5th ed. Opladen, 1982.

Kronenfeld, David. "Kinship Terminology." In *Encyclopedia of Cultural Anthropology* 2, 1996.

Krüger, K. H. *Königsgrabkirchen der Franken, Angelsachsen und Langobarden bis zur Mitte des 8. Jahrhunderts.: Ein historischer Katalog.* Münstersche Mittelalter-Schriften 4. Munich, 1971.

Krumbacher, K. *Geschichte der byzantinischen Litteratur von Justinian bis zum Ende des oströmischen Reiches (527–1453).* Handbuch der klassischen Altertumswissenschaft 9,1. 2d ed. Munich, 1897.

Kruse, G. "Pater." In *Paulys Real-Encyclopädie der classischen Altertumswissenschaft* 18.4, 1949.
Kuhn, H. "Adoption." In *Reallexikon der germanischen Altertumskunde* 1, 1973.
Landau, P. "Asylrecht III: Alte Kirche und Mittelalter." In *Theologische Realenzyklopädie* 4, 1979.
Langgärtner, G. *Die Gallienpolitik der Päpste im 5. und 6. Jahrhundert. Eine Studie über den apostolischen Vikariat von Arles.* Theophaneia 16. Bonn, 1964.
Langlois, P. " Fulgentius." In *Reallexikon für Antike und Christentum* 8, 1972.
Latte, Kurt. "Römische Religionsgeschichte." In *Handbuch der Altertumswissenschaften* V, 4. Munich, 1960. Reprint, 1970.
Latte, Robert de. "Saint Augustin et le baptême: Etude liturgico-historique du rituel baptismal des adultes chez saint Augustin." *Questions liturgiques et paroissiales* 56 (1975): 175–223.

———. "Saint Augustin et le baptême: Étude liturgico-historique du rituel baptismal des enfants chez Saint Augustin. *Questions liturgiques et paroissiales* 57 (1976): 41–55.
Laurent, M. H. "Cavaillon." In *Dictionnaire d'histoire et de géographie ecclésiastique* 12, 1953.

———. "Carpentras." In *Dictionnaire d'histoire et de géographie ecclésiastique* 11, 1949.
Lefas, A. "L'adoption testamentaire a Rome." *Nouvelle revue historique de droit français et étranger* 21 (1897): 721–63.
Lenz, R. "Emotion und Affektion in der Familie der frühen Neuzeit. Leichenpredigten als Quelle der historischen Familienforschung." In *Die Familie als sozialer und historischer Verband. Untersuchungen zum Spätmittelalter und zur frühen Neuzeit*, ed. P. J. Schuler, 121–46. Sigmaringen, 1987.
Levillain, L. "Les comptes de Paris à l'époque franque." *Le Moyen age* 41, 3rd ser. no. 12 (1941): 137–205.
Lévi-Strauss, Claude. *The Elementary Structures of Kinship.* Translated by James Harle Bell, John Richard von Sturmer, and Rodney Needham. Boston, 1969.
Levy, Ernst. *West Roman Vulgar Law: The Law of Property.* Memoirs of the American Philosophical Society 29. Philadelphia, 1951.

———. *Weströmisches Vulgarrecht: Das Obligationenrecht.* Forschungen zum römischen Recht 7. Weimar, 1956.
Longnon, A. *Géographie de la Gaule au 6ᵉ siécle.* Paris, 1878.
Lüdtke, Alf. "What is the History of Everyday Life and Who Are Its Practitioners?" In *The History of Everyday Life,* edited by A. Lüdtke. Princeton, 1995.
Luhmann, Niklas. *Soziale Systeme: Grundriß einer allgemeinen Theorie.* Frankfurt am Main, 1984.
Lynch, Joseph H. *Godparents and Kinship in Early Medieval Europe.* Princeton, N.J., 1986.

———. *Spiritual Kinship and Sexual Prohibitions in Early Medieval Europe,* 271–88. Monumenta iuris canonici, ser. c, subsidia 7. Rome, 1985.

———. "Baptismal Sponsorship and Monks and Nuns, 500–1000." *American Benedictine Review* 31 (1980): 108–29.
Maher, Vanessa. "Possession and Dispossession: Maternity and Mortality in Morocco." In *Interest and Emotion,* 143–78.

Maine, Henry Sumner. *Ancient Law: Its Connection with the Early History of Society and its Relation to Modern Ideas* [1861]. Ed. Frederick Pollack. Boston, 1963.

Manselli, Raoul. "Vie familiale et éthique sexuelle dans les pénitentiels." In *Famille et parenté dans l'occident médiéval*, ed. Georges Duby and Jacques Le Goff, 363–78. Collection de l'école française de Rome 30. Rome, 1977.

Martin, J. *Spätantike und Völkerwanderung*. Oldenbourg Grundriß der Geschichte 4. Munich, 1987.

Mauss, Marcel. *The Gift: The Form and Reason for Exchange in Archaic Societies*. Translated by W. D. Halls. London, 1990.

Medick, Hans, and David Sabean. "Interest and Emotion in Family and Kinship Studies: A Critique of Social History and Anthropology." In *Interest and Emotion*, 9–27.

Memoria: Der geschichtliche Zeugniswert des liturgischen Gedenkens im Mittelalter. Ed. K. Schmid und J. Wollasch. Münstersche Mittelalter-Schriften 48. Munich, 1984.

Meier, C. *Caesar*. Berlin, 1982.

Merzbacher, F. "Nordisches Recht." In *Handwörterbuch der deutschen Rechtsgeschichte* 3, 1984.

Michaud-Quantin, P. *Universitas: Expressions du mouvement communautaire dans le moyen-âge latin*. L'église et l'état au moyen âge 13. Paris, 1970.

Mikat, Paul. *Dotierte Ehe—rechte Ehe: Zur Entwicklung des Eheschließungsrechts in fränkischer Zeit*. Rheinisch-Westfälische Akademie der Wissenschaften: Vorträge G 227. Opladen, 1978.

———. "Zu den Voraussetzungen der Begegnung von fränkischer und kirchlicher Eheauffassung in Gallien." In *Religionsrechtliche Studien: Abhandlungen zum Staatskirchenrecht und Eherecht* 2, ed. J. Listl, 889–913. Staatskirchenrechtliche Abhandlungen 5. Berlin, 1974.

———. "Die Inzestverbote des Konzils von Epaon: Ein Beitrag zur Geschichte des fränkischen Eherechts." In *Religionsrechtliche Studien*, 869–88.

Mintz, Sidney W., and Eric R. Wolf. An Analysis of Ritual Co-parenthood (Compadrazgo)." *Southwestern Journal of Anthropology* 6 (1950): 341–68.

Mitteis, Heinrich. "Adoptionsurkunde vom Jahre 381 n. Chr." *Archiv für Papyruskunde* 3 (1906): 171–84.

———. *Deutsches Privatrecht*. Revised by H. Lieberich. 9th ed. Munich, 1981.

Mitteis, Ludwig. *Reichsrecht und Volksrecht in den östlichen Provinzen des Römischen Kaiserreiches*. Leipzig, 1891, rpt. 1963.

Mittelstrass, J. "Fiktion." In *Enzyklopädie Philosophie und Wissenschaftstheorie* 1, 1980.

Morsel, Joseph. "Geschlecht und Repräsentation. Beobachtungen zur Verwandtschaftskonstruktion im fränkischen Adel des späten Mittelalters." In *Die Repräsentation der Gruppen*, edited by Otto Gerhard Oexle and Andrea von Hülsen-Esch, 259–325. Veröffentlichungen des Max-Planck-Instituts für Geschichte 14. Göttingen, 1998.

Müller, Ernst Wilhelm. *Der Begriff der Verwandtschaft in der modernen Ethnosoziologie*. Mainzer Etnologica 2. Berlin, 1981.

Murray, Alexander C. *Germanic Kinship Structure: Studies in Law and Society in Antiquity and the Early Middle Ages*. Toronto, 1983.

Nagel, E. *Kindertaufe und Taufaufschub: Die Praxis vom 3.–5. Jahrhundert in Nordafrika und ihre theologische Einordnung bei Tertullian, Cyprian und Augustinus*. Europäische Hochschulschriften, Reihe 23, Theologie 144. Berne, 1980.

Nehlsen, Hermann. "Zur Aktualität und Effektivität germanischer Rechtsaufzeichnungen." In *Recht und Schrift im Mittelalter*, ed. P Classen, 449–502. Vorträge und Forschungen 23. Sigmaringen, 1977.

———. *Sklavenrecht zwischen Antike und Mittelalter: Germanisches und römisches Recht in den germanischen Rechtsaufzeichnungen 1: Ostgoten, Westgoten, Franken, Langobarden*. Göttinger Studien zur Rechtsgeschichte 7). Göttingen, 1972.

Nehlsen-von Stryk, K. "Die Freien im Frankenreich als ungelöstes Problem der Rechts-, Sozial- und Verfassungsgeschichte." In *Akten des 26. Deutschen Rechtshistorikertages*, ed. D. Simon, 427–41. *Ius commune*. Sonderheft 30. Frankfurt, 1987.

Neunheuser, Burkhard. *Taufe und Firmung*. Handbuch der Dogmengeschichte 4.2, ed. M. Schmaus et al. Freiburg, 1983.

Noble, Thomas F. X. *The Republic of St. Peter: The Birth of the Papal State, 680–825*. Philadelphia, 1984.

Nonn, U. "Merowingische Testamente: Studien zum Fortleben einer römischen Urkundenform im Frankenreich." *Archiv für Diplomatik* 18 (1972): 1–129.

Norberg, Dag. *La poésie latine rythmique du haut moyen âge*. Studia latina Holmiensia 2. Stockholm, 1954.

Nutini, Hugo G., and Betty Bell. *Ritual Kinship: The Structure and Historical Development of the Compadrazgo System in Rural Tlaxcala*. 2 vols. Princeton, N.J., 1980–84.

Oexle, Otto Gerhard. "Die 'Wirklichkeit' und das 'Wissen': Ein Blick in das sozialgeschichtliche Oeuvre von Georges Duby." *Historische Zeitschrift* 232 (1981): 61–91.

———. "Conjuratio und Gilde im frühen Mittelalter: Ein Beitrag zum Problem der sozialgeschichtlichen Kontinuität zwischen Antike und Mittelalter." In *Gilden und Zünfte: Kaufmännische und gewerbliche Genossenschaften im frühen und hohen Mittelalter*, ed. B. Schwineköper, 151–214. Vorträge und Forschungen 29. Sigmaringen, 1985.

———. "Perceiving Society in the Early and High Middle Ages: A Contribution to a History of Social Knowledge." In *Ordering Medieval Society: Intellectual and Practical Modes of Shaping Social Relations*, edited by Bernhard Jussen. Philadelphia, 2000. Published in German as "Deutungsschemata der sozialen Wirklichkeit im frühen und hohen Mittelalter. Ein Beitrag zur Geschichte des Wissens," in *Mentalitäten im Mittelalter: Methodische und inhaltliche Probleme*, ed. F. Graus, 65–117, Vorträge und Forschungen 35 (Sigmaringen, 1987).

———. "Die funktionale Dreiteilung als Deutungschema der sozialen Wirklichkeit in der ständischen Gesellschaft des Mittelalters." In *Ständische Gesellschaft und soziale Mobilität*, ed. W. Schulze, 19–51. Schriften des historischen Kollegs, Kolloquien 12. Munich, 1988.

———. "Das Evangeliar Heinrichs des Löwen als geschichtliches Denkmal." In *Das Evangeliar Heinrichs des Löwen: Kommentar zum Faksimile*, ed. Dietrich Kötzsche. Frankfurt am Main, 1989.

———. "Die Gegenwart der Toten." In *Death in the Middle Ages*, ed. H. Braet and W. Verbeke, 19–77. Mediaevalia Lovaniensia, series 1, studia 9. Louvain, 1983.

———. "Die mittelalterlichen Gilden: Ihre Selbstdeutung und ihr Beitrag zur Formung sozialer Strukturen." In *Soziale Ordnungen im Selbstverständnis des Mittelalters* 1, ed. A. Zimmermann, 203–26. Miscellanea Mediaevalia 12,1. Berlin and New York, 1979.

———. "Gilden als soziale Gruppen in der Karolingerzeit." In *Das Handwerk in vor- und frühgeschichtlicher Zeit* 1: *Historische und rechtshistorische Beiträge und Untersuchungen zur Frühgeschichte der Gilde*, ed. H. Jankuhn et al., 284–354. Abhandlungen der Akademie der Wissenschaften in Göttingen. Phil. hist. Klasse, 3rd ser., vol. 122. Göttingen, 1981.

———. "Mahl und Spende im mittelalterlichen Totenkult." *Frühmittelalterliche Studien* 18 (1984): 401–20.

———. "Tria genera hominum: Zur Geschichte eines Deutungsschemas der sozialen Wirklichkeit in Antike und Mittelalter." In *Institutionen, Kultur und Gesellschaft im Mittelalter: Festschrift für Josef Fleckenstein zu seinem 65. Geburtstag*, ed. L. Fenske, W. Roesener, and T. Zotz, 483–500. Sigmaringen, 1984.

———. "Peace through Conspiracy." In *Ordering Medieval Society: Intellectual and Practical Modes of Shaping Social Relations*, edited by Bernhard Jussen. Philadelphia, 2000.

Ogris, W. "Aufnehmen des Kindes." *Handwörterbuch der deutschen Rechtsgeschichte* 1, 1971.

———. "Das Erlöschen der väterlichen Gewalt nach deutschen Rechten des Mittelalters und der Neuzeit." In *L'enfant* 2: *Europe médiévale et moderne*, 417–52. Recueils de la société Jean Bodin pour l'histoire comparative des institutions 36. Brussels, 1976.

———. "Munt, Muntwalt." In *Handwörterbuch der deutschen Rechtsgeschichte* 3, 1984.

Ohly, F. "Haus III (Metapher)." *Reallexikon für Antike und Christentum* 13, 1986.

Olberg, Gabriele v. *Freie, Nachbarn und Gefolgsleute: Volkssprachige Bezeichnungen aus dem sozialen Bereich in den frühmittelalterlichen Leges*. Europäische Hochschulschriften, ser. 1, vol. 627. Berne, 1983.

———. "Zum Freiheitsbegriff im Spiegel volkssprachiger Bezeichnungen in den frühmittelalterlichen Leges." Akten des 26. Deutschen Rechtshistorikertages, ed. D. Simon, 411–26. *Ius commune*, Sonderheft 30. Frankfurt, 1987.

———. "Ein sozialgeschichtliches Schlüsselzeugnis im Licht der Textsortenforschung." *Frühmittelalterliche Studien* 20 (1986): 123–36.

Oxford Latin Dictionary. Edited by P. W. G. Glare. Oxford, 1982.

Padberg, L. v. "Heilige und Familie: Studien zur Bedeutung familiengebundener Aspekte in den Viten des Verwandten- und Schülerkreises um Willibrord, Bonifatius und Liudger." Ph.D. diss., Universität Münster, 1981.

Palanque, J. R. "L'époque mérovingienne." In *Le diocèse de Marseille*, 29–33. Histoire des diocèses de France 1, ed. E. Jarry and J. R. Palanque. Paris, n.d.

Pappenheim, Max. "Die Pflegekindschaft in der Graugans." In *Festschrift Heinrich Brunner zum siebzigsten Geburtstag*, 1–15. Weimar, 1910.

Perkow, Ursula. "Wasserweihe, Taufe und Patenschaft bei den Nordgermanen." Ph.D. diss., Universität Hamburg, 1972.

Pietri, L. "Gregor von Tours." In *Theologische Realenzyklopädie* 14, 1985.

———. "Le premier millénaire." In *Le diocèse de Paris* 1. *Des origines à la Revolution*, ed. B. Plongeron, 28–57. Histoire des Diocèses de France 20, ed. B. Plongeron and A. Vauchez. Paris, 1987.

Pitt-Rivers, Julian. "Kinship III: Pseudo-kinship." In *International Encyclopedia of the Social Sciences* 8, 1968.

Pörtschner, W. "Numen." *Gymnasium* 66 (1959): 353–74.

Pontal, Odette. *Die Synoden im Merowingerreich.* Konziliengeschichte Reihe A: Darstellungen, ed. Walter Brandmueller. Paderborn, 1986.

Prinz, Friedrich. *Askese und Kultur. Vor- und Frühbenediktinisches Mönchtum an der Wiege Europas.* Munich, 1980.

———. *Frühes Mönchtum im Frankenreich: Kultur und Gesellschaft in Gallien, den Rheinlanden und Bayern am Beispiel der monastischen Entwicklung (4.–8. Jahrhundert).* Munich, 1965.

———. *Klerus und Krieg: Untersuchungen zur Rolle der Kirche beim Aufbau der Königsherrschaft.* Monographien zur Geschichte des Mittelalters 2. Stuttgart, 1971.

———. "Die Rolle der Iren beim Aufbau der merowingischen Klosterkultur." In *Die Iren und Europa im frühen Mittelalter* 1, ed. H. Löwe, 202–18. Veröffentlichungen des Europazentrums Tübingen, Kulturwissenschaftliche Reih. Stuttgart, 1982.

———. "Die bischöfliche Stadtherrschaft im Frankenreich vom 5. bis zum 7. Jahrhundert." *Historische Zeitschrift* 217 (1975): 1–35.

Rastoul, A. "Aix en Provence." In *Dictionnaire d'histoire et de géographie ecclésiastiques* 1, 1912.

Riché, Pierre. *Éducation et culture dans l'occident barbare. VIe–VIIIe siècle.* Patristica Sorbonnensia 4. Paris, 1962. Translated by John J. Contreni under the title *Education and Culture in the Barbarian West* (Columbia, S.C., 1976).

———. "Bildung IV: Alte Kirche und Mittelalter." In *Theologische Realenzyklopädie* 6, 1980.

Rilinger, R. "Die Interpretation des späten Imperium Romanum als 'Zwangsstaat'." *Geschichte in Wissenschaft und Unterricht* 36 (1985): 321–40.

Roblin, M. *Le terroir de Paris aux époques galloromaine et franque.* 2d ed. Paris, 1971.

———. *Le terroir de l'oise aux époques galloromaine et franque: Peuplement, défrichement, environnement.* Paris, 1978.

Rouche, Michel. *L'Aquitaine des Wisigoths aux Arabes, 418–781: naissance d'une région.* Paris, 1979.

———. "Les baptêmes forcés de juifs en Gaule mérovingienne et dans l'Empire d'Orient." In *De l'antijudaisme antique à l'antisémitisme contemporain*, ed. V. Nikiprowetzky, 105–24. Lille, 1979.

Rubellin, M. "Entrée dans la vie, entrée dans la chrétienté, entrée dans la société: Autour du baptême à l'époque carolingienne." In *Les entrées dans la vie. Initiation et apprentissages*, 31–51. XIIe Congrès de la Société des historiens médiévistes de l'Enseignement supérieur public, Nancy 1981. Nancy, 1982.

Sabean, David. *Kinship in Neckarhausen, 1700–1870.* Cambridge, 1997.

———. *Property, Production and Family in Neckarhausen 1700–1870.* Cambridge, 1990.

Sablonier, Roger. "The Aragonese Royal Family Around 1300." In *Interest and Emotion*, 210–39.

Sachers, E. "Pater familias". In *Paulys Real-Encyclopädie der classischen Altertumswissenschaft* 18.4, 1949.

Sahlins, Marshall. *Stone Age Economics.* Chicago and New York, 1972.

"Saint Vrain." In *Vies des Saintes et des Bienheureux selon l'ordre du calendrier avec l'historique des fêtes* 10, 629–31. Paris, 1952.

Saxer, V. "L'initiation chrétienne du IIe au VIe siècle: Esquisse historique des rites et de leur signification. In *Segni e riti nella chiesa altomedievale occidentale* 1, 173–205. Settimane di studio del centro italiano di studi sull'alto medioevo 33. Spoleto, 1987.

Schäferdiek, K. "Columbans Wirken im Frankenreich 591–612." In *Die Iren und Europa im frühen Mittelalter* 1, edited by H. Löwe, 171–201. Veröffentlichungen des Europazentrums Tübingen, Kulturwissenschaftliche Reihe. Stuttgart, 1982.

Schaff, A. *Stereotypen und das menschliche Handeln.* Vienna, 1980.

Scharbert, J. *Heilsmittler im Alten Testament und im alten Orient.* Quaestiones Disputatae 23/24. Freiburg, 1964.

Scheibelreiter, Georg. *Der Bischof in merowingischer Zeit.* Veröffentlichungen des Instituts für österreichische Geschichtsforschung, vol. 27. Vienna, 1983.

Schenk von Schweinsberg, G. "Reims in merowingischer Zeit: Stadt, Civitas, Bistum. Anhang: Die Geschichte der Reimser Bischöfe in karolingischer Zeit bis zur Bischofserhebung Hincmars (845)." Ph.D diss., Universität Bonn, 1971.

Schieffer, R. "Der Bischof zwischen Civitas und Königshof (4. bis 9. Jahrhundert)." In *Bischofstypus und Bischofsideal im Spiegel der Kölner Kirche: Festgabe für Joseph Kardinal Höffner zum 80. Geburtstag*, edited by P. Berglar and O. Engels, 17–39. Cologne, 1986.

Schindler, A. "Geistliche Väter und Hausväter in der christlichen Antike." In *Das Vaterbild im Abendland* I, edited by H. Tellenbach, 70–82. Stuttgart, 1978.

Schlumbohm, Jürgen. *Lebensläufe, Familien, Höfe. Die Bauern und Heuerleute des Osnabrückischen Kirchspiels Belm in proto-industrieller Zeit, 1650–1860.* Göttingen, 1994.

Schmid, Karl. "Zur Problematik von Familie, Sippe und Geschlecht, Haus und Dynastie beim mittelalterlichen Adel: Vorfragen zum Thema 'Adel und Herrschaft im Mittelalter'." In*Gebetsgedenken und adliges Selbstverständnis im Mittelalter: Ausgewählte Beiträge—Festgabe zu seinem sechzigsten Geburtstag*, 183–244. Sigmaringen, 1983.

———. "Unerforschte Quellen aus quellenarmer Zeit: Zur amicitia zwischen Heinrich I. und dem westfränkischen König Robert im Jahre 923." *Francia* 12 (1984): 119–47.

———. "Welfisches Selbstverständnis." In *Adel und Kirche. Festschrift Gerd Tellenbach*, 389–416. Freiburg, 1968.

———. "De regia stirpe Waiblingensium: Bemerkungen zum Selbstverständnis der Staufer." *Zeitschrift für die Geschichte des Oberrheins* 124 (1976): 63–73.

Schmid, Karl, and Joachim Wollasch. "Societas et fraternitas: Begründung eines kommentierten Quellenwerkes zur Erforschung der Personen und Personengruppen des Mittelalters." *Frühmittelalterliche Studien* 9 (1975): 1–48.

Schmidt, Roderich. "Zur Geschichte des fränkischen Königsthrons." *Frühmittelalterliche Studien* 2 (1968): 45–66.

Schmidt-Wiegandt, R. "Lex Salica." In *Handwörterbuch der deutschen Rechtsgeschichte* 2, 1978.

———. "Die volkssprachigen Wörter der Leges barbarorum als Ausdruck sprachlicher Interferenz." *Frühmittelalterliche Studien* 13 (1979): 56–87.

Schneider, Reinhard. *Brüdergemeine und Schwurfreundschaft. Der Auflösungsprozess des Karolingerreiches im Spiegel der caritas-Terminologie in den Verträgen der karlingischen Teilkönige des 9. Jahrhunderts.* Historische Studien, vol. 388. Lübeck and Hamburg, 1964.

———. *Königswahl und Königserhebung im Frühmittelalter*. Monographien zur Geschichte des Mittelalters 3. Stuttgart, 1972.

Schott, G. "Der Stand der Legesforschung." *Frühmittelalterliche Studien* 13 (1974): 29–55.

Schrenk, G. "pater." In *Theologisches Wörterbuch zum Neuen Testament* 5, 1954, 946–59 and 974–1024.

Schröder, R. "*adfatimire*." In *Deutsches Rechtswörterbuch* 1, 1914–32.

———. "*adfatimus*." In *Deutsches Rechtswörterbuch* 1, 1914–32.

———. *Lehrbuch der deutschen Rechtsgeschichte*. Revised by E. Frh. v. Künßberg. 7th ed. Berlin and Leipzig, 1932.

Schrörs, H. *Hinkmar, Erzbischof von Reims: Sein Leben und seine Schriften*. Freiburg, 1884.

Schuetzeichel, R. *Althochdeutsches Wörterbuch*. 4th ed. Tübingen, 1974.

Sellert, W. "Erbvertrag." In *Handwörterbuch der deutschen Rechtsgeschichte* 1, 1971.

Semmler, Josef. "Episcopi potestas und karolingische Klosterpolitik." In *Mönchtum, Episkopat und Adel zur Gründungszeit des Klosters Reichenau*, edited by A. Borst, 305–95. Vorträge und Forschungen 20. Sigmaringen, 1974.

Seymour-Smith, Charlotte. *Macmillan Dictionary of Anthropology*. London and Basingstoke, 1986.

Simmel, Georg. "Soziologie der Mahlzeit." In *Das Individuum und die Freiheit: Essais*, 205–11. Berlin, 1984.

Sokoll, Thomas. "Familien hausen. Überlegungen zu David Sabeans Studie über Eigentum, Produktion, und Familie in Neckarhausen, 1700–1870." *Historische Anthropologie* 3 (1995): 335–48.

Spangenberg, P. M. "Pragmatische Konzepte als Horizonte von Stilreflexionen im Mittelalter." In *Stil: Geschichten und Funktionen eines kulturwissenschaftlichen Diskurselements*, edited by H. U. Gumbrecht and K. L. Pfeiffer, 68–92. Frankfurt am Main, 1986.

Sprandel, Rolf. "Dux und comes in der Merowingerzeit." *Zeitschrift der Savigny-Stiftung für Rechtsgeschichte: Germanistische Abteilung*. 74 (1957): 41–84.

Staubach, N. "Germanisches Königtum und lateinische Literatur vom fünften bis zum siebten Jahrhundert: Bemerkungen zum Buch von Marc Reydellet, *La royauté dans la littérature latine de Sidoine Apollinaire à Isidore de Séville*." *Frühmittelalterliche Studien* 17 (1983): 1–54.

Staudt, R. "Studien zum Patenbrauch in Hessen." Ph.D. diss., Universität Frankfurt am Main, 1958.

Steidle, Basilius. "Homo Dei Antonius: Zum Bild des 'Mannes Gottes' im alten Mönchtum." In *Antonius magnus eremita, 356–1956: Studia ad antiquam monachismum spectantia*, edited by B. Steidle, 148–200. Studia Anselmiana 38. Rome, 1956.

Thomas, Heinz. "Die Namenliste des Diptychon Barberini und der Sturz des Hausmeiers Grimoald." *Deutsches Archiv* 25 (1969): 17–63.

Thompson, Edward P. *The Making of the English Working Class*. Harmondsworth, 1968.

Der Tod Jesu. Edited by K. Kertelge. Quaestiones Disputatae 74. 2d ed. Freiburg, 1976.

Tolksdorf, U. "Strukturalistische Nahrungsforschung: Versuch eines generellen Ansatzes." *Ethnologica Europea* 9 (1976): 64–85.

Van Molle, M. "Les fonctions du parrainage des enfants en occident: Leur apogée et leur degradation (du VIe au Xe siecle)." *Paroisse et Liturgie* 46 (1964): 121–46.
Verdon, Michael. "Virgins and Widows: European Kinship and Early Christianity." *Man* 23 (1988): 488–505.
Veyne, P. *Did the Greeks Believe in their Myths?: An Essay on the Constitutive Imagination.* Translated by Paula Wissing. Chicago, 1988.
Vittinghoff, F. "Zur Entwicklung der städtischen Selbstverwaltung: Einige kritische Anmerkungen." In *Stadt und Herrschaft: Römische Kaiserzeit und hohes Mittelalter,* edited by F. Vittinghoff, 107–46. Historische Zeitschrift, Beiheft Neue Folge 7. Munich, 1982.
Vivelo, F. R. *Handbuch der Kulturanthropologie: Eine grundlegende Einführung.* Stuttgart, 1981.
Vocabularium iurisprudentiae Romanae auspiciis Savigniani institutum 5. Edited by the Prussian Academy of Sciences. Berlin, 1939.
Vogel, Cyrille. *Introduction aux sources de l'histoire du culte chrétien au moyen âge.* Anastatic reprint with a preface by B. Botte. Bibliotheca degli "Studi medievali" 1. 2d ed. Spoleto, 1981.
———. *Medieval Liturgy: An Introduction to the Sources.* Translated and revised by W. G. Storey and N. K. Rasmussen. Washington, D.C., 1986.
Vollmann, B. K. "Gregor IV (Gregor von Tours)." In *Reallexikon für Antike und Christentum* 12, 1983.
Wackernagel, W. D. "Die rechtliche Stellung der Nachkommen des Adoptivkindes nach schweizerischem Recht: Der Ursprung der Adoption." Ph.D. diss., Universität Basel, 1953.
———. "Adoption." In *Handwörterbuch der deutschen Rechtsgeschichte* 1, 1971.
Wadle, E. "Über Entstehung, Funktion und Geltungsgrund normativer Rechtsaufzeichnungen im Mittelalter: Notizen zu einem Durchblick." In *Recht und Schrift im Mittelalter,* edited by P. Classen, 503–18. Vorträge und Forschungen 23. Sigmaringen, 1977.
Weber, Max. "R. Stammlers 'Ueberwindung' der materialistischen Geschichtsauffassung." In *Gesammelte Aufsätze zur Wissenschaftslehre,* edited by J. Winckelmann, 291–359. 6th ed. Tübingen, 1985.
Weidemann, Margarete. "Zur Chronologie der Merowinger im 6. Jahrhundert." *Francia* 10 (1982): 471–513.
———. *Kulturgeschichte der Merowingerzeit nach den Werken Gregors von Tours.* 2 vols. Römisch Germanisches Zentralmuseum. Monographien 3.1/3.2. Mainz, 1982.
———. *Das Testament des Bischofs Berthramn von Le Mans vom 27. März 616: Untersuchungen zu Besitz und Geschichte einer fränkischen Familie im 6. und 7. Jahrhundert.* Römisch-Germanisches Zentralmuseum. Monographien 9. Mainz, 1986.
Weinstock, S. *Divus Iulius.* Oxford, 1971.
Weiss, E. *Institutionen des römischen Privatrechts* 2. 2d ed. Stuttgart, 1949.
Weitzel, J. *Dinggenossenschaft und Recht: Untersuchungen zum Rechtsverständnis im fränkisch-deutschen Mittelalter* 1. Quellen und Forschungen zur höchsten Gerichtsbarkeit im alten Reich 15.1. Cologne and Vienna, 1985.
Wenger, Leopold. "Adoption." In *Reallexikon für Antike und Christentum* 1, 1950.
———. *Die Quellen des römischen Rechts.* Österreichische Akademie der Wissenschaften. Denkschrift der Gesamtakademie 2. Vienna, 1953.

———. *Die Stellvertretung im Rechte der Papyri*. Leipzig, 1909.

Wenskus, Reinhard. "Bemerkungen zum Thunginus der Lex Salica." In *Festschrift Percy Ernst Schramm* 1, 217–36. Wiesbaden, 1964.

———. "Die germanische Welt am Vorabend des Hunnensturms." In *Europa im Wandel von der Antike zum Mittelalter*, edited by Theodor Schieffer, 95–106. Handbuch der europäischen Geschichte 1, ed. Theodor Schieder. Stuttgart, 1976.

Werner, Karl Ferdinand. "Adel A: Fränkisches Reich, Imperium, Frankreich." In *Lexikon des Mittelalters* 1, 1980.

Weyrauch, Erdmann. "Mahl-Zeiten: Beobachtungen zur sozialen Kultur des Essens in der Ständegesellschaft." In *Leib und Leben in der Geschichte der Neuzeit*, ed. Arthur Imhof, 103–18. Berliner historische Studien 9. Berlin, 1983.

White, Stephen D. *Custom, Kinship and Gifts to Saints: The laudatio parentum in Western France, 1050–1150*. Chapel Hill and London, 1988.

Wieacker, F. *Privatrechtsgeschichte der Neuzeit unter besonderer Berücksichtigung der deutschen Entwicklung*. 2d ed. Göttingen, 1967.

Wielers, Margret. "Zwischenstaatliche Beziehungsformen im frühen Mittelalter (pax, foedus, amicitia, fraternitas)." Ph.D. diss., Universität Münster, 1959.

Winheller, E. *Die Lebensbeschreibungen der vorkarolingischen Bischöfe von Trier*. Rheinisches Archiv 27. Bonn, 1935.

Wlosok, A. "Vater und Vatervorstellungen in der römischen Kultur." In *Das Vaterbild im Abendland* 1: *Rom, frühes Christentum, Mittelalter, Neuzeit, Gegenwart*, edited by H. Tellenbach, 18–54. Stuttgart, 1978.

———. "Römischer Religions- und Gottesbegriff in heidnischer und christlicher Zeit." *Antike und Abendland* 16 (1970): 39–53.

———. *Laktanz und die philosophische Gnosis*. Heidelberg, 1961.

Wolfram, Herwig. *Geschichte der Goten: Von den Anfängen bis zur Mitte des sechsten Jahrhunderts. Entwurf einer historischen Ethnographie*. 2nd ed. Munich, 1980.

Wollasch, J. "Eine adlige Familie des frühen Mittelalters: Ihr Selbstverständnis und ihre Wirklichkeit." *Archiv für Kulturgeschichte* 39 (1957): 150–88.

———. "Kaiser und Könige als Brüder der Mönche: Zum Herrscherbild in liturgischen Handschriften des 9. bis 11. Jahrhunderts." *Deutsches Archiv für Erforschung des Mittelalters* 40 (1984): 1–20.

Wood, Ian N. "Disputes in Late Fifth- and Sixth-Century Gaul: Some Problems." In *The Settlement of Disputes in Early Medieval Europe*, edited by Wendy Davies and Paul Fouracre, 7–22. Cambridge, 1986.

Wormald, Patrick. "*Lex scripta* and *verbum regis*: Legislation and Germanic Kingship, from Euric to Cnut." In *Early Medieval Kingship*, edited by P. H. Sawyer and Ian N. Wood, 105–38. Leeds, 1979.

Zöllner, Erich. *Geschichte der Franken bis zur Mitte des sechsten Jahrhunderts*. Munich, 1970.

Zwahr, Hartmut. *Zur Konstituierung des Proletariats als Klasse: Strukturuntersuchung über das Leipziger Proletariat während der industriellen Revolution*. Akademie der Wissenschaften der DDR: Schriften des Zentralinstituts für Geschichte 56. Berlin, 1978.

Index

Abbanus (holy man), 230
Adalbero of Augsburg, 189
Adam of Bremen, 129
Adelheid (empress), 33
Aethelwalh of Sussex, 43, 205
Affatomie, 59–60
Ageric of Verdun, 101, 156–62, 164, 172, 215, 218, 234, 236
Agnellus of Ravenna, 173, 218, 227, 231–33
Aix, 99
Alais-Arisitum, 99, 102
Alaric II (Visigothic king), 29, 31
Albi, 74, 110
Albinus (governor in Provence) , 94
Alfred the Great, 33
Alcuin, 125
alliances bound by oath (friendships, coalitions, guilds) 56, 84, 180, 215, 218–19
Amalafrida (sister of Theoderic), 29
Amalasuintha (daughter of Theoderic), 31
Amalbert (son of Geremar), 189
Amandus (bishop), 191, 196–97, 212–13, 225–26, 228, 230, 235
Ambrose of Milan, 121
Amelius of Bigorre, 99
amicitia. *See* friendship
Anarawd ap Rhodri (Welsh king), 33
Andelot, 47–48, 63, 69, 80, 83–84, 87, 90–91, 92, 99–101, 111–12, 161, 163, 181, 192–95, 198–204
appropriation, 55–56
Angers, 70, 74, 106–7
Aniane. *See* Benedict of Aniane

Anianenese, Suppl. ad Hadrianum, 188
Arles, 121, 123, 126–28, 131, 144
Arnulf of Carinthia, 189
Attigny, 193, 219
Audoenus/Dado of Rouen, 189, 224–25
Audovera (Chilperic's first wife), 37, 145–46
Augsburg. *See* Adalbero
Augustine, 123–26, 129, 165
Aurelian of Arles, 216, 185
Avignon, 99, 111
Avitus of Clermont, 99
Avitus of Vienne, 127, 130, 143, 281 n. 119
Avranches, 201

Baddo (hired assassin), 194
baptism, baptismal rite: assistance of sponsor, 184–87; deacons and deaconesses, 119, 185; delayed, 120–21, 146, 169–70; birth and adoption metaphors, 135–36; forced, of Jews, 174; healing power, 165; naming, 187–90; representation, 169, 191; site of, 191–93. *See also* naming
Bearn, 99
Beauvais, 198–99, 201
Bede, 43, 61
Benedict of Aniane, 183, 188
Benedict, Saint, Rule of, 134
Berchar (holy man), 231
Bertefred, 157, 160, 172, 179–80, 216, 218, 226, 231–32, 235, 259

357

Berthchramn/Waldo of Le Mans, 151, 187, 199
Bertin (holy man), 214, 230, 233
Bertram of Bordeaux, 187
Berulf *(dux)*, 72, 103
Bigorre, 99
Bladast *(dux)*, 72, 103
Bobo *(dux)*, 72, 103
Boniface (saint), 16, 20, 36, 41
Boniface of Cataqua, 124–25, 129
Bonitus of Clermont, 86–87
Bordeaux, 97, 106, 147
Boris (Bulgarian *khan*), 54, 229
Bourges, 140
Brigid (saint), 231, 234
Brunechildis, 65, 70, 72, 74, 90, 111–12, 129, 145–50, 153–54, 164, 167, 179–80, 188, 198, 200, 216, 218, 231–32, 235
Burchard of Worms, 34, 37

Caesar, Julius, 133
Caesarius of Arles, 121, 123, 126–28, 130–31, 134–35, 185, 215–17, 229–30
Canones Theodori, 103
Caracalla (emperor), 123
Cassius Dio, 133
catechumenate, 42, 116, 118, 126, 133, 229; catechumenate witnesses, 116–19, 134
Catullus, 132
Cavaillon, 166, 200, 225
Châlons-sur-Marne, 99
Châlon-sur-Saône, 38, 99, 206
Charibert, 46, 72, 88, 106–7, 142, 146–47, 199
Charimer (Childebert's referendary), 157
Charlemagne, 44, 183, 193, 205, 207, 218–21
Charles III, 205, 207, 219
Chartres, 72–74, 106, 142, 198–200
Châteaudun, 73, 142
Chellanus/ Kilian (holy man), 223
Childebert (son of Grimoald), 84–88
Childebert (son of Theuderic II), 173
Childebert I, 71, 80, 88, 143, 172, 198
Childebert II, 46, 66, 71, 79, 84, 88, 99, 101, 103, 156, 213
Childeric II, 86, 93

Chilperic, 37, 46–48, 53–54, 66–67, 70–78, 80, 82, 85, 87–88, 100, 102–8, 110, 141, 145–56, 159, 161, 164–65, 168–70, 173–76, 181–82, 187, 191, 194, 200, 204–5, 211, 218, 224, 228, 232–33, 235, 237
Chlodomer, 188
Chlodosinda (sister of Childebert II), 91, 111, 151
Chlodovic, Chlodwig. *See* Clovis
Chlothar I, 79, 109, 141, 143, 146, 157, 203
Chlothar II, 46, 66, 79, 82, 84, 88, 169, 198, 201, 211, 214, 232, 233, 235
Chrodechildis (wife of Clovis I), 29, 188
Chulderic (subject of Gunthchramn), 93
Ciaran (monk), 222
Claudius (emperor), 174
Claudius (scoundrel), 194
Clermont, 86–87, 99, 140, 144, 171, 174; synod of, 144
Clovis, 29, 127, 130, 142, 143, 157, 172, 175, 188, 228, 231
Clovis (son of Chilperic), 145
Colmanus (holy man), 214–15, 222–23
Columbanus (holy man), 167, 168, 188, 222–24, 226
Comminges, 99, 111
Constantinople, 117
Couserans, 201
Cyprian, 120–21

Dado. *See* Audoenus of Rouen
Dagobert I, 59, 174, 189, 191, 196, 213, 224, 228
Dagobert II, 85–86
Dalfinus of Lyon, 61–62
Declanus (holy man), 214–15
Decretum Gratiani, 33–34
Desiderius of Rennes, 72, 103
Deusdedit (pope), 33, 37, 42
Dhuoda, 230, 232
Domigisel (Neustrian nobleman), 107
Domremy, 211
Donatus of Besançon, 188
duty, fulfillment of duty, 32, 43, 45, 91, 116, 118, 124, 131, 137, 149, 153, 155, 156, 158, 175, 183, 185, 189, 196, 220
Dynamius (governor), 94, 99, 101

Eberegisel of Cologne, 97–98
Eberulf, 103, 176–78, 216–17, 224, 226, 235, 237
Egeria (nun), 118
Egidius of Reims, 98, 100, 117, 164
Eligius of Noyon, 225
emotions, 31, 232–33
Ennodius of Pavia, 127, 130–31, 134–35, 232
enthronement at Pompierre, 94–96
Epaon, synod of, 41
Erchinoald *(maior domus)*, 193, 213, 218
Ermoldus Nigellus, 205
Etampes, 198–200
Euspicius (presbyter), 157

Faro of Meaux, 214
father, image of the father: catechumenate witnesses, 117–18; *mos*, 132–33; *pater spiritualis*,128–29; Roman law, 57–58, 132
feasts, 204, 206–7; one-sided hospitality, 205–6, 208
Ferreolus of Uzès, 94, 185, 216
fideiussor, fidepromissor, fidedicto, 123–24
Fidolus (holy man), 230, 234
Fidus (bishop), 120
Flavia (wife of Waldelenus), 222
Flavius of Rouen, 146
Flodoard, 204
Florianus (abbot of *Romenum*), 127, 129, 131, 134–35, 230, 232
foster fatherhood, 59–60, 91–92, 190–92, 220–21
foster son *(alumnus). See* foster fatherhood
Fredegar, 46, 79, 166, 174, 182, 185, 192–93, 198, 203–4, 208, 235
Fredegund, 37, 48, 67, 70, 72–78, 80, 101–4, 107–8, 110–11, 154, 165, 182–83, 185, 189–95, 197–98, 206–7, 214, 220, 227–28, 231
Fregius (holy man), 222–23
Fridolin (holy man), 211–13, 218–19, 222, 226
friendship, 19, 113, 153, 194–95, 214, 231
Fulgentius of Ruspe, 121, 124
Furseus (holy man), 193, 213, 218–19, 224, 226

Galswintha (wife of Chilperic), 188
Gamalbert (holy man), 222, 234
Gelasius I (pope), 127
Gennadius of Marseilles, 121
Genovefa (saint), 127–29
Geremar, 189, 224, 226
Germanus of Paris, 169
Ghaerbald of Liège, 37
gift, gift exchange, 148–51, 154, 204, 206–8; as an explanatory model, 149–50; one-sided gifts, 205–6, 208; role of time in, 208–9, 151–53
Gisela (daughter of Lothar II), 285
Gisela (daughter of Pippin III), 54
Godegisel (Childebert's general), 179
godparenthood. *See* sponsorship
Gordianus (Spanish bishop), 33
Godefrid (Norman leader), 205, 219–20
Gregory of Tours, 28, 45–48, 63, 65–71, 76, 78, 81–82, 88, 92–93, 95–101, 104, 106–7, 121, 127–29, 135–37, 142–48, 151, 153, 156–57, 160, 163–69, 171–73, 175–82, 185, 187–89, 191–92, 194, 199, 203, 205–8, 211, 217, 220, 224, 228–29, 231, 235–36
Gregory I (pope), 144
Gregory II (pope), 37, 229
Grimoald *(maior domus)*, 85–88
guardianship, 67–68, 70–71, 84, 94, 108, 112
Gundobad (Burgundian king), 188
Gundovald, 88, 93, 96, 100, 103, 106, 142, 156
Guldulf *(dux)*, 99
Gunthchramn, 27, 29–30, 46–49, 53–54, 56, 62–112, 142, 151, 156–61, 166–67, 172, 176, 181–85, 187–209, 214–15, 217–18, 220, 226–28, 231–32, 235
Gunthchramn Boso, 101, 156–63, 172, 217, 229, 231, 234, 236–37

Hadrian (pope), 188, 221
Haito of Basel, 40
Harald of Denmark, 205, 220, 229, 232
Hatto of Mainz, 189, 236–37
Henry I, 204
Henry II, 33
Heraclius (Byzantine emperor), 174
Hesychius of Vienne (father of Avitus), 130
Hieronymus, 184

Hincmar of Reims, 130–31, 134
Hippolytus of Rome, 117–18, 137–38
holy man, as godfather, 166–68, 213–15
honor, reputation, 197, 219, 223–24, 226–28, 232–34

Ingismund (*jarl* of Gautland), 61
Innocence of Rodez, 99
Isidore of Seville, 140

James II of Aragon, 31, 77–78
Javols, 99
Jews, baptism of, 173–75
Joan of Arc, 39, 43–44, 211
John (Venetian deacon), 150
John Chrysostom, 117–19, 123
John of Avignon, 99
Jonas of Bobbio, 188
Jovinus (governor in Provence), 94
Julian (priest), 18, 167, 173
Julian of Eclanum, 121
Justinian (Byzantine emperor), 36, 57–58, 61, 123

Kinship (spiritual, fictive, ritual, metaphor), 17–24

Laon, 99, 142
Leon III (Byzantine emperor), 229
Léscar Bearn, 99
Lex Ribuaria, 59–60, 88, 109
Lex Salica, 59–60
Liber mozarabicus, 189
lifting up a child: as a custom signaling acknowledgment of paternity, 103–4, 184–87; from the baptismal font, 184–85
Liutprand (Langobard king), 37
Lothar II, 220
Lothar III, 214
Louis the Child, 188–89
Louis the Pious, 205, 207, 229, 232
love, *caritas, amor:* of banquet companions, 205; of catechumenate witnesses, 118; fraternal, 82–83; in (oath) friendship/brotherhood, 84, 153; parental, 136; in sponsorship, *compaternitas,* 172–73, 218–19, 232–33
Luxeuil, 222

Maastricht, 99
Mâcon, synod of, 99–101
Magneric of Trier, 101, 156, 158, 161–64, 188, 197, 215–17
Mainz, 99, 164
Mamertus of Vienne, 130
Manglieu (Manlieu), 86
Maori society, 156
Marcellus of Uzès, 101
Markulf, 60, 62, 88
Maroveus of Poitiers, 100, 142
Marseilles, 93, 99, 101, 121, 200
Martel, Charles, 142, 237
Martin of Tours (saint), 93, 140, 143, 154, 176–78
Mauss, Marcel, 150–51
Meaux, 99, 103, 199–200, 214
Medardus, 174
Melantius of Rouen, 70
Melun, 143
Merovich (son of Theuderic II), 173
Merovich (son of Chilperic), 145–46, 148–49, 153–55, 165, 175, 211, 232, 235
Metz, 159, 164
Mopsuestia. *See* Theodore
morality, 232–33, 237
mother, *ecclesia* as, 135

naming, 187–190; before baptism, 104
Nanterre, 128, 192
Nantes, 72, 201
Neckarhausen, 19, 35
Nicetius of Trier, 127, 131, 163–64, 230, 232
Nicholas I (pope), 61
Nivard of Reims, 231
Nothelm of Canterbury, 15
Noyon. *See* Eligius

oath: of loyalty, 105; oath-helping (compurgation), 77–78. *See also* alliances bound by oath
Odilia (saint), 211
Oloron, 201
Origen, 117, 121
Orléans, 80–81
Ostrogotho (daughter of Theuderic), 29
Otto I, 33, 42
Otto III, 33, 207

Paris, 66–68, 71–72, 75–77, 81, 92, 102–3, 106, 129, 143–46, 149, 165, 168–70, 174, 181–83, 187–88, 191–94, 196, 198–204, 207, 224, 228; synods of 556 to 573, 77, 144; synods of 561 and 829, 146
Pathir (a Jew baptized by force), 173–75, 188, 232–33
Paul (the apostle), 134–35, 212
Paul I (pope), 54
Pavia. *See* Ennodius and Theodore
Pehthelm (bishop), 15
Petrus Cantor, 38, 41, 223, 230, 235–36
Petrus Orseolo (doge of Venice), 207
Petrus of Metz, 164
Phatyr. *See* Pathir
Pientius of Aix, 99
Pippin II, 33, 37, 41, 54, 87, 109, 221
Pippin III, 87
Pirmin, 213, 219, 226
Poitiers, 66–67, 72, 75, 92, 97, 100, 103, 142, 146, 182, 200–201
Pompierre, 66, 69–70, 80, 82–83, 87–88, 91, 94, 151–52, 181, 204
Praetextatus, 70, 73, 107, 145–56, 159, 161–62, 166, 168, 172, 175, 197, 205–6, 218, 235–37
Priscus (a Jew), 173, 175
proxies, 121–25
Pseudo-Dionysius, 124, 126

Ragnachar (Frankish king), 79
Ragnemod of Paris, 165, 168–70, 188, 197
Rather *(quasi dux)*, 93, 100
Rauching (nobleman), 236–37
Ravenna, 34, 214, 218, 227, 231
Recared (Visigothic king), 90–91, 111, 151
Regino of Prüm, 219–20
Regula Tarnatensis, 196, 216
Reichenau, 213
Reims, 159, 164. *See also* Remigius
Remigius of Reims, 130, 134, 228, 231
Rennes, 70, 74, 106–8
Ressons-sur-Matz, 72, 198–99, 201
Richarius (holy man), 230
Rigunthe (daughter of King Chilperic), 103
Rimbert, 43
Robert (father of William of Dijon), 229

Robert I of France, 204
Rodez, 99
Rodulf (king of the Heruli), 29
Rodulph Glaber, 229
Roer River, 204
Rome, council of, 36
Romenus. *See* Florianus
Rouen, 70, 73–74, 106–8, 145–47, 154, 159, 163, 166, 168–69, 194, 218, 225. *See also* Audoenus
Rueil, 192, 204

Samson (son of Chilperic), 164–65, 211
Sedulius, 174
Séez, 198, 201
Seneca, 133
Senlis, 72, 200–201
Sens, 143, 169, 198, 200
Sidonius Appolinaris, 140–41
Sigebert of Gembloux, 87
Sigibert I, 46–47, 66, 72–74, 81, 99, 142–43, 146, 156, 159, 165, 168–69, 191, 199, 201, 218, 228
Sigibert III, 85–87, 88, 191
Sigismund (Burgundian king), 29
Sigivald the Elder, 171–73, 216
Sigivald the Younger, 171–73, 216, 230, 232
Sigulf *(dux)*, 107
S. Lizier, 99
Soissons, 72, 82, 103, 143, 146, 154, 174
Speyer, 99
sponsor (Latin term), 122–23
sponsorship: *adoptio*, 16–17, 184–85, 204; *amicitia* and *fraternitas* (*see also* friendship), 214–15; banquets and gifts, 204, 208–9, 215, 219; calling in obligations, 156; *caritas*, 38, 172–73, 219, 232–33; catechumenate, 33, 42; at churching, 42; *compaternitas*, 38, 156, 193, 220–21, 223, 227–28; confirmation, 32–33, 41–42; foster-sonship and, 48, 190–92; fulfillment of duties, 158, 161, 178–79, 232-238; holy men as godfathers, 167–68, 213–15; imperial, 43–44, 204–5, 208, 219–20, 228–29; incest, prohibition of, 33–34, 36–42; incest taboos, 39–40; inheritance, 193, 195–96, 199, 202–3; intermediaries, 121–22, 230; kinship terminology and, 17–28; at

sponsorship *(continued)*:
  loosening of the confirmation band, 42; monastic foundations and, 213–14, 225–26; number of godparents, 39, 42–43; obligations to help and assist, 155–56, 234–35; presence of the dead, 229–30; prestige and representation, 169, 175, 228; property, 153; receiving from the font and the Roman *tollere liberum*, 184–87; search for sponsors, 210–13; trickery, 159–61, 236; vassalage and, 43–44, 208, 215, 218–20; vocabulary of, 128–29, 231–32
Stephen II (pope), 33, 221

Tertullian, 120–21, 123
Theodatus (abbot of *Romenum*), 131
Theoderic the Great, 77, 175
Theodore of Mopsuestia, 118–19
Theodore of Marseilles, 93–94, 99–101, 160
Theodore of Pavia, 40–42
Theodulf *(comes)*, 70, 107
Theudebald, 71, 84, 157
Theudebert I, 71, 80, 88, 142, 157, 166, 171–73
Theudebert II, 84, 156, 161–62, 166, 188, 198, 234
Theudebert (son of Chilperic I), 145
Theuderic I, 157, 163, 171–72, 216
Theuderic II, 164, 166, 188
Theuderic III, 87
Theuderic (son of Chilperic I), 168, 188, 228
Thiudigotho (daughter of Theoderic), 29
Thiudimir (father of Theoderic), 29
Thoringus (nephew of Bertram of Le Mans), 199
Tigernach (holy man), 211, 231
time: factor in gift exchange, 151–52, 208; factor in social action, 62–63

Tongeren, 99
Tordis (daughter of Ingismund), 61
Torstein (Nordic ruler), 61
Toul, 99
Toulouse, 102
Tournai, 165
Tours, 66, 72, 75, 93, 100, 103, 146, 154, 160, 176–77, 200–201, 224; synod of, 567, 146
Tribur, synod of 895, 41
Trier, 101, 141, 162–64, 166, 169, 188
Troyes, 69, 96
Trudo (holy man), 212–13, 230, 234
Trullo, council of, 37

Ulpian (Roman jurist), 57
Ursio (nobleman), 157, 179–80

Vannes, 108
vassalage. *See* sponsorship
Velay, 99
Venantius Fortunatus, 99
Venice, doges of, 33
Veranus of Cavaillon, 166–67, 188, 197, 213
Verdun, 156–57, 159–60, 164, 169
Viviers, 99

Waddo (Austrasian nobleman), 160
Waldelenus *(dux)* and Flavia, 222
Waldo. *See* Berthchramn of Le Mans
Waltbert *(comes)*, 214
Warache *(compater* of Fridolin), 211–13
Waroch (Breton leader), 108
Widukind (Saxon leader), 44, 193, 205, 218–20
Widukind of Corvey, 236
Wilfrid of York, 61
William of Aquitaine, 230, 232
William of Dijon, 33, 229
Worms, 99
Wulfhere (king of Mercia), 43, 205, 207

Zachary (pope), 37, 40–42